Victimology

⑤SAGE | 50 YEARS

SAGE was founded in 1965 by Sara Miller McCune to support the dissemination of usable knowledge by publishing innovative and high-quality research and teaching content. Today, we publish more than 850 journals, including those of more than 300 learned societies, more than 800 new books per year, and a growing range of library products including archives, data, case studies, reports, and video. SAGE remains majority-owned by our founder, and after Sara's lifetime will become owned by a charitable trust that secures our continued independence.

Los Angeles | London | New Delhi | Singapore | Washington DC

Victimology

LEAH E. DAIGLE
Georgia State University

LISA R. MUFTIĆ
Sam Houston State University

Los Angeles | London | New Delhi
Singapore | Washington DC

Los Angeles | London | New Delhi
Singapore | Washington DC

FOR INFORMATION:

SAGE Publications, Inc.
2455 Teller Road
Thousand Oaks, California 91320
E-mail: order@sagepub.com

SAGE Publications Ltd.
1 Oliver's Yard
55 City Road
London EC1Y 1SP
United Kingdom

SAGE Publications India Pvt. Ltd.
B 1/I 1 Mohan Cooperative Industrial Area
Mathura Road, New Delhi 110 044
India

SAGE Publications Asia-Pacific Pte. Ltd.
3 Church Street
#10-04 Samsung Hub
Singapore 049483

Printed in the United States of America.

ISBN 978-1-4833-5901-4

This book is printed on acid-free paper.

Acquisitions Editor: Jerry Westby
Editorial Assistant: Laura Kirkhuff
Production Editor: Bennie Clark Allen
Copy Editor: Lana Arndt
Typesetter: C&M Digitals (P) Ltd.
Proofreader: Kris Bergstad
Indexer: Wendy Allex
Cover Designer: Candice Harman
Marketing Manager: Terra Schultz

16 17 18 19 10 9 8 7 6 5 4 3 2

■ ■ BRIEF CONTENTS

■■■■■ DETAILED CONTENTS

Although offender behavior and the impact of crime have long been studied, how victimization shapes the lives of victims was not similarly studied until recently. Now, policymakers, practitioners, academics, and activists alike have recognized the importance of studying the other half of the crime–victim dyad. Indeed, it is an exciting time to study victimology—an academic field that is growing rapidly. Hence, this text fills a void in what is currently available in the market. As noted below, it is a text that includes brief chapters covering the essentials on victimology. Moreover, it uses a consistent framework throughout to orient the reader, while addressing the latest topics within the field of victimology.

We have attempted to incorporate a general framework in each chapter—one that examines the causes and consequences of specific types of victimization and the responses to them. Our intent was to create a comprehensive yet accessible work that examines many types of victimization from a common framework so that similarities and differences can be easily identified.

Within this framework, we pay particular attention to identifying the characteristics of victims and incidents so that theory can be applied to understanding why some people are victims while others remain unscathed. Although the earliest forays into the study of victimology were focused on identifying victim typologies, theory development in this field has lagged behind that in criminology. Aside from routine activities and lifestyles theory, there are few theories that explicitly identify causes of victimization. This is not to say that the field of victimology is devoid of theory—it is just that the theories that have been applied to victimization are largely derived from other fields of study. We have included a chapter that discusses these theories. Furthermore, in each chapter about a specific type of victimization, we have identified the causes and how theory may apply. Knowing this is a critical first step in preventing victimization and revictimization.

We also wanted to include throughout the text emerging issues in the field of victimology. To this end, each chapter discusses current issues germane to its particular topic and the latest research. For example, same-sex intimate partner violence is covered in depth, as are cyberbullying, identity theft victimization, and human trafficking. Other chapters wholly address contemporary issues. Specifically, there is a chapter devoted to the victim–offender overlap; one to recurring victimization; one to victims of homicide; and one to victims who suffer from mental illness, victims who are incarcerated, and victims who have disabilities. We believe that the inclusion of the latest issues within the field of victimology will expose the reader to the topics likely to garner the most attention in the years to come. Further, we include a chapter that specifically addresses issues about victimology around the world. Doing so allows the reader to be exposed to how victimization is defined and measured in different countries and how victims are treated in countries beyond the United States.

This text covers these topics while highlighting empirical research that ties into an issue from each chapter. In addition, each chapter uses a "real-world" news example to connect issues in victimology to current events. Finally, international issues are discussed within each chapter. As such, the book is appropriate for undergraduate students as a primary text and for graduate students as a supplement/resource or as a primary text. Its comprehensive nature will allow the instructor to focus on the issues that are most relevant to him or her and to his or her students. The book is appropriate for classes within criminal justice and criminology programs (e.g., victimology, crime victims, gender and crime) but is also relevant for women's studies, social work, psychology, and sociology courses.

The book contains 15 chapters that were selected because they address the topics typically covered in victimology courses and emerging topics. These chapters include the following:

Chapter 1. Introduction to Victimology

Chapter 2. Extent, Theories, and Factors of Victimization

Chapter 3. The Victim–Offender Overlap

Chapter 4. Consequences of Victimization

Chapter 5. Recurring Victimization

Chapter 6. Victims' Rights and Remedies

Chapter 7. Homicide Victimization

Chapter 8. Sexual Victimization

Chapter 9. Intimate Partner Violence

Chapter 10. Victimization at the Beginning and End of Life

Chapter 11. Victimization of Special Populations

Chapter 12. Victimization at School and Work

Chapter 13. Property and Identity Theft Victimization

Chapter 14. Victimology From a Comparative Perspective

Chapter 15. Contemporary Issues in Victimology

The text also includes a range of features to aid both professors and students:

- Each chapter is summarized in bullet points.
- Discussion questions are included at the end of each chapter.
- A list of key terms is included at the end of each chapter.
- Internet resources relevant for each chapter are provided.
- Each chapter includes graphics pertinent to the topic presented.
- The book has a glossary of key terms.

■■ ACKNOWLEDGMENTS

We would like to thank the editorial and production staff at SAGE Publications for their assistance. Jerry Westby has been wonderfully supportive throughout this process. We appreciate your continued confidence in our work. Laura Kirkhuff, Jerry's editorial assistant, has provided valuable assistance throughout this project. Thanks also to Lana Arndt for her copyediting work and to Terra Schultz for her work marketing the book.

We owe a great debt to a number of students at our respective universities who assisted us in various ways in preparing this text, including Susannah Tapp, Andia Azimi, and Jane Daquin from Georgia State University and Jonathan Grubb, Molly Smith, Ashley Boillot-Fansher, Michael Candler, Susan Hoppe, and Laura Taylor at Sam Houston State University.

From Leah Daigle
It has been my pleasure to work with Lisa Muftić on this project as a coauthor. She is not only a great collaborator, but a great friend. I miss you at work but will take writing together as a small consolation!

From Lisa Muftić
Throughout the years I have been blessed to be surrounded by hardworking, dedicated, and extremely talented individuals, particularly Gaylene Armstrong, Leana Bouffard, Jeff Bouffard, Mary Finn, Wendy Guastaferro, Irma Deljkic, and Almir Maljević: Thank you for making "work" (teaching/research/writing/conferences) fun! I am especially indebted to my coauthor and friend Leah Daigle, who presented me with this wonderful opportunity. Thank you for your support and guidance throughout this process—I am so glad we were in this together! Finally, a special thank you to my familial support system—near and far. To my parents, Doug and Gloria Ryberg and (the late) Ahmet and Hafiza Muftić, who provided the foundation my family is built upon, there are not enough words to express my gratitude and love. A big thank you to my mom who weathered this process with me and provided much needed editorial and proofreading support. To my children, Safia, Rizah, and Meliha, who remind me every day what is really important in life, I love you! And to my husband, Mensur Muftić: I've said it before, but it bears repeating, *Mensure, moje najveće dostignuće će uvijek biti porodica i život koji smo zajedno stvorili. Volim te. Tvoja žena.*

Leah E. Daigle
Georgia State University

Lisa R. Muftić
Sam Houston State University

Victimology

SAGE Publications and the authors gratefully acknowledge the following reviewers:

Dr. Joseph A-Gyamfi, The University of Texas-Pan American

Martha Earwood, University of Alabama at Birmingham

Julie Hibdon, Southern Illinois University

Karol Lucken, University of Central Florida

Jennifer Riggs, Eastern New Mexico University-Ruidoso

Dr. Beverly Ross, California University of Pennsylvania

Lindsey Vigesaa, Ph.D., St. Cloud State University

Isis N. Walton, Ph.D., Virginia State University

Mary West-Smith, Ph.D., University of Northern Colorado

Giselle White-Perry, South Carolina State University

CHAPTER 1

INTRODUCTION TO VICTIMOLOGY

■ WHAT IS VICTIMOLOGY?

The term *victimology* is not new. In fact, Benjamin Mendelsohn first used it in 1947 to describe the scientific study of crime victims. Victimology is often considered a subfield of criminology, and the two fields do share much in common. Just as criminology is the study of criminals—what they do, why they do it, and how the criminal justice system responds to them—victimology is the study of victims. Victimology, then, is the study of the etiology (or causes) of victimization, its consequences, how the criminal justice system accommodates and assists victims, and how other elements of society, such as the media, deal with crime victims. Victimology is a science; victimologists use the scientific method to answer questions about victims. For example, instead of simply wondering or hypothesizing why younger people are more likely to be victims than are older people, victimologists conduct research to attempt to identify the reasons why younger people seem more vulnerable.

■ THE HISTORY OF VICTIMOLOGY: BEFORE THE VICTIMS' RIGHTS MOVEMENT

As previously mentioned, the term victimology was coined in the mid-1900s. Crime was, of course, occurring prior to this time; thus, people were being victimized long before the scientific study of crime victims began. Even though they were not scientifically studied, victims were recognized as being harmed by crime, and their role in the criminal justice process has evolved over time.

Before and throughout the Middle Ages (about the 5th through the 16th century), the burden of the justice system, informal as it was, fell on the victim. When a person or property was harmed, it was up to the victim and the victim's family to seek justice. This was typically achieved via retaliation. The justice system operated under the principle of lex talionis, an eye for an eye. A criminal would be punished because he or she deserved it, and the punishment would be equal to the harm caused. Punishment based on these notions is consistent with **retribution.** During this time period, a crime was considered a harm against the victim, not the state. The concepts of restitution and retribution governed action against criminals. Criminals were expected to pay back the victim through **restitution.** During this time period, a criminal who stole a person's cow likely would have to compensate the owner (the victim) by returning the stolen cow and also giving him or her another one.

Early criminal codes incorporated these principles. The **Code of Hammurabi** was the basis for order and certainty in Babylon. In the code, restoration of equity between the offender and victim was stressed. Notice that the early response to crime centered on the victim, not the state. This focus on the victim continued until the Industrial Revolution, when criminal law shifted to considering crimes violations against the state rather than the victim. Once the victim ceased to be seen as the entity harmed by the crime, the victim became secondary. Although this shift most certainly benefited the state—by allowing it to collect fines and monies from these newly defined harms—the victim did not fare as well. Instead of being the focus, the crime victim was effectively excluded from the formal aspects of the justice system.

Since then, this state-centered system has largely remained in place, but attention—at least from researchers and activists—returned to the crime victim during the 1940s. Beginning in this time period, concern was shown for the crime victim, but this concern was not entirely sympathetic. Instead, scholars and others became preoccupied with how the crime victim contributes to his or her own victimization. Scholarly work during this time period focused not on the needs of crime victims but on identifying to what extent victims could be held responsible for being victimized. In this way, the damage that offenders cause was ignored. Instead, the ideas of victim precipitation, victim facilitation, and victim provocation emerged.

◼ THE ROLE OF THE VICTIM IN CRIME: VICTIM PRECIPITATION, VICTIM FACILITATION, AND VICTIM PROVOCATION

Although the field of victimology has largely moved away from simply investigating how much a victim contributes to his or her own victimization, the first forays into the study of crime victims were centered on such investigations. In this way, the first studies of crime victims did not portray victims as innocents who were wronged at the hands of an offender. Rather, concepts such as victim precipitation, victim facilitation, and victim provocation developed from these investigations. **Victim precipitation** is defined as the extent to which a victim is responsible for his or her own victimization. The concept of victim precipitation is rooted in the notion that, although some victims are not at all responsible for their victimization, other victims are. In this way, victim precipitation acknowledges that crime victimization involves at least two people—an offender and a victim—and that both parties are acting and often reacting before, during, and after the incident. Identifying victim precipitation does not necessarily lead to negative outcomes. It is problematic, however, when it is used to blame the victim while ignoring the offender's role.

Similar to victim precipitation is the concept of victim facilitation. **Victim facilitation** occurs when a victim unintentionally makes it easier for an offender to commit a crime.

A victim may, in this way, be a catalyst for victimization. A woman who accidentally left her purse in plain view in her office while she went to the restroom and then had it stolen would be a victim who facilitated her own victimization. This woman is not

PHOTO 1.1

A bar fight breaks out after a man yells an insult at the other. By yelling an insult, the victim is precipitating the victimization.

blameworthy—the offender should not steal, regardless of whether the purse is in plain view or not. But the victim's actions certainly made her a likely target and made it easy for the offender to steal her purse. Unlike precipitation, facilitation helps understand why one person may be victimized over another but does not connote blame and responsibility.

Contrast victim facilitation with victim provocation. **Victim provocation** occurs when a person does something that incites another person to commit an illegal act. Provocation suggests that without the victim's behavior, the crime would not have occurred. Provocation, then, most certainly connotes blame. In fact, the offender is not at all responsible. An example of victim provocation would be if a person attempted to mug a man who was walking home from work and the man, instead of willingly giving the offender his wallet, pulled out a gun and shot the mugger. The offender in this scenario ultimately is a victim, but he would not have been shot if not for attempting to mug the shooter. The distinctions between victim precipitation, facilitation, and provocation, as you probably noticed, are not always clear-cut. These terms were developed, described, studied, and used in somewhat different ways in the mid-1900s by several scholars.

RIPPED FROM THE HEADLINES

On November 5, 2013, two armed robbers entered a Reading, Pennsylvania, convenience store and stole cash, cigarettes, and lottery tickets. They got more than they bargained for! After leaving the store with their loot, a friend of the owner of the store confronted them, and the two robbers then raised their gun at him. In response, the man then pulled out his own weapon and shot both of the robbers in the chest. Both of the robbers were pronounced dead at the scene. What do you think about this incident? Was the man justified in shooting the robbers? Was this victim facilitation? Precipitation? Provocation? What do you think about one of the friends of the robbers who said, "they should have thought about this before going"?

Source: Adapted from Bayliss, K., & Chang, D. (2013, November 5). Man shoots, kills 2 armed robbers: Police. http://www.nbcphiladelphia.com/news/local/2-Shot-Killed-in-Attempted-Robbery-230539261.html.

Hans von Hentig

In his book *The Criminal and His Victim: Studies in the Sociobiology of Crime*, Hans von Hentig (1948) recognized the importance of investigating what factors underpin why certain people are victims, just as criminology attempts to identify those factors that produce criminality. He determined that some of the same characteristics that produce crime also produce victimization. We will return to this link between victims and offenders in Chapter 3, but for now, recognize that one of the first discussions of criminal victimization connected it to offending.

In studying victimization, then, von Hentig looked at the criminal-victim dyad, thus recognizing the importance of considering the victim and the criminal not in isolation but together. He attempted to identify the characteristics of a victim that may effectively serve to increase victimization risk. He considered that victims may provoke victimization—acting as agents provocateurs—based on their characteristics. He argued that crime victims could be placed into one of 13 categories based on their propensity for victimization: (1) young; (2) females; (3) old; (4) immigrants; (5) depressed; (6) mentally defective/deranged; (7) the acquisitive; (8) dull normals; (9) minorities; (10) wanton; (11) the lonesome and heartbroken; (12) tormentor; and (13) the blocked, exempted, and fighting. All these victims are targeted and contribute to their own victimization because of their characteristics. For example, the young, the old, and females may be victimized because of their ignorance or risk taking, or may be taken advantage of, such as when women are sexually assaulted. Immigrants, minorities, and dull normals are likely to be victimized due to their social status and inability to activate assistance in the community. The mentally defective or deranged may be victimized because they do not recognize or appropriately respond to threats in the environment. Those who are depressed, acquisitive, wanton, lonesome, or heartbroken may place themselves in situations in which they do not recognize danger because of their mental state, their sadness over a lost relationship, their desire for companionship, or their greed. Tormentors are people who provoke their own victimization via violence and aggression toward others. Finally, the blocked, exempted, and fighting victims are those who are enmeshed in poor decisions and unable to defend themselves or seek assistance if victimized. An example of such a victim is a person who is blackmailed because of his behavior, which places him in a precarious situation if he reports the blackmail to the police (Dupont-Morales, 2009).

Benjamin Mendelsohn

Known as the "father of victimology," Benjamin Mendelsohn coined the term for this area of study in the mid-1940s. As an attorney, he became interested in the relationship between the victim and the criminal as he conducted interviews with victims and witnesses and realized that victims and offenders often knew each other and had some kind of existing relationship. He then created a classification of victims based on their culpability, or the degree of the victim's blame. His classification entailed the following:

1. *Completely innocent victim:* a victim who bears no responsibility at all for victimization; victimized simply because of his or her nature, such as being a child

2. *Victim with minor guilt:* a victim who is victimized due to ignorance; a victim who inadvertently places himself or herself in harm's way

3. *Victim as guilty as offender/voluntary victim:* a victim who bears as much responsibility as the offender; a person who, for example, enters into a suicide pact

4. *Victim more guilty than offender:* a victim who instigates or provokes his or her own victimization

5. *Most guilty victim:* a victim who is victimized during the perpetration of a crime or as a result of crime

6. *Simulating or imaginary victim:* a victim who is not victimized at all but, instead, fabricates a victimization event

Mendelsohn's classification emphasized degrees of culpability, recognizing that some victims bear no responsibility for their victimization, while others, based on their behaviors or actions, do.

Stephen Schafer

One of the earliest victimologists, Stephen Schafer (1968) wrote *The Victim and His Criminal: A Study in Functional Responsibility.* Much like von Hentig and Mendelsohn, Schafer also proposed a victim typology. Using both social characteristics and behaviors, his typology places victims in groups based on how responsible they are for their own victimization. In this way, it includes facets of von Hentig's typology based on personal characteristics and Mendelsohn's typology rooted in behavior. He argued that people have a functional responsibility not to provoke others into victimizing or harming them and that they also should actively attempt to prevent that from occurring. He identified seven categories and labeled their levels of responsibility as follows:

1. Unrelated victims—no responsibility

2. Provocative victims—share responsibility

3. Precipitative victims—some degree of responsibility

4. Biologically weak victims—no responsibility

5. Socially weak victims—no responsibility

6. Self-victimizing—total responsibility

7. Political victims—no responsibility

Marvin Wolfgang

The first person to empirically investigate victim precipitation was Marvin Wolfgang (1957) in his classic study of homicides occurring in Philadelphia from 1948 to 1952. He examined some 558 homicides to see to what extent victims precipitated their own deaths. In those instances in which the victim was the direct, positive precipitator in the homicide, Wolfgang labeled the incident as victim precipitated. For example, the victim in such an incident would be the first to brandish or use a weapon, the first to strike a blow, or the first to initiate physical violence. He found that 26% of all homicides in Philadelphia during this time period were victim precipitated.

Marvin Wolfgang studied homicides in Philadelphia and found that about a quarter were victim precipitated. He has been recognized as one of the most influential criminologists in the English-speaking world (Kaufman, 1998).

Photo Credit: University of Pennsylvania.

Beyond simply identifying the extent to which homicides were victim precipitated, Wolfgang also identified those factors that were common in such homicides. He determined that often in this kind of homicide, the victim and the offender knew each other. He also found that most victim-precipitated homicides involved male offenders and male victims and that the victim was likely to have a history of violent offending himself. Alcohol was also likely to play a role in victim-precipitated homicides, which makes sense, especially considering that Wolfgang determined these homicides often started as minor altercations that escalated to murder.

Since Wolfgang's study of victim-precipitated homicide, others have expanded his definition to include felony-related homicide and subintentional homicide. **Subintentional homicide** occurs when the victim facilitates his or her own demise by using poor judgment, placing himself or herself at risk, living a risky lifestyle, or using alcohol or drugs. Perhaps not surprising, a study of subintentional homicide found that as many as three-fourths of victims were subintentional (Allen, 1980).

Menachem Amir

The crime of rape is not immune from victim-blaming today, and it certainly has not been in the past either. **Menachem Amir,** a student of Wolfgang's, conducted an empirical

FOCUS ON RESEARCH

Even though the first study examining victim precipitation and homicide was published in 1957, this phenomenon is being examined in contemporary times as well. In recent research examining 895 homicides that occurred in Dallas, Texas, Muftić and Hunt (2013) found that 48.9% (n = 438) were victim precipitated. They further found that homicides in which the victim had a previous history of offending were more likely to be victim precipitated than homicides in which the victim had no such history.

Source: Adapted from Muftić, L. R., & Hunt, D. E. (2013). Victim precipitation: Further understanding the linkage between victimization and offending in homicide. *Homicide Studies, 17,* 239–254.

investigation into rape incidents that were reported to the police. Like Wolfgang, he conducted his study using data from Philadelphia, although he examined rapes that occurred from 1958 to 1960. He examined the extent to which victims precipitated their own rapes and also identified common attributes of victim-precipitated rape. Amir labeled almost 1 in 5 rapes as victim precipitated. He found that these rapes were likely to involve alcohol, the victim was likely to engage in seductive behavior, likely to wear revealing clothing, likely to use risqué language, and she likely had a bad reputation. What Amir also determined was that it is the offender's interpretation of actions that is important, rather than what the victim actually does. The offender may view the victim—her actions, words, and clothing—as going against what he considers appropriate female behavior. In this way, the victim may be viewed as being "bad" in terms of how women should behave sexually. He may then choose to rape her because of his misguided view of how women should act, because he thinks she deserves it, or because he thinks she has it coming to her. Amir's study was quite controversial—it was attacked for blaming victims, namely women, for their own victimization. As you will learn in Chapter 8, rape and sexual assault victims today still must overcome this view that women (since such victims are usually female) are largely responsible for their own victimization.

■ THE HISTORY OF VICTIMOLOGY: THE VICTIMS' RIGHTS MOVEMENT

Beyond the attention victims began to get based on how much they contributed to their own victimization, researchers and social organizations started to pay attention to victims and their plight during the mid-1900s. This marked a shift in how victims were viewed not only by the public but also by the criminal justice system. As noted, scholars began to examine the role of the victim in criminal events, but more sympathetic attention was also given to crime victims, largely as an outgrowth of other social movements.

FOCUS ON INTERNATIONAL ISSUES

Even though the field of Victimology has moved beyond the early typologies put forth by von Hentig and others, victimology still is concerned with victim precipitation, provocation, and facilitation. Consider the case of Ahmed Hassan, a 24-year-old man, who was shot and killed at a Toronto, Canada, shopping mall on June 2, 2012. Christopher Husbands, aged 23, shot him and injured six others. Although the exact motives behind the murder are not known, it is believed that Husbands and Hassan were members of a gang, known as Sic Thugs. Husbands had previously been attacked by Hassan and other members of Sic Thugs. He was tied up with duct tape and tortured in a bathtub in an empty public-housing apartment. According to the typologies you have learned about, how did Hassan contribute, if at all, to his own victimization?

Source: Adapted from Mertl, S. (2012, June 12). Toronto Eaton Centre shooting shines light on Canada's gang problem. *The Daily Brew.* Retrieved from http://ca.news.yahoo.com/blogs/dailybrew/toronto-eaton-centre-shooting-shines-light-canada-gang-202058661.html.

During the 1960s, concern about crime was growing. This time period saw a large increase in the amount of crime occurring in the United States. As crime rates soared, so too did the number of people directly and indirectly harmed by crime. In 1966, in response to the growing crime problem, the President's Commission on Law Enforcement and the Administration of Justice was formed. One of the commission's responsibilities was to conduct the first-ever government-sponsored victimization survey, called the **National Crime Survey** (which later became the National Crime Victimization Survey). This survey is discussed in depth in Chapter 2. Importantly, it showed that although official crime rates were on the rise, they paled in comparison with the amount of victimization uncovered. This discrepancy was found because official data sources of crime rates are based on those crimes reported or otherwise made known to the police, whereas the National Crime Survey relied on victims to recall their own experiences. Further, victims were asked in the survey whether they reported their victimization to the police and, if not, why they chose not to report. For the first time, a picture of victimization emerged, and this picture was far different than previously depicted. Victimization was more extensive than originally thought, and the reluctance of victims to report was discovered. This initial data collection effort did not occur in a vacuum. Instead, several social movements were underway that further moved crime victims into the collective American consciousness.

The Women's Movement

One of the most influential movements for victims was the **women's movement**. In recognition that victimizations such as sexual assault and domestic violence were a byproduct of sexism, traditional sex roles, emphasis on traditional family values, and economic subjugation of women, the women's movement took on as part of its mission helping female victims of crime. Feminists were, in part, concerned with how female victims were treated by the criminal justice system and pushed for victims of rape and domestic violence to receive special care and services. As a result, domestic violence shelters and rape crisis centers started appearing in the 1970s. Closely connected to the women's movement was the push toward giving children rights. Not before viewed as crime victims, children were also identified as being in need of services, as they could be victims of child abuse, could become runaways, and could be victimized in much the same ways as older people. The effects of victimization on children were, at this time, of particular concern.

Three critical developments arose from the recognition of women and children as victims and from the opening of victims' services devoted specifically to them. First, the movement brought awareness that victimization often entails emotional and mental harm, even in the absence of physical injury. To address this harm, counseling for victims was advocated. Second, the criminal justice system was no longer relied on to provide victims with assistance in rebuilding their lives, thus additional victimization by the criminal justice system could be lessened or avoided altogether. Third, because these shelters and centers relied largely on volunteers, services were able to run and stay open even without significant budgetary support (Young & Stein, 2004).

The Civil Rights Movement

Also integral to the development of victims' rights was the **civil rights movement**. This movement advocated against racism and discrimination, noting that all Americans have rights protected by the U.S. Constitution. The civil rights movement, as it created awareness of the mistreatment of minorities, served as a backdrop for the **victims' rights movement** in that it identified how minorities were mistreated by the criminal justice system, both as offenders and victims. The ideologies of the women's movement and the civil rights movement merged to create a victims' rights movement largely supported by females, minorities, and young persons who pushed forward a victims' agenda that concentrated on making procedural changes in the operation of the criminal justice system (Smith, Sloan, & Ward, 1990).

■ CONTRIBUTIONS OF THE VICTIMS' RIGHTS MOVEMENT

We will discuss the particulars of programs and services available for crime victims today in Chapter 6, but to understand the importance of the victims' rights movement, its contributions should be outlined.

Early Programs for Crime Victims

In the United States, the first crime victims' compensation program was started in California in 1965. Victim compensation programs allow for victims to be financially compensated for uncovered costs resulting from their victimization. Not long after, in 1972, the first three victim assistance programs in the nation, two of which were rape crisis centers, were founded by volunteers. The first prototypes for what today are victim/witness assistance programs housed in district attorneys' offices were funded in 1974 by the Federal Law Enforcement Assistance Administration. These programs were designed to notify victims of critical dates in their cases and to create separate waiting areas for victims. Some programs began to make social services referrals for victims, providing them with input on criminal justice decisions that involved them, such as bail and plea bargains, notifying them about critical points in their cases—not just court dates—and going to court with them. Victim/witness assistance programs continue to provide similar services today.

Development of Victim Organizations

With women and children victims and their needs at the forefront of the victims' rights movement, other crime victims found that special services were not readily available to them. One group of victims whose voices emerged during the 1970s was persons whose loved ones had been murdered—called secondary victims. After having a loved one become a victim of homicide, many survivors found that people around them did not know how to act or how to help them. As one woman whose son was murdered remarked, "I soon found that murder is a taboo subject in our society. I found, to my surprise, that nice people apparently just don't get killed" (quoted in Young & Stein, 2004, p. 5). In response to the particular needs of homicide survivors, Families and Friends of Missing Persons was organized in 1974 and Parents of Murdered Children was formed in 1978. Mothers Against Drunk Driving was formed in 1980. These groups provide support for their members and others but also advocate for laws and policy changes that reflect the groups' missions. The National Organization for Victim Assistance was developed in 1975 to consolidate the purposes of the victims' movement and eventually to hold national conferences and provide training for persons working with crime victims.

Legislation and Policy

In 1980, Wisconsin became the first state to pass a Victims' Bill of Rights. Also in 1980, the National Organization for Victim Assistance created a new policy platform that included the initiation of a National Campaign for Victim Rights, which included a National Victims' Rights Week, implemented by then president Ronald Reagan. The attorney general at the time, William French Smith, created a Task Force on Violent Crime, which recommended that a President's Task Force on Victims of Crime be commissioned. President Reagan followed the recommendation. The President's Task Force held six hearings across the country from which 68 recommendations on how crime victims could be better assisted were made. Major initiatives were generated from these recommendations.

1. Federal legislation to fund state victim compensation programs and local victim assistance programs

2. Recommendations to criminal justice professionals and other professionals about how to better treat crime victims

3. Creation of a task force on violence within families

4. An amendment to the U.S. Constitution to provide crime victims' rights (yet to be passed)

As part of the first initiative, the Victims of Crime Act (1984) was passed and created the Office for Victims of Crime in the Department of Justice and established the Crime Victims Fund, which provides money to state victim compensation and local victim assistance programs. The Crime Victims Fund and victim compensation are discussed in detail in Chapter 6. The Victims of Crime Act was amended in 1988 to require victim compensation eligibility to include victims of domestic violence and drunk-driving accidents. It also expanded victim compensation coverage to nonresident commuters and visitors.

Legislation and policy continued to be implemented through the 1980s and 1990s. The Violent Crime Control and Law Enforcement Act, passed in 1994 by Congress, included the Violence Against Women Act. This law provides funding for research and for the development of professional partnerships to address the issues of violence against women. Annually, the attorney general reports to Congress the status of monies awarded under the act, including the amount of money awarded and the number of grants funded. The act also mandates that federal agencies engage in research specifically addressing violence against women.

In 1998, a publication called *New Directions From the Field: Victims' Rights and Services for the 21st Century* was released by then attorney general Janet Reno and the Office for Victims of Crime. This publication reviewed the status of the recommendations and initiatives put forth by President Reagan's task force. It also identified some 250 new recommendations for victims' rights, victim advocacy, and services. Also integral, during the 1990s, the federal government and many states implemented victims' rights legislation that enumerated specific rights to be guaranteed to crime victims. These rights will be discussed in detail in Chapter 6, but some basic rights typically afforded to victims include the right to be present at trial, to be provided a waiting area separate from the offender and people associated with the offender during stages of the criminal justice process, to be notified of key events in the criminal justice process, to testify at parole hearings, to be informed of rights, to be informed of compensation programs, and to be treated with dignity and respect. These rights continue to be implemented and expanded through various pieces of legislation, such as the Crime Victims' Rights Act, which is part of the Justice for All Act of 2004 signed into law by then president George W. Bush. Despite this push among the various legislatures, a federal victims' rights constitutional amendment has not been passed. Some states have been successful in amending their constitutions to ensure that the rights of crime victims are protected, but the U.S. Constitution has not been similarly amended. Various rights afforded to crime victims through these amendments are outlined in Chapter 6.

■ VICTIMOLOGY TODAY

Today, the field of victimology covers a wide range of topics, including crime victims, causes of victimization, consequences of victimization, interaction of victims with the criminal justice system, interaction of victims with other social service agencies and programs, and prevention of victimization. Each of these topics is discussed throughout the text. As a prelude to the text, a brief treatment of the contents is provided in the following subsections.

The Crime Victim

To study victimization, one of the first things victimologists needed to know was who was victimized by crime. In order to determine who victims were, victimologists looked at official data sources—namely, the Uniform Crime Reports—but found them to be imperfect sources for victim information because they do not include detailed information on crime victims. As a result, victimization surveys were developed to determine the extent to which people were victimized, the typical characteristics of victims, and the characteristics of victimization incidents. The most widely cited and used victimization survey is the National Crime Victimization Survey (NCVS), which is discussed in detail in Chapter 2.

From the NCVS and other victimization surveys, victimologists discovered that victimization is more prevalent than originally thought. Also, the "typical" victim was identified—a young male who lives in urban areas. This is not to say that other people are not victimized. In fact, children, women, and older people are all prone to victimization. These groups are discussed in detail in later chapters. In addition, victimologists have uncovered other vulnerable groups. Homeless individuals, persons with mental illness, disabled persons, and prisoners, all have been recognized as deserving of special attention given their victimization rates. Special populations vulnerable to victimization are discussed in Chapter 11.

The Causes of Victimization

It is difficult to know why a person is singled out and victimized by crime. Is it something he did? Did an offender choose a particular individual because she seemed like an easy target? Or does victimization occur because somebody is simply in the wrong place at the wrong time? Perhaps there is an element of "bad luck" or chance involved, but victimologists have developed some theories to explain victimization. Theories are sets of propositions that explain phenomena. In relation to victimology, victimization theories explain why some people are more likely than others to be victimized. As you will read in Chapter 2, the most widely utilized theories of victimization are routine activities theory and risky lifestyles theory. In the past two decades, however, victimologists and criminologists alike have developed additional theories and identified other correlates of victimization both generally and to explain why particular types of victimization, such as child abuse, occur.

Costs of Victimization

Victimologists are particularly interested in studying victims of crime because of the mass costs they often incur. These **costs of victimization** can be tangible, such as the cost of stolen or damaged property or the costs of receiving treatment at the emergency room, but they can also be harder to quantify. Crime victims may experience mental anguish or other more serious mental health issues such as posttraumatic stress disorder. Costs also include monies spent by the criminal justice system preventing and responding to crime and monies spent to assist crime victims. An additional consequence of victimization is fear of being a victim. This fear may be tied to the actual risk of being a victim or, as you will read about in Chapter 4, with the other consequences of victimization.

Recurring Victimization

An additional significant cost of victimization is the real risk of being victimized again that many victims face. Unfortunately, some victims do not suffer only a single victimization event but, rather, are victimized again and, sometimes, again and again. In this way, a certain subset of victims appears to be particularly vulnerable to revictimization. Research has begun to describe which particular victims are at risk of recurring victimization. In addition, theoretical explanations of recurring victimization have been proffered. The two main theories used to explain recurring victimization are state dependence and risk heterogeneity. Recurring victimization is discussed in Chapter 5.

The Crime Victim and the Criminal Justice System

Another experience of crime victims that is important to understand is how they interact with the criminal justice system. As is discussed in detail in Chapter 4, many persons who are victimized by crime do not report their experiences to the police. The reasons victims choose to remain silent, at least in terms of not calling the police, are varied but often include an element of suspicion and distrust of the police. Some victims worry that police will not take them seriously or will not think what happened to them is worth the police's time. Others may be worried that calling the police will effectively invoke a system response that cannot be erased or stopped, even when the victim wishes not to have the system move forward. An example of such a victim is one who does not want to call the police after being hit by her partner because she fears the police will automatically and mandatorily arrest him. Whatever the reason, without a report, the victim will not activate the formal criminal justice system, which will preclude an arrest and also may preclude the victim from receiving victim services explicitly tied to reporting.

When victims do report, they then enter the world of criminal justice, a world in which they are often seen as witnesses rather than victims, given that the U.S. criminal justice system recognizes crimes as harms against the state. This being the case, victims do not always find they are treated with dignity and respect, even though the victims' rights movement stresses the importance of doing so. The police are not the only ones with whom victims must contend. If an offender is apprehended and charged with a crime, the victim will also interact with the prosecutor and perhaps a judge. Fortunately, many police departments and prosecutors' offices offer victim assistance programs through which victims can receive information about available services. These programs also offer personal assistance and support, such as attending court sessions with the victim or helping submit a victim impact statement. The experience of the crime victim after the system is put into motion is an area of research ripe for study by victimologists. It is important to understand how victims view their interactions with the criminal justice system so that victim satisfaction can be maximized and any additional harm caused to the victim can be minimized. The criminal justice response will be discussed throughout this text, especially since different victim types have unique experiences with the police.

The Crime Victim and Social Services

The criminal justice system is not the only organization with which crime victims may come into contact. After being victimized, victims may need medical attention. As a result, emergency medical technicians, hospital and doctor's office staff, nurses, doctors, and clinicians may all be persons with whom victims interact. Although some of these professionals will have training or specialize in dealing with victims, others may not treat victims with the care and sensitivity they need. To combat this, sometimes victims will have persons from the police department or prosecutor's office with them at the hospital to serve as mediators and provide counsel. Also to aid victims, many hospitals and clinics now have sexual assault nurse examiners, who are specially trained in completing forensic and health exams for sexual assault victims.

In addition to medical professionals, mental health clinicians also often serve victims, as large numbers of victims seek mental health services after being victimized. Beyond mental health care, victims may use the services of social workers or other social service workers. But not all persons with whom victims interact as a consequence of being victimized are part of social service agencies accustomed to serving victims. Crime victims may seek assistance from insurance agents and repair and maintenance workers. Crime victims may need special accommodations from their employers or schools. In short, being victimized may touch multiple aspects of a person's life, and agencies, businesses, and organizations alike may find themselves in the position of dealing with the aftermath, one to which they may not be particularly attuned. The more knowledge people have about crime victimization and its impact on victims, the more likely victims will be satisfactorily treated.

Prevention

Knowing the extent to which people are victimized, who is likely targeted, and the reasons why people are victimized can help in the development of prevention efforts. To be effective, prevention programs and policies need to target the known causes of victimization. Although the offender is ultimately responsible for crime victimization, it is difficult to change offender behavior. Reliance on doing so limits complete prevention, since victimization involves at least two elements—the offender and the victim—that both need to be addressed to stop crime victimization. In addition, as noted by scholars, it is easier to reduce the opportunity than the motivation to offend (Clarke, 1980, 1982). Nonetheless, offenders should be discouraged from committing crimes, likely through informal mechanisms of social control. For example, colleges could provide crime awareness seminars directed at teaching leaders of student organizations how to dissuade their members from committing acts of aggression, using drugs or alcohol, or engaging in other conduct that could lead to victimization.

In addition to discouraging offenders, potential victims also play a key role in preventing victimization. Factors that place victims at risk need to be addressed to the extent that victims can change them. For example, since routine activities and lifestyles theories identify daily routines and risky lifestyles as being key risk factors for victimization, people should attempt to reduce their risk by making changes they are able to make. Other theories and risk factors related to victimization should also be targeted (these are discussed in Chapter 2). Because different types of victimization have different risk factors—and, therefore, different risk-reduction strategies—prevention will be discussed in each chapter that deals with a specific victim type.

As victimology today focuses on the victim, the causes of victimization, the consequences associated with victimization, and how the victim is treated within and outside the criminal justice system, this text will address these issues for the various types of crime victims. In this way, each chapter that deals with specific types of victimization—such as sexual victimization and intimate partner violence—will include an overview of the extent to which people are victimized, who is victimized, why they are victimized, the outcomes of being victimized, and the services provided to and challenges faced by victims. The specific remedies in place for crime victims are discussed in each chapter and also in a stand-alone chapter.

SUMMARY

- The field of victimology originated in the early to mid-1900s, with the first victimologists attempting to identify how victims contribute to their own victimization. To this end, the concepts of victim precipitation, victim facilitation, and victim provocation were examined.
- Hans von Hentig, Benjamin Mendelsohn, and Stephen Schafer each proposed victim typologies that were used to classify victims in terms of their responsibility or role in their own victimization.
- Marvin Wolfgang and Menachem Amir conducted the first empirical examinations of victim precipitation. Wolfgang studied homicides in Philadelphia, and Amir focused on forcible rapes. Wolfgang found that 26% of homicides were victim precipitated. Amir concluded that 19% of forcible rapes were precipitated by the victim.
- The victims' rights movement gained momentum during the 1960s. It was spurred by the civil rights and women's movements. This time period saw the recognition of children and women as victims of violence. The first victim services agencies were developed in the early 1970s.
- The victims' rights movement influenced the development of multiple advocacy groups, such as Mothers Against Drunk Driving, Families and Friends of Missing Persons, and Parents of Murdered Children.

- Important pieces of legislation came out of the victims' rights movement, including the Victims of Crime Act, the Violence Against Women Act, and the Crime Victims' Rights Act. Many states have victims' rights amendments and/or legislation that guarantee victim protections.
- Victimology today is concerned with the extent to which people are victimized, the different types of victimization they experience, the causes of victimization, the consequences associated with victimization, the criminal justice system's response to victims, and the response of other agencies and people. Victimology is a science—victimologists use the scientific method to study these areas.
- As victimologists become aware of who is likely to be victimized and the reasons for this, risk-reduction and prevention strategies can be developed. These should target not only offender behavior, but also opportunity. In this way, victims can play an important role in reducing their likelihood of being victimized.

DISCUSSION QUESTIONS

1. Compare and contrast victim precipitation, victim facilitation, and victim provocation.

2. Why do you think the first explorations into victimization in terms of explaining why people are victimized centered not on offender behavior but on victim behavior?

3. What are the reasons behind labeling crimes as acts against the state rather than against victims?

4. How does the victims' rights movement correspond to the treatment of offenders and rights afforded to offenders?

5. Does examining victim behavior when attempting to identify causes of victimization lead to victim blaming? Is it wrong to consider the role of the victim?

KEY TERMS

victimology

lex talionis

retribution

restitution

Code of Hammurabi

victim precipitation

victim facilitation

victim provocation

Hans von Hentig

Benjamin Mendelsohn

Stephen Schafer

Marvin Wolfgang

subintentional homicide

Menachem Amir

National Crime Survey

women's movement

civil rights movement

victims' rights movement

costs of victimization

INTERNET RESOURCES

An Oral History of the Crime Victim Assistance Field Video and Audio Archive (http://vroh.uakron.edu/index.php)

This website contains information from the Victim Oral History Project, intended to capture the development and evolution of the crime victims' movement. You will find video clips of interviews with more than 50 persons critical to this movement, in which they discuss their contributions to and perspectives of the field.

Crime in the United States (http://www.fbi.gov/about-us/cjis/ucr/crime-in-the-u.s/2013/crime-in-the-u.s.-2013)

The Federal Bureau of Investigation compiles all the information for both the Uniform Crime Reports and National Incident-Based Reporting System. The information is then put into several annual publications, such as *Crime in the United States* and *Hate Crime Statistics*. The data for these statistics are provided by nearly 17,000 law enforcement agencies across the United States. This website provides the crime information for 2013.

Crime Prevention Tips (http://www.crimepreventiontips.org/)

This website provides many tips on how to reduce your chances of becoming a crime victim. There is also a section to help you determine whether you have been a crime victim. Some of the prevention tips specifically address how to be safer when you use public transportation and on college campuses.

The American Society of Victimology (http://www.american-society-victimology.us)

This organization advances the discipline of victimology by promoting evidence-based practices and providing leadership in research and education. The website contains information about victimology and victimologists. This organization looks at advancements in victimology through research, practice, and teaching.

EXTENT, THEORIES, AND FACTORS OF VICTIMIZATION

It was not exactly a typical night for Polly. Instead of studying at the library as she normally did during the week, she decided to meet two of her friends at a local bar. They spent the evening catching up and drinking a few beers before they decided to head home. Since Polly lived within walking distance of the bar, she bid her friends goodnight and started on her journey home. It was dark out, but since she had never confronted trouble in the neighborhood before—even though it was in a fairly crime-ridden part of a large city—she felt relatively safe.

As Polly walked by an alley, two young men whom she had never seen before stepped out, and one of them grabbed her arm and demanded that she give them her school bag, in which she had her wallet, computer, keys, and phone. Since Polly refused, the other man shoved her while the first man grabbed her bag. Despite holding on as tightly as she could, the men were able to take her bag before running off into the night. Slightly stunned, Polly stood there trying to calm down. Without her bag, which held her phone and keys, she felt there was little she could do other than continue to walk home and hope her roommates were there to let her in. As she walked home, she wondered why she had such bad luck. Why was she targeted? Was she simply in "the wrong place at the wrong time," or did she do something to place herself in harm's way? Although it is hard to know why Polly was victimized, we can compare her to other victims to see how similar she is to them. To this end, a description of the "typical" crime victim is presented in this section. But what about why she was targeted? Fortunately, we can use the theories presented in this section to understand why Polly fell victim on that particular night.

■ MEASURING VICTIMIZATION

Before we can begin to understand *why* some people are the victims of crime and others are not, we must first know how often victimization occurs. Also important is knowing who the typical crime victim is. Luckily, these characteristics of victimization can be readily gleaned from existing data sources.

Uniform Crime Reports (UCRs)

Begun in 1929, the **Uniform Crime Report (UCR)** shows the amount of crime known to the police in a year. Police departments around the country submit to the Federal Bureau of Investigation (FBI) monthly law enforcement reports on crimes that are reported to them or that they otherwise know about. The FBI then compiles these data and each year publishes a report called *Crime in the United States,* which details the crime that occurred in the United States for the year. This report includes information on eight offenses, known as the Part I index offenses: murder and nonnegligent manslaughter, forcible rape, robbery, aggravated assault, burglary, larceny-theft, motor vehicle theft, and arson. Arrest data are also listed in the report on Part II offenses, which include an additional 21 crime categories.

Advantages and Disadvantages

The UCR is a valuable data source for learning about crime and victimization. Because more than 90% of the population is represented by agencies participating in the UCR program, it provides an approximation of the total amount of crime experienced by almost all Americans (FBI, 2006). It presents the number of crimes for regions, states, cities, towns, areas under tribal law enforcement, and colleges and universities. It does so annually so that crime trends can be determined for the country and for these geographical units. Another benefit of the UCR is that crime characteristics are also reported. It includes demographic information (age, sex, and race) on people who are arrested and some information on the crimes, such as location and time of occurrence.

Despite these advantages, it does not provide detailed information on crime victims. Also important to consider, the UCR includes information

PHOTO 2.1

Polly, on her way home from the bar.

Photo Credit: iStockphoto.com/Rasmus Rasmussen.

only on crimes that are reported to the police or of which the police are aware. In this way, all crimes that occur are not represented, especially since, as discussed below, crime victims often do not report their victimization to the police. Another limitation of the UCR as a crime data source is that the Part I index offenses do not cover the wide range of crimes that occur, such as simple assault and sexual assaults other than forcible rape, and federal crimes are not counted. Furthermore, the UCR uses the hierarchy rule. If more than one Part I offense occurs within the same incident report, the law enforcement agency counts only the highest offense in the reporting process (FBI, 2009). These exclusions also contribute to the UCR's underestimation of the extent of crime. Accuracy of the UCR data is also affected by law enforcement's willingness to participate in the program and to do so by reporting to the FBI all offenses of which they are aware.

Crime as Measured by the UCR

Nonetheless, the UCR can be used to paint a picture of crime in the United States. In 2012, the police became aware of 1,214,462 violent crimes and 8,975,438 property crimes. According to the UCR data, the most common offense is larceny-theft. Aggravated assaults are the most common violent crime, although they are outnumbered by larceny-thefts. The typical criminal is a young (less than 30 years old), White male (although young, Black, males have the highest offending rates) (FBI, 2012a).

National Incident-Based Reporting System

As noted, the UCR includes little information about the characteristics of criminal incidents. To overcome this deficiency, the FBI began the National Incident-Based Reporting System (NIBRS), an expanded data collection effort that includes detailed information about crimes. Agencies participating in the NIBRS collect information on each crime incident and arrest in 22 different offense categories (Group A offenses) that encompass 46 specific crimes. Arrest data are reported for an additional 11 offenses (Group B offenses). Information about the offender, the victim, injury, location, property loss, and weapons is included (FBI, n.d.-b).

Although the NIBRS represents an advancement of the UCR program, not all law enforcement agencies participate in the system. As such, crime trends similar to those based on national data produced by the UCR are not yet available. As more agencies come online, the NIBRS data will likely be an even more valuable tool for understanding patterns and trends of crime victimization.

The National Crime Victimization Survey

As noted, the UCR and NIBRS have some limitations as crime data sources, particularly when information on victimization is of interest. To provide a picture of the extent to which individuals experience a range of crime victimizations, the Bureau of Justice Statistics (BJS) began, in 1973, a national survey of U.S. households. Originally called the National Crime Survey, it provides a picture of crime incidents and victims. In 1993, the BJS redesigned the survey, making extensive methodological changes, and renamed it the National Crime Victimization Survey (NCVS).

The NCVS is administered by the U.S. Census Bureau to a nationally representative sample of 92,390 households in 2012 (Truman, Langton, & Planty, 2013). Each member of participating households who is 12 years old or older completes the survey, resulting in 162,940 persons being interviewed in 2012 (Truman et al., 2013). Each household selected remains in the study for 3 years and completes seven interviews 6 months apart. Each interview serves a **bounding** purpose by giving respondents a concrete event to reference (i.e., since the last interview) when answering questions in the next interview. Bounding is used to improve recall. In general, the first interview is conducted in person, with subsequent interviews taking place either in person or over the phone (Truman et al., 2013).

The NCVS is conducted in two stages. In the first stage, individuals are asked if they experienced any of seven types of victimization during the previous 6 months. The victimizations that respondents are asked about are rape and sexual assault, robbery, aggravated and simple assault, personal theft, household burglary, motor vehicle theft, and theft. The initial questions asked in the first stage are known as **screen questions,** which are used to cue respondents or jog their memories as to whether they experienced any of these criminal victimizations in the previous 6 months. An example of a screen question is shown in Table 2.1. In the second stage, if the respondent answers affirmatively to any of the screen questions, the respondent then completes an **incident report** for each victimization experienced. In this way, if an individual stated that he or she had experienced one theft and one aggravated assault, he or she would fill out two incident reports—one for the theft and a separate one for the aggravated assault. In the incident report, detailed questions are asked about the incident, such as where it happened, whether it was reported to the police and why the victim did or did not report it, who the offender was, and whether the victim did anything to protect himself or herself during the incident. Table 2.2 shows an example of a question from the incident report. As you can see, responses to the questions from the incident report can help reveal the context of victimization.

Another advantage of this two-stage procedure is that the incident report is used to determine what, if any, incident occurred. The incident report, as discussed, includes detailed questions about what happened, including questions that are used to classify an incident into its appropriate crime victimization type. For example, in order for a rape to be counted as such, the questions in the incident report that concern the elements of rape, which are discussed in Chapter 8 (force, penetration, and consent), must be answered affirmatively for the incident to be counted as rape in the NCVS. This process is fairly conservative in that all elements of the criminal victimization must have occurred for it to be included in the estimates of that type of crime victimization.

The NCVS has several advantages as a measure of crime victimization. First, it includes in its estimates of victimization several offenses that are not included in Part I of the UCR; for example, simple assault and sexual assault are both included in NCVS estimates of victimization. Second, the NCVS does not measure only crimes reported to the police as does the UCR. Third, the NCVS asks individuals to recall incidents that occurred only during the previous 6 months, which is a relatively short recall period. In addition, its two-stage measurement process allows for a more conservative way of estimating the amount of victimization that occurs each year in that incidents are counted only if they meet the criteria for inclusion.

Despite these advantages, the NCVS is not without its limitations. Estimates of crime victimization depend on the ability of respondents to accurately recall what happened to them during the previous 6 months. Even though the NCVS attempts to aid in recall by spanning a short period (6 months) and by providing bounding via the previous survey administration, it is still possible that individuals will not be completely accurate in recounting the particulars of an incident. Bounding and using a short recall period also do not combat against someone intentionally being misleading or lying or answering in a way meant to please the interviewer. Another possible limitation of the NCVS is its treatment of high-frequency repeat victimizations. Called **series victimizations**, these incidents are those in which a person experiences the same type of victimization during the six-month recall period at such a high rate that he or she cannot recall specific details about each incident or even recall each incident. When this occurs, an incident report is only completed for the most recent incident, and incident counts are only included for up to 10 incidents (Truman et al., 2013). As such, estimates of victimization may be lower than the actual amount because the cap for counting series victimizations is 10. On the other hand, even without recalling specific detail, these incidents are included in estimates of victimization. Including series victimizations in this way reveals little effect on the trends in violence estimates (Truman et al., 2013). In addition, murder and "victimless" crimes such as prostitution and drug use are not included in NCVS estimates of crime victimization. Another limitation is that crime that occurs to commercial establishments is not included. Beyond recall issues, the NCVS sample is selected from U.S. households. This sample may not be truly representative, as it excludes individuals who are institutionalized, such as persons in prison, and does not include homeless people. Remember, too, that only those persons ages 12 and over are included. As a result, estimates about victimization of children cannot be determined.

Table 2.1 ■ Example of Screen Question From NCVS

Other than any incidents already mentioned, has anyone attacked or threatened you in any of these ways (exclude telephone threats)?

  a. With any weapon, for instance, a gun or knife

  b. With anything like a baseball bat, frying pan, scissors, or stick

  c. By something thrown, such as a rock or bottle

  d. Include any grabbing, punching, or choking

  e. Any rape, attempted rape, or other type of sexual attack

  f. Any face-to-face threats

OR

  g. Any attack or threat or use of force by anyone at all? Please mention it even if you are not certain it was a crime.

Source: NCVS-1 Basic Screen Questionnaire. Bureau of Justice Statistics, U.S. Department of Justice. Washington, D.C.

Table 2.2 ■ Example of Question From Incident Report in NCVS

Did the offender have a weapon such as a gun or knife, or something to use as a weapon, such as a bottle or wrench?

Source: Crime Incident Report. National Crime Victimization Survey. Bureau of Justice Statistics, U.S. Department of Justice. Washington, D.C.

Extent of Crime Victimization

Each year, the BJS publishes *Criminal Victimization in the United States,* which is a report about crime victimization as measured by the NCVS. From this report, we can see what the most typical victimizations are and who is most likely to be victimized. In 2012, more than 26,465,570 victimizations were experienced among the nation's households (Truman et al., 2013). Property crimes were much more likely to be experienced compared with violent crimes; 6.8 million violent crime victimizations were experienced compared with 19.6 million property crime victimizations. The most common type of property crime reported was theft, while simple assault was the most commonly occurring violent crime (see Figure 2.1).

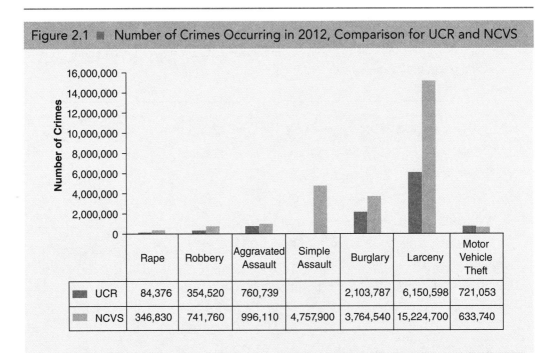

Figure 2.1 ■ Number of Crimes Occurring in 2012, Comparison for UCR and NCVS

	Rape	Robbery	Aggravated Assault	Simple Assault	Burglary	Larceny	Motor Vehicle Theft
■ UCR	84,376	354,520	760,739		2,103,787	6,150,598	721,053
▨ NCVS	346,830	741,760	996,110	4,757,900	3,764,540	15,224,700	633,740

Source: U.S. Department of Justice.

Notes: The UCR includes only forcible rape, while the NCVS includes both rape and sexual assault. The UCR measures only aggravated assault, while the NCVS includes both aggravated and simple assault.

The Typical Victimization and Victim

The typical crime victim can also be identified from the NCVS. For all violent victimizations except for rape and sexual assaults, males are more likely to be victimized than females. Persons who are Black/African American, American Indian/Alaska Native, or two or more races have higher victimization rates than persons who are White, Asian/Native Hawaiian/ other Pacific Islander, or Hipanic/Latino, and those under the age of 24 also have higher victimization rates than older persons (Truman et al., 2013). Characteristics of victimization incidents are also evident. Less than half of all victimizations experienced by individuals in the NCVS are reported to the police. Property crimes are less likely to be reported than are violent crimes, with some crimes being much more likely to come to the attention of police than others. For example, rape and sexual assault are the least likely of all violent crimes to be reported, while aggravated assault is the most likely to be reported. Over three fourths of motor vehicle thefts are reported to the police, but only about one fourth of all thefts are (Truman et al., 2013). This disjuncture in reporting is likely tied to features of the victimization and motivations for reporting. For example, the lack of reporting may be related in part to the fact that most victims of violent crime know their offender; most often, victims identified their attacker as a friend or acquaintance. Strangers perpetrated only about one third of violent victimizations in the NCVS. Reporting, on the other hand, may be tied to wanting to secure property back, especially a car! In addition, when a person has his or her car stolen, a police report is necessary for insurance purposes, so a person may be particularly motivated to report this type of victimization to the police. Returning now to incident characteristics, females are more likely than males to be victimized by an intimate partner. In only 1 in 5 incidents did the offender have a weapon, and about 23% of violent crimes resulted in the victim being physically injured (Truman et al., 2013). Now that you know the characteristics of the typical victimization and the typical crime victim, how do Polly and her victimization compare?

The International Crime Victims Survey

As you may imagine, there are many other self-report victimization surveys that are used to understand more specific forms of victimization, such as sexual victimization and those that occur outside the United States. Many of these will be discussed in later sections. One oft-cited survey of international victimization is the International Crime Victims Survey (ICVS), which was created to provide a standardized survey to compare crime victims' experiences across countries (van Dijk, van Kesteren, & Smit, 2008). The first round of the survey was conducted in 1989 and was repeated in 1992, 1996, 2000, and 2004/2005. Collectively, more than 340,000 persons have been surveyed in more than 78 countries as part of the ICVS program (van Dijk et al., 2008). Respondents are asked about 10 different types of victimization that they could have experienced: car theft, theft from or out of a car, motorcycle theft, bicycle theft, attempted or completed burglary, sexual victimization (rapes and sexual assault), threats, assaults, robbery, and theft of personal property (van Dijk et al., 2008). If a person has experienced any of these offenses, he or she then answers follow-up questions about the incident. This survey has provided estimates of the extent of crime victimization in many countries and regions of the world. In addition, characteristics of crime victims and incidents have been produced from these surveys. Similar to the NCVS and the ICVS, the Crime Survey for England and Wales (CSEW) is conducted to measure the extent and characteristics of victimization in England and Wales. Read the Focus on International Issues box for more information about the CSEW.

■ THEORIES AND EXPLANATIONS OF VICTIMIZATION

Now that you have an idea about who the typical crime victim is, you are probably wondering why some people are more likely than others to find themselves victims of crime. Is it because those people provoke the victimization, as von Hentig and his contemporaries thought? Is it because crime victims are perceived by offenders to be more vulnerable than others? Is there some personality trait that influences victimization risk? All these factors may play at least some role in why victimization occurs to particular people. The following chapters address these possibilities.

The Link Between Victimization and Offending

One facet about victimization that cannot be ignored is the link between offending and victimization and offenders and victims. As mentioned in Chapter 1, the first forays into the study of victims included a close look at how victims contribute to their own victimization. In this way, victims were not always assumed to be innocents; rather, some victims were seen as being at least partly responsible for bringing on their victimization—for instance, by being an offender who is victimized when the victim fights back. Although the field of victimology has moved from trying to place blame on victims, the recognition that offenders and victims are often linked—and often the same person—has aided in the understanding of why people are victimized.

FOCUS ON INTERNATIONAL ISSUES

Victimization surveys are also conducted in other countries. The CSEW is a victimization survey of persons aged 16 and over living in England and Wales. Beginning in 1982, the CSEW, formerly known as the British Crime Survey until April 1, 2012, was conducted every two years until 2001, when it was changed to reflect victimizations during the previous 12 months. Using Computer Assisted Personal Interviewing to aid in personal interviewing, in the 2010/2011 CSEW, 51,000 people were surveyed—47,000 adults and an additional 4,000 children in the 10-15-year-old supplement. Persons are asked about victimizations that their households and themselves experienced. To get the sample, about 1,000 interviews are conducted in each police force area. If individuals answer "yes" to any screen question about victimization, they complete a victim module that includes detailed questions about the event. Findings from the 2010/2011 CSEW indicate that 23% of the sample had experienced a victimization during the previous 12 months. Of these victims, 30% experienced more than one victimization.

Source: Adapted from Crime in England and Wales (2010/2011). Home Office Statistical Bulletin 10/11. Published 14 July 2011.

Victim and Offender Characteristics

The typical victim and the typical offender have many commonalities. As mentioned before in our discussion of the NCVS, the groups with the highest rates of violent victimization are young, Black males. The UCR also provides information on offenders. The groups with the highest rates of violent offending are also young, Black males. The typical victim and the typical offender, then, share common demographics. In addition, both victims and offenders are likely to live in urban areas. Thus, individuals who spend time with people who have the characteristics of offenders are more likely to be victimized than others.

Explaining the Link Between Victimization and Offending

Some even argue that victims and offenders are often one and the same, with offenders being more likely to be victimized and vice versa. It is not hard to understand why this may be the case. Offending can be viewed as part of a risky lifestyle. Individuals who engage in offending are exposed more frequently to people and contexts in which victimization is likely to occur (Lauritsen, Laub, & Sampson, 1992).

There also may be a link between victimization and offending that is part of a broader cultural belief in the acceptability and sometimes necessity of violence, known as the subculture of violence theory. This theory proposes that for certain subgroups of the population and in certain areas, violence is part of a value system that supports the use of violence, in response to disrespect in particular (Wolfgang & Ferracuti, 1967). In this way, when a subculture that supports violence exists, victims will be likely to respond by retaliating. Offenders may initiate violence that leads to their victimization by, for example, getting into a physical fight to resolve a dispute. Recent research shows that the victim–offender overlap does indeed vary across neighborhoods and that this variation is related to the neighborhood's strength of attachment to the "code of the streets" and degree of structural deprivation (Berg & Loeber, 2011; Berg, Stewart, Schreck, & Simons, 2012).

Being victimized may be related to offending in ways that are not directly tied to retaliation. In fact, being victimized at one point in life may increase the likelihood that a person will engage in delinquency and crime later in life. This link has been found especially in individuals who are abused during childhood. As discussed in Chapter 10 on victimization at the beginning and end of life, those who are victimized as children are significantly more likely than those who do not experience child abuse to be arrested in adulthood (Widom, 2000) or to engage in violence and property offending (Menard, 2002).

The reasons why victimization may lead to participation in crime are not fully understood, but it may be that being victimized carries psychological consequences, such as depression, anxiety, or posttraumatic stress disorder, that can lead to coping through the use of alcohol or drugs. Victimization may also carry physical consequences, such as brain damage, that can further impede success later in life. Cognitive ability may also be tempered by maltreatment, particularly in childhood, which can hinder school performance. Behavior may also change as a result of being victimized. People may experience problems in their interpersonal relationships or become violent or aggressive. Whatever the reason, it is evident that victimization and offending are intimately intertwined.

Insomuch as victimization and offending are linked, it makes sense then, as you will see in the following sections, that the same influences on offending may also affect victimization and hence may explain the link between victimization and offending. This is not to say that the only explanations of victimization should be tied to or be an extension of explanations of offending—just remember that when you read about the research that has used criminological theories to explain victimization, it is largely because of the connection between victimization and offending. The link between victimization and offending is more thoroughly explored in Chapter 3.

Routine Activities and Lifestyles Theory

In the 1970s, two theoretical perspectives—**routine activities and lifestyles theory**—were put forth that both linked crime victimization risk to the fact that victims had to come into contact with a potential offender. Before discussing these theories in detail, first, it is important to understand what a **victimization theory** is. A victimization theory is generally a set of testable propositions designed to explain why a person is victimized. Both routine activities and lifestyles theories propose that a person's victimization risk can best be understood by the extent to which the victim's routine activities or lifestyle creates opportunities for a motivated offender to commit crime.

In developing routine activities theory, Lawrence Cohen and Marcus Felson (1979) proposed that a person's routine activities, or daily routine patterns, impact risk of being a crime victim. Insomuch as a person's routine activities bring him or her into contact with **motivated offenders,** crime victimization risk abounds. Cohen and Felson thought that motivated offenders were plentiful and that their motivation to offend did not need to be explained. Rather, their selection of particular victims was more interesting. Cohen and Felson noted that there must be something about particular targets, both individuals and places, that encouraged selection by these motivated offenders. In fact, those individuals deemed to be **suitable targets** based on their attractiveness would be chosen by offenders. Attractiveness relates to qualities about the target, such as ease of transport, which is why a burglar may break into a home and leave with an iPod or laptop computer rather than a couch. Attractiveness is further evident when the target does not have **capable guardianship.** Capable guardianship is conceived as means by which a person or target can be effectively guarded to prevent a victimization from occurring. Guardianship is typically considered to be *social,* when the presence of another person makes someone less attractive as a target. Guardianship can also be provided through *physical* means, such as a home with a burglar alarm or a person who carries a weapon for self-protection. A home with a burglar alarm and a person who carries a weapon are certainly less attractive crime targets! When these three elements—motivated offenders, suitable targets, and lack of capable guardianship—coalesce in time and space, victimization is likely to occur.

When Cohen and Felson (1979) originally developed their theory, they focused on predatory crimes—those that involve a target and offender making contact. They originally were interested in explaining changes in rates of these types of crime over time. In doing so, they argued that people's routines had shifted since World War II, taking them away from home and making their homes attractive targets. People began spending more time outside the home, in leisure activities and going to and from work and school. As people spent more time interacting with others, they were more likely to come into contact with motivated offenders. Capable guardianship was unlikely to be present; thus, the risk of criminal victimization increased. Cohen and Felson also linked the increase in crime to the production of durable goods. Electronics began to be produced in portable sizes, making them easier to steal. Similarly, cars and other expensive items that could be stolen, reused, and resold became targets. As Cohen and Felson saw it, prosperity of society could produce an increase in criminal victimization rather than a decline! Also important, they linked victimization to everyday activities rather than to social ills, such as poverty.

Michael Hindelang, Michael Gottfredson, and James Garofalo's (1978) lifestyles theory is a close relative of routine activities theory. Hindelang and colleagues posited that certain lifestyles or behaviors place people in situations in which victimization is likely to occur. Your lifestyle, such as going to bars or working late at night in relative seclusion, places you at more risk of being a crime victim than others. Although the authors of lifestyles theory did not specify how opportunity structures risk as clearly as did the authors of routine activities theory, at its heart, lifestyles theory closely resembles routine activities theory and its propositions. As a person comes into contact—via lifestyle and behavior—with potential offenders, he or she is likely creating opportunities for crime victimization to occur. The lifestyle factors identified by Hindelang and his colleagues that create opportunities for victimization are the people with whom one associates, working outside the home, and engaging in leisure activities. In this way, a person who associates with criminals, works outside the home, and participates in activities—particularly at night, away from home, and with nonfamily members—is a more likely target for personal victimization than others. Hindelang and colleagues noted that a person's lifestyle is structured by social constraints and role expectations. That is, because of a person's demographic characteristics, he or she may be afforded less opportunity to engage in particular activities. Consider the fact that females are socialized differently from males. Females may be expected to be the caretaker of the home and, when younger, may be supervised more closely than males. Accordingly, females may spend more time at home and spend more time under the supervision of their parents or other guardians. Given these social constraints and role expectations, females may be less likely to engage in activities outside the home that would place them at risk for victimization; hence, explaining why females are at lower risk for victimization than males.

Hindelang et al. (1978) further delineated why victimization risk is higher for some people than others using the **principle of homogamy.** According to this principle, the more frequently a person comes into contact with persons in demographic groups with likely offenders, the more likely it is the person will be victimized. This frequency may be a function of demographics or lifestyle. For example, males are more likely to be criminal offenders than females. Males, then, are at greater risk for victimization because they are more likely to spend time with other males. Now that you know about routine activities theory, do you think Polly's routines or lifestyle placed her at risk for being victimized? Today, researchers largely treat routine activities theory and lifestyles theory interchangeably and often refer to them as the routine activities and lifestyles theory perspectives.

One of the reasons that routine activities and lifestyles theories have been the prevailing theories of victimization for more than 30 years is the wide empirical support researchers have found when testing them. It has been shown that a person's routine activities and lifestyles impact risk of being sexually victimized (Cass, 2007; Fisher, Daigle, & Cullen, 2010a, 2010b; Mustaine & Tewksbury, 1999, 2007; Schwartz & Pitts, 1995). This perspective also has been used to explain auto theft (Rice & Smith, 2002), stalking (Mustaine & Tewksbury, 1999), cybercrime victimization (Holt & Bossler, 2009), adolescent violent victimization (Lauritsen et al., 1992), theft (Mustaine & Tewksbury, 1998), victimization at work (Lynch, 1997), and street robbery (Groff, 2007).

RIPPED FROM THE HEADLINES

At a pre-MTV Video Music Awards party hosted by Chris Brown, multiple gun shots rang out inside a packed club in West Hollywood. Several people were hit, including Suge Knight, the founder of Death Row Records. This was not the first time that Knight has been shot—he was shot at another pre-awards party that was hosted by Kanye West and he was driving the vehicle when Tupac Shakur was shot and killed (and was shot himself). Although the exact motives behind Knight's shooting are unknown, the preliminary investigation has linked the shooting to gang ties. Knight has been connected to the Compton's Bloods gang and several known members were at the party. Knight also has a criminal history, having spent time in prison for violating probation regarding an assault case and for violating parole, when he assaulted a parking-lot attendant. Can you apply lifestyles theory to the shooting that occurred at the party?

Source: Adapted from Branson-Potts, H. (2014, August 24). Suge Knight, 2 others shot at Chris Brown party on Sunset Strip. *LA Times.* http://www.latimes.com/local/lanow/la-me-ln-suge-knight-chris-brown-20140824-story.html.

Structural and Social Process Factors

In addition to routine activities and lifestyles theory, other factors also increase a person's risk of being victimized. Key components of life—such as **neighborhood context,** family, friends, and personal interaction—also play a role in victimization.

Neighborhood Context

We have already discussed how certain individuals are more at risk of becoming victims of crime than others. So far, we have tied this risk to factors related to the person's lifestyle. Where that person lives and spends time, however, may also place him or her at risk of victimization. Indeed, you are probably not surprised to learn that certain areas have higher rates of victimization than others. Some areas are so crime-prone that they are considered to be **hot spots** for crime. Highlighted by Lawrence Sherman (Sherman, Martin, & Buerger, 1989), hot spots are areas that have a concentrated amount of crime. He found through examining police call data in Minneapolis that only 3% of all locations made up most calls to the police. A person living in or frequenting a hot spot will be putting himself or herself in danger. The features of these hot spots and other high-risk areas may create opportunities for victimization that, independent of a person's lifestyle or demographic characteristics, enhance chances of being victimized.

What is it about certain areas that relates them to victimization? A body of recent research has identified many features, particularly of neighborhoods (notice we are not discussing hot spots specifically). One factor related to victimization is **family structure.** Robert Sampson (1985), in his seminal piece on neighborhoods and crime, found that neighborhoods that have a large percentage of female-headed households have higher rates of theft and violent victimization. He also found that **structural density,** as measured by the percentage of units in structures of five or more units, is positively related to victimization. **Residential mobility,** or the percentage of persons 5 years and older living in a different house from 5 years before, also predicted victimization.

Beyond finding that the structure of a neighborhood influences victimization rates for that area, it also has been shown that neighborhood features influence personal risk. In this way, living in a neighborhood that is disadvantaged places individuals at risk of being victimized, even if they do not have risky lifestyles or other characteristics related to victimization (Browning & Erickson, 2009). For example, neighborhood disadvantage and neighborhood residential instability are related to experiencing violent victimization at the hands of an intimate partner (Benson, Fox, DeMaris, & Van Wyk, 2003). Using the notions of collective efficacy, it makes sense that neighborhoods that are disadvantaged are less able to mobilize effective sources of informal social control (Sampson, Raudenbush, & Earls, 1997). Informal social controls are often used as mechanisms to maintain order, stability, and safety in neighborhoods. When communities do not have strong informal mechanisms in place, violence and other deviancy are likely to abound. Such communities are less safe; hence, their residents are more likely to be victimized than residents of more socially organized areas. Recent research has linked self-control with neighborhood disadvantage to victimization risk. Gibson's (2012) research using data from the Project on Human Development in Chicago Neighborhoods revealed that in the most disadvantaged neighborhoods, low self-control's relationship to violent victimization was low, but its effect on violent victimization was higher in neighborhoods that were the least disadvantaged.

PHOTO 2.2

This area may be a "hot spot" due to lots of people milling about at night.

Photo Credit: © Stockbyte/Thinkstock.

Exposure to Delinquent Peers

The neighborhood context is but one factor related to risk of victimization. Social process factors, such as peers and family, are also important in understanding crime victimization. Generally, one of the strongest influences on youth is their peers. Peer pressure can lead people, especially juveniles, to act in ways they normally would not and to engage in behavior they otherwise would not. Having **delinquent peers** places youth not only at risk of engaging in delinquent behavior—juvenile delinquency does, after all, often take place in groups— but also of being victimized ((Lauritsen, Laub, & Sampson, 1991; Schreck & Fisher, 2004). Spending time with delinquent peers places people at risk of being victimized because, as lifestyles and routine activities theory suggests, spending time in the presence of motivated offenders increases risk. Never mind that these would-be offenders are your friends! Another reason having delinquent peers may be related to victimization is that a person may find himself or herself in risky situations (such as being present for a fight) in which being harmed is not unlikely. In this situation, it may not be your friends per se who harm you, but others involved in the fight may attack you, or you may feel the need to come to the aid of your friends. In a specific case of having delinquent peers, being a member of a gang increases a young person's risk of experiencing violence (Taylor, Peterson, Esbensen, & Freng, 2007).

Family

Especially during adolescence, the family also plays an important role in individual experiences. Having strong attachments to family members, particularly parents, is likely to insulate a person from many negative events, including being victimized. Not surprisingly, research has found that weak emotional attachment between family members is a strong predictor of victimization (Esbensen, Huizinga, & Menard, 1999; Lauritsen et al., 1992). This may be due to parents being unable and unwilling to exert control over the behavior of their children, such that they are more likely to end up in risky situations. Family units may also spend more time together when there is strong attachment, thus reducing exposure to motivated offenders. Youth may also be less likely to place themselves in risky situations because they do not want to disappoint their parents, as they place high value on the relationships they have with them. In these ways, emotional attachment to family members serves to reduce risky behavior. At this point, you may be noting that familial attachment may be related to lifestyles and routine activities theory—and you would be right! Research investigating the link between familial attachment and victimization has found that the better a person feels about his or her family, the less likely he or she is to be victimized (Schreck & Fisher, 2004).

Social Learning Theory

According to social learning theory (Akers, 1973), criminal behavior is learned behavior. Specifically, it is learned through differential association (spending time with delinquent or criminal others) whereby imitation or modeling of behavior occurs. A person learns behavior as well as the definitions about behavior, such as whether or not it is acceptable to engage in crime. The likelihood that a behavior will persist depends on the degree of reward or punishment. In this way, behaviors are differentially reinforced, and people continue to engage in behaviors that are rewarded and cease to engage in behaviors that are punished. When a behavior is rewarded, the definitions favorable toward that act will eventually outweigh the definitions against that act. Although this social learning process was originally posited to explain delinquency, it has also been used to explain victimization, especially intimate partner violence in the sense that children who are exposed to violence between parents in the home are more likely to be victims of intimate partner violence than others later in life (see Chapter 9 for a more detailed discussion). Other research has linked social learning theory to stalking victimization (Fox, Nobles, & Akers, 2011).

Control-Balance Theory

A general theory of deviancy, **control-balance theory,** may also apply to victimization. Developed by Charles Tittle (1995, 1997), this theory proposes that the amount of control that people possess over others and the amount of control to which one is subject factor into their risk of engaging in deviancy. When considered together, a **control ratio** can be determined for individuals. Control-balance theory posits that when the control a person has exceeds the amount of control he or she is subject to, that person has a **control surplus.** When the amount of control a person exercises is outweighed by the control he or she is subject to, that person has a **control deficit.** When a person has a control surplus or deficit, he or she is likely to be predisposed toward deviant behavior. The type of deviant behavior to which a person will be predisposed depends on the control ratio. A control surplus is linked to autonomous forms of deviance such as exploitation of others. Control deficits, on the other hand, are linked to repressive forms of deviance such as defiance.

While not expressly a theory of victimization, Piquero and Hickman (2003) used control-balance theory to explain victimization. They proposed that having a control surplus or control deficit would increase victimization risk as compared with having a control balance. Individuals with a control surplus are used to having their needs and desires met and have a desire to extend their control. In short, they engage in risky behaviors (in terms of victimization) because there is little to restrain their actions. They may treat others who have control deficits with disrespect in such a way that those individuals act out and victimize them. Those with control deficits are at risk for victimization for different reasons. So used to having little control at their disposal, they lack the confidence or belief that they can protect themselves and are, thus, vulnerable targets. They may also try to overcome their control deficits by lashing out or victimizing those who exercise control over them. Piquero and Hickman tested control-balance's ability to predict victimization and found that both control deficits and control surpluses predicted general and theft victimization.

Social Interactionist Perspective

Richard Felson (1992) posited that distress may be related to victimization. When experiencing stress, peoples' behavior and demeanor are impacted. People are more likely to break rules and to be generally irritating to others. Distressed individuals, thus, may entice a certain measure of aggression from others given their poor attitudes and rule-breaking behavior. Consider a student who goes to class having just learned that he failed a test in his previous class that effectively ruined his chances of passing that class. This student is likely experiencing a level of stress that will negatively impact his behavior in class. While in class, then, he may explode after a fellow student makes a comment that he finds unreasonable. The student who is the "victim" of the outburst may find the other student's behavior unacceptable and offensive. The attacked student then may, as a result, respond aggressively, effectively starting an aggressive exchange. This distress-and-reaction sequence is at the heart of the **social interactionist perspective.**

Stated more formally, Felson (1992) argues that aggressive encounters occur when distressed individuals break social rules and those who are aggrieved by the breaking of rules respond aggressively. The distressed individual is then placed in a situation in which he or she has to respond to aggression. If this person does so unsatisfactorily, the original aggrieved person is likely to implement punishment—in other words, victimization. The distressed individual then may retaliate, thus continuing the cycle of aggression. In this way, distress is a cause of victimization.

The Life-Course Perspective

Emerging in the 1990s in the field of criminology, the **life-course perspective** considers the development of offending over time. In doing so, it uses elements from biology, sociology, and psychology to explain why persons initiate into, continue with, and desist or move out of a life of crime. Contributing to the growth of this field, in large part due to the overlap between victims and offenders discussed in a section below, victimologists have recently begun applying and testing the principles of life-course criminology to victimization. A summary of these theories is presented in Table 2.3.

The General Theory of Crime

In 1990, Michael Gottfredson and Travis Hirschi published *The General Theory of Crime*. In this seminal work, they proposed their **general theory of crime,** proposing that criminal behavior is caused by a single factor—namely, low self-control. They argued that a person with low self-control, when presented with opportunity, will engage in criminal and other analogous behaviors, such as excessive drinking. When examining the characteristics of persons with low self-control, the reasons this trait might lead to criminal behavior are clear. A person with low self-control will exhibit six elements, the first being inability to delay gratification; a person with low self-control will be impulsive and unable or unwilling to delay gratification. Second, the person will be a risk taker who engages in thrill-seeking behavior without thought of consequence. Third, an individual with low self-control will be shortsighted, without any clear long-term goals. Fourth, low self-control is indicated by a preference for physical as compared with mental activity. This preference may lead an individual to respond to disrespect with violence rather than having a discussion about the finer points of being respectful. Fifth, low self-control is evidenced by low frustration tolerance, which results in a person being quick to anger. Sixth, insensitivity and self-centeredness are hallmarks of low self-control. A person with low self-control will be unlikely to exhibit empathy toward others.

Gottfredson and Hirschi (1990) argue that low self-control is fairly immutable once developed, which occurs during early childhood. They believe that, although self-control is an individual-level characteristic, it is not inherent; rather, it is developed through parental socialization. Once the level is set (around age 8), people will be hard-pressed to develop greater abilities to moderate their behavior. With low self-control, a person will act on impulses and seek personal gratification—often engaging in crime. Importantly, as noted, low self-control will lead individuals to engage in other behaviors that are similar to crime.

In 1999, Schreck applied the general theory of crime to victimization. He was one of the first researchers to apply to victimization what had been conceived as a theory of crime. This innovative approach was rooted in his recognition that persons who engage in crime are also likely to be victimized, a point we return to later. He also noted that since crime and victimization may be closely related, often with the same people engaging in both, the same factors that explain crime participation may also explain crime victimization. He tested his theory and found that low self-control increased the likelihood that a person would experience both personal and property victimization, even when controlling for participation in criminal behavior. This finding suggests that solely being involved in crime does not increase risk of victimization but that low self-control has significant, independent effects on victimization. In a recent meta-analysis, which is a type of study that examines all the research that has been conducted on the link between low self-control and victimization collectively and produces an effect size for the magnitude of this relationship, self-control was found to have a modest effect on victimization. The overall mean effect size for low self-control on victimization is .154, which means that a one standard deviation increase in low self-control corresponds to a .154 standard deviation increase in victimization. The relationship was strongest for victimizations that were noncontact in nature such as online victimization (Pratt, Turanovic, Fox, & Wright, 2014).

Table 2.3 ■ Summary Table of Life-Course Criminological Theories Relevant for Victimization

Theory	Author(s)	Key Factor Related to Outcome
General theory of crime	Gottfredson and Hirschi (1990)	Low self-control
Age-graded theory of adult social bonds	Sampson and Laub (1993)	Social bonds: Marriage and employment; marriage related to desistance

Age-Graded Theory of Adult Social Bonds

Not all criminologists agree that there is a single cause of crime (or victimization) called low self-control. Others noted that people do indeed move in and out of criminal activity, a phenomenon that is difficult to explain with a persistent trait, low self-control. Robert Sampson and John Laub (1993) instead believed that a person's social bonds could serve to insulate him or her from criminal activity. In their **age-graded theory of adult social bonds,** Sampson and Laub identified two key social bonds—marriage and employment—that can aid people in moving out of a life of delinquency and crime as they emerge into young adulthood. If a person enters into marriage and has gainful employment, he or she is developing valuable social capital. In other words, a person who has these two social bonds will have much to lose by engaging in crime, which will promote crime desistance if he or she was previously involved in crime. If that person was not involved in crime, social capital would enable him or her to continue living a crime-free life.

Although this obviously is not a victimization theory, because of the link between victimization and offending, researchers have attempted to connect the attainment of adult social bonds with victimization in that individuals who are married and working will be less likely to be crime victims than those with little to lose. Daigle, Beaver, and Hartman (2008) found that entering into marriage did in fact predict desistance from victimization as individuals moved into early adulthood. They found that employment was not similarly protective; instead, employment reduced the chances that a person would desist from victimization. Looking at routine activities and lifestyles theory, however, this finding is none too surprising! The more time a person spends outside the home, at work or in other activities, the greater the chances of being victimized.

Genes and Victimization

The life-course perspective in criminology has also centered on individual factors, such as genetics, that promote offending. This body of research has found a link between different genetic polymorphisms and behaviors relevant to criminology, such as criminal involvement and alcohol and drug use. A genetic polymorphism is a variant on a gene. Research has shown that sometimes these variations impact the likelihood of engaging in certain behaviors, such as violence, aggression, and delinquency. The genes that have been identified as linked to criminality are those that code for neurotransmitters, such as monoamine oxidase, serotonin, and dopamine. Neurotransmitters are chemical messengers responsible for information transmission. In terms of criminal behavior, relevant neurotransmitters are those linked to behavioral inhibition, mood, reward, and attention deficits. One important aspect of the link between genetics and crime is that possessing a variant for a gene, or having a certain polymorphism for a particular neurotransmitter, appears to "matter" only in certain environments. This is known as a **gene X environment interaction.** Genes tend to be important not for everyone in every circumstance but for particular individuals in particular contexts. For example, a person who is genetically predisposed toward alcoholism will express these alcoholic tendencies only if first exposed to alcohol.

As noted with other life-course perspective approaches, the applicability of genetic factors to the study of victimization has been explored. In fact, a gene X environment interaction for one gene in particular, dopamine, has been found to increase victimization risk. Dopamine is a neurotransmitter linked to the reward and punishment systems of the brain. Dopamine is released when we engage in pleasurable activities, thus reinforcing such behavior. Too much dopamine, however, can be a bad thing. High levels of dopamine are linked to enhanced problem solving and attentiveness, but overproduction of dopamine can be problematic. In fact, it has been linked to violence and aggression. One gene that codes for dopamine is the DRD2 gene, a dopamine receptor gene. Research has found evidence for a gene X environment interaction between DRD2 and having delinquent peers. White males who have delinquent peers and have a certain genetic polymorphism for DRD2 are more likely than others to be violently victimized (Beaver, Wright, DeLisi, Daigle et al., 2007). Genes have also been implicated in the victim–offender overlap. Research has found that genetic factors account for between 54% and 98% of the covariation between delinquency and victimization (Barnes & Beaver, 2012a). The link between genes and victimization is an emerging area of research, and therefore, additional research is certainly needed to understand fully how genes impact victimization.

The Role of Alcohol in Victimization

One of the common elements present in victimization is alcohol. According to data from the NCVS in 2008, 36% of victims perceived their offender to be under the influence of alcohol at the time of the incident (National Crime Victimization Survey, 2004–2008). Alcohol use is commonplace among crime offenders, but many crime victims also report that just prior to their victimizations, they had consumed alcohol. Patricia Tjaden and Nancy Thoennes (2006) found in their National Violence Against Women study that 20% of women and 38% of men who experienced rape in adulthood had consumed alcohol or drugs prior to being victimized. Alcohol use is associated with other forms of victimization as well, such as physical assault. This fact should not be too surprising given the effects of alcohol on individuals. Generally, alcohol is linked to victimization since it reduces inhibition and also impedes people's ability to recognize or respond effectively to dangerous situations. Offenders may also see intoxicated persons as particularly vulnerable targets for these reasons. Where a person consumes alcohol is also important. A person who drinks at home alone or with family is less likely to be victimized than a person who drinks in a bar at night. The latter person is likely interacting with motivated offenders without capable guardianship and may be perceived as a suitable target.

Alcohol use may place a person at risk of being victimized but also may impact how the victim responds to the incident. Research by Ruback, Menard, Outlaw, and Shaffer (1999) shows how alcohol use may be relevant to understanding why victims often do not report their experiences to police. In their study, college students evaluated various hypothetical scenarios that depicted victimization. Study participants were asked whether they would advise a victimized friend to report to the police based on a given scenario. When the friend in the scenario had been drinking, college students were less likely to advise that the police be contacted, and this relationship was particularly strong for victims depicted as being underage and drinking.

As you can see, the explanations of victimization are many. The "hallmark" victimization theory is routine activities and lifestyles theory, which is based on the notion that a person's routines and lifestyle, not social conditions, place him or her at risk. As you have read, however, explanations of victimization have expanded beyond this to include social process and structural factors. The explanations you are drawn to may be tied to the data you are examining, which you now know are impacted by methodology. To understand the causes of victimization, you must first know who the "typical" victim is and what characterizes the "typical" victimization. In some of the following sections, specific types of victims will be examined. Think about what theories can be used to explain their victimizations.

SUMMARY

- The Uniform Crime Report (UCR) is an official measure of the amount of crime known to the police. According to this report, which is published annually by the Federal Bureau of Investigation (FBI), the most common crime type is larceny/theft. The most common type of violent crime is aggravated assault. Criminal offending rates are highest for young, Black males.
- The National Crime Victimization Survey (NCVS) uses a nationally representative sample of U.S. households. Individuals ages 12 and over in selected households are asked questions about victimization experiences they faced during the previous 6 months. According to the NCVS, the typical victim is a young, White male—although Blacks have higher victimization rates than other racial or ethnic groups and females experience higher rates of rape and sexual assault than males.
- The typical victimization incident is perpetrated by someone known to the victim, is not reported to the police, and does not involve a weapon.
- There is a clear link between victimization and offending, as well as between victims and offenders. Persons who live risky lifestyles are more likely to engage in criminal or delinquent activity and also to be victims of crime. Victims and offenders also share similar demographic profiles.
- Routine activities theory suggests that crime victimization is likely to occur when motivated offenders, lack of capable guardianship, and suitable targets coalesce in time and space. Lifestyles theory is closely linked with routine activities theory in proposing that a person who leads a risky lifestyle is at risk of being victimized.
- Neighborhoods are not equally safe. The risk of being victimized, then, differs across geographical areas, and even when controlling for individual-level factors such as risky lifestyle, neighborhood disadvantage predicts victimization.
- Spending time with friends who participate in delinquent activities places a person at risk of being victimized. These "friends" may victimize their nondelinquent peers and also encourage them to participate in risky behaviors that may lead to victimization.
- Strong attachments to family may serve to protect individuals from victimization, while weak attachments may increase victimization risk.
- Victimization may also be a learned process, whereby victims have learned the motives, definitions, and behaviors of victimization and had them reinforced.

- According to control-balance theory, individuals with an unequal control-balance ratio—either having a control deficit or a control surplus—are more prone to victimization than those with a balanced ratio. Those with control deficits may be seen as easy targets. They also may get tired of being targeted and lash out, thus increasing their involvement in situations associated with violent victimization. Those with control surpluses may engage in risky behavior with impunity, which could set them up for being victimized or retaliated against.
- Research on the general theory of crime suggests that those individuals who have low self-control are more likely to be victimized than those with higher levels of self-control.
- Adult social bonds may explain why people who were once victimized are not victimized again as they age into young adulthood. Marriage appears to protect individuals from victimization.
- Genetic factors may also play a role in victimization. One specific genetic polymorphism of the DRD2 gene has been found to increase risk for White males who have delinquent peers. A genetic effect that occurs only under certain environmental conditions is known as a gene X environment interaction.
- Alcohol and victimization appear to go hand-in-hand. Alcohol impacts cognitive ability, and persons who are drinking are less likely to assess and recognize situations as being risky even when they are. In addition, alcohol is linked to behavioral inhibition, such that people may act in ways they otherwise would not, which may incite aggression in others. Alcohol is also linked to victimization when offenders purposefully select intoxicated victims because they are seen as easy targets.

DISCUSSION QUESTIONS

1. Compare and contrast the UCR and the NCVS. What are the advantages and disadvantages of each? Which is the best measure of victimization?

2. Apply the concepts of routine activities and lifestyles theory to evaluate your own risk of being victimized. What could you change to reduce your risk?

3. What are the individual-level factors that place people at risk of being crime victims? What are the structural factors and social process factors that place individuals at risk of being crime victims?

4. How should the criminal justice system handle victimized individuals who may also have been involved in a crime? Do you believe in the idea of truly innocent victims? If so, should they be treated differently?

5. Given what you have read about the theories and factors that influence crime victimization, how can victimization be prevented? Be sure to tie your prevention ideas to what is thought to cause victimization.

KEY TERMS

Uniform Crime Report (UCR)

hierarchy rule

National Crime Victimization Survey (NCVS)

bounding

screen questions

incident report

series victimizations

"code of the streets"

routine activities and lifestyles theory

victimization theory

motivated offenders

suitable targets

capable guardianship

principle of homogamy

neighborhood context

hot spots

family structure

structural density

residential mobility

delinquent peers

control-balance theory

control ratio

control surplus

control deficit

social interactionist perspective

life-course perspective

age-graded theory of adult social bonds

gene x environment interaction

general theory of crime

INTERNET RESOURCES

"Alcohol and Crime" (http://bjs.ojp.usdoj.gov/content/pub/pdf/ac.pdf)

This report by the Bureau of Justice Statistics, in connection with the U.S. Department of Justice, looks at the link between alcohol and crime. It includes several graphs and figures that show the link between crime, specifically violent crime, and alcohol. These statistics also show that alcohol-related crime is generally decreasing.

Bureau of Justice Statistics: Victim Characteristics (http://bjs.ojp.usdoj.gov/index.cfm?ty=tp&tid=92)

The NCVS provides information on characteristics of victims, including age, race, ethnicity, gender, marital status, and household income. For violent crimes (rape, sexual assault, assault, and robbery) the characteristics are based on the victim who experienced the crime. For property crimes (household burglary, motor vehicle theft, and property theft) the characteristics are based on the household of the respondent who provided information about these crimes. Property crimes are defined as affecting the entire household.

Crime in the United States: The Nation's Two Crime Measures (http://www.fbi.gov/about-us/cjis/ucr/crime-in-the-u.s/2010/crime-in-the-u.s.-2010/the-nations-two-crime-measures)

This website is part of the FBI's research on various crimes. This one specifically examines the differences, advantages, and disadvantages of the UCR and the NCVS. Both forms of research are important to the study of crime.

Crime Times (http://www.crimetimes.org)

Crime Times is a quarterly publication of the Wacker Foundation concentrating on the links between brain dysfunction and disordered/criminal/psychopathic behavior. Instead of focusing just on sociological problems, this website looks at brain malfunctions that prevent criminals from benefiting from sociological or psychological interventions. This website addresses several topics, including attention-deficit/hyperactivity disorder, aggression, antisocial behavior, food and chemical sensitivities, hormonal imbalances, maternal smoking or alcohol abuse, and new medical and nutritional interventions.

"Opportunity Makes the Thief: Practical Theory for Crime Prevention" (http://webarchive.nationalarchives.gov.uk/20110218135832/rds.homeoffice.gov.uk/rds/prgpdfs/fprs98.pdf)

This article combines several theories that focus on the "opportunity" of crimes. This includes the routine activities approach, the rational choice perspective, and crime pattern theory. This publication argues that the root cause of crime is opportunity. This allows for prevention techniques to focus on how to lessen the opportunity for crime to occur.

Project on Human Development in Chicago Neighborhoods (http://www.icpsr.umich.edu/PHDCN/about.html)

The Project on Human Development in Chicago Neighborhoods is an interdisciplinary study of how families, schools, and neighborhoods affect child and adolescent development. It was designed to advance understanding of the developmental pathways of both positive and negative human social behaviors. In particular, the project examined the pathways to juvenile delinquency, adult crime, substance abuse, and violence. At the same time, the project also provided a detailed look at the environments in which these social behaviors take place by collecting substantial amounts of data about urban Chicago, including its people, institutions, and resources.

3

THE VICTIM–OFFENDER OVERLAP

One facet about victimization that cannot be ignored is the link that exists between offending and victimization and between offenders and victims. As mentioned in Chapter 1, the first forays into the study of victims included a close look at how victims contribute to their own victimization. In this way, victims were not always assumed to be innocents; rather, some victims were seen as being at least partly responsible for bringing on their victimization— for instance, by being an offender who is victimized when the victim fights back. Although the field of victimology has moved away from placing blame on victims, the recognition that offenders and victims are often linked—and often the same person—has aided in the understanding of why people are victimized.

Take, for instance, the case of Terrance Williams. In the early 1980s while just 18 years of age, Williams murdered two men. He was later tried and convicted for those crimes, receiving a sentence of death for one of the murders in which the district attorney claimed Williams robbed and then brutally killed his victim. Nearly three decades later, new evidence pertaining to the case and, more specifically, Williams' childhood and alleged relationship with his victim, was heard in court as the defense petitioned for a stay of execution. Read the news story to find out more about the possible link between victimization and offending in the Williams case.

WILL PENNSYLVANIA EXECUTE
A MAN WHO KILLED HIS ABUSERS?

Eighteen-year-old Terrance Williams "did not fit the mold of a typical street criminal," the *Philadelphia Inquirer* reported in September of 1984. "He was a bright, talented college student, former star quarterback of the Germantown High School football team. His friends, teachers, coaches and neighbors could not believe that he would be involved in murder, or any sordid activity."

Yet Williams, had committed two grisly killings. One victim, the *Inquirer* reported, was 50-year-old Herbert Hamilton, who had been found naked, with a knife through his throat, on his kitchen floor. The other, Amos Norwood, who led the altar boys and directed the Youth Theater Fellowship at Philadelphia's St. Luke's Episcopal Church, had been beaten with a tire iron, set on fire, and left in a cemetery.

"The problem I find with you, Mr. Williams, is you are a Jekyll and Hyde, apparently," one judge told him. Tried as an adult for the Hamilton murder despite being 17 at the time, Williams was already in prison when he was sentenced to die for killing Norwood. "We were glad we did it," one juror told the press.

Williams, 46, is facing death by lethal injection. In August 2012, Pennsylvania Governor Tom Corbett signed a warrant scheduling his execution for October 3. But in the meantime, the same jurors who sealed his fate have had a dramatic change of heart. At least five say that if they could go back, they would never have sent Williams to death row. That's because they were never told a salient and deeply disturbing detail about his relationship with his victim. Williams, it turns out, had been violently and systematically raped by Norwood, beginning when he was 13 years old.

In fact, behind the image of Williams as a model student athlete was a childhood marred by horrific physical and sexual abuse that began from the time Williams was just 6 years old. Relentlessly beaten by his mother (herself a victim of abuse) and his alcoholic stepfather and gang-raped at a juvenile detention center when he was 16, by the time Williams killed Norwood he was regularly cutting himself, abusing drugs and alcohol, and had endured more than a decade of abuse. Among the others who sexually assaulted him: his other victim, Herbert Hamilton.

At a post-conviction relief hearing in the late 1990s, attorneys argued that Williams had inadequate representation—his original lawyer, who would later be disbarred, did not meet him until one week before trial—and presented proof that, in addition to being raped at age 6 by a neighbor and "repeatedly molested by a [male] teacher" in his early teens, when he was 13, "[he] met and began a relationship with Norwood," who was "cruel and physically abusive at times." Family, friends and teachers attested to the abuse, and a trio of mental health experts would describe him as "suffering from extreme mental or emotional disturbance when he killed Norwood." (Court filings describe how Norwood raped Williams in a parking lot the night before he was killed.)

Among those calling on the state to spare Williams's life are twenty-two former prosecutors, eight retired judges and forty-seven mental health professionals—a highly unusual display of support. Part of this is likely due to an increased public awareness of sexual abuse. While not all victims murder their abusers, Williams's petition argues that his case is largely about devastating effects of that victimization.

Source: Reprinted from Segura, L. (2012, September 12). Will Pennsylvania execute a man who killed his abusers? *The Nation.* http://www .thenation.com/blog/169881/will-pennsylvania-execute-man-who-killed-his-abusers.

◼ THE LINK BETWEEN VICTIMIZATION AND OFFENDING

Ask any social scientist what the major causes of crime and victimization are, and you are bound to get a variety of responses. Often cited are age, sex, low self-control, urbanization, and poverty. While we might not all agree as to what the "facts" are, there are several correlates that have generated a consensus in the field as being top predictors of crime and victimization, and the **victim–offender overlap** is definitely on that list (Berg, 2012). Case in point, a fairly recent review of the literature found 37

Photo Credit: http://murderpedia.org/male.W/w/williams-terrance.htm; Pennsylvannia Department of Corrections.

PHOTO 3.1

Did Terrance Williams's experiences as a victim while a child lead to his violent behavior as an emerging adult? Does his history of victimization mitigate the seriousness of the crimes he committed? Should Terrance be considered a victim or a criminal? These questions are central to the victim–offender overlap. In this chapter, we will discuss the connection between victimization and offending.

empirical studies spanning five decades dedicated to the study of the victim–offender overlap, of which the vast majority (84%) found considerable support for the presence of the overlap within a diversity of samples (see the Focus on International Issues box for a discussion of cross-cultural research on the victim–offender overlap) and across a wide range of criminal behaviors (Jennings, Piquero, & Reingle, 2012). In this chapter, we will discuss a few of these including homicide and intimate partner violence.

Victim and Offender Characteristics

The typical victim and the typical offender have many commonalities. As mentioned before in our discussion of the National Crime Victimization Survey (NCVS) in Chapter 2, the groups with the highest rates of violent victimization are young, Black males. The Uniform Crime Report (UCR) also provides information on offenders. The groups with the highest rates of violent offending are also young, Black males. The typical victim and the typical offender, then, share common demographics. In addition, both victims and offenders are likely to live in urban areas. Thus, individuals who spend time with people who have the characteristics of offenders are more likely to be victimized than others.

Sampson and Lauritsen (1990) have advanced the **principle of homogamy** to better explain demographic similarities between offenders and victims. The premise of this idea is that associating with criminals increases a person's risk of victimization. The connection between victims and offenders makes sense, as offenders are more likely to associate with others who are in close proximity to them—people they live, work, go to school, or spend time with. Therefore, the victims of their crimes will be people who are similar to them (the offenders) on such characteristics as race, socioeconomic status, and neighborhood.

Whereas research has found similarities between offenders and victims (i.e., victim–offender overlap), other research has noted the existence of role differentiation between the two. This has led some researchers to contend that there are actually three distinct types of individuals involved in crime (Mustaine & Tewksbury, 2000). There are **victims** (sometimes referred to as "pure" or "exclusive" victims). These are individuals who have been victimized, but do not engage in crime. There are **offenders** (sometimes referred to as "pure" or "exclusive" offenders). These are individuals who engage in crime but have no victimization history. Lastly, there are victims who are also offenders (aka **victim-offenders**). Victim–offenders are individuals who have histories of both victimization and offending. Research that has examined the possibility of three groupings finds support for Mustaine and Tewksbury's (2000) assertion that while an overlap exists for a majority of victims and offenders, the overlap is not present for all victims or offenders (Muftić & Hunt, 2013). For example, Craig et al. (2009) utilized data on 200,000 children from 40 different countries who participated in the Health Behavior in School-Aged Children survey to assess the victim–offender overlap within bullying. They found that almost 13% of children had been bullied (but had not bullied others), about 11% had bullied others (but had not been bullied themselves), and roughly 4% had bullied others and had been bullied themselves.

■ EXPLAINING THE LINK BETWEEN VICTIMIZATION AND OFFENDING

As you can see, the victim–offender overlap centers around the acknowledgment that victims and offenders share a multitude of characteristics. This is compounded by the fact that involvement in a criminal event, whether as a victim or as an offender, increases *both your offending and victimization risk*. In other words, if you've experienced one type of criminal event (e.g., offending), you're likely to experience the other (e.g., victimization). There are several reasons why this might be. We will discuss a number of them in this section.

Dynamic Causal Perspective

In general, there are two types of theoretical arguments when it comes to explaining the relationship between victimization and offending: the dynamic causal perspective and the population heterogeneity argument (Ousey, Wilcox, & Fisher, 2011). The **dynamic causal perspective** suggests that the linkage between victimization and offending occurs due to the influence and impact of these experiences directly on one another. Essentially this argument is based on the claim that specific negative incidents (e.g., victimization) modifies attitudinal and behavioral patterns, in turn shifting the likelihood for engaging in the other (e.g., offending) (Ousey et al., 2011). There are several theories that fall under the dynamic causal perspective: general strain theory, routine activities and lifestyle theory, subcultural theories, and the victim-rationality perspective. These theories have differing ideas about the temporal ordering of the victim–offender overlap (victimization leads to offending vs. offending leads to victimization).

General Strain Theory

Robert Agnew's general strain theory falls within the dynamic causal perspective because it asserts that victimization can lead to subsequent offending. Simply put, general strain theory proposes that individuals who experience negative emotion, such as stress, strain, frustration, depression, or anger, are likely to commit crime (Agnew, 2006). While negative emotive states can be caused by the failure to achieve a positively valued goal (like failing an exam) or the loss of a positively valued goal (e.g., losing your job), stress and strain can also come about from the presentation of negative stimuli, such as having been the victim of a crime.

Agnew's theory is one of only a few that identifies victimization as a risk factor for offending. Accordingly, Agnew contends that being victimized is a highly stressful experience and can cause negative emotion. In order to cope with the feelings that come from being victimized (e.g., anger, fear, anxiety), victims will rely on coping mechanisms to alleviate the distress they are experiencing. These coping mechanisms may be noncriminal. For instance, victims often find that talking with a trained professional helps them deal with the victimization process. Other victims, however, may find themselves driven to criminal coping behaviors. Retaliatory behavior, brought on by the desire to exact revenge, is a prime example. As we explore other dynamic causal explanations for the victim–offender overlap, you will notice that retaliation is a common thread linking victimization and offending.

Routine Activities and Lifestyles Theory

Probably the most often cited theoretical explanation given for the relationship between victimization and offending is the lifestyles and routine activities perspectives (Cohen & Felson, 1979; Hindelang, Gottfredson, & Garofalo, 1978). It is not hard to understand why this may be the case. Offending can be viewed as part of a risky lifestyle. Individuals who engage in offending are exposed more frequently to people and contexts in which victimization is likely to occur (Lauritsen, Laub, & Sampson, 1992). Hence, a routine activities/lifestyles perspective predicts that offending increases risk for subsequent victimization. Additionally, their status as an offender makes them "legally vulnerable" and hence an attractive target for would-be predators. Take for instance drug dealers. Drug dealers often find themselves the victims of robbery, but due to the illicit nature of their work, can't call the police for fear of incriminating themselves. Read what happens to a couple of drug dealers who call the police after being robbed. Do you think they should have been arrested? Are they victims or offenders? Can they be both?

Subcultural Theories

There also may be a link between victimization and offending that is part of a broader cultural belief in the acceptability and sometimes necessity of violence, known as the subculture of violence theory. This theory proposes that for certain subgroups of the population and in certain areas, violence is part of a value system that supports the use of violence, in response to disrespect in particular (Wolfgang & Ferracuti, 1967). In this way, when a subculture

RIPPED FROM THE HEADLINES

Drug Dealers Report Being Victims of Armed Robbery

In February 2012, two teenage boys, Kyle Hodges and Calvin Williams, called police to report being victims of an armed robbery. Savannah-Chatham (Georgia) Metro Police responded at approximately 11:00 pm.

Upon arrival, the officers found a "large amount of marijuana" (Sanders, 2012) inside Williams' vehicle. The street value was estimated at approximately $10,000. The two individuals, who initially called to report being robbed at gun point, were promptly arrested and charged with Possession of Marijuana with Intent to Distribute and Criminal Attempt to Sell a Controlled Substance, among others.

With the assistance of the Savannah State University Police, authorities located Darius Harper, age 20, as their prime suspect for the armed robbery. Prior to apprehension and arrest, Harper ran from police. Even though Harper could not be clearly linked to the armed robbery, upon arrest he was charged with Loitering, Prowling and Obstruction by Fleeing. Officers searched the area where Harper was originally located and "found clothing matching the description of the armed robber, along with a pistol and marijuana" (Sanders, 2012).

Source: Adapted from http://www.wsav.com/story/21211356/two-accused-drug-dealers-call-police-to-report-armed-robbery.

that supports violence exists, victims will be likely to respond by retaliating. Let's revisit the example of the two drug dealers who called the police to report being robbed. Urban drug dealers are often part of a subculture with values and norms that promote violence as an appropriate response to victimization. Thus, in order to protect their turf and save face, drug dealers are likely to retaliate against the person who robbed them. Thus, similar to routine activities theories, subcultural theories predict that victimization may lead to subsequent offending. Recent research shows that the victim–offender overlap does indeed vary across neighborhoods and that this variation is related to the neighborhood's strength of attachment to the **"code of the streets"** and degree of structural deprivation (Berg & Loeber, 2011; Berg, Stewart, Schreck, & Simons, 2012).

An alternate, albeit plausible argument, is that within street subcultures, a perilous lifestyle acts as a deterrent against victimization. As word spreads that an individual is willing to "fight back" or "seek revenge" following an attack, the less attractive the person becomes as a target (Berg & Loeber, 2011). Research that has utilized longitudinal data to examine the link between offending and victimization has found support for this contention. Specifically, Chen (2009) found that the more enmeshed an individual was in a deviant lifestyle in early adolescence, the greater the decline in victimization over time (Chen, 2009).

Victim-Rationality Perspective

While subcultural theories propose that victimization likely leads to offending, an alternate perspective is that victimization can decrease subsequent offending. This perspective is known as the victim-rationality perspective and rests on the assertion that not all victimizations lead to retaliatory behavior. Essentially the victim-rationality perspective is premised on the hypothesis that the victimization experience can serve as a turning point for some offenders (Jacques & Wright, 2008). This turning point comes about when an offender recognizes that the victimization he or she has experienced is the result of his or her offending and that if he or she stops, or at least drastically reduces, offending, he or she will also reduce the risk of being victimized in the future.

Interviews conducted with drug-involved offenders revealed that victimization is a highly common experience, with 9 out of 10 men having experienced at least one victimization (Vecchio, 2013). Of the men who had been victimized, 2 out of 3 said that after they had been victimized they modified their offending behavior in an effort to avoid subsequent victimization (Vecchio, 2013). In addition, research indicates that some victims make changes to their lifestyle following a victimization experience. These alterations are generally for the better, with these individuals discontinuing their involvement in violent crimes, drug dealing, and different forms of trafficking (Pyrooz, Moule, & Decker, 2014).

Population Heterogeneity Perspective

We have just discussed the dynamic causal perspective used to explain the link between victimization and offending. The second theoretical viewpoint on the victim–offender overlap is referred to as the population heterogeneity perspective. The **population heterogeneity perspective**, or the "noncausal" argument, essentially states that victimization does not cause offending or vice versa but rather that they are both related to a personality characteristic or environment that does not change over time. Consequently, an individual's offending and victimization may be related to having low self-control or living in an environment with a high crime rate. Since offending and victimization are essentially a result of one of these characteristics and/or environments, they do not directly affect each other. In other words, if this perspective is accurate, then personality and environmental factors that do not significantly change over time should completely reduce the relationship between offending and victimization.

General Theory of Crime

Simply put, the general theory of crime states that crime (defined as "an act of force or fraud done in pursuit of self-interest," Gottfredson & Hirschi, 1990) and behavior that is crime-like (smoking, promiscuous behavior, chronic unemployment) can be explained by one trait—an individual's level of self-control. The theory centers around a few key assumptions: (1) crime is easy and exciting; (2) crime requires no special motive; and (3) crime occurs when there is an opportunity. Accordingly, people withstand the lure of crime via their self-control. Self-control, which is a time-stable trait, is developed in early childhood through effective parenting practices (socialization, monitoring, recognition of problematic behavior, and discipline). Studies that have examined the relationship between self-control and crime have generally been supportive, finding that individuals who have low levels of self-control are more likely to be criminal or delinquent. Likewise, research finds that a person's risk of victimization has been linked to low self-control. Increases in victimization risk for persons with low self-control are associated with their involvement in different forms of offending and association with peer delinquents, as well as more generally that they have a higher level of impulsivity (Piquero et al., 2005).

Biosocial Explanations

Biosocial or genetic explanations for the victim–offender overlap is a fairly recent area of exploration. According to this perspective, victimization and offending are influenced by similar genetic factors that lead to an overlap between the two (Barnes & Beaver, 2012a). To test this hypothesis, Vaske, Boisvert, and Wright (2012) used a twin study design to evaluate the influence of genetics on the victim–offender overlap. They compared the victimization and offending experiences of monozygotic (identical) twins to dizygotic (fraternal) twins. Because monozygotic twins share 100% of their genetic material, while fraternal twins only share 50% of their genetic material (making them no more genetically similar than other sibling pairs), one would expect that if the victim–offender overlap is driven, at least partially, by genetic factors, the overlap between offending and victimization would be greater for identical twins than fraternal twins. This is exactly what they found with approximately 20% to 40% of the correlation between violent victimization and delinquency/offending due to shared genetic factors (Vaske et al., 2012).

*Theoretical Integration and the Victim–Offender Overlap**

Integrated theories pull together theories (sometimes in their entirety and sometimes in pieces) into broad explanations of offending. Recently these theories have been preferred

---

Note: This section written by Jonathan A. Grubb.

because they highlight how a variety of different factors come together to explain crime. Integrated theories commonly incorporate concepts such as social bonds between individuals, social support, the influence of deviant peers, the ability to control others (or be controlled), family dynamics, and one's own personality characteristics. These theories provide a variety of different explanations of offending, from why certain groups of individuals might be involved in crime throughout their lives to why coercion might be crucial for recognizing why persons offend. There are relatively few integrated theories and most are relatively new. In addition, the majority only explain offending, with little attention given to victimization.

An example of one such theory is Agnew's (2005) integrated general theory of crime and delinquency. Agnew's integrated theory doesn't provide a new theoretical argument per se, but rather organizes factors that influence offending into specific groupings, which he calls life domains. He proposes a total of five domains that focus on an individual's personality as well as on his or her connections to family, school, friends, and work. According to the theory, these domains have the greatest influence on offending when motivations to offend are high and restraints against offending are low. There is a growing body of evidence beginning to show support of this integrated theory.

Although Agnew (2005) does not focus directly on the victim–offender overlap in his integrated theory, there is reason to believe that the theory can explain why people might be both victims and offenders. For instance, personality characteristics have been found to be significant for understanding why individuals offend and are victimized. The same can be found when considering factors related to a person's family, school, friends, and work environment. While not all factors described by Agnew explain why individuals might offend and also be victimized, the overwhelming majority have been used to explain both experiences. What would be expected then would be that the life domains predict both why an individual offends and is victimized. Agnew would also suggest that victimization comes before offending, and it would serve as a significant motivation for an individual to offend.

To summarize, very few integrated theories have focused on victimization, with none known to examine the victim–offender overlap. One integrated theory that might explain the overlap is Agnew's (2005) integrated theory of crime and delinquency. Because the domains described have separately been used to understand victimization and offending, there is reason to believe they could explain why persons who offend are victimized and vice versa.

■ THE VICTIM–OFFENDER OVERLAP AND SPECIFIC TYPES OF VICTIMIZATION

The reasons why victimization may lead to participation in crime are not fully understood, but it may be that being victimized carries psychological consequences, such as depression, anxiety, or posttraumatic stress disorder, that can lead to coping through the use of alcohol or drugs. Victimization may also carry physical consequences, such as brain damage, that can further impede success later in life. Cognitive ability may also be tempered by maltreatment, particularly in childhood, which can hinder school performance. Behavior may also change as a result of being victimized. People may experience problems in their interpersonal relationships or become violent or aggressive. Whatever the reason, it is evident that victimization and offending are intimately intertwined. We will now focus on examining the victim–offender overlap within specific types of victimization.

Homicide

Homicide (which will be discussed in detail in Chapter 7) involves the killing of one human being by another. Wolfgang (1957) was one of the first to recognize the overlap between offending and victimization within homicide when he studied victim-precipitated homicides in Philadelphia. As discussed in Chapter 1, Wolfgang asserted that a victim can, at times, directly influence the outcome of a violent encounter through his or her own behavior. Defining victim precipitated homicide as an incident in which "the role of the victim is characterized by his having been the first in the homicide drama to use physical force directed against his subsequent slayer" (p. 73), Wolfgang (1957) found that slightly over one quarter of the homicides in his Philadelphia study were victim precipitated. Both concepts, the victim–offender overlap and victim-precipitation, highlight the demographic and behavioral similarities between victims and offenders (Muftić & Hunt, 2013).

Following in this tradition, several researchers have explored the victim–offender overlap within homicide. All together, the homicide research demonstrates that that anywhere up to 50% of homicide victims had previous offending records and that homicide victims and their killers share many similar demographic characteristics, structural environments, and risky behaviors, supporting the victim–offender overlap thesis (Broidy, Daday, Crandall, Sklar, & Jost, 2006; Dobrin, 2001; Ezell & Tanner-Smith, 2009; Muftić & Hunt, 2013; Pizarro, Zgoba, & Jennings, 2011). For instance, in one of the first empirical attempts to determine whether previous offending increases homicide victimization risk, Dobrin (2001) compared homicide victims to nonvictims and found that prior offending was a significant predictor of homicide victimization even after controlling for demographic and socioeconomic factors. In another study, Pizarro et al. (2011) found that criminally-involved victims and offenders were more likely to be involved in homicides associated with criminal events (e.g., drug-related homicides) than victims and suspects with lesser degrees of criminal involvement.

Intimate Partner Violence

On March 9, 1977, Francine Hughes, a housewife from Michigan, killed her ex-husband by pouring gasoline around the bed where he slept and starting it on fire. Hughes, who had endured over a decade of abuse at the hands of her husband, was found not guilty by reason of insanity. Hughes became the poster child for battered women (and the battered woman defense), and her story was recounted in the 1984 book *The Burning Bed* and later a TV movie by the same name. Country artist Martina McBride had a huge hit with her single "Independence Day" in which she tells a very similar story of a woman who escapes abuse by setting her house ablaze with her abusive partner inside.

Despite numerous examples in the media of the overlap between victimization and offending, especially among female victims who exact revenge on their abusers (take for example *Kill Bill, Thelma & Louise, The Girl with the Dragon Tattoo*), only recently has the victim–offender overlap been applied to the empirical study of intimate partner violence (IPV). As will be discussed in Chapter 9, intimate partner violence entails violence that occurs between individuals in a current or former intimate relationship (e.g., husband/wife, boyfriend/girlfriend, dating partner). The lack of attention given to the victim–offender overlap within IPV may be because the victim–offender overlap centers around the argument that victims and offenders are *similar*; however, most people view IPV victims and IPV perpetrators as *dissimilar*. This is due, in part, to feminist researchers' contention that IPV is a unique crime influenced by patriarchy and sexism. Yet, many feminist scholars have acknowledged that there is more than one type of IPV. Predominantly Johnson (2011) has identified three major types. They include situational couple violence, intimate terrorism, and violent resistance. **Situational couple violence** is the most common type of IPV, which occurs when conflict in a relationship escalates to violence, but the violence is not used by either partner as a control tactic, and men and women are equally likely to be perpetrators and victims of this type of IPV. **Intimate terrorism**, also referred to as battering or coercive control, while not the most common type of IPV, is the type likely to be experienced by women who seek assistance from the police or domestic violence shelters and involves a pattern of coercive control that involves the partner's use of physical violence and related tactics (emotional abuse or economic abuse) as a means of maintaining control. The last type, **violent resistance** (also referred to as defensive violence), involves women fighting back against intimate terrorism. What Francine Hughes did to her ex-husband is an example of violent resistance.

FOCUS ON RESEARCH

Using official police data, Muftić, Finn, and Marsh (2013) examined the overlap between victimization and offending within officially recorded incidents of intimate partner violence (IPV) by taking into consideration an individual's role in the initial IPV incident (either victim or offender) and then his or her role in further officially recorded IPV incidents during an 18 to 30 month follow-up period. Individuals were then categorized into four distinct groups: victims (IPV victims in all officially recorded incidents on file), persistent offenders (IPV offenders in all incidents), desistent offenders (IPV offender in original IPV incident with no subsequent IPV offending recorded), or victim-offenders (IPV victims who later became IPV offenders or IPV offenders who later became IPV victims). Taking into consideration an individual's behavior during the follow-up period, results indicated that among the 1,256 individuals, victim-offenders comprised roughly one-quarter of the sample and that men and women were equally represented in this category.

Source: Partially reprinted from Muftić, L. R., Finn, M. A., & Marsh, E. (2013). The victim-offender overlap, intimate partner violence, and sex: Assessing differences among exclusive victims, exclusive offenders, and victim-offenders. *Crime & Delinquency.* Advance Online Publication. doi: 0.1177/0011128712453677.

Johnson's typology lays the groundwork for the possibility that like other types of violent crime, victim-offenders exist within intimate partner violence, particularly within IPV that involves common couple violence and violent resistance. For instance, feminist researchers have long contended that when women perpetuate IPV, they do so defensively as opposed to offensively. Research that has explored the motivations behind women's use of violence against an intimate partner finds that their motivations are typically more defensive in nature, with most women reporting assaulting their intimate partners as a means of self-defense or retaliation for their own victimization (Henning, Renauer, & Holdford, 2006).

Special Case: The Role of Childhood Victimization on Offending and Victimization in Adulthood

Being victimized may be related to offending in ways that are not directly tied to retaliation or part of a risky lifestyle. In fact, being victimized at one point in life may increase the likelihood that a person will engage in delinquency and crime later in life. This link has been found especially in individuals who are abused during childhood. As will be discussed in Chapter 10 on victimization that occurs at the beginning and end of life, those who are victimized as children are significantly more likely than those who do not experience child abuse to be arrested in adulthood (Widom, 2000) or to engage in violence and property offending (Menard, 2002). This is showcased in the story of Terrance Williams at the beginning of this chapter.

THE INCIDENCE OF CHILD ABUSE IN SERIAL KILLERS

Serial killers attract a substantial amount of attention not only in the media but also within academia for the heinous acts that they commit. One fairly common question asked is to what extent do serial killers have a history of abuse? Mitchell and Aamodt (2005) attempted to answer this question when they examined the prevalence of childhood physical, sexual, and psychological abuse among 50 U.S.-born serial killers. Results from their study indicated that a significant portion of serial killers sampled had been maltreated in general (68%), with psychological abuse the most common (50%), followed by physical (36%) and sexual abuse (26%), and to a lesser extent neglect (18%). Only a minority of serial killers reported no type of abuse (32%). Furthermore, their research found that serial killers were more likely to have experienced child abuse than individuals from the general population.

Source: Adapted from Mitchell, H., & Aamodt, M. G. (2005). The incidence of child abuse in serial killers. *Journal of Police and Criminal Psychology,* *20*(1), 40–47.

The effect of maltreatment on crime and delinquency may be gendered in that, in retrospective studies of offenders, the relationship between child maltreatment and offending appears to be more relevant for females than males. In fact, female inmates reported more childhood maltreatment than did male inmates (McClellan, Farabee, & Crouch, 1997). Research has also found that a common precursor to entry into sex work, as a prostitute or sex trafficking victim, is physical and sexual abuse during childhood (Campbell et al., 2003; Wilson & Widom, 2010). And while victimization may originate in childhood, it doesn't appear to end there, with sexually exploited females reporting extensive violent victimization (Briere & Spinazzola, 2005; Farley et al., 2003; Muftić & Finn, 2013; Zimmerman et al., 2008) and offending (Finn, Muftić, & Marsh, 2014) across their lifetimes. Refer to the section "Special Case: Prostitution Courts" for an innovative approach designed to address the unique needs of prostitutes by addressing their victimization histories in an effort to reduce recidivism.

Special Case: Prostitution Courts

For the criminal justice system, women engaged in prostitution represent a complex dichotomy. On one hand, females engaged in prostitution are viewed as offenders, involved in the selling of sex. On the other hand, females engaged in prostitution have commonly reported histories of various forms of abuse, running away from home and becoming involved in prostitution and offending as a method of survival. Moreover, they may have been forced or coerced into prostitution against their will, commonly referred to as sex trafficking. Female sex workers are often differentiated as victims or offenders based upon the amount of agency they are able to exert, with sexually trafficked women having been conceived as victims, while prostitutes have been portrayed as offenders (Finn et al., 2014). The distinction of prostitutes as victims or offenders presents difficulties for how the criminal justice system should treat these persons, with prostitutes identifying dissatisfaction with their treatment by police and court officials (Shdaimah & Wiechelt, 2012). However, recently a specific set of courts and programs has served as a positive outlet for handling prostitution.

Prostitution courts and diversionary programs have emerged as a method to reduce recidivism associated with sex work and to cut down on the number of sexually exploited individuals cycling through the criminal justice system. Such programs draw attention to the heart of the problem, questioning why individuals are continually engaged in prostitution (e.g., being forced, supporting a drug habit) and what avenues might be beneficial to help them exit prostitution (e.g., financial, social, and emotional assistance). A few of these programs include: Services to Access Resources and Safety (STARS), Salt Lake City's Prostitution Diversion Project (PDP), Phoenix Prostitution Diversion Program, and Baltimore City's Specialized Prostitution Diversion program (SPD). These programs have included a variety of components focusing on assisting sex workers through education, counseling, and drug and alcohol treatment. Moreover, these programs have also been utilized to reduce public health concerns (e.g., AIDS) as well as to educate volunteers and individuals working in these programs about prostitution (Wahab, 2006).

Evaluations of prostitution courts have found that prostitutes who have completed a diversionary program are less likely to recidivate for prostitution compared to prostitutes not involved in the diversionary program (Roe-Sepowitz, Hickle, Pérez Loubert, & Egan, 2011). Sex workers have reported the benefits of these courts and programs, commonly feeling empowered as well as socially supported, especially when the persons assisting them had previously been sex workers. A prime example of the benefits of diversionary programs is evident in the story of Lizzie (read box below).

With the assistance of the prostitution court, Lizzie was able to move into a shelter and acquire meaningful employment. Overall, prostitution courts and diversionary programs for sex workers represent a positive alternative to incarceration that tap into the etiology of why these individuals are involved in prostitution, with a focus on victimization.

LIZZIE'S STORY

Lizzie was sexually abused from age 2 to 12 by her stepfather and others, and physically and emotionally abused by her mother. Lizzie was 12 when her mother kicked her out. With no money, no food, and nowhere to go, Lizzie became involved with a pimp and entered the life of prostitution. 20 years later, Lizzie was homeless, struggling with addiction, and had been arrested over 100 times.

For many experts who work with women and girls in prostitution, Lizzie's story is typical. "The multiple experiences of sexual abuse at such a young age ingrained in her a belief that she was worth nothing; this is very common with survivors of childhood sexual abuse," said Miriam Goodman, clinical director at the Midtown

Community Court. Midtown was the first court to treat Lizzie as a victim. The court linked her with mental health and career counseling and helped her get on a path to leave the life of prostitution.

"What made the Midtown Community Court different from the other courts that I've been to is that they offer individual therapy," said Lizzie. "The social workers in the STARS program . . . helped me realize that I needed to make changes in my life."

Lizzie got a job and moved into a reunification shelter for mothers and children. "With the help and the support that I had with Midtown Community Court, I made some wonderful steps," Lizzie said.

Source: Reprinted from Schweig, Malangone, & Goodman (n.d.). Prostitution Diversion Programs.

SUMMARY

- The victim–offender overlap can be conceptualized as a victim who is an offender and vice versa.
- As indicated by recent research, approximately 84% of published studies on the victim–offender overlap since the 1960s have shown support for the concept.
- The victim–offender overlap has been found internationally in Western and non-Western countries.
- The victim–offender overlap has been found for different forms of offending and victimization including those related to violence, property, and substance use. The overlap is most notably exhibited in homicide and intimate partner violence.
- The homicide literature indicates that 50% of victims had previous criminal records.
- Intimate partner violence typologies can be used for understanding the victim–offender overlap.
- Victims and offenders have similar demographic characteristics, commonly being African American and living in urban areas.
- In general, involvement in a criminal event increases the chances of victimization and offending.
- The literature has suggested there are three groups of individuals involved in criminal events: victims, offenders, and victim-offenders.
- There are multiple perspectives why an individual who is victimized might offend (and vice versa), including the dynamic causal perspective and population heterogeneity perspective.
- The dynamic causal and population heterogeneity perspectives attribute social, environmental, and biological factors to explain the overlap.

- While integrated theories have not explicitly tested the overlap, there is substantial reason to believe that they could adequately explain both victimization and offending.
- Victimization early in life might influence delinquency in childhood as well as offending and victimization later in life. This is most relevant for females compared to males, and is common for victims of sexual abuse.
- Prostitutes can be conceptualized as victim-offenders, in that they commonly have a history of abuse (victimization), which influences them to run away from home and become involved in prostitution (offending) as a method of survival.
- Prostitution courts and diversionary programs have produced positive results in reducing recidivism of prostitutes by providing assistance in understanding why individuals might be involve in prostitution and what can be done to them to exit prostitution.

DISCUSSION QUESTIONS

1. Should offenders who have had a history of victimization be treated differently by the legal system than individuals who do not have a history of victimization, and why?

2. Which of the following is more likely, and why: (1) Victimization is more likely to come prior to offending; or (2) Offending is more likely to come prior to victimization?

3. What interventions (aside from the one discussed) might be used to reduce the impact of childhood victimization on offending and victimization later in life?

4. If the population heterogeneity perspective is accurate, and time stable personality and environmental characteristics influence the overlap, what could be done to reduce victimization and offending?

KEY TERMS

victim–offender overlap

principle of homogamy

victim

offender

victim–offender

dynamic causal perspective

"code of the streets"

population heterogeneity

perspective

situational couple violence

intimate terrorism

violent resistance

INTERNET RESOURCES

Prostitution Courts, National Drug Center Court Resource Center (http://www.ndcrc.org/category/types-courts/prostitution-courts)

Contained within the National Drug Center Court Resource Center database, this compilation of reports provides information on prostitution courts and other problem-solving programs.

CONSEQUENCES OF VICTIMIZATION

Let us revisit Polly, the young woman whose victimization was described in Chapter 2. When we left her, Polly was on her way back home after leaving a bar alone at night, and she was robbed and assaulted by two men. But Polly's story does not end there, and although the incident itself ended, Polly dealt with it for quite some time. Polly made it home safely; she entered her apartment, locked her door, and started to cry. She felt scared, alone, and her head was hurting. She told one of her roommates, who was home when she returned, what happened. Her roommate, Rachel, told her she should call the police and have someone look at her head. Polly was hesitant—after all, she did not know what to expect—but she really wanted to make sure that the men were caught, so she called the police and told the dispatcher what had occurred.

The police and emergency personnel arrived. She was taken to the hospital for her head injury and was released after receiving 10 stitches. Before she could go home, though, the police wanted to take her statement. They questioned her for more than an hour, asking minute details about what happened and about the offenders. They also asked her why she was walking home alone at night. The police officers left her with assurances that they would do everything they could to identify her attackers.

The days passed, and Polly had a hard time forgetting about the men and what had transpired. She was having a hard time getting out of bed. In fact, she missed several days of class. She found herself avoiding going out alone at night. She felt as though her life had taken an unexpected, unwanted, and frightening turn—one that she was worried would forever alter her life. Polly's concerns, like others', were most likely not unfounded.

Note: Portions of Chapter 4 are based on Daigle, L. E., & Fisher, B. S. (2013). *The recurrence of victimization: What researchers know about its terminology, characteristics, causes, and prevention.* In R. C. Davis, A. J. Lurigio, & S. Herman (Eds.), *Victims of Crime* (3rd ed.). Thousand Oaks, CA: Sage.

■ PHYSICAL INJURY

Clearly, when people suffer personal victimizations, they are at risk of **physical injury**. These injuries can include bruises, soreness, scratches, cuts, broken bones, contracted diseases, and stab or gunshot wounds. Some of these injuries may be temporary and short-lived, while others can be long-lasting or permanent.

According to data from the National Crime Victimization Survey (NCVS) in 2006, 27% of assault victims sustained physical injuries. Those who experienced robbery were more likely to be injured; 35% of robbery victims suffered physical injury. A larger percentage of female victims were injured than male victims, although the differences were not large. For example, 29% of female assault victims compared with 25% of male assault victims reported being injured. There appears to be a difference in injury for racial groups as well. For both assault and robbery, injuries were present in a larger percentage of Black victims than White victims. The victim–offender relationship was also related to injury—incidents perpetrated by nonstrangers were more likely to result in injury than those perpetrated by strangers (46% for assault compared with 35% for robbery) (Bureau of Justice Statistics [BJS], 2006a).

The most serious physical injury is, of course, death. Although the NCVS does not measure murder—remember, it asks people about their victimization experiences—the Uniform Crime Reports (UCRs) can be used to find out the extent to which deaths are attributable to murder and nonnegligent manslaughter. In 2008, UCR figures showed that 14,180 murders were brought to the attention of the police. The majority of murder victims were male (78%), almost equal percentages were White and Black (49%), and 55% were murdered by an acquaintance. Almost three fourths of the homicides that involved a weapon were gun-related. Most of the homicides for which the circumstances were known resulted from an argument (FBI, 2009).

■ MENTAL HEALTH CONSEQUENCES AND COSTS

People differentially respond to trauma, including victimization. Some people may cope by internalizing their feelings and emotions, while others may experience externalizing responses. It is likely that the way people deal with victimization is tied to their biological make-up, their interactional style, their coping style and resources, and the context in which the incident occurs and in which they operate thereafter. Some of the responses can be quite serious and long-term, while others may be more transitory.

Three affective responses that are common among crime victims are depression, reductions in self-esteem, and anxiety. The way in which **depression** manifests itself varies greatly across individuals. It can include symptoms such as sleep disturbances, changes in eating habits, feelings of guilt and worthlessness, and irritability. Generally, depressed persons will experience a decline in interest in activities they once enjoyed, a depressed mood, or both. For youth, depression is a common outcome for those who are victimized by peers, such as in bullying (Sweeting, Young, West, & Der, 2006). With the advent of technology and the widespread use of the Internet, recent research has explored online victimization and its effects. Online victimization is related to depressive responses in victims (Tynes & Giang, 2009).

Victimization may be powerful enough to alter the way in which a crime victim views himself or herself. Self-esteem and self-worth both have been found to be reduced in some crime victims, particularly female victims. In one study of youths in Virginia, Grills and Ollendick (2002) found that, for girls, being victimized by peers was associated with a reduction in global **self-worth** and that their self-worth was related to elevated levels of anxiety. There may also be a difference in crime's impact on self-appraisals based on the type of victimization experienced. For example, victims of childhood sexual abuse are likely to suffer long-term negative impacts to their **self-esteem** (Beitchman et al., 1992). Sexual victimization also has been linked to reductions in self-esteem (Turner, Finkelhor, & Ormrod, 2010).

Anxiety is another consequence linked to victimization. Persons who suffer from anxiety are likely to experience a range of emotional and physical symptoms. Much like depression, however, anxiety affects people differently. Most notably, anxiety is often experienced as irrational and excessive fear and worry, which may be coupled with feelings of tension and restlessness, vigilance, irritability, and difficulty concentrating. In addition, because anxiety is a product of the body's fight-or-flight response, it also has physical symptoms. These include a racing and pounding heart, sweating, stomach upset, headaches, difficulty sleeping and breathing, tremors, and muscle tension (Dryden-Edwards, 2007).

Although anxiety that crime victims experience may not escalate to a point where they are diagnosed with an anxiety disorder by a mental health clinician, victimization does appear to be linked to anxiety symptoms. For example, adolescents who experience victimization by their peers experience anxiety at higher levels than nonvictimized adolescents (Storch, 2003). The relationship between anxiety and victimization is likely complex in that victimization can lead to anxiety, but anxiety and distress are also precursors to victimization (Siegel, La Greca, & Harrison, 2009). Some victims do experience mental health consequences tied to anxiety that lead to mental health diagnoses.

FOCUS ON RESEARCH

Research on the physical and mental health consequences of victimization has established that victimization can have short- and long-term effects. Bouffard and Koeppel (2014) recently discovered that experiencing repeated bullying before the age of 12 in childhood is linked to poor outcomes in early adulthood. They found that when respondents were between the ages of 18 and 23, those who experienced this specific type of victimization experienced worse negative mental health, were more likely to be homeless during the previous 5 years, and to have poor or fair physical health. What do these findings mean for policy? Given these findings, what should teachers, health care professionals, or others who interact with children do for those who experience bullying?

Source: Adapted from Bouffard, L. A., & Koeppel, M. D. H. (2014). Understanding the potential longterm physical and mental health consequences of early experiences of victimization. *Justice Quarterly, 31,* 568–587.

Posttraumatic Stress Disorder

One of the recognized disorders associated with a patterned response to trauma, such as victimization, is **posttraumatic stress disorder (PTSD)**. Commonly associated with individuals returning from war and combat, PTSD is a psychiatric condition that recently has been recognized as a possible consequence of other traumatic events, such as criminal victimization. Currently classified by the American Psychiatric Association in the *DSM-IV-TR* as an anxiety disorder, PTSD is diagnosed based on several criteria outlined in detail in Table 4.1. A person must have experienced or witnessed a traumatic event that involved actual or threatened death or serious injury to oneself or others, or threat to the physical integrity of oneself or others. The person must have experienced fear, helplessness, or horror in response to the event and then reexperienced the trauma over time via flashbacks, nightmares, images, and/or reliving the event. The person must avoid stimuli associated with the traumatic event and experience numbness of response, such as lack of affect and reduced interest in activities. Finally, PTSD is characterized by hyperarousal.

In order for PTSD to be diagnosed, symptoms must be experienced for more than 1 month and must cause clinically significant distress or impairment in social, occupational, or other functional areas (American Psychiatric Association, 2000). As you may imagine, PTSD can be debilitating and can impact a victim's ability to heal, move on, and thrive after being victimized. About 8% of Americans will experience PTSD, although women are more likely than men to experience this disorder (Kessler, Sonnega, Bromet, Hughes, & Nelson, 1995). The traumatic events most likely to lead to PTSD for men are military combat and witnessing a serious injury or violent death. Women, on the other hand, are most likely to be diagnosed with PTSD related to incidents of rape and sexual molestation (Kessler et al., 1995).

Although it is difficult to know how common PTSD is among crime victims, some studies suggest that PTSD is a real problem for this group. The estimate for PTSD in persons who have been victimized is around 25%. Lifetime incidence of PTSD for persons who have not experienced a victimization is 9% (Kilpatrick & Acierno, 2003). Depression also commonly co-occurs in victims who suffer PTSD (Kilpatrick & Acierno, 2003). Research has shown that victims of sexual assault, aggravated assault, and persons whose family members were homicide victims are more likely than other crime victims to develop PTSD (Kilpatrick & Tidwell, 1989). In support of this link, the occurrence of PTSD in rape victims has been estimated to be almost 1 in 3 (Kilpatrick, Edmunds, & Seymour, 1992). Recent research has explored PTSD as a mediator of outcomes (Ullman, Relyea, Peter-Hagene, & Vasquez, 2013). That is, research has examined the effects of victimization on PTSD and how PTSD may influence other outcomes such as **revictimization** (Risser, Hetzel-Riggin, Thomsen, & McCanne, 2006) and alcohol and drug use (Ullman et al., 2013). For example, while experiencing child sexual abuse was related to PTSD symptomatology, it mediated the relationship between child sexual abuse and adult sexual abuse (Risser et al., 2006). The hyperarousal cluster (of the three symptom clusters of PTSD) was the only significant mediator. This finding suggests the need to intervene after a girl has been victimized, in particular to address mental health needs such as PTSD as a way to potentially reduce revictimization.

Table 4.1 ■ *DSM-IV-TR* Diagnostic Criteria for Posttraumatic Stress Disorder

1. Stressor: A person has been exposed to a traumatic event in which he or she has

   a. experienced, witnessed, or been confronted with an event(s) that involved actual or threatened death or serious injury, or threat to the physical integrity of oneself or others; and

   b. the response to the event included intense fear, helplessness, or horror.

2. Intrusive recollection: The trauma is reexperienced in at least one of the following ways:

   a. Recurrent and intrusive recollections of the event, such as images, thoughts, or perceptions

   b. Recurrent nightmares

   c. Acting or feeling as if the traumatic event were recurring, such as reliving the event, illusions, hallucinations, and flashbacks

   d. Intense psychological distress when exposed to cues that symbolize or resemble a component of the traumatic event

   e. Physiologic reactivity when exposed to cues that symbolize or resemble a component of the traumatic event

3. Avoidance/numbing symptoms: Regular avoidance of stimuli associated with the traumatic event and numbness of response. Three or more of the following symptoms must be present:

   a. Efforts to avoid thoughts, feelings, or conversations about the trauma

   b. Efforts to avoid activities, places, or people that cause the trauma to be remembered

   c. Inability to remember an important element of the trauma

   d. Significant reduced interest or participation in significant activities

   e. Feelings of detachment or estrangement from other people

   f. Lack of affect

   g. Lack of sense of future

4. Hyperarousal: Persistent arousal symptomology. Must experience at least two of the following:

   a. Difficulty falling or staying asleep

   b. Irritability or emotional outbursts

   c. Problems concentrating

   d. Hypervigilance

   e. Exaggerated startle response

In order for PTSD to be diagnosed, the symptoms in Sections 2, 3, and 4 must be experienced for more than one month and must cause clinically significant distress or impairment in social, occupational, or other functional areas.

Source: Reprinted with permission from *The Diagnostic and Statistical Manual of Mental Disorders, Fourth Edition, Text Revision.* Copyright © 2000. American Psychiatric Association.

Self-Blame and Learned Helplessness

Victims of crime may blame themselves for their victimization. One type of **self-blame** is **characterological self-blame,** which occurs when a person ascribes blame to a nonmodifiable source, such as one's character (Janoff-Bulman, 1979). In this way, characterological self-blame involves believing that victimization is deserved. Another type of self-blame is **behavioral self-blame,** which occurs when a person ascribes blame to a modifiable source—behavior (Janoff-Bulman, 1979). When a person turns to behavioral self-blame, a future victimization can be avoided as long as behavior is changed.

In addition to self-blame, others may experience learned helplessness following victimization. **Learned helplessness** is a response to victimization in which victims believe that responding is futile and become passive and numb (Seligman, 1975). In this way, victims may not activate to protect themselves in the face of danger and, instead, put themselves at risk of subsequent victimization experiences.

■ ECONOMIC COSTS

Not only are victimologists concerned with the impact that being a crime victim has on an individual in terms of health, but they are also concerned with the **economic costs** incurred by both the victim and the public. In this sense, victimization is a public health issue. Economic costs can result from property losses; monies associated with medical care; time lost from work, school, and housework; pain, suffering, and reduced quality of life; and legal costs. In 2008, the NCVS estimated the total economic loss from crimes at $17,397 billion. The NCVS also shows that the median dollar amount of loss attributed to crime was $125 (BJS, 2011). Although this number may appear to be low, it largely represents the fact that the typical property crime is a simple larceny-theft.

Direct Property Losses

Crime victims often experience tangible losses in terms of having their property damaged or taken. Generally, when determining **direct property losses,** the value of property that is damaged, taken, and not recovered, and insurance claims and administration costs are considered. According to the NCVS, in 2008, 94% of property crimes resulted in economic losses (BJS, 2011). In one of the most comprehensive reports on the costs of victimization— sponsored by the National Institute of Justice—Miller, Cohen, and Wiersema (1996) estimated the property loss or damage experienced per crime victimization event. These estimates were used by Welsh et al. (2008) in their article on the costs of juvenile crime in urban areas. They found that arson victimizations resulted in an estimated $15,500 per episode. Motor vehicle theft costs about $3,300 per incident. Results from the NCVS show that personal crime victimizations typically did not result in as much direct property loss. For example, only 18% of personal crime victimizations resulted in economic loss. Rape and sexual assaults typically resulted in $100 of property loss or property damage. It is rare for a victim of a violent or property offense to recover any losses. Only about 29% of victims of personal crime and 16% of victims of property crime recover all or some property (BJS, 2011).

Medical Care

To be sure, many victims would gladly suffer property loss if it meant they would not experience any physical injury. After all, items can be replaced and damage repaired. Physical injury may lead to victims needing medical attention, which for some may be the first step in accumulating costs associated with their victimization. **Medical care costs** encompass such expenses as transporting victims to the hospital, doctor care, prescription drugs, allied health services, medical devices, coroner payments, insurance claims processing fees, and premature funeral expenses (Miller et al., 1996).

Results from the NCVS indicate that in 2008, 542,280 violent crime victims received some type of medical care (BJS, 2011). Of those victims who received medical care, slightly more than one third received care in the hospital emergency room or at an emergency clinic, and 9% went to the hospital (BJS, 2011). Receiving medical care often results in victims incurring medical expenses. Almost 6% of victims of violence reported having medical expenses as a result of being victimized (BJS, 2011). About 63% of injured victims had health insurance or were eligible for public medical services (BJS, 2011).

Costs vary across types of victimization. For example, the annual cost of hospitalizations for victims of child abuse is estimated to be $6.2 billion (Prevent Child Abuse America, 2000). Medical treatment for battered women is estimated to cost $1.8 billion annually (Wisner, Gilmer, Saltman, & Zink, 1999). Per-criminal-victimization medical care costs also have been estimated. Assaults in which there were injuries cost $1,470 per incident. Drunk-driving victims who were injured incurred $6,400 in medical care costs (Miller et al., 1996).

Gun violence is associated with substantial medical costs for victims. Although most crime victims do not require hospitalization, even if they are treated in the emergency room, a report on gun violence published by the Office for Victims of Crime showed that gunshot victims make up one third of those who require hospitalization (as cited by Bonderman, 2001). Persons who are shot and admitted to the hospital are likely to face numerous rehospitalizations and incur medical costs throughout their lifetimes. In 2010, the hospital costs associated with firearm assault injuries totaled almost $700 million (Howell, Bieler, & Anderson, 2014). About 60% of these costs is paid by the public either by public insurance such as Medicaid or because persons are uninsured (Howell et al., 2014).

RIPPED FROM THE HEADLINES

Costs of victimization may permeate beyond individuals into the community. That is just what is happening in Memphis, TN where several long-standing businesses are closing their doors and relocating. One business, the Cottage Restaurant, had been operating at its location since 1957, but its owner felt that it simply was not safe any longer to keep open. Instead, it is moving a mile and a half down the road to a safer part of town. Another business owner spent $40,000 to install a surveillance system after losing $10,000 to thefts in the previous year. How can these costs be accounted for when measuring the costs of victimization? What other costs of victimization are there to the community?

Source: Adapted from Preston, E. (2014, August 24). Crime forcing old family business out of neighborhood. News Channel 3, Memphis, TN. http://wreg.com/2014/08/24/crime-forcing-old-family-business-out-of-neighborhood.

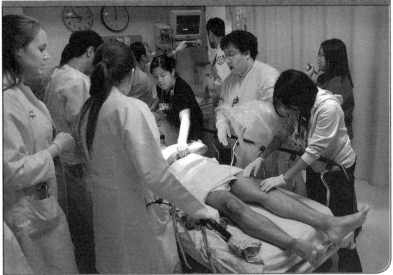

Photo Credit: © Getty Images/Scott Olson.

Mental Health Care Costs

When victims seek mental health care, this also adds to their total costs. It is estimated that
between 10% and 20% of total **mental health care costs** in the United States are related to
crime (Miller et al., 1996). Most of this cost is a result of crime victims seeking treatment
to deal with the effects of their victimization. Between one quarter and one half of rape and
child sexual abuse victims receive mental health care. As a result, sexual victimizations, of
both adults and children, result in some of the largest mental health care costs for victims.
The average mental health care cost per rape and sexual assault is $2,200, and the average for
child abuse is $5,800. Victims of arson who are injured incur about $10,000 of mental care
expenditures per victimization. Secondary victimization, which is discussed in detail in a later
section, is also associated with mental health care costs. The average murder results in between
1.5 and 2.5 people receiving mental health counseling (Miller et al., 1996).

Losses in Productivity

Persons who are victimized may experience an inability to work at their place of employment,
complete housework, or attend school. Not being able to do these things contributes to
the total **lost productivity** that crime victims experience. In 2008, about 7% of persons in
the NCVS who said they were violently victimized lost some time from work (BJS, 2011).
About the same percentage of victims of property offenses lost time from work. Some
victims are more prone to miss work than others. For example, almost one tenth of burglary
victimizations cause victims to miss at least one day of work (BJS, 2011). Data from the NCVS
show that 9% of robbery victimizations resulted in victims missing more than 10 days of
work (BJS, 2011), while victims of intimate partner violence lost almost 8 million paid days
of work annually (Centers for Disease Control and Prevention, 2003). Employers also bear

some costs when their employees are victimized; victimized employees may be less productive, their employers may incur costs associated with hiring replacements, and employers may experience costs dealing with the emotional responses of their employees. Parents also may suffer costs when their children are victimized and they are unable to meet all their job responsibilities as a result of doing things such as taking the child to the doctor or staying home with the child (Miller et al., 1996).

Pain, Suffering, and Lost Quality of Life

The most difficult cost to quantify is the pain, suffering, and loss of quality of life that crime victims experience. When these elements are added to the costs associated with medical care, lost earnings, and programs associated with victim assistance, the cost to crime victims increases 4 times. In other words, this is the largest cost that crime victims sustain. For example, one study estimated the cost in out-of-pocket expenses to victims of rape to be slightly less than $5,100. The crime of rape, however, on average, costs $87,000 when its impact on quality of life is considered (Miller et al., 1996).

Another cost that crime victims may experience is a change in their routines and lifestyles. Many victims report that after being victimized, they changed their behavior. For example, victims of stalking may change their phone numbers, move, or change their normal routines. Others may stop going out alone or start carrying a weapon when they do so. Although these changes may reduce risk of being victimized again, for victims to bear the cost of crime seems somewhat unfair. Did Polly sustain any of these costs?

■ SYSTEM COSTS

The victim is not the only entity impacted economically by crime. The United States in general spends an incredible amount of money on criminal justice. When including **system costs** for law enforcement, the courts, and corrections, the direct expenditures of the criminal justice system are more than $214 billion annually (BJS, 2006b). The criminal justice system employs more than 2.4 million persons, whose collective pay tops $9 billion. Obviously, crime is big business in the United States!

Insurance companies pay about $45 billion annually due to crime (Headden, 1996). The federal government also pays $8 billion annually for restorative and emergency services for crime victims (Headden, 1996). There are other costs society must absorb as a result of crime. For example, it costs Americans when individuals who are not insured or are on public assistance are victimized and receive medical care. The U.S. government covers about one fourth of health insurance payouts to crime victims. Gunshot victims alone cost taxpayers more than $4.5 billion dollars annually (Headden, 1996). These costs are not distributed equally across society. Some communities have been hit especially hard by violence—gun violence in particular. Some 96% of hospital expenses associated with gun violence at King/Drew Medical Center in Los Angeles are paid with public funds (as cited by Bonderman, 2001). To understand how expensive gun violence medical fees can be to the public, read the box item about James, who was shot and survived. We will discuss in Chapter 6 just how these costs are paid and who pays them.

THE STORY OF JAMES

James, 45, was shot in the knee on Sept. 9 as he sat in a car with another man, who died of his wounds at the scene. James' injuries, which also included a hole in the arm and fragments in the eye, were not near vital organs.

His knee looked bad when he came into Froedtert's trauma center, but that turned out to be just the beginning. The next day, he aspirated as a breathing tube was being inserted during surgery, and contents from his stomach got into his lungs.

"It is kind of like a chemical burn," trauma surgeon James Feeney said.

James had to stay in intensive care on a ventilator and be heavily sedated for almost two weeks, while his hospital charges ballooned.

For about a week, he was on drugs that essentially paralyzed most of his muscles. When he began to regain consciousness, he suffered another setback, called ICU psychosis. The maddening disorder is believed to be caused by a variety of factors in intensive care, including breathing tubes, lights, beeping noises, a lack of sleep and sensory deprivation or overload. It can make patients temporarily insane.

"His agitation was so severe every time we tried to take him off (the ventilator), he would get crazy and wild," Feeney said.

James eventually got out of intensive care and has improved dramatically. Doctors say they think they have saved his leg, although they don't know how functional it will be. They also don't know how much vision he lost. He is likely to need more surgeries on both the knee and the eye. James also will need extensive physical therapy.

"The truth is, a lot of these guys would have died 20 years ago before we had an organized system of trauma care," Feeney said.

After a call that started off as a man shot in the leg, he spent nearly six weeks in Froedtert. When he was discharged Oct. 20, the hospital charges—which will be billed to Medicare—topped $277,000.

Medicare caps reimbursement for shooting cases at $36,000, said Blaine O'Connell, Froedtert's chief financial officer. Medicaid and Milwaukee County's General Assistance Medical Program also pay only a fraction of the hospital's charges.

And for many uninsured patients, the hospital may collect even less, he said.

Ultimately, the losses on all those cases are factored into the rates the hospital must charge private insurers.

Source: "Gunshot costs echo through economy. From hospitals to jails, price of violence adds up quickly." By John Diedrich and John Fauber (2006). *Milwaukee Wisconsin Journal Sentinel Online,* http://www.jsonline.com/news/milwaukee/29205944.html.

■ VICARIOUS VICTIMIZATION

It is not only the victim and the system that are saddled with costs. The effects that victimization has on those close to the victim are also critical in understanding the total impact of crime. So far, we have discussed how a victim may need medical care, may seek mental health counseling, may lose time from work, and may have a less full life after being victimized. But what happens to those who love and care about these victims? Does witnessing a loved one go through victimization also exact a price?

The effects that victimization has on others are collectively known as **vicarious victimization.** Vicarious victimization has been most widely studied in regard to **homicide** survivors—people whose loved ones have been murdered—given the profound effect that homicide has on family members, even when compared with nonhomicide deaths. Homicide deaths are almost exclusively sudden and violent. Surviving family members often experience guilt about not being able to prevent the death. The involvement of the criminal justice system also adds an element to the response family members have, and there is often a feeling that others view the death as at least partly the victim's fault.

The studies on homicide survivors have largely found that they experience many of the same posttrauma symptoms that crime victims themselves experience. One study found that almost one quarter of homicide surviving family members developed PTSD after the murder of their family member (as cited in Kilpatrick, Amick, & Resnick, 1990). The disorder and PTSD symptomology are often not transient, with homicide survivors exhibiting PTSD symptoms for up to 5 years following the murder (Redmond, 1989). Being a homicide survivor also may be related to greater PTSD symptoms than being a victim of a crime such as rape (Amick-McMullan, Kilpatrick, & Veronen, 1989). Also interesting, homicide survivors experience higher levels of PTSD than do family members who lose a loved one through means other than homicide, such as accidentally (Applebaum & Burns, 1991). PTSD is not the only psychological response that homicide survivors show. They also have higher levels of distress, depression, anxiety, and hostility than persons who have not experienced trauma (Thompson, Kaslow, Price, Williams, & Kingree, 1998).

In addition to psychological responses, homicide survivors may exhibit behavioral consequences. Parents whose children die via homicide are more likely to exhibit suicidal ideation than parents whose children commit suicide or die accidentally (Murphy, Tapper, Johnson, & Lohan, 2003). Other homicide survivors may exhibit lifestyle changes by avoiding places and activities—either because they are fearful or anxious, or because they no longer feel able to participate in activities that are reminiscent of times spent with their now-deceased

PHOTO 4.2

A support group for family members of murdered people.

Photo Credit: © iStockphoto.com/Alina Solovyova-Vincent.

loved one. Homicide survivors also evince feelings of vulnerability, loss of control, loss of meaning, and self-blame. As you can now be certain, criminal victimization has wide-reaching effects on the victim, the system, and others.

Another form of vicarious victimization occurs when a person is traumatized by the coverage violent acts receive through media or other outlets that provide information. This type of vicarious victimization is likely to occur when seven factors are present: (1) realistic threat of death to all members of the community; (2) extraordinary carnage; (3) strong community affiliation; (4) witnessing of event by community members; (5) symbolic significance of victims to community; (6) need for rescue workers; and (7) significant media attention (Young, 1989). Given these factors, traumatic events that do not directly affect a person or a person's loved ones may also cause harm such as PTSD. Events such as the terrorist attacks on September 11, 2001, are prime examples of traumas that can produce lasting, harmful consequences to people exposed to them. Other events, such as a serial killer operating in a community, may also be a form of vicarious victimization that can produce PTSD in community members (Herkov & Biernat, 1997).

■ REPORTING

All the consequences and outcomes we have discussed thus far are impacted by the victim **reporting** the offense to the police. Reporting may intensify some of these consequences, may temper some of the impact, or may be somewhat unrelated to the victim's experiences after the incident occurs. Reporting is important for several reasons. One important factor about reporting to the police is that it is the first essential step in activating the formal criminal justice system. Without a report to the police, the victim is left to deal with the aftermath through other channels, and the police will never begin an investigative process. Without this first critical step, it is extremely unlikely that an offender will ever be caught. When an offender "gets away" with crime, it can have important consequences. When this occurs, the offender is learning that he or she can continue to freely offend—perhaps even against the same person or household. Conversely, an arrest or real threat of arrest may deter potential offenders.

Victims may also be negatively impacted if they do not report. Many victims' services, as will be discussed in Chapter 6, are available only for victims who notify the police about their incident. For example, many district attorney's offices have victim advocates, whose job it is to help victims navigate the criminal justice system and assist them with other programs such as receiving victim compensation. The ability to utilize these services is typically conditioned on reporting, since the district attorney's office would not even know about a crime victim who did not first come forward. To highlight the lack of use of victims' services, in 2012, only 8% of individuals who experienced a violent crime according to the NCVS indicated that they received assistance from a victim service agency (Truman, Langton, & Planty, 2013). A greater percentage of rape and sexual assault victims receive such services (22%) than other types of violent crime victims (Truman et al., 2013).

With all these benefits to reporting, it is easy to forget that slightly less than half of all violent crime victims and just more than one third of property crime victims notify the police (Truman et al., 2013). In 2012, slightly more than half of all robbery victims, 62% of aggravated assault victims, and 28% of all rape and sexual assault victims reported their incidents to the police.

Reporting varies by crime type, but it also varies according to other characteristics (Hart & Rennison, 2003). Generally, violence against women and violence against older persons is more likely to come to the attention of the police than violence against men and younger persons. Victimizations that result in the victim suffering an injury are more likely to be reported than those that do not result in injury. When an offender is armed, perceived to be under the influence of alcohol and/or drugs, a stranger, and a non-gang member, the victim is more likely to call the police (Hart & Rennison, 2003).

Besides these incident characteristics, victims also give tangible reasons for not reporting their incidents to the police. Overall, the most common reasons given by victims of violence for why they do not report include that the victimization was a private or personal matter, that it was reported to another official, that the object was recovered/the offender was unsuccessful, or for fear of reprisal (BJS, 2006a). Table 4.2 shows the reasons victims give for not reporting to the police for different victimization types. But some victims do in fact bring their incidents to the attention of the police. Most commonly, victims of violence report their incidents to prevent future violence, to stop the offender, because it was a crime, and to protect others (BJS, 2006a). Table 3.4 shows the common reasons that victims do report for different victimization types.

For victims of property crime, the most common reasons given for not bringing the incident to the attention of the police are that the object was recovered/the offender was unsuccessful, feeling the police would not want to be bothered, or lack of proof. Property crime victims were motivated to report because they wanted to recover stolen property, because it was a crime, and to prevent further crimes against them by the offender (BJS, 2006a).

■ FEAR OF CRIME

Another cost associated with victimization is fear. Fear is an emotional response to a perceived threat (Ferraro & LaGrange, 1987). Physiologically, when people experience fear, their body activates to alert them to danger. These bodily responses are associated with the autonomic nervous system being activated—heart rate increases, pupils dilate, digestion slows, blood supply to muscles increases, breathing rate increases, and sweating increases (Fishbein, 2001). These physiological changes occur so that in the face of danger, a person can fight or flee. **Fear of crime** is different than **perceived risk** of being a victim. Perceived risk is the perceived likelihood that a person feels that he or she will become a crime victim. Perceptions of risk are related to fear in that those people who perceive their risk to be high generally have higher levels of fear of crime than those who do not perceive their risk of victimization to be high (May, Rader, & Goodrum, 2010; Warr, 1984).

As you may imagine, fear is difficult to measure. How do you know whether someone is more fearful of crime than another person? Would you simply ask someone, or do you think looking for other indications of fear would be better? One of the most common ways to measure fear of crime is by asking individuals on surveys, "How safe do you feel or would you feel being out alone in your neighborhood?" (Ferraro & LaGrange, 1987). One problem with this question is that the respondent is not asked specifically about fear or being afraid. In addition, asking about how safe someone feels being alone in his or her neighborhood at

Reasons for Not Reporting	Type of Crime						
	Rape/ Sexual Assault	Robbery	Assault	Purse Snatching/ Pocket Picking	Household Burglary	Motor Vehicle Theft	Theft
Reported to another official	9.4	5.4	14.2	14.8	5.2	3.4	8.3
Private or personal matter	24.5	12.2	21.8	18.0	7.0	7.9	5.3
Object recovered; offender unsuccessful	10.0	11.2	18.5	17.5	21.4	16.3	28.7
Not important enough	2.0	1.9	7.1	3.7	6.2	0.0	4.4
Insurance would not cover	0.0	0.7	0.0	0.0	3.4	3.4	2.6
Not aware crime occurred until later	0.0	2.1	0.2	2.3	7.1	4.7	5.1
Unable to recover property; no ID number	0.0	0.0	0.2	7.4	4.8	1.0	6.5
Lack of proof	0.0	10.2	2.1	21.0	12.1	13.1	9.9
Police would not want to be bothered	4.8	11.4	5.8	3.3	10.9	3.1	10.5
Police inefficient, ineffective, or biased	0.0	17.8	3.1	0.0	6.9	15.3	3.8
Fear of reprisal	17.0	5.8	7.3	0.0	1.0	1.3	0.5
Too inconvenient or time-consuming	6.5	7.5	4.2	3.8	3.5	6.4	4.1
Other	25.9	13.8	15.6	8.3	10.3	24.2	10.4

Table 4.2 ■ Percentage of Reasons for Not Reporting Victimization to the Police

Source: Criminal Victimization in the United States 2006, Statistical Tables; National Crime Victimization Survey. Washington, D. C.: U.S. Department of Justice, Bureau of Justice Statistics.

Table 4.3 ◼ Percentage of Reasons for Reporting Victimization to the Police

Reasons for Reporting	Type of Crime						
	Rape/ Sexual Assault	Robbery	Assault	Purse Snatching/ Pocket Picking	Household Burglary	Motor Vehicle Theft	Theft
Stop or prevent incident	15.4	8.6	28.5	10.3	11.3	5.3	9.3
Needed help due to injury	7.3	1.6	2.9	6.0	0.1	0.0	0.6
To recover property	2.4	15.2	0.3	30.9	18.0	35.5	23.6
To collect insurance	0.0	1.5	0.5	0.0	3.0	6.2	4.0
To prevent further crimes by offender against victim	16.8	20.0	21.9	10.7	12.3	5.4	8.0
To prevent crime by offender against anyone	2.5	13.2	8.2	3.3	7.9	6.8	6.5
To punish offender	13.8	5.9	6.6	0.0	5.5	5.0	4.5
To catch or find offender	11.6	9.3	4.2	9.9	8.6	6.7	6.6
To improve police surveillance	4.1	3.3	2.7	8.4	9.3	5.3	7.1
Duty to notify police	4.1	7.4	4.8	5.7	6.8	4.9	7.3
Because it was a crime	12.8	11.1	14.2	14.8	15.2	19.1	20.7
Other reason	4.1	2.1	3.9	0.0	1.5	0.9	2.1

Source: Criminal Victimization in the United States 2006, Statistical Tables; National Crime Victimization Survey. Washington, D. C.: U.S. Department of Justice, Bureau of Justice Statistics.

night may not capture the types of criminal behavior of which a person is fearful. Another common question asked of survey participants is, "Is there any area around here—that is, within a mile—where you would be afraid to walk alone at night?" Although this question does ask specifically about being afraid, it does not ask the respondent to consider being afraid of crime. Also, the question vaguely references "around here within a mile," which covers a wide range. Finally, many people may be unlikely to walk alone at night, therefore the question may fail to capture events that an individual is likely to face. A better question that has been commonly used in more frequent research is, "How afraid are you of becoming the victim of [separate offenses] in your everyday life?" (Warr & Stafford, 1983). This question asks about how afraid the respondent is, makes a specific reference to crime, and uses the phrase "in your everyday life" so that respondents will reference their daily routines and realities.

Now that you know how fear is measured, let's now consider who is fearful of being a victim of crime. One thing to consider is that persons do not have to be victims of crime to be fearful. In fact, research shows that some groups who are actually less likely to be victimized than others have higher levels of fear of crime than those with higher risks of victimization. For example, females (Ferraro, 1995, 1996; Haynie, 1998; May et al., 2010; Rountree, 1998) and older persons (Ferraro, 1995) have higher levels of fear of crime than males and younger people. Older adults are likely fearful because they are less likely to feel that they can fend off attackers or otherwise protect themselves (Fuentes & Gatz, 1983). For females, this elevated fear of crime has been attributed to their overarching fear of sexual assault. What is interesting is that, in general, women note that their real risk of being raped or sexually assaulted is actually low compared to other crimes, but that they fear rape at greater levels. Known as the "shadow hypothesis," this fear of sexual assault actually serves to increase females' fears of other types of crimes (Ferraro, 1995, 1996; Warr, 1985; Wilcox, Jordan, & Pritchard, 2006). Not all women are fearful of course. Those women who feel as though they are unable to defend themselves from rape and sexual violence, who believe that sexual violence comes with serious negative consequences, and who thought that becoming a victim of sexual violence was likely were most fearful (Custers & Van den Bulck, 2013).

Other factors have been tied to experiencing fear of crime. One element that has been linked to fear is the level of **incivilities** in an area. Incivilities are low-level breaches of community standards that indicate erosion of conventionally accepted norms and values (LaGrange, Ferraro, & Supancic, 1992). Incivilities can be **physical**, which are disordered physical surroundings such as litter, trash, and untended property. They can also be **social**, which are untended people or behavior such as rowdy youth, loiterers, and people drinking. Research on incivilities shows that incivility is related to people's perceived risk of crime, and risk of crime is related to fear (LaGrange et al., 1992). Other research on incivilities shows that incivilities predict fear of burglary, vandalism, and panhandling (Ferraro, 1996). It may be crime itself that influences fear of crime. Research shows that burglary rates within a neighborhood influence fear of crime in the United States (Taylor, 2001) as do crime rates in a person's own neighborhood among New Zealanders (Breetzke & Pearson, 2014), and crime rates on fear of crime in the United Kingdom (Brunton-Smith & Sturgis, 2011).

Being fearful may be good if it leads people to protect themselves while still enjoying their life. Research on fear of crime shows that people, in response to fear, may engage in avoidance behaviors. **Avoidance behaviors** (also called **constrained behaviors**) are restrictions that people place on their behavior to protect themselves from harm, such as staying home at night. Others may engage in **defensive behaviors** or **protective behaviors** to guard themselves from victimization, such as purchasing a gun or installing security lights (Ferraro & LaGrange, 1987). To read about how fear of crime has impacted people's behavior see the Focus on International Issues box. Although having some level of fear is likely good, as it serves to properly activate people in the face of danger and to caution people to engage in protective behaviors, exaggerated levels of fear can be problematic. People may effectively sever themselves from the outside world and not engage in activities they find enjoyable—in short, fear may paralyze some people. What also may happen is that engaging in avoidance behaviors may increase a person's fear levels (Ferraro, 1996). What this means is that the behaviors that people engage in to protect them from harm may actually serve to make them feel *less* safe.

FOCUS ON INTERNATIONAL ISSUES

Fear of victimization can cause persons to engage in avoidance behaviors. Some family members of England's soccer team's players who are black decided to not travel to the European Championship for fear of racist abuse and violence. The British government and human rights organizations warned about the possibility of such abuse and violence in Poland and Ukraine, the nations who were co-hosting the Championship. Do you think it is sad that the fear of victimization causes people to not engage in behaviors that they would like to, like travel with their families?

Source: Adapted from Black families fear racism at Euros. (2012, May 25). Retrieved from http://www.iol.co.za/sport/soccer/cup-competitions/black-families-fear-racism-at-euros-1.1305217#.T-ndXmXwKHg.

SUMMARY

- The potential consequences and costs to crime victims are plenty and occur over the short and long term. These costs include economic costs as well as costs to their functioning and health.
- A small proportion of crime victims experience physical injury, and most do not receive medical care. Victims of violence, particularly gun violence, are likely to need medical assistance. Female victims, Black victims, and those victimized by a nonstranger are more likely than other victims to experience an injury.
- Beyond physical injury, victims may need mental health care. Victims often experience mental health issues such as depression, anxiety, and posttraumatic stress disorder following their victimization. Victims of sexual assault, rape, and child abuse are the most likely to seek mental health care as a direct result of being victimized. Treatment for mental health issues is yet another cost that victims face.
- There are direct economic costs to victims as well. National Crime Victimization Survey data show that more than 90% of property crimes involve some economic loss to the victim. These economic costs include direct property losses in which a victim's property is stolen or damaged. They also include expenses related to medical care. Slightly less than

1 in 10 victims of violence incur medical expenses. Victims also lose money and productivity when they are unable to work, go to school, or complete housework. Almost 20% of victims of rape and sexual assault miss 10 or more days of work. Finally, victims may experience pain, suffering, and a reduced quality of life, all of which are difficult to quantify.

- Crime and victimization create costs to the system. The United States spends more than $214 billion annually on direct expenditures to operate the criminal justice system. Other elements of the economy are also hit by crime. Insurance companies make large payouts each year due to crime.

- It is not just the victim himself or herself who is pained by the event. Friends and family members may also experience costs when their loved ones are harmed. This is known as secondary victimization. Homicide survivors are more likely than others to experience posttraumatic stress disorder, distress, depression, and anxiety. They may find themselves unable or unwilling to participate in ordinary activities.

- Most criminal victimizations are not reported to the police, and crime reporting varies across crime type. Robbery and aggravated assault are the most common personal victimizations reported to the police. Females, older persons, and those injured are more likely than other victims to notify the police.

- Incident characteristics such as use of a weapon, the offender being under the influence of alcohol and/or drugs, and the offender being a non-gang member are related to reporting.

- Common reasons given for reporting are to stop the incident, to prevent the offender from offending again, and because it was a crime. Nonreporting is linked to the event being considered a personal/private matter, feeling the police would not want to be bothered, and being worried about reprisal.

- Another potential cost of victimization is being fearful of becoming a crime victim. Females and older people tend to have higher levels of fear than males and younger persons. Females tend to have higher levels of fear due to their fear of sexual assault, which shadows their fear of crime more generally. People who perceive their risk of victimization to be high also tend to have high levels of fear. Some levels of fear are probably good in that they lead people to protect themselves by engaging in avoidance or defensive behaviors. Too much fear, however, can be bad if fear leads to anxiety or isolation.

DISCUSSION QUESTIONS

1. We will discuss in a later section who pays for the costs of victimization and how victims can be compensated. What do you think we should do for victims? Should their medical bills be paid? What about other costs? Who should be held accountable for paying those?

2. Why do people not report their victimizations to police? What barriers to reporting exist for crime victims? What are the implications of reporting or failure to report?

3. What costs did Polly experience as a result of her victimization? What long-term consequences do you think she may have to deal with?

4. Think about your own life and try to recall a time when you were victimized. Identify all the costs that came with your victimization. What short-term and long-term costs did you experience? Did you report the incident to the police?

5. How fearful of crime are you? Of what specific types of crimes do you fear becoming the victim? Do you think your fear is rational (e.g., tied to actual risk), or is it linked to something else? Why?

KEY TERMS

physical injury

depression

self-worth

self-esteem

anxiety

posttraumatic stress disorder (PTSD)

revictimization

stressor

intrusive recollection

avoidance/numbing symptoms

hyperarousal

self-blame

characterological self-blame

behavioral self-blame

learned helplessness

economic costs

direct property losses

medical care costs

mental health care costs

lost productivity

system costs

vicarious victimization

homicide survivors

reporting

fear of crime

perceived risk

incivilities

physical incivilities

social incivilities

avoidance or constrained behaviors

defensive behaviors

protective behaviors

INTERNET RESOURCES

"Addressing Predisposition Revictimization in Cases of Violence Against Women" (http://www.nij.gov/topics/crime/violence-against-women/workshops/pages/revictimization.aspx)

This website includes summary information on a workshop hosted by the National Institute of Justice. This workshop was conducted to examine strategies, policies, and principles in place in 2005 and to focus research on victimization in the time period of predisposition (postarrest and prior to trial and/or sentencing).

Coping with Trauma and Grief (http://www.victimsofcrime.org/help-for-crime-victims/coping-with-trauma-and-grief)

This website is part of the National Center for Victims of Crime and includes recent information on coping with trauma and grief, particularly as they relate to victimization. It discusses issues such as how children cope with tragedies such as school shootings and losing loved ones. It provides links to resources for victims, including information about resilience.

Help for Crime Victims (http://www.ovc.gov/pubs/helpseries/pdfs/HelpBrochure_Homicide.pdf)

The Office for Victims of Crime has collected a list of websites that lend support and encouragement to homicide survivors and covictims. There is also information about homicide and what to expect if a loved one is murdered.

National Center for PTSD (http://www.ptsd.va.gov/index.asp)

This website contains information on PTSD in relation to the U.S. Department of Veterans Affairs. The center aims to help U.S. veterans and others through research, education, and training focused on trauma and PTSD. The website also has information for providers, researchers, and the general public on PTSD and its treatment.

5

RECURRING VICTIMIZATION

Another cost of victimization often not discussed or known is the real possibility that a person who is victimized once will be victimized again. In fact, persons who have been victimized are *more* likely to be victimized again than others who have not experienced *any* victimization. For example, a home that has been burgled is 4 times more likely to be burgled a second time than a home that has not experienced any burglary at all (Forrester, Chatterton, & Pease, 1988). At first, this reality probably does not make sense. After all, if you were victimized, you may be likely to implement crime reduction strategies. For example, if you had your car broken into because you had valuables in plain view, would you keep such items in your car again? You probably are shaking your head no. So, why then are some people prone to being victimized not once, but again, and sometimes, again and again and again? Before we can address that question, let us first define terms related to recurring victimization and find out the extent to which people are victimized more than once.

■ TYPES OF RECURRING VICTIMIZATION

To know the extent to which people experience more than one victimization, let us first identify what we mean by recurring victimization. As seen in Table 5.1, **recurring victimization** occurs when a person or place is victimized more than once by any type of victimization. **Repeat victimization** occurs when a person or place is victimized more than once by the same type of victimization. **Revictimization** is commonly referred to when a person is victimized more than once by any type of victimization but across a relatively wide span of time—such as from childhood to adulthood. Revictimization has been most widely studied in terms of childhood sexual abuse and sexual assault in adulthood. **Poly-victimization** is another form of recurring victimization. Poly-victimization is a term that is generally used for childhood recurring victimization, when a person has experienced multiple forms of victimization (Finkelhor, Ormrod, & Turner, 2007a, 2007b). For example, a child who is beaten by his or her parents and who experiences sexual abuse by a neighbor is a poly-victim.

The last term to be familiar with is **near-repeat victimization**. A near-repeat victimization occurs when a place is victimized that is close by or near in proximity to a place that was previously victimized. Near repeats occur because of crime displacement within a relatively small geographical area after an initial victimization has occurred (Johnson et al., 2007). Near repeats are often studied in reference to burglary incidents. Consider a home that experiences a burglary. The homeowner decides to install an alarm and security lighting after the burglary, thus "hardening" the home from future burglary. Other homes without alarms, however, are not similarly protected. As a result, a burglar who returns to the location may find the first home an unattractive target and choose to burglarize a nearby home instead. In this way, near-repeat victimization happens to a new place but is considered recurring victimization, because it is believed that the initial place that was victimized would have been targeted again had it not been for its target hardening.

■ EXTENT OF RECURRING VICTIMIZATION

Now that we know what the terms mean, let's find out how often people and places are victimized more than once. Although most people and households in a given year are not victimized at all, some experience more than one victimization. Large-scale national victimization surveys reveal that many people who are victimized are unfortunate enough to experience recurring victimization. A victimization survey similar to the National Crime Victimization Survey (NCVS), the British Crime Survey (BCS) that you read about in Chapter 2, showed that of those individuals who experienced any type of victimization, 28% experienced two or more incidents during the same year (Crime in England and Wales, 2010/2011). Forty-four percent of domestic violence victims and 19% of acquaintance violence victims experienced more than one incident (Crime in England and Wales, 2010/2011). Results from the NCVS also indicate that recurring victimization is occurring. For example, in 2012, about 1% of the victimizations were series victimizations ((Truman, et al., 2013). Findings from the General Social Survey on Victimization in Canada also highlight the occurrence of recurring victimization. Results from the 2004 survey show that 38% of victims experienced more than one incident (Perrault, Sauve, & Burns, 2010).

You may be wondering if all types of victimizations are likely to happen to victims more than once. Although some types are more likely to recur than others, research shows that victims of intimate partner violence, rape, assault, and property victimization are all at risk of experiencing a subsequent incident following their initial victimization. For example, between 1992 and 2004, about 15% of households surveyed in the NCVS experienced multiple family violence incidents involving the same victim (Goodlin & Dunn, 2010). Other research on intimate partner violence supports this finding. Findings from the National Violence Against Women Survey (discussed in detail in Chapter 9) shows that female victims of intimate partner physical assault reported being assaulted on average 6.9 times by the same partner, while men reported experiencing an average 4.4 assaults by the same intimate partner (Tjaden & Thoennes, 2000a).

Table 5.1 ■ Terminology Related to Recurring Victimization

Type of Victimization	Type of Incidents Experienced	Length of Time Between Incidents
Recurring victimization	A victimization of any type followed by a victimization of any type Ex. A theft followed by an assault	Can be any time between incidents
Repeat victimization	A victimization followed by another victimization of the exact same type Ex. A theft followed by a theft	Generally, incidents occur relatively close to each other temporally in the same developmental period. Ex. A college student is assaulted in May and assaulted in June of the same year.
Revictimization	A victimization of any type followed by a victimization of any type Ex. A theft followed by an assault	Can be any time between incidents; generally refers to incidents that occur in different developmental time periods Ex. A person is abused as a child and then is raped as an adult.
Poly-victimization	A victimization of any type followed by a victimization of a different type Ex. A sexual abuse followed by a physical assault	Generally, during childhood, but must be during the same developmental time period Ex. A child is hit by his parents and bullied by students at school.
Near-repeat victimization	A victimization that occurs in one location followed by the same type of victimization at a nearby location Ex. A burglary at one home followed by a burglary at a neighbor's home	No set time frame in between incidents, but generally relatively close to each other. More important is the geographical closeness of incidents.

Rape and other sexual victimizations also recur. Women in the National Violence Against Women Study who had been raped averaged 2.9 rapes during the previous 12 months. In addition, research on college students shows that they too are at risk of experiencing recurring sexual victimization. In fact, 7% of college students in the National Women Sexual Victimization Study had experienced more than one sexual victimization incident during the previous academic year (Daigle, Fisher, & Cullen, 2008). There is a strong correlation between sexual victimization in childhood and sexual victimization later in life as well. Women who had experienced childhood sexual abuse were six times more likely to experience sexual abuse as adults by a current intimate partner than women without a childhood sexual abuse history (Desai, Arias, Thompson, & Basile, 2002). Others have estimated that childhood sexual abuse increases the risk of adult sexual victimization by 2 to 3 times (Fleming, Mullen, Sibthorpe, & Bammer, 1999; Wyatt, Guthrie, & Notgrass, 1992).

Assault and property victimizations are other types of victimizations that may recur. Findings from the National Youth Survey revealed that almost 60% of youth who had been assaulted were actually repeat victims (Lauritsen & Davis Quinet, 1995)! Although not quite as prevalent, a proportion of burglary victims in the BCS were repeat victims—14% in 2004 (Nicholas, Povey, Walker, & Kershaw, 2005).

Another interesting feature of recurring victimization is that these recurring victims also experience a disproportionate share of all victimization events. For example, 6% of the respondents in the BCS over 10 years experienced 68% of all the thefts that occurred (Pease, 1998). Other research on property victimization also supports this finding. Research on university students in the East Midlands of England showed that 10% of the victims of property crime accounted for 56% of all of the property crime incidents (Barberet, Fisher, & Taylor, 2004). Recurring violent crime victims also experience more than their "fair share" of victimization events. The 2% of respondents in Canada's General Social Survey who were recurring violence victims had experienced 60% of all of the violent victimizations (Perrault et al., 2010). Similarly, 3% of personal crime victims in the BCS accounted for 78% of all personal crime victimizations (Pease, 1998). Lauritsen and Davis Quinet's (1995) research on youth found that 18% of them experienced almost 90% of the assaults. Finally, sexual assault recurring victims also experience an inordinate amount of all sexual victimization incidents. In their study of college women, Daigle, Fisher, and Cullen (2008) found that 7% of college women experienced more than one sexual victimization incident during the previous academic year and that these women experienced almost three fourths of all of the sexual victimizations that occurred.

■ CHARACTERISTICS OF RECURRING VICTIMIZATION

In addition to knowing to what extent recurring victimization occurs, two other features of recurring victimization have been examined—the time between recurring incidents and the type of incident a person is likely to experience after the initial victimization. The first characteristic is known as the **time-course** of recurring victimization, while the latter is referred to as **crime-switching** patterns and **victim proneness**. We will discuss each in turn.

The Time-Course of Recurring Victimization

Researchers have been interested in knowing how soon a victim is likely to experience a subsequent victimization. What this body of research has generally found is that recurring victimization is likely to happen quickly. When examining the time between incidents, researchers have found that, often, little time transpires between incidents. Specifically, research on residential burglary shows that a subsequent burglary is likely to happen within a month after the initial burglary incident! In fact, one study showed that half of the second residential burglaries in Canada that were reported to the police occurred within 7 days of the first burglary (Polvi, Looman, Humphries, & Pease, 1991)! Research within the United States also confirms that the time immediately following an initial burglary is the key period of risk for households—25% of repeat burglary incidents occurred within a week and just more than half occurred within a month in a study that examined police call data in Tallahassee, Florida (Robinson 1998).

This period of heightened risk holds true for domestic violence, sexual victimization, and near repeats as well. Of the households that had called the police for domestic violence once, 35% had done so again within 5 weeks (as cited by Farrell & Pease, 2006). For college women's sexual victimization, one study found that most subsequent incidents happened within the same month or 1 month after the initial incident (Daigle et al., 2008). Near repeats are most likely to occur within 2 weeks. Research on shootings in Philadelphia discovered that near repeats were likely to occur within 2 weeks and one city block after previous shootings (Ratcliffe & Rengert, 2008). This elevated risk also occurs for near-repeat burglaries. After a burglary occurs, burglaries within 200 meters of the burgled home are at greatest risk of being burgled for a 2-week period (Johnson et al., 2007). What is also interesting is that across victimization types, this heightened risk period declines over time. For example, in the study of college women's experiences of sexual victimization by Daigle, Fisher, and Cullen (2008), only 21% of rape incidents occurred within 3 months or more after the initial rape incident.

Others have studied the amount of time that transpires between successive incidents of victimization. Intimate partner violence has been investigated in this manner to see how long victims go without being victimized. In her study of repeat intimate partner violence, Mele (2009) found that, over time, the median number of days between successive incidents of intimate partner violence decreases. The median number of days between the first and second incident was 62, and the median number of days between the third and fourth incident was 37. This finding shows that the frequency of recurring intimate partner violence actually accelerates over time.

You may have noticed that the research on the time course of repeat victimization has also pin-pointed a spatial element to this phenomenon. Indeed, there appears to be a clustering of incidents in that near-repeat incidents are likely to recur within a relatively small geographic space from an initial victimized target. In other words, the risk of a near-repeat is not random, but rather concentrated in particular areas within a city or neighborhood. This pattern holds true for near-repeat burglaries as well as gun violence (Wells, Wu, & Ye, 2011). Importantly, knowing that repeat victimization is likely to recur within a close proximity should aid in prevention efforts (Johnson & Bowers, 2004).

Crime-Switch Patterns and Victim Proneness

Do recurring victims always experience the same type of victimization when they experience more than one victimization? You may wonder what type of victimization victims are likely to experience if they experience more than one. Research examining this issue concludes that, most likely, when a person is victimized a subsequent time, he or she will experience the same type of victimization previously experienced (Reiss, 1980). For example, a theft victim is likely to experience another theft if victimized a second time. One of the first investigations that examined crime-switch (or proneness) patterns found evidence for victim proneness for victims of larceny, burglary, household larceny, and assault (Reiss, 1980). More recent research examining crime-switching within types of sexual victimization also found evidence of victim proneness. For example, in a sample of sexual victimization incidents occurring among college women, rape incidents were likely to be followed by rape incidents, and sexual coercion incidents were likely to be followed by sexual coercion incidents (Daigle et al., 2008).

■ RISK FACTORS FOR RECURRING VICTIMIZATION

We know that recurring victimization is likely to happen quickly and is likely to be of the same type of victimization, but what factors place a person or place at risk of experiencing recurring victimization? These risk factors can be individual-level risk factors or characteristics of the area or household.

Individual-Level Risk Factors

Let's first consider those factors that are tied to the individual that place a person at risk of being victimized more than once. Demographic characteristics are examples of individual-level risk factors that may place a person at risk for recurring victimization. Indeed, the recurring victimization literature has found that males are more likely to be victims repeatedly than females (for all types of victimizations except sexual victimization) (Lauritsen & Davis Quinet, 1995; Mukherjee & Carcach, 1998). In addition, younger people are at a greater risk for recurring victimization than are older persons (Gabor & Mata, 2004; Lauritsen & Davis Quinet, 1995; Mukherjee & Carcach, 1998; Outlaw, Ruback, & Britt, 2002; Perrault et al., 2010; Tseloni, 2000; Wittebrood & Nieuwbeerta, 2000). Single (Lasley & Rosenbaum, 1988; Perrault et al., 2010), separated (Mukherjee & Carcach, 1998), and divorced (Tseloni, 2000) persons face greater risks of repeat victimization than others. Socioeconomic and employment status are two additional demographic characteristics that have been linked to recurring victimization. Low, as compared to high, socioeconomic status is a risk factor for personal recurring victimization (Lauritsen & Davis Quinet, 1995), although having high socioeconomic status actually places you at greater risk of repeat property victimization (Lauritsen & Davis Quinet, 1995; Outlaw et al., 2002). Finally, unemployed persons are more likely than employed persons to be victimized more than once (Mukherjee & Carcach, 1998).

Demographics are not the only type of individual-level characteristics that may increase risk for recurring victimization. Think back to Chapter 2 and risky lifestyles/routine activities theory. Given what these theoretical perspectives say about victimization risk, what other factors may increase risk for recurring victimization? Research indicates that people who spend nights away from home more frequently face greater chances of being repeatedly victimized than those who spend less time away from home at night (Lasley & Rosenbaum, 1988; Tseloni, 2000). Using public transportation after 6 PM also places people at risk for repeat victimization (Mukherjee & Carcach, 1998). Other features of risky lifestyles theory that have been linked to repeat victimization are spending time with delinquent peers and involvement in delinquency (Lauritsen & Davis Quinet, 1995). Participating in dangerous activities has been linked to repeat victimization for adults (Outlaw et al., 2002), and frequency of offending has been linked to repeat victimization for people in the Netherlands (Wittebrood & Nieuwbeerta, 2000). Alcohol use has also been linked to recurring victimization. Specifically, the link between alcohol use and recurring victimization has been found for sexual victimization. Among adolescent women, using alcohol within the past year was predictive of sexual revictimization (Raghavan, Bogart, Elliott, Vestal, & Schuster, 2004). Others have found a link between alcohol use and sexual revictimization among persons with a history of childhood sexual assault (Messman-Moore & Long, 2002; Siegel & Williams,

2003). When these factors are considered together, it is likely then that participating in a risky lifestyle or having routine activities increases the likelihood that a person will experience more than one victimization.

Why might some people engage in these risky lifestyles or routine activities? Some research has linked recurring victimization to genetic factors that may be related to involvement in risky behaviors. Remember from Chapter 2 that genes in and of themselves do not cause criminal behavior, but rather they influence how a person responds to his or her environment. Genetic factors have been linked to victimization and, more recently, to recurring victimization. One recent study revealed that genetic factors account for 64% of the variance in repeat victimization (Beaver, Boutwell, Barnes, & Cooper, 2009). Another study on recurring victimization has attempted to identify what specific genetic factor is linked to recurring victimization risk. This study found that the 7-repeat allele of the DRD4 gene distinguishes those individuals who have been victimized a single time from those who have been victimized more than once (Daigle, 2010). DRD4 codes for the production of dopamine receptors located in postsynaptic neurons (DeYoung et al., 2006). The 7-repeat allele produces less efficient receptors and has been linked to attention-related problems (Faraone, Doyle, Mick, & Biederman, 2001), novelty seeking (Benjamin et al., 1996; Ebstein et al., 1996), and conduct disorder (Rowe et al., 2001). DRD4 has also been linked to aggression (Schmidt, Fox, Rubin, Hu, & Hamer, 2002) and serious violence for males who also have the A1 allele of DRD2 (Beaver, Wright, DeLisi, Walsh, et al., 2007). Because of its impact on these characteristics, DRD4 may be related to recurring victimization because individuals may be less attuned to risk and likely to actually seek out novel or risky situations, perhaps even after being victimized.

The last set of individual-level risk factors that have been explored are psychological and cognitive factors. Much of this research has focused on the sexual revictimization of women. What this research has shown is that women who have been revictimized often experience high levels of psychological distress and posttraumatic stress disorder (PTSD) symptoms, and these levels are higher than in women who have experienced a single sexual victimization incident (Banyard, Williams, & Siegel, 2001; Gibson & Leitenberg, 2001; Murphy et al., 1988). PTSD may play an important role in revictimization in that it may inhibit women's ability to quickly identify risk. In fact, one study found that PTSD reduced latency in recognizing risk in an audiotape of a date-rape situation among revictimized women (Wilson, Calhoun, & Bernat, 1999).

Neighborhood or Household-Level Risk Factors

The last set of risk factors for recurring victimization to consider are those tied to the neighborhood or household. Neighborhoods that are dangerous place the residents who reside in them at risk for recurring victimization. That is, living in urban areas places people at risk for repeat victimization (Tseloni, 2000; Wittebrood & Nieuwbeerta, 2000), and living in areas with a high concentration of single-parent households puts people at risk for recurring victimization as well (Osborn, Ellingworth, Hope, & Trickett, 1996). A third characteristic, neighborhood disorder, has also been linked to recurring victimization. It has been linked to an increase in the number of assault, larceny, and vandalism victimizations experienced by youth (Lauritsen & Davis Quinet, 1995) and to repeat property victimizations experienced by adults (Outlaw et al., 2002). Why is it, though, that these factors would impact risk for recurring victimization? It is likely that urban areas are simply those areas where more crime happens; therefore, a person who lives there is at greater risk of experiencing recurring victimization. In addition, areas with lots of single-parent households may not have high levels of supervision or capable guardianship and may be indicative of an area's socioeconomic status. Finally, areas that are highly disordered are likely low in socioeconomic status, low in capable guardianship, and beacons for motivated offenders.

Household characteristics such as living in a low-income household, having children, having four or more cars, participating in neighborhood watch, and having security devices installed in the home are related to an increase in the number of personal victimizations (Tseloni, 2000). However, higher incomes have been linked to recurring property victimization (see Perrault et al., 2010). In addition, work with the BCS has found that younger households, having two or more adults in the household, having more children in the household, and having more than one car increased the number of crime victimizations (Osborn & Tseloni, 1998). The shorter the time people have lived in a residence, the greater the likelihood of repeat victimization (Mukherjee & Carcach, 1998; Osborn & Tseloni, 1998). Renting a residence is also linked to recurring victimization (Mukherjee & Carcach, 1998; Osborn et al., 1996; Osborn & Tseloni, 1998; Perrault et al., 2010).

■ THEORETICAL EXPLANATIONS OF RECURRING VICTIMIZATION

We know, then, that recurring victimization is a reality many victims face, that it is likely to recur rather quickly if it does happen, and that the same type of victimization is likely to follow. But this picture of what recurring victimization looks like does not address why some people are victimized a single time and others find themselves victimized again.

There are two theoretical explanations that have been proffered to explain recurring victimization. The first is called **risk heterogeneity** or the **"flag" explanation.** This explanation of recurring victimization focuses on qualities or characteristics of the victim. Those qualities or characteristics that initially place a victim at risk will keep that person at risk of experiencing a subsequent victimization if unchanged (Farrell, Phillips, & Pease, 1995). For example, remember Polly? Is there any quality or characteristic that placed her at risk for being accosted by the two men in the alley? You are probably thinking that her walking home at night may have been a risk factor for her. This was discussed in Chapter 2 about lifestyles and routine activities. Polly quite likely was victimized, at least in part, because she was seen by the two men as being a vulnerable target. In this way, walking home at night by herself placed her at risk. If Polly walks home at night by herself on other nights, she is again at risk of being victimized. In this way, Polly's walking home at night by herself placed her at risk of being victimized the first time, and it also places her at risk of being a victim in the future. What if she walked home because she could not afford a car? In other words, what if her social status or class placed her in a position that increased her vulnerability to crime victimization because she had to walk home at night rather than drive? This quality or characteristic would also fall into the explanation of risk heterogeneity. Also, remember other factors, discussed in Chapter 2, that place individuals at risk of victimization more generally—living in disadvantaged neighborhoods and exposure to delinquent peers, for example. These factors, if left unchanged, will keep individuals at risk of subsequent victimization.

In contrast to the risk heterogeneity argument, the second theoretical explanation of recurring victimization is known as **state dependence, event dependence,** or the **"boost" explanation.** According to state dependence, it is not the qualities or characteristics of a victim that are important for recurring victimization so much as what happens during and after the victimization (Farrell et al., 1995). How the victim and the offender act and react to the victimization event will predict risk of becoming a recurrent victim. In this way, the victim and offender are learning key information that will impact the likelihood of subsequent victimizations. For example, a victim of rape or other sexual victimization who resists or uses self-protective actions is less likely than those who do not to be victimized again (Fisher, Daigle, & Cullen, 2010b). This reduction in risk is likely due to the victim learning that she has agency and control over her life. Protecting herself may even serve to empower her so that in the future she is able to identify and avoid risk. Likewise, the offender is likely learning that she is not an "easy" target and that victimizing her will not pay off in the future. In both scenarios, the victim is less likely to find herself the target of an offender. In Polly's case, it is difficult to know if she is likely to be victimized again based on a state-dependence explanation. Since she tried to resist and she called the police, she certainly is learning that she has some control over her life. If doing so empowers her, she likely will be less attractive as a target to offenders, and she may be less likely to find herself in risky situations—such as walking home at night alone. To be clear, neither of these explanations should be used to blame the victim or place responsibility for the victimization on the victim. The offender is responsible for his or her actions, and blame should rest there. These explanations are, however, tools to help understand why some people are targeted over and over again.

RIPPED FROM THE HEADLINES

Robert Keller went to the Smoke Land Outlet and Mini Mart on January 17, 2014, wearing dark clothing and a hood pulled over his head. Carrying a gun, he demanded money and threatened to kill the clerk who was working behind the counter. He was able to get away with money and left in a black vehicle. On January 24, the same cashier was working at the Smoke Land Outlet and Mini Mart when he noticed on video surveillance a black vehicle parked in the lot. The person who got out of the vehicle was dressed similar to the man who robbed him the previous week. When the man entered the store, the cashier confronted him, they struggled, and the man pulled a handgun out of his jacket before fleeing to his vehicle. The clerk chased the man into the parking lot, carrying his own weapon and shot his gun twice, hitting the vehicle. The car then ran into a parked tow truck, whose driver gave the registration information of the car to a state trooper. After connecting Keller to both of the robberies, the police were able to search Keller's residence and take him into custody. How do you think these incidents can be explained by the theories of recurring victimization?

Source: State police: Man robbed Ogletown business once, then tried again. (2014, January 25). *The News Journal.* Retrieved from http://www.delawareonline.com/story/news/crime/2014/01/25/state-police-man-robbed-ogletown-business-once-then-tried-again/4895479.

■ CONSEQUENCES OF RECURRING VICTIMIZATION

As you read about in Chapter 4, victimization can take a toll on individuals. What happens to individuals, then, when they experience multiple victimization incidents? Do the consequences of victimization accumulate and cause even more destruction in victims' lives? It is not clear that experiencing more than one victimization necessarily causes more negative outcomes for victims, but some research does suggest that experiencing more than one victimization can be particularly bad for victims (Finkelhor, Ormrod, & Turner, 2007a, 2009; Ford, Elhai, Connor, & Frueh, 2010; Snyder, Fisher, Scherer, & Daigle, 2012). For example, Finkelhor, Ormod, and Turner (2009) found that youth who experience poly-victimization also experience significantly more distress than those youth who experience a single type of victimization. Research using the National Violence Against Women Survey also found support for the link between experiencing more than one victimization and worse outcomes. The number of sexual assaults experienced during a woman's lifetime was predictive of current depressive symptoms, current PTSD symptoms, poor health, and binge drinking (Casey & Nurius, 2005). In this way, experiencing more than one victimization may in fact carry negative outcomes for individuals that a single victimization experience does not.

FOCUS ON RESEARCH

Youth who experience poly-victimization in Canada have also been shown to experience negative consequences. In a study of caregivers of children who were between the ages of 2 and 11, caregivers were asked about 32 different forms of direct and indirect victimization that a child could have experienced. Almost half of the children had experienced more than one type of victimization. The number of different types of victimization experienced (poly-victimization) was related to an increase in depression, anxiety, and anger/aggression. Given these findings, what do you think can be done to intervene in the lives of young children to reduce the effects of poly-victimization?

Source: Adapted from Cyr, K., Clement, M., & Chamberland, C. (2014). Lifetime prevalence of multiple victimizations and its impact on children's mental health. *Journal of Interpersonal Violence, 29,* 616–634.

■ RESPONSES TO RECURRING VICTIMIZATION

In as much as recurring victimization is tied to specific risk factors that can be identified, prevention efforts can be undertaken that target these risk factors to reduce recurring victimization. Most of the recurring victimization efforts have targeted specific types of recurring victimization. The first type of recurring victimization that has been targeted for programs is repeat burglary. Recall that one of the explanations of repeat victimization is state dependence, which notes that offenders are learning valuable information when they victimize. In the case of burglary, a burglar learns how to get into a home, what valuables there are to steal, whether a home has an alarm, and whether it seems that the police were called and able to track the offender down. All this information makes the home more or less likely to be targeted again, either by the same burglar or by a fellow burglar to whom the offender has divulged this information. Consider research that examined repeat burglary incidents in Dallas and San Diego. In this research, it was discovered that in **delayed repeat victimizations**—those incidents that took place 30 days or more after the initial incident—the same items were taken more often than expected from the home (Clarke, Perkins, & Smith, 2001). This finding suggests that either the same offender is returning or a "colleague" of the offender knows that the home has stuff worth stealing! Although research has supported both the risk heterogeneity and the state dependence perspectives, you may be asking yourself, to what extent are houses or people victimized by the same perpetrator more than once? Although not all repeat victimization research has been able to address this question directly, some research on burglary shows that those burglaries that occur close in time and space are more likely to be perpetrated by the same offender than incidents that occur more distally in time and space (Bernasco, 2008). In addition, a substantial proportion of burglars admit to burglarizing the same home more than once! It should make sense, then, that houses that have been burglarized are ripe targets for burglary prevention.

To read about a successful burglary prevention program in England, see the Focus on International Issues box. Although this program was effective at preventing repeat burglary in Kirkholt, programs implemented in the United States have generally been less successful. In fact, a review of burglary prevention programs in Dallas, San Diego, and Baltimore found that burglary rates were not reduced in any of the cities. Instead, there was actually an increase in burglary rates in two of the cities compared to the control groups (Weisel, Clarke, & Stedman, 1999). It is instructive to examine what was done in these cities to attempt to reduce burglary as compared to what was done in Kirkholt. In these programs, prevention was attempted through the police providing information and advice to people who had experienced a burglary. This tactic was different than what was done in the Kirkholt program, where funds were used to assist individuals in making their homes more secure.

A second type of recurring victimization that has been targeted in prevention efforts is sexual recurring victimization. The majority of these prevention programs have been delivered to college students, probably because college students face high risks of sexual victimization and recurring victimization and because they are "easy" to target for interventions given that you can readily administer a program on a college campus. Evaluations of these programs have found that after attending them, women are more knowledgeable about sexual assault and show improvement in psychological functioning (Gidycz et al., 2001; Marx, Calhoun, Wilson, & Meyerson, 2001). But can these programs reduce the risk of experiencing subsequent sexual victimization incidents? Although evaluations of one intervention program (Hanson & Gidycz, 1993) and a revised version of it were found not to reduce sexual revictimization (Breitenbecher & Gidycz, 1998), the same intervention was found to be effective in a later program when expanded to two 2-hour sessions (Gidycz et al., 2001). In this evaluation, it was found that women receiving the intervention who had been moderately sexually victimized 2 months after the intervention were less likely to experience repeat sexual victimization at the 6-month follow-up than those who did not receive the intervention. This intervention was later expanded to include an emphasis on risk recognition skills and delivered to college students. It too was found to be effective at reducing risk of recurring victimization, with women in the program being less likely to report being raped than women who were in the control group (Marx et al., 2001). You may be wondering if prevention programs can be administered to noncollege students. As previously mentioned, they are not as widespread, but researchers are trying. The program used in the Marx study has been adapted and implemented for an urban sample, although an evaluation of the program did not find reductions in revictimization risk, knowledge about sexual assault, attributions for the sexual assault, self-efficacy, or improvement in psychological functioning for program participants (Davis, O'Sullivan, Guthrie, & Ross, 2006). Obviously, developing and implementing such programs for college students as well as community members at large continues to be a need for sexually victimized individuals.

The third type of recurring victimization that prevention programs have targeted is intimate partner violence. Most of these prevention programs have centered on reducing repeat offending rather than focusing on ways to intervene with victims. For example, you will read about the Minneapolis Domestic Violence Experiment in Chapter 9, which was an experiment designed to evaluate the effectiveness of arrest on recidivism for domestic violence offenders. In essence, it was an evaluation of the ability of arrest to prevent repeat domestic violence. Other programs such as domestic violence courts and anger management also target offenders in hopes of reducing their violent behavior toward their intimate partners. One type of program designed to assist victims is the second responder program. This program involves a team—usually a police officer and victim advocate—who follow-up with a victim after an initial police response. During this follow-up, the team provides the victim with information on services and legal options, such as obtaining a protective order; information about the cyclical nature of domestic violence; providing assistance in relocating or providing placement in a shelter; and aid in developing a safety plan. Some teams may also have as their goals to refer victims to social services and get them job training and public assistance to facilitate their independence. An evaluation of 10 studies on second responder programs, however, found that this intervention does not affect the likelihood that a victim suffers additional family violence incidents (Davis, Weisburd, & Taylor, 2008). When these interventions are considered together, it is evident that more work needs to be done to prevent recurring victimization. Doing so is especially important considering that preventing recurring victimization would result in the reduction of a large percentage of all victimizations since recurring victims experience a disproportionate share of all victimization incidents.

FOCUS ON INTERNATIONAL ISSUES

When Rochdale, England, suffered from high burglary rates in the late 1980s, the Kirkholt Burglary Prevention Project was spawned. The project was designed to target burglary victims; hence, one of its goals was to reduce repeat victimization. The program involved three components. First, homes in this area at the time had prepayment meters that were prime targets for burglary. Part of the program entailed having the

(Continued)

utility company replace these meters with token-fed meters upon request. Second, "cocoon" watches were instituted between burglary victims and nearby neighbors. Victims and the six or seven houses or flats near them were encouraged to watch out for suspicious activity. Neighbors who joined the cocoon were given the same security upgrades given to burgled residents. Third, persons who had their homes burgled were given security upgrades. The program also had a second phase that targeted not just victims but also offenders and the community to reduce the motivation to offend. To do so, a credit union, work program, school-based crime prevention program, group meetings for offenders, and better information for probation officers and courts were implemented. Research on the effectiveness of the program revealed that burglary fell to 40% of its preimplementation rate after the first phase in the treatment area.

Source: Adapted from Pease, K. (1992). The Kirkholt Project: Preventing burglary on a British Public Housing Estate. *Security Journal, 2,* 73–77.

SUMMARY

- One startling reality is that many victims will not suffer just one victimization but will find themselves victimized again in the future—becoming recurring victims. These victims may be particularly hard hit by the costs of victimization as they accumulate over time.
- There are many terms associated with recurring victimization. Victims can be recurring victims, repeat victims, revictims, poly-victims, or near-repeat victims.
- A small percentage of people are victimized in any given time period. A portion of these victims will experience more than one incident. What is notable is that these recurring victims experience a disproportionate share of all victimization incidents that occur.
- Research on recurring victimization shows that it is likely to recur fairly quickly and that a person is prone to experiencing the same type of victimization as previously experienced.
- There are many risk factors for recurring victimization. Individual-level risk factors include demographic characteristics, risky lifestyles/routine activities theory variables, and genetic factors. Household and neighborhood characteristics also distinguish single victims from recurring victims.
- Two explanations have been developed to explain why someone is victimized more than once: state dependence and risk heterogeneity.
- Although any victimization can be traumatizing for a victim, experiencing multiple incidents can be particularly harmful. Research suggests that experiencing more than one victimization may carry more serious consequences for victims than experiencing one incident or a single type of victimization.
- Prevention efforts should be targeted at the factors that cause recurring victimization. Most prevention programs have been directed at preventing repeat burglary, sexual victimization, and domestic violence with varying degrees of effectiveness.

DISCUSSION QUESTIONS

1. How does routine activities/lifestyles theory fit within the state dependence and risk heterogeneity explanations of recurring victimization? How is it different?

2. Given the risk factors identified for recurring victimization, what should be targeted in intervention programs to reduce risk? Are these elements good targets for change? Why or why not?

3. Think of you or someone you know who has been a victim. Have you or that person been victimized more than once? If so, what type of recurring victim are you or is he or she? Why? What factors led to you or him or her becoming this type of recurring victim? What could have been done to prevent you or him or her from becoming a recurring victim?

4. Why do you think that recurring victimization is likely to happen so quickly when it does occur? Why does risk of recurring victimization decline over time from the last victimization incident?

KEY TERMS

recurring victimization

repeat victimization

revictimization

poly-victimization

near-repeat victimization

time-course

crime-switching

victim proneness

risk heterogeneity (the "flag" explanation)

state dependence

"boost" explanation

delayed repeat victimization

INTERNET RESOURCES

Oxford Bibliography on Repeat Victimization (http://www.oxfordbibliographies.com/view/document/obo-9780195396607/obo-9780195396607-0119.xml)

This website provides brief descriptions and links to online resources for repeat victimization. It covers historical overviews as well as current topics germane to the field of repeat victimization. It is a great overview resource for students as they get started on research projects!

The Kirkholt Burglary Prevention Project (http://www.popcenter.org/library/scp/pdf/71-Kirkholt.pdf)

To read about the implementation and effects of the Kirkholt Burglary Prevention Project, which was discussed in the Focus on International Issues Box, visit this website, which takes you to the report from the Home Office about the project.

"Violent Repeat Victimization: Prospects and Challenges for Research and Practice" (http://www.nij.gov/multimedia/presenter/presenter-lauritsen/pages/presenter-lauritsen-transcript.aspx)

Go to this website to view a transcript as well as to view the presentation "Violent Repeat Victimization: Prospects and Challenges for Research and Practice" by Dr. Janet Lauritsen, who gave it at the National Institute of Justice as part of its *Research for the Real World* series.

6

VICTIMS' RIGHTS AND REMEDIES

Let's revisit Polly now that it has been a few days since she was victimized. Remember that Polly is a young undergraduate student who was accosted by two offenders as she was walking home. Her school bag was stolen, and she was assaulted. Unlike most victims, Polly called the police to report what had happened to her. She had to have 10 stitches at the hospital. Clearly a victim, she was still questioned by the police about why she was walking home alone at night. She very well may have felt victimized by this questioning—and we know that she had a hard time emotionally after being victimized. She found it hard to get out of bed, and she missed several classes—she even altered her schedule and stopped going out alone at night.

In Chapter 3, you considered the toll this victimization took on Polly—on her emotions and her lifestyle, and of course financially. As you know, Polly is not alone in suffering these costs. Many victims experience real costs and consequences. But how do victims deal with these outcomes? Are they left to recover on their own, or are services available to them? Whose responsibility is it to help crime victims? What happens when crime victims do not get the help they need and deserve? All these questions will be addressed in this chapter, and as you will see, a variety of rights and resources are available to crime victims today.

■ VICTIMS' RIGHTS

Once essentially ignored by the criminal justice system and the law, victims are now granted a range of rights. These rights have been given to victims through legislation and, in 32 states, through **victims' rights** amendments to state constitutions (National Center for Victims of Crime, 2009). The first such law that guaranteed victims' rights and protections was passed in Wisconsin in 1979; now, every state has at least some form of victims' rights legislation (Davis & Mulford, 2008). Despite each state having laws that afford victims' rights, they differ in whom the law applies to, when the rights begin, what rights victims have, and how the rights can be enforced. Common to all these state laws, however, is the goal of victims' rights—to enhance victim privacy, protection, and participation (Garvin, 2010).

Common Victims' Rights Given by State

Slightly less than half of U.S. states give *all* victims rights (Howley & Dorris, 2007). In all states, the right to compensation, notification of rights, notification of court appearances, and ability to submit victim impact statements before sentencing are granted to at least some victim classes (Deess, 1999). Other common rights given to victims in the majority of states are the right to restitution, to be treated with dignity and respect, to attend court and sentencing hearings, and to consult with court personnel before plea bargains are offered or defendants released from custody (Davis & Mulford, 2008). Other rights extended to victims are the right to protection and the right to a speedy trial. Importantly, some states explicitly protect victims' jobs while they exercise their right to participate in the criminal justice system. These protections may include having the prosecutor intervene with the employer on behalf of the victim or prohibiting employers from penalizing or firing a victim for taking time from work to participate (National Center for Victims of Crime, 2009). Some of these rights are discussed in more detail below, and others are discussed in separate parts of this section. To see an example of what rights a state grants, see Box 6.1 on victims' rights in Virginia.

VICTIMS' RIGHTS IN VIRGINIA

The Victim Services Unit provides the following services to victims of crime:

- Advocacy on behalf of crime victims
- Notification of changes in inmate transfers, release date, name change, escape and capture
- Explanation of parole and probation supervision process
- Accompaniment to parole board appointments when requested by the victim
- Provide victims with ongoing support, crisis intervention, information, and referrals
- Training, education, and public awareness initiatives on behalf of victims of crime

Victims can register to be notified through Victim Information and Notification Everyday (VINE).

VINE is a toll-free, 24-hour, anonymous, computer-based telephone service that provides victims of crime two important features, information and notification. Victims may call VINE from any touch-tone telephone, any time, to check on an inmate's custody status. For inmate information, call 1-800-467-4943 and follow the prompts.

Victims may register with VINE for an automated notification call when an inmate is released, transferred, escapes, and to learn of an inmate's parole status if the inmate is parole eligible.

Victims of crime can address the Parole Board if they have any concerns regarding the release of an offender. Victims have the option of voicing their concerns through letters or through an in-person appointment with the Parole Board.

If victims would like a staff member of the Department of Corrections, Victim Services Unit to accompany them to the appointment, they can contact the Department of Corrections, Victim Services Unit.

Source: Virginia Department of Corrections (2010).

Notification

The right to **notification** allows victims to stay apprised of events in their cases. Notification is important for victims at various steps in the criminal justice process. In some jurisdictions, victims have the right to be notified when their offender is arrested and released from custody after arrest, such as on bail. Victims may also have the right to be notified about the time and place of court proceedings and any changes made to originally scheduled proceedings. Notification may also be given if the offender has a parole hearing and when the offender is released from custody at the end of a criminal sanction. Notification responsibilities may be placed on law enforcement, the prosecutor, and the correctional system. To make notification more systematic and reliable, some jurisdictions use automated notification systems to update victims (through letters or phone calls) about changes in their cases. These systems are often also set up so that a victim can call to receive updates. Some states have also moved to allowing e-mail updates for notification purposes. For instance, Maryland recently passed such legislation in 2014 (Basu, 2014). Victims of federal crimes can register to participate in the national automated victim notification system.

Participation and Consultation

One of the overarching goals of the victims' rights movement was to increase **participation and consultation** by victims in all stages of the criminal justice system. One way victims are encouraged to participate is by submitting or presenting a victim impact statement, which is discussed later in this section under "Remedies and Rights in Court." Other ways victims may participate is by consulting with judges and/or prosecutors before any plea bargains are offered or bail is set. Consultation may also occur before an offender is paroled or sentenced (Davis & Mulford, 2008). Read about how sexual assault victims in Canada are provided a new right to have evidence kept for up to a year as they decide whether or not to pursue charges in the Focus on International Issues box.

FOCUS ON INTERNATIONAL ISSUES

In Calgary, located in Alberta, Canada, sexual assault victims who go to a health centre for services now have the option (called the Third Option) of having materials such as underwear and swabs taken during a medical exam stored if they are unsure about reporting their incident to the police. The evidence is stored for a year, giving victims time to think about whether they would like to formally move forward with their case. At least 58 victims have utilized the Third Option during the inception of the one-year pilot program. Police like that it at least gives victims the option of proceeding with a criminal investigation.

Source: Adapted from Schneider, K. (2012, June 3). Dozens of Calgary sex assault victims opt to wait. *Calgary Sun.* Retrieved from http://www.torontosun.com/2012/06/03/doezns-of-calgary-sex-assault-victims-opt-to-wait.

Right to Protection

Victims may also need protection as they navigate the criminal justice process. Victims may be fearful of the offender and the offender's friends and family. Participation in the criminal justice system may, in fact, endanger victims. In response to this potential danger, many states include safety measures in their victims' rights, falling under the category of **right to protection.** For example, victims may be able to get no-contact or protective orders that prohibit the defendant from having any contact with the victim. Victims may also be provided with secure waiting facilities in court buildings. Victim privacy is also protected ever-increasingly in states; some disclose only minimal victim information in criminal justice records—such as law enforcement and court records (Davis & Mulford, 2008).

Right to a Speedy Trial

You have probably heard of offenders having a **right to a speedy trial,** but did you know that about half of all states also provide victims with this right? Although not as explicit as an offender's right, this right given to victims ensures that the judge considers the victim's interests when ruling on motions for continuance. In other words, in states that give victims this right, decisions about postponing a trial cannot be made without consideration of the victim. Some states also explicitly provide for accelerated dispositions in cases with disabled, elderly, or minor children victims (Davis & Mulford, 2008).

Issues With Victims' Rights

Although victims' advocates have hailed the adoption of legislation and state-level amendments that give victims rights, the adoption of victims' rights has also come with problems. There has been some resistance to states and the federal government giving victims formal rights. Remember that criminal law is written in such a way as to make crimes harms against the state rather than the victim. Also think about how the U.S. Constitution provides widespread rights to those persons suspected of committing crimes. The U.S. Constitution

---

RIPPED FROM THE HEADLINES

Similar to the program mentioned in the Focus on International Issues box, victims of sexual assault in Wisconsin also now have the ability to have DNA evidence stored and tests conducted free of charge at a state crime lab, whether or not they decide to move forward with a criminal case. This change in procedure will provide victims the ability to have tests conducted without feeling the pressure to report their assault to the police or to continue on with the case after an initial report. It also protects the evidence once collected and disallows police departments or the lab from destroying it. Victims will be given a consent form indicating them of this new right.

Source: Simmons, D. (2014, August 20). Sexual assault evidence will be stored in state crime lab in Madison. *Wisconsin State Journal.* Retrieved from http://www.madison.com.

does not currently include any language that provides victims with rights—but it does for persons suspected of committing crimes. Although this omission has been identified by some as deserving remedy, others argue that victims' rights do not have a place in our Constitution (Wallace, 1997). Concerns have also been expressed that providing victims with rights will create a burden on our already overburdened criminal justice system (Davis & Mulford, 2008).

Also problematic is what to do when victims' rights are not protected. What happens if a victim is not notified? Who is responsible? Does the victim have any recourse, legal or otherwise, when a right is violated? Many states do not have specific enforcement strategies in place in their victims' rights legislation, although states that have constitutional amendments generally have enforceable rights in the event that a state official violates a victim's constitutional rights. Victims may also seek a writ of mandamus, which is a court order that directs an agency to comply with a law (National Center for Victims of Crime, 2009). For other victims, although they are given rights on paper, there is little they can do if their rights are not protected. To remedy this, some states—such as California, in its passage of Marsy's Law—have legislation that is more comprehensive and includes language that gives victims the right to enforce their rights in court, called legal standing (National Victims' Constitutional Amendment Passage, n.d.). Some states have set up a designated agency to handle crime victims' complaints (National Center for Victims of Crime, 2009). Despite these developments, many state victims' bills of rights specifically note that when victims' rights are violated, the crime victim does not have the ability to sue civilly a government agency or official. Whatever the redress allowed to victims, you can probably see that for victims, not having their rights protected may feel like an additional victimization and one that they can do little about—at least not easily.

Federal Law

Thus far, we have discussed common rights that states grant to victims of crime, but the federal government has also recognized the importance of protecting the rights of crime victims. (See Table 6.1 for a timeline and brief description of key pieces of federal legislation related to victims' rights.) In 1982, the President's Task Force on Victims of Crime published a report that included 68 recommendations for how victims could receive recognition and get the rights and services they deserve. These recommendations led, in part, to the development of legislation that would grant victims their first federal rights. The first such piece of legislation passed was the **Federal Victim Witness Protection Act** (1982). This act mandated that the attorney general develop and implement guidelines that outlined for officials how to respond to victims and witnesses. Two years later, the **Victims of Crime Act** (1984) was passed to create the Office for Victims of Crime and to provide funds to assist state victim compensation programs. The funds are generated from fines and fees and from seized assets of offenders who break federal law. A critical step in victims' rights also occurred in 1990 with passage of the **Child Victims' Bill of Rights,** which extended victims' rights to child victims and witnesses. Child victims and witnesses were granted rights to have proceedings explained in language they can understand; to have a victims' advocate present at interviews, hearings, and trials; to have a secure waiting area at trials; to have personal information kept private unless otherwise specified by the child or guardian; to have an advocate to discuss with the court their ability to understand proceedings; to be given information about and referrals to agencies for assistance;

and to allow other services to be provided by law enforcement. Also in 1990, the **Crime Control Act** and the **Victims' Rights and Restitution Act** were passed, creating a federal bill of rights for victims of federal crime and guaranteeing that victims have a right to restitution. Specifically, victims of federal crimes were given the right to

a. be reasonably protected from the accused;

b. reasonable, accurate, and timely notice of any public proceeding involving the crime or any release or escape of the accused and to not be excluded from such proceedings;

c. be reasonably heard at any public proceeding involving release, plea, or sentencing;

d. confer with the attorney for the government in the case;

e. full and timely restitution as provided by law;

f. proceedings free from unreasonable delay;

g. be treated with fairness and with respect for the victim's dignity and privacy.

The acts also provide that the court ensures that crime victims are afforded these rights.

The 1990s also saw the adoption of the **Violent Crime Control and Law Enforcement Act** (1994), which included the implementation of the **Violence Against Women Act** (VAWA) that gave more than $1 billion to programs designed to reduce and respond to violence against women. It also increased funding for victim compensation programs and established a national sex offender registry (Gundy-Yoder, 2010). In 1996, the **Antiterrorism and Effective Death Penalty Act** was passed, making restitution mandatory in violent crime cases and further expanding compensation and assistance to victims of terrorism. Victims were given the right to provide victim impact statements during sentencing in capital and noncapital cases, and the right to attend the trials of their offenders was clarified via the **Victims' Rights Clarification Act** (1997).

Victims' rights were further expanded in the first part of the 21st century. The **Violence Against Women Act** (2000) was signed into law as part of the Victims of Trafficking and Violence Protection Act of 2000. It reauthorized some previous VAWA funding. This legislation also authorized funding for rape prevention and education, battered women's shelters, transitional housing for female victims of violence, and addressed violence against older women and those with disabilities. This act also expanded the federal stalking statute to include stalking over the Internet. The VAWA was reauthorized in 2013; among other provisions, it expands housing protections for victims of domestic violence in all federally subsidized housing programs and protects victims of sexual assault; adds additional protections for dating violence on college campuses; and it protects LGBT survivors of violence from discrimination so that they can receive services. In 2004, Congress passed the **Justice for All Act,** thus strengthening federal crime victims' rights and providing enforcement and remedies when there is not compliance. It also provided monies to test the backlog of rape kits.

Despite the provision and expansion of victims' rights at the federal level, there is still not a federal constitutional amendment. This lack of adoption may be somewhat surprising since the National Victims' Constitutional Amendment Network and Steering Committee was

PHOTO 6.1

Former U.S. President George W. Bush shakes hands with Sen. Pat Leahy (D-VT) (second from right), and Sen. Arlen Specter (R-PA) (right), during a bill-signing ceremony for the Violence Against Women and Department of Justice Reauthorization Act of 2005 at the White House on January 5, 2006.

formed in 1987 and federal victims' rights constitutional amendments were introduced in both the House and the Senate in 1996. Additional victims' rights constitutional amendments were introduced in 1997, 1998, 1999, 2000, 2003, and 2004 (Maryland Crime Victims' Resource Center, 2007). To date, such an amendment has not been adopted.

■ FINANCIAL REMEDY

In Chapter 4, you read about the substantial costs that victims face after being victimized. Some of these costs are financial. Victims may lose time from work, have hospital bills, seek and pay for mental health care, need a crime scene cleaned, or lose income from a loved one's death. To help assuage some of these costs, victims can apply for financial compensation from the state, receive restitution from the offender, or seek remedy civilly.

Victim Compensation

One way victims can receive financial compensation for their economic losses is through state-run **victim compensation** programs. First begun in 1965 in California, victim compensation programs now operate in every state. Money for compensation comes from a variety of sources. In many states, a large portion of funding comes from criminals themselves—fees and fines are collected from people who are charged with criminal offenses. These fees are attached to the normal court fees that offenders are expected to pay. In addition, the Victims of Crime Act of 1984 (VOCA) authorized funding for state compensation and assistance programs. Today, the VOCA Crime Victims Fund provides more than $700 million annually to states to assist victims and constitutes about one third of each program's funding (National Association of Crime Victim Compensation Boards, 2009). Not only did VOCA increase funding for state programs,

Table 6.1 ■ Federal Legislation Pertaining to Victims' Rights

Legislation Timeline	Key Provisions
Federal Victim Witness Protection Act (1982)	• Provided for the punishment of anyone who tampers with a witness, victim, or informant • If victim provided address and telephone number, required notification for arrest of the accused, times of court appearances at which victim may appear, release or detention of accused, and opportunities for victim to address the sentencing court • Recommended federal officials consult with victims and witnesses regarding proposed dismissals and plea negotiations • Required that officials not disclose the names and addresses of victims and witnesses
Victims of Crime Act (1984)	• Established the Crime Victims Fund, which promoted state and local victim support and compensation programs • In 1998, amended to require state programs to include survivors of victims of drunk driving and domestic violence in eligibility for federal funds
Child Victims' Bill of Rights (1990)	Children who are victims or witnesses are provided these rights: • That proceedings be explained in language children can understand • A victim's advocate can be present at interviews, hearings, and trial • A secure waiting area at trial • Certain personal information kept private unless otherwise specified by the child or guardian • An advocate to discuss with the court their ability to understand proceedings • Information provided about agencies for assistance and referrals made to such agencies
Victims' Rights and Restitution Act (1990)	Provided victims with the right to: • Be reasonably protected from the accused • Reasonable, accurate, and timely notice of any public proceeding involving the crime or any release or escape of the accused and to not be excluded from such proceedings • Be reasonably heard at any public proceeding involving release, plea, or sentencing • Confer with the attorney for the government in the case • Be given full and timely restitution as provided by law • Have proceedings free from unreasonable delay • Be treated with fairness and with respect for the victim's dignity and privacy

Legislation Timeline	Key Provisions
Violent Crime Control and Law Enforcement Act (1994)	• Allocated $1.6 billion to fight violence against women • Included money for victims' services and advocates and for rape education and community prevention programs
Violence Against Women Act (1994)	• Provided $1 billion to programs designed to reduce and respond to violence against women • Increased funding for victim compensation programs and established a national sex offender registry
Antiterrorism and Effective Death Penalty Act (1996)	• Made restitution mandatory in violent crime • Expanded compensation and assistance to victims of terrorism
Victims' Rights Clarification Act (1997)	• Gave victims the right to provide victim impact statements during sentencing in capital and noncapital cases, and the right to attend the trial of their offender was clarified
Violence Against Women Act (2000)	• Provided additional protections for immigrant victims of domestic violence • Authorized funding for rape prevention and education, battered women's shelters, transitional housing for female victims of violence, and addressed violence against older women and those with disabilities
Justice for All Act (2004)	• Provided additional federal protections of crime victims' rights • Provided funding to test the substantial backlog of DNA samples collected from crime scenes and convicted offenders
Violence Against Women Act (2013)	• Gives tribal courts authority to prosecute offenders in their communities even if not Native American • Prohibits survivors of domestic violence as well as sexual assault from being evicted from federally subsidized housing programs • Requires colleges and universities to record incidents of dating violence, to implement programs to prevent its occurrence, and to provide resources to victims • Prohibits discrimination of LGBT survivors of violent crimes when seeking assistance from victim services and/or protection • Strengthens provisions for immigrant survivors

but it also required states to cover all U.S. citizens victimized within the state's borders, regardless of the victim's residency. It also required that states provide mental health counseling and that victims of domestic violence as well as drunk driving be covered.

Not all victims, however, are eligible for compensation from the Crime Victims Fund. Only victims of rape, assault, child sexual abuse, drunk driving, domestic violence, and homicide are eligible, since these crimes are known to create undue hardship for victims

(Klein, 2010). In some states, victims must have experienced physical injury, while in others, if they experienced serious emotional trauma from the victimization, they are also eligible (Evans, 2014). In addition to the type of victimization, victims must meet other requirements to be eligible:

- Must report the victimization promptly to law enforcement; usually within 72 hours of the victimization unless "good cause" can be shown, such as being a child, incarcerated, or otherwise incapacitated
- Must cooperate with law enforcement and prosecutors in the investigation and prosecution of the case
- Must submit application for compensation that includes evidence of expenses within a specified time, generally 1 year from the date of the crime
- Must show that costs have not been compensated by other sources such as insurance or other programs
- Must not have participated in criminal conduct or significant misconduct that caused or contributed to the victimization

Victims can be compensated for a wide variety of expenses, including medical care costs, mental health treatment costs, funeral costs, and lost wages. Some programs have expanded coverage to include crime scene clean-up, transportation costs to receive treatment, moving expenses, housekeeping costs, and child-care costs (Klein, 2010). Other expenses for which victims may be able to be compensated include the replacement or repair of eyeglasses or corrective lenses, dental care, prosthetic devices, and forensic sexual assault exams. Note that property damage and loss are not compensable expenses (Office for Victims of Crime, 2012), and only three states currently pay for pain and suffering (Klein, 2010). States have caps in place that limit the amount of money a crime victim may receive from the Crime Victims Fund, generally ranging from $10,000 to $25,000 per incident. On average, the maximum victims can receive is $26,000 (Evans, 2014). Some states also allow for monies for catastrophic injuries and permanent disability, ranging from $5,000 to $150,000 (Evans, 2014).

Although compensation clearly can provide a benefit for victims, there are some problems with current compensation programs. One problem is that only a small portion of victims who are eligible for compensation actually receive monies from these funds. In addition, even when people do apply for compensation, there is no guarantee that they will receive benefits. Data from victim compensation claims in 2012 showed that about one fourth of claims were denied (Office for Victims of Crime, 2013). The programs also do not seem to encourage participation in the criminal justice system. There is little evidence that persons who receive compensation are any more satisfied than others (Elias, 1984) or that they are more likely to participate in the criminal justice process (Klein, 2010).

Restitution

Unlike monies from crime victims' funds, **restitution** is money paid by the offender to the victim. Restitution is made by court order as part of a sentence—the judge orders the offender to pay the victim money to compensate for expenses. Much like compensation programs, expenses that may be recovered through restitution include medical and dental bills, counseling, transportation, and lost wages. Restitution can also be ordered to cover costs of stolen or damaged property, unlike in crime victim compensation programs. Restitution cannot be ordered to cover costs associated with pain and suffering; it is limited to tangible and documentable expenses.

Restitution has its benefits. It is based on the notion of restorative justice, which seeks to involve the community, the offender, and the victim in the criminal justice system. Paying restitution helps restore both the offender and the victim to their precrime status. Problematic, however, is that the offender must first be caught for restitution to be ordered. Often, crimes go unreported and offenders remain free from arrest. Even if an offender is arrested, it may be difficult for the court to determine an appropriate amount for restitution. How much money should be paid in restitution to a victim whose mother's engagement ring was stolen? The ring's worth to the victim may far outweigh the dollar amount a judge would require the offender to pay in restitution. In addition, many offenders lack sufficient funds to pay victims immediately, even when court ordered. As a result, restitution may not be met.

Civil Litigation

Although compensation and restitution programs may significantly aid victims in recouping crime victimization costs, not all economic costs may be covered. Recall, too, that neither program addresses pain and suffering costs (except for the three states that allow compensation for pain and suffering). To seek redress for these uncompensated costs, victims may pursue **civil litigation** against the offender. There are some key advantages afforded to a plaintiff (the person filing the lawsuit) in a civil suit. That person is a party to the lawsuit and is allowed to make key decisions regarding whether to accept a settlement—unlike in criminal court, where it is the state versus the defendant (National Crime Victim Bar Association, 2007). Persons can seek money for emotional as well as physical harm.

In addition, the burden of proof is different in the civil justice system. Liability must be proved by a fair preponderance of the evidence, not beyond a reasonable doubt, which is the standard of proof in the criminal justice system. If the court finds that the defendant is in fact liable, then the offender is held financially accountable for the harm caused to the defendant.

Much like with restitution, however, the likelihood of the victim actually receiving the money awarded is tied to the offender being identified and the offender's ability to pay. Accordingly, it may be quite difficult for the victim to recover damages awarded. Also, the costs of entering into a civil lawsuit must be borne by the victim and can be quite expensive. The victim may have to hire an attorney, and civil lawsuits can sometimes drag on for years.

■ REMEDIES AND RIGHTS IN COURT

Rights are also afforded to crime victims in other phases of the criminal justice system. Although not discussed in detail in this section, police are often the first level of criminal justice with which crime victims interact. The response that victims receive from them may shape how they view the criminal justice system as a whole and may impact their future dealings (or not) with the system should they be victimized again. It seems that when police meet victims' expectations, they report high levels of satisfaction. When victims' expectations are not met, however, victims report lower levels of satisfaction (Chandek & Porter, 1998). That is, it is expectation in conjunction with what the police do that impacts overall satisfaction with the police. In addition to the police, the prosecutor and the courts also provide crime victims with rights. These rights are discussed below.

Victim Impact Statements

As previously discussed, the criminal trial involves two parties in an adversarial system that reflects crime as a harm against the state. As such, historically, victims seldom played more than the role of witness in the criminal trial. Not until the 1970s did victims receive rights that guaranteed them at least some voice in the criminal trial process. One of these rights was first adopted in 1976 in Fresno, California, and it gave the victim an opportunity to address the court through a **victim impact statement (VIS).** The VIS can be submitted by direct victims and by those who are indirectly impacted by crime, such as family members. The VIS is either submitted in writing or presented orally (victim allocution).

In the VIS, the harm caused is typically detailed, with psychological, economic, social, as well as physical effects included. Depending on the jurisdiction, the victim or others

PHOTO 6.2

A victim delivers her victim impact statement in court during sentencing.

Photo Credit: © iStockphoto.com/Rich Legg.

presenting a VIS may also provide a recommendation as to what the offender's sentence should be. Take a look at the "Sample Victim Impact Statement Guide" box to see what kind of information victims include in a victim impact statement. Not only may the victim enter a VIS at sentencing, but most states allow for the victim to make a VIS at parole hearings as well. In some cases, the original VIS is included in the offender's file and will be considered during the parole process. In others, the victim is allowed to update the original VIS and include additional information that may be pertinent to the parole board. Less common, the victim may be allowed to make a VIS during bail hearings, pretrial release hearings, and plea bargaining hearings (National Center for Victims of Crime, 1999). Importantly, despite the victim's wishes, the VIS is used only as information and may impact the court's decision, but not always. As noted by the Minnesota Court of Appeals in *State v. Johnson* (1993), although the victim's wishes are important, they are not the only consideration or determinative in the prosecutor's decision to bring a case to trial.

There are many reasons to expect VISs to benefit victims. They give victims a right to be heard in court and allow their pain and experience to be acknowledged in the criminal justice process. As such, VISs may be therapeutic, especially if a victim's statement is referred to by the prosecutor or judge and if the victim's recommendation is in accordance with the sentence the offender receives. In addition to this potential therapeutic benefit, VISs may also provide valuable information to the court and criminal justice actors that allows them truly to understand the impacts criminal behavior has on victims. It may help the judge give a sentence that is more reflective of the true harm caused to the victim. Also, it may prove beneficial to offenders to hear the impact of their crimes. Hearing the extent to which their actions hurt another person makes it more difficult for offenders to rationalize their behavior.

Despite these proposed benefits, not all victims utilize the right to make a VIS. For example, recent data from Texas show that only 22% of VIS applications distributed to crime victims were returned to district attorney's offices (Yun, Johnson, & Kercher, 2005). The type of victimization for which VISs were submitted was most commonly sexual assault of a minor, followed by robbery (Yun et al., 2005).

Nonetheless, the reasons that victims in general do not make VISs are varied. They may not feel comfortable putting their feelings in writing or going to court and making a public statement; they may fear the offender and being retaliated against. Others may not be fully aware of their right to make a VIS or not know how to go about utilizing this right. Although it is certainly a victim's choice to make or not make a VIS, it may have an impact on the sentence the offender receives. Recent research shows that when VISs are made in capital cases, there is an increased likelihood that the offender will be sentenced to death (Blumenthal, 2009). Although a clear impact on noncapital offenses is not evident, research suggests that when VISs do impact sentencing, they do so in a punitive fashion (Erez & Globokar, 2010). Although speculative, the reason behind this influence may be tied to the influence that hearing from the victim and his or her family has on a jury member's emotions. Research shows that being exposed to VISs may increase feelings of hostility, anger, and vengefulness toward offenders (Paternoster & Deise, 2011). Other research has found that not all jury members respond the same to VISs. Rather, it is those who have a tendency to approach emotions who are likely to respond with hostility and, as a result, recommend longer sentences (Wevodau, Cramer, Kehn, & Clark, 2014).

This may be good for the victim, but it does raise the issue of equal justice for offenders. Does an offender deserve a more severe penalty because a VIS is made? Conversely, do victims not deserve to have their offenders penalized as severely as others if they are not able or willing to make a VIS? This issue underlies some of the debate surrounding the use of VISs.

The constitutionality of VISs has been questioned, particularly in capital cases. Current case law makes it constitutional for VISs to be made in capital cases. In *Payne v. Tennessee* (1991), the U.S. Supreme Court found that how the victim is impacted does not negatively impact the rights of the defendant—VISs are a way to inform the court about the harm caused. This decision allowed states to decide whether to allow VISs in capital cases.

The positive benefit for victims may be overstated in that making a VIS can be traumatizing for victims (Bandes, 1999). Victims may also be dissatisfied if their recommendations are not followed (Davis, Henley, & Smith, 1990; Erez, Roeger, & Morgan, 1994; Erez & Tontodonato, 1992). Furthermore, victims who make a VIS may not be likely to use and participate in additional criminal proceedings if they are victimized again, one of the key considerations in granting victims' rights (Erez & Globokar, 2010; Kennard, 1989).

SAMPLE VICTIM IMPACT STATEMENT GUIDE*

1. Please describe how this offense has affected you and your family.

2. What was the emotional impact of this crime on you and your family?

3. What was the financial impact of this crime on you and your family?

   (NOTE: Add "physical impact" for personal crimes.)

4. What concerns do you have, if any, about your safety and security?

5. What do you want to happen now?

6. Would you like an opportunity to participate in victim/offender programming (such as mediation/dialogue or victim impact panels) that can help hold the offender accountable for his/her actions? (NOTE: Only utilize this question if such programs are in place, and ensure that the victim has written resources that fully describe such programs.)

7. If community service is recommended as part of the disposition or sentence, do you have a favorite charity or cause you'd like to recommend as a placement?

8. Is there any other information you would like to share with the court regarding the offense, and how it affected you and your family?

Please check here if you would like to be notified about the status and outcome of this case.

*Allow as much space as is needed to complete the victim impact statement.

Source: Seymour, A. (2001). National Crime Victim Advocate, Washington, DC. Retrieved from http://justicesolutions.org.

Victim/Witness Assistance Programs

Victim/witness assistance programs (VWAPs) provide victims with assistance as they navigate the criminal justice system. These programs are designed to ensure that victims know their rights and have the resources necessary to exercise these rights. At their heart, however, is a goal to increase victim and witness participation in the criminal justice process, particularly as witnesses, with the notion that victims who have criminal justice personnel assisting them will be more likely to participate and to be satisfied with their experience.

These programs first began in the 1970s, with the first program established in St. Louis, Missouri, by Carol Vittert (Davies, 2010). Although not sponsored by the government, Vittert and her friends would visit victims and offer them support. Two years later, the first government victim assistance programs were developed in Milwaukee, Wisconsin, and Brooklyn, New York. Not long after, in 1982, the Task Force on Victims of Crime recommended that prosecutors better serve victims. Specifically, the task force noted that prosecutors should work more closely with crime victims and receive their input as their cases are processed. It also noted that victims need protection and that their contributions should be valued—prosecutors should honor scheduled case appearances and return personal property as soon as possible. To this end, VWAPs have been developed, most commonly administrated through prosecutors' offices but also sometimes run through law enforcement agencies. At the federal level, each U.S. attorney's office has a victim witness coordinator to help victims of federal crimes.

Today, these programs most commonly provide victims with background information regarding the court procedure and their basic rights as crime victims. Notification about court dates and changes to those dates is also given. They also provide victims with information regarding victim compensation and aid them in applying for compensation if eligible. A victim who wishes to make a VIS can also receive assistance from the VWAP in doing so. Another service offered by VWAPs is making sure the victims and witnesses have separate waiting areas in the courthouse for privacy. In some instances, VWAP personnel will attend court proceedings and the trial with the victim and his or her family.

Despite the efforts of VWAPs, research shows that some of the first of these programs did little to improve victim participation. The Vera Institute of Justice's Victim/Witness Assistance Project, which ran in the 1970s, provided victims with a wide range of services—day care for children while parents were in court, counseling for victims, assistance with victim compensation, notification of all court dates, and a program that allowed victims to stay at work rather than come to court if their testimony was not needed—to little "success" (Herman, 2004). An evaluation of the project showed that victims were no more likely to show up at court than those without access to these services. It was not until the Vera Institute developed a new program that provided victim advocates to go to court with victims that positive outcomes emerged. This program did, in fact, then have a positive influence on attendance in court (Herman, 2004). Few of the programs provide services identified in the research literature as most critical; instead, VWAPs are largely oriented toward ensuring that witnesses cooperate and participate in court proceedings rather than that crime victims receive needed services (Jerin, Moriarty, & Gibson, 1996).

Family Justice Centers

Family Justice Centers have recently begun opening throughout the United States to better serve crime victims. Because crime victims often need a variety of services, family justice centers are designed to provide many services in "one stop." These centers often provide counseling, advocacy, legal services, health care, financial services, housing assistance, employment referrals, and other services (National Center on Domestic and Sexual Violence,

2011). The advantages of providing these services in one place are many—primarily, victims can receive a plethora of services without having to navigate the maze of health and social service agencies in their jurisdiction.

Restorative Justice

The traditional criminal justice system is adversarial, with the state on one side and the defense on the other attempting to determine if the offender did in fact commit a crime against the state. It is largely offender centered—the offender's rights must be protected from investigation to conviction—and the victim traditionally has not been recognized as having a role beyond that of a witness, since crimes are considered harms against the state. Beginning in the 1970s, as discussed in Chapter 1, the victims' rights movement sought to garner a larger role for victims in the justice process and to ensure that victims are provided the services they deserved from the state and community agencies. Also during the 1970s, there was a movement in the criminal justice system to get "tough on crime." In doing so, more people were sentenced to prison and for longer, and our correctional system moved away from a rehabilitation model to a justice model. No longer was the correctional system dedicated to "fixing" offenders—rather, its main focus became public safety by reducing crime. This reduction was thought to be achieved through the use of tough criminal sanctions rather than treatment for the offender. Although this experiment in incarceration is not over, another movement less focused on being punitive toward offenders within the criminal justice system also emerged during the 1970s—the **restorative justice** movement.

The restorative justice movement formally began in Canada in the 1970s, but some of its principles were in place long before. Our first "systems" of justice did not define crimes as harms against the state. As such, if a person was victimized, it was up to him or her or the family to seek reparation from the offender (Tobolowsky, 1999). It was essentially a victim-centered approach. As crimes were redefined as harms against the state (or the king), the system of justice that emerged was more offender focused. Such a system was in place until the 1970s in the United States, when people began to advocate for an increased role for the victim and for victims to receive rights similar to those of offenders. The restorative justice movement was an outgrowth of the attention given to the need for victims' rights and also the push-back from adoption of a crime-control model exclusively focused on punishment.

The restorative justice movement is based on the belief that the way to reduce crime is not by solely punishing the offender or by adhering to a strict adversarial system that pits the defendant against the state. Instead, all entities impacted by crime should come to the table and work together to deal with crime and criminals. In this way, the restorative justice movement sees crime as harm to the state, the community, and the victim (Johnstone, 2002). Accordingly, instead of offenders simply being tried, convicted, and sentenced without the victim and community playing more than a cursory role, the system should develop and adopt strategies to deal with crime that include all relevant parties. Instead of a judge or jury deciding what happens to the offender, the restorative justice movement allows for input from the offender, the victim, and community members harmed by the offense in making a determination of how to repair the harm caused by the offender. In this way, justice is not just handed down and does not just "happen"; it is a cooperative agreement. Simply stated, restorative justice is a process "whereby parties with a stake in a specific offence collectively resolve how to deal with the aftermath of the offence and its implications for the future" (Marshall, 1999, p. 5).

What types of programs meet this objective? Many of the programs in use today in the United States and throughout the world were adapted from or based on traditional practices of indigenous people, who, given their communal living situation, often have a stake in group members' ability to collaboratively resolve issues (Centre for Justice and Reconciliation, 2008). The most common types of programs are victim–offender mediation or reconciliation programs and restitution programs. Victim–offender mediation is discussed below, and restitution was discussed earlier in this chapter as a financial remedy for victims. Another program that is restorative in nature is face-to-face meetings between the victim and offender that do not involve formal mediation. **Family or community group conferencing** is also restorative. In this type of program, the victim, offender, family, friends, and supporters of both the victim and offender collectively address the aftermath of the crime, with the victim addressing how the crime impacted him or her, thus increasing the offender's awareness of the consequences of the crime (Centre for Justice and Reconciliation, 2008). Because supporters of both sides are present, it allows additional people with a stake in the process and outcome to give input. Victims and offenders report high levels of satisfaction with group conferencing (Centre for Justice and Reconciliation, 2008). Restorative justice is also practiced through **peacemaking** or **sentencing circles.** A circle consists of the victim, the offender, community members, victim and offender supporters, and sometimes members of the criminal justice community such as prosecutors, judges, defense attorneys, police, and court workers. The goals of the circles are to "build community around shared values" and to "promote healing of all affected parties, giving the offender the opportunity to make amends" and giving all parties a "voice and shared responsibility in finding constructive resolutions" (Centre for Justice and Reconciliation, 2008, p. 2). The circles are also designed to address the causes of criminal behavior. In sentencing circles, the parties work together to determine the outcome for the offender, while peacemaking circles are more focused on healing.

Victim–Offender Mediation Programs

Some victims may not wish to sit in the background and interact only on the periphery of the criminal justice system. Instead, they may wish to have face-to-face meetings with their offenders. As a way to allow such a dialogue between victims and offenders, **victim–offender mediation programs** have sprouted up throughout the United States, with more than 300 such programs in operation today (Umbreit & Greenwood, 2000). With the American Bar Association endorsing the use of victim–offender mediation and what appears to be widespread public support for these programs, victim–offender mediation is likely to become commonplace in U.S. courts (Umbreit & Greenwood, 2000). Victim–offender mediation is already widely used in other countries, with more than 700 programs operating in Europe (Umbreit & Greenwood, 2000).

Mediation in criminal justice cases most commonly occurs as a **diversion** from prosecution. This means that if an offender and victim agree to complete mediation and if the offender completes any requirements set forth in the mediation agreement, then the offender will not be formally prosecuted in the criminal justice system. In this way, offenders receive a clear benefit if they agree to and successfully complete mediation. Mediation can also take place as a condition of probation. For some offenders, if they formally admit guilt and are adjudicated, they may be placed on probation by the judge with the condition that they participate in mediation. In all instances, the decision to participate in victim–offender mediation programs is ultimately up to the victim (Umbreit & Greenwood, 2000). Most victims who are given the opportunity to participate in victim–offender mediation do so (Umbreit & Greenwood, 2000).

Victim–offender mediation programs are designed to provide victims—usually those of property crimes and minor assaults—a chance to meet with their offenders in a structured environment. The session is led by a third-party mediator whose job it is to facilitate a dialogue through which victims are able to directly address their offenders and tell them how the crime impacted their lives. The victim may also ask questions of the offender. To achieve the objectives of restorative justice, mediation programs in criminal justice use humanistic mediation, which is dialogue driven rather than settlement driven (Umbreit, 2000). The impartial mediator is there to provide unconditional positive concern and regard for both parties, with minimal interruption. As noted by Umbreit (2000), humanistic mediation emphasizes healing and peacemaking over problem solving and resolution. He notes,

> the telling and hearing of each other's stories about the conflict, the opportunity for maximum direct communication with each other, and the importance of honoring silence and the innate wisdom and strength of the participants are all central to humanistic mediation practice. (p. 4)

One tangible outcome often but not always stemming from victim–offender mediation is a restitution plan for the offender. The victim plays a central role in its development. This agreement becomes enforceable in court, whereby an offender who does not meet the requirements can be held accountable.

What happens after an offender and victim meet? Do both offenders and victims benefit? What about the community? It is important to evaluate programs in terms of their effectiveness in meeting objectives, and victim–offender mediation programs have been assessed in this way. Collectively, this body of research shows many benefits to victim–offender mediation programs. Participation in victim–offender mediation has been shown to reduce fear and anxiety among crime victims (Umbreit, Coates, & Kalanj, 1994), including posttraumatic stress symptoms (Angel, 2005), and desire to seek revenge against or harm offenders (Sherman et al., 2005; Strang, 2002). In addition, both offenders and victims report high levels of satisfaction with the victim–offender mediation process (McCold & Wachtel, 1998; McGarrell, Olivares, Crawford, & Kroovand, 2000; see also Umbreit & Greenwood, 2000). Victims who meet with their offenders report higher levels of satisfaction than victims of similar crimes whose cases are formally processed in the criminal justice system (Umbreit, 1994a). In addition to satisfaction, research shows that offenders are more likely to complete restitution required through victim–offender mediation (Umbreit et al., 1994). More than 90% of restitution agreements from victim–offender mediation programs are completed within 1 year (Victim–Offender Reconciliation Program Information and Resource Center,

2006). Reduction in recidivism rates for offenders also has been found (Nugent & Paddock, 1995; Umbreit, 1994b). As you can see, our system has changed from victim centered to entirely offender focused and is now bringing the victim back into focus. Crime victims are afforded many rights in the criminal justice system. But, as you have seen, it is sometimes difficult for victims to exercise these rights, and they often have little recourse if their rights are not protected. These issues will certainly continue to be addressed as victims' voices are heard and their needs met.

SUMMARY

- All states give the right to compensation, notification of rights, notification of court appearances, and ability to submit victim impact statements before sentencing.
- Other states may give the right to restitution, to be treated with dignity and respect, to attend court and sentencing hearings, and to consult with court personnel before plea bargains are offered or defendants released from custody. Other rights will also protect victims' employment status so they can testify against their offenders.
- There has been some resistance to states and the federal government giving victims formal rights. Although numerous federal acts have been passed with victims' rights in mind, there still is no victims' rights amendment in the U.S. Constitution.
- To help assuage some of the financial costs of a crime, victims can apply for financial compensation from the state, can receive restitution from the offender, or can seek remedy in civil court.
- A victim impact statement can be submitted by direct victims and by those who are indirectly impacted by crime, such as family members. In the victim impact statement, the harm that was caused is typically detailed, with psychological, economic, social, as well as physical effects included.
- Victim/witness assistance programs provide victims with guidance as they navigate the criminal justice system. These programs are designed to ensure that victims know their rights and have the resources necessary to exercise these rights. Another goal of these programs is to increase the likelihood that a witness or victim will interact with the criminal justice system.
- The restorative justice movement is based on the belief that the way to reduce crime is not solely by punishing the offender or by adhering to a strict adversarial system that pits the defendant against the state. Instead, all entities impacted by crime should come to the table and work together to deal with crime and criminals.
- To increase dialogue between offenders and victims, victim–offender mediation programs have emerged throughout the United States.

DISCUSSION QUESTIONS

1. Do you think it is the role of the criminal justice system to provide victims with rights? How else could we ensure that victims receive help?

2. What rights does the state in which you reside provide to crime victims? What rights do you think are most important?

3. Why would offenders be more likely to complete restitution in victim–offender mediation? Could it be used for other types of programs? Why or why not?

4. What types of services would Polly be eligible to receive? Explain.

KEY TERMS

victims' rights

notification

participation and consultation

right to protection

right to a speedy trial

Federal Victim Witness Protection Act (1982)

Victims of Crime Act (1984)

Child Victims' Bill of Rights (1990)

Crime Control Act (1990)

Victims' Rights and Restitution Act (1990)

Violent Crime Control and Law Enforcement Act (1994)

Violence Against Women Act (1994)

Antiterrorism and Effective Death Penalty Act (1996)

Victims' Rights Clarification Act (1997)

Violence Against Women Act (2000)

Justice for All Act (2004)

victim compensation

restitution

civil litigation

victim impact statement (VIS)

victim/witness assistance programs (VWAPs)

restorative justice

family or community group conferencing

peacemaking circle

sentencing circle

victim–offender mediation programs

diversion

INTERNET RESOURCES

Guidelines for Victim-Sensitive Victim–Offender Mediation (https://www.ncjrs.gov/ovc_archives/reports/96517-gdlines_victims-sens/ncj176346.pdf)

Published by the Office for Victims of Crime, this is a compilation of six documents that covers issues related to restorative justice, including victim–offender mediation and family group counselling. It provides guidelines and criteria to enhance the quality of such restorative justice initiatives and to make them more victim-sensitive.

National Association of Crime Victim Compensation Boards (http://www.nacvcb.org/links.html)

This website provides links to federal agencies and resources, national victim organizations, national and state criminal justice victim-related organizations, victim-related education links, state crime victim compensation boards, federal and state correctional agencies, victim service units, sex offender registries, and other resources. It is your go-to website for links related to crime victims.

National Center for Victims of Crime Resource Library (http://www.victimsofcrime.org/library)

The Center disseminates information online for crime victims and people working with crime victims or in the area of policy. In its resource library, you can find information on victim impact statements, statistics regarding the extent of various kinds of victimization, and information on how to assist lesbian, gay, bisexual, transgender, and queer victims, among other topics.

Restorative Justice Online (http://www.restorativejustice.org/)

The restorative justice movement is concerned with repairing harm caused by crime. Restorative Justice Online provides information for criminal justice professionals, social service providers, students, teachers, and victims. It includes links to research as well as more general information. It also provides information for restorative justice around the world.

CHAPTER 7

HOMICIDE VICTIMIZATION

On the surface, Justin Lopez is your typical American college student. The child of divorced parents, Justin is the first person in his family to attend college. To make ends meet, he works full time while attending a local state university. In his limited free time, he enjoys watching football and hanging out with friends. Justin has one other responsibility, however, that sets him apart from most of his peers; he's raising his 14-year-old sister Porsha. Justin became Porsha's legal guardian after their mother was brutally murdered by her ex-boyfriend in 2012. This is their story:

THE STORY OF JUSTIN AND PORSHA

On September 15th, 2012, Justin Lopez, 22, was driving down Texas Highway 6 on his way to a football game when he received a frantic call from his mother's neighbor. The news was devastating: His mother had been shot and was en route to the hospital. With very few details of the event, he turned around and drove the 200 miles to the hospital as fast as he could. Upon arrival, he found his 12-year-old sister Porsha outside in tears. He was too late. Their mother was dead: a victim of intimate partner homicide.

Angela (Angie) Renee Lopez, 42, had been killed by her ex-boyfriend, William (Billy) Ray Parker, 44. Just a few weeks prior to the incident, Angie had ended their 3-year relationship. Angie had never indicated that Billy

(Continued)

(Continued)

was abusive. Friends said she left the relationship over differences in parenting styles (Billy had three kids from a previous relationship).

On that fatal day, Billy pulled up in the driveway of the apartment duplex Angie had recently moved into, parked his truck, and finished off a bottle of liquor. After about 30 minutes, he walked up to Angie's front door and knocked. Angie opened the door to find Billy drunk. She asked him to leave, and they began to argue. Porsha, asleep upstairs, woke to the sounds of arguing and came down to see what was going on.

It wasn't long after that, when Billy fired the first shot. The gun misfired, and Porsha ran toward Billy, knocking him off balance. This gave Angie and Porsha the opportunity to run. Billy fired again, hitting Angie in the left shoulder.

Injured, terrified, and in pain, Angie ran out the front door and into a neighbor's lawn screaming for help. Billy followed, continuing to fire his gun. Angie was shot three more times before she fell to the ground. Then, in front of seven eyewitnesses, including Angie's daughter, Billy got on top of her and fired off the fifth and final shot before a neighbor tackled Billy, beat, and restrained him until the police arrived. Angie was life-flighted to the hospital in Galveston, but succumbed to her injuries in the helicopter.

On September 27, 2013, Billy was convicted of murder and sentenced to 99 years in state prison, the maximum sentence allowable under Texas state law.

Source: Adapted from http://www.kbtx.com/home/headlines/Bryan-Man-Raises-Awareness-About-Domestic-Violence-After-Moms-Murder-231998721.html.

■ DEFINING HOMICIDE VICTIMIZATION

According to various legal dictionaries, **homicide** is a general term referring to "the killing of one human being by another." There are generally three types of homicide: excusable, justifiable, and criminal homicide/murder.

PHOTO 7.1

Justin and Porsha Lopez and their mom, Angela (Angie) Lopez. Angie was murdered in 2012 in a domestic violence incident, and since then, Justin has become an outspoken advocate of victim's rights, creating "Angie's Awareness Angels" to increase support for domestic violence victims.

Photo Credit: Justin Porsha Lopez.

Excusable Homicide

With **excusable homicide**, there is no guilt. These are accidental or unintentional killings. The Uniform Crime Reports' (UCR) definition of homicide inserts the phrase "willful (non-negligent) killing" to focus their definition solely on criminal homicide and does not, therefore, count accidental or excusable homicides. An example of excusable homicide occurred when two children were being taught to swim by a swim instructor. One of the children had an asthma attack and needed his inhaler. The instructor told the other child to stay out of the pool even though she was a good swimmer. While the instructor was retrieving the inhaler, the girl got back in the pool and drowned.

Justifiable Homicide

Justifiable homicides are judged to be acceptable because they occur in defense of life or property. The UCR identifies justifiable homicides as being limited to "the killing of a felon by a peace officer in the line of duty," or "the killing (during the commission of a felony) of a felon by a private citizen." The UCR makes a distinction between its definition and any legal action, thus, the UCR's definition is not based on a claim of self-defense or the actions of a prosecutor, judge, etc. An example of justifiable homicide would be homicides that occur under stand your ground laws and the castle doctrine. **Stand your ground laws** are laws stating that individuals are not required to retreat from their location prior to using force in self-defense. More specifically, stand your ground laws can be enforced regardless of where an event occurs (e.g., in your residence, on a public street). Somewhat similar to stand your ground laws is the **castle doctrine.** The castle doctrine also states that there is no duty to retreat prior to using force in self-defense, but these events are limited only to those occurring within or on an individual's personal property (such as a residence [house and yard]). In states without stand your ground laws or the castle doctrine, the law requires that an individual flee to safety, if this may reasonably be achieved, prior to using force in self-defense.

Criminal Homicide

The legal definition of **criminal homicide** is, more specifically, "the purposeful, knowing, reckless, or negligent killing of one human being by another." Thus, any death resulting from injuries pursuant to a fight, quarrel, argument, or commission of a crime falls under the umbrella of criminal homicide. Criminal homicide (specifically murder or manslaughter) does not include justifiable or excusable homicides, attempted murder, deaths stemming from accidents and traffic-related incidents, or suicides. Moreover, instances whereby an individual dies from medical issues (e.g., heart attack) while involved or witnessing a crime also do not fit into the categorization of criminal homicide. Again, aside from justifiable homicide, this is the only type of homicide that the UCR includes in its statistics. There are four types of criminal homicide: first degree murder, second degree murder, felony murder, and manslaughter.

First Degree Murder

First degree murder is murder committed with deliberate premeditation and malice. **Premeditation** means the act was considered beforehand. **Deliberation** indicates the act was planned after careful thought (not on impulse). The planning does not need to take a long time. UCR's definition also includes malice that goes to intent, proving that a person intended to cause harm. **Express malice** is actual malice, such as when a person in a fight shoots the other person, showing that he or she intended to cause serious injury. **Implied/constructive malice** exists when death occurs due to negligence rather than intent. First degree murder is the only type of murder eligible for the death penalty. A prime example of this is evident in the opening story involving William (Billy) Ray Parker.

Second Degree Murder

Second degree murder involves murder committed with malice, but without premeditation and deliberation. In other words, the offender intended to cause harm but the murder was not planned. This type of murder is considered to be a less serious offense. For example, John returns home early to find his wife, Rebecca having an affair. Without thinking, John grabs his semiautomatic handgun out of the nightstand, shoots and kills both Rebecca and Jeff. Since the murders were fueled by rage and were not premeditated, this would be considered second degree murder.

Felony Murder

Felony murder is the often unintentional killing during the commission of another felony, such as striking someone on the head during a robbery, and he dies. This type of murder is usually considered first degree murder. Let's use an example to illustrate. Tom breaks and enters into a residential house owned by Mary and Bill. As Tom begins to steal jewelry from the master bedroom, Bill walks in. Startled, Bill screams at Tom to leave. Rather than fleeing the scene, Tom comes after Bill with a knife and stabs him. If Bill dies from stab wounds inflicted by Tom, this would be considered a felony murder since Tom was in the act of burglary (a felony charge), that resulted in the death of Bill.

Manslaughter

Manslaughter deems the degree of responsibility is less than for murder; however, it is still an unlawful killing. This killing can include **voluntary manslaughter**, which is the intentional infliction of injury that is likely to and actually does cause death. It could also include excessive use of force in self-defense. An example of this would be if at a party one evening, Luis got into a verbal confrontation with Tony. Tony punches Luis in the face, but did not use any other physical force. As Tony was walking away from the confrontation, Luis gets up, pulls out a gun, and shoots Tony in the back repeatedly until he dies. In this case, Luis used excessive force, so this scenario would be classified as voluntary manslaughter.

Manslaughter can include **involuntary/negligent manslaughter**, which is death resulting from gross negligence (ignoring the possible danger or potential harm to other people). The Federal Bureau of Investigation (FBI) defines negligent manslaughter as "the killing of another person through negligence, with no willful intent. Included in this offense are killings resulting from hunting accidents, gun cleaning, children playing with guns, etc. Not included are deaths of persons due to their own negligence, accidental deaths not resulting from gross negligence, and accidental traffic fatalities" (FBI, 2013b). One such scenario would be when a young college student, Kevin, decides to drive home from the bar while under the influence of alcohol. On the way home, Kevin blacks out and strikes Veronica with his vehicle, instantly killing her. This case would be considered negligent manslaughter since Kevin did not intend to kill Veronica, but was deemed negligent since he was operating a vehicle while under the influence.

■ MEASUREMENT AND EXTENT OF HOMICIDE VICTIMIZATION

Homicide Victimization in the United States

Homicide victimization data are not available through victimization surveys, such as the National Crime Victimization Survey. However, in the United States, there are a few methods for measuring murder. They include the Uniform Crime Report, the Supplementary Homicide Reports, and the National Center for Health Statistics.

Uniform Crime Report (UCR)

As discussed in Chapter 2, the UCR provides a yearly summation of crime data collected by law enforcement agencies across the United States. This measurement tool includes both aggregate murder rates and clearance rates (a measure of crimes solved by the police) for murder, similar to other offense types. The UCR reported 12,765 murders in 2012. This is a rate of 4.7 homicides per 100,000 people. Murders constitute about 1% of all violent index crimes reported to police.

Supplementary Homicide Reports (SHR)

Beginning in the 1960s, the UCR included the Supplemental Homicide Reports (SHR), which provide case-specific information for each murder reported in the UCR. The SHR includes the age, race, and sex of victims and offenders (if caught), as well as information pertaining to weapon used and situational information such as the relationship between the victim and offender and the circumstance leading up to the murder. Table 7.1 shows the circumstance codes used in the SHR.

It is important to point out that the SHR is one of the few sources of official data that provide detailed information on crime victims. According to the SHR, victims of homicide share certain characteristics with their perpetrators. Specifically, homicide *victims and offenders* are likely to be male (men are 6 times more likely than females to be the victim and 9 times more likely to be the offender), young (highest rates of victimization and offending are between the ages of 16 and 24), and intraracial (90% of murders are comprised of victims and offenders from the same race). Murders also typically occur between people who know each other, and this relationship has interesting differences by the sex of the victim. Nearly one third (33%) of female murder victims were killed by a husband or boyfriend. This phenomenon is labeled as intimate partner homicide (and discussed in further detail in the section on Intimate Partner Homicide in this chapter), while only 3% of male victims were killed by a wife or girlfriend.

National Center for Health Statistics (NCHS)

The National Center for Health Statistics (NCHS) is another source of nationwide mortality data collected since the early 1930s. These data are derived from death certificates that are forwarded to the Vital Statistics Division of the NCHS by coroners and medical examiners. While all types of deaths are reported, there are specifics codes for homicides

Table 7.1 ■ Circumstance Codes in the SHR

Circumstance	Definition
Argument over Money/Property	A dispute, quarrel, or conflict over money or property led to the homicide.
Argument (Influence of Alcohol)	A dispute, quarrel, or conflict where impairment of the offender and/or the victim by alcohol led to homicide.
Argument (Influence of Drugs)	A dispute, quarrel, or conflict where impairment of the offender and/or the victim by drugs led to homicide.
Drug-Related Transaction	Drug dealing (buying or selling) is suspected to have played a role in the homicide.
Other Argument	A quarrel or other interpersonal conflict such as abuse, insult, grudge, or personal revenge precipitated the killing. Exclude arguments over money, property, or drugs, arguments under the influence of alcohol or drugs, or lovers' triangle, because these choices are listed separately.
Arson	The homicide resulted from an act of arson.
Burglary	The homicide occurred during the commission of a burglary.
Child Killed by Babysitter	Homicide due to abuse or neglect. The victim is a child and the suspect is a person hired to take care of the child in the temporary absence of a parent or guardian.
Inappropriate Caregiving	Homicide precipitated by abuse or neglect of a victim who requires care. Include all caregivers other than babysitter (e.g., nursing home worker, home health aide, parent, etc.).
Gang/Organized Crime Related	Suspected organized crime or gang activity resulted in the homicide.
Youth Gang Activity	Youth gang activity is suspected to have led to the homicide.
Gambling	Illegal gambling is suspected to have played a role in the homicide.
Larceny	The homicide occurred during the commission of a larceny.
Lovers' Triangle	Jealousy or distress over a current or former intimate partner's relationship or suspected relationship with another person leads to the homicide.
Motor Vehicle Theft	The homicide occurred during the commission of a motor vehicle theft.
Murder-Suicide	An individual murdered another individual and then killed himself or herself.
Prostitution/Commercialized Vice	Prostitution or other commercialized vice led to the homicide (e.g., a pimp or a john kills a prostitute).

Circumstance	Definition
Rape	The homicide was preceded by forcible rape of a female. The FBI limits the definition of rape to the forcible rape of a female victim by a male suspect.
Other Sex Offense	The homicide was preceded by the sexual assault of a male or female.
Robbery	The homicide occurred during the commission of a robbery.
Other Felony—Not Specified	The homicide occurred during the commission of a suspected felony that is not listed above.
Other (provide description)	Use if none of the other choices fits the situation.
Unknown	The circumstance that precipitated the homicide is unknown (e.g., a body is discovered underneath an embankment and foul play is suspected).

Source: New York Department of Criminal Justice. (2013). Retrieved from http://www.criminaljustice.ny.gov/crimnet/ojsa/crimereporting/forms/homicide.pdf.

Table 7.2 ■ Expanded Homicide Data

	Victims				Offenders			
Sex	Total	Male	Female	Unknown	Total	Male	Female	Unknown
	12,765	9,917	2,834	14	14,581	9,425	1,098	4,058
Race	White	Black	Other	Unknown	White	Black	Other	Unknown
	5,855	6,454	326	130	4,582	5,531	240	4,228
Age	0-8		501		0-8		1	
	9-16		391		9-16		346	
	17-24		3,363		17-24		3,831	
	25-34		3,396		25-34		2,763	
	35-44		2,044		35-44		1,306	
	45-54		1,518		45-54		867	
	55-64		825		55-64		391	
	65+		612		65+		209	
	Unknown		115		Unknown		4,867	

Source: Federal Bureau of Investigation. 2014. "Expanded Homicide Data Table 2" Retrieved October 31, 2014 (http://www.fbi.gov/about-us/cjis/ucr/crime-in-the-u.s/2012/crime-in-the-u.s.-2012/offenses-known-to-law-enforcement/expanded-homicide/expanded_homicide_data_table_2_murder_victims_by_age_sex_and_race_2012.xls).

(with distinctions between justifiable homicides and criminal homicides) that allow for the estimation of trends and patterns at the national level by selected characteristics (age, sex, Hispanic origin, race, and state of residence). In 2010, homicide dropped from among the top 15 leading causes of death for the first time since 1965. The vast majority of deaths (68%) classified as homicides in 2010 involved a firearm.

Homicide Victimization Across the Globe

Unlike other types of criminal victimization, homicide victimization is one of the few types of criminal victimization that can be compared across countries. This ability to compare is due to a general consensus between countries regarding what constitutes homicide. High rates of reporting and recording of murders are evident across countries due to (1) the ease of identifying whether a homicide occurred (i.e., finding a body or not) and (2) a relatively uniform moral opposition across societies pertaining to homicide, resulting in a significant amount of agency attention being placed on this type of crime.

United Nations Office on Drugs and Crime (UNODC)

Since 2000, the United Nations Office on Drugs and Crime (UNODC) collects data on intentional homicides from 219 countries and territories across the globe from criminal justice and public health agencies as part of the Homicide Statistics Dataset. Information from this dataset is currently being utilized for the UNODC's Global Study on Homicide, which provides information on intentional homicides from a global perspective.

According to the most recent report, nearly half a million people (437,000) across the globe fell victim to homicide in 2012 (UNODC, 2013). This equates to a global average murder rate of 6.2 per 100,000 inhabitants. Roughly 1 in 3 (36%) of all intentional homicides occurred in the Americas, followed by Africa (31%), Asia (28%), Europe (5%), and Oceania (0.3%). Similar to homicide patterns in the United States, globally victims are disproportionately male (79% of all homicide victims are male) and young (almost half of all homicide victims were aged 14–29).

World Health Organization (WHO)

Since 1951, mortality data are collected for 120 countries from individual death certificates and reported in aggregate form annually by the World Health Organization (WHO). While

Table 7.3 ■ Number of Homicides Victims From 2004 to 2013									
Year	2004	2005	2006	2007	2008	2009	2010	2011	2012
Number of Homicides	14,121	14,860	14,990	14,831	14,180	13,636	12,996	12,664	12,765

Source: Federal Bureau of Investigation. 2014. "UCR Publications" Retrieved October 31, 2014 (http://www.ucrdatatool.gov/Search/Crime/State/RunCrimeStatebyState.cfm).

information is collected for homicides, there is no distinction made between intentional and unintentional homicides. Additionally, because of changes in definitions over time, earlier inclusion of war-related casualties in homicide-related deaths, and capabilities of nation states to participate, caution is warranted when making comparisons of WHO data over time.

■ RISK FACTORS FOR AND CHARACTERISTICS OF HOMICIDE VICTIMIZATION

Risk for homicide victimization is not evenly distributed among the population. Rather, your risk is dependent upon a number of characteristics including your age, your sex, your race, where you live, and how much money you make. Across the globe, homicide is the 16th leading cause of premature death (UNODC, 2013). In the United States, homicide is one of the foremost causes of the death for young, African American males.

Socio-Demographic Characteristics of Victims and Offenders

Sex

Sex is an important characteristic when investigating homicide victimization, because, as previously stated, males are overrepresented as both homicide victims and offenders (Muftić & Moreno, 2010). In the United States, data collected by the police indicate that males are nearly 4 times more likely to be murdered and 7 times more likely to be the murderer than females (Cooper & Smith, 2011). Similar patterns are found globally. Homicide research has consistently found victim sex correlated with homicide type (e.g., intimate partner homicide), motive, and method, not to mention various demographic characteristics of both homicide victims and perpetrators. For instance, Muftić and Moreno (2010) studied 360 homicide incidents involving juvenile victims that took place in Dallas, Texas, and found that male homicide victimization in later adolescence was linked to overall involvement in criminal networks. In other words, male homicide victims (compared to female victims of the same age) were more likely to have been killed while committing another crime (e.g., during a robbery) or as a result of a dispute (e.g., during a fight). Male victims were also more likely to have prior offending histories, gang ties, and to have used alcohol and/or drugs prior to their death. In contrast, female victims in later adolescence were most likely to be killed as a result of family or sexual violence, indicating that female homicide victimization is an extension of family violence.

Age

Homicide is also a relatively young offense with victims and perpetrators likely to be between the ages of 18 and 24 (Cooper & Smith, 2011). As such, homicide is one of the leading causes of death of juveniles in the United States. Yet, very little is known about these victims. Who are they? Why are they victimized? Copeland (1985) conducted one of the first published research articles that examined the phenomenon of juvenile homicide victimization. Using data acquired from the Dade County Medical Examiner, Copeland (1985) provided a descriptive profile of 263 juvenile homicide victims who were killed in Metro-Dade County, Florida, between 1973 and 1982. Overall, the majority of victims were between the ages of

17 and 19 (70%), were male (76.8%), were Black (53.2%), and were killed by a firearm (78.7%). In cases where alcohol and/or drug use could be detected via the autopsy, one third of juvenile victims had been drinking and a little over one fourth of juvenile victims tested positive for drugs at the time of their death.

Race

In terms of race, homicide is an overwhelmingly intraracial event. According to official records, homicide victimization and perpetration is unevenly distributed by race with Black people having higher victimization and perpetration rates than White people (Smith & Cooper, 2013). Additionally, it has been suggested that a victim's race may be related to the type of homicide to which he or she falls victims. For instance, one study found that stranger killings were significantly more common among White women than Black women (Moracco, Runyan, & Butts, 1998) and that Asian women were far more likely to fall victim to intimate partner homicide than White or Black women (Frye, Hosein, Waltermaurer, Blaney, & Wilt, 2005).

Urbanity and Socioeconomic Status

Homicide victimization rates are highest in urban areas, compared to suburban and rural areas. While the murder rate has declined across community type (i.e., large and small cities, suburban areas, and rural areas), rates continue to remain highest where population is greatest. For example, the homicide rate in large cities with 500,000 or more residents was 10.9 per 100,000 individuals in 2011. For the same year, the homicide rate was 1.8 per 100,000 in cities with fewer than 99,999 residents (Smith & Cooper, 2013). Moreover, the highest victimization rates are generally found in families located in the lowest socioeconomic bracket. In other words, as family income increases, victimization rates decrease. For example, research by Levitt (1999) has indicated that an increase of $1,000 in median household income decreases the homicide rate by 0.7 homicides per 100,000 persons.

Victim–Offender Relationship

When the police are able to determine the relationship between the victim and the offender in a homicide case, most homicides (roughly 3 out of 4) involve people who knew each other; referred to as nonstranger homicides. Within nonstranger homicides, more than half (56%) of victims were acquaintances of the perpetrator, while another quarter (22%) were killed by a spouse or other family member (Cooper & Smith, 2011). Although most murders involve people known to one another, your risk of being killed by a loved one is drastically higher if you are female. Among nonstranger homicides, nearly one third of murder victims who were female were killed by a husband or boyfriend. In contrast, less than 3% of murder victims who were male were killed by a wife or girlfriend (Cooper & Smith, 2011).

Incident Characteristics

Weapon Usage

Firearm involvement is especially common in homicides and official statistics indicate they comprise about 70% of homicide cases known to the police (FBI, 2013b). Interestingly, firearms are more likely to be used in homicides involving male victims (73%) than homicides with female victims (35%). When firearms are used, handguns are the most common (71.9%). Other weapons, such as knives, hands and feet, and blunt objects, are less commonplace.

Circumstance

Because there are many different reasons for homicide, understanding the circumstances that surround the homicide event is an important component of the homicide investigation. For about 1 out of every 3 homicides, the police are unable to determine the circumstances surrounding the murder. For the cases in which they are, 2 out of 5 victims were murdered during an argument (FBI, 2013b). In 1 out of 4 murders, felony circumstances such as rape, robbery, or burglary were involved (FBI, 2013b).

Location

The location of the homicide is another important consideration in the homicide investigation. Homicides are likely to occur in private dwellings, such as the victim's residence, especially if the homicide is domestic in nature or involves a victim that is elderly.

Substance Use

The relationship between substance use and homicide is complex. Though not all homicides involve substance use, studies have found that murderers and their victims are likely to have consumed alcohol, drugs, or both prior to the homicide incident. One study found that two thirds of men who either killed or attempted to kill their intimate partners had used alcohol, drugs, or both during the incident (Sharps et al., 2003). Another study found that one third of victims and one fourth of suspects had consumed alcohol at the time of the murder (Muftić & Hunt, 2013).

■ DIFFERENT TYPES OF HOMICIDE VICTIMIZATION

Filicide

Filicide refers to the killing of a child by a parent or a caretaker. Infanticide, a type of filicide, involves homicides in which the victim is under one year of age. Both filicide and infanticide are, by definition, a type of child abuse. Determining the number of fatalities attributable to child abuse is difficult. When a child dies, his or her death may be explained as an accident or the result of sudden infant death syndrome (SIDS).

Official reports typically indicate that the younger the child, the greater the risk of being a victim of homicide. During the period 1980–2008, infants under the age of 1 had the highest rate of victimization of all children under the age of 5 (Cooper & Smith, 2011). When a child under 5 is killed, it is most likely to be killed by a parent (63%), followed by a male (23%) or female (5%) acquaintance, or other relative (7%) (Cooper & Smith, 2011). It is rare for a young child to be killed by a stranger, with only 3% of children under the age of 5 being murdered by a perpetrator unknown to the child (Cooper & Smith, 2011).

Parricide

Parricide refers to the murder of one's parent. Within parricide, **patricide** is the killing of one's father while **matricide** is the killing of one's mother. Both are rare events, although patricide is more common than matricide (Dantas, Santos, Dinis-Oliveira, & Mahalhaes, 2014). Parricide is more likely to occur in families that are characterized as being dysfunctional and where the child has experienced maltreatment at the hands of his or her father, mother, or both (Heide, 2013).

Eldercide

Eldercide is a type of homicide categorized by the age of the victim. In other words, eldercide is a murder that involves a victim who is 65 years of age or older. In the United States, only about 5% of all homicide victims are elderly (Cooper & Smith, 2011). As with other types of homicide, males comprise the largest proportion of eldercide victims accounting for nearly 6 out of every 10 elderly homicide victims (Cooper & Smith, 2011). While eldercide includes the homicide of individuals over the age of 65, the category can be subdivided into multiple age categories. Addington (2013) describes the youngest category of elderly as "young old" and between the ages of 65 and 74. Aside from this category, elderly between the ages of 75 and 84 are labeled as "aged," while persons older than 85 are deemed the "oldest old."

Felonious Homicide Risk and the Elderly

For most of us, our risk of being the victim of homicide decreases as we age. However, in the last four decades, the proportion of felony homicides has increased for elderly victims compared to victims in other age categories (Cooper & Smith, 2011). Read more about the felonious homicide risk and the elderly in the Grandma's at Risk? box.

GRANDMA'S AT RISK?

Most of us find it comforting to know that our grandparents' risk of violent victimization, including being murdered, generally declines with age. However, recent research has found that the elderly may be at an *increased* risk of being the victim of a felony-related murder. The very factors that decrease an older individual's risk of violent victimization in general (i.e., isolated lifestyles, such as living alone) may increase their risk of being the victim of felonious murder.

In fact, two researchers found just that when they examined felony- and argument-related homicides involving elderly victims using data from 195 cities contained within the FBI's Supplementary Homicide Reports. They found the rate of felonious eldercide was significantly influenced by the robbery rate (per 100,000 persons), the proportion of elderly individuals living alone, and the proportion of elderly persons with disabilities.

Source: Adapted from Roberts & Willits. (2013). Lifestyle, routine activities, and felony-related eldercide. *Homicide Studies, 17*(2), 184–203.

Intimate Partner Homicide

According to the World Health Organization (2013), 1 out of every 7 murders around the world is the result of domestic violence. As previously stated in Chapter 9, in the United States, intimate homicides comprised 14% of all homicides (Catalano, Smith, Snyder, & Rand, 2009). **Intimate partner homicide** is defined as a homicide involving spouses, ex-spouses, persons in current or de facto relationships, boyfriends or girlfriends, or partners of same-sex relationships.

Intimate partner homicide is a gender-differentiated offense that most likely involves a male offender and a female victim. Current victimization rates of intimate partner homicide for females are approximately 6 times the rate for male victims globally (Stöckl et al., 2013) and 4 to 5 times the rate for male victims in the United States (Cooper & Smith, 2011). When women are the perpetrator, they have often killed a husband or boyfriend who was abusive to them in the past.

FOCUS ON RESEARCH

A National Institute of Justice review of risk factors for intimate partner homicide highlights important findings that are predictive of a lethal outcome amongst intimate partners (Block, 2003). Several of the key findings include:

- Women who experienced violence in the past are more at risk for intimate partner homicide.
- The type of violence previously experienced can be an indicator of what is to come. For example, attempts of strangling or choking is considered to be a risk factor for severe or fatal violence. In one quarter of the homicides of a woman by a man, she was strangled or smothered to death.
- The number of days since the last violent episode is also a predictor of homicide risk for abused women. Regardless of the severity of the last episode, if it happened recently, the woman is at greater risk for homicide victimization. Block (2003) found that half of the women

killed by their intimate partners in Chicago had experienced violence within 30 days of the homicide.

- For some women (1 in 5), the first act of violence by their intimate partner is lethal. The risk factors for these women are slightly different. They include a partner who exhibits controlling behavior or jealousy, a partner who abused drugs, and/or a partner who is violent outside of the home.
- Risk factors for women who perpetrated intimate partner homicide were also assessed. Women who killed their partners, compared to abused women who did not, were more likely to have experienced more severe and increasing violence, had fewer resources (such as employment or education), were in more traditional relationships (for example they were married to, had children with, and were in longer relationships with their abuser), and were more likely to have called the police after a violent incident against them.

Source: Partially reprinted from Block, C. R. (2003). How can practitioners help an abused woman lower her risk of death? (pp. 5–7). Intimate Partner Homicide. NIJ 2003 (Issue No. 250).

Over the last three decades, we have witnessed a general decline in intimate partner homicides. However, this decline has not been experienced equally by all victims. When we look at rates of intimate partner homicide by the sex of the victim, what is evident is that the number of male victims has decreased, but the number of female victims has remained relatively stable. Why the difference? As discussed in Chapter 6, since the 1980s, there has been a shift in policy as to how the criminal justice system responds to domestic violence as well as a growing number of resources made available to intimate partner victims. As a result, more women are finding help within the community (social service agencies, programs, and domestic violence shelters), rather than resorting to homicide in an attempt to end an abusive relationship. These resources may have resulted in fewer incidents of intimate partner homicide involving female perpetrators and male victims. For male offenders, their motivations for intimate partner homicide are generally not addressed by resources that are, for the most part, designed for female victims, and this may be why we are not seeing comparable decreases in the number of female victims.

Intimate Partner Homicide Followed by Suicide

Some intimate partner homicides are characterized by the perpetrator killing himself after murdering his intimate partner, referred to as homicide followed by suicide or homicide-suicide. In the United States, homicide-suicide is a relatively rare event with an estimated rate of 0.19–0.46 per 100,000 individuals (Morton, Runyan, Moracco, & Butts, 1998). The most prevalent type of homicide-suicide involves males killing their female intimate partners and then themselves. An evaluation of 1,108 homicide-suicide deaths in 2007 found that almost three quarters of such events involved intimate partners of which the vast majority were committed by males using a firearm in

Table 7.4 ■ Victim and Offender Relationship by Race and Sex

	Race of Offender			
Race of Victim	White	Black	Other	Unknown
White	2,614	431	36	47
Black	193	2,412	12	31
Other	42	36	103	2
Unknown	26	17	1	5
	Sex of Offender			
Sex of Victim	Male	Female	Unknown	
Male	3,725	421	62	
Female	1,609	124	18	
Unknown	41	3	15	

Source: Federal Bureau of Investigation. 2014. "Expanded Homicide Data Table 5" Retrieved October 31, 2014 (http://www.fbi.gov/about-us/cjis/ucr/crime-in-the-u.s/2012/crime-in-the-u.s.-2012/offenses-known-to-law-enforcement/expanded-homicide/expanded_homicide_data_table_6_murder_race_and_sex_of_vicitm_by_race_and_sex_of_offender_2012.xls).

the home (Violence Policy Center, 2008). Various motives for intimate partner homicides followed by the suicide of the perpetrator have been cited in the literature, including amorous jealousy, declining health (resulting in what may be viewed as a mercy killing), precipitating crisis (e.g., job loss, divorce, financial emergency), and psychosis (Harper & Voigt, 2007).

Femicide

Across the globe, women and girls are at risk for violence because of their gender; a phenomenon referred to as **gender-based violence**. Gender-based violence can take various forms, ranging from the relatively minor (e.g., being pushed, grabbed, or shoved), to the severe (e.g., being kicked, punched, or raped). In some instances, the violence inflicted upon a victim, often at the hands of an intimate partner or family member, results in her death; an act researchers and activists have started to label as **femicide**.

While femicide can mean different things to different individuals, Diana Russell is largely credited with having shaped the most commonly used definition. Russell defines femicide as "the killing of females by males because they are female" (Russell & Harmes, 2001, p. 3). This definition revolves around two general understandings: (1) that femicide is the end product of misogyny and sexism and (2) the gender of the victim mattered to the perpetrator. Thus, not all murders involving women are acts of femicide. For example, a woman killed during a robbery is not necessarily a victim of femicide.

So what exactly comprises femcide? At its most basic, femicide is any form of gender-based violence that results in the death of a female victim. The United Nations, in their Vienna 2013 Declaration on Femicide, outlined the various forms femicide can take. Read this declaration in the next box. What each of these types of gender-based violence has in common is that they involve the murder of women and/or girls *because* of the victim's gender, and thus are considered femicide.

Gauging the extent of femcide is a bit more difficult. As previously discussed, while we are getting a better understanding of the extent of females killed by their intimate partners (sometimes labeled as intimate partner femicide), there is less data that exist that measure the

VIENNA 2013 DECLARATION ON FEMICIDE

Femicide is the killing of women and girls because of their gender, which can take the form of, inter alia (1) the murder of women as a result of intimate partner violence; (2) the torture and misogynist slaying of women; (3) killing of women and girls in the name of "honour"; (4) targeted killing of women and girls in the context of armed conflict; (5) dowry-related killings of women; (6) killing of women and girls because of their sexual orientation and gender identity; (7) the killing of aboriginal and indigenous women and girls because of their gender; (8) female infanticide and gender-based sex selection foeticide; (9) genital mutilation-related deaths; (10) accusations of witchcraft; and (11) other femicides connected with gangs, organized crime, drug dealers, human trafficking, and the proliferation of small arms.

Source: Reprinted from http://www.unodc.org/documents/commissions/CCPCJ_session22/ECN152013_NGO1_eV1380536.pdf.

magnitude of other forms of femicide (e.g., honor killings) in the United States and elsewhere. What is known is that femicide is a complex phenomenon that is dependent upon a number of key victim and offender characteristics. Overall, research indicates that femicide victims and perpetrators typically resemble each other in terms of race, educational background, and employment status (Frye et al., 2005; Moracco et al., 1998; Mouzos, 1999; Muftić & Baumann, 2012).

Table 7.5 ■ Murder by Relationship,[1] Percent Distribution,[2] Volume by Relationship, 2012

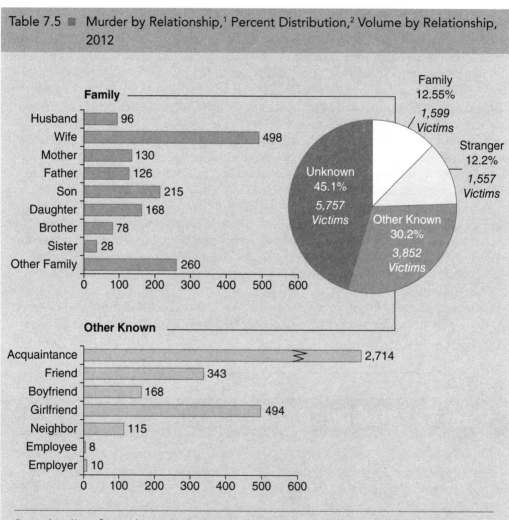

Source: http://www.fbi.gov/about-us/cjis/ucr/crime-in-the-u.s/2011/crime-in-the-u.s.-2011/offenses-known-to-law-enforcement/expanded/expanded-homicide-data.

1. Relationship is that of victim to offender.

2. Due to rounding, the percentages may not add to 100.0.

Note: Figures are based on 12,765 murder victims for whom supplemental homicide data were received and include the 5,757 victims for which the relationship was unknown.

Honor Killings

From a cultural standpoint, the construct of honor varies in the importance attached to it. Most cultures place value on honor, which is defined as "virtuous behavior, good moral character, integrity, and altruism" (Vandello & Cohen, 2003, p. 997). In some cultures, however, there is additional social significance having to do with status, precedence, and reputation. As such, honor "is based on a person's (usually a man's) strength and power to enforce his will on others or to command deferential treatment" (Vandello & Cohen, 2003, p. 998). In such cultures, it is deemed justifiable for violence. These incidents are often referred to as honor violence or honor killings.

Honor violence against females is usually committed with the idea that the perpetrator is protecting or regaining his honor, or that of the family or community. Victims of honor violence are targeted because how they behave or seem to behave is considered shameful or a violation of cultural or religious norms. For instance, Human Rights Watch lists a variety of reasons including "refusing to enter an arranged marriage, being the victim of a sexual assault, seeking a divorce (even from an abusive husband), or (allegedly) committing adultery" (HRW, 2001). While men, often homosexuals, can be the victim of an honor killing, women and girls comprise the majority of victims.

It is very difficult to determine if an incident is, indeed, an **honor killing**. Data on this type of violence are not collected systematically. Furthermore, the killings may be falsely reported as suicides by families and recorded as such. To read about India's efforts to collect such data, see the Focus on International Issues Box. In spite of the notion that honor killings are often associated with Asia, especially South Asia and the Middle East, they actually occur all over the world. For example, in Canada, honor killings have become such a concern that the Canadian citizenship study guide mentions them specifically, saying, "Canada's openness and generosity do not extend to barbaric practices that tolerate spousal abuse, honor killings, female genital mutilation, forced marriage or other gender-based violence" (Weese, 2011).

FOCUS ON INTERNATIONAL ISSUES

The National Criminal Records Bureau of India keeps detailed criminal justice data on the number of homicide victims by sex, age, and motive. In 2009, out of a total 33,159 recorded homicide victims in India, 8,718 (26 percent) were female, about the same as in previous years. Some of these killings relate to disputes over dowry payments or violent demands for higher payments from the families of brides or brides-to-be. While the payment of a dowry has been illegal in India since 1961, the practice remains common.

Among all female victims of recorded homicides, about 15 per cent (1,267) were recorded as dowry-related murders. In addition to the data recorded as homicide, the police records "dowry deaths" under a separate section of the Indian Penal Code.[1] These are deaths of women within seven years of their marriage

(Continued)

for which circumstantial evidence provides a strong suspicion of a dowry-related killing. In 2009, the police recorded 8,383 such deaths of women and girls, and it can be calculated that the total number of dowry-related killings in 2009 amounted to 9,650,[2] which corresponds to 56 percent deaths (17,101).

The reported number of such killings has been increasing for many years. While homicide levels have steadily decreased by 31 percent over the last 15 years, the rate of recorded dowry deaths has increased by more than 40 percent in the same period. This increase might partly be due to more accurate recording by the police when suspicious deaths are notified and increased awareness and determination to address the issue. On the other hand, it is likely that, in addition to officially recorded dowry-related homicides and dowry deaths, an unknown number of deaths related to dowry remain undetected as they are often recorded as accidents or suicides.

Source: Reprinted from United Nations Office on Drugs and Crime. (2011). *Global study on homicide: Trends, contexts, data.* Retrieved from http://www.unodc.org/documents/data-and-analysis/statistics/Homicide/Global_study_on_homicide_2011_web.pdf.

Notes:

1. Section 304B of the Indian Penal Code specifies that "where the death of a woman is caused by any burns or bodily injury or occurs otherwise than under normal circumstances within seven years of her marriage and it is shown that soon before her death she was subjected to cruelty or harassment by her husband or any relative of her husband for, or in connection with, any demand for dowry, such death shall be called 'dowry death' and such husband or relative shall be deemed to have caused her death."

2. This is given by the sum of dowry-related killings (1,267) and dowry deaths (8,383) for 2009.

Homicides Involving Multiple Victims

One of the most heinous examples of homicide victimization within recent history is evident in the Sandy Hook Massacre committed by Adam Lanza. Read about the details of the Sandy Hook Massacre box in the next box.

What makes this homicide especially heinous is the number of victims involved and their age. Homicides that involve multiple victims are often referred to as serial murder, mass murder, or spree murder.

- **Serial murder** is defined by federal law as "a series of three or more killings, not less than one of which was committed within the United States, having common characteristics such as to suggest the reasonable possibility that the crimes were committed by the same actor or actors" (Protection of Children from Sexual Predator Act of 1998, Title 18, US Code, Chapter 51, Section 1111).
- **Mass murder** involves the killing of four or more victims in one location in one incident.
- A **spree murder**, such as the Sandy Hook Massacre, is the killing of multiple victims at two or more separate locations but with no cooling-off period in between, each event is emotionally connected.

The key definitional distinction is usually time and place. That being said, it is often difficult to distinguish who falls into which category, more so between spree and serial. Roughly 1 out of 10 homicides committed in the United States involve multiple victims (FBI, 2013).

RIPPED FROM THE HEADLINES

Sandy Hook Massacre

In the early morning hours of December 14, 2012, 20-year-old Adam Lanza murdered his mother in the home they shared in Newtown, Connecticut. Nancy Lanza, age 52, was shot dead by her son with a .22 caliber rifle.

Neighbors later reported that they heard gunshots but dismissed it as nearby hunters. A delivery driver left a package at the front door of the residence prior to 10 a.m. He had no way of knowing what horror had happened inside the peaceful-looking residence.

But the story didn't end there. Adam entered Sandy Hook Elementary by shooting out a window after finding the front doors to the school locked. Armed with multiple firearms including a semi-automatic rifle and two handguns, he shot and killed Principal Dawn Hochsprung and May Sherlach, the school psychologist. Two other staff members were also shot, but survived.

Adam turned his attention toward the main office, which he entered, but he did not kill any of the staff members who were hiding. Although the exact events following Adam's exit of the main office remain unclear, what is known is that he eventually entered classrooms 8 and 10 (the order is unknown), which contained first graders and their teachers. Between the two classrooms, a total of 20 children and four adults were killed. At approximately 9:40 a.m. upon the arrival of first responders, Adam Lanza shot himself in the head.

Source: Adapted from Sedensky, S. J. (2013). *Report of the State's Attorney for the Judicial District of Danbury on the Shootings at Sandy Hook Elementary School and 36 Yogananda Street, Newtown, Connecticut on December 14, 2012.* Retrieved from the State of Connecticut website http://www.ct.gov/csao/lib/csao/Sandy_Hook_Final_Report.pdf.

■ VICTIM PRECIPITATION

Now that you know about the different types of homicide, let's consider how a person's own actions may influence the risk that he or she dies at the hands of another. As previously defined in Chapter 1, **victim precipitation** is typically defined as "the extent to which a victim is responsible for his or her own victimization." The concept of victim precipitation is rooted in the notion that, although many victims are not responsible for their victimization, other victims are.

Marvin Wolfgang is credited with coining the term victim precipitation when, in his seminal work on homicide, he argued that, in some instances, the victim may initiate the behavior of the perpetrator. To test his claim, Wolfgang collected official homicide data over the course of 4 years in Philadelphia. Of 588 homicide incidents, almost 26% corresponded with Wolfgang's definition of victim precipitation. Subsequent studies have found that victim precipitated violent crimes are most likely to occur between a victim and offender who know each other, with one or both parties having consumed alcohol prior to the incident (Muftić & Hunt, 2013).

Victim Precipitation Theories

Victim precipitation theories generally involve an explanation of how an individual's behavior may contribute to his or her own victimization. For instance, Luckenbill (1977) talks about violence and homicide as a "situated transaction." In his study of criminal homicide in California, he examined in detail how each incident played out. The majority of homicides involved some type of "character contest" (also referred to as "honor contest" or "confrontational homicides") with an identifiable pattern of "give and take" (involving insults, verbal and physical challenges, and use of violence) between the actors involved that eventually resulted in the death of one of the parties involved.

Similarly, Polk (1999) found that confrontational homicides are likely to involve young males engaging in a complex interaction, which he labels as an "honor contest," that begins with some type of provocation, such as an insult, joke, or shove, and in a sequential chain, results in a challenge, acceptance of the challenge, and a fight. The fight may or may not result in death. These honor contests are more likely to occur in leisure settings (e.g., a bar) and within the presence of a social audience, which serves two purposes: It makes the challenge public, and the response of the audience reaffirms the perception of the actors. Finally, Polk found that the presence of alcohol was also a major contributor to the honor contest as it influences judgment and impulsivity of the parties involved.

This understanding fits with what we know about the facts of murder. The SHR indicates that murder most frequently occurs as the result of a fight or an argument. Nearly 40% of homicides are argument related. Many homicides involve some degree of victim precipitation. The victim may have been the first person to use physical force or start the violence that eventually resulted in his or her own death. For instance, Muftić and Hunt (2013) found that 1 in 4 homicides involving adult victims and adult offenders over a 10-year time span in Dallas, Texas, were clearly victim precipitated.

Interestingly, Luckenbill points out that this explanation can also be useful in understanding situations in which parents kill their children. Often the child is challenging the parent's authority, and the parent feels he or she must save face. Any question of the victim's intent is irrelevant, only the killer's interpretation is important. Can these situations be classified as victim precipitated?

As the last question demonstrates, the examination of victim precipitation, while important in understanding the context surrounding victimization, is not without controversy. Victim precipitation theories have been accused of being indirect attempts at victim blaming. In addition, studies that have examined the concept of victim precipitation have been criticized for relying on poor methodology.

■ INDIRECT (SECONDARY) VICTIMIZATION

Remember Angie from the beginning of the chapter? Angie was the victim of a brutal act of intimate partner homicide. Angie, is not, however, the only victim from that incident. If you recall, her death profoundly impacted the lives of the children she left behind, Justin and Porsha. The survivors of homicide victims are referred to as **indirect or secondary homicide victims**. While indirect victimization most often applies to close family and friends of the primary homicide victim, such as Justin and Porsha, it can also be applied to individuals who witness a homicide and professionals who, because of their occupation, deal with a homicide's after effects (e.g., law enforcement) (Morrall, Hazelton, & Shackleton, 2011).

Common Reactions to Homicide

Once notified of a loved one's murder, a survivor's reaction to the homicide is dependent on a number of factors including the suddenness of the event, the survivor's ability to comprehend what has taken place, his or her state of mind leading up to the homicide, as well as homicide type (e.g., stranger homicide, domestic homicide, act of terrorism, etc.).

Bereavement

Bereavement is typically defined as the state of being sad after an individual you have cared for has passed. Typical reactions for grieving individuals include crying, insomnia, and loss of appetite. The bereavement process is influenced by the manner in which a person dies. When a death is caused by something sudden and unexpected, such as homicide, the bereavement process may be prolonged. Because homicide causes severe personal suffering, reactions to the loss may be more acute than those of "normal" mourning. Take for instance, Justin. Bombarded by requests to "update" family members and friends on Facebook of the proceedings of the murder trial, he posted this "update" after a particularly long day in court:

PHOTO 7.2

Social media post made by Justin Lopez on September 24, 2013, during the murder trial of William (Billy) Ray Parker who was convicted of killing Justin's mother, Angela Renee Lopez in 2012.

> **Angie's Awareness Angels**
> September 24, 2013 ·
>
> I know a lot of you are dying to know how it is going! Well, ITS A EMOTIONAL HORRIBLE HORRIBLE EXPERIENCE FOR EVERYONE INVOLVED! I can not and will not post daily updates about what happened in court room! I just can't.... I'm very tired and overwhelmed! Thank you to everyone who came, you have no idea how much I appreciate all of your presence! The court room was PACKED! Also thank you to those of you who are thinking about us and praying and unable to be here! Love you all GOODNIGHT!
>
> Like · Comment · Share

Source: Angies's Awareness Angels Facebook page, September 24, 2013. Retrieved from https://www.facebook.com/AngiesAwarenessAngels.

Homicide survivors may find themselves experiencing intense feelings of anger, rage, and/or terror, flashbacks, and nightmares (Morrall et al., 2011). Research has also indicated that traumatic loss may trigger panic attacks, anxiety, depression, or obsessive behaviors in homicide survivors (Morrall et al., 2011).

Additional Stressors

Having to deal with the murder of a loved one is especially stressful and is usually aggravated by other stressors unique to the situation. Take for instance the notification process. Many homicide survivors remember the notification process as a severely traumatic event (Parents of Murdered Children, 2014). **Death** or **casualty notification** is the process by which family members of the deceased are notified of their loved one's passing. Whenever possible, this is done in person, in time, and by a team of at least two trained law enforcement officers. Notifications that are done over the phone, with incomplete or inaccurate information, or via the media compound an already difficult situation.

The criminal justice system provides another source of stress for homicide survivors. When a loved one is murdered, involvement with the criminal justice system may be unavoidable. For many secondary victims, this experience may be especially traumatic if they perceive they are being treated unfairly, insensitively, or inappropriately by agents of the system. For instance, secondary victims may be banned from entering the crime scene in an effort to preserve evidence. They may be asked about their whereabouts when the murder occurred. If the police are unable to solve the murder, which happens in about 1 out of 3 cases, secondary victims may feel a lack of closure. If a perpetrator is identified and the case goes to trial, details of the murder presented in court, the inability to defend the victim, the length of the trial, and the outcome of the trial (e.g., hung jury) provide additional sources of anxiety for homicide survivors, magnifying their original trauma.

■ LEGAL AND COMMUNITY RESPONSES TO HOMICIDE VICTIMIZATION

Throughout history, homicide has been viewed as one of, if not the most significant forms of victimization a person can experience. Homicide victimization has been seen as violating moral and societal norms and has been conceptualized in a variety of different ways, such as first or second degree murder. Regardless of the type of homicide, the event can have a substantial impact on family members of the victim as well as the community as a whole. At an individual level, family members who have lost loved ones to homicide have experienced significant issues related to homicide, including posttraumatic stress syndrome (e.g., Amick-McMullan, Kilpatrick, & Resnick, 1991). The community is also impacted by homicide, with violence taking a significant toll on the emotional and psychological well-being of children, while also escalating the risk of issues related to substance use and cognitive functioning (Aisenberg & Herrenkohl, 2008). These problems suggest that the criminal justice system, as well as the community, might benefit from the use of specific tactics to respond to homicide victimization.

Police Responses

From the perspective of law enforcement officers, a few different responses have been used to reduce homicide victimization. Some of the most popular methods to reduce homicide occurred during the 1990s in Boston and New York City, titled Operation Ceasefire and CompStat, respectively (Rosenfeld, Fornango, & Baumer, 2005). Moreover, each program represented a unique technique to reduce homicide, with Operation Ceasefire having addressed gun-related gang violence. On the other hand, CompStat, which functioned as an organizational system centered on the dissemination of crime data and promoting unique problem-solving practices, centered on reducing crime and disorder more generally (Weisburd, Mastrofski, McNally, Greenspan, & Willis, 2003). Research has found that both programs were not entirely successful at reducing homicide victimization. Overall, data indicated that Operation Ceasefire did not result in a significant drop in the rate of firearm-related youth homicides during or after the intervention period compared to the average trend across 95 cities examined. On the other hand, CompStat achieved a significant yet minimal decline on the homicide rate during the intervention compared to the average homicide rate across all cities. However, once other factors, such as population density and police size were taken into account, the decline was no longer significantly different from the rate of homicides for the rest of the included cities (Rosenfeld, Fornango, & Baumer, 2005).

Court Responses

Within the legal environment, a number of different tactics have been incorporated to respond to homicide. A third intervention highlighted by Rosenfeld et al. (2005), titled Project Exile (in Richmond Virginia), focused on increasing federal sentences for firearm-related drug and violent offenses. Compared to Operation Ceasefire and Compstat, the findings for Project Exile were relatively successful. Specifically, the intervention had a significant impact on decreasing the firearm-related homicide rates compared to the sample average after the previously identified factors were included. Thus, while the other two law enforcement strategies previously mentioned did not produce the intended results, this program did significantly decrease homicide rates.

A similar example focusing on a specialized homicide prosecution unit (Operation Hardcore) focused on gang-related incidents in Los Angeles during the mid to late 1970s has also produced positive results (Pyrooz, Wolfe, & Spohn, 2011). Following the incorporation of the specialized unit, results suggested that cases processed through nonspecialized units were significantly more likely to be rejected than cases prosecuted through a specialized unit. As a whole, court responses to gun and gang-related homicides have been successful in decreasing homicide rates.

Community Responses

One increasingly used community response to homicide victimization has been **fatality reviews**. In general, fatality reviews are community-based programs that seek to review the circumstances of the homicide to gain a better understanding of the cause of death. In the United States, there have generally been two different types of fatality reviews: child and domestic. Child fatality reviews (also discussed in Chapter 10) have become an increasingly popular tool used in almost every state, with such reviews commonly having focused on inquiry into most types of child death. Recent work on child fatality reviews has indicated that the majority of these programs included members from various criminal justice agencies (e.g., law enforcement officers, prosecutors), the medical and public health community (e.g., medical examiner, public health representative, and emergency medical personnel), and members of child protective services (Shanley, Risch, & Bonner, 2010). Although the majority of states have legislation in place pertaining to child fatality reviews, the majority do not review all cases of juvenile deaths, but rather only those occurring because of maltreatment or neglect or those that could possibly have been prevented.

The second type of fatality review that has become popular has focused on homicides occurring as the result of domestic violence. Similar to fatality reviews used to examine juvenile deaths, those focusing on domestic violence incorporate various members of the community that focus on identifying "relevant social, economic, and policy realities that compromise the safety of battered women and their children" (Websdale, 2003, p. 27). Domestic fatality reviews can be beneficial for showcasing deficiencies in various criminal justice and political strategies, underscoring the need for change in both of these domains. As a whole, both of these fatality reviews provide a positive outlet whereby members of the community come together to provide a more comprehensive examination of specific types of homicide.

One specific example of a community-based program to examine homicides is evident in the work of the Milwaukee Homicide Review Commission. In general, the commission was structured as a multi-agency intervention effort focused on homicide preventative and intervention initiatives (Azrael, Braga, & O'Brien, 2013). A range of different groups from various sectors, including the criminal justice system, community service organizations, and domestic violence agencies, have been involved in the review commission. Evaluation of the intervention indicated a significant decrease (52%) in the number of homicides during the intervention period in specific areas receiving the intervention. As a whole, this review commission was relatively successful in reducing homicides in areas that had received the intervention.

In some communities, bereavement centers have been established. Bereavement centers are designed to assist homicide survivors primarily dealt with the emotional difficulties that result from the death of homicide victims, however, some centers provide support related to financial, social, and legal problems related to the homicide. To read about a successful community-based bereavement center in Cambridge, Massachusetts, see the box item about the Center for Homicide Bereavement.

CENTER FOR HOMICIDE BEREAVEMENT

Extending clinical care and support to individuals and families who have lost loved ones to murder defines the programmatic mission of the Center for Homicide Bereavement (CHB). The CHB is a community-based component of the Victims of Violence Program of the Cambridge Health Alliance in Cambridge, Massachusetts. Since its inception in 2002, the CHB's trilingual, tricultural staff have served over 700 parents, siblings, children, and extended family members of homicide victims in the greater Boston/Cambridge area and developed a wide range of services including crisis intervention, acute and long-term traumatic grief therapy, victim advocacy, psychiatric triage, short-term and ongoing homicide bereavement groups, and community outreach. Additionally, CHB staff offers community-based commemorative and self-care forums for survivors and extends crisis response services to community settings traumatized by acts of homicide. All CHB services are free of charge, supported by Victims of Crime Act funds awarded by the Massachusetts Office for Victim Assistance.

Source: Reprinted from H. Aldrich & D. Kallivayalil (2013). The impact of homicide on survivors and clinicians. *Journal of Loss and Trauma: International Perspectives on Stress & Coping, 18*(4), 362–377.

A final example of a community-based program focusing on homicide victims and their family members that has had a strong media presence is Mothers Against Drunk Driving (MADD). Although the organization focuses broadly on drunk driving, a range of different materials are provided on emotional issues (i.e., grief, guilt, mourning, and healing), financial concerns (as well as victim compensation), and legal rights of victims and their family members (i.e., Victims of Crime Act) affected by homicide victimization. Moreover, the organization has information focusing on the prevention of drunk driving and the possible deaths that might be associated with such activities. From a service standpoint, the organization is one of the largest in the United States, providing a range of different services through 1,200 victim advocates who have focused on assisting persons with emotional and legal support. MADD represents a unique avenue of response by the community to assist family members (as well as victims/survivors in general) of drunk driving homicide victimization through a variety of available literature and services.

Restorative Justice Efforts

Although restorative justice efforts might seem unreasonable for homicide victims, one avenue is victim–offender mediation efforts between the family members of a homicide victim and the offender(s). One of the most compelling examples is evident in the mediation process that occurred between the family members of homicide victims and their perpetrators who were on death row in Texas (Umbreit & Vos, 2000). Different reasons for participation in the mediation process were evident between the family members and offenders. In general, family members of the deceased wished to physically see the offender as well as to gain more information in general and pertaining to the event. In contrast, the offenders participated as part of a healing process and the increasing importance of religion in their lives. All participants, both the family members and the offenders, explained that the mediation process they experienced was beneficial and served as a healing process.

SUMMARY

- Homicide is defined as "the killing of one human being by another" and can be subdivided into excusable, justifiable, and criminal homicide.
- Excusable homicides are killings that are either unintentional or accidental. Guilt is not a factor in cases of excusable homicide.
- Justifiable homicides represent killings occurring in defense of property or life. However, the UCR defines a justifiable homicide as the killing of a felon by a police officer (in the line of duty) or a private citizen (if the felon is in the act of committing a felony).
- Criminal homicides represent "the purposeful, knowing, reckless, or negligent killing of one human being by another." This form of homicide can be divided into first degree murder (premeditated and malicious), second degree murder (malicious but not premeditated), felony murder (a homicide committed during the commission of a felony), and manslaughter (reduced responsibility compared to a murder). Manslaughter can also be subdivided into voluntary (intentional) and involuntary/negligent (not necessarily intentional but based on neglect).

- Homicide victimization in the United States is measured with the Uniform Crime Report (UCR), which includes the Supplementary Homicide Reports (SHR), as well as through the National Center for Health Statistics (NCHS). In general, there are 4.7 homicides per 100,000 people in the United States.
- Homicide victimization across the globe is measured by the United Nations Office on Drugs and Crime (UNODC) and the World Health Organization (WHO). At the international level, the homicide rate was 6.2 homicides per 100,000 persons, with the largest proportions coming from the Americas and the smallest from the Oceania region.
- Information available on socio-demographic characteristics indicates that homicide offenders and victims are likely to be demographically similar. Data indicate that males are more likely than females to be victims and perpetrators of homicides. Younger individuals (18–24 years) are likely to be both homicide victims and perpetrators. The majority of homicides that occur are intraracial (within a racial group, e.g., White offender and White victim). The homicide rate is highest in urban environments, with a homicide rate of 10.9 per 100,000 persons in cities with a population over half a million. In addition, the majority of homicides occur between victims and offenders who know one another and not between strangers.
- Incident characteristics indicate that weapons are used in the majority of homicides. While circumstances around homicides are not always entirely clear, research highlights that homicides are likely to occur during an argument or commission of another felony. Private residences are common locations for elderly and domestic-related homicides. Moreover, although not all homicides involve drugs or alcohol, a moderate proportion of victims and offenders have been found to have used these substances prior to the event.
- Filicide represents a parent or guardian killing a child, while infanticide represents the killing of an infant by these same individuals. In the majority of filicides, the parent is most likely the offender.
- Parricide represents the killing of a parent, with more specific definitions present for the killing of a mother (matricide) and father (patricide).
- Eldercide refers to the killing of an individual over the age of 65.
- Felonious homicide risk for the elderly is significantly influenced by an area's robbery rates, as well as the proportion of elderly living alone and who have disabilities.
- Intimate partner homicide (IPH) involves the killing of a current or former partner or spouse regardless of sexual orientation. In the majority of situations, the offender is male and victim is female.
- A number of risk factors exist for intimate partner homicide for women, notably if they have been violently victimized in the past and time since the last violent incident. IPH perpetration by females is likely to occur for these individuals based on the extent and type of violence, lack of educational and financial resources, married and had children, and notified police following violent events.
- Suicide of a perpetrator following an instance of IPH is a relatively rare event. When a homicide-suicide does occur, it is likely the male who is the perpetrator and occurs with a firearm.
- Femicide represents "the killing of females by males because they are female," and might occur for a variety of reasons (e.g., honor killings, sexual orientation, witchcraft). Although the prevalence of femicide is hard to estimate, the practice has been present on an international level.
- Homicides containing multiple victims is relatively rare in the United States, with only 1 out of 10 homicides involving multiple victims in 2011. Homicides that involve multiple victims include serial murder, mass murder, and spree murders.
- Honor killings are homicides that are perpetrated by males against females to ensure that honor (which can be his own, his family's, or his community's) is maintained. These killings are justified on the grounds that in some way the females who they are victimizing have gone against cultural or moral values.
- Victim precipitation is "the extent to which a victim is responsible for his or her own victimization." This process may occur based on an escalation of verbal to physical violence when protecting one's honor.

- Indirect or secondary homicide victimization is commonly viewed as being a relative or a friend of the homicide victim.
- A wide range of reactions to homicide have been found for family members of victims. While bereavement is common after the death of a family member or friend, individuals may also feel a sense of anger. Stress might additionally be brought on by the criminal justice system if family members and friends of the victim do not feel as though justice has been served or they have been treated unfairly.
- Although specialized police responses have been utilized to combat homicide (and gang-related gun violence), the impact of these programs on decreasing homicide have been mostly minimal.
- A number of court responses exist to combat homicide. The most effective methods have been specialized units to combat gang and firearm violence as well as increases in federal sentences.
- A variety of different community responses are evident for homicides.
- Restorative justice efforts for homicide victims are present in a mediation process between the family members of homicide victims and their offenders.

DISCUSSION QUESTIONS

1. Can you think of an example (aside from the one provided) in which a homicide is excusable (not justifiable)?

2. What preventative methods might be reasonable for reducing the occurrence of intimate partner homicide?

3. How does a victim-precipitated homicide fit into the victim–offender overlap?

4. What additional police and court responses might be beneficial in reducing homicide victimization?

5. What are the possible advantages and disadvantages of a mediation process between family members of a homicide victim and their offender?

KEY TERMS

homicide

excusable homicide

justifiable homicide

stand your ground laws

castle doctrine

criminal homicide

first degree murder

premediation

deliberation

express malice

implied/constructive malice

second degree murder

felony murder

manslaughter

voluntary manslaughter

involuntary/negligent manslaughter

filicide

infanticide

parricide

patricide

matricide

eldercide

intimate partner homicide

homicide-suicide

gender-based violence

femicide

honor violence

honor killings

serial murder

mass murder

spree murder

victim precipitation

indirect/secondary victimization

bereavement

death/casualty notification

fatality reviews

Global Study on Homicide (http://www.unodc.org/gsh/)

Contained within the United Nations Office on Drugs and Crime, the Global Study on Homicide (GSH) represents an international picture focusing explicitly on homicides. In general, the website has information on criminal justice responses to homicide, drug- and firearm-related factors influencing homicide, as well as changing trends in the rate of homicide. In addition to graphics and a basic overview of homicide on an international level, a publication providing a comprehensive review of homicide is available.

Mothers Against Drunk Driving (http://www.madd.org/)

The Mothers Against Drunk Driving (MADD) website has a number of different publications and services available to survivors of drunk driving as well as for family members of individuals who have passed away after being victims of a drunk driver. Publications focus on the bereavement process, grief, coping, survivor guilt, and legal concerns. Also important are a variety of services offered by the organization focusing on assistance throughout the criminal justice process as well as dealing with emotional issues.

Supplementary Homicide Reports (http://www.fbi.gov/about-us/cjis/ucr/nibrs/addendum-for-submitting-cargo-theft-data/shr) (http://ojjdp.gov/ojstatbb/ezashr/)

Contained within the Federal Bureau of Investigation (FBI), the Supplementary Homicide Reports (SHR) represent data on homicides victims and offenders. At the first website, you can find the variety of demographic and situational factors associated with the homicide event. The second website provides easy access to data from the Supplementary Homicide Reports.

Vital Statistics Division of the NCHS (http://www.cdc.gov/nchs/deaths.htm)

Within the National Vital Statistics System (which is contained within the Centers for Disease Control and Prevention [CDC]), data are available on factors related to causes of death and to mortality trends more generally. In addition, the statistics allow for cross country comparisons to gain a better understanding pertaining to mortality on an international level. This website lists a variety of different publications generally pertaining to mortality.

World Health Organization (http://www.who.int/violence_injury_prevention/surveillance/databases/mortality/en/)

The World Health Organization (WHO) website contains data similar to the CDC's but focuses more generally on an international level. Mortality information for causes of death and demographics is available for approximately 120 countries. More narrowly, the website offers an online database as well as raw data dating back to 1979 to specifically investigate mortality on an international level.

SEXUAL VICTIMIZATION

On March 5, 2010, a woman reported to the police,

We went downtown to Velvet Elvis, where we first saw our friends. We then saw Ben [Roethlisberger] and his friends/bodyguards. We went to take pictures (group) with him and then we left him alone. We went to The Brick where they happened to be, and we continued to have casual conversation, he even made crude, sexual remarks. They ended up leaving, and we went to Capital, where they also were. Ben asked us to go to his "VIP" area (back of Capital). We all went with him. He said there were shots for us, numerous shots were on the bar, and he told us to take them. His bodyguard came and took my arm and said come with me, he escorted me into a side door/ hallway, and sat me on a stool. He left and Ben came back with his penis out of his pants. I told him it wasn't OK, no, we don't need to do this and I proceeded to get up and try to leave. I went to the first door I saw, which happened to be a bathroom. He followed me into the bathroom and shut the door behind him. I still said no, this is not OK, and he then had sex with me. He said it was OK. He then left without saying anything. I went out of the hallway/door to the side where I saw my friends. We left Capital and went to the first police car we saw.

The complaint of rape against Pittsburgh Steelers quarterback Ben Roethlisberger was investigated, but not less than 2 weeks later, a lawyer for the woman asked the prosecutor to drop the investigation into the events of March 5. He said,

What is obvious in looking forward is that a criminal trial would be a very intrusive personal experience for a complainant in this situation, given the extraordinary media attention that would be inevitable. The media coverage to date, and the efforts of the media to access our client, have been unnerving, to say the least. (*The Smoking Gun*, 2010)

(Continued)

Subsequently, Ben Roethlisberger was not criminally charged in this case. But what really happened that night? Was the woman raped? Did she willingly engage in sex? This case is a common example of the inherent problems with knowing, defining, and proving when a rape or other type of sexual victimization occurs. The ways in which law enforcement and the media reacted to the victim are also telling of the challenges that victims face when coming forward. This chapter covers these issues—it defines what sexual victimization is, describes the extent and effects of sexual victimization, and details how the criminal justice system deals with victims.

Source: Milledgeville Police Department - Statement Form For Witness. The Smoking Gun, 2010. http://www.thesmokinggun.com/file/ben-roethlisbergers-bad-play?page=0.

■ WHAT IS SEXUAL VICTIMIZATION?

A unique form of victimization that has been widely studied because of its pervasiveness and negative effects is sexual victimization. Generally speaking, sexual victimization encompasses any type of victimization involving unwanted sexual behavior perpetrated against an individual. These behaviors can range from forced penetration to surreptitiously videotaping an individual undressing. Sexual victimization can take a toll on victims, with effects ranging from physical injury to psychological trauma to risk of additional sexual victimizations.

Rape

Originally defined in common law as unlawful carnal knowledge (i.e., vaginal penetration) of a woman by a man who is not the perpetrator's wife by force and against her will, more contemporary definitions of rape have been developed. Rape can now be perpetrated by and against both females and males, and it includes other types of penetration such as oral, digital, and anal. Most states' laws no longer exclude husbands.

Each state has its own legal definition of what behavior constitutes rape, but most states share some commonalities. First, rape occurs when there is nonconsensual contact between the penis and the vulva or anus, or when there is penetration of the vulva or anus. Rape also occurs when there is contact between the mouth and penis, vulva, or anus, or penetration of another person's genital or anal opening with a finger, hand, or object. Second, in order to be considered rape, force or threat of force must be used. Third, contact or penetration must occur without the consent of the victim or when the victim is unable to give consent—such as when asleep or under the influence of drugs or alcohol.

There are different types of rape, including forcible rape, drug or alcohol facilitated rape, incapacitated rape, and statutory rape—all of which involve unique circumstances. A forcible rape is one in which the offender uses or threatens to use force to achieve penetration (Fisher, Daigle, & Cullen, 2010a). Another type of rape is drug or alcohol facilitated rape, which occurs when a person is raped while under the influence of drugs or alcohol after being deliberately given alcohol, a drug, or other intoxicant without his or her knowledge or consent (Fisher et al., 2010a). A third type of rape is incapacitated rape. This type of rape occurs when a victim cannot consent because of self-induced consumption of alcohol, a drug, or other intoxicant. Incapacitated rape also occurs when a person is unable to consent due to being unconscious or asleep (Fisher et al., 2010a).

Another type of rape, statutory rape, is somewhat unique in that it does not involve force. Rather, **statutory rape** occurs when a person who is under the proscribed age of consent engages in sex. Because the person is legally unable to give consent to have sex, such activity is illegal. The minimum age that most states set is between 14 and 18 years old.

Some states also consider the difference in age between the offender and the victim in determining whether it is statutory rape (Daigle & Fisher, 2010). In this way, some statutory rape laws are age graded; that is, offenders have to be a certain number of years older than victims to activate the laws. For example, in Alabama, statutory rape occurs if the offender is at least 16 years old, the victim is less than 16 but more than 12, and the offender is at least 2 years older than the victim (Sexual Assault Laws of Alabama, n.d.). Statutory rape laws that allow offenders who are close in age—such as two students enrolled in high school—to be convicted of sex offenses have recently come under fire in some states as not targeting sexual predators. For example, in the following box, the case of Genarlow Wilson is discussed. Georgia has since revamped its laws so that a case like Wilson's will not be handled in the same way. These new laws are commonly referred to as "Romeo and Juliet" laws.

Genarlow Wilson was a 17-year-old star athlete and honors student in 2003 when he attended a New Year's Eve Party in Douglasville, Georgia, and had consensual sex with a 15-year-old girl. He was found guilty of felony child molestation and sentenced to 10 years in prison. This case sparked public outrage, and as a result, Georgia lawmakers changed the law, which now makes consensual sex between teens a misdemeanor. The change, however, was not retroactive, so Wilson remained behind bars.

A judge overturned Wilson's case and he was going to be set free, but Georgia Attorney General Thurbert Baker announced he would appeal that decision, which effectively kept Wilson incarcerated. Baker said he filed the appeal to resolve "clearly erroneous legal issues," saying that the judge did not have the authority "to reduce or modify the judgment of the trial court."

On July 20, 2007, the Georgia Supreme Court heard the appeal. It wasn't until October 27 that the court ruled in a 4–3 decision that the new law "represents a seismic shift in the legislature's view of the gravity of oral sex between two willing teenage participants." The justices talked about a "sea change" in attitudes on sex, and they concluded the 10-year sentence was "grossly out of proportion to the severity of the crime." This led to Genarlow Wilson's release after 2 years in prison for child molestation.

Source: Adapted from http://www.theipinionsjournal.com/2007/06/forget-paris-keeping-genarlow-in-prison-constitutes-a-gross-miscarriage-of-justice/ and http://sports.espn.go.com/espn/news/story?id=3081047.

Sexual Victimization Other Than Rape

Although rape is a sexual offense that garners widespread media attention, there are other types of sexual victimization. Perhaps surprisingly, these other forms are much more common than rape. They include sexual coercion, unwanted sexual contact, and noncontact sexual abuse. Each of these has unique elements, but all have been shown to cause negative outcomes for victims. See Table 8.1 for a description of the major types of sexual victimization discussed in this chapter.

Sexual Coercion

Similar to rape, **sexual coercion** involves intercourse or penetration with the offender's penis, mouth, tongue, digit, or object. The key difference between rape and sexual coercion has to do with the means the offender uses. Instead of using force or threats of force, the offender coerces the victim into having sexual intercourse. Coercion entails emotional or psychological tactics, such as promising reward, threat of nonphysical punishment, or pressuring/pestering for sex (Fisher & Cullen, 2000). For example, if the offender threatens to end the relationship unless the victim engages in sex, the offender is sexually coercing the victim. If a professor threatens to lower a student's grade if the student does not engage in sex, the student is being sexually coerced. If a person uses continued "sweet talk" and sexual advances, sufficiently pressuring the victim into compliance, the victim is being sexually coerced. In each of these scenarios, if the offender was unsuccessful, the behavior would be classified as an attempted sexual coercion.

Unwanted Sexual Contact

Not all sexual victimizations involve force or penetration. **Unwanted sexual contact** occurs when a person is touched in an erogenous zone, but it does not involve attempted or completed penetration. It may or may not involve force. What kinds of actions may be classified as unwanted sexual contact? Unwanted contact such as touching, groping, rubbing, petting, licking, or sucking of the breasts, buttocks, lips, or genitals constitutes unwanted sexual contact (Fisher & Cullen, 2000). This contact can be above or under clothing. If the offender uses psychological or emotional coercion, then the unwanted sexual contact is **coerced sexual contact.** If the offender uses force or threatens to use force, the behavior is classified as **unwanted sexual contact with force.**

Noncontact Sexual Abuse

Not all actions that people may consider victimizing involve touching or penetration. Other forms of sexual victimization, categorized as **noncontact sexual abuse,** are visual or verbal. **Visual abuse** occurs when a perpetrator uses unwanted visual means. The perpetrator may send pornographic images or videos via text messaging or e-mail or may post images to social networking sites or the Internet (Fisher & Cullen, 2000). **Verbal abuse** occurs when a perpetrator says something or makes sounds that are intentionally condescending, sexual, or abusive (Fisher & Cullen, 2000). For example, a perpetrator may make sexist remarks, may make catcalls or whistles in response to a victim's appearance, or may make noises with sexual overtones. Asking inappropriate questions about another person's sex or romantic life is also considered verbal abuse.

■ MEASUREMENT AND EXTENT OF SEXUAL VICTIMIZATION

Uniform Crime Reports

As previously discussed, one of the most widely used sources of data on crime and victimization is the Uniform Crime Reports (UCR), which show the amount of crime known to law enforcement in a given year. To be included in the UCR, a victim must report his or

Table 8.1 ■ Definitions of Different Types of Sexual Victimization

Type of Sexual Victimization	Definition
Forcible rape	The offender uses or threatens to use force to achieve penetration.
Drug or alcohol facilitated rape	A person is raped while under the influence of drugs or alcohol after being deliberately given alcohol, a drug, or other intoxicant without his or her knowledge or consent.
Incapacitated rape	A victim cannot consent because of self-induced consumption of alcohol, a drug, or other intoxicant. Incapacitated rape also occurs when a person is unable to consent due to being unconscious or asleep.
Statutory rape	A person who is under the proscribed age of consent engages in sex. Because the person is legally unable to give consent to have sex, such activity is illegal.
Sexual coercion	The offender coerces the victim into having sexual intercourse. Coercion entails emotional or psychological tactics, such as promising reward, threat of nonphysical punishment, or pressuring/pestering for sex.
Unwanted sexual contact	A person is touched in an erogenous zone, but it does not involve attempted or completed penetration. It may or may not involve force.
Coerced sexual contact	The offender uses psychological or emotional coercion to touch, grope, rub, pet, lick, or suck the breasts, lips, or genitals of the victim.
Unwanted sexual contact with force	The offender uses force or threatens to use force to touch the victim in an erogenous zone.
Visual abuse	A perpetrator uses visual means. These may include showing the victim pornographic materials, sex organs, or taking photographs or video of the victim while she or he is nude or having sex, without the victim's consent.
Verbal abuse	A perpetrator says or makes sounds that are intentionally condescending, sexual, or abusive.

her victimization or the police must somehow become aware that a crime has occurred. As we will discuss below, rape and other forms of sexual victimization are often not reported to the police. In addition, the UCR uses a fairly restrictive definition of rape. Up until 2013, rape in the UCR was limited to forcible rape, which is defined as the carnal knowledge of a female forcibly and against her will (Federal Bureau of Investigation [FBI], 2009). Attempts and assaults to commit rape by force or threat of force are also included. Note that only females could be the victims of forcible rape and that sexual assaults other than rape (e.g., forced touching) are not included. Just less than 85,000 rapes were reported to law enforcement in 2012. The rate of rape in 2012 was 52.9 offenses per 100,000 female inhabitants (FBI, 2012a). Beginning in January 2013, data collected through the UCR were done so with a new definition of rape. The new definition is "penetration, no matter how slight, of the vagina or anus with any body part or object, or oral penetration by a sex organ of another person, without the consent of the victim." This new definition includes both males and females as victims and includes forms of penetration other than rape (FBI, 2011).

National Crime Victimization Survey

Because many persons do not report being raped or sexually victimized to the police, a more accurate portrayal of the extent of rape and other sexual victimizations can be found from the National Criminal Victimization Survey (NCVS). This survey of households is used to find out about individuals' victimization experiences, including rape and sexual assault. The NCVS is different from the UCR in regard to rape and sexual victimization in several ways. First, the NCVS includes estimates of the extent of sexual assault as well as rape. Second, the NCVS is a self-report survey; its estimates include incidents that have been reported to the police and also those that were not. Third, both male and female victims of rapes and sexual assault are included. According to the NCVS, in 2012, there were 346,830 rapes and sexual assaults. This number equates to a rape/sexual assault rate of 1.3 per 1,000 persons 12 years old and older (Truman, Langton, & Planty, 2013).

National Violence Against Women Survey

Another source of information on the extent of rape is the National Violence Against Women Survey (NVAWS) (Tjaden & Thoennes, 2000a). Conducted between November 1995 and May 1996, 8,000 men and 8,000 women were surveyed via telephone about abuse they experienced in the previous 12 months and during their lifetimes. The NVAWS included questions about rape, and both men and women were asked about their rape experiences. For the survey, rape was defined as "an event that occurred without the victim's consent, that involved the use or threat of force to penetrate the victim's vagina or anus by penis, tongue, fingers, or objects, or the victim's mouth by penis" (Tjaden & Thoennes, 1998, p. 13). Results from the NVAWS revealed that 18% of women had been raped (completed or attempted) during their lifetime and 0.3% had experienced a rape (completed or attempted) during the previous 12 months. Men were less likely to report being raped—3% of men reported a rape (completed or attempted) during their lifetime and 0.1% had been raped (completed or attempted) in the previous 12 months (Tjaden & Thoennes, 2000a).

Sexual Experiences Survey

Other research has examined college females and their experiences of sexual victimization and rape. The first national-level study of college women's sexual victimization was conducted by Mary Koss and her colleagues (Koss, Gidycz, & Wisniewski, 1987). To measure the extent to which females were sexually victimized, Koss developed the Sexual Experiences Survey (SES), a 10-item survey designed to measure rape, sexual coercion, and sexual contact. The survey items used to measure these sexual victimizations were behaviorally specific. Behaviorally-specific questions are those that include descriptive language and examples of the behaviors that constitute rape or sexual victimization. The survey did not rely on the victim to know whether she had been raped; instead, she was asked whether certain behaviors occurred.

Koss found that more than half the women in the study had experienced some form of sexual victimization since the age of 14. More than 27% of the women had been raped (attempted or completed), almost 15% had experienced a sexual contact, and almost 12% had been sexually coerced. She also found that 16.6% had been raped (attempted or completed) during the previous 12 months, showing that college women faced a real risk of being raped. The SES underwent a redesign in 2007 (Koss et al., 2007).

National College Women Sexual Victimization Study

Conducted in the spring of 1997 by Bonnie Fisher, Francis Cullen, and Michael Turner (1998), the **National College Women Sexual Victimization Study (NCWSV)** is a nationally representative study of college women. In this study, 4,446 college females were asked about their experiences of rape and sexual victimization since school began in fall 1996. The types of sexual victimization asked about included completed and attempted rape, attempted and completed sexual coercion, attempted and completed unwanted sexual contact with and without force, threats, and stalking. Two important methodological aspects of the NCWSV should be discussed. First, the study used a two-step measurement strategy, similar to the one employed by the NCVS. In the first stage, individuals were asked a set of behaviorally-specific screening questions designed to capture the experience of rape and sexual victimization. For example, women were asked, "Since school began in fall 1996, has anyone *made* you have sexual intercourse by using *force or threatening to harm* you or someone close to you? Just so there is no mistake, by intercourse, I mean putting a penis in your vagina" (Fisher, Cullen, & Turner, 2000, p. 6). If a woman affirmatively responded to any of the screening questions, she then continued to the second stage to fill out an incident report. Incident reports were filled out for each incident of rape or sexual victimization that she indicated had occurred. The incident report, similar to the NCVS, included detailed information about the incident, such as the relationship of the offender to the victim, whether alcohol or drugs were used by the victim or offender, the location of the incident, and victim responses such as reporting and using self-protective action, among other things.

In total, 15.5% of the women had experienced at least one sexual victimization during the academic year. Rape was the least likely to occur, although 2.5% experienced either a completed or an attempted rape. Unwanted sexual contact was most common—10.9% reported experiencing at least one incident. College women also reported experiencing noncontact sexual abuse. More than half the women in the study reported having general sexist remarks made in front of them, and slightly more than 1 in 5 reported receiving obscene telephone calls or messages. Just more than 6% were exposed to pornographic pictures or materials when they did not consent to see them.

National Study of Drug or Alcohol Facilitated, Incapacitated, and Forcible Rape

Kilpatrick, Resnick, Ruggiero, Conoscenti, and McCauley (2007) recently conducted a national-level study of three types of rape: the **National Study of Drug or Alcohol Facilitated, Incapacitated, and Forcible Rape.** Forcible rapes involve unwanted oral, anal, or vaginal penetration. Drug or alcohol facilitated rapes also involve unwanted oral, anal, or vaginal penetration, but the victim must also have stated that she thought the offender purposefully gave her alcohol or drugs without her permission or attempted to get her drunk. This type of rape also could occur if the victim was too drunk to control her behavior or if she was unconscious (Kilpatrick et al., 2007). Incapacitated rapes also involve unwanted oral, anal, or vaginal penetration, but the victim must have voluntarily used drugs or alcohol or have been passed out or too drunk or high to control her behavior.

The study included almost 5,000 adult women between the ages of 18 and 86, with two subsamples—one sample of 3,001 U.S. women that was a national sample (1,000 of whom who were 35+ years and 2,000 between the ages of 18 and 34 years) and another that was a national sample of 2,000 women attending college and universities in the United States who were between the ages of 18 and 34 years. Asking about incidents that occurred in the past year and during their lifetime, the study found that 18% of women had been raped during their lifetime. Most of the rapes, 14.5%, were forcible rapes, and 5% were drug or alcohol facilitated or incapacitated rapes. Twelve-month estimates were 0.52% for forcible rape and 0.42% for drug or alcohol facilitated or incapacitated rape.

National Intimate Partner and Sexual Violence Survey

Conducted by the Centers for Disease Control National Center for Injury Prevention and Control in 2010, the National Intimate Partner and Sexual Violence Survey (NISVS) is an ongoing nationally representative survey of adult men and women living in the United States. Survey data were collected from 9,086 women and 7,421 men via random digit dial telephone surveys to measure the prevalence and characteristics of intimate partner violence, stalking, and sexual violence. The types of sexual violence that were measured in the NISVS were rape, being made to penetrate someone else, sexual coercion, unwanted sexual contact, and noncontact unwanted sexual experiences. Individuals were asked about these experiences during the past 12 months and also across their lifetimes.

According to the NISVS, almost 1 in 5 women had been raped during their lifetime, and 1% had been raped during the previous 12 months. Males also experienced rape, but at lower levels. One in 71 men, which equates to 1.4%, of men had been raped during their lifetime. The number of men reporting rape during the previous 12 months was too low to produce a reliable estimate. Other types of sexual violence were also experienced by respondents of the survey. About one third of women indicating experiencing noncontact unwanted sexual experiences, 27% experienced unwanted sexual contact, and 13% experienced sexual coercion during their lifetime. For the previous 12 months, 3% reported noncontact unwanted sexual experiences, 2.2% experienced unwanted sexual contact, and 2% experienced sexual coercion. Males in the NISVS also reported experiencing noncontact unwanted sexual experiences at higher levels than the other types of sexual violence: 12.8% indicated this type of sexual violence over their lifetime, and 2.7% experienced it during the previous 12 months. Unwanted sexual contact was experienced by 11.7% of men over their lifetime and 2.3% during the previous 12 months. Finally, 6% of men experienced sexual coercion during their lifetime, with 1.5% of men saying this occurred during the previous 12 months. Notice that the 12-month prevalence estimates for noncontact unwanted sexual experiences, unwanted sexual contact, and sexual coercion are fairly similar for males and females. Also of note is that

4.8% of males said that they had been made to penetrate someone else over the course of their lifetime, and 1.1% had been forced to do this action in the past 12 months.

■ RISK FACTORS FOR AND CHARACTERISTICS OF SEXUAL VICTIMIZATION

Although anyone can be sexually victimized, some people are at greater risk than others. As you probably surmise, females are more likely than males to be sexually victimized at all stages of life. Males are relatively unlikely to be sexually victimized, but when they are, they are likely to be under the age of 12 (Tjaden & Thoennes, 2006). Females face the greatest risk of being sexually victimized during their late teens and early 20s—often spanning the years women are enrolled in college. For both genders, risk of being sexually victimized wanes over time. Besides gender and age, socioeconomic status and location of residence are also related to risk of sexual victimization. Persons of lower socioeconomic status and persons who are unemployed face a greater risk of being sexually victimized than others (Rennison, 1999). Between 2005 and 2010, data from the NCVS revealed that persons living in rural areas faced greater risks of rape and sexual victimizations than those residing in urban or suburban areas (Planty, Langton, Krebs, Berzofsky, & Smiley-McDonald, 2013). Black persons have higher rates of sexual victimization than others (Planty et al., 2013).

Beyond these demographic characteristics, other factors differentially place persons at risk of being sexually victimized. As discussed in Chapter 2, one of the prevailing theories of victimization is lifestyles/routine activities theory. According to this theory, victimization is ripe to occur when motivated offenders, lack of capable guardianship, and suitable targets coalesce in time and space. This theory applies to sexual victimization as well as other predatory victimizations. Remember that motivated offenders are thought to be omnipresent—but a person has to be in proximity to these motivated offenders to be victimized. For sexual victimization, this can be achieved through dating (being alone with a potential offender), going to parties (particularly those with a high concentration of males, such as fraternity parties), or frequenting bars. Lack of capable guardianship also places people at risk for sexual victimization. Capable guardianship can come in the form of social guardianship and physical guardianship. Social guardianship is created when persons are present who can protect a person from being sexually victimized. Having a roommate or going out at night with others can provide social guardianship. Possessing Mace, pepper spray, or an alarm system can provide physical guardianship. When people lack social guardianship and physical guardianship, they are more likely to be victimized. Finally, victims who are deemed suitable by offenders are more likely than others to be sexually victimized. What factors do you think would make a person "suitable"? Factors such as being female, visibly intoxicated, and alone may increase risk of sexual victimization.

A risky lifestyle also has been linked to sexual victimization risk. What constitutes a risky lifestyle is up for debate, but participating in particular activities certainly increases risk for sexual victimization. For example, alcohol use has been intimately linked to sexual victimization. According to data from the NVAWS, almost 20% of women who were raped as adults had used alcohol and/or drugs at the time of the victimization. Offenders are also likely to be under the influence of alcohol or drugs when perpetrating sexual victimizations

(Tjaden & Thoennes, 2006). For college women, alcohol also plays an important role. College females who have a greater propensity for substance use are more likely to be sexually victimized than others (Fisher et al., 2010a). Binge drinking has also been linked to alcohol-related sexual assault among college students (Howard, Griffin, & Boekeloo, 2008). Alcohol places women at risk for victimization because it makes them suitable targets for would-be offenders (Abbey, 2002). These offenders may see intoxicated women and specifically select them for victimization, thinking that they will be easy to victimize. In addition, alcohol reduces a person's ability to recognize risk cues in the environment, thus a person who is drinking may be less diligent and aware of risk that is present (Abbey, 2002). Alcohol also reduces inhibition (Abbey, 2002). A college woman who is drinking may engage in behaviors that she would not otherwise, which then may increase her risk for victimization. For example, she may go home with a man from a party or engage in levels of consensual sexual activity that then place her at risk for sexual victimization.

FOCUS ON RESEARCH

Altough research has linked risky lifestyles to sexual victimization risk, the factors that lead people to engage in these risky lifestyles are just beginning to be explored. In their research of 913 mothers and their college-bound daughters, Testa, Hoffman, and Livingston (2011) found that mothers who had experienced sexual victimization after the age of 14 were perceived by their daughters to have lower perceived monitoring of their behavior and to have greater perceived approval of sex, and that these factors increased the risk of sexual victimization among the adolescent girls. They also found that the mother's communication effectiveness, mother's monitoring, and mother's experiencing childhood sexual assault were related to daughter's risk of sexual victimization. These findings suggest that mothers may play a key role in the risk of sexual victimization for young women. What do you think can be done in terms of intervention, given these findings?

Source: Adapted from Testa, M., Hoffman, J. A., & Livingston, J. A. (2011). Intergenerational transmission of sexual victimization vulnerability as mediated by parenting. *Child Abuse & Neglect, 35,* 363–371.

Beyond demographic characteristics and risky lifestyles, it may be that some people are less able to identify, recognize, and respond to risk. The body of research that has investigated risk perception has done so in several ways, but most of it has centered on having women (1) listen to audiotaped vignettes "in which a man and a woman act out a hypothetical scenario in which the man's behavior becomes increasingly coercive, and the woman's verbal resistance becomes increasingly forceful until the scenario ends in date rape" (Rinehart & Yeater, 2013, p. 2); (2) read written vignettes with different levels of risks and outcomes that were ambiguous—not leading to sexual assault or rape; and (3) watch videotaped vignettes in which the outcome was ambiguous as to whether it would lead to sexual assault. For the audiotaped vignette studies, women are generally asked to identify the point at which the man should stop making additional sexual advances. For the written vignettes, women are asked to identify when they feel uncomfortable, how likely it is the man would engage in a variety of sexually coercive behaviors, or to identify how they would react in various scenarios (e.g., on guard, seriously at risk). For the video vignettes, women are asked to identify different scenarios on their levels of risk or to identify what made them uncomfortable in the video.

This body of research has uncovered several interesting findings regarding risk perception, mainly as they relate to women who have experienced a victimization. Some of this research has found that women who have been victimized take longer to indicate that a man has gone too far in the vignette than women who have not been victimized (Soler-Baillo, Marx, & Sloan, 2005). The time it takes to indicate this is called **response latency**. Other research has found that women who had been previously victimized needed greater levels of ambiguous risk factors to feel on guard than women without victimization histories (Norris, Nurius, & Graham, 1999). Not all of this research has found a link between victimization and response latency or risk recognition, but it is interesting that at least some studies have found this link. Does it make sense that someone who has experienced a victimization would take longer or not identify a risky situation as such?

Characteristics of Sexual Victimization

In addition to knowing what factors place an individual at risk of being sexually victimized, it is also instructive to know what the "typical" sexual victimization and rape looks like. This is not to discount the seriousness of such victimizations but to understand the commonalities that many of them share.

Offenders

There is not one template for rape and sexual victimization offenders—they can be anyone. Data from the UCR indicate that those arrested for committing forcible rape are most commonly White males between the ages of 18 and 30 years old (FBI, 2009). Females compose less than 2% of all those arrested for forcible rape.

Even more studied is the victim–offender relationship. Researchers have wanted to know whether people are more likely to be raped or sexually victimized by strangers or by people who are known to them. In doing so, researchers found that rape and sexual victimization was relatively unlikely to be perpetrated by a stranger. Indeed, they found that rape rarely begins with an offender jumping out of the dark in a secluded place in a blitz-style attack, identified as "real rape" (Estrich, 1988). Instead, most rape and sexual assaults are perpetrated by someone known to the victim. Data from the NCVS from 2005 to 2010 show that about 1 in 3 rapes and sexual assaults were perpetrated by an intimate partner and another third were perpetrated by a well-known or a casual acquaintance (Planty et al., 2013).

Injury

Although being raped or sexually victimized can be traumatizing, fortunately most victims do not suffer serious physical injury. Slightly more than one third of rape victims in the NVAWS reported that they experienced some type of physical assault in addition to the rape, such as being slapped or hit (Tjaden & Thoennes, 2006). Even when such injuries are incurred, only about one third of those victims who report injury seek medical treatment for their injuries (Rand, 2008).

Offenders are also relatively unlikely to have or use a weapon during the perpetration of a rape or sexual assault. Between 2005 and 2010, in only about 11% of rapes or sexual assaults did the offender have a weapon (Planty et al., 2013). When a weapon is used, it is most likely to be a firearm (Rand, 2009).

■ RESPONSES TO SEXUAL VICTIMIZATION

Acknowledgment

After experiencing a rape, a victim may go through various emotions—anger, fear, and sadness, just to name a few. As a victim copes with the rape, one of the things he or she may do is think about the event itself and attempt to define it. A victim may feel immediately that he or she was raped (referred to as acknowledgment); on the other hand, a victim may see the incident as a horrible misunderstanding. It may not make sense that a person who is raped may not define it as such, but research shows that, in fact, many victims do not label their experience as rape. In fact, less than half the women (47.4% of completed rape victims) who participated in the NCWSV discussed earlier and who met a legal definition of rape labeled the incident a rape (Fisher, Cullen, & Turner, 1998).

Labeling an incident as rape may be important for several reasons. A victim may not get help from family, friends, or professionals if she or he does not think what happened was rape. The police are also unlikely to be notified of the incident if the victim does not think what happened was a crime. So why, then, do some victims not label or define their rape as such? It may be that victims are unsure how to label the incident (Littleton, Axson, Breitkopf, & Berenson, 2006), see it as a miscommunication (Layman, Gidycz, & Lynn, 1996), or think it was a crime other than rape (Layman et al., 1996). Women may also be less likely to label their experiences as rape when the perpetrator is someone they know, such as their date or boyfriend (Koss, 1985). In Koss's (1988) study, only 10.6% of college women who were raped believed that they were not victimized. In other words, almost all rape victims felt that what had happened to them was "wrong" or victimizing, even if they did not label it as rape.

Reporting

Acknowledgment of rape is likely closely tied to reporting rape or sexual victimization to the police. As previously noted in the discussion about the extent of rape and sexual victimization, rape is one of the most underreported crimes. In fact, results from the NCVS suggest that less than half of persons who are raped and sexually assaulted report their experiences to the police (Rennison, 2002). Rapes and sexual assaults of college women are also unlikely to come to the attention of the police. In the NCWSV, less than 5% of the rapes were reported to the police (Fisher et al., 1998). In the study by Kilpatrick et al. (2007), it was found that 10% of college women who experienced a drug or alcohol facilitated or incapacitated rape reported their incident to police. Slightly more (18%) victims of forcible rape told the police about what happened.

Why would a person who has experienced such a serious crime not report the incident to the police? One reason may be tied to acknowledgment: Victims who are not sure the incident was a crime are unlikely to report (Fisher, Daigle, Cullen, & Turner, 2003). Similarly, victims may be unsure that harm was intended on the part of the offender. Another reason victims do not report may be that they want to keep the event private (Rennison, 2002). Other victims have noted fear of the offender seeking reprisal (Rennison, 2002). Suspiciousness of the police and fear that they may be biased also drive victims' decisions not to report to the police (Rennison, 2002).

Resistance/Self-Protective Action

Not all victim responses happen after the incident has been completed. Instead, many victims of rape and other sexual attacks report that they tried to do something during the course of the incident either to stop it from occurring or being completed or to protect themselves. When this occurs, it is said that the victim used a **resistance strategy** or some type of **self-protective action.** Self-protective actions generally are classified into one of four types: forceful physical, nonforceful physical, forceful verbal, or nonforceful verbal (Ullman, 2007). **Forceful physical strategies** include actions such as shoving, punching, or biting the offender. **Nonforceful physical strategies** are passive actions, such as fleeing or pulling away. Self-protective actions may also be verbal. **Forceful verbal strategies,** such as yelling, are active and are used either to scare the offender or to attract the attention of others. Pleading with, talking to, and begging the offender are examples of nonaggressive, **nonforceful verbal strategies** (Ullman, 2007).

You may wonder whether it is wise to fight an attacker who is trying to rape or sexually victimize you. Although it is not effective in every situation, research shows that most women do use some type of self-protective action. In about two thirds of all rape and sexual assault victimizations recorded in the NCVS in 2007, the victim used some type of self-protective action (Bureau of Justice Statistics, 2010). Rape and sexual assault victims were most likely to say that they resisted their offender, scared or warned their offender, or ran away or hid from their offender. Generally, nonforceful verbal strategies have been shown to be ineffective in reducing the chances of a rape being completed (Clay-Warner, 2002; Fisher, Daigle, Cullen, & Santana, 2007). The type of self-protective action used is important. Research shows that if a victim is trying to stop the incident from occurring (i.e., keep it from being completed) and prevent injury, then the level of self-protective action should match the offender's efforts (Fisher et al., 2007). This concept, known as the **parity hypothesis,** states that a victim's use of self-protective action should be on par with the offender's attack. In other words, if the offender is using physical force, the victim's most effective defense will be forceful physical self-protective action.

■ CONSEQUENCES OF SEXUAL VICTIMIZATION

One reason that rape and sexual victimization have received so much attention in research and in the media is because of their often pernicious effects. Victims frequently experience serious consequences, some temporary and others long lasting. How a victim responds to being sexually victimized varies according to numerous factors, such as age and maturity of the victim, social support for the victim, the relationship of the offender to the victim, how the victim defines the incident, whether the victim reports to the police and how the system responds, whether the victim discloses to others and how they respond, the severity of the victimization, the level of injury, and the overall view of the community regarding sexual victimization.

Physical, Emotional, and Psychological Effects

As previously noted, most people who are sexually victimized do not suffer serious physical injury; however, possible physical effects include pain, bruises, cuts, scratches, genital/anal tears, nausea, vomiting, and headaches (National Center for Victims of Crime, 2008c). Victims may experience these effects immediately following the event or as long-term consequences.

In addition to physical effects, victims may experience emotional and psychological effects related to their sexual victimization. Some victims experience depression, which may lead to suicidal ideation (Stepakoff, 1998). They may experience anger, irritability, feelings of guilt and helplessness. Posttraumatic stress disorder also has been linked to sexual victimization—victims may have nightmares, flashbacks, exaggerated startle responses, and difficulty concentrating. Victims also may experience reductions in self-esteem or become more negatively self-focused (McMullin, Wirth, & White, 2007). Research on women who have experienced forced or coerced sex shows that they are at greater risk than women who have not experienced these events to have pain that interferes with their normal work, and to have physical health or emotional problems interfere with social activities (Jozkowski & Sanders, 2012).

Behavioral and Relationship Effects

Sexual victimization may also impact a person's behavior. Sexual victimization has been linked to delinquency and criminal behavior (Widom, 1989b), compulsive behavior, as well as substance use and abuse (Knauer, 2002). Some victims change their lifestyles by becoming more isolated and spending more time alone. Victims may also exhibit self-mutilating behavior or attempt suicide (Minnesota Department of Health, 1998).

Persons who are sexually victimized may also find that they have a difficult time navigating their personal relationships and have problems in their sexual functioning. Victims may find it difficult to enter into or maintain intimate relationships and to engage in parenting and other nurturing behaviors. Finally, victims may also evince changes in their sexuality—they may avoid sex, have difficulty becoming aroused, experience intrusive thoughts, and have difficulty reaching orgasm (Maltz, 2001). Conversely, some victims may increase their levels of sexual activity.

Costs

A detailed account of the costs that victims of crime may incur was presented in Chapter 4, so all the costs associated with sexual victimization will not be reviewed here. It should be noted, however, that sexual victimization carries with it many costs. As a consequence of the problems—physical, emotional, psychological, behavioral, and relationship—that victims experience, many seek assistance from mental health professionals. About one third of the female victims and one fourth of the male victims who reported rape in the NVAWS sought mental health counseling (Tjaden & Thoennes, 2006). About 12% of victims of rape and sexual assault in the NCVS missed time from work as a result of their victimization (Maston, 2010).

Data from the NCVS (Klaus & Maston, 2008) show that 18% of rape and sexual assault victims missed more than 10 days of work following the incident. Between one quarter and one half of all rape and child sexual abuse victims receive mental health care. As a result, sexual victimizations of both adults and children result in some of the largest mental health care costs for victims. The average mental health care loss per rape or sexual assault is $2,200, and the average for child abuse is $5,800. All told, the estimate of total economic loss a rape victim experiences is $87,000 on average when impact on quality of life is considered (Miller, Cohen, & Wiersema, 1996).

Recurring Sexual Victimization

As noted in Chapter 5, persons who are victimized once are at increased risk of experiencing subsequent victimizations. This relationship holds true for victims of sexual victimization. Research shows that individuals who experience childhood sexual abuse are at risk of being sexually victimized in adolescence and adulthood (Breitenbecher, 2001). Subsequent victimization may also occur relatively quickly. Research on college women shows that they are at risk of being repeatedly sexually victimized even during the course of a single academic year. In fact, data from the NCWSV show that more than 7% of the college women surveyed experienced more than one sexual victimization incident over the approximate 7-month recall period (Daigle, Fisher, & Cullen, 2008). These women experienced more than 72% of all sexual victimizations reported by the sample. What is especially alarming is that when a subsequent sexual victimization did occur, it was likely to occur within the same month or in the month immediately following the initial incident.

■ SPECIAL CASE: SEXUAL VICTIMIZATION OF MALES

Although most rape victims are female, males can also be the victims of rape. This realization only occurred recently, indicated by changes in the law to include males as potential victims of rape and by attention given to male rape by researchers. Estimates of the extent of male rape vary, but as noted, the NVAW study indicates that approximately 3% of males are raped during some point in their lifetime (Tjaden & Thoennes, 2006), while the NCVS shows that 8% of rape/sexual assault victims were male in 2010 (Truman, 2011). The experience, however, of rape for males is often somewhat similar to that of females.

Men often experience psychological trauma following a rape. They too may experience depression, self-blame, sexual dysfunctions, PTSD, and anger. Problematic, though, is that male victims often do not receive helpful support when they disclose their experience to friends and family (Brochman, 1991). Instead, male victims often are not believed and fault is often attributed to them rather than the offender (Brochman, 1991). As a result, male victims are particularly unlikely to report their rape to the police (National Center for Victims of Crime, n.d.-a). Male victims may also be afraid of being labeled homosexual because of being raped.

Particularly problematic for males is the confusion they may experience if they had a physiological response during the rape (RAINN, 2009a). Men may become sexually aroused during rape, not because of pleasure, but because of an uncontrollable physiological response. As a result, males may feel shame and confusion if their body responded in a way that is contrary to how they internally experienced the event (National Center for Victims of Crime, n.d.-a). Feeling this way reduces the likelihood that a male victim would seek assistance from the police. Also problematic is that rape crisis centers, which are designed to provide emergency assistance to victims of rape, were designed around a feminist philosophy and meant to address the needs of female rape victims, although this identity has changed over time as centers have collaborated with more mainstream organizations (Maier, 2008). Male victims may still be reluctant to seek help from such centers and, if they do, may find that the atmosphere is less open to males.

■ LEGAL AND CRIMINAL JUSTICE RESPONSES TO SEXUAL VICTIMIZATION

Legal Aspects of Sexual Victimization

Up until the mid-1960s and 1970s, traditional legal definitions of rape limited the offense to forceful unlawful carnal knowledge of a woman without her consent. What, then, did such definitions exclude? These definitions limited rape to incidents perpetrated against women and involving vaginal penetration. Under common law, husbands could not be charged with raping their wives. Calls for rape law reform resulted in changes to these laws: Now, both males and females can be victims and perpetrators of rape; other forms of penetration, such as digital and anal penetration, are included; and the marital exemption has been removed in all 50 states. This movement to change laws also applied to other criminal sexual victimizations: Such victimizations can be perpetrated by both genders, and married persons can be held liable for offending against their partners.

Before rape law reform, victims were often required to produce corroborating evidence for the incident to be prosecuted in court. Because rape is often a crime that occurs in private without additional witnesses, it can be difficult for victims to prove that they did not consent to have sex. For this reason, victims were often asked to provide corroborating evidence—such as injury, presence of a weapon, presence of semen, timely reporting to the police, and proof that the victim provided at least some degree of physical resistance. Remember, however, that a relatively small portion of victims are seriously physically injured, few incidents involve a weapon, and the most common perpetrator of such an offense is an acquaintance or someone known to the victim. These types of rape are the most difficult to prove, and the victim is likely to have difficulty proving, beyond her or his word, that a rape took place. Corroboration is no longer a requirement.

To further reduce the stress the victim may feel in the criminal justice process; rape shield laws also have been enacted. **Rape shield laws** prohibit the defense from using a victim's previous sexual conduct in court. In some circumstances, a victim's past may be used, but this is determined in a closed hearing, not in front of a jury. Generally, such information can be used only if doing so is necessary to establish the facts of the case. Another recent change involves prohibiting the use of polygraph examinations of victims. Some police departments and prosecutors have required that rape and sexual assault victims submit to a polygraph examination before they will investigate their claims or initiate prosecution. A few states have passed legislation to prohibit law enforcement officers and prosecutors from requiring these tests.

Violence Against Women Act (1994)

As part of the Omnibus Crime Bill of 1994, Congress passed the **Violence Against Women Act (VAWA)**, which was designed to provide women protection from systematic violence, including sexual violence. The act provided $1.6 billion in funding for education, research, treatment of victims, and improvement of state criminal justice system responses to female victims of violence. It also provided funding to improve victim services and to create more shelters for female victims of domestic violence, among other services. Through VAWA, the collection of crime statistics on violence against women was stressed, as well as the protection of college women and immigrant women and children. Interstate domestic violence and sexual assault crimes were identified as prosecutable federal offenses, and guarantees of interstate enforcement of protection orders were included.

The VAWA legislation was renewed in 2000. This renewal identified dating violence and stalking as additional crimes against women deserving of legal protections, created a legal assistance program for victims of domestic violence and sexual assault, promoted supervised visitation programs for families affected by violence, and granted additional protections to immigrants experiencing intimate partner violence, sexual violence, and stalking. The VAWA legislation was further reauthorized in 2005, with several key additions. It continued to focus on serving underserved populations, such as immigrant women and women with disabilities, and created cultural and language-specific services in communities to this end. It broadened services to include children and teenagers instead of just adults, created the first federal funding stream for rape crisis centers, protected victims from being evicted based on their victimization status, and emphasized prevention of violence. Related to policing and prosecution, it included a provision that polygraph examinations not be required of sexual assault victims as a condition of charging or prosecution. In 2013, VAWA was again reauthorized. It strengthened many of the provisions that were provided in the original bill, along with those that were added in the 2005 reauthorization. In addition, it expanded the housing protections provided for victims of domestic violence and sexual violence so that all persons residing in federally subsidized housing programs would be protected. In addition, it added additional protections for college students related to dating violence on campus and expanded protections for LGBT victims of violence so that they can be free from discrimination in receiving services. Although elements of the VAWA legislation have been met with some resistance from the courts, its impact on the way in which the criminal justice system responds to violence against women is evident.

HIV and STD Testing

A common fear among victims of rape is that they may contract HIV or other sexually transmitted diseases (STDs) from their attackers. This fear is particularly elevated when a person is raped by a stranger (Resnick, Monnier, & Seals, 2002). To assuage this fear, most states have implemented policies that allow for or require convicted sex offenders to submit to HIV testing. Some states, such as Wisconsin and Georgia, allow for testing if the victim requests it and if probable cause for the victim's exposure is established (RAINN, 2009a; Ritsche, 2006). See Table 8.2 for a detailed description of Georgia's policy on HIV testing for criminal offenders. Other states allow for pretrial testing. The Centers for Disease Control and Prevention has estimated the likelihood of contracting HIV from an HIV-positive person. When consensual vaginal sexual intercourse occurs, there is between a 0.1% and 0.2% chance of contracting HIV. Estimates are higher for consensual rectal sexual intercourse—between 0.5% and 3.0% (Centers for Disease Control and Prevention, 2006). Risk of exposure is likely higher for nonconsensual activity; however, those people who are most likely to be infected with HIV (men who have sex with men, intravenous drug users) are not the most likely rape offenders.

Sex Offender Registration and Notification

In 1996, the U.S. Congress passed Megan's Law, which requires that sex offenders convicted in federal court register a current address with criminal justice agencies. Following this enactment at the federal level, all states now have laws that require at least some types of sex offenders to register with state agencies in order for these agencies to keep track of where sex offenders live (Chon, 2010). With this registration also come restrictions on where sex offenders can live. Registered sex offenders often cannot live within a certain distance—such as 1,000 feet—of a school or other place where children congregate (Chon, 2010). Notification also allows for potential employers, community residents, organizations, and people who work with potential victims to be notified that a person living in the community is a sex offender. Notification does not always have to be overt; it can be achieved by making registries readily available and accessible, such as through the Internet or through a law enforcement agency (Chon, 2010). Notification can also occur through the distribution of fliers, door-to-door visits, and letters. Information such as the offender's name, address, description, and the charged offense is typically provided (Chon, 2010).

Police Response

The way in which police respond to victims of sexual assault and rape is critical to how the victims interact—or not—with the criminal justice system. As previously noted, victims of rape and sexual assault are unlikely to report their victimizations to the police. One common reason victims do not report is a lack of trust in the police or a belief that the police will not take the incident seriously. Unfortunately, events shown in the media suggest that this fear is not completely unfounded. For example, as reported by Barton and Vevea (2010), Gregory Below was arrested and charged in 2010 with 32 counts relating to sexual assault, stalking, kidnapping, and assault involving seven different women. One of the women reported to the police that Below met her at a club and directed her to take him to find crack cocaine and then to a vacant apartment. She told the police that, while in the apartment, he beat her with a closet rod and sexually assaulted her. She said he threatened to kill her and throw her body in the river if she did not comply with his orders. One of the officers ran a background check on her that showed a recent drug charge, and that officer admitted that he did not believe her claims, despite her visible injuries. It would be 2 years and several more victims later before Below was finally arrested. Those victims may have been spared had the police responded differently to the earlier victim's claims.

The above case speaks to a larger issue with which police and victims must deal—suspicion of victims making **false allegations.** For a report to be considered false, sufficient evidence must establish that a sexual assault did not happen. An allegation is not considered false if the investigation fails to prove that a sexual assault occurred or

Table 8.2 ■ Georgia's Law Regarding HIV Testing for Sex Offenders

Crimes and offenders	Individuals arrested or convicted of rape, sodomy, aggravated sodomy, child molestation, incest, or statutory rape, or other sexual offense that involves significant exposure
Is testing required or available?	Testing is available (but not mandatory) upon arrest of offender of enumerated offenses at the request of the victim upon showing of probable cause that person committed the crime and that significant exposure occurred. Testing is required upon a verdict or plea of guilty or nolo contendere to any AIDS-transmitting crime.
When does testing occur?	Upon court order after arrest or within 45 days following a guilty verdict or plea
What is the process?	In the case of an arrest, the victim, or the parent or legal guardian of a minor or incompetent victim, makes a request to the prosecuting agency to request that the alleged offender voluntarily submit to a test. If the person arrested declines, the court, upon a showing of probable cause, may (but is not required) to order the test to be performed.
To whom is the information disclosed?	To the victim, or to any parent or guardian of any such victim who is a minor, by the Department of Community Health
What other services for victims are available in connection with the testing?	None specified
Other	The cost of the test shall be borne by the victim or by the person arrested, in the discretion of the court.
Source and/or applicable references	Ga. Code Ann. §§ 17-10-15, 24-9-47, 31-22-9.1

Source: Reprinted by permission of RAINN, Rape, Abuse and Incest National Network through the support of Hogan Lovells.

Note: This information in this chart is intended to be current through December, 2013. The information is not presented as a source of legal advice. You should not rely for legal advice on statements or representations made within the Web site or by any externally referenced Internet sites. If you need legal advice upon which you intend to rely in the course of your legal affairs, consult a competent, independent attorney.

if there is a lack of evidence to prove it occurred. Such cases would be deemed **baseless allegations**—not false (Lonsway, Archambault, & Berkowitz, 2007). Unfortunately, statistics of false allegations often erroneously use baseless cases as evidence. In the UCR program, police departments label baseless and false allegations using one term—**unfounded.** To know what percentage of rape and sexual assault complaints are actually false, researchers need to determine if a claim is merely baseless or actually false. In using this standard, a study of complaints of sexual assault in Portland, Oregon, showed that

1.6% were false. This percentage was less than that for stolen vehicles, 2.6% (Raphael, 2008). Estimates provided by the San Diego, California, police show that 4% of their reports for sexual assault were false, while a study of British police showed that only 2% of reported sexual assault cases were false (Lonsway et al., 2007). It seems, then, that false reports of rape and sexual assault are not typical.

Quite likely a larger problem than false allegations is the lack of action police may take in cases or their not responding to victims in a sensitive manner. To deal with victim concerns and encourage positive police response, many police departments have implemented new policies and practices. Many police departments now have special investigatory **sex crime units.** These units staff officers who are specially trained in how to respond to victims of sex crimes, including training in crisis counseling and in investigatory techniques germane to such cases. Police departments sometimes have **victim/witness assistance programs (VWAPs)** that provide guidance to victims during the investigation and criminal justice process. People working in these programs may go with the victim to the hospital for an exam, accompany her or him to court, provide transportation to court, assist with filing compensation claims, and assist her or him in receiving counseling. Another important function they may serve is providing notification when the offender is released from police custody. The way in which police respond to victims is particularly important given that research has shown that when victims are treated with empathy and receive support, they are more likely to cooperate with criminal justice personnel, to remember more details about the incident, and to receive psychological benefit (Meyers, 2002). See the Focus on International Issues box to read about how rape victims from other cultures respond to being victimized and how officials deal with rape.

FOCUS ON INTERNATIONAL ISSUES

Not all rape victims around the world feel safe seeking help, for being a rape victim can lead to being killed. Lal Bibi faces this possibility after being repeatedly raped and beaten. She was kidnapped, chained to a wall, beaten, and raped repeatedly by members of the Afghan Local Police. It is thought that she was targeted because one of her cousins started a relationship with a girl and either unsuccessfully tried to elope with her or he could not pay the bride price to marry her, thus causing dishonor to her father. Tribal justice provided that one way to settle this dishonor would be to give Lal Bibi to the wronged girl's family as payment. Armed men came to Lal Bibi's home and took her to one of the subcommander's homes where she was tortured. Lal Bibi spoke out about her abuse and her family has asked that justice be done, with all of the men who harmed her being brought to justice. Instead, Lal Bibi's mother said, "If nobody wants to solve our problem, then they should behead her; we don't want her." In Afghanistan, a woman who is not a virgin is not fit for marriage and is a dishonor to her family.

Source: Adapted from Rubin, A. J. (2012, June 1). Rape case, in public, cites abuse by armed groups in Afghanistan. *The New York Times.* Retrieved from http://www.nytimes.com/2012/06/02/world/asia/afghan-rape-case-is-a-challenge-for-the-government.html?pagewanted=all.

Medical-Legal Response

Victims of rape and sexual assault may find themselves at the hospital either to seek medical treatment for their injuries or to receive a forensic examination. This process can be quite daunting. In the past, rape victims would often find that they were not given priority in emergency rooms and were forced to wait for long periods of time in crowded waiting rooms, unable to eat, drink, or urinate until after they were examined. Staff at the hospital often were not trained in how to conduct forensic evidence collection and were sometimes insensitive regarding the special needs of sexual assault victims (Littel, 2001). To combat these problems, the **sexual assault nurse examiner (SANE)** program was developed in the mid- to late 1970s (Campbell, Patterson, & Lichty, 2005). SANEs are forensic, registered nurses. They perform forensic examinations of sexual assault victims that include collecting information about the crime, performing a physical examination to evaluate and inspect the victim's body, collecting and preserving all evidence, collecting urine and blood samples, providing the victim with prophylactic medications for the prevention of sexually transmitted diseases, and providing the victim with referrals (Buschur, 2010). Evidence is collected through swabbing, debris collection, and photo documentation (Buschur, 2010). For example, at least two photos of external injuries should be taken and swabs should be collected if body fluids are present on the victim (Buschur, 2010). The release of evidence to the police is done at the consent of the victim in cases that already have been reported to the police or if the victim agrees to report (with the exception of cases in which medical personnel must mandatorily report, such as child abuse cases). SANEs may also conduct evidentiary exams of suspects in sexual assault and rape cases. Research on the effectiveness of SANEs has shown that victims report that they feel respected and safe, that they were cared for by people with expertise, and were informed (Ericksen et al., 2002). Other research shows that evidence collected by SANEs was more thorough and had fewer errors than evidence collected by non-SANEs (Sievers, Murphy, & Miller, 2003) and that conviction rates are higher for SANE cases than non-SANE cases (Crandall & Helitzer, 2003).

In addition to SANEs, many communities have **sexual assault response teams (SARTs)** that work to coordinate responses to sexual assault and rape victims. Started in the early to mid-1970s, these teams often consist of individuals who work together to ensure that victims of sexual assault receive assistance in navigating the medical and criminal justice systems. Most SARTs include individuals from the prosecutor's office, local law enforcement agency, advocacy groups, and forensic examiners as core members (Howton, 2010). When a victim seeks medical treatment or reports his or her incident to a law enforcement agency, the SART in that jurisdiction (if one exists) is notified and activated. Individuals then work to ensure that the victim receives appropriate medical care, including a forensic medical exam, and is treated with dignity and respect by individuals in the criminal justice system. They further assist the victim in receiving additional services such as counseling.

Prosecuting Rape and Sexual Assault

The prosecutor is the key actor in charging and trying any criminal case. The prosecutor has discretion in deciding what cases to charge and in which cases to offer plea bargains to the defendant. Historically, prosecutors tend to move forward with prosecuting those cases that are easiest to prove legally—those that have a clear victim and strong evidence to prove the

The contents of a "rape kit," what investigators and medical personnel use to collect evidence in cases of rape and sexual assault, is pictured here.

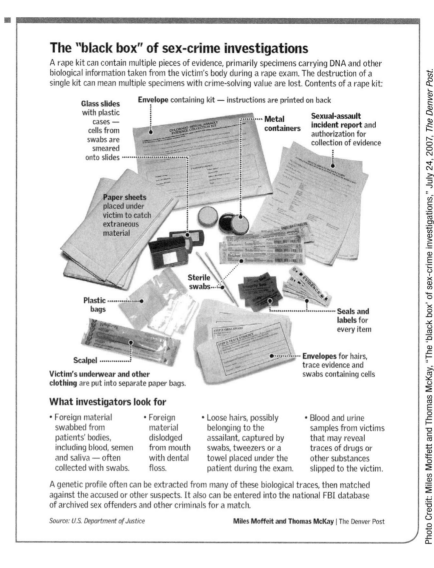

The "black box" of sex-crime investigations

A rape kit can contain multiple pieces of evidence, primarily specimens carrying DNA and other biological information taken from the victim's body during a rape exam. The destruction of a single kit can mean multiple specimens with crime-solving value are lost. Contents of a rape kit:

Glass slides with plastic cases — cells from swabs are smeared onto slides

Envelope containing kit — instructions are printed on back

Metal containers

Sexual-assault incident report and authorization for collection of evidence

Paper sheets placed under victim to catch extraneous material

Sterile swabs

Plastic bags

Seals and labels for every item

Scalpel

Envelopes for hairs, trace evidence and swabs containing cells

Victim's underwear and other clothing are put into separate paper bags.

What investigators look for

- Foreign material swabbed from patients' bodies, including blood, semen and saliva — often collected with swabs.
- Foreign material dislodged from mouth with dental floss.
- Loose hairs, possibly belonging to the assailant, captured by swabs, tweezers or a towel placed under the patient during the exam.
- Blood and urine samples from victims that may reveal traces of drugs or other substances slipped to the victim.

A genetic profile often can be extracted from many of these biological traces, then matched against the accused or other suspects. It also can be entered into the national FBI database of archived sex offenders and other criminals for a match.

Source: U.S. Department of Justice

Miles Moffeit and Thomas McKay | The Denver Post

Photo Credit: Miles Moffett and Thomas McKay, "The 'black box' of sex-crime investigations," July 24, 2007, *The Denver Post.*

defendant's guilt. It may not be surprising, then, to learn that prosecutors have been reluctant to try rape and sexual assault cases since they often involve a lack of evidence and are "he said, she said"-type cases. Although the decision to charge or not is most commonly impacted by legal factors, characteristics of the victim also play a role. This may be the case even more so in rape and sexual assault cases, in which eyewitnesses and physical evidence are uncommon. As such, prosecutors may evaluate how a jury or judge will perceive the victim in terms of his or her background, character, and behavior.

In a recent study on charging decisions of prosecutors on sexual assaults, Spohn and Holleran (2004) found that in cases in which the perpetrator was a nonstranger, prosecutors were less likely to charge when the victim had engaged in risk-taking behavior at the time of the incident. Similarly, prosecutors were unlikely to charge if the victim's character or reputation was questioned and if the victim and offender had been or were intimate partners. For incidents involving strangers, on the other hand, victim characteristics and behaviors did not predict charging decisions. Rather, stranger-perpetrated sexual assaults were charged based on legal factors, such as the presence of physical evidence and whether the perpetrator used a gun or knife. As noted by Shepherd (2002), prosecutors are not the only ones who make tough decisions in rape cases. She discusses her own experience of being a juror for a rape trial in Alaska. She notes that jurors' beliefs in rape myths impact the way in which they evaluate information presented at trial and make decisions regarding guilt. Rape myths are stereotypes or false beliefs that people hold about rape offenders, victims, and rape in general that serve to justify male sexual aggression against females (Lonsway & Fitzgerald, 1994). An example of a rape myth is that women lie about consensual sex afterward and call it rape.

■ PREVENTION AND INTERVENTION

Most programs designed to reduce the occurrence of rape and sexual victimization target college students. One reason for this is an amendment to the Clery Act (discussed in detail in Chapter 12) that requires colleges and universities to develop sexual assault prevention policies. Another reason is the attention that has been given to sexual victimization among college students and the ability to target this at-risk population easily.

Some of the most effective programs include teaching women how to assess situations as risky, how to acknowledge situations as potentially leading to rape, and how to act with resistance. These programs often include self-defense training. Self-defense training has been shown to reduce the likelihood that college women will be raped. It also increases their use of self-protective behaviors, use of assertive sexual communication, and belief in their ability to resist offenders (for a review, see Daigle, Fisher, & Stewart, 2009). Increasing college women's ability to recognize risk also appears to be effective in reducing rape (Marx, Calhoun, Wilson, & Meyerson, 2001). Bystander programs are another type of prevention programs that look promising. These programs focus on training men and women to be agents of change. People are taught

Photo Credit: © Washington Post/Getty Images.

■ ■ ■ ■ ■ ■ ■ ■ ■ ■

PHOTO 8.2

A self-defense class is pictured here. Some prevention programs incorporate self-defense, building on the knowledge that using resistance has been shown to thwart the completion of sexual victimization.

to intervene when they hear sexist comments or see high-risk behavior and are instructed on how to react after a rape occurs (Banyard, Plante, & Moynihan, 2007). Early research on bystander intervention programs does show their promise. College students who have completed Green Dot, a bystander interevention program, had lower rape myth acceptance scores than students without training (Coker et al., 2011). Similarly, persons going through bystander intervention have shown improvement in attitudes, knowledge, and behavior related to sexual violence (Banyard, Moynihan, & Plante, 2007). Bystander intervention has also been shown to reduce males' sexual aggression and positive reinforcement for engaging in sexually aggressive behaviors (Gidycz, Orchowski, & Berkowitz, 2011). With the development of prevention programs, reducing the occurrence of sexual victimization may be possible, but targeting the reasons why offenders engage in this type of behavior also will be necessary. Until the individual and societal causes can be addressed, it is imperative that the extent, characteristics, and causes of sexual victimization be understood so that victims can be responded to in helpful ways and potential victims can minimize their risk of being victimized.

RIPPED FROM THE HEADLINES

One particular concern among college students is the use of date rape drugs, particularly that someone puts a drug into a beverage without them knowing. Four male students at North Carolina State University have developed a product that may reduce the likelihood that females would drink such a beverage. The students have developed a new type of nail polish, called Undercover Colors, that changes color when it comes into contact with date rape drugs, such as Rohypnol, gamma hydroxybutyric (GHB), and ketamine. The men hope that knowing that this type of nail polish can be worn by women will prevent would-be perpetrators from attempting to spike a person's drink and that women can protect themselves by dipping a finger into the drink to make sure it does not contain a drug. The product is currently under development. Do you think this is an effective strategy at reducing the incidence of rape? Why or why not?

Source: Adapted from Students invent nail polish that could detect date rape drugs. (2014). Retrieved from http://www.foxnews.com/health/2014/08/25/students-invent-nail-polish-that-could-detect-date-rape-drugs.

SUMMARY

- Sexual victimization is any type of victimization that involves sexual behavior perpetrated against an individual. There are many types of sexual victimization, such as forcible rape, drug or alcohol facilitated rape, incapacitated rape, statutory rape, sexual coercion, unwanted sexual contact, coerced sexual contact, unwanted sexual contact with force, visual abuse, and verbal abuse.

- Rape is measured using both Uniform Crime Reports (UCRs) and the National Criminal Victimization Survey (NCVS). The UCR is dependent on people reporting rape as a crime. The UCR also does not measure other types of sexual victimization, such as unwanted sexual contact or sexual coercion. About 85,000 rapes were reported to law enforcement in 2012.
- The NCVS looks at both male and female victims and both rape and sexual assault. The NCVS does not rely on victims to report the crime. According to the NCVS, in 2012, there were 346,830 rapes and sexual assaults.
- Another source of information on the extent of rape is the National Violence Against Women Survey (NVAWS). It was conducted via telephone, with 8,000 males and 8,000 females interviewed.
- The Sexual Experiences Survey is a 10-item survey designed to measure rape, sexual coercion, and sexual contact.
- The National College Women Sexual Victimization Study is a nationally-representative study of college women. About 16% of college women reported experiencing some type of sexual victimization during the academic year.
- The National Study of Drug or Alcohol Facilitated, Incapacitated, and Forcible Rape is a national-level study of those three types of rape.
- Certain risk factors may place a person at higher risk of victimization. Females are more likely to be sexually victimized than males. Age can also determine when a person is at the highest risk of victimization. A person's socioeconomic status and where he or she lives are also related to risk of sexual victimization. Persons who are Black have higher rates of sexual victimization than others.
- Lifestyles/routine activities theory relates to sexual victimization. According to this theory, victimization is ripe to occur when motivated offenders, lack of capable guardianship, and suitable targets coalesce in time and space. For sexual victimization, this can be achieved through dating (being alone with a potential offender), going to parties (particularly those where many males are present, such as fraternity parties), or frequenting bars. Victims may also be less likely to identify situations as risky than nonvictims.
- White, young males are the most common perpetrators of sexual victimization according to the UCR and NCVS.
- Sexual victimization is traumatic, but most victims do not suffer physical injury and few of those who do suffer injuries seek medical help. Rapes that involve a stranger are more likely to result in injury. Offenders are also unlikely to use or have a weapon during the perpetration of a rape or sexual assault.
- It is hard sometimes for a victim to feel and acknowledge that he or she is the victim of rape. However, it is an important first step to label the incident as rape so the victim can receive necessary help from family, friends, and professionals.
- Rape is one of the most underreported crimes. There are several reasons that reporting of rape is so low, including fear of reprisal or belief that the police will be biased. Victims also cite wanting to keep the matter private as a reason not to report.
- A resistance strategy or self-protective action is something victims of rape or other sexual attacks do during the course of the incident either to stop it from occurring or being completed or to protect themselves. There are four types of self-protective action: forceful physical strategies, nonforceful physical strategies, forceful verbal strategies, and nonforceful verbal strategies.
- There are many physical, emotional, psychological, behavioral, and relationship effects caused by rape and sexual victimization. There are also significant financial costs associated with rape.
- Repeat sexual victimization occurs when people who have been victimized once experience a subsequent victimization.
- Males may also be sexually victimized. When they are, they may experience similar negative consequences. Some of what they may experience may, however, be unique to being male and how males often experience sexual victimization.
- Several legal reforms have been enacted to help rape victims. Rape shield laws, the Violence Against Women Act (1994), sex offender registration, and required HIV testing of offenders are all laws that help victims of sexual crimes navigate the criminal justice system. Certain entities such as sexual assault nurse examiners and sexual assault response teams work to assist victims as they deal with the medical and legal system.

DISCUSSION QUESTIONS

1. What are some issues with requiring HIV testing of offenders? Do you agree with this reform?

2. Investigate your state's laws for rape and sexual assault. How are rape and sexual assault defined? Who can be a victim? Who can be an offender? What are the proscribed punishments for committing these acts?

3. Why is measurement so important in determining accurate estimates of the extent of rape and other types of sexual victimization?

4. With the widespread use of the Internet and technology, how might the nature of sexual victimization change?

5. Given what you know about reporting, use of self-protective actions, and recurring sexual victimization, how can we prevent sexual victimization?

KEY TERMS

sexual victimization

rape

forcible rape

drug or alcohol facilitated rape

incapacitated rape

statutory rape

sexual coercion

unwanted sexual contact

coerced sexual contact

unwanted sexual contact with force

noncontact sexual abuse

visual abuse

verbal abuse

Sexual Experiences Survey (SES)

National College Women Sexual Victimization Study (NCWSV)

National Study of Drug or Alcohol Facilitated, Incapacitated, and Forcible Rape

response latency

resistance strategy

self-protective action

forceful physical strategies

nonforceful physical strategies

forceful verbal strategies

nonforceful verbal strategies

parity hypothesis

rape shield laws

Violence Against Women Act (1994)

false allegations

baseless allegations

unfounded

sex crime units

victim/witness assistance programs (VWAPs)

sexual assault nurse examiner (SANE)

sexual assault response team (SART)

INTERNET RESOURCES

Male Survivor: Overcoming Sexual Victimization of Boys & Men (http://www.malesurvivor.org/default.html)

While sexual victimization is widely studied as a problem women face, this website examines and provides resources and support for men who were sexually victimized as children, adolescents, or adults. It examines common myths of sexual victimization, such as the belief that males cannot be victims and that sexual crimes committed against males are always perpetrated by homosexual males. The website also includes survivor stories and publications from researchers examining the topic of male sexual victims.

National Sexual Violence Resource Center (http://www.nsvrc.org/)

This is a comprehensive collection and distribution center for information, statistics, and resources related to sexual violence. It serves as a resource for coalitions, rape crisis centers, allied organizations, and others working to eliminate sexual assault. The Center does not provide direct services to sexual assault victims but, rather, supports those who do.

RAINN: Rape, Abuse, and Incest National Network (http://www.rainn.org/)

RAINN is the nation's largest antisexual assault organization. Its website provides information about local counseling centers and how to help a loved one who may be the victim of sexual abuse. The website also lists statistics, reporting, and tips on how to reduce the risk of becoming a victim of sexual assault or rape. You can also learn about volunteering for RAINN, donating money, and becoming a student activist.

The Date Safe Project (http://www.datesafeproject.org)

This website provides information for parents and students on how to be safe while dating. There is also information about curricula and classroom exercises on dating, hooking up, and parties. There are also sexual assault survivor stories. The Date Safe Project provides parents, educators, educational institutions, students, military installations, community organizations, state agencies, and federal government with resources, educational materials, and programming addressing consent, healthy intimacy, sexual education, sexual assault awareness, bystander intervention, and support for sexual assault survivors.

The Sexual Victimization of College Women (http://www.ncjrs.gov/pdffiles1/nij/182369.pdf)

One of the most at-risk groups for sexual victimization is college women, and this report—put together by Bonnie Fisher, Francis Cullen, and Michael Turner—discusses findings from the NCWSV. They also discuss stalking, since that is a crime seen frequently on college campuses. This is a comprehensive report on the sexual victimization of college women and provides a wide range of information on the topic.

University of Pittsburgh at Johnstown: Sexual Victimization (http://www.upj.pitt.edu/en/campus-life/campus-police/sexual-assault-services/

This website is part of the University of Pittsburgh at Johnstown's counseling center and provides information about the types of rape, the definition of rape, and how consent is defined. It also discusses the steps a person should take if he or she is raped and some of the side effects of rape, including posttraumatic stress disorder. The website also links to other articles by the college's center: two on date rape drugs, including the use of alcohol as a drug that leads to incapacitated rapes, and another on sexual assault prevention.

CHAPTER 9

INTIMATE PARTNER VIOLENCE

For most of us, what goes on behind closed doors in our intimate relationships remains private. Except for the details we choose to share with others, the give-and-take, the ups and downs, and the good and bad times are largely shared by only us and our partners. For others, these details are sometimes made public and, in some circumstances, are widely broadcast for the world to know. Unfortunately, it is usually those times involving fighting that become public fodder. For Mel Gibson, an Oscar-winning actor and director, his "rants" at then live-in girlfriend Oksana Grigorieva were exposed. Several phone conversations between him and Oksana were taped and then posted to the Internet, where anyone with an Internet connection could listen to what was said by both parties. Below is a transcript from one of their conversations. It was edited lightly to censor profanity, and some lines were omitted.

M: I'm sick of your bull****! Has any relationship ever worked with you? Nooo!

O: Listen to me. You don't love me, because somebody who loves does not behave this way.

M: Shut the f*** up. I know . . . *(cross-talking)* because I know absolutely that you do not love me and you treat me with no consideration.

O: One second. One second. Can I please speak? . . .

O: You just enjoy insulting me, that's all.

M: F*** you, I so f***** do, because you hurt me so bad.

(Continued)

(Continued)

O: I didn't do . . . I don't . . .

M: You insult me with every look, *(garbled)* every f***** heartbeat, you selfish harpy.

O: I did not do anything, and I apologized for nothing . . .

O: I wanted to peace. I wanted to have peace.

M: Keep peace.

O: Because you are unbalanced!

O: You need medication! . . .

M: I need a woman! . . . I need a f***** woman. *(panting)* I don't need medication. You need a f***** bat in the side of the head. All right? How 'bout that? You need a f***** doctor. You need a f***** brain transplant. You need a f*****, you need a f***** soul. I need medication. I need someone who treats me like a man, like a human being. With kindness, who understands what gratitude is, because I f***** bend over backwards with my balls in a knot to do it all for her and she gives me sh**, like a f***** sour look or says I'm mean. Mean? What the f*** is that? This is mean! Get it? You get it now? What mean is? Get it? *(panting)* You f***** don't care about me. I'm having a hard time, and you f***** yank the rug, you b****, you f***** selfish b****. *(panting)* Don't you dare hang up on me.

O: I can't listen to this anymore.

M: You hang up, I'm coming over there.

O: I'll call the police.

M: What?

O: I'll call the police.

M: You f***** c***. I'm coming to my house. You're in my house, honey.

O: Yes, but you, honey, don't call me honey. You just . . .

M: *(screaming)* You're in my house! So I'll call the police and tell them there's someone in my house. How 'bout that?

Now that you have read this transcript, think about how you would characterize their conversation to others. Is this just a typical, everyday fight that any couple might have? Is it abusive? Are both parties contributing equally? What kind of effect might this kind of conversation have on Oksana? On Mel? On their young child? This section will discuss the variations of intimate partner violence, its causes and effects, and how the criminal justice system and other agencies respond to victims.

Source: Mel Gibson and Oksana Grigorieva phone transcript, July 12, 2010.

■ DEFINING INTIMATE PARTNER VIOLENCE AND ABUSE

In order to understand intimate partner violence (IPV), we must first define what it entails. First, we must identify what an intimate partner is. An **intimate partner** can be a husband or wife, an ex-husband or ex-wife, a boyfriend or girlfriend, or a dating partner. **Violence**—the intentional physical harm of another person—that occurs between these people includes overt **physical violence** such as hitting, slapping, kicking, punching, and choking. Throwing objects at another person is also physical violence. In short, any intentional physical harm that results in pain is physical violence. When it comes to intimate partners, however, physical violence may not encompass all the harm done. For example, yelling at and verbally degrading a partner may also be seen as violent—or at least as **emotional abuse** (Payne & Gainey, 2009). The transcript from Mel Gibson's phone conversation is, quite likely, indicative of emotional abuse. This emotional form of violence also includes threats of harm, restraint of normal activities or freedom, and denial of access to resources (National Research Council, 1996). Violence within intimate relationships can also be sexual in nature. **Sexual violence** includes unwanted sexual contact, sexual coercion, and rape. As discussed in Chapter 6, sexual violence often involves someone known to the victim, including current or former intimate partners. Given these varied forms of IPV and abuse, examples of this type of victimization are plenty. Is it abusive when a man does not provide his wife any mode of transportation and insists that she stay at home during the day, calling throughout the day to ensure that she is home and alone? Many would consider this isolating and controlling behavior abusive, although not violent. What about when a couple is fighting and the woman shoves her boyfriend? Even though the shoving may not have created serious injury or even really hurt her boyfriend, the woman did, in fact, use physical violence.

These are not the only ways in which IPV has been defined and described. Michael Johnson (2006), for instance, put forth that there are two major types of IPV. The first type, called **intimate terrorism,** is rooted in the need for power and control, of which the abuse is but one element. Intimate terrorism involves severe, persistent, and frequent abuse that tends to escalate over time. This type of IPV is likely to result in serious injury and to be seen by criminal justice professionals and social service agencies. It is the type of IPV that has been viewed as most problematic and deserving of money and research attention to reduce its occurrence and pernicious effects. The second type of IPV is called **situational couple violence,** or common couple violence. Instead of resulting from a desire for power and control, situational couple violence occurs when conflict gets out of hand and results in violence. It could start with a "run-of-the-mill" disagreement and then turn violent. This type of IPV tends not to result in serious injury or to be a part of a larger pattern of persistent and frequent abuse; it also is unlikely to come to the attention of criminal justice and social service agencies. Two additional types of IPV also have been identified: violent resistance and mutual violent control. Violent resistance occurs when a person is violent but not controlling; instead, the person's partner is the violent and controlling one in the relationship. In mutual violent control, both people are violent and controlling.

These descriptions and definitions show how IPV is currently viewed. Historically, however, IPV was not viewed in these terms. Originally, IPV was defined only as physical violence perpetrated by husbands against their wives, but this definition has evolved over the past 40 years to include emotional and sexual violence. We also now recognize that IPV is not exclusive to married couples and that both men and women can be perpetrators and victims. But let's discuss how we got to this point. There is a bit of controversy regarding just how tolerant or intolerant society has been toward men's violence against their wives. Some have argued that such violence was essentially tolerated, if not condoned, given that males were considered dominant (Dobash & Dobash, 1979). The man was the head of the family and was able to use power and control, even violence, to control his wife and children. Presumably, minor forms of violence were permitted as long as they were used by men to maintain their positions of dominance. It is not apparent, however, just how pervasive IPV was during this time. As you may imagine, there were no national-level studies conducted in which people reported victimization and perpetration. Instead, we can look to laws and their usage during this time as a guide. Importantly, there have been laws in place since the 1600s that specifically prohibited violence against wives in America. By the 1870s, most states had adopted such laws. Punishment of wife abusers was generally informal, with vigilante groups often taking the matter into their own hands. In addition, punishments such as public shaming were often used. For example, a man who assaulted his wife in Portland, Oregon, during the early 20th century could face flogging (as cited in Felson, 2002).

Despite these laws, it does appear that some trial and appellate courts tolerated minor forms of violence by husbands against their wives (Pleck, 1987), but most courts did not tolerate physical violence in any form (Felson, 2002). When courts failed to convict or uphold convictions of men who had abused their wives, it was mainly done not with the view that violence against women by their husbands was acceptable but with the view that the courts should not intervene based on the principle of privacy (Felson, 2002). In the same vein, females were rarely arrested or brought to court for abusing their husbands. As a whole, then, courts have routinely rejected the notion that men have the right to physically assault their wives. See the Focus on International Issues box for a discussion about domestic violence in West Africa and how it has just recently been outlawed.

As with many other forms of victimization, IPV really took center stage in policy and research in the 1970s. The women's rights movement was central in focusing attention on women as victims of IPV. During this time, feminists argued that IPV was a reflection of the subjugation of women and that the male-dominated criminal justice system did little to protect women. In response to these claims, an outgrowth of the women's rights movement was to open domestic violence shelters for battered women and to provide women with the assistance they needed to get out of abusive relationships. Since then, efforts to identify, describe, prevent, and respond to IPV have expanded dramatically. Specific responses by the criminal justice system and other social service agencies are discussed later in this section.

FOCUS ON INTERNATIONAL ISSUES

In 2007, Sierra Leone, a country located in western Africa, passed a domestic violence act that established basic rights for women in the home and provides victims free medical care and other entitlements. Perpetrators of domestic violence can be punished by a fine of up to 5m leones ($1144) and up to two years in prison. This law was passed in response to the growing threat to women of violence in their homes committed by their husbands. In Ivory Coast and Liberia, laws against domestic violence do not exist.

Source: Adapted from Ford, T. (2012, May 22). Domestic violence is biggest threat to west Africa's women, IRC says. *The Guardian.* Retrieved from http://www.guardian.co.uk/global-development/2012/may/22/domestic-violence-west-africa-irc.

■ MEASUREMENT AND EXTENT

Now that you know what IPV is, you are probably wondering how common it is for partners, who supposedly care about each other, to engage in violence against each other. As you might imagine, it can be difficult to know exactly how frequently such behavior occurs given that it often occurs in private. In addition, people may be reluctant to call the police when the perpetrator is someone close to them; thus, official data sources may underestimate the extent to which violence between intimate partners occurs. Much like for other types of victimization, one of the most widely used research methodologies is to employ surveys that ask people to self-report their victimizations and perpetrations. The findings from such studies are addressed in this section.

National Crime Victimization Survey

Remember from our discussion in Chapter 2 that the **National Crime Victimization Survey (NCVS)** is a survey of U.S. households in which individuals are asked about their victimization experiences during the previous 6 months. Individuals who report experiencing a victimization event complete an incident report for each event. Within this detailed incident report, individuals are asked to identify their relationship with the perpetrator. Violent incidents perpetrated by spouses or ex-spouses, boyfriends or girlfriends, and former boyfriends or girlfriends are considered in the NCVS to be IPV. Data from the NCVS indicate that the rate of IPV declined from 1993 to 2008 (Catalano, Smith, Snyder, & Rand, 2009). Nonetheless, in 2008, females experienced 552,000 nonfatal IPV victimizations, making the IPV rate for females 4.3 victimizations per 1,000 females age 12 or older. Males were less likely to report IPV victimizations. Males experienced 101,000 nonfatal IPV victimizations. This equates to a rate of 0.8 victimizations per 1,000 males age 12 or older (Catalano et al., 2009). For both males and females, the most common type of IPV reported in the NCVS was simple assault, which composes more than half of all IPV victimizations (Catalano et al., 2009).

Conflict Tactics Scale

Developed in the 1970s, the **Conflict Tactics Scale (CTS)** is designed to measure levels and use of various conflict tactics. Created by Murray Straus, this scale was constructed to examine conflict in intimate relationships. The CTS since has been revised into the revised Conflict Tactics Scale (CTS-2) (Straus, Hamby, Boney-McCoy, & Sugarman, 1996). Conflict was seen by Straus (1979) as being inevitable in close interpersonal interactions; however, it is not conflict itself that matters but the ways in which couples resolve it. The ways in which couples resolve conflict are known as conflict tactics, and the CTS-2 examines the use of conflict tactics in three domains: physical assault, psychological aggression, and negotiation. It also includes items to measure injury and sexual coercion of and by an intimate partner.

The CTS-2 comprises 78 questions that measure these domains. Respondents are asked about the frequency of occurrence of each item during the past year and are given eight response options, ranging from *never* to *more than 20 times in the past year*. Items are presented in pairs so that individuals are asked about victimization and perpetration of the same item together. An example of a question from the CTS-2 is shown in the following box. Respondents are asked about how often their partners push or shove them. Although this item is designed to measure physical assault, other items ask about the other domains. Since its development, the CTS (and now the CTS-2) has become the most widely used survey instrument to measure the occurrence of IPV.

EXAMPLE OF CTS-2 QUESTIONS

Please circle how many times you did each of these things in the past year, and how many times your partner did them in the past year. If you or your partner did not do one of these things in the past year, but it happened before that, circle "7."

How often did this happen?

1 = Once in the past year

2 = Twice in the past year

3 = 3–5 times in the past year

4 = 6–10 times in the past year

5 = 11–20 times in the past year

6 = More than 20 times in the past year

7 = Not in the past year, but it did happen before

0 = This has never happened

My partner pushed or shoved me.

1 2 3 4 5 6 7 0

My partner punched or hit me with something that could hurt.

1 2 3 4 5 6 7 0

Source: Copyright 1995 Straus, Hamby, Boney-McCoy, & Sugarman. Revised Conflict Tactics Scale.

Straus and Gelles used the CTS in the National Family Violence Surveys in 1978 and 1985, both national samples. They found that in about 1 in 8 couples, the husband perpetrated at least one violent act in the previous 12 months. Females were also found to perpetrate violence—with females perpetrating IPV in 12% of couples in the study (Straus & Gelles, 1990). This finding that males and females were essentially equally likely to use violence in their relationships is one of the major contributions of Straus and Gelles's work. This finding goes against conventional wisdom that males are violent and females are passive in their relationships. You are probably not surprised, then, to learn that the CTS has been criticized. It does not include spousal homicide, which does not reflect sexual symmetry (Payne & Gainey, 2009). In addition, critics point out that checklists such as the CTS do not consider the motives, meanings, and consequences of violence. Females may be using violence in relationships in response to initial violent acts by males. Moreover, even when women hit or strike their partners, they are less likely to cause serious injury compared with a male hitting or striking a female. Even without considering the context, the CTS can be used to uncover the extent to which partners use various conflict tactics, even if the underlying processes that create the conflict and response are not captured (Straus, 2007). Other concerns surround the underreporting of male violence and the overreporting of female violence by survey participants, which could contribute to the gender symmetry found (Dragiewicz, 2010), although a meta-analysis of studies using the CTS found that males are more likely to underreport (Archer, 1999). Despite these concerns, the CTS has made major contributions to the field.

National Violence Against Women Survey

Recall from Chapter 6 that the National Violence Against Women Survey (NVAWS) was a telephone survey of 8,000 women and 8,000 men aged 18 and older (Tjaden & Thoennes, 2000b). In the study, participants were asked about violence they had experienced. Specifically, they were asked about psychological and emotional abuse perpetrated by current or former spouses and cohabitating partners, and rape, physical assault, and stalking they had experienced during their lifetime. The survey was conducted, in part, to focus on violence against women and on the victim–offender relationship. Of those surveyed, 22% of the women and 7% of the men said they had been physically assaulted by their current or former intimate partner during their lifetime. Respondents were also asked about IPV occurring in the 12 months prior to the survey. More women (1.3%) than men (0.09%) experienced IPV during that time period. Other gender differences emerged in the NVAWS: Women were more likely than men to report being injured and to report their victimizations to the police. Moreover, women reported experiencing a greater number of physical assaults by the same partner (recurring victimization) than did men. Women who were victimized averaged 6.9 physical assaults by the same partner compared with an average of 4.4 assaults for male victims.

National Intimate Partner and Sexual Violence Survey

In 2010, the Centers for Disease Control and Prevention's National Center for Injury Prevention and Control launched the National Intimate Partner and Sexual Violence Survey (Black et al., 2011). This nationally representative telephone survey is conducted through random digit dial. In 2010, interviews were completed with 16,507 individuals aged 18 and over (9,086 women and 7,421 men). The survey is designed to collect information about intimate partner violence, stalking, and sexual violence. According to findings from the 2010 survey, 35.6% of women and 28.5% of men in the United States have experienced physical violence, rape, and/or stalking by an intimate partner in their lifetime. Severe physical intimate partner violence is experienced by 24.3% of women and 13.8% of men during their lifetime.

■ WHO IS VICTIMIZED?

IPV is experienced by people in all walks of life; however, certain people are at greater risk than others. For example, age is a factor in IPV risk. Younger adults are more likely to experience IPV than are older adults, although IPV perpetrated against older women has received particular attention recently. Race is also a characteristic that has been studied. Findings from the NCVS indicate that Black females are at a greater risk of experiencing IPV than are White females. The data show that the rate of IPV against Black females is 2.5 times higher than that against women of other races (Rand & Rennison, 2004). When examining race and age in the NCVS, this difference appears to be driven by the difference in rates across race for women between the ages of 20 and 24, where the variation between rates for Black and White women is most marked. It should be noted that the NVAWS data also revealed higher rates of victimization among Black women but that this difference was eliminated when other variables, such as socio-demographic and relationship variables, were included (Tjaden & Thoennes, 2000b). In other words, factors such as low income, unemployment, and marital status account for the relationship between IPV and race. Finally, much research shows that females are more likely to experience IPV than are males, although this finding has been a point of debate and deserves special attention.

PHOTO 9.1

Anyone can be a victim of intimate partner violence—but most victims do not have their pictures plastered on the news. This picture shows the injuries that singer Rihanna suffered at the hands of her then-boyfriend singer Chris Brown. How do you feel about victims having their injuries displayed and written about in this manner?

Gender and Intimate Partner Violence

Who is more likely to perpetrate and who is more likely to be victimized by IPV—males or females? A close reading of the previous sections on the extent of IPV indicates mixed findings. The NCVS, police records, emergency room data, and the NVAWS all show that females are more likely than males to be victims of IPV and that males are the dominant perpetrators. Results from other studies using the CTS suggest that this gender gap in IPV perpetration and victimization is not so evident. In a meta-analysis examining gender differences in IPV, women were found to be slightly more likely than men to engage in IPV and to do so more frequently (Archer, 2000). So, which is correct? Let's examine the findings a little more closely.

Criminal victimization survey data, police records, and emergency room data all measure more severe forms of IPV, while the CTS includes measures of slapping and pushing, which are relatively unlikely to cause injury. Serious, injurious IPV, which males are more likely to engage in than females, is rare and unlikely to be revealed through surveys. Reliance on surveys, particularly those using the CTS to measure IPV, may underestimate serious physical violence. In addition, men are less likely to seek medical attention and are less likely to report their victimization to police. Men are also less likely to define their victimization as criminal—which hinders reporting. Insofar as studies depend on males defining their experiences as criminal or on reporting to the police or seeking medical assistance, the extent of IPV victimization for males is likely to be underestimated.

So, where else are gender differences evident? First, when women are violently victimized it is more likely to be by someone they know and by intimate partners. Males are more likely to experience violence at the hands of strangers and nonintimates (Catalano, 2013). Keep in mind that males are more likely to be violently victimized—but males are generally "safe" from violence in the home or with their dating partners. Females, on the other hand, are "safe" in general—females are simply less likely to experience any type of violent victimization. When they do, however, it is more likely to be IPV than it is for males. Second, it seems that severe IPV is more a male enterprise. Males are more likely to cause serious injury in IPV incidents (Catalano, 2013). This may be because men are generally bigger and stronger than women and can more easily physically harm their partners when engaging in violence. Third, males also may use tactics in IPV incidents that are more likely to result in violence. Women are likely to throw objects at their partners, push, and shove—all behaviors that may, indeed, cause injury. Keep in mind, however, that these behaviors are less likely to cause serious damage than punching and using weapons. Although data from the 2002–2011 NCVS show that a larger percentage of IPV victimizations involving males compared with females involved a weapon (Catalano, 2013), other research shows that in these IPV incidents that involve weapons, women are more likely to cause injury to their partner than are men (Felson, 2006). Felson (2006) interpreted this finding to indicate that the reason that females are injured more often in IPV victimizations is largely due to the relative differences between males and females in size and power, and when these differences are neutralized with weapons, that males are more likely to be injured. Fourth, males are more likely to engage in intimate terrorism—the kind of violence that is rooted in power and control and that often results in serious physical injury. As a particular case, females are more likely to be victims of homicide at the hands of their intimate partners than are males (Catalano, 2013). Women are more likely to be participators in situational or common couple violence. Indeed, gender differences are greatest for physical aggression and less so for verbal aggression (Bettencourt & Miller, 1996).

Special Case: Same-Sex Intimate Partner Violence

So far, we have discussed IPV within heterosexual relationships, but people in homosexual relationships are also at risk of experiencing IPV. The kinds of behavior that are classified as IPV are largely the same for homosexual and heterosexual people. One act, however, is unique to homosexual persons: "outing an individual." If a person is not out to family, friends, coworkers, or in the community, an abuser may threaten to reveal this secret.

Although there is now an awareness of same-sex IPV, it is difficult to measure and hard to know exactly to what extent it occurs. Most of the research relies on small convenience samples rather than large-scale representative samples. Renzetti and Miley (1996) estimate that between 22% and 46% of lesbians have been in an abusive relationship, although this could mean that lesbians experienced IPV in a heterosexual relationship. Data from the NVAWS show that about half of lesbians experienced physical violence in their current intimate relationships (Neeves, 2008). Homosexual men are also at risk of being the victims of IPV, and some estimate that homosexual men are more likely than homosexual women and heterosexual men to experience IPV (Tjaden, Thoennes, & Allison, 1999) and that homosexual men experience IPV at rates similar to those of heterosexual women (Baum & Moore, 2002).

Even with the awareness of same-sex IPV, victims may still be treated differently than victims of opposite-sex IPV. There is a real fear among homosexual victims of not being believed or being demeaned or insulted by law enforcement (Jaquier, 2010). For these reasons, victims of same-sex IPV may be more reluctant to report than others. In addition, resources that are now widely available to victims, especially female victims, of IPV are not necessarily available for same-sex IPV victims. In some states, laws are written such that the partners must be opposite-sex, married, or civilly united; thus, same-sex couples who live together or are dating may find they are not protected under the same domestic violence laws (Allen, 2007). Same-sex IPV victims may be able to secure an order of protection, but doing so requires that a police report is filed—something victims may be particularly unwilling to do—and some states do not grant lesbians and gay men this remedy (Allen, 2007). Gay male victims of IPV may also have difficulty seeking shelter, since most domestic violence shelters admit only females. Finally, most domestic violence programs do not offer programming specifically designed to address same-sex IPV (Allen, 2007).

Special Case: Stalking

In recent years, a special type of victimization often tied to discussions of IPV is stalking. Although definitions of stalking vary across jurisdictions, a working definition for this term is a course of conduct that is unwanted and harassing and would cause a reasonable person to be fearful (National Center for Victims of Crime, n.d.-b). Not recognized as a crime until the 1980s in the United States, stalking is now recognized in all 50 states and by the federal government as a criminal act. State stalking laws differ, but generally, a victim must show that the behavior constitutes a course of conduct; in other words, the offending behavior must have occurred more than once. Also, the behavior must be unwanted and harassing and must cause some level of emotional distress without a legitimate purpose. Finally, the offender must be a credible threat to the victim, the victim's family, or the victim's friends (Mustaine, 2010). To this end, stalkers may show up at the victim's home or work; follow or track the victim; send unwanted letters, cards, or e-mails; damage the victim's property or home; monitor Internet, computer, and phone use; post information on the Internet or spread rumors; or threaten to hurt the victim, the victim's family, or the victim's pet (National Center for Victims of Crime, n.d.-b).

Estimates from the CDC's NISVS indicate that 1 in 6 women and 1 in 19 men have been the victim of stalking during their lifetime (Black et al., 2011). Each year, 3.4 million adults are stalked, with more than three fourths of these victims being stalked by someone they know. Young adults aged 18 and 19 are the most common victims of stalking, with individuals between 20 and 24 also experiencing high rates (Baum, Catalano, Rand, & Rose, 2009). Persons who are divorced or separated are at the highest risk for being stalked, as are persons who are poor (Baum et al., 2009). Almost 30% of stalkers are current or former intimate partners (Baum et al., 2009). Females are more likely to be stalked by current or former intimate partners than are males, with two thirds of female victims having this perpetrated by their current or former intimate partners compared to 41% of males (Black et al., 2011). Stalking can be long-term and involve frequent contact—almost half of all stalking victims experience at least one unwanted contact per week, and 11% of stalking victims have been stalked for 5 years or more, although victims most commonly report being stalked for 6 months or less (Baum et al., 2009).

The types of behaviors that stalkers engage in vary. Almost two thirds of victims received unwanted phone calls, voice or text messages. About one third of victims had rumors spread about them, received unwanted letters or e-mails, were followed or spied on, had the offender show up at various places, or had the offender wait for them (Baum et al., 2009). About one fourth of stalking victims reported being stalked through some type of technology, such as e-mail or instant messaging. Global positioning systems (GPS) can be used to monitor victims (10% of victims report), and video and digital cameras or listening devices are also used in a small percentage of stalking cases (8% of victims report) (Baum et al., 2009).

Given the unique circumstances of stalking, it often carries significant consequences for victims. Many victims fear the uncertainty that comes with being stalked, not knowing what will happen from one moment to the next. They also report fearing that the stalking will not stop (Baum et al., 2009). In addition to fear, stalking victims experience higher levels of anxiety, insomnia, social dysfunction, and severe depression than do members of the general population (Blaauw, Winkel, Arensman, Sheridan, & Freeve, 2002). As with other victims, stalking may result in loss of time at work and changes in behavior. For example, about 1 in 8 victims of stalking miss time from work, and 1 in 7 change their residence as a result of the stalking (Baum et al., 2009). About 21% of stalking victims reported changing their day-to-day activities, 13% changed their route to school or work, and 2.3% altered their appearance (Baum et al., 2009). Victims also took action to protect themselves. More than 17% changed their phone number, while 8% installed caller ID or call blocking (Baum et al., 2009). More than 13% changed their locks or installed a security system (Baum et al., 2009). Stalking also can come with economic costs. About 3 in 10 stalking victims report expenses related to dealing with their stalking, with 13% spending more than $1,000 (Baum et al., 2009).

◼ RISK FACTORS AND THEORIES FOR INTIMATE PARTNER VIOLENCE

You may be wondering at this point why people are victimized by their intimate partners. Keep in mind that there is not a singular reason why IPV occurs, but researchers have identified many factors that produce IPV. The most common factors are discussed below.

Stress

While the family and the home are seen as places of sanctuary, the family also can cause stress. Given the close physical interaction that families share, it is probably not hard to imagine scenarios that involve stress—money is tight, children are fussy, schedules are hectic. Although stress does not always result in IPV, it certainly can. How couples deal with stress and conflict can dictate the couples' likelihood of experiencing IPV.

Cohabitation

Although IPV is commonly thought of as occurring within marital relationships, it most commonly occurs within **cohabitation** relationships. In fact, the rate of IPV is highest among couples living together, and these couples experience more severe forms of violence (Wallace, 2007). There are several reasons why cohabitating couples experience more incidents of and more severe IPV. One is that individuals in these relationships may be less committed and perceive less stability—two qualities that may increase the amount of conflict in the relationship (Buzawa, 2007). Another explanation may be that these couples feel more social isolation, and abuse may be more likely to occur and continue without the support of family and friends (Stets & Straus, 1990).

FOCUS ON RESEARCH

Based on data from surveys of over 24,000 women between the ages of 15 and 49 in Bangladesh, Brazil, Ethiopia, Japan, Namibia, Peru, Republic of Tanzania, Samoa, Serbia and Montenegro, and Thailand, researchers found that alcohol abuse, being young, cohabiting, having attitudes supportive of wife beating, having partners who have outside sexual partners, having children from a previous relationship, experiencing childhood abuse, witnessing mother being beaten by partner, and being a victim or perpetrating other types of violence in adulthood were related to an increased risk of intimate partner violence. What do these findings suggest about the risk factors for intimate partner violence around the world? What are the policy implications?

Source: Adapted from Abramsky, T., Watts, C. H., Garcia-Moreno, C., Devries, K., Kiss, L., Ellsberg, M., Jansen, H. A. F. M., & Heise, L. (2011). What factors are associated with recent intimate partner violence? Findings from the WHO multi-country study on women's health and domestic violence. *BMC Public Health, 11.*

Power and Patriarchy

Power can be defined as a person's ability to impose his or her will on another. For couples, this likely involves everyday life decisions. Both men and women usually have power in relationships—for example, a man may make more money and a woman may make more decisions about the household. It is when power is abused that it may result in IPV. Power can be used to isolate and scare and take advantage, which is abusive. Patriarchy is defined as a form of social organization in which men are dominant and are allowed to control women and children. Patriarchy may allow IPV by men and even encourage it by giving men a "green light" to exercise their dominance. The research on power and patriarchy and how it relates to IPV is mixed (Coleman & Straus, 1986). There is some evidence that patriarchal norms and structural inequality are positively related to IPV rates (Yllo & Straus, 1990). Men who hold patriarchal values have been shown in other research to be more violent against women (Sugarman & Frankel, 1996). Some research shows that when couples share power and are egalitarian, there is less IPV. Conversely, other research shows that men who believe in traditional sex roles are less likely to be abusive toward their intimate partners (Bookwala, Frieze, Smith, & Ryan, 1992; Rosenbaum, 1986). In fact, Felson (2002) contends that patriarchy has little applicability to the dyadic relationships between intimate partners.

Social Learning

According to the traditions of social learning theorists, criminal behavior is learned behavior. People can learn by observing others engaging in crime and by having their own criminal behavior reinforced. Social learning theory can help understand why IPV occurs. People who grow up in homes where IPV occurs are more likely than others to be both perpetrators and victims of IPV (Foshee, Bauman, & Linder, 1999; Riggs, Caulfield, & Street, 2000). It is not just witnessing IPV that can have negative effects on later behavior; individuals who are abused or neglected as children have been shown to be more likely to engage in IPV later in life (Heyman & Smith, 2002; Widom, 1989a; Widom, Czaja, & Dutton, 2014) and to be victimized (Riggs et al., 2000; Widom et al., 2014). Widom et al. (2014) found that child abuse and neglect among children ages 0–11 was related to an increase in the odds of suffering an injury via intimate partner violence victimization in adulthood. Beyond exposure to and experiencing violence, social learning theory also addresses how definitions, values, and norms favorable to IPV play a role in IPV. Individuals who have positive expectations about the use of violence are more likely to perpetrate IPV (Foshee et al., 1999).

Disability Status

As you will read in Chapter 11, having a disability places individuals at an increased risk for victimization. Recent research has found that this increase in risk for victimization holds true for IPV victimization as well. In a study using data from two waves of the National Epidemiologic Survey on Alcohol and Related Conditions, it was found that adults having physical health impairments or mental health impairments increased the risks of IPV victimization (Hahn, McCormick, Silverman, Robinson, & Koenen, 2014). Other research conducted by the CDC has confirmed that women with disabilities are more likely than those without disabilities to be the victims of IPV (Barrett, O'Day, Roche, & Carlson, 2009; Smith, 2008).

Risky Lifestyle

According to lifestyles theory, those individuals who engage in **risky lifestyles** expose themselves to people and situations that are likely to increase their victimization risk (Hindelang, Gottfredson, & Garofalo, 1978). Although this theory has been used to explain risk of victimization, it has been less widely adopted by researchers studying IPV. Two ways in which risky lifestyles have been linked to IPV are through associating with known criminals and using alcohol and drugs.

Associating With Known Criminals

According to lifestyles theory, the more time people spend in the company of offenders, the more likely they are to become victims themselves. Although females are generally less likely to be victimized than males, when they spend time with criminal others, their risk of victimization increases—similar to how it increases for males. As noted by Carbone-Lopez and Kruttschnitt (2010), females who have criminal mates are more likely to be the victims of IPV than are females with prosocial intimate partners.

Alcohol and Drugs

In Chapter 2, we discussed the role that alcohol plays in victimization. It should come as no surprise, then, to learn that alcohol also has been studied in connection with IPV. A wealth of research shows that IPV offenders use illegal drugs and/or drink excessively more than others (Scott, Schafer, & Greenfield, 1999). Findings from the NVAWS show that binge drinkers (people who have five or more drinks in a setting) are 3 to 5 times more likely to engage in IPV against a female than those who abstain from drinking (Tjaden & Thoennes, 2000b). Some researchers argue that the relationship between alcohol use and IPV perpetration is mediated by attitudes that support the use of IPV (Buzawa, 2007).

Alcohol use by the victim is also important to examine. Alcohol use is related to IPV victimization in several ways. First, women who have histories of IPV have higher rates of substance abuse than women without such histories (Coker, Smith, Bethea, King, & McKeown, 2000). Second, many victims report having used alcohol or drugs prior to being victimized (Greenfeld & Henneberg, 2000). Using drugs or alcohol may make them more vulnerable or may affect them cognitively and behaviorally such that they initiate or respond to conflict differently than they would when not under the influence. Third, alcohol and drug use may be likely after an IPV victimization. In this way, alcohol or drug use may be a consequence of IPV rather than a cause (Devries et al., 2014).

■ CONSEQUENCES OF INTIMATE PARTNER VIOLENCE

Negative Health Outcomes

One of the most obvious physical effects of IPV is, of course, **injury.** IPV is one of the most common reasons why women present in the emergency room (ER). More than one third of women who seek care in the ER for violence-related injuries do so because they were victimized by a current or former spouse, a boyfriend, or a girlfriend (Rand, 1997). Often, these injuries that bring women to ERs are quite serious; in one study of women who sought care in a metropolitan ER, almost 3 in 10 required hospital admission and more than 1 in 10 required major medical treatment (Berios & Grady, 1991). In addition to injury, female victims of IPV are more likely to experience frequent headaches and to suffer from gastrointestinal problems (Family Violence Prevention Fund, 2010). IPV may also result in back pain, gynecological disorders, pregnancy difficulties, sexually transmitted diseases, central nervous system disorders, and heart or circulatory conditions (Centers for Disease Control and Prevention, 2010b).

Death

Although it may seem surprising, in 2007, intimate partners committed 14% of all homicides (Catalano et al., 2009). The risk of being murdered by an intimate partner is greater for females than for males—70% of victims killed by an intimate partner are female. A sizeable portion of fatalities of women are caused by IPV (Catalano, 2013). In recent years, between one third and four tenths of female murder victims were killed by an intimate partner (Catalano, 2013). In contrast, of those men who were murdered, only 3% were killed by their current or former spouse or boyfriend (Catalano, 2013). Fatal outcomes of IPV are also found for abused women who are pregnant. IPV is the leading cause of homicide and injury-related deaths among pregnant women (Frye, 2001). Also of note is that Black females are more likely than White females to be murdered by a spouse, boyfriend, or girlfriend (Catalano et al., 2009).

Psychological/Emotional Outcomes

IPV also commonly carries significant psychological and emotional consequences. Remember that IPV can come in the form of emotional or psychological abuse—by definition, it creates emotional and psychological harm. Being physically abused can also cause such harm. Victims of IPV are likely to experience depression, anxiety, sleep disorders, and posttraumatic stress disorder (Centers for Disease Control and Prevention, 2010b). Some of the psychological consequences are quite severe—battered women have higher rates of suicide than do nonbattered women (Stark, 1984). Attempting suicide and considering suicide are also more common among women experiencing IPV than among other women (Coker et al., 2002). Suicide ideation and attempt was about 6 to 9 times more likely for adolescent girls who had been sexually or physically hurt by a dating partner than for girls who did not report such harm (Silverman, Raj, Mucci, & Hathaway, 2001).

Revictimization

One of the consequences of being a victim of IPV is that additional IPV events commonly occur, called **revictimization.** As noted in the discussion of the NVAWS, the typical victim of IPV experiences more than one victimization. Women in the study reported experiencing, on average, 6.9 physical assaults by the same partner. Males also experienced revictimization—averaging 4.4 assaults by the same partner. Research using official records of rearrest, victim interviews, offender interviews, court records, probation records, and shelter records has supported this finding that many victims are abused again and that many offenders reoffend (see Cattaneo & Goodman, 2005). For example, in a study that examined victims of arrested batterers, 28% experienced physical abuse, threats, or unwanted contact during the 3-month follow-up period (Cattaneo & Goodman, 2003). In a study of men convicted of domestic violence, 16% were rearrested or had a complaint made against them by the same victim (Taylor, Davis, & Maxwell, 2001).

This pattern of revictimization is not a new revelation. The **cycle of violence** was first described by Lenore Walker in 1979. Through interviews with battered women, she identified a common pattern of abuse that involves different phases. In the first phase, the **tension-building phase,** the abuser and victim interact in a close relationship that likely involves positive and charming behavior on the part of the abuser. This period of tranquility does not last as day-to-day pressures and more serious events generate tension. These periods of tension and stress precede what may at first be minor violence. The woman is likely to attempt to appease the abuser, "tiptoeing" around and trying not to incite the abuser's violence. This tension, though, continues until the abuser explodes into a fit of rage. When this occurs, the second phase begins. The **acute battering phase** involves the abuser engaging in major and often serious physically assaultive behavior. This phase is followed by the **honeymoon phase.** The abuser is calm and loving and most probably begging his partner for forgiveness. He likely is making promises not to engage in violence again. If the relationship continues, Walker proposes that the cycle of violence is likely to start over. Remember, though, not all abuse is repetitive and most abuse is not the explosive type of violence that Walker's cycle of violence concerns.

■ WHY WOMEN DO NOT LEAVE ABUSIVE RELATIONSHIPS

The cycle of violence is but one reason why women do not leave abusive relationships. The ups and downs of these relationships, which often include some positive "high" points, can be confusing emotionally. Remember that often the person who is abused sees positive traits in the abuser—probably loved and maybe still loves him. Even when women do make a decision to leave, many return to their abusers. In fact, women leave an average of six times before permanently severing their relationships (Okun, 1986). But many women do, in fact, eventually leave.

Why is leaving so difficult? As mentioned, people in relationships often feel a love for and commitment to the other person that they define as important. This commitment may be even more important if the two are married, and marriage and relationships may be defined as more important than personal safety, especially for women (Barnett & LaViolette, 1993). They may also share children; thus, leaving may mean splitting the family and taking children away from the other parent.

Some women may not be financially capable of leaving their abusers. Women may be economically dependent on their abusers and feel that they are unable to leave for financial reasons. They may not be employed and may lack the resources necessary to establish independence. In addition, abused women may be isolated from their friends and family and lack a support system that could help them as they try to leave. Abusers often purposefully isolate their partners from social networks, thus making it difficult for them to leave (National Center for Victims of Crime, 2008a). Finally, women may be embarrassed, ashamed, and scared. Feeling scared may be warranted. Abused women often have been living a life characterized by a pattern of abuse. Even if they want to leave, research shows that women are more likely to be killed after leaving their husbands than while living with them (Wilson & Daly, 1993).

■ CRIMINAL JUSTICE SYSTEM RESPONSES TO INTIMATE PARTNER VIOLENCE

As noted, the major developments in recognizing and responding to IPV first occurred in the 1970s. Between 1975 and 1980, 44 states passed laws concerning IPV, mainly focusing on the prevention of and protection from IPV and providing victims needed resources (Escobar, 2010). Today, every state has some type of IPV law. These laws and how they impact criminal justice and social service agency responses are discussed in the following subsections.

The Police Response

Traditionally, police were reluctant to become involved in IPV cases. They often did not make arrests in these types of cases, instead allowing privacy to trump police involvement. The reasons for this lack of formal response are varied. Police may not want to intervene in IPV cases because of their perception that such a case will not result in a conviction (Buzawa & Buzawa, 1993). They also may view what happens behind closed doors and within families as beyond the purview of the criminal justice system. Police also may not want to respond to or make arrests in these cases since they are thought to be quite dangerous for the police (Kanno & Newhill, 2009), although others have disputed this claim (Hirschel, Dean, & Lumb, 1994; Pagelow, 1997). Also, victims may request that officers not make an arrest or may tell officers that they will not follow through with charges; hence, police have been reluctant to arrest (Wallace, 2007).

The ability of police to make arrests, even when they are willing to do so, may also be limited. Historically, police have been unable to make an arrest for a misdemeanor without a warrant. A **misdemeanor** is a crime that usually is less serious than a felony and carries a maximum penalty of a year in jail. Police could make an arrest for a misdemeanor only if they had a warrant or if they had witnessed the event. As you might imagine, police often do not arrive on the scene of a crime until after the violence occurs and, thus, would not be able to make an arrest without first getting an arrest warrant. This inability of police to make arrests changed during the 1980s, when research was conducted on the utility of arrests in IPV cases.

In 1984, Lawrence Sherman and Richard Berk conducted the **Minneapolis Domestic Violence Experiment** to examine the deterrent effect of arrest on domestic violence perpetrators. To make it a true experiment, the researchers set up the study so that the police randomly responded to calls for domestic violence in one of three ways: The police could make an arrest that would result in one night of incarceration, separate the parties for a period of 8 hours, or advise the couple using the officer's judgment. For eligible calls, the officer would take a color-coded card indicating which of the three response options he or she was to use for the call. The study ran from March 17, 1982, to August 1, 1982, and covered 314 eligible domestic violence calls. For each call, biweekly follow-up interviews were conducted with the victims for 6 months, although only 62% of the victims participated in the initial follow-up interview and slightly less than half participated in all 12 interviews. The researchers also collected police reports during the 6-month follow-up to check for additional domestic violence incidents.

What did the researchers find? From both the victim interviews and police records, the researchers concluded that those who were arrested were less likely than others to commit additional domestic violence offenses. Only 10% of those who were arrested committed a subsequent offense, according to police records, as compared with 24% of those who were separated and 19% of those who were advised. Interview data also indicated that arrest was most effective, with only 19% of those arrested committing additional domestic violence. One third of those who were separated and 37% of those advised by officers committed additional offenses, according to victim interviews.

Based on these findings and lawsuits against the police for negligence and unequal treatment of female victims, advocates for mandatory arrest in domestic violence cases were given ample evidence for their position. Not long after, many states began revamping their domestic violence laws to allow police to make arrests in misdemeanor domestic violence cases without a warrant. Other states enacted mandatory arrest policies. **Mandatory arrest policies** are those that prescribe arrest by police officers when there is probable cause that a crime was committed and enough evidence exists for an arrest. Note that mandatory arrest policies may create a situation in which a victim does not want the offender to be arrested and the police make an arrest regardless. By 1992, seven states had adopted mandatory arrest policies (Dobash & Dobash, 1992). Today, more than 20 states have mandatory arrest policies (Iyengar, 2007).

It is interesting that mandatory arrest policies began to be adopted so quickly following the Minneapolis Domestic Violence Experiment because replication studies conducted in five jurisdictions—Charlotte, Dade County, Colorado Springs, Milwaukee, and Omaha— provided different results. In only one location, Dade County, did police records show that arrest had a deterrent effect. In Omaha, Charlotte, and Milwaukee, arrest deterred offenders initially but caused an escalation of domestic violence over time. One of the most important findings from the replication studies was that arrest differentially impacted offenders. Specifically, it was found that arrest of employed offenders did produce a deterrent effect, likely because these offenders had a lot to lose. Conversely, unemployed offenders were more likely to engage in

Photo Credit: © Thinkstock/Comstock.

PHOTO 9.2

Minneapolis, Minnesota, was the location of the famous **Minneapolis Domestic Violence Experiment** that effectively changed the way that domestic violence cases were policed throughout the country.

violence (Maxwell, Garner, & Fagan, 2001). From the replication studies, it was concluded that mandatory arrest policies may not be a "one-size-fits-all" solution. Instead, they may be beneficial for some offenders and actually detrimental for others in terms of recidivism.

As states look to adopt policies for their law enforcement officers' responses to IPV, they have other options in addition to requiring arrest. Some states have **pro-arrest** or **presumptive arrest policies**. These policies require arrest but limit this requirement to specific situations in which certain criteria are met. That is, there is a presumption of arrest. These policies are similar to mandatory arrest policies in that the decision to arrest may be independent from the desires of the victim. Consent on the victim's part is not required. When deciding not to make an arrest, an officer may be required to provide a written justification for doing so (Payne & Gainey, 2009).

Less strict policies on policing IPV are **permissive arrest policies**. These policies do not mandate or presume that an arrest will be made by law enforcement when warranted. Rather, they allow police to use their discretion to best determine how they should respond in IPV situations.

In addition to these policies used by police departments, another outgrowth of the movement to handle IPV incidents differently has been for officers to make dual arrests. In a **dual arrest**, both the offender and the victim are arrested. This practice of arresting both the victim and the offender is tied to the belief that many offenders are also victims and that IPV is part of mutual, common-couple violence. When officers arrive on the scene and there is evidence that both parties engaged in violence, they can make a dual arrest. Many states have guidelines as to how and when dual arrests can be made so that victims are not erroneously arrested. Some states have policies that require the officer to arrest only the aggressor; others require that police officers provide written justification for making a dual arrest (Hirschel, Buzawa, Pattavina, Faggiani, & Reuland, 2007). Although dual arrest does not always occur, a large-scale study of dual arrest using National Incident-Based Reporting System data found that it does appear to be more common in homosexual intimate partner incidents and when the offender is female (Hirschel, 2008). As you might imagine, arresting a victim may create a situation in which the victim is afraid to call for assistance if needed in the future for fear of being arrested again. Moreover, victims may not want to participate in the prosecution of the offender if they were also arrested (Bui, 2001).

Court Responses

Law enforcement officers are not the only ones who have an important job in responding to and dealing with incidents of IPV. After an incident has been reported to and investigated by the police, the prosecutor is then given the police file to determine whether formal charges will be brought against the offender. Early criticisms of the prosecutor's job as it relates to IPV centered on the belief and research showing that prosecutors rarely brought formal charges against IPV offenders, even after arrest (Chalk & King, 1998; Hartman & Belknap, 2003). Some have concluded that there is a "widespread underprosecution of domestic violence cases" (Sherman, 1992, p. 244). The current rate of prosecution for these types of cases is in dispute, but a recent review of more than 135 studies in more than 170 jurisdictions found that on average about one third of reported offenses and more than 60% of arrests resulted in the filing of charges by the prosecutor. In addition, about one third of the arrests and more than half the prosecutions resulted in the defendant being found guilty (Garner & Maxwell,

2009). The authors noted that there was a large amount of variation across jurisdictions in terms of prosecution and conviction rates, which implies that making blanket statements regarding prosecution and conviction of all IPV cases is troublesome. Additional research is also clearly needed in this area to help resolve the conflicting viewpoints about prosecution and conviction rates.

What factors do prosecutors consider when deciding whether to prosecute a person for IPV? Research shows that prosecutors are most likely to move forward with prosecution when the victim has been visibly physically injured (Jordan, 2004). Other research has shown that prosecutors consider whether the victim or the defendant had been drinking or under the influence of drugs at the time of the incident (Jordan, 2004; Rauma, 1984; Schmidt & Steury, 1989) and the history between the victim and the offender (Schmidt & Steury, 1989). Finally, victim willingness to participate in the process has been shown to be related to prosecutorial decision making in IPV cases (Dawson & Dinovitzer, 2001).

Let's discuss victim participation and how it impacts prosecution. As it may seem, one reason that prosecution and subsequent conviction may be difficult to achieve is lack of participation on the part of the victim. The victim may not want to testify against the offender. He or she may still be involved with the offender. They may share children. The victim may be fearful of what will happen if he or she testifies in court. The victim may have calculated that he or she cannot "afford" to move forward in the criminal justice process. Whatever the reason, some jurisdictions have **no-drop prosecution** policies—the victim is not able to drop the charges against the offender, and the prosecutor's discretion in deciding to charge is curtailed. After adoption of such policies, rates of dismissal have dropped (Davis, Smith, & Davies, 2001). Despite this seemingly positive result of no-drop prosecution policies, there is concern that they may be harmful to victims in that the offender may retaliate against the victim and forced participation may be victimizing. Also concerning is that victims may be reluctant to call the police if they are aware of the no-drop policy. In some states, victims may not have to testify against their abusers if they are legally married to them. The laws that provide this exception are known as **spousal or marital privilege laws**. In states that have these laws, the number of times the option not to testify against the abuser can be used varies—in Maryland, it can be used only once (Bune, 2007).

More recently, the court system has responded to IPV by adopting special courts that handle domestic violence cases. Designed to increase coordination among criminal justice and social service agencies, these courts hold criminals accountable and consider the needs of victims (Gover, MacDonald, & Alpert, 2003). These courts often have a therapeutic focus, which allows for the offender to get help identifying the causes of his or her abusive behavior and controlling this behavior in the future (Gover et al., 2003). Although evaluations of domestic violence courts are not widespread, evidence suggests that participating in the court and its associated programs generally reduced recidivism against the same victim (Goldkamp, Weiland, Collins, & White, 1996) and rearrests (Gover et al., 2003).

■ LEGAL AND COMMUNITY RESPONSES

The criminal justice system is not the only entity that addresses the needs of victims of IPV. Legal and community services also have been developed to assist victims.

Protective Orders

One way victims can seek protection from their abusers is by obtaining a **protective order** or a restraining order. Both types of order are designed so that victims will be protected from their offenders. Victims of IPV may get an order in hopes of ensuring their protection. These orders may include stay-away orders, no-contact orders, or peaceful contact orders. Some states differentiate between protective and restraining orders, with the criminal court issuing protective orders and the civil court issuing restraining orders. This is not the arena to attempt to differentiate how every state operates in this area, but commonalities will be discussed.

Once an offender is arrested, the judge in a criminal court may issue a no-contact order at the offender's arraignment or first court appearance. Some states require the issuance of a no-contact order in IPV cases. The order stays in effect for a specified amount of time (typically 2 weeks) or until it is amended by the court, sometimes at the request of the victim and agreement of the prosecutor (Hartman & Alligood, 2010). If a victim would like to acquire a restraining order against the offender, the victim is generally required to go before the court and ask for a temporary order in an "emergency hearing." The judge determines whether an order should be issued. If the victim would like to extend the order, then a second, more comprehensive hearing is conducted (Hartman & Alligood, 2010). Even though a defendant (the offender) may be unaware of a hearing for a temporary order, the offender is notified if the victim requests a more permanent order. Depending on the state, if the order is granted, it stays in place for the length of time set by statute. For example, in the California Superior Court, a civil restraining order in IPV situations can stay in place for up to 5 years.

Similar to the disparate procedures and orders states have in place, enforcement of protective orders and restraining orders varies from state to state. Despite this, states are mandated under the 1994 Violence Against Women Act to receive full faith and credit from courts for orders granted in other states. Most states have also passed their own full faith and credit laws that require enforcement of other states' protective orders as though they were enacted in that state. So what do states do when a person violates a protective order? Most states have criminal sanctions that can be implemented when an offender violates an order. A person who violates an order may be charged with a felony, a misdemeanor, or contempt of court (Office of Justice Programs, 2002). Some states have laws that make a violation a new offense, and some require that anyone found guilty of violating a protective order serve time in confinement (Office of Justice Programs, 2002). In other states, a violator may face bail forfeiture or revocation of bail, pretrial release, or probation (Office of Justice Programs, 2002).

Although protective orders are available in all states for the protection of IPV victims, most eligible victims do not secure protective orders. Research from the NVAWS shows that 17.1% of female victims of assault perpetrated by intimate partners received protective orders and 36.6% of female victims of intimate partner-perpetrated stalking received protective orders (Tjaden & Thoennes, 2000b). Women who get orders of protection may be different from those who do not—they are more likely to be employed full-time, to have been injured by the abuse, to have experienced sexual coercion by the offender, and to be severely depressed, with more serious symptoms of mental health problems (Wolf, Holt, Kernic, & Rivara, 2000). Research shows that women tend to seek orders of protection after long periods of abuse that they view as escalating (Fischer & Rose, 1995). Women tend to make the decision to get an order of protection when they had had "enough" (Fischer & Rose, 1995).

Also important to consider is the effectiveness of protective orders. A body of research shows that protective orders reduce recidivism. Even so, these studies show that orders are violated between 20% and 40% of the time (Jordan, 2004). Victims also report a variety of feelings regarding protective orders, with some feeling satisfied and having a sense of security after receiving a protective order (Keilitz, Hannaford, & Efkeman, 1997). Others report being frustrated with the timely and confusing process they had to go through in order to secure a protective order (Ptacek, 1999). These feelings may be tied to the fact that victims often have to be the ones to notify the police if a protective order is violated—meaning that decision making and enforcement is largely up to victims. This, quite understandably, may be a role that few victims relish.

RIPPED FROM THE HEADLINES

Current federal law prohibits persons who have been convicted of domestic violence from possessing a firearm. There is proposed federal legislation, however, that would expand this law to cover dating partners and persons who are similarly situated as a spouse, if that person is protected by the domestic or family violence laws of the state or tribal jurisdiction in which the incident occurred or where the victim lives. The legislation would prohibit the sale of a firearm or ammunition to a person convicted of misdemeanor stalking. It also expands the definition of misdemeanor domestic violence to include the use or attempted used of physical force or a deadly weapon. The National Rifle Association (NRA) has sent a letter to at least two different senators' offices opposing the legislation. In the letter, the NRA argued that the legislation would turn "disputes between family members and social acquintances into lifelong firearm prohibitions" (Bassett, 2014) and that the bill would simply cast too wide a net for federal gun restrictions. What do you think about this proposed legislation? Should it be passed?

Sources: S.1290-Protecting Domestic Violence and Stalking Victims Act of 2013 Bill Summary. Retrieved from http://www.congress.gov. Bassett, L. (2014, June 25). NRA fights for convicted stalkers' gun rights. Retrieved from http:// www.huffingtonpost.com.

Domestic Violence Shelters

Another resource available to victims of IPV is domestic violence shelters. First opened for women in 1974 in Minnesota, domestic violence shelters offer a place of refuge for victims. They provide a range of services, including short-term room and board, emergency clothing and transportation, counseling, assistance with the legal process, 24-hour crisis lines, programs for children, and help with seeking employment. Most domestic violence shelters allow residents to stay more than 30 days in residence, and about one third allow stays of 60 days or more (Lyon & Lane, 2009). It appears that domestic violence shelters are indeed meeting the needs of victims. In a recent study, it was found that almost three fourths of domestic violence victims reported that the assistance they received from shelters was very helpful (Lyon, Lane, & Menard, 2008).

The services shelters offer may be lacking when it comes to some victims. Lesbian women are more likely to believe that shelters are for heterosexual women and to have negative experiences with shelters than are other women (Lyon et al., 2008). Men also are unlikely to seek assistance from domestic violence shelters as compared with women; shelters were traditionally designed to service only female victims, although recent efforts to assist male victims have been made. The first domestic violence shelter exclusively for men opened in Minnesota in 1993. This shelter housed 50 men within the first 6 months of opening (Cose, 1994). Minority women may also be reluctant to utilize domestic violence shelters. They may perceive that their particular needs are not met, especially if the staff is largely White (Lyon et al., 2008). More generally, victims may experience problems with other residents, and the lack of privacy may be difficult (Lyon & Lane, 2009).

Health Care

Protective orders and domestic violence shelters are common resources for victims of IPV, but health care professionals are also in a unique position to help. Recall that IPV is one of the major reasons that women seek medical assistance from ERs and is a key reason why women become the victims of homicide. Because of the injuries caused by IPV and the fact that health care professionals see women on a regular basis, they are in a position to help women who are victimized, even if the violence is not the reason the woman is seeking medical treatment. As such, many health care organizations recommend that patients be screened for IPV (Waalen, Goodwin, Spitz, Petersen, & Saltzman, 2000). Screening can allow for victims to be identified and then subsequently referred to services. Screening typically involves the medical professional asking questions either from a screening instrument or other instrument designed to assess whether a patient is a victim of IPV. Despite this innovative approach, screening rates remain low. One study found that only 13% of victims of acute IPV were asked by a doctor or nurse about violence, even though they had presented at the emergency department (Krasnoff & Moscati, 2002).

Can you think of ways in which improved screening by health care professionals may be achieved? This holistic approach to IPV intervention appears to be a critical link, so improving health care screening is needed, particularly for women. It may be a way for victimizations that often remain hidden to be revealed in a safe, controlled environment. It may be the step victims need to get assistance or referrals to resources that can help them stop the cycle of violence.

SUMMARY

- There are two major types of intimate partner violence (IPV)—intimate terrorism and situational or common couple violence. Within these types, IPV can be physical, emotional/psychological, or sexual.
- Since IPV often occurs in private, it is somewhat difficult to measure. That being the case, it is hard to know the true extent to which people are victimized by intimate partners.

- Three commonly used resources on IPV statistics are the National Crime Victimization Survey (NCVS), the Conflict Tactics Scale (CTS), and the National Violence Against Women Survey (NVAWS). Depending on the resource, estimates of IPV vary. Both the NCVS and NVAWS indicate that more females than males are victimized. Research using the CTS shows that gender symmetry may exist.
- Young people, Black women, and those with lower socioeconomic status are the most likely to be victimized.
- IPV can also occur in same-sex relationships. By some estimates, homosexual men experience higher rates of IPV victimization than do homosexual women or heterosexual men.
- Stalking is a special type of victimization. Stalking is a course of conduct that is unwanted and harassing and that would cause a reasonable person to be fearful. The three most common types of stalking are unwanted phone calls or messages, unwanted letters or e-mails, or stalking using new technology such as e-mail or instant messaging. The main fear with stalking is the uncertainty of what will come next.
- Female victims of IPV tend to experience more severe and more frequent violence than do male victims.
- Stress, cohabitation, power and patriarchy, social learning, risky lifestyles, and alcohol use and/or drug use are all risk factors for IPV victimization.
- In addition to injury and death, victims of IPV may also experience psychological and emotional consequences. Posttraumatic stress disorder, depression, suicide ideation, suicide attempts, suicide completion, anxiety, and sleep disorders all have been linked to IPV victimization.
- Revictimization can also occur. Court reports, victim surveys, and official records all demonstrate that victims of IPV are at risk of experiencing additional IPV incidents.
- Police historically have been reluctant to deal with IPV cases. The Minneapolis Domestic Violence Experiment changed how police respond to IPV cases. Results from the study showed that arresting offenders reduced recidivism, although replication studies did not find this clear result. Instead, the replication studies showed that arrest impacted offenders differentially, with those who were employed being deterred but others not.
- Courts have responded to the problem of IPV by instituting no-drop prosecution policies and adopting domestic violence courts.
- Processes of obtaining a protective order vary from state to state, but in all states, protective orders against offenders can be obtained by victims of IPV.
- Domestic violence shelters also serve victims of IPV by providing safe and secure living arrangements. These shelters also link victims with other social services to help them transition out of abusive relationships.
- Health care professionals also may be able to help victims of IPV. Screening instruments have been developed to help health care officials identify and refer patients who have been victimized.

DISCUSSION QUESTIONS

1. On what side of the gender symmetry debate do you fall? When females are offenders, do you think it is largely in response to male aggression? When female victims do not apply for protective orders, do you think it encourages recurring IPV? Why or why not?

2. What measures should the criminal justice system, social service agencies, and the health care community take to reduce IPV victimization?

3. Given the fact that females traditionally have been considered the "true" victims of IPV, how do you think this affects the criminal justice system's response when males report crime, especially in instances where there are few or no visible physical injuries?

4. What are the advantages and disadvantages of mandatory arrest policies for IPV?

KEY TERMS

intimate partner
violence

physical violence

emotional abuse

sexual violence

intimate terrorism

situational couple violence

National Crime Victimization Survey
(NCVS)

Conflict Tactics Scale (CTS)

National Violence Against Women
Survey (NVAWS)

cohabitation

power

patriarchy

social learning

risky lifestyles

injury

revictimization

cycle of violence

tension-building phase

acute battering phase

honeymoon phase

misdemeanor

Minneapolis Domestic Violence
Experiment

mandatory arrest policies

pro-arrest policies

presumptive arrest policies

permissive arrest policies

dual arrest

no-drop prosecution

spousal or marital privilege laws

protective order

screening

INTERNET RESOURCES

Menweb (http://www.menweb.org/battered/)

Men can also be the victims of intimate partner violence. One Internet resource for men is Menweb, which provides information for men who have experienced intimate partner violence. It also includes links to news items and research that highlight intimate partner violence perpetrated by women against men. Men's stories of victimization are also presented.

Office on Violence Against Women (http://www.ovw.usdoj.gov/index.html)

Housed in the U.S. Department of Justice, the Office on Violence Against Women administers both financial and technical assistance to help communities develop programs, policies, and practices with the goal of ending domestic violence, dating violence, sexual assault, and stalking. On its website, you can find information on these types of violence against women, information about grant opportunities and funded projects, and help for persons who have been victimized. It also provides up-to-date information about federal legislation and policies directed at violence against women.

"Teen Dating Violence" (http://www.cdc.gov/violenceprevention/intimate partnerviolence/teen_dating_violence.html)

Recently, research on intimate partner violence has uncovered that teens are at risk of experiencing violence within their dating relationships. For information on teen dating violence, including what it is, facts about teen dating violence, why it occurs, and its consequences, visit the Centers for Disease Control webpage on teen dating violence. Also, included are links to various resources for more information on and assistance with teen dating violence.

WomensLaw.org (http://www.womenslaw.org/)

This website is a resource for persons who are experiencing or who have experienced intimate partner violence. It includes links and information about state and federal laws addressing intimate partner violence as well as how victims can better navigate the criminal justice system. People can find information on how to apply for protective orders, how to prepare for court, and how to find assistance safely in their communities.

10

VICTIMIZATION AT THE BEGINNING AND END OF LIFE

CHILD AND ELDER ABUSE

Rosienell Adams, a 27-year-old woman, was recently convicted of aggravated child abuse against her 22-month-old son. The son had scars, burns, and other injuries, but one burn was particularly gruesome: a third-degree burn on his hand in the exact shape of an iron. In court, a woman with the Children's Hospital Intervention and Prevention Services Clinic testified that if the burn had been accidental, the scar would show evidence of a "glancing" burn rather than the outline of the iron, which is consistent with the iron being held on the child's hand. After the burn occurred, the mother did not seek medical care for her son, even though the child's father drove her to the hospital. She simply pretended to get medical attention ("Gadsden Mother Convicted," 2011).

This case is an example of child abuse. Had it occurred to a person over the age of 60, it would qualify as a case of elder abuse. This section is devoted to these special victims—those who are very young and those who are older. These two types of victimizations are discussed in the same section because they are defined by the victim's position in the life course. Accordingly, the ways in which policy and actors respond to the victim and victimization are tied to the stage in the life course. Also, the causes and consequences of child abuse and elder abuse have a direct tie to the victim's stage in the life course.

Source: Adapted from *The Gadsden Times*, 2011.

■ CHILD MALTREATMENT

If the case of physical child abuse perpetrated by Rosienell Adams had occurred prior to the late 19th century, it might have gone without intervention. In fact, child maltreatment was not much of a concern to the public or the justice system until an 1875 case involving a 9-year-old girl, Mary Ellen. She was abused and neglected by her caregivers, but a concerned neighbor intervened to get her help. This neighbor, Mrs. Wheeler, quickly found that no policies or laws were in place to address issues of child maltreatment. As such, she did not receive the assistance she had hoped for. She turned to Henry Bergh, the founder and president of the Society for the Prevention of Cruelty to Animals (SPCA). He intervened on her behalf in court and was able to get Mary Ellen removed from the custody of her abusers and placed in a children's home. After this case, Bergh formed the New York Society for the Prevention of Cruelty to Children (Payne & Gainey, 2009; Pfohl, 1977). This development, coupled with the House of Refuge movement—which called for institutions to provide care for maltreated children—and the development of the first Juvenile Court in 1899 in Cook County, Illinois, served to create services that would address, at least in part, maltreated children.

It would take another 50 years, during the 1940s and 1950s, for child maltreatment to again receive meaningful attention. This time, the attention came from the medical community. Pediatric radiologists began to notice in X-rays broken bones that they believed were attributable to child abuse. These X-rays provided empirical evidence to support the occurrence of child abuse. In the 1960s, the *Journal of the American Medical Association* published a set of presentations on battered child syndrome, further contributing to the recognition of child abuse as a real issue and a medical condition (Payne & Gainey, 2009). During the 1970s, these developments spurred widespread concern about child maltreatment that led to the passage of the first federal legislation addressing child abuse.

What Is Child Maltreatment?

Child maltreatment can take two major forms: abuse and neglect. Abuse occurs when a person causes harm to a child (a person under the age of majority in a state, usually 18 years). It consists of actions done to a child rather than what a person fails to do for a child. Abuse can be physical, but it can also be emotional or sexual. What distinguishes these three types of abuse? Physical abuse may at first appear to be self-explanatory, but it merits some discussion to distinguish the differences between physical abuse and punishment. **Physical abuse** involves injury or physical harm of a child. Examples of physical abuse include hitting, punching, burning, slapping, and cutting. It may result from a person's intention to hurt a child, but it also may result from a misuse of discipline, such as a person using a belt to punish a child (Saisan, Smith, & Segal, 2011). When physical discipline is used not to teach a child right from wrong but, instead, out of anger and to make a child live in fear, it crosses the line from discipline into abuse (Saisan et al., 2011). Table 10.1 displays examples of physical abuse.

Emotional abuse may not carry physical marks, but it also can be quite harmful for children. When you think of **emotional abuse,** what first comes to mind likely is name calling, yelling, threatening, or bullying. These are overt and aggressive acts of emotional abuse. Emotional abuse can take less aggressive forms. For example, belittling, shaming, and humiliating a child are forms of emotional abuse. In addition, ignoring, rejecting, or limiting physical contact with a child constitutes emotional abuse (Saisan et al., 2011). As you may imagine, these behaviors can cause psychological harm for a child and may be detrimental to the child's social development. For a detailed description of emotional abuse, see Table 10.1.

Table 10.1 ■ Types of Child Maltreatment	
Physical	Deliberate attempt to harm a child. It can be distinguished from discipline by one question: Is the action intended to teach the child right from wrong or to create a life of fear for the child? Examples: • Hitting • Burning • Slapping (Saisan, Smith, & Segal, 2011)
Emotional	Damaging to the child's mental health and/or social development; often leaves psychological marks Examples: • Belittling, shaming, and humiliating a child • Name calling and making negative comparisons to others • Telling a child he or she is "no good," "worthless," "bad," or "a mistake" • Frequent yelling, threatening, or bullying • Ignoring or rejecting a child as punishment—using the silent treatment • Withholding hugs, kisses, and other forms of physical contact from the child • Exposing the child to violence or the abuse of others (Saisan et al., 2011)
Neglect	Parents or caregivers do not provide the child's basic needs, such as adequate food, clothing, hygiene, and supervision. Examples: • Physical: failure to provide necessary food or shelter, or lack of appropriate supervision • Medical: failure to provide necessary medical or mental health treatment • Educational: failure to educate a child or attend to special education needs • Emotional: inattention to a child's emotional needs, failure to provide psychological care, or permitting the child to use alcohol or other drugs (Child Welfare Information Gateway, 2008b)
Sexual	Rape, sexual assault, molestation, prostitution, or sexual exploitation of a child; also includes incest with children. Involving children in sexually explicit conduct or simulation for the purpose of producing a visual depiction of conduct is also child sexual abuse (The Child Abuse Prevention and Treatment Act).

Source: Reprinted with permission from Helpguide.org © 2001–2010. All rights reserved. For HelpGuide's series on Abuse, visit www.Helpguide.org.

The third type of abuse is sexual abuse of a child. Child sexual abuse can be active and involve physical touching but does not have to involve touching. Exposing children to sexual content or situations can be sexually abusive, as can involving children in pornography or prostitution. See Table 10.1 for a description of what child sexual abuse includes. The Child Abuse Prevention and Treatment Act defines child sexual abuse as

> the employment, use, persuasion, inducement, enticement, or coercion of any child to engage in, or assist any other person to engage in, any sexually explicit conduct or simulation of such conduct for the purpose of producing a visual depiction of such conduct; or the rape, and in cases of caretaker or inter-familial relationships, statutory rape, molestation, prostitution, or other form of sexual exploitation of children, or incest with children. (Sec. 111.42 U.S.C. 5106g)

See the Focus on International Issues box for a description of the types of abuse to which children are subjected beyond the United States.

FOCUS ON INTERNATIONAL ISSUES

Child maltreatment can include behaviors beyond abuse and neglect as we think of them in the United States. To recognize the suffering of children from aggressive acts over the world, June 4 is the International Day of Innocent Children Victims of Aggression. First celebrated in 1983, this day is a time to reflect on the fact that violence around the world impacts too many children. Two of the latest reports on the effects of armed conflict on children have noted that the conflict in Colombia between the government and guerilla forces has resulted in about 150,000 displaced children. This displacement is due to violence, threats of violence, landmines, the recruitment of child soldiers, and a lack of access to basic human services. As many as 14,000 children have been recruited into the conflict in Colombia. In addition, children in the Democratic Republic of the Congo and South Sudan continue to be impacted by the Lord's Resistance Army (LRA). As of May 2012, over 600 children have been recruited, girls have been reported to be sexually violated, 45 children have been killed, and 39 maimed.

Source: Adapted from International Day of Innocent Children Victims of Aggression. (2012). Retrieved from http://www.soschildrensvillages.ca/news/news/child-protection-news/child-rights-news/pages/innocent-children-aggression-298.aspx.

Another way children can be maltreated is not abuse in that it is not active and does not result from the direct, intentional, and active harming of a child. Neglect results when a child's basic needs are not met. Children are, by definition, reliant on their caregivers for almost everything—food, shelter, transportation, love, and care. Legally, caregivers are required to meet these basic needs and are bound by law to make sure that children are getting a certain level of care. When this does not happen, children are said to be neglected. As such, neglect can be physical, medical, educational, or emotional, depending on the required need not being met. For example, if food is not being provided to a child, that is physical neglect. If a child routinely misses school because of a parent, it is educational neglect. See Table 10.1 for a description of the types of neglect.

Measurement and Extent of Child Maltreatment

It is difficult to know the true extent of child maltreatment in the United States. Child maltreatment is hard to detect for several reasons. Children may be too young to verbalize what is happening to them, even if they are capable of understanding that they are being maltreated. This is one of the reasons why child abuse goes undetected—children are not likely to tell anyone that they are being harmed. Another is that parents, caregivers, and other family members are often the perpetrators. These people are unlikely to tell the police or other authorities that abuse or neglect is occurring if they are the perpetrators. Others who may be concerned about the child may not know that maltreatment is occurring, so they may not report either.

Nonetheless, what we do know about the extent of child maltreatment mainly comes from official data sources. Because, as you will read later in this section, all states require that certain people report suspected child maltreatment to authorities, official statistics reflect these reports. The **National Child Abuse and Neglect Data System (NCANDS)** provides an analysis of annual data on child abuse and neglect reports made to state child protective service agencies, including those in the District of Columbia and Puerto Rico (U.S. Department of Health and Human Services [DHHS], 2010). Once a referral is made to the child protective service agency, the agency determines whether the case will be screened in to determine if maltreatment has occurred or if a child is at risk (DHHS, 2010). The case can also be screened out if the agency determines that no maltreatment has occurred or that the child is not at risk (DHHS, 2010).

Another resource for data on maltreated children is the **National Incidence Study (NIS)**. Most recently, data from the fourth NIS (NIS-4) were released. This study includes information on cases investigated by Child Protective Services but also cases that were

Photo Credit: © Bettmann/Corbis.

identified by professionals in the community. To receive information on these cases, 10,791 professionals (called sentinels) submitted data forms on children with whom they had contact who were victims of abuse and/or neglect during the study period (3-month reference period in either 2005 or 2006) (Sedlak et al., 2010).

According to the NCANDS, in 2012, there were about 3.4 million referrals in the United States. These referrals dealt with the alleged maltreatment of about 6.3 million children (DHHS, 2012). Of the referrals, about one fifth resulted in a substantiated disposition, which means the child was a victim of some form of maltreatment (DHHS, 2012). In over half of the cases, a professional made the report of suspected child abuse (DHHS, 2012). Results from the NIS-4 study indicate that more than 1.25 million children during 2005–2006 experienced maltreatment that resulted in demonstrable harm (Sedlak et al., 2010). When using a less restrictive definition, the NIS-4 study estimated that 1 in 25 children experienced maltreatment (even if they were not yet harmed by maltreatment but the sentinel thought the maltreatment endangered the child or if a child protective services investigation indicated maltreatment) (Sedlak et al., 2010). Neglect accounted for the majority of cases reported in the NCANDS—more than three fourths suffered from neglect. Next most common was physical abuse (18.3%), followed by sexual abuse (9.3%) (DHHS, 2012).

As with other official data sources, these estimates of child maltreatment are probably low since child abuse and neglect are likely to go undetected and unreported to Child Protective Services and/or law enforcement. One way to tap into this "dark figure of crime" is through surveys. As noted before, children may not be able to identify whether they have been victimized. To address this problem, researchers in one study asked questions directly of children aged 10 years and older, but asked the caregiver who was "most familiar with the child's daily routine and experiences" questions about victimization experiences of children younger than 10 (Finkelhor, Turner, Ormrod, & Hamby, 2009, p. 2). Results from this study showed that 10.2% of the children had been maltreated by a significant adult in their life during the previous year (Finkelhor, Turner, Ormrod, & Hamby, 2009).

The most serious consequence of child maltreatment is death. Fortunately, most cases of child maltreatment do not result in fatalities, but some children lose their lives far too early at the hands of an abuser. In 2012, an estimated 1,640 children died as a result of child maltreatment (DHHS, 2012). Unlike maltreatment reported to NCANDS, generally, about one third of child fatalities were attributed exclusively to neglect, while one third were caused by multiple forms of maltreatment (DHHS, 2010).

Who Are Victims of Child Maltreatment?

Based on reports to child protective service agencies, the "typical" victim of child maltreatment is quite young. In fact, victims from birth to 1 year old had the highest rate of victimization (DHHS, 2012). More than 80% of children who died from child maltreatment were under the age of 4 (DHHS, 2010). Victims were almost equally likely to be males as females (48.7% compared to 50.9%). As you may imagine, however, female children are more likely than male children to be the victims of child sexual abuse (Sedlak et al., 2010). Male children, on the other hand, are at greater risk of dying from child maltreatment than are female children (DHHS, 2010). White children made up the largest percentage of reports (44.0%), but African American (21.0%) and Hispanic (21.8%) children were disproportionately represented in reports, given their composition in the population (DHHS, 2012). Similarly, the NIS-4 study revealed rates of maltreatment for Black children to be higher than those for both White and Hispanic children (Sedlak et al., 2010).

Who Perpetrates Child Maltreatment?

To understand the causes of child maltreatment, it is particularly instructive to identify the perpetrator of the abuse. Data from the NCANDS show that biological parents are the most likely perpetrators of child maltreatment reported to Child Protective Services (DHHS, 2012). More than 80% of child maltreatment incidents in 2012 were perpetrated by parents. Mothers are more likely to be perpetrators of child maltreatment than are fathers, except in cases of child sexual abuse (DHHS, 2010). This difference may be attributable to the fact that mothers are likely to be responsible for the majority of caregiving responsibilities. Of the incidents not perpetrated by parents, other relatives make up the largest group, followed by unmarried partners of parents (DHHS, 2010). Most perpetrators are White (48.5% in 2009) and between the ages of 20 and 39 (66.4% in 2009) (DHHS, 2010).

It may be difficult to imagine that a parent could take the life of a child, but of the child maltreatment incidents that resulted in death, more than three fourths were perpetrated by one or both parents (DHHS, 2010). Of these, 27.3% were perpetrated by a mother acting alone, 14.8% by a father acting alone, and 22.5% by both a mother and father (DHHS, 2010). Slightly less than 5% of child fatalities were caused by a parent's partner (DHHS, 2010).

Risk Factors for Child Maltreatment

For other types of victimization, we have examined risk factors tied to the victim that place him or her at more risk of being victimized as compared with others. The very nature of being a child may place children at risk. That is, children's vulnerability in terms of size and not being able to protect themselves may make them targets. In addition, children who are "fussy" and who have difficult temperaments are more prone to abuse than other children (Rycus & Hughes, 1998). Examining the family structure and caregivers for factors tied to an increased risk for child abuse is also instructive, since traditional explanations of victimization such as routine activities and lifestyles theory do not apply.

Familial Risk Factors

Several factors about a child's family are tied to increased risk of maltreatment. One key factor consistently found in the lives of children who are maltreated is that they come from families living in poverty. This is not to say that all maltreated children live in poverty, but poverty and child maltreatment are correlated. Poverty is often tied to unemployment and a lack of general resources needed to meet the needs of children, often creating stress that leads to violence and neglect (Bond & Webb, 2010). In the NIS-4 study, children with parents who were unemployed and who lived in low socioeconomic status households had higher rates of maltreatment than other children (Sedlak et al., 2010).

In addition to poverty, the structure of the family impacts risk of child maltreatment. Children who live with two biological parents are at lowest risk of being maltreated, while children who live with a single parent who has a cohabiting partner are at greatest risk (Sedlak et al., 2010). Those children who live with a single parent with a cohabiting partner have a rate of abuse more than 10 times that of other children (Sedlak et al., 2010). In particular, boyfriends of mothers are responsible for a disproportionate share of child maltreatment. One study found that boyfriends account for half of all child abuse committed by nonparents (Margolin, 1992). In addition, family size is connected to maltreatment. Children who live in households with four or more children are at greater risk of maltreatment than children who live in households with two children (Sedlak et al., 2010).

Individual Risk Factors

Factors specific to the individual also relate to risk of child abuse. According to social learning theory, abusive behavior is learned behavior. In this way, people abuse or neglect their children because they experienced or witnessed such behavior when they were younger. Age is also a factor. Research shows that young fatherhood is a risk factor for child maltreatment (Guterman & Lee, 2005) and that young teen mothers are particularly vulnerable to abusing and neglecting their children (Afifi & Brownridge, 2008). This relationship may be due to the fact that young mothers do not have the resources to meet the needs of their children. Also, they may not have the maturity to deal with the stresses of full-time parenthood. Both factors may lead to abuse and neglect.

Particularly in regard to neglect, parents may also simply lack the knowledge of what children need. In this way, they may not be equipped to provide the nurturing, food, and medical care required (Cantwell, 1999). In addition, parents may lack judgment for making good parenting choices, such as deciding when a child is old enough to be left alone (Cantwell, 1999). Under these circumstances, parents' behavior may meet the definitions of neglect.

Other individual risk factors include substance use by parents. Like criminal behavior and aggression, generally, child abuse and neglect are often linked to substance abuse. Between one third to two thirds of all child maltreatment cases involve substance use (DHHS, 1999). Substance abuse is tied to violent behavior but is also linked to an inability or unwillingness to provide physical or emotional support to children (Wilcox & Dew, 2008). Parents with addictions often fail to place their children before their addiction and may leave their children alone and unsupervised or in the care of untrustworthy people (Bond & Webb, 2010). Substance abuse often co-occurs with other problems such as mental illness, unemployment, stress, and impaired family functioning, all of which may increase risk for child maltreatment (Child Welfare Information Gateway, 2009). Parental mental illness may also place children at risk. Depression, particularly, has been linked to child maltreatment (Conron, Beardslee, Koenen, Buka, & Gortmaker, 2009). Depression may lead to poor parenting in that parents suffering from depression may be emotionally unavailable to their children (Weinberg & Tronick, 1998).

Children may also have certain characteristics that place them at increased risk of experiencing maltreatment. Data from NCANDS show that children who have a disability are more likely to be maltreated than other children (DHHS, 2012). Children with behavioral problems and medical problems are also at an increased risk for maltreatment (DHHS, 2012).

Consequences of Child Maltreatment

It is often said that children are resilient—that they bounce back from adversity to overcome even the worst of situations. This is often the case. For some children, being abused or neglected will seemingly not leave lasting scars. But for others, the effects of maltreatment are deeply rooted and long lasting, impacting multiple areas of their lives.

Physical, Cognitive, and Developmental Effects

We have already discussed that abuse and neglect may cause death, but there are other physical effects that could be present. One outcome that has recently garnered attention is **shaken baby syndrome,** which causes brain hemorrhages, skull fractures, and retinal hemorrhages (U.S. National Library of Medicine, 2011). It is estimated that between 1,200 and 1,400 children in the United States alone are injured or killed each year by shaking (U.S. National Library of Medicine, 2011).

Shaken baby syndrome is a specific consequence of a specific action—shaking a baby—but other outcomes of maltreatment can impact development for children. Depending on the severity of abuse and neglect, it may cause impairments to brain development, which can affect cognitive, language, and academic abilities (Watts-English, Fortson, Gibler, Hooper, & De Bellis, 2006). Children who are neglected may not have their basic developmental needs met and may suffer from developmental delays. Consider that parents who are neglectful are less likely to provide an enriched environment that would allow children to flourish. Moreover, neglected children are less likely to be getting the necessary food and nutrients that a brain needs to develop normally. Accordingly, neglected children are more likely to experience developmental delays (Child Welfare Information Gateway, 2008a).

Psychological Effects

It is common for victims of all types of child maltreatment to experience guilt, shame, fear, and anger in response to their victimization. Children may blame themselves for the abuse or neglect or, if their family dissolves, for the breakup of their family unit. At least in some children, abuse and neglect have been associated with panic disorder, anxiety, depression, posttraumatic stress disorder, attention-deficit/hyperactivity disorder, reactive attachment disorder, anger, and dissociative disorders (Child Welfare Information Gateway, 2008a).

Although all types of maltreatment may cause psychological harm, they are associated more commonly with different types of outcomes. For example, physical abuse may lead to internalizing emotions, which may lead to anxiety and depression (Bond & Webb, 2010). Neglect is commonly associated with children being unable to trust and being socially withdrawn (Bond & Webb, 2010). The psychological effects of sexual abuse often evince themselves in interpersonal relationships later in life. Sexually abused children often have difficulty developing and maintaining healthy sexual relationships (Browne & Finkelhor, 1986). In addition, child sexual abuse victims are more likely to experience anxiety, depression, anger, and problems with substance abuse than nonabused children (Browne & Finkelhor, 1986). Child sexual abuse is also linked to suicidal ideation (Martin, Bergen, Richardson, Roeger, & Allison, 2004).

Effect on Criminality and Other Behaviors

As discussed in Chapter 2, research has uncovered a victim–offender overlap in that people who are victims are often criminal and vice versa. In this way, one of the risk factors for criminality is being a crime victim. This relationship holds true for being a victim of child abuse as well. Research consistently has shown that persons who suffer child abuse are more likely to be involved in delinquent and criminal behavior than others. Being abused and neglected increases the risk of arrest for violent and general juvenile offenses by 1.9 times (Widom, 2000). This effect carries over to adulthood—abused and neglected children are 1.6 times more likely to be arrested as adults (Widom, 2000). Being sexually abused as a child increases the chances that a person will offend later in life as well. Sex offenders are more likely to have a history of sexual abuse than non-sex offenders (Jesperson, Lalumiere, & Seto, 2009).

The effect of maltreatment on crime and delinquency may be gendered in that, in retrospective studies of offenders, the relationship between child maltreatment and offending appears to be more relevant for females than males. In fact, female inmates reported more childhood maltreatment than did male inmates (McClellan, Farabee, & Crouch, 1997).

Criminal and delinquent behaviors are just one type of maladaptive behavior that is associated with child maltreatment. Many other behavioral consequences have been linked to child maltreatment. There appears to be a clear link between abuse and neglect in childhood and later use of alcohol and illegal drugs. It is not surprising, then, to learn that a large proportion of people in drug treatment programs report that they were abused as children (Kang, Magura, Laudet, & Whitney, 1999; Rounds-Bryant, Kristiansen, Fairbank, & Hubbard, 1998). Generally, abused and neglected children are more likely to have problems in school (Kelley, Thornberry, & Smith, 1997). In addition, these children are more likely to experience teen pregnancy (Kelley et al., 1997). Children who are sexually abused are more likely to engage in risky sexual behavior and to contract a sexually transmitted disease (Johnson, Rew, & Sternglanz, 2006). Beyond consequences tied to sexual health, child sexual abuse victims are more likely to have eating disorders (Smolak & Murnen, 2002), to engage in self-mutilating behaviors (Fliege, Lee, Grimm, & Klapp, 2009), and to experience revictimization (Classen, Pales, & Aggarwa, 2005).

Effect on Adult Poverty

The link between child maltreatment and later delinquency and criminal behavior has been explored, but other outcomes have also been investigated. Generally, this research has highlighted that child maltreatment can have long-lasting negative effects. Being maltreated as a child has been shown to increase a person's chances of living in poverty and being unemployed. In one study, adults who had experienced maltreatment in childhood had two times the risk of being unemployed (Zielinski, 2009). Physical abuse in childhood was linked to a 60% increase in the risk of living in poverty in adulthood (Zielinski, 2009).

Responses to Child Maltreatment

Legislation

As previously noted, the landmark federal legislation defining child maltreatment, the **Child Abuse Prevention and Treatment Act** (Pub. L. 93-247), was passed in 1974. This act provided definitions of child abuse and neglect and, as noted below, required states to pass mandatory reporting laws for suspected cases of child maltreatment in order to receive certain federal funding. It also established a national clearinghouse for information on child abuse, promoted research on child abuse and neglect, and provided grant and other monies to support research and programs designed to address child maltreatment.

FOCUS ON RESEARCH

In a prospective study, children who had a case of child abuse or neglect reported prior to the age of 12 were compared to matched samples of children who did not and followed into early adulthood, it was found that children with abuse reports had higher rates of perpetrating intimate partner violence (IPV) than other children. In addition, gender differences were found. Men who were maltreated were more likely to perpetrate IPV than maltreated women. What do these findings suggest about social learning theory? Why would this effect be different for males and females?

Source: Adapted from Millett, L. S., Kohl, P. L., Jonson-Reid, M., Drake, B., & Petra, M. (2013). Child maltreatment victimization and subsequent perpetration of young adult intimate partner violence: An exploration of mediating factors. *Child Maltreatment, 18,* 71–84.

The mandatory reporting requirement was especially important given the difficulty in detecting child abuse. Currently, every state in the United States has some form of **mandatory reporting law** for suspected child abuse cases. These laws require that certain individuals report to authorities (e.g., law enforcement, a child protective agency, Department of Health and Human Services) if they suspect that a child is a victim of maltreatment. Mandatory reporters typically include individuals who work with children, such as teachers, day-care workers, law enforcement, mental health care providers, social workers, and school personnel. Some states require film developers to report. States differ regarding the standard of knowledge that triggers the duty to mandatorily report. In some states, it is a "reasonable suspicion"; in others, it is a "reasonable cause to believe"; and in others, a person is required to "know or suspect" (Child Welfare Information Gateway, 2010b). When a person does not report suspected child maltreatment when required to do so, he or she could be held criminally liable. Most typically, this is a misdemeanor that carries a fine as punishment (Child Welfare Information Gateway, 2010b). Civil liability, however, can attach for nonreporting. To further encourage reporting, the Child Abuse Prevention and Treatment Act requires states to have legislation that provides immunity from prosecution, both criminally and civilly, for individuals who report suspected child abuse in "good faith." See the following box for Kentucky's mandatory reporting law for suspected cases of child abuse. In 2009, most reports were made by legal and law enforcement professionals (16.7%) and education personnel (16.6%) (DHHS, 2012). The next most common reporters were social services personnel (11.1%) (DHHS, 2012).

Another approach to reducing child abuse through legislation has been through **safe haven laws.** These laws allow mothers or custodial parents who are in crisis to relinquish their babies anonymously to designated places so that their babies are protected and can receive medical care until a permanent home is found. The mother or custodial parent is protected from criminal prosecution if he or she follows the requirements of the safe haven laws. As of May 2010, 49 states and Puerto Rico had adopted safe haven laws (Child Welfare Information Gateway, 2010a). Most states allow infants (up to 72 hours old in some states, up to 1 month in others, and other ages stipulated in other states) to be dropped off at hospitals, health care facilities, law enforcement agencies, emergency service providers, or fire stations (Child

KENTUCKY MANDATORY REPORTING REQUIREMENTS REGARDING CHILDREN

Who must report?	Any person must report abuse or neglect of a child.
Standard of knowledge	Any person who knows or has reason to believe that a child is being neglected or abused must report.
Definition of applicable victim	An "abused or neglected child" is any person who is under the age of 18, and whose health or welfare is harmed or is threatened with harm when his parent, guardian, or other person exercising custodial control or supervision of the child

- inflicts physical or emotional injury or allows such to be inflicted;
- creates or allows to be created a risk of physical or emotional injury;
- engages in conduct that makes the parent unable to care for the needs of the child (e.g., alcohol or drug abuse);
- continuously or repeatedly fails or refuses to provide essential parental care and protection for the child, considering the age of the child;
- commits or allows to be committed sexual abuse, exploitation, or prostitution of the child;
- creates or allows to be created a risk of sexual abuse, exploitation, or prostitution of the child;
- abandons or exploits the child;
- fails to provide the child with adequate care, supervision, food, clothing, shelter, and education or medical care necessary to the child's well-being (exemption is made for parents who elect not to provide medical treatment for religious reasons); or
- fails to make sufficient progress on a court-approved case plan that would allow the child to be returned to the custody of the parent such that the child remains in foster care for 15 of the most recent 22 months.

Who to report to?	• Local law enforcement: Department of Kentucky State Police • Department of Social Services of the Cabinet for Human Resources • State or County Attorney

Source: Reprinted by permission of RAINN, Rape, Abuse and Incest National Network through the support of Hogan Lovells.

Note: This information in this chart is intended to be current through December, 2013. The information is not presented as a source of legal advice. You should not rely for legal advice on statements or representations made within the Web site or by any externally referenced Internet sites. If you need legal advice upon which you intend to rely in the course of your legal affairs, consult a competent, independent attorney.

Welfare Information Gateway, 2010a). As you may imagine, the goal of these laws is to reduce infanticide and abandonment of babies and to ensure that parents who feel they are incapable of caring for their infants know they can, without penalty to themselves, leave their children in the safe hands of others.

Criminal Justice System Response

Despite the difficulty in detecting child abuse, when the criminal justice system is made aware of suspected cases of child abuse, the cases are often treated seriously. Recent research analyzing 21 studies on prosecutions of child abuse cases revealed that they are treated similarly to other violent crimes (Cross, Walsh, Simone, & Jones, 2003). For cases that were carried forward with charges, conviction rates averaged 94% (Cross et al., 2003).

One reason why conviction rates may be high is because of the protections afforded to victims in the courtroom. Recognizing the special care that maltreated children may need from the criminal justice system, courtroom assistance is provided to them in the form of a **guardian ad litem (GAL).** A GAL appears on behalf of the child in court to represent the child's best interests. In child abuse and neglect cases involving allegations against a parent, GALs are often required since, by definition, the child's interests conflict with those of the parent. Many times the GAL will be a court-appointed special advocate, a volunteer with the National Court Appointed Special Advocates Association (2010). In addition to having court-appointed advocates, children may also be allowed to testify through videotape, closed-circuit television, or a two-way mirror rather than testify in the courtroom with the suspect present (Bennett, 2003). In addition, the judge may choose to clear the courtroom of all observers or of the suspect during the child's testimony (National Center for Prosecution of Child Abuse, 2010). Anatomically correct dolls may also be used to facilitate testimony so that the child can use the doll to demonstrate abusive behavior (National District Attorneys Association, 2008). In addition, the courtroom's furniture may be reorganized to make it more comfortable for testifying (Chon, 2010).

■ ELDER MALTREATMENT

What Is Elder Maltreatment?

Maltreatment of the elderly is discussed in the same section as maltreatment of children because victimization of these two groups is similar in many ways. Both children and the elderly can be abused because of their status—they rely on others for their care. Because of this special status, persons who are charged with their care bear a special responsibility. When they do not meet this responsibility, they may be committing abuse or neglect.

Generally, maltreatment of a person over the age of 60 is considered elder maltreatment. Similar to child maltreatment, elder maltreatment comes in many forms. **Physical elder abuse** is nonaccidental harm against an elderly person that causes pain, injury,

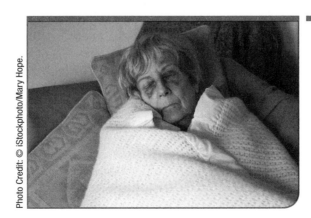

Photo Credit: © iStockphoto/Mary Hope.

PHOTO 10.2

An 83-year-old woman who was physically abused by her home health assistant rests at home after being released from the hospital.

or impairment (National Center on Elder Abuse, 2011). Hitting, beating, pushing, shoving, slapping, kicking, punching, and burning are examples of physical abuse. In addition, it is elder physical abuse to force-feed, inappropriately administer drugs, inappropriately use physical restraints, and use physical punishment against elderly persons (National Center on Elder Abuse, 2011). It is also elder maltreatment to emotionally abuse an elderly person. **Emotional or psychological elder abuse** occurs when emotional pain or distress is caused by intimidation, humiliation, ridicule, blaming, verbal assaults, insults, and harassment (National Center on Elder Abuse, 2011). Less direct forms of emotional or psychological elder abuse include treating an elderly person like an infant; isolating an elderly person from family, friends, or activities; and refusing to engage or speak with the elderly person (National Center on Elder Abuse, 2011). Older adults can also be sexually abused. Unlike children, who cannot give consent to engage in sexual conduct, adults can as long as they are cognitively able to do so. **Sexual elder abuse** takes place when sexual contact occurs with an elderly person without his or her consent. This contact can be physical touching (e.g., penetration, kissing) but can also be nonphysical, such as showing an elderly person pornographic images against his or her will or coercing a woman to undress against her will (National Center on Elder Abuse, 2011).

Neglect of elderly persons is also a form of maltreatment. When an elderly person is under someone's care and that person fails to fulfill a caretaking obligation, it is **neglect** (National Center on Elder Abuse, 2011). One of these obligations may be fiduciary in that persons may be responsible for paying for an elderly person's care. In addition, in-home service providers may be neglectful if they fail to provide necessary care (National Center on Elder Abuse, 2011). Neglect at its most extreme comes in the form of abandonment. **Abandonment** occurs when an elderly person is deserted by a person who has assumed responsibility to provide his or her care or by a person who has physical custody of the elderly person (National Center on Elder Abuse, 2011).

Two additional types of maltreatment are specific to elderly persons. One is **financial exploitation,** which involves the illegal or improper use of an elderly person's property, assets, or funds (National Center on Elder Abuse, 2011). This misuse can be carried out by anyone, not just a caretaker. Examples of financial exploitation include cashing an elderly person's check without permission, stealing money, coercing an elderly person into signing a document such as a will, and forging an elderly person's signature (National Center on Elder Abuse, 2011). Elderly persons are also at risk of having a conservatorship, guardianship, or power of attorney misused. A power of attorney is a legal document that grants a person the ability to act on another's behalf (Stiegel, 2008). An example of **power of attorney abuse** is provided in the following box. Seniors should also be wary of health care fraud and abuse. This type of elder maltreatment is perpetrated by nurses, doctors, health care workers, and professional care workers. It includes such behaviors as not providing health care but charging as though it were provided, double-billing or overcharging for medical services, overmedicating, undermedicating, recommending fraudulent remedies, and Medicaid fraud (Robinson, de Benedictis, & Segal, 2011).

Although not a form of maltreatment committed by others, you should also be aware that older adults may self-neglect. **Self-neglect** occurs when elderly persons refuse or fail to provide the care they need for themselves or to take appropriate safety precautions. Examples of self-neglect are not eating or drinking, refusing to take necessary medication, and lack of personal hygiene (National Center on Elder Abuse, 2011).

ABUSE OF DURABLE POWER OF ATTORNEY: CASE EXAMPLE

Helen was an 85-year-old woman who was in poor health. Her daughter, Susan, was designated as her durable power of attorney, but Susan took advantage of this role. She sold Helen's home and placed the money from the sale into bank accounts in Helen's name, but a year later, she withdrew all the money. Instead of using the money for Helen's care, Susan used it for her own business ventures and personal expenses. Once Helen realized that the money was gone, she contacted the civil courts, but she could not afford a civil attorney and did not find much help with the free legal services program for elders. She also received little help from the Adult Protective Service Agency. Helen lost all hope. Six weeks later, Helen died.

Source: Stiegel, L. A. (2008). Durable power of attorney abuse: A National Center on Elder Abuse fact sheet for criminal justice professionals. Copyright © American Bar Association, 2008.

Measurement and Extent of Elder Maltreatment

It is difficult to know to what extent elderly people are maltreated in the United States each year. One reason that a true picture of elder maltreatment is hard to paint is because many elderly persons may not report their victimization to law enforcement. This lack of reporting can be due to several reasons (Hodge, 1999). Elderly persons may not want to report if the perpetrator is a family member or loved one. They also may be dependent on the care of the perpetrator and be fearful that if they report, the person will retaliate against them. A real worry may also be that they will not have anyone to care for them and will be forced to live in an institutionalized setting. In addition, they may be unaware of the abuse, especially in cases of financial or medical abuse. It is also possible that elderly persons feel shame, humiliation, and embarrassment regarding their maltreatment that impedes their seeking assistance. Finally, they may be poor witnesses in that they may not recall specific details, may be confused about what happened, and may forget about their victimization (Hodge, 1999).

Reports From Adult Protective Services

Because reporting to the police is limited, to understand the extent of elder maltreatment, we must look to resources outside of police reports, although official reports to other agencies are often used. For example, similar to what is done for child abuse, if elder maltreatment is suspected, some people are required to report this suspicion to Adult Protective Services in their jurisdiction. Others may use Adult Protective Services as a reporting resource even if not required to report (e.g., a concerned neighbor). The National Elder Abuse Incidence Study was conducted in 1996 using reports made to Adult Protective Services Agencies in a sample of 20 counties in 15 states and reports from sentinels—trained individuals who have frequent contact with the elderly (Tatara,

Kuzmeskus, Duckhorn, & Bivens, 1998). It measured the extent to which domestic elder maltreatment (maltreatment of elderly persons in noninstitutionalized settings) occurred against individuals aged 60 or older during 1996.

From this study, it was estimated that 449,924 elderly persons experienced abuse and/or neglect (Tatara et al., 1998). Few of these victims (16%) had their cases reported to and substantiated by Adult Protective Services (Tatara et al., 1998). In 1996, there were 236,479 reports of suspected maltreatment made to Adult Protective Services (actual reports, not including reports from sentinels). Almost half the cases were substantiated after Adult Protective Services investigated (Tatara et al., 1998). Most of these cases involved maltreatment by another (62%), as opposed to self-neglect (Tatara et al., 1998).

Also using information from Adult Protective Services, Teaster et al. (2006) produced estimates of elder maltreatment for the 2003 fiscal year. These estimates were produced based on survey responses of Adult Protective Services contacts in each state, who responded about elder maltreatment cases in their records. In 2003, 253,426 reports of maltreatment against persons aged 60 and older were made to Adult Protective Services. Of these reports, 76% were investigated and 35% were substantiated (Teaster et al., 2006).

Estimates Derived From Surveys

Elder maltreatment estimates also have been derived through survey research. In the first large-scale random sample survey of elder maltreatment, Pillemer and Finkelhor (1988) found that the prevalence rate of elder maltreatment was 32 persons per 1,000. The National Crime Victimization Survey is not the best resource for elder maltreatment victimization statistics. Although it does include elderly persons in its sample, it asks questions only of persons who are not institutionalized, reports only estimates broken down for persons in certain age groups, and measures only criminal victimization. To examine elder victimization, the latest survey provides estimates for persons aged 65 and older. Using these data, the violent victimization rate in 2007 for persons aged 65 and older was 3.3 per 1,000, and the property crime victimization rate was 75.0 per 1,000 (Bureau of Justice Statistics, 2010). Persons in this age category had the lowest victimization rates.

Other efforts have been made to produce estimates of the extent of elder maltreatment in the United States using surveys. One national-level study was conducted using the **National Social Life, Health, and Aging Project.** This sample included 3,005 individuals aged 57 to 85 who lived in the community. They were asked if they had experienced verbal, financial, or physical maltreatment during the previous year. The results of the study do not provide estimates of maltreatment perpetrated by nonfamily members, but 9% of the sample reported verbal maltreatment, 3.5% reported financial maltreatment, and 0.02% reported physical maltreatment by family members (Laumann, Leitsch, & Waite, 2008).

Special Case: Elder Maltreatment in Institutions

Slightly more than 5% of the population aged 65 and older live in nursing homes or assisted living facilities (Orel, 2010). Although these facilities are charged with caring for people who cannot find this care in their own homes, sometimes people are abused or neglected there. According to Adult Protective Services records, the majority of incidents of elder maltreatment occur in domestic settings. Only 6% of substantiated reports of elder maltreatment occurred in long-term care settings, and 2% occurred in other locations, which included assisted living facilities (Teaster et al., 2006). Another source of data regarding elder maltreatment in long-term care facilities is the **Long-Term Care Ombudsman Program.** Every state is required to have an ombudsman program under the federal Older Americans Act. The Long-Term Care Ombudsman Program receives complaints about elder maltreatment in long-term care facilities. In 2012, more than 193,000 complaints about long-term care were made to the program. Of these complaints, 9,999 were for abuse, gross neglect, or exploitation (Administration on Aging, 2012). Institutions with high percentages of residents suffering from dementia (Talerico, Evans, & Strumpf, 2002) and that have low staff-to-patient ratios and frequent staff turnover (as cited by Bachman & Meloy, 2008) are at risk of having high levels of elder maltreatment.

Special Case: Intimate Partner Violence of Older Women

As women get older, if they remain in abusive relationships, it makes sense that these relationships will remain abusive without intervention. It is also possible that women enter into new relationships that are abusive. Although research shows that older women are less likely to experience intimate partner violence than their younger counterparts, older women do still face some risk. One study reported that almost 2% of women over the age of 55 in the sample reported physical abuse in their intimate relationships (Zink, Fisher, Regan, & Pabst, 2005). Similar percentages reported experiencing sexual abuse (Zink et al., 2005). Most commonly, the person who perpetrated the abuse was the woman's spouse (Zink et al., 2005). This research suggests that older women may be at risk of elder maltreatment not only at the hands of family members but also by their intimate partners.

Special Case: Financial Exploitation of the Elderly

Elder persons may be at particular risk of being financially exploited given their age. In a recent study of adults aged 60 and older in Arizona and Florida, researchers discovered that older adults were at risk of fraud. In fact, 60% of the respondents in their survey indicated being targeted by fraud in the previous year, with 14% saying the fraud had been completed. In terms of what older adults are likely to experience, 10% experienced a type of shopping or purchasing fraud—they had someone attempt to sell them a phony subscription to a magazine or something else. Financial fraud was also experienced by the sample. Slightly more than 16% had someone attempt to trick them into providing financial information. A greater percentage of the sample was targeted for consumer fraud. Almost one quarter had someone try to get them to pay money to claim a phony prize, while 22% had someone try to get them to give money to a phony charity or religious organization (Holtfreter, Reisig, Mears, & Wolfe, 2014).

Who Are Victims of Elder Maltreatment?

Adult Protective Services reports and survey data show that females make up a greater proportion of victims of elder maltreatment than do males (Bureau of Justice Statistics, 2010; Tatara et al., 1998; Teaster et al., 2006). This disproportionate representation of females in victimization statistics is unlike most types of victimization. Why do you think this is the case? There may be several reasons. One reason is that people may be more watchful over older women and may be more likely to report suspected cases of maltreatment. Another reason may be due to the longer life expectancy of women—they make up a larger proportion of the elderly population than do males (Zink et al., 2005). Another reason may be tied to the victim–offender relationship. As you will learn in the following section, perpetrators of elder maltreatment are often spouses, and elderly females are at risk of experiencing domestic violence at the hands of their partners. Some of the maltreatment presented in the statistics may be domestic violence. This overrepresentation of females was not found in the large study of financial fraud victimization, however. In that study, being male was associated with a greater chance of being targeted for fraud (Holtfreter et al., 2014).

As mentioned, elder maltreatment includes maltreatment of individuals over the age of 60; however, not all persons in this age group share similar risks of experiencing maltreatment. From Adult Protective Services reports, it seems that older persons are at greatest risk. In fact, slightly less than half (43%) of substantiated cases of maltreatment were against individuals who were 80 years old or older (Teaster et al., 2006). Along with gender and age, another demographic characteristic to consider is race. In both surveys and in official Adult Protective Services data reports, White elderly persons are shown to be the majority of the victims (Bureau of Justice Statistics, 2010; Laumann et al., 2008; Teaster et al., 2006).

Characteristics of Elder Maltreatment Victimization

Most cases of investigated and substantiated elder maltreatment are of self-neglect (Teaster et al., 2006). Next most common are caregiver neglect cases, followed by financial exploitation cases (Teaster et al., 2006). Results from the National Incidence Study were slightly different. Although self-neglect cases were most common, physical abuse cases were the next most commonly substantiated, followed by abandonment, emotional/psychological abuse, financial/material abuse, and neglect (Tatara et al., 1998). These differences are likely due to temporal differences in study time period and in study design. From the National Social Life, Health, and Aging Project, it was found that verbal maltreatment committed by family members was more common than both financial maltreatment or physical maltreatment perpetrated by family members; physical maltreatment was the least commonly experienced type of elder maltreatment out of the three types examined (Laumann et al., 2008).

Who perpetrates elder abuse? Adult Protective Services data show that females make up the majority of suspected perpetrators, although these statistics were based on reports from only 11 states (Teaster et al., 2006). Most often, an adult child was the perpetrator, constituting one third of all alleged perpetrators in substantiated elder maltreatment cases (Teaster et al., 2006). Other family members were the alleged perpetrators in 22% of the cases, and 11% of the alleged perpetrators were spouses or intimate partners (Teaster et al., 2006). More than three fourths of the alleged perpetrators were under the age of 60; about one fourth were between the ages of 40 and 49 (Teaster et al., 2006).

Risk Factors for Elder Maltreatment

Although it may be hard to imagine how anyone could harm or neglect an elderly person, certain risk factors place a person at risk of being a perpetrator or a victim of elder maltreatment.

Perpetrator Risk Factors

If the family has suffered from domestic violence, elder maltreatment may be an outgrowth of this domestic violence pattern. As persons age and roles change, the parents who were once the abusers may become the abused by children who hold resentment. In this way, the children may be continuing a cycle of violence (Fedus, 2010). Even if abuse was not present in the family's history, adult children who have taken on a caregiving role may find it to be quite stressful. This stress may overwhelm them to the point that they become abusive or neglectful (Bonnie & Wallace, 2003). This explanation is rooted in **dependency theory**—as dependency of the elderly person increases, stress will increase, as will the risk of abuse and neglect (Bonnie & Wallace, 2003). Children who take on this caretaker role may think it entitles them to access their parents' financial resources, even if they do not legally have access to these resources. In this way, financial exploitation may occur.

Risk factors for institutional abuse are also tied to the perpetrator. Research on abuse in nursing homes shows that nursing aides compose the largest group of abusers (Payne & Cikovic, 1995). Nursing aides typically work long shifts, often for little pay. They usually have to care for many patients on their shift—elderly persons who require high levels of supervision and who have high needs—even though they may have received minimal training. The demands placed on them are, indeed, great. Without the necessary training and skills, abuse and neglect are likely unfortunate consequences.

Routine Activities Theory

Older persons typically do not have risky lifestyles. They may, however, be seen as vulnerable or suitable targets. They may be unable to physically protect themselves from victimization and, thus, may be easily harmed. Likewise, some older people may be suitable targets for scam artists, given their waning cognitive ability or lack of technological sophistication. In this way, people may take advantage of them. These risk factors have been linked in research to elder maltreatment. Elders who are unable to care for themselves are more likely to be abused than others (Tatara et al., 1998). Similarly, about 60% of substantiated elder abuse victims experienced some degree of confusion (Tatara et al., 1998). Persons in nursing homes are also likely to experience cognitive deficits, and about half of them are confined to a bed or wheelchair (Orel, 2010). These characteristics make these elderly persons more vulnerable to abuse but also increase the burden of caring for them. That is, the stress of caring for individuals who are unable to care for themselves or who have cognitive impairments is likely high; thus, caretakers who are not equipped to care for these people are more likely than others to become frustrated and respond in abusive and aggressive ways.

Older persons, especially if they live alone, also may lack capable guardianship. Consider that family members make up a large portion of perpetrators of elder maltreatment—even if elderly persons do have guardianship, it may not be capable if the people who are supposed to be providing guardianship are the ones mistreating them. Regarding financial fraud, individuals who remotely purchase goods (e.g., online purchase, telemarketing purchase, e-mail-order purchase, infomercial purchase, e-mail-order purchase) are at an increased risk of being targeted for fraud (Holtfreter et al., 2014). In this way, routine activities theory may be applicable to elder maltreatment. When motivated offenders, suitable targets, and lack of capable guardianship coalesce in time and space, elder maltreatment is likely to occur.

Responses to Elder Maltreatment

In recognition of elder maltreatment as a serious form of victimization that warrants special consideration in the law and the criminal justice system, special laws and criminal justice programs have been developed.

Legislation

The **Older Americans Act of 1965** (amended in 2006, Pub. L. 109-365) provided protection of rights for older Americans, among other things. One of these protections involved the creation of the State Long-Term Care Ombudsman Program discussed earlier. In addition, in order to receive certain funds, state agencies must develop and enhance programs to address elder maltreatment. It also provides grants for states to create elder justice systems. More recently, the **Elder Justice Act** (Pub. L. 111-148) was signed into law in 2010. This law provides $400 million over 4 years for Adult Protective Services, monies for grants to detect and prevent elder abuse, to establish and support forensic centers relating to elder maltreatment, to support the Long-Term Care Ombudsman Program, and to enhance long-term care staffing.

States also have legislation to protect elderly persons. Most abuse perpetrated against elderly persons is illegal in all states because existing statutes make these behaviors illegal regardless of the victim's age. Emotional/psychological abuse and neglect are also illegal, depending on the behavior of the perpetrator, the outcome for the victim, and the nature of the relationship between the perpetrator and the victim. For example, most states impose a legal duty on adult children to care for and protect their elderly parents (Stiegel, Klem, & Turner, 2007). Once a person has taken on the role of caregiver, that person has a duty to provide care or seek assistance in providing care. Failing to do so can lead to that person being held criminally liable (Stiegel et al., 2007).

Along with criminalizing abuse and neglect, all states have Adult Protective Services agencies to which people can report suspected cases of elder maltreatment. Forty-eight states require at least some persons to report suspected elder maltreatment, while the other two (Colorado and South Dakota, as of December 2009) encourage but do not mandate reporting (RAINN, 2011b). States vary as to who is a mandatory reporter, but people who have regular contact with older adults, such as physicians and health care workers, are mainly mandatory reporters. Reports can be made to Adult Protective Services or to other agencies such as law enforcement. See the Alabama's Mandatory Reporting Requirements Regarding Elders/ Disabled box for Alabama's mandatory reporting law for elder maltreatment.

ALABAMA'S MANDATORY REPORTING REQUIREMENTS REGARDING ELDERS/DISABLED

Who must report?	• Physicians • Other practitioners of the healing arts • Caregivers
Standard of knowledge	Reasonable cause to believe that any protected person has been subjected to physical abuse, neglect, exploitation, sexual abuse, or emotional abuse
Definition of applicable victim	A "protected person" is anyone over 18 years of age • who has an intellectual disability or developmental disability (including but not limited to senility); or • who is mentally or physically incapable of adequately caring for himself or herself and his or her interests without serious consequences to himself or herself or others.
Who to report to?	• The county department of human resources or the chief of police of the city and county, or • The sheriff of the county if the observation is made in an unincorporated territory

Reports of a nursing home employee who abuses, neglects, or misappropriates the property of a nursing home resident shall be made to the Department of Public Health.

Source: Reprinted by permission of RAINN, Rape, Abuse and Incest National Network through the support of Hogan Lovells.

Note: This information in this chart is intended to be current through December, 2013. The information is not presented as a source of legal advice. You should not rely for legal advice on statements or representations made within the Web site or by any externally referenced Internet sites. If you need legal advice upon which you intend to rely in the course of your legal affairs, consult a competent, independent attorney.

Criminal Justice System Response

The criminal justice system has also responded to the problem of elder maltreatment. The criminal justice community has joined forces to develop multidisciplinary and multiagency teams to investigate and prosecute elder maltreatment. For example, the Northeast Healthcare Law Enforcement Association (NHLEA) consists of law enforcement managers from federal, regional, and state elder, patient abuse, and health care fraud law enforcement units. The NHLEA enforces, investigates, and prosecutes maltreatment against elderly persons and has developed a criminal offender elder abuse database to track offenders convicted of elder and patient abuse (Hodge, 1999). Other jurisdictions have Financial Abuse Specialist Teams designed to investigate financial exploitation of elderly persons. Specialized prosecution units also have been instituted. San Diego has an Elder Abuse Prosecution Unit that specializes in the prosecution of elder maltreatment and provides training to law enforcement in how to investigate elder abuse and training to banks in how to identify financial exploitation (Hodge, 1999).

As you can see, the causes and consequences of both child maltreatment and elder maltreatment are situated in the life course, but child abuse has garnered more widespread attention than has elder abuse. Nonetheless, with the passage of the Elder Justice Act and the aging of the population, coupled with longer life spans, elder maltreatment may become a policy and programmatic hot bed.

SUMMARY

- The two major forms of child maltreatment are abuse and neglect.
- The difference between physical abuse and discipline of a child is the intent to harm versus the intent to teach the child right from wrong.
- Because children often cannot verbalize how they are being abused and their parents or caregivers often are the abusers, it is difficult to know the extent of child maltreatment in the United States.
- Data sources such as the National Child Abuse and Neglect Data System and National Incidence Study (NIS) provide most of the information known about child maltreatment.
- Results from the NIS-4 indicate that more than 1.25 million children experienced maltreatment during 2005–2006 that resulted in demonstrable harm.
- Death is the most serious outcome of child maltreatment, and one third of child fatalities in 2009 were attributed to neglect.
- Victims of child maltreatment are almost equally likely to be male and female, with children under age 4 making up 80% of fatalities in 2009.
- White children made up the largest percentage of reports of child maltreatment, but African American and Hispanic children were disproportionately represented in reports, given their composition in the population.
- Biological parents of the child are most likely to be the abusers, with mothers more likely than fathers to be the perpetrator.
- Risk factors for child maltreatment include child's temperament and vulnerability. Family risk factors include living in poverty, stress, single-headed households, and living with a single parent with a cohabiting partner. Parenting risk factors include witnessing or experiencing violence as a child or adolescent, substance use/abuse, depression, and mental illness.
- There are many consequences of child maltreatment. Children who are maltreated are at heightened risk of experiencing cognitive and developmental disorders and suffering from psychological disorders. They also may

experience problems in school and have problems in their sexual relationships. Later in life, maltreated children are at risk of living in poverty and being unemployed.

- Children who are victims of maltreatment are likely to be involved in criminal behavior, delinquency, and to use alcohol and drugs.
- The Child Abuse Prevention and Treatment Act made it mandatory for states to report suspected cases of child maltreatment in order to receive certain federal funding.
- Mandatory reporting laws require certain people to report suspected cases of child abuse.
- Safe haven laws protect mothers and custodial parents from criminal prosecution so they can give their babies up if they feel they cannot raise them.
- The criminal justice system recognizes that children need special attention and certain court-appointed advocates when they testify in court.
- In addition to abuse and neglect, financial exploitation is a form of maltreatment specific to the elderly. Elderly persons are also at risk of having conservatorship, guardianship, or power of attorney misused.
- Elders are also capable of self-neglect when they refuse or fail to provide care for themselves, such as not eating or drinking, refusing to take necessary medication, and lack of personal hygiene.
- The Long-Term Care Ombudsman Program is mandatory in every state, allowing for elder maltreatment complaints to be reported.
- In 1996, Adult Protective Services received 236,479 reports of suspected maltreatment.
- In 2006, only 6% of substantiated reports of elder maltreatment occurred in long-term care settings, and 2% occurred in other locations, which included assisted living facilities.
- Females make up a greater proportion of victims of elder maltreatment than do males.
- Females are also the most likely perpetrators of elder maltreatment. Adult children are most likely to be the perpetrators of elder abuse.
- Most cases of investigated and substantiated elder maltreatment are cases of self-neglect. Next most common are caregiver neglect cases, followed by financial exploitation cases.
- As dependency of the elderly person increases, stress will increase, as will the risk for abuse and neglect.
- Research on abuse in nursing homes shows that nursing aides compose the largest group of abusers.
- Elderly persons may be unable to physically protect themselves from victimization and, thus, may be easily harmed. Some older people may be suitable targets for scam artists, given their waning cognitive ability or lack of technological sophistication.
- Almost all states have mandatory reporting laws for suspected cases of elder abuse.
- The Elder Justice Act, signed into law in 2010, provides $400 million to Adult Protective Services for detection and prevention of elder abuse and/or maltreatment.
- The criminal justice system has the Northeast Healthcare Law Enforcement Association, which consists of officers and officials who enforce, investigate, and prosecute maltreatment offenders.
- Overall, child and elder maltreatment share some similarities, such as the types of abuse and risk factors, and show some differences in responses by the criminal justice system and typical perpetrators.

DISCUSSION QUESTIONS

1. What are some issues with generating accurate estimates of the extent of child maltreatment and elder maltreatment?

2. Why do you think parents are the most likely to be perpetrators of their children's maltreatment? Why are adult children the most likely perpetrators of elder maltreatment?

3. What is the victim–offender overlap as it pertains to child maltreatment?

4. Why do you think child maltreatment has been linked with adult poverty?

5. Why do you think females are more likely to be victims of elder maltreatment than are males? Why are male children more likely to be killed through child maltreatment than are female children?

KEY TERMS

physical abuse

emotional abuse

child sexual abuse

neglect

National Child Abuse and Neglect Data System (NCANDS)

National Incidence Study (NIS)

shaken baby syndrome

Child Abuse Prevention and Treatment Act

mandatory reporting law

safe haven laws

guardian ad litem (GAL)

physical elder abuse

emotional or psychological elder abuse

sexual elder abuse

abandonment

financial exploitation

power of attorney abuse

self-neglect

National Elder Abuse Incidence Study

National Social Life, Health, and Aging Project

Long-Term Care Ombudsman Program

dependency theory

Older Americans Act of 1965

Elder Justice Act

INTERNET RESOURCES

Child Welfare Information Gateway (http://www.childwelfare.gov)

This website provides a great deal of information about child maltreatment. It includes data, statistics, and laws on child maltreatment, along with information on how child maltreatment can be prevented. It also has links to resources in Spanish.

National MCH Center for Child Death Review (http://www.childdeathreview.org/)

This is a resource center for state and local death review teams that investigate child deaths. Links for each state's child mortality data are provided so that you can see the most common causes of death, including those attributable to child maltreatment.

National Center on Elder Abuse (http://www.ncea.aoa.gov)

This website provides background information about elder maltreatment, including definitions and statistics. Nursing home abuse, a type of elder maltreatment, is discussed. Links to information about how to report elder maltreatment and about Adult Protective Services are also provided.

National Committee for the Prevention of Elder Abuse (http://www.preventelderabuse.org/)

This website provides information about the different types of elder maltreatment, including sexual violence, domestic violence, and financial exploitation. Links to publications and current news items related to elder maltreatment are also included.

11

VICTIMIZATION OF SPECIAL POPULATIONS

On February 1, 2011, it was reported that a Swiss social worker had confessed to sexually assaulting 114 disabled children and adults. The man, working as a therapist, assaulted these people in nine different institutions over a 28-year span. He confessed to sexually abusing these people, all of whom were mentally disabled—72 of them were under the age of 18, and one was only 1 year old! He went so far as to videotape or photograph 18 of the incidents ("Gadsden Mother Convicted," 2011). You probably are wondering what could possess a person to do this to individuals under his care. But consider the victims here—these are mentally disabled individuals in institutions. These people may have been especially vulnerable to victimization given their reliance on others for care and their diminished mental capacity.

This chapter is dedicated to such vulnerable victims. It begins with a discussion of persons who are mentally disabled and then turns to a discussion of persons who are mentally ill. Victimization of persons who are incarcerated is then covered. You may wonder why incarcerated victims are included in the same chapter as mentally disabled and mentally ill victims, but as you will read below, these three groups are at particular risk of being victimized, given their status and unique vulnerability.

Source: Adapted from Swiss authorities: Social worker admits to 114 sexual assaults. By the CNN Wire Staff. February 2, 2011. http://www.cnn.com/2011/WORLD/europe/02/01/switzerland.sex.charges/.

■ VICTIMIZATION OF PERSONS WITH DISABILITIES

Another group of individuals who are especially vulnerable to victimization are people who have disabilities. It may seem odd, at first, to discuss persons with disabilities in the same section as those who are incarcerated. But let's consider the fact that both groups of people, given their status, are likely targets of would-be offenders. Given what we know about lifestyle and routine activities theory, being a vulnerable target is a key factor in a person's risk for victimization. For some people, their personal characteristics will place them at particular risk of being victimized while incarcerated. Predators and offenders in prison will target them. The same is true for people with disabilities. Predators and offenders will likely see them as easy marks for a variety of reasons. Because of this, persons with disabilities who are victimized deserve special attention.

Defining Persons With Disabilities

When you first began reading this section, an image of a person with a disability may have come to you. This image may have been of a person with a physical disability or an intellectual disability. Both of these are, in fact, examples of persons with disabilities. But what do these terms mean? A physical disability is present when a person is unable to perform daily activities such as walking, climbing stairs, bathing, getting dressed, and taking care of himself or herself. An intellectual disability falls under the broader category of **developmental disability.** Developmental disabilities include such things as cerebral palsy, epilepsy, severe learning disabilities, mental retardation, and autism (Petersilia, 2001). See Table 11.1 for descriptions of common developmental disabilities. A developmental disability manifests before the age of 22, is long-lasting, and causes severe impairment in at least three of five areas of activity—self-care, language, learning, mobility, and capacity for independent living (Centers for Disease Control and Prevention, 2010a). In this section, we will mainly discuss persons with physical disabilities, which can occur at any point in life, and persons with developmental disabilities. If the research or study being referenced does not distinguish between developmental and physical disability, the term *disability* will be used.

Extent of Victimization of Persons With Disabilities

As with most types of victimization, the first place we turn for a snapshot of the extent of victimization is the National Crime Victimization Survey (NCVS). For persons with disabilities, this is no different. The Crime Victims with Disabilities Awareness Act of 1998 mandated that the NCVS begin to collect information about the victimization of people with disabilities. To do so, the NCVS incorporated questions asking people if they have a hearing limitation, a vision limitation, a cognitive limitation, an ambulatory limitation, a self-care limitation, or an independent living limitation (Harrell, 2014). For instance, persons are asked if "because of a physical, mental, or emotional condition, do you have serious difficulty concentrating, remembering, or making decisions?" (Harrell, 2014, p. 10). If a person reported that he or she did have such a condition that person would be considered to suffer from a disability (Harrell, 2014). Notice that the NCVS's definition of disability includes a wide range of limitations on behavior and interaction.

Based on this definition, according to findings from the 2012 NCVS, there were 1,346,900 violent crime victimizations perpetrated against persons with disabilities. The most common type of victimization was simple assault—the same type of violent victimization most commonly experienced by persons without disabilities. Comparing victimization rates of persons with disabilities with those of persons without disabilities in the NCVS shows that people with disabilities have higher victimization rates. The victimization rate of people with disabilities is 60.4 per 1,000 compared with 22.3 per 1,000 people without disabilities (Harrell, 2014).

The NCVS is, of course, not the only source of victimization statistics for persons with disabilities. It is the only source for national-level survey-derived estimates in the United States, but other research has been conducted on smaller samples and in other countries. Much of the research was conducted in the 1980s and early 1990s. Not to say that these estimates are unreliable, but it should be noted that this area of research has not received as much attention as others. Also of importance, because most of these studies have been conducted on nonrepresentative samples, it is hard to say how generalizable the findings are. In fact, there is actually some debate in terms of the extent to which people with disabilities are more likely to be victimized than persons without, given the methodological weaknesses of the research studies (Marge, 2003).

From these studies, other pictures of the extent of victimization against persons with disabilities are revealed. In Australia, the Bureau of Statistics administered a version of their Victims of Crime Survey to adults with intellectual handicaps. From this survey, it was found that these individuals had higher rates of victimization than persons without intellectual handicaps (Petersilia, 2010). An oft-cited study by Wilson and Brewer (1992), in which they studied 174 adults with intellectual disabilities in South Australia, found that the relative risk of victimization was highest for violent victimizations—persons with intellectual disabilities were 12.8 times more likely to be robbed, 10.7 times more likely to be sexually assaulted, and 2.8 times more likely to be assaulted (as cited in Petersilia, 2001). Other research has found that persons with disabilities are at risk of being victimized by their personal care attendants (Ulicyn, White, Bradford, & Matthews, 1990).

Official data sources also can be used to glean information about abuse of persons with disabilities. In one study, McCartney and Campbell (1998) reviewed records of 9,400 men and women with mental retardation living in 23 institutional facilities in six states. They found that 5% of them had experienced abuse by a staff member over a 22-month period. Most typically, the victim had been neglected or physically abused.

Table 11.1 ■ Description of Common Developmental Disabilities	
Cerebral palsy	A condition that involves the brain and nervous system functions. Persons with cerebral palsy have damage to the area of the brain responsible for muscle tone, resulting in difficulty in movement, balance, and posture.
Epilepsy	A disorder in the brain that typically causes various spontaneous seizures.
Severe learning or intellectual disability	Limited ability to perform daily functions (i.e., communication, self-care, and getting through basic and often very simple learning/education courses) and below-average score on mental ability or intelligence.
Mental retardation	Intellectual level is significantly below average; person lacks basic skills for everyday living. This condition is generally diagnosed before a person reaches age 18.
Autism	Within the first 3 years of a child's life, this developmental disorder appears and affects brain development (usually disrupting the child's social and communication skills).

Source: Centers for Disease Control and Prevention. (2010). Developmental disabilities: Topic home. Retrieved from http://www.cdc.gov/ncbddd/dd/default.htm.

■ WHO IS VICTIMIZED?

Among those persons with disabilities surveyed in the NCVS, women were more likely to be the victims of a violent crime than were men (Harrell, 2014). This is unlike the patterns we see for violent crime victimization in general, in which men are more likely than women to be violently victimized for all types of victimization except rape and sexual assault. White persons with disabilities have higher rates of violent victimizations than Black persons with disabilities and persons of other races with disabilities (American Indian or Alaska Native; and Asian, Native Hawaiian, or other Pacific Islander) (Harrell, 2014). All in all, even when disaggregating different racial groups (White, Black, other race) and examining Hispanics and non-Hispanics, persons with disabilities have higher rates of violent victimization than do persons without disabilities.

When examining the types of disabilities separately, it does seem that not all disabilities impact victimization risk similarly. Persons with cognitive disabilities have the highest rates of violent victimization, compared with the other disabilities measured in the NCVS (Harrell, 2014). In 2012, over half of nonfatal violent victimizations occurred against people who had multiple disability types (Harrell, 2014).

Violence Against Women With Disabilities

Special attention has been given to studying women with disabilities. In one study of physically disabled women who used personal assistants, Powers et al. (2002) discovered these women had experienced a wide range of abusive behavior. Many women reported that their personal assistants had stolen money or items from them (35.5%) and that their checks had been misused or forged (30%). Neglect and physical abuse were also experienced by the women—19.5% had their physical needs neglected, 14% had been physically abused, and 11% reported unwanted sexual touching. Other studies estimate that 2% of women with disabilities (physical, mental, or emotional) have been physically abused in the past year (Martin et al., 2006), 10% of women with physical disabilities have experienced abuse within the past year (McFarlane et al., 2001), and 36% of women with disabilities have experienced physical assault abuse during their lifetimes (Young, Nosek, Howland, Chanpong, & Rintala, 1997).

When we discuss victimization against women, we must, of course, give attention to rape and sexual victimization. Like other women, women with disabilities are at risk of being sexually victimized. Women with developmental disabilities are 4 to 10 times more likely to be sexual assault victims than women in the general population (National Council on Disability, 2007). When only rape is examined, between 15,000 and 19,000 people with developmental disabilities are raped each year in the United States (Sobsey, 1994). It is estimated that more than 80% of women with a disability will be sexually assaulted over their lifetime (Wisconsin Coalition Against Sexual Assault, 2003). Research on women who use personal assistance services has revealed that women may be abused by people employed by these services. In fact, Powers et al. (2002) found that in their study, women with physical disabilities and those with both physical and intellectual disabilities were more likely to report being sexually abused in general by persons employed by personal assistance services.

Most of the research on sexual victimization of women with disabilities has been largely descriptive—identifying the extent to which it occurs. Little research has identified the characteristics that place certain women with disabilities at risk. It does appear, though, that women who are younger, non-White, unmarried, employed, and less-educated are more likely than other women with disabilities (physical, mental, or emotional problems that limit activity) to be sexually assaulted (Martin et al., 2006). Also important, research on women with disabilities shows that repeat sexual victimization is also quite common. Some estimate that almost half of women with developmental disabilities who are victims of sexual victimization will experience at least 10 incidents during their lives (Valenti-Hein & Schwartz, 1995). Past sexual victimization also has been shown to increase the likelihood of being sexually assaulted 2.5 times for this population (Nannini, 2006). Although this section refers to female victims, males with disabilities are also at risk for experiencing sexual assault. In one study, 32% of males with developmental disabilities reported being sexually assaulted by an intimate partner (Johnson & Sigler, 2000).

Along with sexual victimization, women with disabilities are at risk of being violently victimized by their intimate partners. They have indicated through surveys a particular worry about intimate partner violence, naming it one of their top five concerns (Grothaus, 1985). Given the prevalence of intimate partner violence among women with disabilities, this concern does not appear to be unfounded. One study of Canadian women found that women with disabilities (long-term physical, mental, or health problems that limit home, school, work, or other activities) were 39% more likely to experience partner violence within the previous 5 years than were women without disabilities (Brownridge, 2006).

Victimization of Youth With Disabilities

Children with disabilities may be especially vulnerable to victimization. Young people in general are at risk of victimization because they may be unable to defend themselves, thus being attractive targets. Children with disabilities may be around caretakers who become frustrated with them and are less emotionally invested in them than their parents. They also may be targets of peers at school. For these reasons, their victimization patterns have been examined. Professionals working with youth with disabilities perceive that children with intellectual disabilities have higher rates of maltreatment than children without them (Verdugo, Bermejo, & Fuertes, 1995). Formal school records also support this contention (Sullivan & Knutson, 2000).

FOCUS ON RESEARCH

Recent research using the General Social Survey (a population based survey of Canadian residents), shows that mental health-related activity limitations (having your daily activities at home, work, school, or other area be limited by a psychological, emotional, or mental health condition) may also be a risk factor for women.

Women with more frequent mental health-related activity limitations (AL) had higher rates of violent intimate partner victimization, emotional intimate partner victimization, and financial intimate partner victimization than others. Why would mental health-related AL be related to IPV?

Source: Adapted from Du Mont, J., & Forte, T. (2014). Intimate partner violence among women with mental health-related activity limitations: A Canadian population based study. *BMC Public Health,* 14.

Bullying, although not necessarily reaching levels that would be considered criminal, may also be a problem facing youth with disabilities. Bullying—discussed in detail in Chapter 12—is harmful behavior directed at a youth that occurs more than once and is characterized by a power imbalance (Olweus, 1993a).

A study of children with disabilities compared to other children found that they were more likely than other children to be bullied at school—half of them reported being bullied during the school term (Dawkins, 1996). Similarly, when mothers were asked whether their children with Asperger's syndrome or other nonverbal learning disabilities had experienced victimization by their peers, more than 90% responded "yes" (Little, 2002). We have already learned that many children are bullied and victimized by their peers, but it seems that children with disabilities are particularly vulnerable.

Another type of victimization of children with disabilities that appears to be especially problematic is sexual abuse. Children with disabilities are estimated to be 4 to 10 times more likely than the general population to be sexually abused. As noted by Baladerian (1991), an estimated 25% of the general population of females is sexually victimized before reaching adulthood; thus, girls with disabilities are particularly vulnerable (it is estimated that almost all of them will experience a sexually abusive event). Also, between 16% and 32% of boys with developmental disabilities are believed to be at risk for sexual abuse before the age of 18 (Badgley et al., 1984; Hard, 1986).

■ PATTERNS OF VICTIMIZATION

The NCVS provides interesting information about each incident of victimization that occurred against persons with disabilities. Individuals were asked if they believed they were victimized because of their disability; about 15% of violent crime victims with disabilities indicated that they thought so (Harrell & Rand, 2010). About one third of victims with disabilities noted they were unsure if they were victimized because of their disability (Harrell & Rand, 2010). Victims were also asked if they did anything during the victimization to resist or try to stop it. Persons with disabilities were less likely than persons without disabilities to attempt to employ any measure of resistance during a violent victimization (Harrell & Rand, 2010). We will return to the use of resistance below, but for now, think about the use of resistance, or lack thereof, and how it may factor into victim selection by offenders.

Violent victimizations against persons with disabilities most commonly do not involve a weapon (only 20% do), and about one fourth of victims with disabilities suffer injury as a result (Harrell & Rand, 2010). About half of violent crime victims with disabilities reported their experiences to the police, a finding similar to violent crime victims overall. They were, however, more likely than violent crime victims without disabilities to seek assistance from victim advocacy agencies (Harrell & Rand, 2010). Property crime victims with disabilities were less likely to report their victimizations to police (Harrell & Rand, 2010).

Who is likely to perpetrate these victimizations? One of the unique features of victimization of persons with disabilities is that they often rely on others for support and care. Adults may receive care from friends and family and/or formal personal care assistance services. The victim-offender relationship, then, is worthy of discussion, because for this type of victimization, exposure to motivated offenders is likely to be different than for other potential victims. It is difficult to say exactly who is most likely to offend against victims with disabilities because many studies have exclusively asked about certain types of offenders. That is, some surveys have explicitly asked victims only about whether care providers have victimized them and not asked about other types of offenders. Nonetheless, these studies have revealed a startling picture of persons who are charged with caring for individuals actually harming them. For example, one study compared individuals with severe cognitive impairment receiving in-home supportive services in California with individuals having no severe cognitive impairment. Those with severe impairment had significantly higher rates of neglect, injury, being yelled at, suspected theft, threats by their providers, physical abuse, and sexual advances (Matthias & Benjamin, 2003). In another study, researchers reviewed the records of 9,400 institutionalized women and men with mental retardation living in 23 residential facilities in six U.S. states. They found that about 5% had experienced some form of abuse by a member of the facility staff during a 22-month period (McCartney & Campbell, 1998). Other studies have included questions about who the perpetrator is or have located in official records who the offender was. These studies revealed that persons are most likely to be victimized by family members, intimate partners, and personal assistance/health care providers (McFarlane et al., 2001; National Council on Disability, 2007).

■ RISK FACTORS FOR VICTIMIZATION FOR PERSONS WITH DISABILITIES

As noted, there are a number of reasons why persons with disabilities are at risk of being victimized. Let's discuss these factors in a bit more detail so that the risk of victimization can be better understood. First, persons with disabilities are likely seen as vulnerable, especially if they rely on others for care. They may, by necessity, allow other people access to their money, bank accounts, checking accounts, and other financial records. As you may imagine, doing so places them at risk for theft. Having home health care and personal assistants requires allowing strangers access to their homes and personal effects. According to routine activities theory, these people could be providing capable guardianship, but they may be motivated offenders instead.

Second, people with intellectual or developmental disabilities may not be able to recognize and process risk. They may not, despite doing all the "right" things to protect themselves, realize that they are in the wrong place or with the wrong people. Unfortunately, they also may not realize that a victimization has occurred. Even when they do, some research shows that they are less likely to report their victimization to police than are other victims. The decision not to report could be a result of several factors. They may have limited communication skills, which could make reporting difficult and frightening (Nettelbeck & Wilson, 2002). They may be unaware that money has been taken if they typically do not control their own finances. They may not know that sexual activity that has occurred is inappropriate and illegal if they have never been exposed to sex education (Petersilia, 2001). Reporting may also be unlikely if the offender is a family member or someone else who is caring for them. Victims may fear retaliation for reporting (National Council on Disability, 2007). Reporting may mean that the victim will have to move into a more restrictive living situation, an option that may be worse than saying nothing (Petersilia, 2001). For victims of intimate partner violence, they may not have access to shelters that can accommodate persons with disabilities, or similar to other victims of intimate partner violence, they may feel they lack the financial resources to leave (Petersilia, 2001).

Third, persons with disabilities are more likely to live in poverty than people without disabilities. At least one in every three adults with disabilities lives in households with an income totaling less than $15,000 per year. Overall, only 12% of those without disabilities live in households in this income range (as cited in Petersilia, 2001). Poverty is a risk factor for victimization in that people living in poverty are likely to live in crime-ridden neighborhoods in areas that are unlikely to be diligently patrolled by law enforcement.

Fourth, victimization of persons with disabilities has been linked to a **dependency-stress model**, especially for victimization of younger persons with disabilities. That is, because children with disabilities tend to be more dependent than other children on their parents and caregivers, it creates more stress, which may result in abuse if their parents and caregivers cannot appropriately deal with the stress of their responsibilities (Petersilia, 2001). Some have argued that persons with disabilities display behaviors that may promote victimization— without suggesting a victim-blaming model. Persons with disabilities may misinterpret social cues, want to please others, and think that people want to be their friends (Petersilia, 2001). In this way, they may comply with inappropriate requests, resulting in victimization (Nettelbeck & Wilson, 2002). In addition, victims with disabilities may evoke aggressive responses with their behaviors. In one study that compared nonvictims to victims matched on age, IQ, and adaptive behavior, Wilson, Seaman, and Nettelbeck (1996) found that victims were more likely to react with inappropriately angry or aggressive responses in everyday situations with strangers, indicating that poor social competence (anger and aggression in interpersonal interactions) rather than intellectual disability was a contributing factor in victimization.

■ RESPONSES TO VICTIMS WITH DISABILITIES

Remember that much research shows that crime victims with disabilities are unlikely to seek assistance from the police (Focht-New, Clements, Barol, Faulkner, & Service, 2008). This low level of reporting may be due to several reasons. They may be unaware, especially in cases of property victimization (Petersilia, 2001) or because of not receiving appropriate sex education, that a crime ever occurred (Nosek, 1996). In addition, persons with disabilities may be particularly dependent on the person who perpetrated the incident; thus, reporting a crime may make their day-to-day living difficult (Nosek, 1996). Even when crime victims with disabilities do come forward, there is evidence that police may be hesitant to treat the cases the same as they do when other victims come forward (Petersilia, 2010). These victims may be seen as less legitimate and as unreliable witnesses due to their diminished intellectual capacity. Law enforcement may not realize that persons with mental retardation and autism have good memories and can be reliable witnesses (Petersilia, 2010). Indeed, in Petersilia's (2001) review of research on crime victims with developmental disorders, she notes that much research shows that people with mental retardation forget information at rates similar to those of persons without mental retardation and that they recall with similar accuracy to others their age (in studies of children). Children with mental retardation are, however, highly impressionable and eager to please; thus, interviewers and attorneys should take special precautions in criminal justice settings (Petersilia, 2001). Prosecutors also may be hesitant to pursue these cases for similar reasons.

Research on people with disabilities who have been sexually abused is particularly instructive. It has shown that victims rarely report (Wacker, Parish, & Macy, 2008). Even when victims do report, offenders are rarely charged—this may be due to a number of reasons, one of which is that perpetrators are commonly acquaintances and intimate partners (Wacker et al., 2008). In one study, of the 22% of alleged offenders charged with sexual abuse, only 38% were ultimately convicted (Sobsey & Doe, 1991). This lack of reporting, charging, and conviction is not unique to victims with disabilities, but the rates do appear to be particularly low for female victims of sexual abuse/violence with disabilities.

Recognizing the difficulties victims with disabilities face, the **Federal Crime Victims with Disabilities Awareness Act of 1998** required the collection of statistics on the victimization of persons with disabilities (Pub. L. 105-301). Also proposed was the **Federal Crime Victims with Disabilities Act of 1998,** which would require reporting of abuse to law enforcement; provide training for law enforcement, prosecutors, rape crisis counselors, and health care providers; require victim/witness assistance programs to cover victims with disabilities; and develop continued reform for working with victims with disabilities (Assembly Bill 2038). This act was proposed by then senator Biden but had not been reintroduced as of January 2011.

Without federal legislation requiring reporting and victim assistance, some states have specifically addressed victims with disabilities. For example, Ohio has a mandatory reporting law requiring that a mandatory reporter who has a "reason to believe that a person with mental retardation or a developmental disability has suffered or faces a substantial risk of suffering any wound, injury, disability, or condition of such a nature as to reasonably indicate abuse or neglect of that person" (RAINN, 2009b) must report. Table 11.2 provides the specifics of Ohio's law. Other states have amended their criminal codes so that persons with cognitive disabilities are afforded similar protections as those afforded to children when testifying in court, such as videotaped testimony, testimony via closed-circuit television, the use of breaks during testimony, allowing the presence of support persons in the courtroom, and adjusting the seating arrangements in the courtroom to be less intimidating (Petersilia, 2001).

Even without legislation, victim service providers are already faced with addressing the needs of victims with disabilities, although some jurisdictions are likely better able to do this than others. Nonetheless, victim service providers should be able to assist victims with disabilities in finding suitable housing, applying for victim compensation, receiving counseling, getting legal services, having someone attend court with them, and navigating the criminal justice system (National Council on Disability, 2007). Beyond victim services, there are training videos, classes, and pamphlets available for law enforcement and other criminal justice professionals preparing to respond to crime victims with disabilities. Most of the training, however, has primarily focused on victims with mental illness, discussed in the next section.

Table 11.2 ▨ Ohio's Mandatory Reporting Law for Crime Victims With Mental Disabilities	
Who is disabled?	Persons with mental retardation and persons with developmental disabilities
Who is the mandatory reporter?	Any physician (including a hospital intern or resident); dentist; podiatrist; chiropractor; practitioner of a limited branch of medicine; hospital administrator or employee; licensed nurse; ambulatory health facility employee; home health agency employee; adult care facility employee; community mental health facility employee; school teacher or authority; social worker; psychologist; attorney; peace officer; coroner; residents' rights advocate; superintendent, board member, or employee of a county board of developmental disabilities; administrator, board member, or employee of a residential facility; administrator, board member, or employee or any other public or private provider of services to a person with mental retardation or a developmental disability; MR/DD employee; member of a citizen's advisory council established at an institution or branch institution of the department of developmental disabilities; a person who is employed in a position that includes providing specialized services to persons with disabilities, and a clergyman who is employed in a position that includes providing specialized services to persons with disabilities and who renders spiritual treatment through prayer in accordance with the tenets of an organized religion
Who is reported to?	Law enforcement agency or the county board of developmental disabilities
	State highway patrol if the individual is an inmate in a state correctional institution
	Law enforcement agency or the department of developmental disabilities if the report concerns a resident of a facility operated by the department
Standard of knowledge	Reason to believe that person with disability has suffered or faces substantial risk of suffering wound, injury, disability, or condition as to reasonably indicate abuse or neglect of that person

Source: Reprinted by permission of RAINN, Rape, Abuse and Incest National Network through the support of Hogan Lovells.

Note: This information in this chart is intended to be current through December, 2013. The information is not presented as a source of legal advice. You should not rely for legal advice on statements or representations made within the Web site or by any externally referenced Internet sites. If you need legal advice upon which you intend to rely in the course of your legal affairs, consult a competent, independent attorney.

■ VICTIMIZATION OF PERSONS WITH MENTAL ILLNESS

Mental illness may also put individuals at risk of being victimized, for many of the same reasons that people with disabilities find themselves at risk. What, though, constitutes mental illness? You may think of mental illness as being debilitating, and sometimes it is. But many people live with mental illness—they go to work, they go to school, they are, by all accounts, productive members of society. Others do, however, face severe challenges. For many, one of these challenges is an increased chance of being victimized. Before we begin a discussion of this risk, let's first discuss what mental illness is.

Defining Mental Illness

Much of the research examining the link between mental illness and victimization has focused on persons with severe mental illness. Persons with severe mental illness often have symptoms of "impaired reality testing, disorganized thought processes, impulsivity, poor planning, and poor problem solving" (Teplin, McClelland, Abram, & Weiner, 2005, p. 911). In terms of operationalization, severe mental illness is often specified when persons have taken psychoactive medications for extended periods of time (e.g., 2 years) or have been hospitalized for psychiatric reasons (Teplin et al., 2005). But people can suffer from mental illness that may not meet these criteria. In addition, classifying severe mental illness as such does not identify the type of mental disorder diagnosis. There is, of course, a range of mental illnesses. Some of the most common ones that have been studied and linked to victimization are found in Table 11.3. Substance abuse issues such as alcohol and marijuana dependence are also mental disorders identified by the *Diagnostic and Statistical Manual* (4th edition, text revision), which is a diagnostic manual published by the American Psychiatric Association. This manual is used by mental health professionals to diagnose and treat patients.

Extent and Type of Victimization of Persons With Mental Illness

When persons in criminal justice first paid attention to persons with mental illness, it was not out of concern for their victimization. Instead, persons with mental illness were perceived to be violent offenders rather than victims (Silver, Arseneault, Langley, Caspi, & Moffitt, 2005). What research has found, however, is that persons with mental illness are more likely to be victims of violence than perpetrators (Levin, 2005). In terms of the extent to which persons with mental illness are victimized, it is important to note the methodology of the study. There are some studies that have examined the victimization of persons who are or have been institutionalized, while others have used samples drawn from those living in the community. We would expect to find different rates of victimization for persons living in the community than for those who are institutionalized.

When comparing persons with mental disorders in the community to persons in the community without mental disorders, it becomes clear that mental disorder is a risk factor for victimization. When comparing persons with severe mental illness to those in the general population, those with mental illness are 2.5 times more likely to be violently victimized (Hiday, Swartz, Swanson, Borum, & Wagner, 1999). Indeed, studies on persons with mental disorders have consistently found high rates of victimization—studies have found estimates of victimization from 8% (sexual assault victimization in the past year for males with severe mental illness; Goodman et al., 2001) to more than 50% (physical abuse in the past year for females with severe mental illness; Goodman et al., 1999).

One way to determine if persons with mental illness are in fact more prone to victimization is to compare their victimization rates with those of the general population. One rich national-level data source is, as you know, the NCVS. It provides data with which researchers can compare their estimates—with national data or with data for smaller areas such as central cities. Doing just this, Teplin et al. (2005) used the NCVS instrument to measure victimization experiences of persons with severe mental illness who were receiving psychiatric services in Chicago from January 31, 1997, to October 4, 1999, and to compare victimization incidence and prevalence to the NCVS. They discovered that more than one fourth of those with severe mental illness in the sample had experienced either a completed or attempted violent crime in the past year. This was 11.8 times higher than the prevalence rate in the NCVS. If this finding is extrapolated to the population of persons with severe mental illness in the United States, almost 3 million persons with severe mental illness are violently victimized each year! In addition, the researchers found that almost 28% had experienced a property crime, rates that were about 4 times higher than the NCVS. Also important, they found that females with severe mental illness were more likely to experience completed violent victimization, rape/ sexual assault, personal theft, and motor vehicle theft than were males with severe mental illness. Males with severe mental illness experienced robbery at higher rates than did females with severe mental illness. For some types of victimization, African Americans had higher rates, but rates were generally similar and high for all racial and ethnic groups.

These findings that victimization risk is higher for persons with mental illness are not specific to the United States. In a study examining a birth cohort of males and females born in Dunedin, New Zealand, Silver et al. (2005) found that 34% of persons with any mental disorder had been physically assaulted during the previous year, compared with 21% of persons without a mental disorder. They also examined specific types of mental disorders— persons with schizophreniform disorders had the highest odds of completed physical assault and threats of physical assault. Persons with anxiety disorders were the most at risk for sexual assault victimization.

Table 11.3 ■ Common Mental Illnesses, *DSM-IV-TR* Definitions and Diagnostic Criteria

Disorder	Definition	Diagnostic Criteria
Depressive	Five or more of the following symptoms have been present during the same 2-week period or represent a change from previous functioning; at least one of the symptoms is either (1) depressed mood or (2) loss of interest or pleasure. • Depressed mood most of the day, nearly every day	• Cause clinically significant distress or impairment in social, occupational, or other important areas of functioning • Are not due to the direct physiological effects of a substance or a general medical condition

Disorder	Definition	Diagnostic Criteria
	• Markedly diminished interest or pleasure in all, or almost all, activities most of the day, nearly all day • Significant weight loss when not dieting or weight gain • Insomnia or hypersomnia nearly every day • Psychomotor agitation or retardation nearly every day • Fatigue or loss of energy nearly every day • Feelings of worthlessness or excessive or inappropriate guilt (which may be delusional) nearly every day • Diminished ability to think or concentrate, or indecisiveness, nearly every day • Recurrent thoughts of death, recurrent suicidal ideation without a specific plan, or a suicide attempt or a specific plan for committing suicide	• Are not better accounted for by bereavement • Persist for longer than 2 months or are characterized by marked functional impairment, morbid preoccupation with worthlessness, suicidal ideation, psychotic symptoms, or psychomotor retardation
Anxiety	Characterized by excessive worry, but such worries are distinguished from obsessions by the fact that the person experiences them as excessive concerns about real-life circumstances.	Ranging from worrying about losing one's job to the intrusive distressing idea that "God" is "dog" spelled backward
Schizophreniform	The essential features of Schizophreniform disorder are identical to those of Schizophrenia except for two differences: the total duration of the illness (including prodromal, active, and residual phases) is at least 1 month but less than 6 months and impaired social or occupational functioning during some part of the illness is not required (although it may occur).	• Onset of prominent psychotic symptoms within 4 weeks of the first noticeable change in usual behavior or functioning • Confusion or perplexity at the height of the psychotic episode • Good premorbid social and occupational functioning • Absence of blunted or flat affect

Source: Data from American Psychiatric Association (2000).

Why Are Persons With
Mental Illness at Risk for Victimization?

Beginning in the 1950s, the United States implemented policies of **deinstitutionalization** that closed many institutions for mentally disordered persons, releasing them into the community (Silver, 2002). Intended to be a more humane approach to care as well as a cost-saving device, deinstitutionalization has had negative consequences. For example, even for people who may benefit from inpatient care, there may not be beds available. In 1970, there were 200 beds available for every 100,000 civilians, but that number had declined to less than 50 by 1992 ("Deinstitutionalization," 2011). The lack of beds has led to shorter stays when inpatient care is received—on average less than 10 days (Teplin et al., 2005). Consequently, persons with mental disorders, even severe mental disorders, may not receive necessary treatment or medicine. Without treatment or medicine, victimization risk actually increases. In fact, research shows that when individuals who have been hospitalized are released under outpatient commitment rather than without any outpatient commitment, they are less likely to be criminally victimized (Hiday, Swartz, Swanson, Borum, & Wagner, 2002).

Persons with mental disorders also have high rates of homelessness (Teasdale, 2009), poverty (Hudson, 2005), and substance abuse (Teasdale, 2009), all of which are risk factors for victimization. These factors place persons with mental disorders at risk for victimization much in the same manner as they do for others—they become easy targets, without capable guardianship. It has been argued that persons with mental illness also may be less likely to report their victimizations to law enforcement because they fear not being believed or taken seriously (Silver et al., 2005). If this is the case, then motivated offenders may target them if the offenders believe they can commit crime with a lower probability of detection (Silver et al., 2005).

Along with lacking capable guardians, persons with mental disorders may be less diligent in their environment and less able to engage in meaningful and effective self-protection (Silver et al., 2005). Also, would-be offenders may perceive that the mentally ill are less able to defend themselves (Silver et al., 2005). This may explain why persons with mental illness who are institutionalized are also at risk. Thus far, we have mainly discussed the victimization of persons with mental illness who reside in the community, but being in a care facility or hospital may also place people at risk. The rates of violent victimization in institutions are "often as high or higher than those in the community at large" (Petersilia, 2010, p. 2). Given their unique vulnerability and perceived or real inability to defend themselves, institutionalized persons may be at a great risk for victimization. Also, there may be little oversight as to the care provided in these institutions. In addition, patient-on-patient abuse may occur.

Exposure to motivated offenders also places persons at risk of being victimized. Persons with mental disorders may very well be exposed to motivated offenders since they engage in violence at higher rates than people without mental disorders (Arseneault, Moffitt, Caspi, Taylor, & Silva, 2000). This is similar to what we expect generally for people who engage in more violent lifestyles, remembering that these individuals are more likely to be around people who are also violent. Also, people may find that their aggressive and violent behavior evokes aggressive and violent responses.

Why are persons with mental illness more violent? Are they naturally aggressive? Research suggests that violence and victimization are linked to **symptomology.** Exhibiting psychological symptomology, such as delusions and hallucinations, is linked to violent behavior (Appelbaum, Robbins, & Monahan, 2000; Link, Monahan, Stueve, & Cullen, 1999). When persons are exhibiting these symptoms, they are also likely to be victimized because they may cope with their symptoms by becoming aggressive and violent. They are hence likely to evoke similar responses in others (Teasdale, 2009).

Others have argued that when people are exhibiting heightened symptomology, they may act in bizarre ways to which others may not know how to respond (Hiday, 1997). People may act to control a person who is mentally disordered, and this action may be victimizing. In this way, persons with mental disorders may find themselves in conflicted relationships. Consider how stressful it can be to care for persons who are mentally disordered! Although it is not excusable to abuse anyone, caring for a mentally ill person may at times be overwhelming. In support of this, some research has found that involvement in conflicted relationships drives the relationship between mental disorder and violent victimization (Silver, 2002). This suggests that it may not be the mental disorder per se that places a person at risk but the fact that persons with mental disorders are often involved in relationships characterized by conflict that produces victimization.

Responses to Victims With Mental Illness

It is likely that victims with mental illness face particular challenges. As previously noted, they may be less likely than others to report their victimizations to police for fear that they will not be believed or will not be taken seriously. For women, this risk may be especially germane. Females with mental illness may be unlikely to be taken seriously and may be blamed for being complicit in their own victimization (Salasin & Rich, 1993).

This lack of reporting is especially problematic since victimization is likely to bear psychological costs that may be particularly traumatizing for persons with mental illness. Mental illness severity and symptomology may be exacerbated by victimization—in this way, mental illness may be a contributory factor and a consequence of victimization (Goodman et al., 2001). The correlation between victimization and substance abuse among the mentally ill may indicate the need to use these substances as a coping mechanism (Goodman et al., 2001). Again, it is likely both a risk factor for and a consequence of victimization. As previously noted, treatment providers and victim service agencies should be

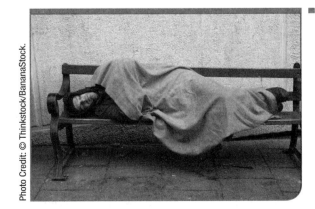

Photo Credit: © Thinkstock/BananaStock.

PHOTO 11.1

A mentally ill man sleeps on a city bench, clearly vulnerable to victimization.

aware that victims with mental illnesses may need special care, treatment, and services to ensure that they can reduce their chances of being revictimized.

Also interesting to note is that a wide range of programs are geared specifically toward addressing the needs of offenders with mental health issues and disorders, such as mental health and drug courts, crisis-intervention training for law enforcement officers, and limited mental health treatment in programs. Of course, participation in and funding for these programs is mandated, which may explain why they abound, but similar attention to the needs of crime victims with mental illness has not been given.

■ VICTIMIZATION OF THE INCARCERATED

Incarceration is, by definition, punishment. It includes loss of freedom, loss of dignity, loss of heterosexual relationships, and loss of liberty. Despite what you may have heard, what happens to prisoners while they are incarcerated is not just part of being in prison. Being victimized is not part of the punishment. In fact, the state or federal government, depending on the type of facility in which an inmate is housed, is supposed to protect inmates from any type of victimization—those perpetrated by staff or other inmates. It is actually part of the correctional staff's and administration's jobs to make sure that the jail or prison environment is safe. Why, then, is there a whole section in this text dedicated to victimization of persons who are incarcerated? Because, despite this charge to protect and to keep a secure and safe environment, prisons are, in fact, dangerous places. This section discusses the extent to which victimization occurs to inmates, the types of victimizations that are most prevalent, the risk factors for victimization, and responses to victimizations that occur.

The Extent of Victimization of People in Jail and Prison

As you may imagine, determining how much victimization occurs in jails and prisons is difficult. Much victimization goes unreported—inmates may be fearful of retaliation if they report, they may be scared to report if the perpetrator was a staff member, and they may feel that nothing will be done if they report. As a result, official data sources may underrepresent the true amount of victimization that occurs. Instead, survey data may be a better source of information to reveal the "dark figure of crime."

Results from surveys indicate that victimization is more prevalent in prisons than in the general population (Wolff, Shi, & Siegel, 2009b). In one study of inmates housed in three prisons in Ohio, it was found that half of all inmates had experienced some type of victimization during the previous 6 months (Wooldredge, 1998). Different types of victimization can also be examined separately. In this same study of inmates in Ohio prisons, 10% of inmates had been physically assaulted (Wooldredge, 1998). In an even larger study of about 7,500 prison inmates in 12 adult male and 1 adult female prison, Wolff, Shi, and Siegel (2009a) found that 34% had experienced a physical victimization during the previous 6 months. Of course, the most serious type of physical victimization that can occur behind bars is homicide. In 2007, three inmates in local jails (Noonan, 2010a) and 57 inmates in state prisons were the victims of homicides (Noonan, 2010b). For jail inmates, homicide is most likely to occur in the largest jails, to the most violent offenders, and within 7 days of admission (Noonan, 2010a). For prison inmates, homicide rates are greatest for males (99% of victims) and for Whites (46%) (Noonan, 2010b). Physical assault, however, is not the only type of victimization that inmates experience. Inmates may also have their personal effects taken. In the same study of Ohio inmates introduced above, it was found that 20% had reported a theft in the previous 6 months (Wooldredge, 1998), while other studies of property victimization indicate that one fourth of inmates experienced a property victimization in the past 12 months (Lahm, 2009). Sexual victimization also occurs in prison, but we will discuss that separately in a later section.

FOCUS ON INTERNATIONAL ISSUES

Videos from a prison in Russia's eastern Amur region surfaced on the Internet on October 24, 2011, showing Deputy Warden Sergei Zychkov viciously beating female detainees, prompting Russian officials to investigate. This is certainly not the first instance of victimization of prisoners occurring in Russia. In fact, Russia's penal system is known for abuse. A 2003 World Organisation Against Torture noted that women in Russia's prisons are often subjected to violence and forced to live in overcrowded and unsanitary conditions. These conditions led Lev Ponomaryov, a Russian human rights activist, to say "I think some of Russia's prisons can be compared to World War II era concentration camps." He notes that often it is other prisoners who are ordered by guards to mete out physical abuse in exchange for privileges.

Source: Adapted from Karmodi, O. (2011, October 31). Hit, kicked and bruised: Beatings at Russian women's prison caught on video. Retrieved from http://observers.france24.com/content/20111031-russia-amur-hit-kicked-bruised-beatings-women-prison-caught-video.

Who Is Victimized?

After researchers recognized that inmates are, in fact, at risk of being victimized while incarcerated, attention was given to identifying who is most at risk. Although little research has been done comparing males and females in terms of risk, it does appear that a greater percentage of male inmates experience physical victimization compared with females (Wolff et al., 2009a). A gendered difference discovered in physical victimization is that when females are physically victimized, they are more likely to be victimized by another inmate than are males; males are more likely to be victimized by a staff member (Wolff et al., 2009a). In addition, younger, White inmates are more likely to experience physical victimization perpetrated by other inmates than by staff (Wolff et al., 2009b). Being non-White, however, is associated with an increased risk of physical assault perpetrated by a staff member (Lahm, 2009; Wolff et al., 2009b). Other research has shown that Mexican American inmates are more likely to be victims of both personal and property crimes compared with White or Black inmates (Wooldredge, 1998). Education and income also have been examined in terms of risk for victimization. Higher-income, more-educated inmates are more at risk for being victimized by theft (Wooldredge, 1998), although lower-income inmates face greater risk of physical assault victimization (Wooldredge, 1998). See the Focus on International Issues Box for a description of the abuses faced by women in Russia's prisons.

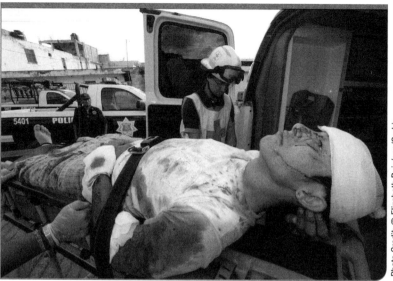

PHOTO 11.2

An inmate involved in a fight is pictured here being taken to a hospital.

Risk Factors for Victimization While Incarcerated

Although the demographic characteristics of gender, age, and race give us a picture of the typical victim of prison or jail assaults, they do not identify additional risk factors that can be used to help staff and administrators identify who may be at risk in their jails and prisons. These risk factors can generally be classified into one of two different perspectives, the **importation** and **deprivation** perspectives. According to the importation perspective, inmates have characteristics that place them at risk of becoming victimized. These factors may be things like having a previous victimization history, stature, or personality. The deprivation perspective, on the other hand, suggests that the prison environment is depriving, and this depriving environment produces victimization. For example, dangerousness of a particular facility (e.g., security level) may play a role in whether an inmate is at risk for victimization. Let's now consider the risk factors that have been studied in the literature.

Previous History of Victimization

Remember from Chapter 2 that one of the risk factors for victimization is having been victimized in the past and that many victims are actually revictimized. This also is true for prisoners. Incarcerated individuals are more likely to be physically victimized if they have been physically victimized in the past (Wolff et al., 2009b). About two thirds of all inmates in Wolff et al.'s study (2009a) who had been victimized in prison also had been physically victimized before the age of 18. Of those who had been victimized before the age of 18, about half had been victimized in prison during the past 6 months, suggesting a relationship between past victimization and victimization in prison. A relationship between sexual victimization in prison and prior sexual victimization history also was found (Wolff et al., 2009a). Specifically, inmates who come into prison with a victimization history are more likely than other inmates to be victimized in prison (Wolff et al., 2009a).

Mental Illness

Those who are vulnerable may be seen as easy targets in prison. As such, having a serious mental illness may impact people's cognitive abilities and behavior, which may make them prone to victimization (Baskin, Sommers, & Steadman, 1991). In addition, if they have affective disorders such as depression, anxiety, or posttraumatic stress disorder, they may be withdrawn or act in ways that suggest defenselessness, hence producing an increased risk for victimization (Wolff et al., 2009b). Some prisons separate persons with severe mental illness so that they can be treated for their disorders. One of the benefits of doing so is that they can be isolated from other prisoners who may otherwise harm them.

Risk Taking/Self-Control

One criminological theory that has been used to explain victimization is Gottfredson and Hirschi's (1990) **theory of low self-control.** In this theory, they propose that persons with low self-control are likely to become involved in delinquency, crime, and other analogous behaviors. In Chapter 2, you read about how Schreck (1999) utilized self-control to explain victimization. Building on this work, Kerley, Hochstetler, and Copes (2009) used the theory of self-control to explain prison victimization. In partial support of the theory of low self-control (remember that self-control encompasses six constructs), they found that inmates who like to take risks are more likely to be victimized than other inmates.

Institutional Factors

Aspects of institutional life such as sentence length, type of crime for which an inmate is in prison, security level, proportion of non-White inmates, and lifestyles also play a role in victimization risk. Inmates closer to the beginning of their sentence are more likely to be property crime victims than other inmates (Wooldredge, 1998). Inmates serving time for sexual offenses find themselves at increased risk of being victimized by fellow prisoners, while inmates serving time for violent offenses are especially at risk of being physically assaulted by staff (Wolff et al., 2009b). Security level also matters. Although some of the most dangerous inmates are housed in maximum-security facilities due to the seriousness of their offenses and sentence length, inmates housed in these facilities are less likely to experience both physical and property victimization (Lahm, 2009). Racial composition also is important. As the proportion of non-White inmates increases in prisons, the likelihood of experiencing property and personal victimization also increases (Lahm, 2009). Although speculative, this finding could be due to a lack of prison management keeping housing units' racial composition in balance. Finally, feelings that inmates have about other inmates and staff may also impact their risk of being victimized. **Social distance** also increased physical and theft victimization risk (Wooldredge, 1998), while the number of friends at the facility decreased personal crime victimization risk (Wooldredge, 1998). Social distance may indicate an unwillingness to incorporate oneself into the prison culture, which may signal to other inmates that others will not protect that person or that person's property (Wooldredge, 1998). Institutions in which inmates report higher levels of dissatisfaction with officers had higher rates of physical victimization than other facilities (Wolff et al., 2009b). Perceptions of correctional officers' fairness also seems to matter in terms of victimization risk. When inmates perceive correctional officers as unfair, their risk of victimization is higher (Wooldredge & Steiner, 2013).

Lifestyle and Routine Activities

The lifestyles and routine activities perspective also has been used to explain victimization in prison. Based on the activities in which inmates routinely engage in prison and the social distance inmates feel in relation to other inmates, it may be possible to identify who is more likely to be victimized. In one study, inmates who spent more hours in education programs and more time studying were less likely to be violently victimized but were more likely to become the victims of theft (Wooldredge, 1998). Spending time in recreation hours and the more visits an inmate had per month also increased physical assault risk. Time spent in recreation was also positively related to theft victimization (Wooldredge, 1998). Why does spending time in these structured activities increase risk? If you think about lifestyles and routine activities theory, it may make sense. Time spent in these activities may leave a person's things vulnerable and without capable guardianship, while placing them in the presence of potential offenders.

Special Case: Sexual Victimization of Incarcerated Persons

With the passage of the Prison Rape Elimination Act of 2003 (Pub. L. 108-79), even more attention has been given to the sexual assault and rape of prisoners than to physical victimization or property victimization. This piece of legislation requires that the Bureau of Justice Statistics, the research arm of the Department of Justice, annually statistically analyze the incidence and effects of prison rape in at least 10% of all state, county, and federal prisons and a representative sample of municipal jails. This means that data about the occurrence and outcomes of prison rape must be collected and analyzed each year from more than 8,700 of our nation's prisons. From these data, a report is submitted annually that lists institutions and identifies them, in order, in terms of incidence of prison rape. This is one list an institution would not want to be at the top of!

Since this act has required data collection, we now have a better idea as to how much sexual victimization occurs in prisons and jails. The data collected for the National Inmate Survey on adult inmates by the Bureau of Justice Statistics was done through self-report surveys, so it did not rely on inmates to make formal reports of their victimizations to institutional authorities. They did, however, have to admit to the victimization during the interview process, which was conducted via an audio computer-assisted self-interview using a touch screen and instructions delivered through headphones (Beck & Harrison, 2010).

From these data, it was found that 4.4% of inmates in prison and 3.1% of jail inmates experienced a sexual victimization by another inmate or someone working at the facility during the past 12 months or since they were admitted (Beck & Harrison, 2010). A slightly greater percentage of inmates in both prisons and jails reported experiencing sexual victimization perpetrated by staff rather than by other inmates (Beck & Harrison, 2010).

Who Is Sexually Victimized?

Similar to sexual victimization outside prison, female inmates are more likely to be sexually victimized than male inmates. According to findings from the National Inmate Survey, 4.7% of female prison inmates and 3.1% of female jail inmates had been sexually victimized by another inmate during the previous 12 months or since admission (Beck & Harrison, 2010). This rate is more than twice that of inmate-on-inmate sexual victimization experienced by male inmates. When males are sexually victimized, they are more likely to be victimized by staff. Almost 3% of male prisoners and 2.1% of male jail inmates reported staff-perpetrated sexual victimization (note that consensual sexual activity with staff is considered victimization) compared with 2.1% of female prisoners and 1.5% of female jail inmates (Beck & Harrison, 2010). White prison and jail inmates were more likely to be sexually victimized by other inmates than were Black or multiracial inmates, although Black inmates were more likely to experience staff-perpetrated sexual victimization (Beck & Harrison, 2010). In addition to gender and race, education and age are factors related to sexual victimization experience. More-educated inmates report higher levels of inmate-on-inmate and staff-on-inmate sexual victimization than do less-educated inmates (Beck & Harrison, 2010). Inmates aged 20 to 24 years are more at risk of being sexually victimized by staff than are inmates aged 25 years and older (Beck & Harrison, 2010).

Adults, however, are not the only inmates we house. Juveniles are also kept in correctional facilities in the United States. Their potential sexual victimization in these facilities is also being studied as part of the requirements of the Prison Rape Elimination Act. Between 2008 and 2009, the Bureau of Justice Statistics completed the first **National Survey of Youth in Custody** (Beck, Harrison, & Guerino, 2010). This survey covered 166 state-owned or state-operated and 29 locally or privately operated facilities that house adjudicated juveniles for at least 90 days. From this study, it was discovered that 12% of youth in these facilities had experienced at least one incident of sexual victimization in the past 12 months or since admission (Beck et al., 2010). Similar to the patterns seen with adult inmates, youth were more likely to be victimized by staff than by other inmates. More often than not, however, the sexual contact was achieved without any force, threat, or explicit form of coercion, although it was still illegal (Beck et al., 2010). Almost all youth (95%) who said they had been sexually victimized said that a female staff member was the perpetrator. Males were more likely than females to report being victimized by staff (10.8% vs. 4.7%), while a greater percentage of females than males indicated they had unwanted sexual activity with other inmates (9.1% vs. 2.0%) (Beck et al., 2010).

Risk Factors for Sexual Victimization in Prison and Jail

In addition to demographic characteristics, other qualities seem to place inmates at an increased risk for being targeted for sexual victimization. One of these risk factors is having experienced a sexual victimization before the current incarceration. In the National Inmate Survey, those inmates who had experienced a sexual victimization prior to coming to the facility were more likely to be sexually victimized by staff and other inmates than were inmates without a previous sexual victimization history (Beck & Harrison, 2010). Similar links between previous sexual victimization history and in-prison sexual victimization have been found (Wolff et al., 2009a). These findings are similar to what other research on the risk of revictimization has found—being victimized at one point in a person's life places him or her at risk of later revictimization.

Another risk factor for sexual victimization is sexual orientation. Specifically, inmates who have a sexual orientation other than heterosexual are more often targets for sexual victimization than are heterosexual inmates (Beck & Harrison, 2010; Hensley, Koscheski, & Tewksbury, 2005). Being vulnerable may also place inmates at risk. For example, being small in stature has been identified in some research as a risk factor for sexual victimization in prisons (Chonco, 1989; Smith & Batiuk, 1989; Toch, 1977). Other research has found that body types, such as having a small build, may also put inmates at risk, perhaps because they cannot defend themselves (Hensley, Tewksbury, & Castle, 2003). Inmates who suffer from mental disorders are also at an elevated risk of experiencing sexual victimization while incarcerated, and females with mental disorders are 3 times as likely to be sexually victimized as males with mental disorders (Wolff, Blitz, & Shi, 2007).

Responses to Victimization in Prison

Inmate Response

The very real likelihood of being victimized while in prison carries consequences with it. Many inmates spend their days in prison fearful of this potential threat. This fear leads some to request placement in **protective custody,** which involves placement in secure housing where an inmate is often kept alone in a cell for 24 hours a day, maybe only getting out for an hour for recreation or showering. Even then, the inmate will be isolated (McCorkle, 1992). Protective custody further impedes inmates from participating in programming such as education, treatment, or vocation training. It hardly seems fair, then, that a common response, albeit for the inmate's "own good," is one that is also used for punishment (solitary confinement) for inmates who have violated institutional policy.

Other inmates may use avoidance strategies such as not going to areas in the prison that they perceive to be dangerous (Irwin, 1980). Research shows that inmates who have been robbed and who are fearful are, indeed, more likely to spend more time in their cells, to avoid areas of the prison, and to avoid activities (McCorkle, 1992). Even more risky, inmates may carry "shanks"—crude, often handmade weapons—as a way to protect themselves should other inmates try to harm them or to take on a tough persona so that others will not target them (McCorkle, 1992). In addition, having been assaulted, threatened, or robbed and being fearful increase the likelihood of using aggressive precautionary behaviors such as using a "get-tough attitude," lifting weights, and keeping a weapon nearby (McCorkle, 1992).

Institutional Response

Given the factors that place inmates at risk of being victimized while in prison, there are many things that institutions do to increase safety and security. Some of these things are done out of response to judicial mandates and constitutional requirements; others are out of recognition of the dangers inherent in prison. Let's first discuss legal and constitutional requirements.

The Eighth Amendment to the United States Constitution, which prohibits cruel and unusual punishment, has been interpreted by the Supreme Court to prohibit inhumane treatment of prisoners (*Farmer v. Brennan*, 1994). As the court noted in *Farmer v. Brennan* (1994), not only do prison officials have to provide a humane environment, but failing to do so can make a prison official liable if he or she acts with **deliberate indifference** to inmate health or safety or if he or she knows that the inmate faces a substantial risk of serious harm and disregards that risk by failing to take reasonable measures to halt it (for a discussion of the facts of this case, see the Case of *Farmer v. Brennan* box).

In addition to these legal requirements, prisons have also put into place policies to reduce victimization. Because physical victimization cannot occur if inmates are not in contact with one another, one way to reduce victimization is through effective classification. Classification is the process through which offenders are screened and placed in facilities that match both their needs and characteristics, both good and bad. For instance, a prisoner who has a substance abuse problem should, theoretically, be placed in a facility that offers substance abuse treatment. Likewise, a prisoner who has anger management issues, who has demonstrated an inability to control impulses, and who has victimized staff and inmates in previous incarcerations should be placed in a maximum-security facility or one that can effectively respond to violent inmates.

Administrators and staff may reduce movement in prisons and reduce prisoner interaction, thus reducing opportunity for victimization to occur. Moreover, because race appears to be a risk factor for victimization and the racial composition of the prison is related to victimization rates, some prisons track the number of White and non-White inmates living in housing units and try to keep a particular balance (Lahm, 2009).

One way prisons have responded to the deprivation of heterosexual relationships that inmates face is through the use of conjugal visits. Conjugal visits are those in which a married inmate is allowed to spend time with his or her partner, usually in prison quarters—such as in a trailer or separate housing unit—overnight or for a weekend. During these visits, the couple is afforded more privacy than the inmate normally receives, although they are regularly checked on. Currently, only six states allow conjugal visits, however, and these visits serve to reduce only consensual sexual activity and forced sexual activity borne out of the lack of access to heterosexual relationships, not sexual activity motivated by a desire to exercise power and control (Knowles, 1999). In this way, conjugal visits are unlikely to be an effective strategy to reduce rape and sexual victimization. In addition, remember that many sexual victimizations are perpetrated by prison staff, not other inmates. As such, prison staff need to be screened, rotated on different assignments throughout the prison, and trained in ethics and law. One study on correctional officers revealed that they are likely to engage in victim blaming in regard to the sexual victimization of inmates (Eigenberg, 1989), thus suggesting a need for continued education. These are but a few of the ways that prison staff and administrators may work to reduce victimization in prisons. As you may imagine, given the unique culture and environment in prisons, seriously curtailing victimization may mean that the prison culture itself—one that involves not just inmates but the relationship between inmates and staff—needs to be addressed. This is not a task so easily undertaken.

Many people are at risk of being victimized, but certain people are more vulnerable to victimization because of qualities or characteristics they possess. In this section, persons with disabilities, persons with mental illness, and persons who are incarcerated were discussed because they are all vulnerable to victimization, given their status. You should consider what responsibility we have to people who are uniquely vulnerable to victimization. What should we do to protect these people?

THE CASE OF *FARMER V. BRENNAN*

Farmer was a preoperative transsexual with feminine characteristics who was incarcerated with other males in an all-male federal prison. During his imprisonment, he was sometimes in the general population but was more often in segregation. He was transferred from a correctional institute to a penitentiary, which is generally a higher-security facility with more serious offenders. After the transfer, he was placed in the general population. He was subsequently beaten and raped by other prisoners. He sought damages and an injunction against further confinement. The Supreme Court eventually heard the case and ruled that "a prison official's 'deliberate indifference' to a substantial risk of serious harm to an inmate violates the Eighth Amendment" (*Farmer v. Brennan*). It is the prison officials' duty under the Eighth Amendment to provide humane conditions for all prisoners; this means adequate food, clothing, shelter, medical care, and protection from violence at the hands of other prisoners.

Source: FindLaw for Legal Professionals. (2011). *Farmer v. Brennan*, U.S. 1994. Retrieved from http://caselaw.lp.findlaw.com/cgi-bin/getcase.pl?court=US&vol=000&invol=U10394.

SUMMARY

- In order to get an accurate measure of the victimization of people with disabilities, the Crime Victims with Disabilities Awareness Act of 1998 mandated that the National Crime Victimization Survey (NCVS) begin to collect information about the victimization of people with disabilities.
- Research suggests that persons with disabilities are more likely than persons without disabilities to be victimized.
- The fact that victims with disabilities and disorders are often in the care of various people who recognize their vulnerability makes them targets for violence.
- Women with disabilities face particular risks of being victimized. According to the NCVS, women with disabilities are more likely to be victimized by their intimate partners than are men. Sexual victimization is also prevalent. It is estimated that women with developmental disorders are between 4 and 10 times more likely to be sexually assaulted than women in the general population (National Council on Disability, 2007).
- Often, victims with mental disorders and/or disabilities are unsure of their victimizations and, therefore, may not receive assistance.
- Children and adolescents with disabilities are also vulnerable to victimization. They face increased risks for bullying, maltreatment, and sexual abuse.
- Risk factors for victimization of persons with disabilities include relying on others for assistance (routine activities/lifestyles theory); inability to recognize, process, and/or respond to risk; living in poverty; and the dependency-stress model.
- When mental disorders were first considered in the criminal justice system, persons with mental disorders were expected to be the offenders and not generally expected to be victims.
- A testable way to find out if victims with mental illness are more prone to victimization is to compare them with victimizations of the general population. Findings from such research suggest that mental illness is linked to an increased risk for violent and property victimization.

- The severity of one's mental illness could make it more likely that he or she will be victimized and revictimized.
- Deinstitutionalization, homelessness, poverty, and substance abuse contribute to victimization of persons with mental illness. Symptomology also has been linked to an increase in victimization risk for persons with mental illness.
- Some estimate that up to half of all prisoners are victimized while incarcerated.
- Male, young, non-White inmates appear to be most at risk for victimization in prison.
- Previous victimization, suffering from mental illness, and having low self-control increase risk for victimization in prison. Institutional factors also play a role in prison victimization.
- Quite a bit of prison victimization goes unreported due to the inmate's fear of being caught reporting.
- Prisoners' sentence length, sexual orientation, physical size, age, lifestyle while incarcerated, and even what they were convicted for may or may not make them suitable targets for sexual victimization.
- Inmates serving time for sexual offenses find themselves at increased risk of being victimized by fellow prisoners, while inmates serving time for violent offenses are especially at risk of being physically assaulted by staff.
- A response to victimization in prison and being fearful is increased likelihood of using aggressive precautionary behaviors such as a "get-tough" attitude, lifting weights, and keeping a weapon nearby.
- It is the prison officials' duty to separate those prisoners who are more vulnerable and likely to be victimized from the general population. In this way, crime within the prison should be reduced.

DISCUSSION QUESTIONS

1. Given that exposure to motivated offenders is a direct cause of victimization of disabled persons and those with mental disorders, do you think that offenders are initially motivated or that they become motivated once they recognize how vulnerable these special populations are? What would Cohen and Felson say?

2. What special services do victims with mental illness and victims with disabilities need from criminal justice professionals and agencies? Do we currently have enough resources in place to address their special needs? What about other social service agencies that help crime victims?

3. Think about the *Farmer v. Brennan* (1994) case. Do you feel special prison conditions should be available for members of the LGBT community who are more likely to be victimized in male or female prisons?

4. As the laws for people in the United States change, do our prison communities also need to evolve so we are providing humane living conditions as defined in our U.S. Constitution?

5. Put yourself in one of the incarcerated victim's position. Would being victimized in prison make you more likely to continue being a victim or would you use other coping strategies? What are the consequences of prison victimization?

KEY TERMS

developmental disability

dependency-stress model

Federal Crime Victims with Disabilities Awareness Act of 1998

Crime Victims with Disabilities Act of 1998

deinstitutionalization

symptomology

dark figure of crime

importation

deprivation

theory of low self-control

social distance

Prison Rape Elimination Act of 2003

National Inmate Survey

National Survey of Youth in
Custody

protective custody

deliberate indifference

classification

conjugal visits

INTERNET RESOURCES

Centers for Disease Control and Prevention (http://www.cdc.gov)

This website offers full definitions of the developmental diseases as well as their symptoms, all of which could make a person a more suitable target for victimization. The site provides some safety and health tips for parents and caregivers of people who have developmental disorders. Most helpful are the emergency preparedness and response topics listed on the website.

"Promising Practices in Serving Crime Victims With Disabilities" (http://www.ovc.gov/publications/infores/ServingVictimsWithDisabilities_bulletin/crime.html)

This page on the Office for Victims of Crime website outlines patterns and responses of victimization. Resources are listed for caregivers or the victims themselves to prevent victimization. There are statistics for how often this type of victimization occurs as well as recommendations for coordinating with law enforcement to stop victimization of persons with disabilities.

State of the USA (http://www.stateoftheusa.org/content/44-percent-of-prison-inmates-s.php)

This website provides a report about prison inmate victimization, with statistics from the Bureau of Justice Statistics. The charts on the website provide an in-depth breakdown of what types of prison victimization occur based on what incidents are actually reported. This page also offers data on variations and circumstances surrounding prison inmates' victimization. Prison facilities are ranked based on inmates' reports of victimization.

"Violence and Mental Illness: The Facts" (http://promoteacceptance.samhsa.gov/publications/facts.aspx?printid=1)

This webpage is a very specific information source on the common stigmas and stereotypes associated with people who have mental health issues as they pertain to violence. This page does well explaining why certain discriminations exist and why people typically have a hard time being caregivers for them. Believing that persons with mental illness are always the suspects in violent situations does not help prevent their victimization.

CHAPTER 12

VICTIMIZATION AT SCHOOL AND WORK

Polly, the young woman first introduced in Chapter 2, was walking home from a local bar when she was accosted by two men. She was shoved by one of the men, and they were able to take her bag and its contents. Polly suffered several negative consequences from her victimization—most obviously, the 10 stitches in her head. But she also had a hard time coping with what happened. She found herself staying in bed when she should have been going to class. As a college student, this negative consequence could have prevented her from successfully completing the semester. So far, you have considered Polly's victimization in terms of why she was victimized, whether she meets the criteria for being a "typical" victim, and the types of services to which Polly should have access. What you should also consider, however, is whether Polly's victimization would be included in school victimization statistics. She is, after all, a college student. Is this designation enough for her victimization to be classified or counted as a victimization at school? Does it matter that she was not in class at the time? Would she need to be on campus for it to count as a school victimization? What would the college have to do if this was considered a school victimization? These issues will be discussed in this section along with another special case of victimizations, those that occur while people are at work or on duty.

■ VICTIMIZATION AT SCHOOL

We often think of school as being a safe place. Schools are designed as places where young people come together to learn and grow. Attendance is not voluntary; instead, children are required to go to school, and it is the place where they spend a great deal of their lives. Parents assume that when they send their children off to school, they will willingly go and that, even if they do not love school, they are at least safe. For the most part, this is true, but not all students matriculate through school without experiencing some type of victimization. When they are victimized in the school building, on school grounds, while riding a school bus, or while attending or participating in a school function, it is termed school victimization. This type of victimization can take the form of any other victimization—property victimization or personal victimization that can include theft, robbery, simple assault, aggravated assault, rape, and murder. Other victimizations may include harassment or bullying—a focus of recent research that is discussed in more detail below.

■ VICTIMIZATION AT SCHOOL: GRADES K–12

The type of victimization that likely comes to mind when you think about children being harmed at school is a school shooting. When a school shooting—such as the one at Columbine in 1999—does occur, it is difficult to watch the news or read the newspaper without hearing about the incident. Indeed, the media pay close attention when young people are shot at school. Although they get heightened media attention, fortunately school shootings are very rare. But how do we know this? The information on victimizations that occur at school comes from a variety of resources. Remember that the National Crime Victimization Survey (NCVS) asks individuals aged 12 and over about their victimization experiences during the previous 6 months. If a person has been victimized, he or she is then asked detailed questions about the victimization, including where it occurred. From the NCVS, then, it is possible to generate estimates of the extent of victimization occurring at school for people at least 12 years of age. To supplement the NCVS, the School Crime Supplement Survey is a national survey of about 6,500 students aged 12 to 18 enrolled in schools in the United States. Students are asked about victimizations they experienced in the previous 6 months (Robers, Zhang, Truman, & Snyder, 2010). Keep in mind, though, that students younger than 12 are not included in this survey. In addition, other nationally representative surveys are commonly used to determine the extent to which students, staff, and teachers are victimized at school. For example, a survey has been implemented to assess safety and crime at schools and is filled out by school principals or those knowledgeable about discipline (School Survey on Crime and Safety 1999–2000, 2003–2004, 2005–2006, 2007–2008, and 2009–2010 school years); another is filled out by teachers in elementary, middle, junior, and high schools (Schools and Staffing Survey 1993–1994, 1999–2000, 2003–2004, 2007–2008, and 2011–2012 school years); and another is completed by students enrolled in Grades 9 through 12 in public and private schools (Youth Risk Behavior Surveillance System, 1993–2011 biennially).

From these surveys and other official data sources, we have a fairly good idea as to what types of victimization experiences occur at school. In 2012, about 1,364,900 million nonfatal victimizations occurred against children aged 12 to 18 at school (Robers, Kemp, Rathbun, & Morgan, 2014). Importantly, more nonfatal violent crimes occurred against this age group *at* school than *away* from school (Robers et al., 2014). It is estimated that 4% of students experienced some type of victimization in the previous 6 months. The most common type of victimization they experienced was theft (3% of students)—1% experienced a violent victimization (Robers et al., 2014). For students enrolled in Grades 9 through 12, violent victimization was more common—in 2013, 8% reported being in a physical fight on school property, and 7% reported being threatened or injured with a weapon on school property (Centers for Disease Control and Prevention, 2014). Although relatively uncommon, violent

PHOTO 12.1

On April 20, 1999, Columbine High School experienced one of the worst school shootings in U.S. history. Twelve students and one teacher were shot dead by two students who also took their own lives. Although the reasons behind the shootings cannot be known for certain, both boys experienced bullying at school.

death also can occur at school. Between July 1, 2010, and June 30, 2011, 11 students were victims of homicide and 3 were victims of suicide at school. Violent deaths at schools are tracked through the School-Associated Violent Deaths Surveillance Study, the Supplementary Homicide Reports, and the Web-Based Injury Statistics Query and Reporting System.

Who Is Victimized?

Similar to most other types of victimization, except for sexual assault and rape, male students are more likely to be victimized at school than are female students. Almost 8% of male students in Grades 9 through 12 reported being threatened or injured with a weapon on school property during the previous year, compared to only 6% of female students (Centers for Disease Control and Prevention, 2014). Males experience greater rates of victimization at school than do females (Robers et al., 2014). Age is another correlate of school victimization that we can examine. Violent victimization appears to be most common among younger school children than those in high school. For example, in the Youth Risk Behavior Surveillance System survey, it was found that students in 9th grade had higher rates of fighting than did students in 10th through 12th grade (Centers for Disease Control and Prevention, 2014). In addition, students aged 12 to 14 have the highest victimization rate (Robers et al., 2014). Race/ethnicity is another important correlate in examining any type of victimization. More than half of victimizations at school are experienced by White youth, but data from 2011 show that there are no differences in risk of victimization at school for White, Black, Hispanic, and Asian students (Robers et al., 2014). Where students live also influences risk of being victimized at school. Students who live in urban or suburban areas face greater risks of being victimized at school than students in rural areas (Robers et al., 2014). A final factor to consider is household income of the student. For theft, there is little difference in victimization rates across household income levels; however, violent victimization impacts children who reside in households with annual incomes less than $15,000 at the highest rate (Robers et al., 2010).

Not only are students at risk of being victimized at school, but teachers, administrators, and staff may also become victims. Technically, this type of victimization would be victimization at work, but since it occurs at schools, we will discuss it here. Fortunately for them, teachers, administrators, and staff are fairly unlikely to be victimized while working at school. As discussed later in the section on workplace victimization, persons working in service and retail occupations, law enforcement/corrections, and mental health have much higher rates of workplace victimization than do educators and persons employed at schools. Nonetheless, victimization does occur, but risk is not constant for all teachers. Special education teachers are more likely to be violently victimized than are other teachers (May, 2010). Data from the Schools and Staffing Survey show that 5% of teachers report being physically attacked by a student during 2011–2012, and 9% said that they had been threatened with injury by a student at school during this time period (Robers et al., 2014). A larger percentage of elementary school teachers are physically attacked as compared to secondary school teachers (Robers et al., 2014). Risk of victimization also varies depending on the location of the school. Teachers employed in public schools are at greater risk of being threatened with injury and being physically attacked than those working in private schools (Robers et al., 2014).

As with students, teachers are more likely to be victims of theft than of violent offenses (Robers et al., 2010).

Risk Factors for School Victimization

Much like with other types of victimization, victimologists and others have attempted to discover what causes school victimization. Why are some school children victimized while others are not? Why are some schools safe and others riddled with crime? It is difficult to determine the exact reasons why school victimization occurs, but it is likely a combination of structural forces as well as individual factors. For example, much attention has been paid to the school's location and its relationship to the amount of victimization that occurs there. As you may expect, schools located in crime-ridden neighborhoods are often likely to have high levels of violence and other types of victimization (Laub & Lauritsen, 1998). But there are high-performing and safe schools in these same neighborhoods, so it is not enough to locate "bad" neighborhoods to identify unsafe schools. It is also possible that the factors that place youth at risk for victimization outside school are similar to the ones that place them at risk of being victimized in school—such as low self-control, lack of capable guardianship, and having deviant or delinquent peers. In addition, adolescence is a period marked by biological changes; hormones run amuck and bodies change. Both males and females go through transitions, both physically and emotionally, and they navigate new social situations. This time can be pressure filled and stressful, which may lead to outbursts, aggression, bullying, and other maladaptive behaviors.

Consequences

We require youth to attend school in the United States, and in turn, we should be providing them a safe, productive learning environment. When this does not occur and students are victimized, many negative outcomes may arise. Results from the 2011 School Crime Supplement to the NCVS show that 4% of students were afraid of being attacked or harmed at school, compared with 2% who were afraid of being attacked or harmed away from school (Robers et al., 2014). Victims reported higher levels of fear than nonvictims, which shows the powerful effects that victimization has on school-aged youth. Victims are also likely to skip or avoid school. The Youth Risk Behavior Surveillance System study data revealed that 7% of students did not attend school at least 1 day during the 30 days prior to the survey because they felt they were unsafe at or on their way to school (Centers for Disease Control and Prevention, 2014). Victimized students also indicated that they avoided school activities and specific places inside school buildings, such as certain hallways, the school entrance, parts of the cafeteria, and restrooms, at higher levels than did nonvictims (Robers et al., 2014). In 2011, about 6% of students admitted to avoiding school activities or certain places because they feared harm (Robers et al., 2014).

Bullying

One specific type of victimization that can occur at school and has garnered recent attention is bullying. **Bullying** is the intentional infliction of injury or discomfort (or the attempt to do so) on another person repeatedly over time when there is a power imbalance between the perpetrator and the victim (Olweus, 2007). Bullying can be both direct and indirect. **Direct bullying** involves both physical and verbal actions in the presence of the victim. **Physical bullying** can include hitting, punching, shoving, pulling the chair out from under another person, tripping, and other physical actions. **Verbal bullying** includes direct name calling and threatening. **Indirect bullying** can be more subtle and harder to detect. It is often referred to as social bullying and includes actions such as isolating individuals, making obscene gestures, excluding from activities, and manipulation. Even though it is often said that "kids will be kids" and bullying is simply a natural part of children's interactions, research suggests that it can have pernicious effects and that ignoring bullying in schools may be dangerous.

Before discussing the consequences of bullying, let's first uncover the extent to which bullying occurs in schools. Bullying appears to be more common than other types of victimization. In 2011, 28% of children aged 12 to 18 said they had been bullied at school during the school year (Robers et al., 2014). A report published by the National Institute of Child Health and Human Development found that 1.6 million children are bullied at least weekly and that 17% of children in Grades 6 through 10 have been bullied (Ericson, 2001). Most commonly, students reported being made fun of (18%), but 81% reported having been pushed, shoved, tripped, or spit on, and 5% said they had been threatened with harm (Robers et al., 2014).

Like school victimization more generally, bullying differentially impacts some youth. In the 2001 World Health Organization's Health Behavior in School-Aged Children Study, it was found that Black youth are less likely to be bullied than are White or Hispanic children (Nansel et al., 2001). Data from the School Crime Supplement show that a greater percentage of White students reported being bullied compared with Black, Hispanic, and Asian students (31% vs. 27%, 22%, and 15% respectively) (Robers et al., 2014). Males were more likely than females to be bullied (Nansel et al., 2001). Research shows, however, that females are more likely to be the targets of verbal and indirect bullying whereas males are more likely to experience physical bullying (Robers et al., 2014). Other recent research has shown that certain groups are more at risk of being bullied than others. Youth who have learning disabilities, those who have attention-deficit/hyperactivity disorder, those with physical disabilities, obese children, and those who stutter experience higher rates of bullying victimization (Miller & Miller, 2010). Recently, attention has been given to the fact that gay youth are more likely to be targeted by bullies than are other youth and that this bullying often occurs on a daily basis (Miller & Miller, 2010). The largest group of victims tends to be slight or frail. They tend to be average or poor students and are generally passive socially (Olweus, 1993a). This is not to say, however, that all bullied victims "look" the same. Other victims tend to be more assertive and hot-tempered; they react aggressively when they are bullied. They start fights in addition to being picked on (Pellegrini, 1998). Both types of bullied youth are unlikely to be in the "popular" groups in school.

As with other forms of victimization, research in bullying has uncovered the fact that there is a subset of individuals who are bully/victims—they bully and are bullied (Haynie et al., 2001). What is important about this group of youth is that they seem to fare even worse in terms of psychosocial or behavioral functioning than do those who are either bullies or victims.

FOCUS ON RESEARCH

Research conducted on children in Finland found that children who experience both social anxiety and are rejected by their classmates are at great risk of being bullied. This research also looked at classroom effects on bullying and found that victimization risk was highest in classrooms where students believed that there were negative social outcomes to defending the victim of bullying. Bullying was also most typical in classrooms and schools where students perceived their teachers to be less disapproving of bullying.

Source: Adapted from Saarento, S., Karna, A., Hodges, E. V. E., & Salmivalli, C. (2013). Student-, classroom-, and school-level risk factors for victimization. *Journal of School Psychology, 51,* 421–434.

Psychosocial Effects of Bullying Victimization

Although, as mentioned, bullying sometimes has been treated as "normal" behavior for children, its effects can be quite serious. It has been linked to poor psychosocial adjustment—students who are bullied more often report greater levels of unhappiness (Arseneault et al., 2006) and lower self-worth (Egan & Perry, 1998). Bullying during adolescence has been linked to anxiety and depression both contemporaneously and later in life (Bond, Carlin, Thomas, Ruin, & Patton, 2001; Olweus, 1993b). Being bullied also has been shown to be linked to health symptoms in children. Children who reported being bullied were more likely to report not sleeping well, bed wetting, and getting occasional headaches and tummy aches (Williams, Chambers, Logan, & Robinson, 1996). In addition to these consequences, being bullied also has negative outcomes on school adjustment and performance. Bullied youth are more likely to say they dislike school than are nonbullied youth (Kochenderfer & Ladd, 1996; Rigby & Slee, 1993), are more likely to report absenteeism from school (Rigby, 1997; Zubrick et al., 1997), and have higher levels of school avoidance (Kochenderfer & Ladd, 1996). See the Focus on International Issues box for a description of a case of bullying that occurred in South Korea in which the victim committed suicide and the perpetrators were found to be criminally responsible for his death.

Bullying is not unique to the United States. It occurs in other countries as well and criminal justice systems and schools are faced with dealing with the consequences. A recent case in South Korea highlights a severe case of bullying in which the perpetrators were held to account by the criminal justice system. Two 15-year-old boys bullied a classmate in a variety of ways—they forced him to play online games on their behalf and took his winnings, beat him, took food from his house, forced him to eat biscuits off the ground, and pushed his head into the sink. The bullying lasted over a period of time until the victim jumped off a building, killing himself. The victim named the two assailants in his suicide note. The two boys were sentenced to 3 years and 3 and half years in prison for their actions.

Source: Adapted from Hancocks, P. (2012, February 20). 2 teens sent to prison for S. Korean bullying suicide. Retrieved from http://articles.cnn.com/2012-02-20/asia/world_asia_south-korea-bullying-sentence_1_prison-terms-suicide-note-on line-games?_s=PM:ASIA.

Violent Effects of Bullying Victimization

Perhaps the most serious outcome of being bullied is acting out in response. Bullying victimization has been linked to violent behavior by the *victim*. A report by the Secret Service revealed that 71% of school shooters whose friends, families, and neighbors were interviewed had been the targets of a bully (Espelage & Swearer, 2003). It should be noted, however, that if bullying caused school shootings, we would see many more than we do. As such, it may be a contributing factor in some instances but by no means can be considered a cause. Recently, the media have given widespread attention to several young people who have committed suicide after being bullied by their peers in various ways. With the widespread use of the Internet and cell phones, bullying methods have expanded to include what is known as cyberbullying. Cyberbullying is bullying behavior that takes place via mobile phones, the Internet, and/or digital technologies. It can involve threats or harassment sent over the phone, threatening and insulting comments posted on a social networking site, and vulgar or scary text messages. Children can do the bullying themselves or enlist their friends or family. Cyberbullying can be particularly harmful given its ease of use and the fact that people can bully without having to be in the presence of the victim. They can even do it anonymously. As noted by Aftab, "The schoolyard bullies beat you up and then go home. The cyberbullies beat you up at home, at grandma's house, wherever you're connected to technology" (as quoted in Nies, James, & Netter, 2010). In the following box read the heartbreaking story of Phoebe Prince, a young teen who committed suicide after being cyberbullied. The School Crime Supplement to the NCVS began including questions regarding bullying behavior through electronic means in 2007. In 2011, almost 9% of students surveyed reported experiencing cyberbullying during the previous school year (Robers et al., 2010). Research on the effects of cyberbullying show that it is related to an increase in delinquency, self-harm, and suicidal ideation (Hay, Meldrum, & Mann, 2010).

THE STORY OF PHOEBE PRINCE

Phoebe Prince, a recent Irish immigrant, hanged herself January 14, 2010, after nearly 3 months of routine torment via text message and through Facebook by students at South Hadley High School. Police believe she was the victim of cyberbullying from multiple "girls at the school who had an unspecified beef with her over who she was dating" (Kotz, 2010). Her case has been called "the culmination of a nearly 3-month campaign of verbally assaultive behavior and threats of physical harm" (as quoted in Goldman, 2010). In at least one instance, she was physically attacked when a girl pelted her with a soft drink can. As of January 28, 2010, "nine students have been indicted on charges ranging from statutory rape to civil rights violations and stalking. It appears that Phoebe may finally get her justice" (Kotz, 2010). As a result of the attention that bullying has garnered through cases like Phoebe's and others, "forty-five states now have anti-bullying laws; in Massachusetts, which has one of the strictest, anti-bullying programs are mandated in schools" (Bennett, 2010).

Source: Adapted from Kotz, P. (2010). Phoebe Prince, 15, Commits suicide after onslaught of cyber-bullying from fellow students. Retrieved from http://www.truecrimereport.com/2010/01/phoebe_prince_15_commits_suici.php. Bennett, J. (2010). From lockers to lockup: School bullying in the digital age can have tragic consequences. But should it be a crime? Retrieved from http://www.newsweek.com/2010/10/04/phoebe-prince-should-bullying-be-a crime.html?GT1=43002.

Responses to School Victimization

In response to victimization and bullying at schools, many schools have instituted security measures. Most commonly, schools have hired law enforcement officers, installed metal detectors, installed security cameras, begun to lock entrances and exits during school hours, and implemented supervision of hallways during the school day (Devoe, Bauer, & Hill, 2010). According to a survey of principals, 43% of public schools in 2009–2010 had security guards, law enforcement, or School Resource Officers (Robers et al., 2014). Over 60% of public schools used security cameras and 5% used random metal detector checks (Robers et al., 2014). The School Crime Supplement Survey also indicates that many students report that schools are implementing security measures. Almost one fourth of students reported that they were required to wear picture identification at school, and 95% indicated that visitors were required to sign in at their school (Robers et al., 2014).

In addition to school security measures, laws and policies are in place to address violence within schools. Current federal law, under the **Gun-Free Schools Act,** mandates that each state that receives federal funding must suspend for at least 1 year any student who brings a firearm to school. As such, most states have laws to address bullying, harassment, and hazing that occurs at school (Olweus Bullying Prevention Program, 2011)—some of which are **zero-tolerance policies** that mandate specific punishments for fighting and violence along with bringing weapons to school—which may serve to limit school victimization and bullying. Fortunately, most states have instituted a broad range of policies that attempt to address school victimization more holistically. For example, see the next box, which provides a description of Florida's laws. Although it remains to be seen how effective these laws are at reducing the amount of victimization that occurs at school, many of the laws also require mandatory reporting of suspected victimization, mandate that schools have programs and resources to reduce school victimization, and require that people are in place to oversee these programs (Limber & Small, 2003).

Most school-based programs are targeted at reducing school violence and/or bullying specifically. The most effective of these programs are proactive and involve parents, students, and the community (Ricketts, 2010). A common type of a violence-reduction program is peer mediation. Peer mediation programs train a group of students in interest-based negotiation skills, communication skills, and problem-solving strategies so they can help their peers settle disagreements peacefully and without violence (Ricketts, 2010). Findings from evaluations of peer mediation programs show that they can change the school climate over time (Ricketts, 2010). To specifically attack bullying, some schools have adopted bullying prevention programs. One of the most widely adopted of these programs, the Olweus Bullying Prevention Program, has shown promising reductions in bullying perpetration and victimization in both the United States and Norway (Olweus, 1991).

FLORIDA'S BULLYING/HARASSMENT, CYBERBULLYING, AND HAZING LAWS

Bullying/Harassment

Statute 1006.147 (2008) prohibits bullying or harassment of any student or employee of a public K–12 educational institution, during any program or activity conducted by a public K–12 educational institution, during any school-related or school-sponsored program or activity, or through the use of data or computer software accessed through a computer, computer system, or network of a public K–12 educational institution. Specific definitions of bullying and harassment are outlined in the statute.

Statute 1006.147 (2008) provides immunity from a cause of action to a school employee, school volunteer, student, or parent who promptly reports in good faith an act of bullying or harassment to the appropriate school official.

Statute 1006.147 (2008) requires school districts to adopt a policy prohibiting bullying and harassment of any student or employee of a public K–12 educational institution. The policy must substantially conform to the model policy of the state Department of Education, and must afford all students the same protection regardless of their status under the law. Requirements of the policy are outlined in the statute.

Statute 1006.07(6) requires district school boards to provide for the welfare of students by using the Safety and Security Best Practices to conduct a self-assessment of the district's current safety and security practices. The self-assessment includes indicators for districts to develop and enforce policies regarding antibullying, antiharassment, and due process rights in accordance with state and federal laws. The assessment also includes indicators of schools surveying students on school climate questions related to discipline, bullying, threats perceived by students, and other safety or security related issues.

Statute 1006.07(2) also requires a student to be subject to in-school suspension, out-of-school suspension, expulsion, or imposition of other disciplinary action by the school and possibly criminal penalties for violating the district's sexual harassment policy.

State Board of Education Administrative Rule 6A-19.008 (1985) requires schools to have environments that are free of harassment and prohibit any slurs, innuendos, or other verbal or physical conduct reflecting on one's race, ethnic background, gender, or handicapping condition, which creates an intimidating, hostile, or offensive educational environment, or interferes with

(Continued)

students' school performance or participation or other educational opportunities.

Cyberbullying

Statute 1006.147 (2008) prohibits bullying and harassment of any student or employee of a public K–12 educational institution through the use of data or computer software that is accessed through a computer, computer system, or computer network of a public K–12 educational institution. The definition of harassment in the statute includes any threatening, insulting, or dehumanizing gesture, use of data or computer software, or written, verbal, or physical conduct directed against a student or school employee that does one of the following: (1) places them in reasonable fear of harm to his or her person or damage to his or her property; (2) substantially interferes with a student's educational performance, opportunities, or benefits; or (3) substantially disrupts the orderly operation of a school. The definition of "bullying and harassment" includes perpetuation of actions by an individual or group with intent to demean, dehumanize, embarrass, or cause physical harm to a student or school employee by accessing or knowingly causing or providing access to data or computer software through a computer, computer system, or computer network within the scope of the district school system.

Hazing

Statute 1006.135 (2005), referred to as the Chad Meredith Act, defines hazing and makes the hazing of students at a high school with Grades 9–12 a criminal offense as defined within the statute. The bill prohibits the following defenses to a charge of hazing: obtained consent of the victim; the conduct or activity that resulted in the death or injury was not part of an official organizational event or was not otherwise sanctioned or approved by the organization; the conduct or activity that resulted in the death or injury was not done as a condition of membership in an organization.

Source: National Association of State Boards of Education (2010). The NASBE Healthy Schools Policy Database is a comprehensive set of state-level laws and policies from 50 states on more than 40 school health topics that includes hyperlinks to the actual policies whenever possible.

■ VICTIMIZATION AT SCHOOL: COLLEGE

You may have been wondering whether college students are similarly at risk for victimization while attending school. Most parents send their children to college feeling pretty confident that they will be safe—most college students report feeling safe at school. Are these feelings justified?

Who Is Victimized?

You will be happy to learn that college students actually have lower average annual rates of victimization than their similarly aged nonstudent counterparts (Baum & Klaus, 2005). The difference for students and nonstudents was not significant, however, for rape and sexual assault. When college students are victimized, they are most likely to experience a nonviolent victimization, such as theft. In a study of college students enrolled in 12 institutions of higher learning, Fisher, Sloan, Cullen, and Lu (1998) found 169.9 theft victimizations per 1,000 students. Of those who are violently victimized, the most common victimization is simple assault (63% of all violent victimizations) (Baum & Klaus, 2005). Most violent victimizations are committed by strangers, at night, without a weapon, and off-campus (Baum & Klaus, 2005). In fact, college students experience violent victimizations off-campus at 20 times the rate they experience them on campus (Hart, 2007). Most violent victimizations of college students do not result in physical injury (75%) (Baum & Klaus, 2005).

In addition to these incident-level characteristics, college students who are victimized share common characteristics. White college students have higher violent victimization rates than do students of other races (Baum & Klaus, 2005). White students and students of other races have lower violent victimization rates than nonstudents, while Hispanic students have similar violent victimization rates to Hispanic nonstudents (Baum & Klaus, 2005). Violently victimized college students also tend to be male. Male college students are twice as likely as female college students to be violently victimized (Baum & Klaus, 2005). The only type of violent victimization that female college students experience at higher rates than males is sexual victimization. Female college students have an average annual rape/sexual assault rate of 6 per 1,000 persons ages 18 to 24, compared with a rate of 1.4 for males. Male college students, on the other hand, have an average annual rate of violent victimization of 80.2, compared with 42.7 for female college students (Baum & Klaus, 2005). For a detailed account of sexual victimization of college students, see Chapter 8 on sexual victimization.

Less attention has been given to property victimization of college students; however, we do have an idea as to who the "typical" college property victim is. Males tend to be property victims more so than female college students (Fisher, Sloan, Cullen, & Lu, 1998). In addition, younger students, aged 17 to 20, are at greater risk of property victimization than are older college students (Fisher et al., 1998). Employed students report higher levels of property victimization than do unemployed students or those who work part-time (Johnson & Kercher, 2009).

Risk Factors for Victimization at College

Although college students are not at a greater risk than nonstudents of being violently victimized, they do still experience a great deal of violent victimization. With over 10 million 18-to-24-year-olds enrolled in college in 2009 (National Center for Higher Education Management Systems, 2009), a violent crime rate of 60.7 per 1,000 persons equates to 607,000 violent victimization incidents each year. So, why do this many victimizations occur?

Lifestyle/Routine Activities

Recall from Chapter 2 that routine activities theory is one of the hallmark theories of victimization. According to this theoretical perspective, risky lifestyles and daily routines place individuals at risk of being victimized. When persons engage in risky lifestyles and routines that bring them together in time and space with would-be offenders, and they are without capable guardians—thus making them suitable targets—they are likely to be victimized. Let's consider how college students may engage in routine activities and risky lifestyles that could place them at risk.

Spending time in the presence of potential offenders increases the risk of being victimized. It is instructive that, for college students, the most common offender is another college student (Fisher et al., 1998). Students who spend more time away from home in the evening are at risk of being victimized (Mustaine & Tewksbury, 2007b). Spending many nights on campus during the week has been found to increase theft victimization for college students (Fisher et al., 1998). For college females, spending time in places where men are seems to increase risk, particularly for sexual victimization. That is, women who spend more time in fraternity houses are more likely than other women to be sexually victimized (Stombler, 1994). Being a member of a fraternity or sorority also has been linked to an increased risk of property victimization (Johnson & Kercher, 2009). Another way that college students may be exposed to potential offenders is through engaging in victimizing behavior. Those who do are more likely to be victimized than others (Tewksbury & Mustaine, 2000).

Being a suitable target also increases risk of victimization for college students. A person can be deemed "suitable" for a variety of reasons. A person may have items that are valuable and easy to steal, and if these items are carried in public, he or she is at greater risk of being victimized than others (Johnson & Kercher, 2009). A person may be walking alone and not seem as though he or she is able to protect himself or herself. Or, as is quite relevant for college students, a person may be visibly intoxicated and, thus, may be seen as easy to victimize and unable to resist an attack; the offender may not fear that the person will fight back or even recall enough details about the event to make a reliable police report. We will return to alcohol and its role in college students' victimization below.

The last element relevant to routine activities theory is lack of capable guardianship. College students who live in settings with high levels of transience and low levels of cohesion—for example, student apartments where residents move year to year and change roommates frequently—are at greater risk of victimization than students who live at home or in campus dorms (Mustaine & Tewksbury, 2007b). Guardianship can also be created through physical means such as carrying a weapon, Mace, or pepper spray or by attending prevention or crime awareness seminars. Attending crime prevention or crime awareness seminars has been found to reduce the risk of violent victimization among college students (Fisher et al., 1998). On the other hand, some research shows that the use of physical guardianship is actually related to an increase in victimization, but this may be due to people purchasing and carrying these items after being victimized (see Fisher, Daigle, & Cullen, 2010b).

Alcohol

In addition to the three elements of routine activities theory, college students also often engage in behaviors that likely increase their risk of victimization. The first risky behavior we should consider is the use of alcohol and drugs. As you are well aware, the use of alcohol is pervasive among college students. Research on the use of alcohol by college students shows that between 75% and 96% of college students consume alcohol (National Institute on Drug Abuse, 1995, 1998). Students also engage in binge drinking, which is defined as having 4 or more drinks in one sitting for a female and having 5 or more drinks in one sitting for a male. Almost half of college students binge drink and drink specifically to get drunk (O'Malley & Johnston, 2002). One of the most serious consequences of alcohol use among college students is criminal victimization. In fact, "college students who drink heavily are more likely to be both criminal offenders and victims of crimes" (Tewksbury & Pedro, 2003, p. 32).

Why does alcohol increase college students' risk of being victimized? Well, as noted in Chapter 2, alcohol impairs cognitive functioning and reduces a person's ability to assess situations as risky. Even if a person can see that a situation is dangerous, he or she may not be physically capable of warding off a potential attacker if inebriated. A person may also have lowered inhibitions and say and do things that he or she would not normally do; thereby, a person can find herself or himself in a situation with a potential offender. Given the effects of alcohol, a person may say or do things to anger others, thus unintentionally getting into a fight or argument. Not to blame the victim, but when alcohol is involved, the victim's actions or words may set in motion a series of events that lead to victimization.

Responses to Campus Victimization

Legislation

No parents ever want to get a phone call informing them that the child they dropped off at college was harmed, but that is just what the parents of Jeanne Clery experienced. They received the worst phone call of all: Their daughter had been raped and murdered while attending Lehigh University. She was sleeping in her dorm room when Joseph Henry entered through propped-open and unlocked doors (Clery & Clery, 2008). In response to their daughter's death, the Clerys sued the university after they found out that the university knew about the propped-open and unlocked doors and did not tell the students about the potential dangers lurking on their campus. In addition to filing a lawsuit, they pushed for legislation that would require college campuses to better inform students about crime. As a result, the Student Right-to-Know and Campus Security Act of 1990, renamed in 1998 the **Jeanne Clery Disclosure of Campus Security Policy and Campus Crime Statistics Act** [20 USC 1092 (f)], was passed (hereafter referred to as the Clery Act).

The Clery Act applies to all institutions of higher learning that are eligible to participate in student aid under Title IV of the Higher Education Act of 1965. Enforced by the Department of Education, the act has three main requirements. First, by October 1 of each year, schools must publish an annual campus security report with crime statistics and a security policy that includes information about sexual assault policies, the authority of campus security officers, and where students should go to report a crime. The security report must include information about the three most recent calendar years and must be made available to all current students and employees. The crimes that must be included in the report are homicide, sex offenses, robbery, aggravated assault, burglary, motor vehicle theft, and arson. If an arrest or disciplinary referral was made, the report must also include liquor law violations, drug law violations, and illegal weapons possession. The location of the incident must be provided in terms of occurring on campus, in residential facilities for students on campus, in noncampus buildings, or on public property immediately adjacent to or running through the campus.

Second, colleges and universities are required to disclose incidents in a timely fashion through crime logs and warnings about ongoing threats. A crime log must be kept by the campus police or security department. Within two days of being made aware of a crime, the police or security must include the offense in the crime log, including the nature, date, time, and location of each crime. This crime log is public record—it is to be made publicly available during normal business hours and kept open for 60 days. Along with the crime log, warnings must be provided about those crimes that are required to be disclosed or those believed to represent an ongoing threat to students and employees. Warnings are commonly delivered through e-mails, phone calls, and text messages.

Third, the Clery Act requires that certain rights for both accusers and victims are protected in cases of sexual assault handled on campus. Both parties are given the same opportunity to have other people present at campus disciplinary hearings. Both parties have the right to be informed of the outcome of disciplinary hearings. Victims have the right to notify law enforcement and also have the right to be notified about counseling services available to them and options for changing academic and living situations.

Despite these requirements, there are some limitations to the Clery Act. Not all crimes that occur are required to be disclosed in the security report, not all crimes are reported to the police, and only those crimes that occur on campus property or public property adjacent to the campus are required to be in the report; thus, individuals who look to the security report for guidance about their campus safety may be getting only a partial picture of the true amount of crime that occurs. In addition, although the Clery Act mandates that colleges and universities comply with its requirements, research shows that not all schools are doing so (Fisher, Karjane et al., 2007).

In addition to the Clery Act, other federal legislation has been passed that allows for the tracking of sex offenders who have been convicted and who are required to register if they are enrolled in an institution of higher learning or volunteering on campus (Carter & Bath, 2007). In addition, at least 19 states have Clery-type legislation (Sloan & Shoemaker, 2007).

Building off of the Clery Act, more recent legislation has been passed that requires universities and colleges to record and disclose dating violence, domestic violence, and stalking in its annual crime report. The Campus Sexual Violence Elimination (SaVE) Act of 2013 (as part of the Violence Against Women Reauthorization Act) also requires colleges to provide those reporting victimization with written information regarding their rights, disciplinary procedures, victim assistance, and safety planning. In addition, new students and employees must be offered primary prevention and awareness programs regarding rape, sexual assault, domestic violence, dating violence, and stalking.

Campus Police and Security Measures

Of those 4-year colleges and universities that have 2,500 students or more, almost 75% have sworn law enforcement officers (Reaves, 2008). Almost all public institutions have sworn

RIPPED FROM THE HEADLINES

Legislation is currently being considered in the U.S. Senate that would increase the penalties for colleges and universities that do not comply with the requirements of the Clery Act, Title IX, and the SaVE Act. If passed, the Bill would increase the penalty from $35,000 to $150,000 per violation. This bill comes at a particularly important time, as the Department of Education is currently investigating 71 different schools for violations.

Source: Adapted from Westerholm, R. (2014, July 31). U.S. Senate announces anticipated bill toughening penalties on schools that mishandle campus sexual assault. Retrieved from http://www.universityherald.com/articles/10687/20140731/u-s-senate-announces-anticipated-bill-toughening-penalties-on-schools-that-mishandle-campus-sexual-assault.htm.

personnel, while less than half of private campuses have sworn officers (Reaves, 2008). Instead, campuses that do not have sworn personnel have nonsworn security officers. Those that do have sworn personnel grant these officers full arrest powers. Campuses

PHOTO 12.2

Howard and Connie Clery, sitting on the bed of their daughter, Jeanne Clery, who was brutally murdered at Lehigh University. Howard and Connie are the heads of Security on Campus, Inc.

differ greatly in terms of the number of officers they employ. As you may imagine, institutions of higher learning that have a large student body and are located in large, urban centers tend to have larger police and security forces than do smaller and more traditional rural institutions (Reaves, 2008). For a list of the campuses with the largest number of sworn law enforcement officers, see Table 12.1.

Almost all college campuses have a three-digit emergency telephone number that persons can call for assistance or to report a crime (Reaves, 2008). Those who are on campus and need assistance can use blue-light emergency campus phones that provide direct access to campus law enforcement. More than 90% of 4-year institutions of higher learning that enroll at least 2,500 students have these phones (Reaves, 2008). In addition to these security measures, most institutions of higher learning have written terrorism plans, written emergency response plans, and provide students with access to crime prevention programs (Reaves, 2008).

Table 12.1 ▦ Largest Number of Full-Time Sworn Officers for Colleges, 2004–2005 School Year	
Campus Served	**Full-Time Sworn Officers**
Howard University	166
Temple University	119
University of Pennsylvania	100
University of Medicine and Dentistry of New Jersey	97
George Washington University	95
University of Florida	86
Georgia State University	79
Yale University	78
University of Maryland—College Park	76
Vanderbilt University	76

Source: Reaves, B. A. (2008). Campus law enforcement, 2004-05.*Bureau of Justice Statistics Special Report*, February 2008, NCJ 219374.

■ VICTIMIZATION AT WORK

So far, we have discussed victimization that occurs when people are attending school, despite the fact that schools should provide a safe environment to encourage active learning. The work environment, you would think, should be similarly safe—and there are strict rules and laws in place, discussed below, that attempt to ensure it is just that. Nonetheless, people are not always safe from harm while they try to earn a living. But just how often are people victimized on the job? Why does it happen, and how can it be prevented? These questions and more will be addressed in this section.

Definition of Workplace Victimization

Before we address the extent to which victimization occurs to people at work, let's address what victimization at work encompasses. Obviously, if a person is victimized while physically at work—say, in his or her office—that constitutes a **workplace victimization.** But what if a person is victimized in the parking garage at work? Would this too be "counted" as a workplace victimization? What if a victimization occurs when a person is traveling for work or doing official work business, such as making a delivery? In short, if a person is working or on duty and victimized, the incident is considered a workplace victimization. Workplace victimizations can be violent—ranging from threats and simple assaults to homicide—or can be nonviolent—such as theft.

Much of the research that has examined workplace victimization has focused on violence that occurs in the workplace, as opposed to nonviolent victimizations. You may be surprised to learn that the concept of workplace violence has been studied for many years. In fact, the first discussions of workplace violence in the literature occurred in 1892 (Jenkins, 2010). Data on workplace violence, though, were not collected and criminologists did not begin to consider seriously the etiology and causes of workplace victimization until the 1970s and 1980s (Jenkins, 2010). Since then, however, widespread attention has been given to violence that occurs in the workplace. One useful tool that has been developed to understand workplace violence is a typology of workplace violence (Jenkins, 2010). The first type is **criminal intent incidents,** which include incidents in which the perpetrator has no legitimate relationship to the business at which the crime occurs. Most commonly, the perpetrator in this type commits a crime in conjunction with the violence, such as a person who robs a gas station and shoots the attendant. The second type is **customer/client incidents.** These incidents occur when the perpetrator has a legitimate relationship with the business and becomes violent when receiving services from the business. An example of this second type would be a person at a doctor's office who is quite agitated and begins punching the doctor. The third type is **worker-on-worker incidents.** In these incidents, the perpetrator is a current or former employee of the business and aggresses against another employee. The fourth, and last, type of incident is **personal relationship incidents,** in which the perpetrator has a personal relationship with the intended victim, who is targeted while at work. An example of this type would be a domestic violence incident in which a man shows up at his ex-wife's place of employment and shoots her. Now that you have an idea of the types of victimization that constitute workplace victimization, let's find out how much of this occurs each year.

Extent of Workplace Victimization

As with victimization at school, most people can safely go to work each day and be free from victimization. But some people do, in fact, experience victimization. We can get an idea of the extent of workplace victimization from a variety of data sources. As with most types of victimization, one rich source of data is the NCVS. Recall that when a person indicates in the NCVS that he or she experienced a victimization, an incident report is then completed. In the incident report, if persons indicate they were at work or on duty at the time of the victimization, the incident is counted as a workplace victimization incident. Between 1993 and 1999, an average of 1.7 million violent victimizations occurred at work or while people were on duty, accounting for 18% of all violent crime during this time period (Duhart, 2001).

According to findings from the NCVS, the most common type of victimization experienced by people at work, however, is personal theft—between 1987 and 1992, more than 2 million personal thefts, on average, were experienced at work each year (Bachman, 1994). Almost a quarter of all thefts reported in the NCVS occurred at work or while persons were on duty (Bachman, 1994). The second most common type of victimization measured in the NCVS is simple assault, a violent victimization. Between 1993 and 1999, an average of 1,311,700 simple assaults occurred against people at work or while on duty (Duhart, 2001). When aggravated assaults are included, almost 19 of every 20 workplace violent incidents were aggravated or simple assaults, which shows that other forms of violent workplace victimization are relatively uncommon (Duhart, 2001). In fact, during this same time period, only 6% of all workplace violent crime was rape/sexual assault, robbery, or homicide (Duhart, 2001).

Who Is Victimized at Work?

Demographic Characteristics of Victims

By now, you could probably guess that males are more likely than females to be violently victimized at work or while on duty, except for rape and sexual assault (Duhart, 2001). There is no difference, however, in the rates of theft victimization for males and females—they are equally likely to be the victims of theft while working (Bachman, 1994). Although the patterns for workplace violent victimization for gender follow the trends for victimization more generally (i.e., males have higher rates than do females), the trends for race do not. Rates of workplace violent victimization are highest for Whites. In fact, from 1993 to 1999, the average workplace violent victimization rate was 25% higher for White workers than for Black workers (Duhart, 2001). The rate for workplace violent victimization was similar for Black and Hispanic workers (Duhart, 2001).

The last two demographic characteristics to consider are age and marital status. Young adults aged 20 to 34 had the highest rates of workplace violent victimization. Persons who were married or widowed had lower workplace violent victimization rates than those who were never married, divorced, or separated. The last three groups all have similar rates of victimization (Duhart, 2001).

Occupations With Greatest Risk

Knowing what demographic characteristics are correlated with workplace victimization does little to inform us what jobs are most risky. You would be right if you thought that some jobs are replete with danger. Data from the NCVS show that law enforcement jobs are the most dangerous. Persons working in this field, which includes police, corrections, and private security officers, experience 11% of all workplace violent victimizations (Duhart, 2001). Fortunately for your professor, college and university teachers have the lowest rates. Other occupational fields that face the highest risk (in order) are mental health, retail sales, teaching, transportation, and medicine. Within these broad categories, police, taxicab drivers, corrections workers, private security, bartenders, custodians in mental health settings, professionals in mental health settings, special education teachers, and gas station attendants have some of the highest violent victimization rates at work (Duhart, 2001). As you might imagine, persons in retail sales have the highest robbery victimization rates, while people in law enforcement have the highest assault rates (Duhart, 2001). Persons working in government jobs are also at risk of workplace violence (Lord, 1998).

Special Case: Fatal Workplace Victimization

Of course, the most serious outcome of victimization is when a person loses his or her life. Unfortunately, this sometimes does occur when a person is at work—and it is not just caused by people "going postal." In fact, homicide is not the leading cause of occupational injury deaths of postal workers (Jenkins, 2010). How do we know this? To track the number of fatal injuries for various occupations, the National Census of Fatal Occupational Injuries program was initiated in 1992. Each year, the Bureau of Labor Statistics publishes its findings about the extent of fatal injuries from this program so that a picture of the extent and types of fatal occupation injuries can be drawn (Bureau of Labor Statistics, 2011).

In 2012, a total of 4,628 people suffered fatal occupational injuries. Of these, 767 persons died in the workplace or while on duty as a result of violence and other injuries by persons or animals (Bureau of Labor Statistics, 2014). Of these 767 people, 463 were homicide victims and 225 died as a result of self-inflicted wounds. Of the 463 homicide victims, most (81%) were the victims of shootings in the workplace (Bureau of Labor Statistics, 2014). The most common type of workplace homicide is criminal incident, with robberies alone accounting for 40% of the cases in 2008 (Bureau of Labor Statistics, 2010). Coworkers and former coworkers (worker-on-worker type) accounted for only 12% of incidents in the same year (Bureau of Labor Statistics, 2010).

Demographic Characteristics of Victims

As with workplace violence in general, males are more likely to be murdered at work than are females. What is notable, though, is that a greater percentage of fatal workplace injuries that involve females are from homicide compared to fatal workplace injuries that involve males (Bureau of Labor Statistics, 2014). In 2012, 28% of all fatal workplace injuries of females were from homicide compared to only 9% of nonfatal workplace injuries from homicide for males (Bureau of Labor Statistics, 2014). Another interesting difference between men and women, however, is who the perpetrator is when homicide at work does occur. Although males and females are equally likely to be the victims of workplace robbery and have other assailants, females are more likely to be murdered at work by a relative or personal acquaintance than are males (Bureau of Labor Statistics, 2010). In addition to males having higher rates of workplace homicide, minorities face a greater risk of becoming victims of this specific type of workplace victimization than do others (Sygnatur & Toscano, 2000). Adults aged 25 to 44 account for the greatest percentage of workplace homicides, while persons under the age of 18 have the lowest rates (Sygnatur & Toscano, 2000).

Occupations and Workplaces With Greatest Risk

You have already learned that workers in some occupations face greater risk of being victimized than do others. Do you think that the same types of occupations pose the same dangers in terms of fatal workplace violence? You may be surprised to learn that, although law enforcement jobs are "risky" in terms of nonfatal violence, they are not the most risky in terms of fatal workplace violence. Taxicab drivers and chauffeurs face the greatest risk of being murdered of any type of worker in the United States (Sygnatur & Toscano, 2000). They face 36 times the risk of all employed individuals. Consider this fact: Taxicab drivers and chauffeurs compose only 0.2% of employed workers but account for 7% of all work-related homicides (Sygnatur & Toscano, 2000). They account for a disproportionate share of workplace homicide. Law enforcement officers have the next highest rate of workplace homicide.

It is also instructive to consider workplaces that have high rates of occupational homicide. Retail trades have the highest rates of workplace homicide, while services, public administration, and transportation also have high rates. Retail establishments that have the most homicides include liquor stores, gas stations, grocery stores, jewelry stores, and eating/drinking establishments. Services include hotels and motels, for example. Public administration includes detective and protective order services as well as justice and public order establishments. Finally, transportation includes taxicab establishments, which, as previously mentioned, contain the most risky occupation for workplace homicide (National Institute for Occupational Safety and Health, 1995).

Risk Factors for Victimization at Work

Now that you know what types of occupations and workplaces have the highest risks of workplace victimization and workplace homicide, the next thing to consider is why these jobs and places are so dangerous. What is it about working in retail or law enforcement, for instance, that poses a risk? Generally, a number of characteristics of certain jobs place workers at risk of being victimized (Jenkins, 2010; National Institute for Occupational Safety and Health, 1995; Sygnatur & Toscano, 2000).

- Working in contexts that involve the exchange of money with the public
- Working with few people or alone
- Working late at night or during the early morning
- Working in high-crime areas
- Working in the community (such as police or taxicab drivers)
- Working with criminal, unstable, or volatile persons

- Having a mobile workplace
- Working in delivery of goods, passengers, or services
- Guarding valuables or property

Special Case: Sexual Harassment

Another special type of victimization at work is sexual harassment. Legally, sexual harassment can occur in two ways. First, **quid pro quo sexual harassment** occurs when a person's compliance with request for sexual favors dictates employment-related outcomes, such as raises and promotion. Second, **hostile work environment sexual harassment** occurs when sex-related conduct creates an intimidating, hostile, or offensive working environment, or unreasonably interferes with an individual's work performance (Sexual Harassment, 29 C.F.R. § 1604.11[a][2][3]]). These are the legal definitions of sexual harassment, but a person may be considered a victim if he or she feels as though he or she was harassed, thus meeting a psychological definition (O'Leary-Kelly, Bowes-Sperry, Bates, & Lean, 2009). A behavioral definition of sexual harassment is that it includes sex-related behaviors that cause psychological discomfort or are illegal (O'Leary-Kelly et al., 2009). A psychological definition would be that sexual harassment occurs when sex-related behavior at work is considered by the recipient as offensive, exceeding a person's resources, or threatening a person's well-being (as cited by O'Leary-Kelly et al., 2009). Research shows that women are more likely to be the victims of sexual harassment than men (O'Leary-Kelly et al., 2009), especially when they exhibit more masculine personalities and when they are working in fields that are traditionally more masculine (Berdahl, 2007). Research also shows that sexual harassment is most common for people working in jobs where organizational tolerance for sexual harassment is high and when there is a small proportion of women in a workgroup (Willness, Steel, & Lee, 2007).

PHOTO 12.3

A day at work can prove to be very dangerous for taxicab drivers, who face some of the greatest risks of violence at work.

Photo Credit: © Thinkstock/Creatas.

Consequences of Workplace Victimization

One of the most obvious consequences of workplace victimization is that people may not be able to go to work. They may be injured and need to receive medical attention and, as a result, may need to take time off from work. They may be fearful and scared to return to work. Persons who participated in the NCVS indicated that they missed some 1,751,100 days of work each year as a result of workplace victimization (Bachman, 1994). On average, each workplace victimization incident cost 3.5 days of missed work, which resulted in more than $55 million in lost wages annually, not including days missed that were covered by sick and annual leave (Bachman, 1994).

Workplace homicide also is associated with a whole host of costs. When examining medical expenses, future earnings lost, and household production losses that include child care and housework, workplace homicides between 1992 and 2001 cost $6.5 billion (Hartley, Biddle, & Jenkins, 2005). Each workplace homicide costs an average of $800,000 (Hartley et al., 2005).

Responses to Workplace Victimization

We know the extent to which workplace victimization occurs, the occupations and workplaces at greatest risk of experiencing workplace victimization, and the risk factors for experiencing workplace victimization. But what have places of business, the government, and the legislature done to prevent victimization at work?

Prevention Strategies

For prevention strategies to be most effective, they should be tied to risk factors. That is, to prevent workplace victimization, the factors that place particular occupations or places of work at risk should be targeted and altered to effect change. In doing this, preventing workplace victimization has typically occurred in three main areas. The first prevention strategy is targeting **environmental design.** These strategies focus on ways to make a workplace more secure and a less attractive target. See Table 12.2 for examples of this type of prevention. The second type of prevention strategy, **organizational and administrative controls,** focuses on strategies that administrators and agencies can implement to reduce the risk of workplace victimization in their organizations. Although these controls can be varied, common strategies are identified in Table 12.2. The third type of prevention strategy is behavioral. **Behavioral strategies** are actions that workers can take to reduce their risk of workplace victimization. These include the behaviors identified in Table 12.2.

Employers can also do their part to reduce workplace violence perpetrated by current or former workers by being careful about who they hire and by being watchful of suspicious behavior from their employees. One thing employers should do is carefully screen their employees to uncover any issues with alcohol or drugs, violence, or issues with coworkers in the past (Morgan, 2010). They should also try to identify persons who tend to externalize blame for their problems, who are hostile, and who frequently change jobs, as all these characteristics are indicators of a person who may become violent at work (Morgan, 2010). Employers should also watch for warning signs of violence such as when a person is obsessed with weapons or brings weapons to work, when a person recently has been written-up or fired, when a person has made a threat, when a person is intimidating or has made others fearful, when a person has demonstrated romantic interest in a coworker that is not reciprocated, when a person is paranoid, when a person cannot accept criticism, when a person has experienced personal problems, or when a person begins changing work habits (e.g., showing up to work late when usually on time) (Morgan, 2010).

Table 12.2 ■ Types of Workplace Prevention Strategies		
Strategy	**Definition**	**Examples**
Environmental	Focuses on ways to make a workplace more secure and a less attractive target	Install better lighting, install security cameras and bullet-proof barriers or enclosures, post signs stating that only small amounts of cash are on hand, make high-risk areas visible to more people, install silent alarms, have police check on workers, etc.
Organizational and administrative	Focuses on strategies that administrators and agencies can implement to reduce the risk of workplace victimization in their organizations	Providing training on maintaining a safe work environment; instituting ban on working alone; recording verbal abuse incidents and suspicious behavior; policies that define what is considered workplace victimization/violence and methods for defusing volatile situations; training on how to use security equipment; access to psychological counseling and/or support to reduce likelihood of acting out at work; and access to services following acts of workplace victimization
Behavioral	Actions that workers can take to reduce their risk of workplace victimization	Training in nonviolent response and conflict resolution, training on how to anticipate and respond to potential violence, training on how to resist during a robbery

Source: U.S. Department of Justice, Bureau of Justice Statistics, School Crime Supplement (SCS) to the National Crime Victimization Survey (NCVS), 2007.

Legislation and Regulation

You may be surprised to learn that there is not a national set of standards specific to the prevention of workplace violence (Jenkins, 2010; OSHA, n.d.). There are, however, federal agencies that provide legislative guidance for workplace safety and health. The **Occupational Safety and Health Administration (OSHA)** in the U.S. Department of Labor has occupational safety and health legislative responsibility, while the National Institute for Occupational Safety and Health in the U.S. Department of Health and Human Services is responsible for research in this area (Jenkins, 2010). Both agencies, along with others in the federal government, provide publications and recommendations regarding workplace violence prevention. In addition to these federal guidelines, 25 states, Puerto Rico, and the Virgin Islands have standards and enforcement policies to address workplace violence as well as plans that have been approved by OSHA (n.d.). Some states have standards or policies that are different from the guidelines put forth by OSHA. More generally, all employers are required to provide a safe work environment that is free of recognizable hazards likely to cause death or serious bodily harm (Occupational Safety and Health Act of 1970, Pub. L. 91-596). If workers are harmed while on duty, employers may be liable if they failed to disclose the dangers workers face or if they negligently ignored the threat of workplace violence (Smith, Gambrell & Russell, LLP, 2005).

SUMMARY

- Males are the most likely targets for victimization in schools, much the same as research shows them to be for most other crimes.
- The most commonly occurring type of school victimization is theft.
- More violent acts of victimization typically happen in lower grade levels than in Grades 10 through 12.
- Individual, school, and structural forces all play a role in school victimization.
- Though extreme cases of school victimization, such as school shootings, that would get increased media attention have occurred, this type of victimization is very rare.
- When looking at school victimization, it is important to note that some teachers are also the targets of aggressive or criminal behavior. The typical teacher-victim is the instructor of a special-education class.
- Though bullying can have some serious psychological effects on people, it often is considered a normative behavior in the socialization process among students.
- Bullying can be indirect or direct, and can be social, physical, or verbal. Cyberbullying—in which people use the Internet, mobile phones, and other digital technologies to bully others—has received recent attention in the news.
- The most typical victimization a college student experiences is theft.
- College students who experience victimization, specifically violent victimization, often engage in risky lifestyles and routine activities (i.e., participating heavily in the college partying culture, binge drinking, and going to events alone and late at night).
- The Jeanne Clery Disclosure of Campus Security Policy and Campus Crime Statistics Act requires most universities to have widely accessible campus crime reports, to keep crime logs and deliver warnings about crime threats, and to protect the rights of both victims and those who are accused of sexual assaults handled on campus.
- Campuses have also responded to the threat of crime by employing campus police or security officers and providing other safety precautions and programming for students.
- In the workplace, younger adults and children are, of course, at less risk for being victimized, while the age range at greatest risk for violent and even fatal victimization is 25 to 44.
- The typology of workplace violence classifies incidents into criminal, customer/client, worker-on-worker, and personal relationship incidents.
- Thefts are the most common type of workplace victimization. Males and White workers have higher rates of workplace victimization than do females and non-White workers.
- The Census of Fatal Occupation Injuries program tracks all cases of fatality in the workplace.

- Taxicab drivers have the highest rates of workplace homicide; law enforcement officers have the highest rates of nonfatal workplace victimization.
- Working at night, alone, with money, with the public, in high-crime areas, in a mobile workplace, or in the community places people at risk for workplace victimization.
- Workplace victimization may also take the form of sexual harassment. Quid pro quo and hostile work environment are two types of sexual harassment. Women are more likely to be the victims of sexual harassment than men.
- Though there is no standard set of workplace prevention guidelines, it is the employer's responsibility to provide a safe work environment for all employees (i.e., screening potential employees before hiring, making sure the physical work space is free from hazardous material or anything that could cause bodily harm, etc.).
- Much like school victimization, the most extreme cases of fatality in the workplace, which would get media attention, are not the most common. Personal theft of belongings is more likely to occur than a workplace shooting or any other physically violent act.

DISCUSSION QUESTIONS

1. Assess your risk of being victimized at college. Are you at high risk? Why or why not? How could you reduce your risk of being victimized?

2. Based on what you have read about workplace violence, assess your risk of being a victim at your current or former place of work. If you do not work, consider your parent's place of employment. Does your job have risk factors for violence? If yes, why? How could your place of employment reduce its risk?

3. Why do you think males and minorities have higher rates of workplace victimization than do females and nonminority workers?

4. In the workplace, do you think you would be at less risk being employed as a police officer or as a taxicab driver? Why? What does the research say?

5. How important is it for you personally to protect yourself and your belongings at work if personal theft is the most common form of victimization in the workplace? How can your own routine activities in the workplace contribute to or prevent you from being a victim of theft?

KEY TERMS

school victimization

bullying

direct bullying

physical bullying

verbal bullying

indirect bullying

cyberbullying

Gun-Free Schools Act

zero-tolerance policies

Jeanne Clery Disclosure of Campus Security Policy and Campus Crime Statistics Act

workplace victimization

criminal intent incidents

customer/client incidents

worker-on-worker incidents

personal relationship incidents

quid pro quo sexual harassment

hostile work environment sexual harassment

environmental design

organizational and administrative controls

behavioral strategies

Occupational Safety and Health Administration (OSHA)

INTERNET RESOURCES

"Fact Sheet: Workplace Shootings" (http://www.bls.gov/iif/oshwc/cfoi/osar0014.htm)

The Bureau of Labor Statistics website provides a workplace shootings fact sheet listing statistics on the year's fatalities, injuries, and illnesses. Charts separate the shootings by workplace industry. The links on the page offer information to victims of workplace violence about how to receive compensation and benefits for their losses.

"Harassment-Free Hallways" (http://history.aauw.org/files/2013/01/harassment_free.pdf)

This article discusses ways in which sexual harassment can be prevented in schools. It provides information for students, parents, and school personnel. It also includes a brief survey that you can take to learn whether you have been a victim of sexual harassment.

Olweus Bullying Prevention Program (http://www.olweus.org/public/index.page)

This website is a helpful tool for understanding the types of bullying that exist as more technology develops. There is a host of information for teachers, parents, and students who may be affected by some form of school victimization, and headlining news videos about bullying that has occurred in various states. This is a website with the facts and harsh realities about school victimization but also with tips and testimonials that could prevent it in the future.

Stop Cyberbullying (http://www.stopcyberbullying.org/index2.html)

This website offers valuable information on how serious this technologically advanced form of bullying is and explains what the law says and does when this type of bullying is reported. This is more of a "take action" website that explains to victims and people who want to help exactly what can be done. The site also explains how cyberbullying works and why people choose to do it so readily.

"Workplace Violence" (www.osha.gov/SLTC/workplaceviolence/)

The U.S. Department of Labor's Occupational Safety and Health Administration webpage defines and outlines the standards, rules, and regulations for workplace/office violence. The key resource this website offers is a detailed list of references for workplace/hazard awareness. A lengthy list of PDFs provides information on preventing victimization and being more aware of routines at work that could make you a suitable target for violence.

CHAPTER 13

PROPERTY AND IDENTITY THEFT VICTIMIZATION

So far, we mainly have discussed violent or personal victimizations. These are the types of victimization that commonly make the news—murders, rapes, assaults, and child abuse, to name a few. We tend to think about these when we hear the word *victimization*. But these are not the most common types of victimization. Instead, the most common type is property victimization. In fact, it is theft! Although this is not the type of victimization most commonly shown on the evening news, it is what will most likely happen to you if you are unfortunate enough to become a crime victim. There are, of course, other types of property victimization, and we will discuss those as well. In today's world, criminals are acting in innovative ways. No longer does an offender need to be in your presence to victimize you. Indeed, the Internet has opened up numerous ways for you to have your money taken, your privacy violated, and even your identity stolen. In this section, we will discuss these two types of victimization that generally receive less attention in the field of victimology, but nonetheless impact numerous persons each year.

■ PROPERTY VICTIMIZATION

Victimization is generally discussed in two categories: personal victimization and property victimization. Personal victimization, as measured in the National Crime Victimization Survey (NCVS), includes simple assault, aggravated assault, rape and sexual assault, and robbery. Property victimization as measured in the NCVS includes theft, motor vehicle theft, and household burglary. There are other types of property victimization, but we will limit our discussion to these three types.

Theft

Theft, also called larceny-theft, is defined by the Federal Bureau of Investigation (FBI, 2009) as the "unlawful taking, carrying, leading, or riding away of property from the possession or constructive possession of another." To be classified as a theft, the item cannot be taken by force, violence, or fraud. As such, if items are taken via embezzlement, confidence games, check fraud, or forgery, it is not considered larceny-theft (FBI, 2009). If these types of action are excluded, what, then, would be considered theft? Stealing a bicycle, shoplifting, pick-pocketing, or stealing any item or property, so long as it is not achieved through force, violence, or fraud, as noted, is theft (FBI, 2009).

Extent of Theft

Theft is the most common crime victimization experienced by Americans. This is supported by statistics from the Uniform Crime Reports (UCRs) and those from the NCVS. According to the UCR, in 2012, there were more than 6 million larceny-thefts, resulting in a rate of 1,959.3 per 100,000 persons in the United States (FBI, 2012a). Larceny-thefts composed almost 69% of all property crimes that occurred in 2009 (FBI, 2012a). The extent of theft is also captured in the NCVS. For 2012, the NCVS estimates that there were 2.5 times the number (15,224,700) of thefts (not including attempted and completed purse snatching and pocket picking) compared with the UCR data (Truman, Langton, & Planty, 2013). Theft composed 58% of all victimizations in the NCVS (Truman, et al., 2013). Why do you think the estimates from the NCVS are so much higher for theft compared with those from the UCR?

Characteristics of Theft

The UCR and the NCVS also describe the characteristics of theft in the United States. According to the UCR, the average larceny costs the victim $987 in lost property, which amounts to over $6 billion in total losses for all larcenies in 2013 (FBI, 2009). According to the NCVS, losses for larceny are somewhat lower, with a mean dollar loss of $403 (BJS, 2007). You are probably not surprised to learn that most thefts go unreported to police. In fact, only about 26% of all thefts were reported to the police in 2012 (Truman et al., 2013). The low reporting rates probably contribute to the low recovery rates of stolen property. In more than 86% of larceny victimizations reported in the NCVS, the victim noted that none of his or her property was recovered (BJS, 2007).

You may wonder what items people most commonly steal. In about a quarter of larcenies reported to the police (remember that the UCR includes only those crimes the police know about) were thefts of motor vehicle parts, accessories, and contents (FBI, 2009). When persons were asked in the NCVS what was stolen, almost 36% indicated that personal effects such as portable electronics, photographic equipment, jewelry, and clothing were taken (BJS, 2007). See the Focus on International Issues box to read about another type of theft that is common in today's world: cell phone theft.

Who Are Theft Victims?

Although virtually any possession can be stolen, theft rates do differ according to household characteristics measured in the NCVS. Rates of theft are highest for households headed by persons who are White, while Hispanics have higher theft victimization rates than do non-Hispanics (BJS, 2007). Households headed by younger people (12–19 years of age) report higher rates of theft victimization than households headed by older persons (BJS, 2007). Households that have a total income less than $7,500 annually have the highest theft rates (BJS, 2007). Also, as the number of people in the household increases, so does the risk of theft. In fact, households with six or more people were 3 times more likely to experience a theft than were single-person households (Truman & Rand, 2010).

Risk Factors for Theft Victimization

Theft is so common, at least in terms of victimization, that it may seem as though risk is ubiquitous and theft amounts to little more than having your property in the wrong place at the wrong time. Remember, though, that researchers have linked victimization risk to certain qualities and characteristics, often due to a person's lifestyle and routine activities. Theft victimization also has been explained using this perspective. In fact, Cohen and Felson, in their routine activities theory, linked increases in property crime to the production developments that made goods smaller, more durable, and easier to move. At the individual level, exposure to delinquent or criminal others increases the chances that a person will become the victim of theft. In a study of college students, Mustaine and Tewksbury (1998) found that smoking marijuana increased the risk of minor theft victimization, while threatening another with a gun or threatening without a weapon increased the risk of minor and major theft victimizations. Living in a neighborhood that had too much crime or was too noisy also positively impacted minor victimization risk (Mustaine & Tewksbury, 1998). In addition, having capable guardianship decreased the chances of theft. College students who had a dog in their residence and who lived in rural areas were less likely to experience minor larceny victimization (Mustaine & Tewksbury, 1998). Installing extra locks also decreased the chances of major larceny victimization for college students (Mustaine & Tewksbury, 1998).

College students may be deemed suitable targets for theft as well. Students who eat out frequently found themselves at a greater risk of minor theft victimization than did others (Mustaine & Tewksbury, 1998), likely because these students were exposing themselves to many people and displaying their wallets and money. Students who left their homes often to study were also more likely to be theft victims than were others, likely because they were exposing their personal items to would-be offenders (Mustaine & Tewksbury, 1998). Beyond this study of routine activities theory and theft among college students, the research on the reasons why some people become victims of theft has not been fully explored. Can you think of other theories or explanations that could eludicate why certain people have their possessions stolen?

Motor Vehicle Theft

Anyone who has a car has probably thought about the possibility of having it stolen, but motor vehicle theft can also occur with other self-propelled vehicles that run on land, such as sport utility vehicles, trucks, buses, motorcycles, motor scooters, all-terrain vehicles, and snowmobiles (FBI, 2009). When we discuss motor vehicle theft, it covers the theft or attempted theft of the vehicle itself. If a car is broken into, for example, and the contents taken, it is a larceny-theft, not a motor vehicle theft. When auto theft involves the taking of a car by an offender who is armed and the vehicle is occupied, it is called carjacking. In this section, we limit our discussion to the nonviolent victimization of motor vehicle theft.

Extent of Motor Vehicle Theft Victimization

In 2012, 721,053 motor vehicle thefts were reported to the police—this number of reported thefts equates to a motor vehicle theft rate of 229.7 per 100,000 persons in the United States (FBI, 2012a). For motor vehicle theft, the number of reports to the police, as shown in the UCR, is not too different from the estimate in the NCVS. In 2013, there were 633,740 motor vehicle thefts according to the NCVS (Truman et al., 2013). Why are motor vehicle theft estimates so close for the UCR and NCVS, while estimates for theft, as you read above, are so divergent? The answer is probably tied to the nature of the victimization. If your car were stolen, don't you think you would be quite likely to report it to the police? You would want to get the police on the case so your car could be found. You also need a police report for insurance purposes. These reasons likely contribute to the similar estimates.

Characteristics of Motor Vehicle Theft Victimization

Along with knowing the extent to which motor vehicles are stolen, we also have an idea of the characteristics of motor vehicle thefts that occur in the United States. The costs associated with motor vehicle theft are high. According to the UCR, each stolen vehicle costs, on average, $6,019 (FBI, 2009), and the average is $6,286 according to the NCVS (BJS, 2007). For the nation as a whole, motor vehicle theft costs almost $4.3 billion annually (FBI, 2009). However, financial costs are not the only ones that victims incur when their motor vehicles are stolen. More than one fifth of victims report missing at least 1 day of work due to motor vehicle theft (BJS, 2007).

As previously mentioned, motor vehicle theft is widely reported to the police (more than 80%). About half the victims of motor vehicle theft report that all their property (in this case, their vehicle) was recovered (BJS, 2007). Motor vehicle theft is most likely to occur at night, near the victim's home (BJS, 2007), and in urban areas (FBI, 2009). Almost half of motor vehicle thefts occur when the victims are sleeping (BJS, 2007).

As you may imagine, though, not all vehicles are equally likely to be stolen. To determine the cars most likely to be stolen, the National Insurance Crime Bureau (NICB) compiles a list using National Crime Information Center data based on police reports (Insurance Information Institute, 2011). See Table 13.1 for a list of the cars that were most stolen in 2013. After you examine the list, consider that the costs of these cars when stolen may not be that much compared with the costs of more expensive cars. When insurance claims rates and the size of insurance payments are considered together, the Highway Loss Data Institute has identified that the Ford F-250 crew 4WD has the highest theft-claim rate for passenger vehicles of 2010–2012 vehicles in the United States, followed by the Chevrolet Silverado 1500 crew, the Chevrolet Avalanche 1500, and the GMC Sierra 1500 crew (Insurance Institute for Highway Safety, 2013). The average loss payment per claim for the Ford F-250 crew 4WD was $7,060. When the number of these vehicles that are stolen, along with the costs associated with their loss, are totalled and compared with the number of each make and model insured, their theft costs the insurance industry the most. These values take into account the value of the contents of the vehicles as well, so it does not include just the cost of the vehicle.

Along with certain types of cars being prime targets, certain cities have higher-than-average rates of motor vehicle theft. In 2012, the Modesto, California, Metropolitan Statistical Area had the highest motor vehicle theft rate per capita in the United States, according to data compiled by the NICB (Insurance Information Institute, 2011). All the top 10 cities for highest motor vehicle theft rates are in the Western part of the United States. See Table 13.2 for the list.

Table 13.1 ■ Top 10 Most Frequently Stolen Passenger Vehicles in 2013

Rank	Make/Model (includes all years)
1	Honda Accord
2	Honda Civic
3	Chevrolet Pickup (Full Size)
4	Ford Pickup (Full Size)
5	Toyota Camry
6	Dodge Pickup (Full Size)
7	Dodge Caravan
8	Jeep Cherokee/Grand Cherokee
9	Toyota Corolla
10	Nissan Altima

Source: Reprinted by permission of the National Insurance Crime Bureau.

Table 13.2 ■ Top 10 U.S. Metropolitan Areas With Highest Motor Vehicle Theft Rates in 2012			
Rank	Metropolitan Statistical Area	Vehicles Stolen	Rate
1	Bakersfield, CA	6,267	725.24
2	Fresno, CA	6,750	706.61
3	Modesto, CA	3,565	678.41
4	San Francisco-Oakland-Hayward, CA	29,326	649.34
5	Stockton-Lodi, CA	4,463	633.61
6	Redding, CA	1,120	625.77
7	Spokane-Spokane Valley, WA	3,205	598.26
8	Vallejo-Fairfield, CA	2,540	597.95
9	San Jose-Sunnyvale-Santa Clara, CA	10,925	569.12
10	Yuba City, CA	930	551.31

Source: Reprinted by permission of the National Insurance Crime Bureau.

Who Are Motor Vehicle Theft Victims?

Anyone can have their car stolen—do you know someone who has had this happen? Does this person have the common characteristics of the "typical" car theft victim? Read below to answer this question. Households headed by persons between the ages of 12 and 19 and the ages of 20 and 34 have the highest rates of motor vehicle theft (Truman & Rand, 2010). Households headed by persons who are Black or by persons of two or more races have higher rates of motor vehicle theft than do others (Truman & Rand, 2010). Households that rent rather than own their home, have total incomes of $7,500 per year or less, and have more people in them (single-person households have the lowest rates) experience higher rates of motor vehicle theft than do other households (Truman & Rand, 2010).

Risk Factors for Motor Vehicle Theft Victimization

Routine activities theory provides an excellent underpinning for understanding why some motor vehicles are stolen while others remain in the possession of their rightful

Photo Credit: © John Lamm/Transtock/Corbis.

PHOTO 13.1

The Cadillac Escalade had the highest theft-loss rate for passenger vehicles that are 1 to 3 years old in the United States.

owners. Remember, the three constructs relevant to this theoretical perspective are motivated offenders, suitable targets, and lack of capable guardianship. Motivated offenders are assumed to be present. What makes a vehicle a suitable target, though? Vehicles that are easy to steal are going to be deemed more suitable than those that are more difficult to steal. Vehicles with keys in the ignition are definitely suitable targets. Similarly, vehicles left unlocked are more suitable than locked vehicles. Cars parked on streets with poor lighting are suitable targets, while those parked in locked garages are not suitable targets. Also consider why a person would be compelled to steal a car. One reason is to sell the parts. A suitable target, then, would be a vehicle whose parts are easy to sell. A suitable vehicle would be a popular model, in that there would be a resale market for its parts. Common vehicles would be easier to sell parts from than more rare models that hardly anyone drives. In addition, vehicles that do not have Vehicle Identification Numbers (VINs) etched in the windows are more suitable than vehicles with these numbers. Thieves will not want to replace the windows after stealing the vehicle.

Capable guardianship is also an important concept to consider. Guardianship for vehicles can be physical—those things that physically provide protection from theft. For cars, this can be locks, steering wheel column locks, car alarms, ignition cut-off systems, and electronic tracking devices. It is a bit more difficult to provide social guardianship for a vehicle, as people are bound to leave their cars unattended at some point. That is why it is imperative that vehicles are left locked at all times, with personal belongings and electronics stowed out of sight.

Building on routine activities theory, additional factors have been used to identify ways in which motor vehicle theft can be understood and perhaps prevented. Five situational factors have been identified: watchers, activity nodes, location, lighting, and security (W.A.L.L.S.). Watchers are capable guardians at the auto theft location, activity nodes are locations that draw heavy use for legal and illegal activity, location refers to the characteristics of the location that make it a suitable target for selection, lighting refers to the quality and amount of lighting near the auto theft location, and security refers to environmental cues that dissuade a person from committing auto theft (Levy & Tartaro, 2010).

Response to Motor Vehicle Theft

As previously discussed, motor vehicle theft has one of the highest reporting rates of all crimes. Even so, only 12% of motor vehicle thefts are cleared by police (FBI, 2012a). When a case is cleared by police, it means the police either made an arrest in the case or cleared the case exceptionally. To clear a case exceptionally, the police agency must know who the offender is, be able to support an arrest, and know where the offender is, but be unable to make an arrest and have the charges filed (FBI, 2012a). These low clearance rates suggest that many motor vehicle thieves are not being apprehended. In addition to police actions, other efforts have been undertaken to reduce motor vehicle theft victimization.

Several key pieces of federal legislation have been passed to deal with motor vehicle theft. The Motor Vehicle Theft Law Enforcement Act (1984; Pub. L. 98-547) required manufacturers to stamp identification numbers on parts in high-theft major passenger car lines (the impetus for the VIN) to make it easier to trace parts that are stolen from vehicles. Penalties for altering or removing these numbers were also increased. Investigators believe that requiring the marking of vehicle parts aids in the arrest of individuals who steal parts or vehicles (Finn, 2000). This act also made interstate trafficking in stolen vehicles part of the federal racketeering statutes (Insurance Information Institute, 2011). In 1992, the **Anti-Car Theft Act** (Pub. L. 105-119) made carjacking a federal crime and provided funding to link all state motor vehicle departments. This funding was created in hopes that states would be able to share title, registration, and salvage information to make it more difficult for stolen vehicles to be easily titled and registered (SmartMotorist.com, n.d.). This led to the development of the National Motor Vehicle Title Information System. It also expanded the parts-marking identification number requirement to include more than just high-theft passenger car line parts. Vans and utility vehicles that have higher-than-average theft rates and half of passenger cars, vans, and SUVs with lower-than-average theft rates were also required to have their major parts (engines, transmissions, and 12 other major parts) marked (SmartMotorist.com, n.d.). As part of the Violent Crime Control and Law Enforcement Act, 2 years later, the **Motor Vehicle Theft Prevention Act of 1994** authorized the development of a national, voluntary motor vehicle theft prevention program. Those people who wished to participate could place on their vehicles a decal alerting police that their car is not normally operated between the hours of 1 AM and 5 AM (Federal Grants Wire, 2011). In 1996, the ability of states and the federal government to determine if a car was stolen was strengthened by the **Anti-Car Theft Improvements Act of 1996.** This act served to upgrade state motor vehicle department databases that contain title information (SmartMotorist.com, n.d.).

Federal legislation is not the only way to combat motor vehicle theft victimization. In many states, anti-car theft groups have formed that comprise law enforcement, insurers, and consumers. These groups work together to promote awareness of motor vehicle theft and to pass state and local legislation to reduce motor vehicle theft (Insurance Information Institute, 2011). Many states attach fees to car registration or car insurance policies that go toward funding such groups. For example, Michigan has a program called Help Eliminate Auto Theft (HEAT), funded through auto insurance policies ($1 from each policy), that has created a hotline for people to report thefts and "chop shop" operations. In 25 years of operation, the program has aided in the recovery of more than 4,200 vehicles (Insurance Information Institute, 2011).

Other ways to reduce motor vehicle theft are centered on target-hardening approaches. **Target hardening** is the process whereby a target is made more difficult for an offender to attack. This approach is likely to be successful in reducing motor vehicle theft. In fact, it has been argued that "the most promising preventive approach is through the manufacture of more secure vehicles" (Clarke & Harris, 1992, p. 1). Locking car doors and installing security devices can be quite beneficial in reducing motor vehicle theft. In addition, installing a steering wheel column lock, such as The Club, can reduce the likelihood that a motor vehicle will be stolen. In the event that your car is stolen, you can increase your chances of recovering it by having an electronic tracking device. One such device, called LoJack, uses a radio transmitter. If your car is stolen, the police can track your car via the radio signal to locate it. LoJack (2011) reports a 90% recovery rate for stolen vehicles equipped with this system. Electronic immobilizers can also be used that disable the ignition, starter, and fuel systems until the system is activated by a computer-coded key (Linden & Chaturvedi, 2005). Research conducted in Canada and Australia indicates that these electronic immobilization systems are quite successful—theft rates for vehicles that have these systems are low (Potter & Thomas, 2001; Tabachneck, Norup, Thomason, & Motlagh, 2000).

Household Burglary

Perhaps one of the scariest things you could think of is to be alone, in the privacy of your own home, when an intruder comes in with a weapon—stealing whatever he or she wants and threatening you. If this were to occur, you would be the victim of a household or residential burglary. The FBI (2009) defines **burglary** as "the unlawful entry of a structure to commit a felony or theft." To understand this definition, you must understand what constitutes a structure. The FBI's definition recognizes structures to include houses, apartments, house trailers, houseboats when used as a permanent dwelling, barns, offices, railroad cars, vessels, and stables. Also important to note, entry into the structure does not have to occur forcefully. Entry can be achieved either via (1) forceful entry or (2) unlawful entry without force. Forceful entry includes such things as breaking a window or forcing a door open, while unlawful entry without force would occur if an offender used an unlocked or opened door to enter the structure. Attempted forceful entry of a structure can also constitute a burglary. Residential or household burglary—those burglaries of structures where persons live, make up 74% of all burglaries reported to the police in 2009 (FBI, 2013a).

You may also have heard the term **home invasion** used to refer to household burglary. This term is most commonly used to refer to a specific type of residential burglary that occurs when someone is home and the offender intends to harm, use force, or use violence against the residents, as in the example presented above. Most typically, a home invasion involves forceful entry. The term *home invasion* has been incorporated into some state laws, where such an offense is a specific crime. For example, in Florida, a home invasion robbery occurs when a person enters a dwelling with the intent to commit a robbery of the persons inside and does, in fact, do so (Fla. Stat. § 812.135). For household burglary to occur more generally, however, intent on the part of the offender to harm the occupants or rob them is not needed, just that the offender enters the dwelling to commit a felony or theft.

Extent of Household Burglary

According to the UCR, in 2013 there were 1,854,167 burglaries, 1,381,122 of which were burglaries of dwellings (FBI, 2013a). Of all property crimes during that year, almost 24% were burglaries (including nonresidential burglary). Most household burglary occurred during the day, perhaps because this is the time when people are at work and their homes are left unguarded. We will return to this point again. On average, each residential burglary resulted in a loss of $2,188. Remember, however, from our discussion in Chapter 2, that the UCR includes only information about crimes that are known to law enforcement—typically because the crime is reported to the police. About half of all crimes go unreported. As such, the UCR likely underrepresents the true amount of crime victimization that occurs in the United States. Also, the UCR provides only limited information about the offense, criminal, and victim. To find out about victimizations that are reported and not reported to the police and to understand the patterns and characteristics of victims and victimization events, we often use the NCVS. So, let's discuss residential burglary using statistics from the NCVS.

According to the NCVS, in 2009, there were 3,134,920 household burglaries, which does not include household burglaries in which someone became a victim of a violent crime or was threatened (Truman & Rand, 2010). According to NCVS classification rules, those incidents would be classified as personal victimizations according to what occurred (e.g., rape/sexual assault, simple assault). If a household burglary occurred and no one was home or no one was hurt or threatened, it would be classified as a property victimization. It is interesting to examine both types of incidents, however, and the BJS has recently published a report analyzing victimization that occurs during household burglary (Catalano, 2010). When taking into account all household burglaries, it is estimated that there were almost 3.4 million burglaries in 2011 (Walters, Moore, Berzofsky, & Langton, 2013). When a burglar is successful, most typically a household appliance or portable electronic device is stolen (Walters et al., 2013). In 2011, among households that experienced at least $1 in loss due to burglary, the median dollar value of items and cash stolen was $600 (Walters et al., 2013).

Characteristics of Household Burglary

On average, between 1994 and 2011, most household burglaries were achieved through unlawful entry through an unlocked or open door or window rather than forceful entry (Walters et al., 2013). When forceful entry was used or attempted, most typically, a door was damaged or removed or a window pane was damaged or removed (Catalano, 2010). In about 28% of household burglaries, someone was present during the incident, and 7% of households that were burglarized had someone injured as a result (Catalano, 2010). Most typically, the type of violence that occurred was a simple assault (15%), followed by a robbery (7%), and rape/sexual assault (3%) (Catalano, 2010). For those burglaries that occurred when no one was home, one fourth of victims said they were at work at the time and slightly less than one fourth said they were participating in a leisure activity away from home (Catalano, 2010). About 40% of household burglaries occurred between 6 AM and 6 PM (Catalano, 2010). A larger percentage of burglaries occurred during this time period when no one was home, as compared with burglaries that occurred when someone was present (Catalano, 2010). Even though burglary might seem to be one crime that would be perpetrated by a stranger, almost two thirds (65%) of household burglaries that involved violence were perpetrated by someone known to the victim (Catalano, 2010).

What Households Are Burglarized?

If a burglar is intent on entering a house, which house does he or she choose? Is it random or more systematic? Well, it appears that some houses are at greater risk than others for burglary. Households composed of married couples without children have the lowest rates of burglary (Walters et al., 2013). When examining households with children, single-female-headed households had the highest burglary rates (Walters et al., 2013).

Race, income, age, and type of housing unit are also risk factors for burglary. Households that have a person of two or more races as head of household had the highest rates of burglary, followed by households headed by a person who is American Indian/Alaska Native or Black (Walters et al., 2013). Lower-income households (those with an income of $14,999 or less) and those headed by younger persons (aged 12–19) had higher rates of burglary than did higher-income households and those headed by older persons (Walters et al., 2013). Finally, burglary rates were highest for households residing in rental properties (Walters et al., 2013).

Risk Factors for Household Burglary

As with most types of victimization, researchers have attempted to identify why some households are more likely to be burglarized compared with others. This line of inquiry has mainly focused on the decision making of burglars—why they select certain homes to break into but leave others alone. This body of research has concluded that, at least to some degree, household burglars choose suitable targets that lack capable guardians (Cromwell, Olson, & Avary, 1991; Tunnell, 1992; Wright & Decker, 1994). In other words, routine activities theory is a viable explanation for burglary victimization. Remember from Chapter 2 that routine activities theory suggests victimization is likely to occur when motivated offenders, suitable targets, and lack of capable guardianship coalesce in time and space. Let's consider household burglary from this perspective.

Motivated offenders do not need to be explained, according to routing activities theory (Cohen & Felson, 1979). Given opportunity, then, motivated offenders will burgle homes. The selection of homes is what is interesting. What makes a home a suitable target? Ethnographic research conducted via interviews on burglars shows that they tend to target middle- or high-income neighborhoods (Rengert & Wasilchick, 1985), and quantitative research predicting burglary indicates that expensive homes are most prone to burglary (Fishman, Hakim, & Shachmurove, 1998)—even though statistics from the NCVS (that do not control for other factors) indicate that lower-income households are more prone to household burglary (Catalano, 2010). A target also becomes suitable to a burglar when it lies on a familiar route that is also along major arterial routes (Rengert & Wasilchick, 1985).

Households that lack capable guardians are also most likely to be burgled. For instance, homes are most likely to be burgled during the day, when people are at work, and most burglaries occur when no one is home (Catalano, 2010). Because burglars seek out unoccupied homes, research shows that one way to reduce the chances of having your home burglarized is by making it appear that someone is home. Ways to do this are by keeping a car in your driveway, keeping lights on outside and inside, and keeping a television or radio on even if you are not home (Fishman et al., 1998).

In addition, houses located on quiet residential streets are more prone to burglary than others (Fishman et al., 1998), whereas households in high-density areas are less likely to be burglarized (Catalano, 2010). Homes on quiet streets are less likely to have watchful eyes, and burglars may feel that they can successfully get away with their crime. Although it is difficult to change the location of your home, simply having a burglar alarm reduces the chances that your house will be burglarized (Fishman et al., 1998). In addition, findings from the NCVS show that homes that are located in gated or walled communities have burglary rates that are lower than homes that are not located in such communities (Walters et al., 2013). Also of note, residences with restricted access such as having doormen or a reception desk were targeted less frequently by burglars than other residences without restricted access (Walters et al., 2013).

■ IDENTITY THEFT

As technology advances, the means by which a person's property and money are taken also change. Especially with the widespread use of computers and the ready access people have to

FOCUS ON RESEARCH

We often think of college students being at risk for very serious forms of victimization like rape and sexual assault. Research shows, however, that they also face the risk of experiencing property victimization. In recent research of 481 students enrolled at one university, Gardella and colleagues found that 21% had experienced a property victimization. They also found that freshman and sophomores were less likely to be victims of property crime than juniors and seniors. Also students in Greek-letter organizations were less at risk than other students.

Source: Adapted from Gardella, J. H., et al. (2014). Beyond Clery Act statistics: A closer look at college victimization based on self-report data. *Journal of Interpersonal Violence.* doi: 10.1177/0886260514535257.

them, it is easier today than ever for people to access other people's money illegally. With key pieces of identifying information, criminals can assume your identity and either access your existing accounts or open new accounts in your name. Collectively, these actions are known as identity theft, and this section describes its occurrence, its effects, and the system's response.

Generally, **identity theft** is defined as the use of personal identifying information by a person to commit some type of fraud (Federal Deposit Insurance Corporation [FDIC], 2004). According to the FDIC (2004), it is one of the fastest-growing types of consumer fraud. Identity theft became a federal offense in 1998 when the **Identity Theft and Assumption Deterrence Act** was passed. It made it a crime for anyone to

> knowingly transfer or use, without lawful authority, a means of identification of another person with the intent to commit, or to aid or abet, any unlawful activity that constitutes a violation of Federal law, or that constitutes a felony under any applicable State or local law. (FDIC, 2004, pp. 4–5)

Identity theft covers taking over an existing account (**account hijacking**), creating new accounts, or creating a synthetic identity to obtain services or benefits fraudulently (FDIC, 2004).

What are the common ways identity theft occurs? Computers have allowed criminals easy access to your information, but they do not necessarily need computers to steal your personal information. One way they can steal your information is by **shoulder surfing.** Shoulder surfing involves criminals watching while you input numbers such as a telephone calling card number or credit card number. They also can listen while you say your credit card number over the telephone, such as, while you are placing an order or booking a trip (U.S. Department of Justice, n.d.). Account numbers can be stolen via **skimming** devices placed on automated teller machines (ATMs) that record a person's debit account number, password, account information, and other data that can then be used to imprint a new card and withdraw funds (Berg, 2009).

PHOTO 13.2

This ATM has a mini-camera installed so that pin codes can be stolen.

Your physical mail is also a valuable resource for offenders wanting to steal your identity. Criminals may dumpster dive, going through garbage cans or communal dumpsters or bins in hopes of finding documents with account numbers on them, checks, or bank and credit statements (U.S. Department of Justice, n.d.). Criminals may find in your trash or in your mailbox preapproved credit card offers that they can send off in your name. You may not even know that there are open credit lines in your name that others are using.

The Internet is also widely used for identity theft. One common way of executing account hijacking is through phishing. When phishing occurs, deceptive e-mails or fake websites are used to get people to provide usernames, passwords, and sometimes account numbers to perpetrators who then are able to use this information to access accounts (FDIC, 2004). For example, an e-mail is sent to a person indicating a problem with his account and he is asked to log in to his account through a hyperlink included in the e-mail. Unfortunately, the hyperlink takes the person to a spoofed website. If the person does, indeed, go to the site through the hyperlink and enter his username and password, the information is then collected and the account can be hijacked (FDIC, 2004). You may wonder how often phishing occurs. In 2006, more than 109 million adults in the United States reported receiving a phishing e-mail (Gartner, 2006). Between 5% (FDIC, 2004) and 22% (Gartner, 2006) of the people who receive such phishing e-mails respond to them (FDIC, 2004). Account hijacking can also occur when people hack into financial institutions or service providers and access customers' information (FDIC, 2004). Accounts also may be hijacked using software, called spyware, that collects information from unsuspecting persons' computers. This software is surreptitiously loaded when a person opens an e-mail attachment or clicks on a pop-up advertisement. The software then tracks keystrokes and information such as usernames, passwords, and account information and sends it to the defrauder (Berg, 2009). It may not take sophisticated software, however, to hijack an account. It is estimated that 65% to 70% of identity theft is committed by employees who have access to sensitive personal data (as cited in FDIC, 2004). See the box for an example of a real case of identity theft.

Extent of Identity Theft Victimization

It is quite difficult to know exactly how much identity theft victimization occurs each year in the United States. It is possible that you could have your identity stolen and be completely unaware—or if you did become aware, it could be weeks, months, or even years after it initially

30-year-old Anthony Eugene Vaughn was arrested for at least 1,000 counts of second-degree identity theft and two counts of first-degree identity theft. More than 1,000 people had their driver's licenses, credit cards, and Social Security numbers stolen by this Thurston County criminal, who is said to have committed the largest identity theft this country has ever seen! Detectives believe that other thieves, who aided in opening several fraudulent bank accounts in victims' names, accompanied Vaughn. Stolen ATM cards and credit cards were traced back to illegal purchases. More than 40 boxes of evidence were seized, which included driver's licenses, credit cards, credit card swipers, and Social Security cards/numbers. This case has been traced back to a motor vehicle rummage on the Capitol Campus. The vehicle, which belonged to a state employee, held thousands of people's names and Social Security numbers. Further, Vaughn was identified as a suspect in the burglary of a safe belonging to a construction company in Mason County. A detective found that Vaughn used his home phone number to open a fraudulent account using the stolen documents from the Mason County burglary.

Source: Adapted from Pawloski, J. (2011). Thurston sees largest identity theft case in the county's history. From *The Olympian*, 1/8/2011 © 2011, The McClatchy Company. All rights reserved.

occurred. Even if you were aware your identity had been stolen, you might not notify the police. And the UCR does not neatly measure identity theft; it is not one of the eight index crimes that the FBI includes in its yearly report. To begin to understand the extent and characteristics of identity theft, an identity theft victimization supplement to the NCVS was collected for the first time in 2008. Unlike the NCVS, only persons over the age of 16 participated in the survey, and persons were asked about experiences of identity theft they experienced in the previous 2 years (Langton & Planty, 2010). Persons completing the **Identity Theft Supplement** (ITS) were also people participating in the NCVS. The final sample in the ITS included 56,480 persons.

The ITS collected data on the use or attempted use of existing accounts (account hijacking), use of personal information to open a new account, or misuse of personal information for other fraudulent purposes (Langton & Planty, 2010). Existing accounts that a person may hijack could include a credit card account, savings account, mortgage account, loan, or checking account. Persons may want to use personal information to obtain a job, for medical care, when interacting with law enforcement, to rent an apartment, or for government benefits (Langton & Planty, 2010). Based on findings from the 2012 ITS, it was estimated that 16.6 million people (6.7% of persons 16 years old or older) were the victims of identity theft during the previous 12 months (Harrell & Langton, 2013). Slightly more than one fifth experienced more than one identify theft incident (Harrell & Langton, 2013). Most commonly (85%), victims reported that they had an existing credit card account or a bank account information misused or attempted to be misused, equating to about 16.5 million victims (Harrell & Langton, 2013). About 1.1 million persons reported that someone had fraudulently used their information to open a new account, and about 833,600 people said that their personal information had been used for other fraudulent purposes (Harrell & Langton, 2013). There are other ways to assess the extent to which people are victimized by identity theft. One of these ways is to look to agencies where people report their victimizations. The Federal Trade Commission (FTC) publishes a report of complaints it and other agencies (The Internet Crime Complaint Center, the Better Business Bureau, Canada's PhoneBusters, United States Inspection Service, Identity Theft Assistance Center, and the National Fraud Information Center, among others) receive regarding fraud and identity theft. In this report, the Consumer Sentinel Network Databook, identity theft was the number one complaint received by the FTC in 2013, with 14% of all the complaints (FTC, 2014). There were 290,056 identity theft complaints made to the FTC. Of these complaints, 34% were government documents/benefits fraud and 17% was credit card fraud. (FTC, 2014).

Who Is Victimized by Identity Theft?

Identity theft can happen to anyone, but results from the ITS show to whom identity theft is most likely to occur. Females make up the majority of identity theft victims. Fifty-two percent of victims were female (Harrell & Langton, 2013). Remember that young people (ages 12–24 and 25–34) are the typical victims of most property and personal victimizations (Truman et al., 2013). Younger persons are actually less likely than persons between the ages of 25–34 and 35–49 to experience identity theft (Harrell & Langton, 2013). In fact, once accounting for credit card ownership, persons aged 16 to 24 are actually the least likely to report having their credit card misused (Harrell & Langton, 2013). Reports to the FTC also indicate that younger persons are more often victims of identity theft than are older persons. About a quarter of complaints filed with the FTC were by persons 29 years old or younger (FTC, 2014). Differences across race and ethnic groups were also found in the ITS. Persons of more than one race (10.4% of persons) were more likely than others to report experiencing identity theft (Langton & Planty, 2010). A greater percentage of White non-Hispanics experienced identity theft than did Hispanics and Black non-Hispanics. There also was a difference in the types of identity theft experienced. Income is also relevant for understanding who is likely to be victimized by identity theft. As household income increases, so too does a person's likelihood of being victimized. Persons living in households with incomes of $75,000 or more were more likely than others to be identity theft victims (Langton & Planty, 2010). Locales also differed in their rates of reports of identity theft. The states with the five highest rates of identity theft reports for 2013 are, in order, (1) Florida, (2) Georgia, (3) California, (4) Michigan, and (4) Nevada. For an example of a state's 2013 occurrences of identity theft, see Table 13.3, which shows the extent of reports in Arizona for 2013.

Characteristics of Identity Theft Victimizations

One of the interesting things about identity theft victimization is that people may be unaware that they have been victimized. Others may not have any idea as to how the offender was able to victimize them. Not knowing how the offender stole your identity can be especially problematic for prevention. In the ITS, victims were asked if they knew how the identity theft had occurred. About 40% of victims indicated that they knew how their identity had been stolen. Of those victims, about 1 in 3 believed that their identity had been stolen during a purchase or transaction, and about 1 in 5 indicated that they thought their identity had been stolen from a wallet or checkbook. About 14% thought that their personal information had been stolen from personnel or other files at their office, and 8% thought that friends or family had accessed their personal information (Langton & Planty, 2010).

What do victims of identity theft do after realizing that their identities have been stolen? According to findings from the ITS, of those who indicated whether they had contacted law enforcement, 74% of identity theft victims notified a law enforcement agency about the incident (Harrell & Langton, 2013). Victims who had offenders try to open a new account in their name (28%) and who had offenders misuse their personal information (26%) were more likely than victims whose offenders tried to use an existing account (13%) to report the incident to the police. If victims do not tell the police, are they telling others? Results from the ITS indicate that they often do disclose the incident. Sixty-eight percent of victims contacted a credit card company or bank to report that their account or personal information had been misused, about 15% notified a credit bureau, 7% contacted a credit monitoring service, 3% told a government consumer affairs agency or similar consumer protection agency (e.g., Better Business Bureau), 4% notified an agency that issues identification documentation, and 1% reported the incident to the FTC (Langton & Planty, 2010).

Risk Factors for Identity Theft Victimization

Routine activities theory helps us understand who is vulnerable to identity theft. Motivated offenders are, by definition, present. It is when motivated offenders come into contact with suitable targets in time and space without capable guardianship that identity theft is likely to occur. Suitable targets are likely to be those who are easily victimized. Why would a person be an easy target for identity theft? Consider the mechanisms by which offenders steal a person's identity. Leaving personal identification intact in the trash, making phone calls in public places to discuss personal information, and using public Internet connections to access personal

Table 13.3 ■ Reports of Identity Theft in Arizona, 2009 (complaints n = 6,043)			
Rank	**Identity Theft Type**	**Complaints**	**Percentage**
1	Government documents or benefits fraud	1,431	24
2	Employment-related fraud	930	15
3	Credit card fraud	875	14
4	Phone or utilities	653	11
5	Bank fraud	490	8
6	Loan fraud	246	4
	Other	1,608	27
	Attempted	407	7

Source: Consumer Sentinel Network Data Book. Federal Trade Comission (2014, p. 24). Retrieved from http://www.ftc.gov/sentinel/reports/sentinel-annual-reports/sentinel-cy2009.pdf.

accounts all make a person a suitable target. A novice to the Internet or a person who does not understand the intricacies of how secure Internet sites work will also be a more suitable target than a savvier Internet user. Notably, even persons who are aware of the dangers are still likely at risk. What is interesting about identity theft achieved via the Internet is that potential victims will not or cannot curtail their Internet usage, even if they fear victimization (Cox, Johnson, & Richards, 2009). Capable guardianship, then, is a particularly important concept for identity theft, especially when considering online accounts, usernames, and passwords (Cox et al., 2009). Guardianship often comes in the form of warning e-mails, antivirus software, and firewalls (Cox et al., 2009). But simply having bank accounts, credit card accounts, and a Social Security number puts you at risk of having this personal information stolen. For this reason, as discussed in a later section, everyone should take precautions to protect these pieces of information.

Consequences of Identity Theft

Reporting is not the only consequence victims face after being victimized by identity theft. One consequence is the financial cost that being a victim of identity theft carries. The majority of victims incurred some financial cost associated with their victimization. These costs can be direct or indirect. **Direct costs** are monies and the value of goods and services taken. **Indirect costs** consist of things such as legal bills, phone calls, bounced checks, and notary fees (Langton & Planty, 2010). The ITS estimates that identity theft costs from 2007 to 2009 totaled $17.3 billion (Langton & Planty, 2010). Of those victims who suffered a loss, the average was $2,400, and 23% suffered an out-of-pocket cost that was not reimbursed (Langton & Planty, 2010). In addition to financial costs, 27% of victims noted that they had to spend more than a month trying to clear up problems resulting from having their identities stolen. Most victims, however, were able to resolve their problems in a day or less (Langton & Planty, 2010).

Finally, identity theft may take an emotional toll on victims, similar to other victimizations. About 1 in 5 victims of identity theft in the ITS indicated that they experienced severe emotional stress, 6% reported they had significant problems with relationships between family members or friends as a result of the incident, and 3% reported that they experienced significant problems at work or school as a result of being victimized (Langton & Planty, 2010). Although fewer identity theft victims reported problems with relationships at work and school and having severe emotional distress as compared with violent crime victims, it should be evident that identity theft does carry consequences for many victims.

Responses to Identity Theft Victimization

As noted in the first part of this chapter, the Identity Theft and Assumption Deterrence Act of 1998 (Pub. L. 105-318) introduced identity theft into the federal criminal code. It made it a crime for anyone to

> knowingly transfer or use, without lawful authority, a means of identification of another person with the intent to commit, or to aid or abet, any unlawful activity that constitutes a violation of Federal law, or that constitutes a felony under any applicable State or local law. (Pub. L. 105-318)

The **New Fair and Accurate Credit Transactions Act of 2003** (Pub. L. 108-159) enacted several provisions to reduce identity theft and also to help identity theft victims. This act

- mandated that the three major credit reporting bureaus provide a free copy of credit reports to consumers once every 12 months;
- created the National Fraud Alert System, which allows persons who reasonably suspect that they are or will become a victim of identity theft, or who are on active duty in the military, to place an alert on their credit file;
- provided that credit card receipts must have shorter account numbers and developed rules for financial institutions and creditors for the disposal of sensitive credit report information;
- noted that if a person establishes that she or he has been a victim of identity theft, credit reporting agencies are required to stop reporting the fraudulent account information;
- established that creditors and businesses must provide copies of records of fraudulent accounts or transactions related to them so that victims can attempt to prove their victimization; and
- provided for victims to report accounts affected by identity theft directly to creditors. (FTC, 2004)

The **CAN-SPAM Act of 2003** also addressed identity theft. This act made it a federal crime to send spam e-mail under certain circumstances (Pub. L. 108-187). For the specifics of this act, see the boxed item below. In 2004, the **Identity Theft Penalty Enhancement Act** (Pub. L. 108-275) was passed and created the crime of aggravated identity theft, which added 2 years to the sentence of anyone convicted of unlawful identity theft during and in relation to specified felony violations. It also created an additional 5-year prison term enhancement for unlawful identity theft related to terrorist acts. In addition to these federal laws, each of the 50 states and the District of Columbia all have laws addressing identity theft. See the boxed item on the next page for the law in Illinois.

Not only can laws reduce the occurrence of identity theft, but there are many things individuals can do to reduce their chances of having their identities stolen. When going out of town, you should have your mail held at the post office or have a trusted friend or family member remove it from your mailbox. Do not discuss your personal information (address, telephone number, Social Security number) at an open telephone booth or on a phone in public near people who can hear you and possibly intercept your information (U.S. Department of Justice, n.d.). Do not give out your personal information to people who *call you* on the telephone, even if they say they are from your bank or work for a business with whom you have an account. If they do, in fact, work with one of these businesses, they should have your information. If you *call them*, however, you should expect to be asked to verify your identity (U.S. Department of Justice, n.d.). Your personal checks should display the least amount of personal information possible—do not put your Social Security number or your phone number on your checks. Phone calls notifying you of exciting prizes you have won that require you to give your Social Security number, credit card number, or bank account number may be fraudulent. Ask for these offers to be sent to you in writing (U.S. Department of Justice, n.d.). Shred all documents that display your account numbers or personal information before discarding them.

As you can tell, as technology advances, the ways in which your property and goods can be stolen also expand. It will take new prevention strategies to reduce your chances of being victimized. Nonetheless, the connections between the types of property victimization and the factors that place individuals and homes at risk are evident. Although property crimes may not always make the news, these types of offenses are the ones you are most likely to experience.

CAN-SPAM ACT OF 2003

IN GENERAL—Whoever, in or affecting interstate or foreign commerce, knowingly—

1. accesses a protected computer without authorization, and intentionally initiates the transmission of multiple commercial electronic mail messages from or through such computer,

2. uses a protected computer to relay or retransmit multiple commercial electronic mail messages, with the intent to deceive or mislead recipients, or any Internet access service, as to the origin of such messages,

3. materially falsifies header information in multiple commercial electronic mail messages and intentionally initiates the transmission of such messages,

4. registers, using information that materially falsifies the identity of the actual registrant, for five or more electronic mail accounts or online user accounts or two or more domain names, and intentionally initiates the transmission of multiple commercial electronic mail messages from any combination of such accounts or domain names, or

5. falsely represents oneself to be the registrant or the legitimate successor in interest to the registrant of five or more Internet Protocol addresses, and intentionally initiates the transmission of multiple commercial electronic mail messages from such addresses, or conspires to do so, shall be punished as provided in subsection.

Source: Federal Trade Commission. (2004). The CAN-SPAM Act: A compliance guide for business. Retrieved from http://business.ftc.gov/documents/bus61-can-spam-act-compliance-guide-business.

IDENTITY THEFT LAW, ILLINOIS

A person commits the offense of identity theft when he or she knowingly uses any personal identifying information or personal identification document of another person to fraudulently obtain credit, money, goods, services, or other property. Penalties for identity theft depend on the value of the theft.

If the value of the credit, money, goods, services, or other property is less than $300, the crime is a Class 4 felony, punishable by one to three years in prison and a fine up to $25,000. Subsequent offenses are upgraded to a Class 3 felony, punishable by two to five years in prison, as is the penalty for people who have previously been convicted of certain crimes, including burglary, theft, or fraud. If the amount is between $300 and $2,000, it is a Class 3 felony; between $2,000 and $10,000 is a Class 2 felony (punishable by two to seven years in prison); between $10,000 and $100,000 is a Class 1 felony (punishable by four to fifteen years in prison); and over $100,000 is a Class X felony (punishable by six to thirty years in prison).

Penalties are increased one step (with the exception of a Class X felony) if the victim of the offense is an active duty member of the Armed Services or Reserve Forces of the United States or of the Illinois National Guard serving in a foreign country.

Source: Reprinted by permission of the National Conference of State Legislatures (2010).

SUMMARY

- Theft made up more than half the reported cases of property crime in the National Crime Victimization Survey (NCVS) and 69% of all property crimes in the Uniform Crime Reports (UCRs) in 2013.
- The characteristics of your household contribute to your chances of property crime victimization—persons living in households headed by persons who are White, young, and with a total income less than $7,500 have the highest theft victimization rates, according to the NCVS.
- There are characteristics that make certain vehicles' and cities' motor vehicle theft rates exceed the rates of others.
- Within households, there are even certain races of people who are more likely to be burglarized and/or experience some form of property victimization.
- In discussing motor vehicle theft, routine activities theory provides that some vehicles are more suitable targets than others.
- Motor vehicle theft is one of the most reported crimes to the police.
- In response to the fact that many motor vehicle thieves are not apprehended, federal legislation has been passed to reduce, eliminate, and protect potential victims and those who already have been victimized.
- Target hardening is the process whereby targets are made more difficult for offenders to attack.
- Household burglary is not always achieved through forceful entry; it can also be accomplished through unlawful entry.
- Most household burglary is committed during the day, when no one is home, via unlawful entry, and by someone known to the victim.
- Routine activities theory can be used to explain why some households are burglarized and others are not. Those houses that are well guarded are less likely to be burglarized than others. Also, houses that are deemed suitable targets are more likely to be burglarized.

- The advancement of technology has made it easier for criminals to steal other people's identities.
- Common methods of identity theft include shoulder surfing, skimming, dumpster diving, phishing, and using spyware.
- The UCR does not neatly measure identity theft, but both the Federal Trade Commission and the Identity Theft Supplement to the NCVS measure the extent to which people's identities are stolen.
- It is estimated that 6.7% of persons between the ages of 25 and 34 had their identities stolen in 2012.
- A person's income and race are indicators of the likelihood that the person's identity will be stolen. A person with more income is a more suitable target for criminals.
- As with other forms of victimization, identity theft can cause more than just financial loss. Victims of identity theft often suffer emotional stress as well.
- To reduce your chances of becoming a victim of identity theft, certain precautions should be taken, such as destroying old mail and credit information rather than simply tossing it in the garbage.
- Though many people do not report their crimes to the police, the NCVS indicates that they contact other entities, such as a credit bureau, to inform them of their victimization.
- The fact that laws for identity theft have been outlined in the federal criminal code signifies the increasing seriousness of this issue, which continues to plague many people. The enhancement of severity of punishment is now addressed in the CAN-SPAM Act of 2003.

DISCUSSION QUESTIONS

1. What about the top 10 most frequently stolen passenger vehicles makes them the most likely to be stolen?

2. Why are theft rates so high in the top 10 U.S. metropolitan areas for motor vehicle theft? Why are motor vehicle theft rates so high in the Western United States?

3. Why do the states with the five highest rates of identity theft reports for 2009 have such high rates?

4. What are some things one can do in order to make his or her house less likely to be burglarized?

5. What makes a person a more likely target for identity theft?

KEY TERMS

theft

motor vehicle theft

carjacking

Motor Vehicle Theft Law Enforcement Act (1984)

Anti-Car Theft Act (1992)

Motor Vehicle Theft Prevention Act of 1994

Anti-Car Theft Improvements Act of 1996

target hardening

burglary

home invasion

identity theft

Identity Theft and Assumption Deterrence Act (1998)

account hijacking

shoulder surfing

skimming

dumpster dive

phishing

spyware

Identity Theft Supplement (ITS)

direct costs

indirect costs

New Fair and Accurate Credit Transactions Act of 2003

CAN-SPAM Act of 2003

Identity Theft Penalty Enhancement Act (2004)

"Auto Theft" (http://www.iii.org/media/hottopics/insurance/test4/)

The Insurance Information Institute website contains statistics from the Federal Bureau of Investigation's Uniform Crime Reports about the types of cars that are most likely to be stolen and in which cities/states cars are most likely to be stolen, as well as the car models least likely to be stolen and the cities/states in which cars are least likely to be stolen. The website also provides this information as it pertains to motorcycle theft. A historical background information section addresses antitheft laws as well.

"Burglary of Single-Family Houses" (http://www.popcenter.org/problems/burglary_home/)

The Center for Problem-Oriented Policing provides a webpage dedicated to the topic of burglary. This webguide provides information about burglary, the types of housing units that are at risk, risk factors for burglary, and the types of goods typically stolen. There is also a discussion about burglars.

Edmunds Inside Line (http://www.insideline.com/)

This website is a great source for information on theft complaints for particular popular motor vehicles. The site not only lists the newest vehicles, but it also lists the issues/complaints that buyers can expect. Recent news articles regarding motor vehicle theft, including new technologies to prevent motor vehicle theft, are also highlighted.

Fighting Back Against Identity Theft (http://www.ftc.gov/bcp/edu/microsites /idtheft/)

The Federal Trade Commission's identity theft website provides introductory information about identity theft for consumers, businesses, law enforcement, and persons in the military. It also includes ways to report identity theft victimization. Data about identity theft and ways to prevent identity theft are also discussed.

"Preventing Auto Theft" (http://www.geico.com/information/safety/auto/preventing-auto-theft/)

This Geico webpage provides several tips to prevent you from becoming the next victim of auto theft. There is a breakdown of what types of auto thieves exist most commonly, as well as the various types of antitheft systems available and what those systems do.

CHAPTER 14

VICTIMOLOGY FROM A COMPARATIVE PERSPECTIVE

Let's revisit what happened to Polly in Chapter 2.

It was not exactly a typical night for Polly. Instead of studying at the library as she normally did during the week, she decided to meet two of her friends at a local bar. They spent the evening catching up and drinking a few beers before they decided to head home. Since Polly lived within walking distance of the bar, she bid her friends goodnight and started on her journey home. It was dark out, but since she had never confronted trouble in the neighborhood before—even though it was in a fairly crime-ridden part of a large city—she felt relatively safe.

As Polly walked by an alley, two young men whom she had never seen before stepped out, and one of them grabbed her arm and demanded that she give them her school bag, in which she had her wallet, laptop, keys, and phone. When Polly refused, the other man shoved her while the first man grabbed her bag. Despite holding on as tightly as she could, the men were able to take her bag before running off into the night. Slightly stunned, Polly stood there trying to calm down. Without her bag, which held her phone and keys, she felt there was little she could do other than continue to walk home and hope her roommates were there to let her in.

What if this scenario left out one important detail: that Polly was participating in a study abroad program, thus her victimization occurred not in her home country, but in a foreign country in which she was a visitor, not a permanent resident or citizen? Does the location matter? What should she do in this situation? Who should she contact? Who can help her? Does she have any rights? These are questions we will explore in this chapter, as we trace the development of victimology across the globe and highlight victims' rights and assistance programs from an international perspective.

■ VICTIMOLOGY ACROSS THE GLOBE

Considering that the birth of the field of victimology is often attributed to the early work of German criminologist Hans Von Hentig and Romanian lawyer Benjamin Mendelsohn (their work was discussed in detail in Chapter 1), two men from two different countries, it shouldn't be surprising that over the last three decades victimology has become a subject studied across the globe (Kirchhoff, 2010). The development of this field of study has not been evenly distributed with some countries being more advanced than others (Fattah, 2010). For example, in some parts of the world, victimology is considered a subdiscipline of criminology, while in other parts, it is its own distinct discipline and students can receive degrees in victimology and/or victim studies. Likewise, in some countries, victimization surveys are carried out and in other countries they are not. We will discuss several of these surveys a little later in this chapter. It should also be noted that in some countries, victims benefit from well-developed and comprehensive victim assistance programs, and in other countries, these types of programs are sorely lacking or do not exist (Lehner-Zimmerer, 2011). We will end this chapter with a brief description of some of these programs.

The development of the field of victimology outside of the United States (and primarily in Europe) has been largely collaborative in nature and supported by the work of several key organizations including the World Society of Victimology, Max Planck Institute of Foreign and International Criminal Law, and International Victimology Institute Tilburg (INTERVICT). Each of these organizations and their contributions to the study of victimology will be discussed briefly.

The **World Society of Victimology (WSV)** was conceived from the *First International Symposium on Victimology* in Israel in 1973. Since its inception, the symposium has been hosted by WSV every 3 years in locations all over the world with a mission of "Advancing research, services, and awareness for victims" (WSV, 2014). According to the WSV website, the five goals of the organization are "(1) to promote research in victimology and on victim needs; (2) to provide services for victim service providers and victimologists; (3) to provide education and training; (4) to advance advocacy and rights; and (5) to provide member opportunities" (WSV, 2014).

The society boasts members from a variety of agencies and academic disciplines. The international nature of the WSV allows for active networking and collaboration with governmental agencies in many countries and the United Nations (UN). Through research and program development, the WSV has successfully advocated for reforms such as the Declaration of Basic Principles of Justice for Victims of Crime and Abuse of Power, which is essentially a victims' rights charter. Aside from the UN, the WSV has active projects through the Council of Europe, the National Organization for Victim Assistance in the USA, and Victim Support in the United Kingdom. As of 2014, the WSV was affiliated with agencies and governments worldwide, providing international advocacy and counseling and sponsoring a variety of training activities for policymakers and practitioners.

Physically located in Germany, the **Max Planck Institute of Foreign and International Criminal Law** is made up of a department of criminal law and a department of criminology, both active in conducting research that brings about a diverse array of academics from across Europe. Historically, the original iteration of the institute came into existence in the late 1930s stemming from the work of Dr. Adolf Schönke (Max Planck Institute for Foreign and International Criminal Law, 2013). Originally titled Seminar for Foreign and International Criminal Law, in 1947 the institute was retitled as the Institute for Foreign and International Criminal Law and shifted into a branch of the Max Planck Society (a research organization) in 1966.

While the primary focus of the institute is comparative law, since the early 1990s the institute has also been promoting victimological research, including examining:

- "What information is available on the type, extent and application of victim rights and on regulations governing compensation in the particular countries?
- What information exists on the attitudes of different parties involved in the criminal procedure (victims, judges, public prosecutors) towards the goals of the criminal procedure, the situation of the victim and regulations governing compensation?" (Würger, 2013)

Like the Max Planck Institute, **The International Victimology Institute Tilburg (INTERVICT)** engages in **comparative research**; however, unlike the Max Planck Institute whose primary focus remains on criminal law, INTERVICT is dedicated solely to the study and advancement of victimology. Physically located at Tilburg University in the Netherlands, the mission of the INTERVICT is to "promote and execute interdisciplinary research that can contribute to a comprehensive, evidence-based body of knowledge on the empowerment and support of victims of crime and abuse of power" (International Victimology Institute Tilburg, 2014).

■ MEASUREMENT AND EXTENT OF VICTIMIZATION ACROSS THE GLOBE

While victimology's roots are quite cosmopolitan, only fairly recently has victimological research been comparative in nature. According to Elder (1976), comparative research is "an approach to knowing social reality through the examination for similarities and differences between data gathered from more than one nation" (p. 210). Comparative victimological research, in the form of international crime victimization surveys, provides us with a tool for not only measuring but also for understanding victimization across the globe.

As previously discussed in Chapter 2, victimization studies can take different forms. We will now highlight the forms victimization studies can take from a comparative perspective. **International victimization studies** utilize randomized samples from several countries that are representative of populations from which they are taken (Schneider, 2001). The International Crime Victims Survey (ICVS) and the International Self Report Delinquency Study (ISRD) are examples of international victimization studies that we will discuss in this section. International victimization studies allow for comparisons across countries to be made. **National victimization studies** are similar to international victimization studies in that they, too, utilize representative random samples; however, a national victimization survey collects data in only one country. Such surveys are conducted in many countries annually, including Andalusia (Spain), Australia, England and Wales, France, Italy, the Netherlands, Scotland, Sweden, Switzerland, and the United States (Schneider, 2001). Because of the differences in definitions and methodology employed, it is usually not possible to use national victimization surveys to make comparisons between countries. **Local victimization studies** involve surveys that are restricted to the population of a specific region or city (Schneider, 2001). Finally, victimization studies may focus on a specific type of victimization, such as sexual violence or violence against women. Take, for example, the International Violence Against Women survey, which is designed to exclusively measure violence experienced by women at the hands of their male partners. These types of studies are referred to as **specialized victimization surveys** (Schneider, 2001).

International Crime Victims Survey (ICVS)

One oft-cited survey of international victimization is the **International Crime Victims Survey (ICVS)**, which was created to provide a standardized survey instrument to compare crime victims' experiences across countries (van Dijk, van Kesteren, & Smit, 2008). The first round of the survey was conducted in 1989 and was repeated in 1992, 1996, 2000, and 2004/2005. Collectively, more than 340,000 persons have been surveyed in more than 78 countries as part of the ICVS program (van Dijk et al., 2008). Respondents are asked about 10 different types of victimization that they could have experienced: car theft, theft from or out of a car, motorcycle theft, bicycle theft, attempted or completed burglary, sexual victimization (rapes and sexual assault), threats, assaults, robbery, and theft of personal property (van Dijk et al., 2008). If a person has experienced any of these offenses, he or she then answers follow-up questions about the incident. This survey has provided estimates of the extent of crime victimization in many countries and regions of the world. In addition, characteristics of crime victims and incidents have been produced from these surveys. According to the last round of surveys completed, almost 16% of the population of the 30 participating countries has been the victim of a crime (van Dijk et al., 2008).

International Self Report Delinquency Study (ISRD)

While initially designed to collect comparative data on juvenile delinquency among adolescents residing primarily in Europe, the **International Self Report Delinquency Study (ISRD)** has been expanded to include questions pertaining to victimization. The ISRD has undergone three waves of data collection. The first sweep of the ISRD (ISRD-1) was conducted in 1990–1991 among 12 European countries and the United States. The second sweep (ISRD-2) was conducted in 2006–2008 and included 31 countries. The third sweep of the ISRD has recently been completed with field work completed in the spring of 2014.

The ISRD is administered to adolescents in the seventh, eighth, and ninth grade via pencil-and-paper surveys or eletronically via computers (Marshall & Maljevic, 2013). A total of 67,883 questionnaires were collected as part of the ISRD-2 study (Junger-Tas et al., 2010). While the ISRD-1 did not include questions on victimization, four questions were added to the ISRD-2 questionnaire. Students are asked to recall victimization experiences that happened to them in the past 12 months. Specifically, they are asked the following:

Table 14.1 ■ International Self Report Delinquency Study (ISRD)

- Thinking back over the last 12 months, did any of the following happen to you . . .

  ✓ Someone wanted you to give him/her money or something else (watch, shoes, mobile phone) and threatened you if you did not do it?
  ✓ Someone hit you violently or hurt you so much that you needed to see a doctor?
  ✓ Something was stolen from you (such as a book, money, mobile phone, sport equipment, bicycle)?
  ✓ You were bullied at school (other students humiliated you or made fun of you, hit or kicked you, or excluded you from their group)?

Source: Reprinted from Gruszczynska, B., Lucia, S., & Killias, M. (2012). Juvenile victimization from an international perspective. *Many faces of youth crime* (pp. 95–116). New York, NY: Springer.

To see what the ISRD-2 found, read the Focus on Research box.

FOCUS ON RESEARCH

Key findings using data from the ISRD-2 regarding juvenile victimization include:

- The four examined victimization types—robbery, assault, theft, and bullying—affect on average almost one-third of the surveyed population of the 30 countries included.
- Students were most often victims of theft (20%) and bullying (14%) and less often of robbery (about 4%) and assault (4%).

- In most countries, boys were more often victims of violence and theft than girls. The exception was bullying: in some countries bullying affected girls more frequently.
- Factors associated with lower victimization risks included family bonding, sound neighborhoods, and order at schools.

Source: Reprinted from Gruszczynska, B., Lucia, S., & Killias, M. (2012). Juvenile victimization from an international perspective. In J. Junger-Tas, I. H. Marshall, D. Enzmann, M. Killias, M.Steketee, & B. Gruszczynska (Eds.), *Many faces of youth crime* (pp. 95–116). New York, NY: Springer.

Building off the ISRD-2, seven questions pertaining to victimization were included in the ISRD-3 questionnaire. Of these questions, three are carryovers from the ISRD-2 questionnaire (Someone wanted you to give him/her money or something else . . . ; Someone hit you violently or hurt you . . . ; and Something was stolen from you . . .), and four questions are new.

These new questions are intended to measure hate crimes, cyberbulling/harassment, and child abuse. The questions include:

- ✓ Someone threatened you with violence or committed physical violence against you because of your religion, the language you speak, the color of your skin, your social or ethnic background, or for similar reasons?
- ✓ Has anyone made fun of you or teased you seriously in a hurtful way through e-mail, instant messaging, in a chat room, on a website, or through a text message sent to your mobile phone?
- ✓ Has your mother or father (or your stepmother or stepfather) ever hit, slapped, or shoved you?
- ✓ Has your mother or father (or your stepmother or stepfather) ever hit you with an object, punched or kicked you forcefully, or beat you up?

Results from the ISRD-3 are forthcoming.

British Crime Survey (BCS)*

Similar to the NCVS and the ICVS, the **British Crime Survey (BCS)** is conducted to measure the extent and characteristics of victimization in England and Wales. The BCS is a type of national victimization study. The BCS is a victimization survey of persons aged 16 and over living in England and Wales. Beginning in 1982, the BCS was conducted every 2 years until 2001, when it was changed to reflect victimizations during the previous 12 months. Beginning April 1, 2012, the BCS changed its name to the **Crime Survey for England and Wales**. Using Computer Assisted Personal Interviewing to aid in personal interviewing, in the 2010/2011 BCS, 51,000 people were surveyed—47,000 adults and an additional 4,000 children in the 10–15 year old supplement. Persons are asked about victimizations that their households and themselves experienced. To get the sample, about 1,000 interviews are conducted in each police force area. If individuals answer "yes" to any screen question about victimization, they complete a victim module that includes detailed questions about the event. Findings from the 2010/2011 BCS indicate that 23% of the sample had experienced a victimization during the previous 12 months. Of these victims, 30% experienced more than one victimization.

International Violence Against Women Survey (IVAWS)

The **International Violence Against Women Survey (IVAWS)** is another international survey that, similar to the National Violence Against Women Survey (NVAWS) conducted in the United States, is designed to collect information specific to violence against women. Coordinated by the UN Interregional Crime and Justice Research Institute, the European Institute for Crime Prevention and Control, and Statistics Canada, the IVAWS collects data from women on violence they have experienced at the hands of men, including the details and consequences of their victimization, as well as background information on the survey

---

*Source: Crime in England and Wales 2010–2011 Home Office Statistical Bulletin 10/11. Published July 14, 2011.

participants and their male partners (Johnson, Ollus, & Nevala, 2008b). The IVAWS was initiated in 1997, and since then 11 countries have participated in the IVAWS.

■ JUSTICE SYSTEM RESPONSES TO VICTIMIZATION

Victims and the United Nations

The United Nations is a collection of countries that was established on October 24, 1945. It was created in the wake of World War II and was created to promote peace, security, and strengthening of friendship between nations. The United Nations is designed to help countries solve their economic, social, and humanitarian problems. Fifty-one countries joined in the beginning, and now that number has increased to 193 sovereign nations.

On November 29, 1985, the United Nations met to discuss crime victims and the dangers of rampant crime and its effects. The committee was pleading to instill several efforts to promote the safety and well-being of victims around the globe. The committee wanted to create both national and international laws to protect the rights of the victims. The United Nations then adopted the Declaration of Basic Principles of Justice for Victims of Crime and Abuse of Power. This Declaration created a basic standard on how victims of crime need to be treated. Victims are defined via the Declaration as "Persons who, individually or collectively, have suffered harm, including physical or mental injury, emotional suffering, economic loss or substantial impairment of their fundamental rights, through acts or omissions that are in

---

Table 14.2 ■ Questions Asked on the IVAWS Survey

Questions pertaining to physical violence:	Questions pertaining to sexual violence:
✓ **Threatened** to hurt you physically in a way that frightened you	✓ **Forced you into sexual intercourse** by threatening, holding you down or hurting you
✓ **Threw something** at you or **hit you with something** that hurt or frightened you	✓ **Attempted to force you into sexual intercourse** by threatening, holding you down or hurting you
✓ **Pushed** or **grabbed** you or **twisted your arm, pulled your hair** in a way that hurt or frightened you	✓ **Touched you sexually** in a way that was distressing
✓ **Slapped**, **kicked**, **bit** or **hit with a fist**	✓ Forced or attempted to force you into sexual activity **with someone else**, including being forced to have sex for money or in exchange for goods
✓ Tried to **strangle** or **suffocate**, **burn** or **scald**	✓ Sexually violent towards you in a way that I have not already mentioned
✓ Used or threatened to use a **knife or gun**	
✓ Physically violent in any other way	

Source: Johnson, H. (2008a, February, 28). "Getting the facts to make the change: The International Violence Against Women Survey." Presentation. Retrieved from http://www.un.org.

violation of criminal laws operative within Member States, including those laws proscribing criminal abuse of power" (UN, 1985).

Under this Declaration, victims have a universal right to receive fair treatment and true justice under the letter of the law. It established several ideals to receive justice for the victims. These ideals included restitution, compensation, and victim assistance programs. Restitution is the idea that offenders make some sort of payments to the victims of their crimes to balance the scales of justice. This includes when the government harms its people and creates victims. Compensation is the principle that states if the offender is unable to give monetary support to the victim the government should try to provide that to the victim. Victim assistance programs were created to grant medical, mental, and social help from organizations to aid in the recovery of the victims. These programs need to be available and accessible in order to provide improvements to recovery of the victims.

The United Nations created a **Handbook on Justice** that is used to help guide the creation of victim service programs. It also aided in establishing policies for workers in the justice system that come into contact with victims. These policies are victim-sensitive to ensure the well-being of everyone affected by crime. Workers that these policies target include anyone in the court system, law enforcement, doctors, prison personnel, and even members of the clergy.

The International Court of Justice

In 1945, the United Nations created the International Court of Justice (ICJ), which is currently located in The Hague, the Netherlands (International Court of Justice, n.d.-a). The ICJ serves two primary purposes, including (1) the resolution of issues presented to the court by countries under the jurisdiction of the United Nations, and (2) to provide assistance in the form of legal opinions sought by various branches of the United Nations as well as other specific agencies. Countries not under the jurisdiction of the United Nations, may not present a case to the ICJ. Furthermore, countries that can bring cases before the ICJ must agree to adhere, prior to the trial, to any ruling that could be handed down by the court (International Court of Justice, n.d.-a). Lastly, the ICJ cannot prosecute specific individuals, only countries (Human Rights Watch, 2012).

A few points relating to the structure as well as trial and advisory process of the ICJ should be made. In regard to structure, a total of 15 judges (from different countries) serve terms of 9 years (can be reelected), and are put in place by the Security Council and General Assembly (International Court of Justice, n.d.-a). Moreover, the judges function independently from their respective countries, providing unbiased opinions and rulings. Pertaining to the trial process in the ICJ, the first stage occurs when parties provide written pleas to one another (International Court of Justice, n.d.-b). Following the plea, oral proceedings occur, after which a final decision is handed down by the court. Transitioning focus to advisory opinions handed down by the ICJ, the first step taken by the court is to identify specific countries and organizations that would have knowledge on the question at hand and then obtain written information pertaining to the inquiry. Although considered confidential, written statements provided by the countries to the ICJ are commonly revealed in public announcements alongside the advisory opinions. It should be noted that such opinions are advisory and are not necessarily binding nor require adherence (International Court of Justice, n.d.-b).

The general characteristics of the court, procedural aspects, and how victims are impacted by the ICJ are all very important. A prime example of how victims are influenced by the ICJ is evident in the case of Hissène Habré, an ex-dictator from Chad. During his time in power throughout the 1980s, Hissène Habré was believed to have been involved in the torture and killing of thousands of individuals (Human Rights Watch, 2012). While Belgium sought extradition multiple times since 2005, nothing came from the situation, and Habré has remained in exile in Senegal since the early 1990s. In 2012, the ICJ ruled in favor of Belgium (which brought the case against Senegal) stating that Habré be extradited to Belgium or be tried in Senegal immediately. The ruling provides the beginning stages of justice for victims of Habré by requiring swift justice be imposed on the former dictator either through extradition or an immediate trial (Human Rights Watch, 2012).

The International Criminal Court (ICC)

Located in The Hague, which is one of the largest cities in the Netherlands, the International Criminal Court (ICC) has functioned as a dominant and independent legal body that handles significant international crimes occurring between countries. The ICC came into existence following the adoption (1998) and subsequent ratification (2002) of an international treaty labeled the Rome Statute. The Rome Statute indicated that the ICC could prosecute specific individuals for four serious international offenses, including (1) genocide, (2) crimes against humanity, (3) war crimes, and (4) crimes of aggression (see Table 14.3 for specifics). However, for individuals to be prosecuted, two conditions must have been met, specifically (1) the offender must be a citizen of a country that ratified the Rome Statute, and (2) jurisdiction must be granted by the country where the offender is from.

Table 14.3 ■ How Are the Crimes Under the Court's Jurisdiction Defined?

Genocide: The Rome Statute defines the crime of genocide as any of the following acts committed with intent to destroy, in whole or in part, a national, ethnical, racial or religious group:

- Killing members of the group
- Causing serious bodily or mental harm to members of the group
- Deliberately inflicting on the group conditions of life calculated to bring about its physical destruction in whole or in part
- Imposing measures intended to prevent births within the group
- Forcibly transferring children of the group to another group.

Crimes Against Humanity: Crimes against humanity are defined as any of the following acts when committed as part of a widespread or systematic attack directed against any civilian population, with knowledge of the attack:

- Murder
- Extermination
- Enslavement

- Deportation or forcible transfer of population
- Imprisonment or other severe deprivation of physical liberty in violation of fundamental rules of international law
- Torture
- Rape, sexual slavery, enforced prostitution, forced pregnancy, enforced sterilization, or any other form of sexual violence of comparable gravity
- Persecution against any identifiable group or collectivity on political, racial, national, ethnic, cultural, religious, gender, or other grounds that are universally recognized as impermissible under international law
- Enforced disappearance of persons
- The crime of apartheid
- Other inhumane acts of a similar character intentionally causing great suffering, or serious injury to body or to mental or physical health.

War Crimes: Under the Rome Statute, war crimes are any of the following breeches [sic] of the Geneva Conventions of 12 August 1949, perpetrated against any persons or property:

- Willful killing
- Torture or inhuman treatment, including biological experiments
- Willfully causing great suffering, or serious injury to body or health
- Extensive destruction and appropriation of property, not justified by military necessity and carried out unlawfully and wantonly
- Compelling a prisoner of war or other protected person to serve in the forces of a hostile power
- Willfully depriving a prisoner of war or other protected person of the rights of fair and regular trial
- Unlawful deportation or transfer or unlawful confinement
- Taking of hostages.

Source: Reprinted from Eberhardt, S. (n.d.). *Core crimes defined in the Rome statute of the International Criminal Court.* Coalition for the International Criminal Court. Retrieved from http://www.iccnow.org/documents/FS-CICC-CoreCrimesinRS.pdf.

Aside from general characteristics of the ICC, a few other important details about the court should be highlighted. First, while the ICC has served as an international legal body, the court is not governed by the United Nations. Second, the ICC is composed of four different branches, including the presidency, judicial divisions, office of the prosecutor, and the registry. The first three of these branches have concentrated on judicial aspects of the court such as administration (presidency), legal proceedings (judicial divisions), and prosecution (office of the prosecutor), while the last branch has focused on assisting the court (registry). Third, the judicial division can be subdivided into different divisions including appeals (containing at least five judges, one being the president), trial, and pre-trial (both having no less than six judges) stages. Fourth, areas currently being focused on by the ICC can be subdivided into: (1) situations under investigation, which include (but are not limited to) Uganda, Darfur, Kenya, Mali, and the Democratic Republic of the Congo, and (2) preliminary examinations, which include (but are not limited to) Colombia, Nigeria, Georgia, Iraq, and Afghanistan.

The ICC has also provided information regarding the role of victims in the court setting. In 2005, the ICC set up the Office of Public Counsel for Victims (OPCV), which has provided two different forms of assistance to victims. First, the office has sought to increase participation of victims during all parts of court proceedings, part of which has allowed for legal representation to be freely selected by victims. Second, the office also has focused on providing reparations to victims, which may include financial compensation for both past and future problems associated with victimization as well as rehabilitation. Moreover, reparations

PHOTO 14.1

Taking action: Bosnian Muslims are suing the Dutch government claiming they should have been protected during the 1995 massacre in Srebrenica.

Photo Credit: AP Photo/Peter DeJong

VICTIMS' RIGHTS AND ASSISTANCE PROGRAMS

Two friends were on holidays in a Member state other than their own. They stayed in a hotel in the center of the country's capital city. On the fifth day of their stay, there was a burglary in their hotel room during dinner time. Their camera, money and jewelry were taken. As the two women didn't speak the local language, they decided not to report the crime to the police. They were not aware of the possibility to call a Victim Support organization. With her credit card one of them had with her during dinner, they booked an earlier flight home. Back home, the travel insurance refused to give the women compensation because they didn't report the crime in the Member State where the crime took place. It cost the women a lot of money and it ruined their holiday.

Source: Reprinted from Victim Support Europe. (2014). *Victim of crime in another EU country? What you need to know.* Retrieved from http://www.victimsupport.im/wp-content/uploads/2014/05/Victim-of-crime-in-another-country.pdf.

can be paid to multiple victims that have been impacted by an incident or to a single victim. Financial compensation for these victims may come from the Trust Fund for Victims (TFV), which contains funds given by private entities, countries, various forfeitures as well as fines. In total, the TFV is currently assisting approximately 80,000 victims. Between both of these forms of assistance provided by the OPCV, there has been a dramatic increase in the number of victims being provided representation and assistance, which between 2006 and July of 2010 increased from 65 to 1,252 victims.

Has this ever happened to you? If so, you are a victim of cross border crime. A **cross border victim** is "anyone who has suffered directly from a crime that took place in a country different than one the victim lives in" (VSE, 2014). As a cross border victim, you are afforded certain rights, and there are agencies you can turn to for support. This section will highlight these organizations, as well as describe some innovative victims' rights programs in various countries across the globe.

European Union

The European Union (EU) is comprised of 28 nation states that together encompass roughly 7% of the world's population, which resides predominantly in Europe. To safeguard free movement (the ability to move about safely within and across borders of EU member states), the EU has placed emphasis on protecting victims' rights. The EU therefore acts to ensure that victims are recognized and treated with respect and dignity; are protected from further victimization and intimidation from the offender, and further distress when they take part in the criminal justice process; receive appropriate support throughout proceedings and have access to justice; and have appropriate access to compensation (EU, 2014).

Additionally, the EU ensures that victims benefit from these rights "without discrimination across the EU, irrespective of their nationality or country of residence, and whether minor or serious crime is involved, whether they have reported the crime, and whether they are the victim or a family member" (*Directive Establishing Minimum Standards on the Rights, Support and Protection of Victims of Crime,* 2012).

Within the EU, victims of crime are afforded certain rights as outlined in several key documents including the *Directive Establishing Minimum Standards on the Rights, Support and Protection of Victims of Crime, EU Framework Decision on the Standing of Victims in Criminal Proceedings,* and the *Council Directive 2004/80/EC Relating to Compensation to Crime Victims.* According to these documents, victims of crime have the following rights: the right to respect and recognition, to be heard, to information, to reimbursement of expenses, to protection, to support, to compensation, to interact with trained professionals, and cross-border assistance.

If you have fallen victim to a crime within a member state of the EU, you may turn to **Victim Support Europe,** which has been providing victim support services for over 30 years. It is the parent network for all national victim support organizations in Europe. Its members provide universal support services for all victims of crime, regardless of the type of crime committed. The types of help that victim support organizations that are members of Victim Support Europe can offer are the following:

- Information on our rights as a victim;
- Emotional support before, during, and after the criminal justice processes;
- Assistance to solve financial and practical issues following the crime;
- Assistance and support for the preparation and attendance of a trial;
- Assistance in applying for state compensation for criminal injuries;
- Information and advice in respect to health care, home security, employment, privacy, finance, education and support services. (Reprinted from Victim Support Europe, 2014)

Different Approaches in Different Locales

The victims' rights movement has not garnered the same amount of attention across the globe as it has in Western countries such as Australia, Canada, Germany, the United Kingdom, and the United States. For instance, France has a long history of providing victims with financial restitution. In 1977, France became one of the first countries to establish a victim compensation law (Kastsoris, 1990). Although this early incarnation only allowed victims to seek financial remedy by pressing charges against the individual who victimized them, more recent efforts have substantially increased French victims' access to victim compensation (Max-Planck-Institut für Strafrecht, 2014; Ministére de la Justice, n.d.). Currently, victims of crime who are either French nationals or citizens of the European Union are able to apply for state-sponsored compensation by bringing their case before an independent tribunal (Ministére de la Justice, n.d.). The amount of compensation that victims are capable of receiving depends on the seriousness of the crime; with victims of seriously violent offenses being eligible for total reimbursement, while victims of less serious crimes, such as theft, only being eligible for partial reimbursement (Ministére de la Justice, n.d.).

France's commitment to victims' rights is further emphasized by the fact that it does not require victims to personally apply for victim compensation. Instead, police agencies are capable of applying on victims' behalf (The Advocates for Human Rights, 2010). By allowing this, victims in France are less likely to be exposed to secondary victimization because they are not required to appear in court to receive funding.

In some countries, specific legislation has been passed that protects individuals should they fall victim of a crime. In Australia, each state/territory has passed legislation that provides victims with a host of fundamental rights that ensure that their information is kept confidential, that they are treated fairly by the criminal justice system, and that the likelihood of secondary victimization is limited (Victim Support Australia, 2003). First and foremost, victims throughout Australia have the right to timely notification of available victim services, such as counseling, legal help, welfare, and medical care. They also have the right to be kept informed of the status of the criminal case against their attacker, including whether or not the offender has been caught, their name, the crime they are being charged with, and whether or not they have posted bail. If the case goes to trial, prosecutors are charged with explaining the court process to victims, letting them know if and when they must appear in court, and keeping victims informed of the offender's final disposition and sentence.

Victims of violent crimes, such as those that involve death or bodily injury, are furthermore entitled to additional rights. Such victims, as well as the victims of non violent crimes in some jurisdictions, are given the opportunity to sign up for the Victims Register; a database that allows victims to stay informed of offender's status after they are incarcerated. This includes being made aware of how long their sentence is, if they escape from jail, and when they are expected to be released. Certain states, such as Queensland, also allow for victims to make comments at an offender's parole hearing (Victims of Crime Assistance Act 2009).

Throughout Australia, victims of violent crimes also have the ability to prepare a victim impact statement, which can be presented to the court between an offender's conviction and sentencing, as well as receive victim compensation to cover medical expenses, psychiatric help, and economic losses. The requirements necessary for the receipt of victim compensation funds vary according to state/territory; often according to the seriousness of the crime. In the State of Victoria, for instance, primary victims are eligible to receive up to $60,000 (State Government of Victoria, 2013), while victims from the State of Western Australia can receive up to $75,000 (Department of the Attorney General, 2006).

In Canada, Canadian Prime Minister Stephen Harper revealed new legislation on April 3, 2014, designed to provide crime victims a more effective voice in the Criminal Justice System. The Victims Bill of Rights Act is a historic piece of legislation that seeks to create clear federal statutory rights for victims of crime for the first time in Canada's history. This legislation establishes statutory rights to information, protection, participation, and restitution, and ensures a complaint process for breaches of these rights.

Each province has set up a method for victims of violent crime to receive financial assistance. The assistance must be applied for by the victim, it is not an automatic recompense. For purposes of this legislation, a victim of a violent crime is defined as any individual who has suffered physical or emotional harm, property damage, or economic

CANADIAN VICTIMS BILL OF RIGHTS

Prime Minister Stephen Harper announced on April 3, 2014, the introduction of legislation to create a Canadian Victims Bill of Rights that would transform the criminal justice system by creating, at the federal level, clear rights for victims of crime—a first in Canadian history. The legislation would create the following statutory rights for victims of crime:

- **Right to information:** Victims would have the right to general information about the criminal justice system and available victim services and programs, as well as specific information about the progress of the case, including information relating to the investigation, prosecution, and sentencing of the person who harmed them.

- **Right to protection**: Victims would have the right to have their security and privacy considered at all stages of the criminal justice process, to have reasonable and necessary measures to protect them from intimidation and retaliation, and to request their identity be protected from public disclosure.

- **Right to participation:** Victims would have a right to convey their views about decisions to be made by criminal justice professionals and have them considered at various stages of the criminal justice process, and to present a victim impact statement.

- **Right to restitution:** Victims would have the right to have the court consider making a restitution order for all offences for which there are easy-to-calculate financial losses.

Source: Adapted from Harper, S. (2014, April 3). "PM announces historic legislation to create a Canadian Victims Bill of Rights" Prime Minister of Canada, Stephen Harper, Mississauga, Ontario. Retrieved from http://www.pm.gc.ca/eng/news/2014/04/03/pm-announces-historic-legislation-create-canadian-victims-bill-rights#sthash.XxHkKWsX.dpuf.

loss as a result of an offense committed under the Criminal Code, the Youth CJ Act, the Crimes Against Humanity and War Crimes Act, and also applies to some offenses under the Controlled Drugs and Substances Act and the Immigration and Refugee Protection Act. The proposed rights would be available only to a victim living in Canada, a permanent resident of Canada, or a Canadian citizen. The Victims Bill of Rights Act also proposes that clearly defined individuals may act as representatives for a victim who is deceased or incapable of acting on his or her behalf. These individuals are defined as follows: "The victim's spouse or an individual cohabitating with the victim in a conjugal relationship for at least 1 year prior to the victim's death; a relative or dependant of the victim; and anyone who has custody of the victim or of the victim's dependant" (Prime Minister of Canada, 2014).

As previously discussed, **Victim Support** is a continent-wide network of agencies throughout Europe with the goal of coordinating agency goals, increasing victim resources, and setting standards on how to assist victims of crime (Victim Support, 2014). Victim Support provides services across and within Europe. For instance, Victim Support in the United Kingdom specifically includes England, Wales, Northern Ireland, and also provides witness services for individuals presenting evidence in criminal trials. The organization classifies itself as a national charity, offering free and confidential services to victims and witnesses. While Victim Support is not officially part of the criminal justice system, the agency is highly influential among different criminal justice agencies. Victims are provided with advocacy, not legal advice or counseling. This includes helping with housing and acting as a liaison between the victim and police, among other services (Dunn, 2004).

The first conceptualization of Victim Support was seen in Bristol (located in South England) in 1974 by a local probation officer and a police officer. The organization now boasts over 1,000 staff members and over 4,000 volunteers among 374 different offices. Volunteers are required to complete 40 hours of basic training, then continue with more specialized training over the following months (e.g., domestic violence) (Dunn, 2004). Victim Support now helps over one million victims and almost 200,000 witnesses a year in England, Wales, and Northern Ireland alone (Victim Support, 2004). As of 2004, over half of the victims referred were for property crime and approximately one fourth for violent crimes. The vast majority of victims are referred by the police, but an agency goal is to target referrals from other agencies to catch victims who do not report their crimes to the police (Dunn, 2004).

In many parts of the world, victim services get their start through the provision of specialized services for women and children who have been the victims of violence (Lindgren & Nikolić-Ristanović, 2011). This is the case in Bosnia and Herzegovina where the victims' rights movement is a fairly recent phenomenon and largely accredited to the country's troubled past. The first victim services in the country were established by women's group activists to meet the needs of war refugees and women and children who were the victims of violence. Take for example Medica Zenica. Created in the midst of brutal conflict in the 1990s, Medica Zenica is one of the first and longest running nongovernmental organizations in Bosnia and Herzegovina dedicated to providing services to female victims of war and postwar violence, including victims of war rape and other forms of war torture,

Photo Credit: © Muhamed Tunović / Association "Medica" Zenica.

PHOTO 14.2

On March 28, 2014, Hollywood actress Angelina Jolie and the Secretary of State for Foreign and Commonwealth Affairs from Great Britain William Hague, visited Medica Zenica.

sexual violence in general, domestic violence survivors, as well as victims of trafficking in human beings (Medica Zenica, 2014). Services provided by Medica Zenica include crisis intervention, temporary shelter and related services, individual and group counseling, occupational therapy and economic empowerment, legal aid, medical support and assistance, and an emergency telephone hotline.

The state of Tamil Nadu in southern India has taken a rather innovative approach to dealing with female victims of crime. All-female police stations, referred to as "women helpline" units, have been established in most districts of Tamil Nadu (Natarajan, 1996). These all-women units are tasked with handling cases pertaining to premarital problems, marital problems, and general problems (see Table 14.4 for description of the nature of these cases) with the main objective being "reconciliation between the parties without going to court" (Natarajan, 1996, p. 67).

Table 14.4 ■ Nature of Cases Dealt With by the All-Women Police Units

Premarital Problems

- False promise of marriage
  - With sexual intimacy
  - Without any illicit intimacy
- Breach of engagement

Marital Problems

- Maladjustment between husband, in-laws, and the wife
- Harassment by husband and in-laws without demand of dowry
  - Physical and mental harassment
- Dowry harassment
- Extra-marital relations
  - Bigamy
  - Concubine
- Temporary separation
  - Abduction of children
- Desertion by husband
- Maintenance
- Return of sridhan or dowry

General Problems

- Petty quarrels
- Cheating
- Civil dispute

Source: Reprinted from Natarajan, M. (1996). Women police units in India: A new direction..*Police Studies, 19*(2), 63–75.

SUMMARY

- Comparative victimology allows for a method of both measuring and understanding victimization around the world.
- Victimology has expanded to a variety of different countries in the last 30 years; however, this line of research has not been equally distributed across all countries.
- Outside of the United States, victimology has been significantly influenced by the World Society of Victimology (WSV), the Max Planck Institute of Foreign and International Criminal Law, and the International Victimology Institute Tilburg (INTERVICT).
- The World Society of Victimology seeks to promote advocacy, research, education, and services for victims of crime on the international level.
- The Max Planck Institute of Foreign and International Criminal Law provides a moderate level of attention toward victimological research, including on attitudes, rights, and compensations for victims.
- The International Victimology Institute Tilburg centers solely on conducting victimological research.
- From a comparative perspective, victimization surveys can be conducted on three different levels, including: (1) internationally, (2) nationally, and (3) locally.
- International victimization surveys include the (1) International Crime Victims Survey (ICVS) and (2) the International Self Report Delinquency Study (ISRD, specifically the ISRD-2), both of which investigate violent and property offenses between countries.
- One example of a national victimization survey is the British Crime Survey (BCS; recently changed to the Crime Survey for England and Wales), which measures household and individual victimization. The survey found that approximately 23% of the sample experienced victimization in the past year.
- Aside from general victimization surveys, specialized victimization surveys tap into specific types of victimization, such as the International Violence Against Women Survey (IVAWS), which investigates violence against women.
- A variety of different international justice system responses exist that are part of (1) the United Nations (UN), (2) the International Court of Justice (ICJ), and (3) The International Criminal Court (ICC).
- The UN has identified ideals of assistance programs for victims, restitution, and compensation.
- The ICJ was created (and functions) as part of the UN and serves two purposes, including (1) to resolve issues between countries under the court's jurisdiction, and (2) to provide legal opinions regarding legal matters.
- The International Criminal Court is an independent international court that came into existence with the ratification of the Rome Statute. While the court focuses specifically on four international crimes, the ICC legally assists victims through the Office of Public Counsel for Victims (OPCV) and financially through the Trust Fund for Victims (TFV).
- Victims' rights significantly vary by country, with some notable examples of these rights present in Western countries (Australia, Canada, Germany, United Kingdom, and the United States).
- In France, financial compensation for victims (of various types of crime) has been in existence for over 30 years, and can be applied for by victims or by police on behalf of the victims.
- In Australia, victims of crime have their personal information kept confidential, are notified of victims' services, and are notified about trial proceedings, in additional to other specific rights for victims of violence (information about the offender while in prison and when released).
- In Canada, the Victims Bill of Rights Act has provided (at the federal level) victims with the right to (1) information, (2) protection, (3) participation, and (4) restitution.
- In the United Kingdom, victim support provides crime victims with different types of advocacy and assistance, such as housing assistance.
- In Bosnia and Herzegovina, specialized victim assistance programs are provided, such as Medica Zenica (a nongovernmental organization), to assist victims of violence during and following the war.
- In certain parts of India, female victims of crime are assisted by all-female police departments.

DISCUSSION QUESTIONS

1. Aside from the three main areas of criminal justice systems across the majority of societies (law enforcement, courts, and corrections), should victim services/assistance be considered a fourth area? Should this be a mandatory part of the criminal justice system? Why or why not?

2. Between the ICVS and ISRD, which provides a more comprehensive investigation of victimization between countries? Which would be better for investigating juveniles? Which would be better for investigating multiple types of victimization?

3. Would the model described in certain parts of India, regarding the use of all-female police departments to handle issues related to victimization of females, be reasonable to use in certain locations in the United States? Why or why not? What might the benefits and drawbacks of this model be if used in the United States?

KEY TERMS

World Society of Victimology (WSV)

Max Planck Institute of Foreign and International Criminal Law

The International Victimology Institute Tilburg (INTERVICT)

comparative research

international victimization studies

national victimization studies

local victimization studies

specialized victimization surveys

International Crime Victims Survey (ICVS)

International Self Report Delinquency Study (ISRD)

British Crime Survey (BCS)

Crime Survey for England and Wales

International Violence Against Women Survey (IVAWS)

Declaration of Basic Principles of Justice for Victims of Crime and Abuse of Power

cross border victim

Victim Support Europe

Victims Bill of Rights Act

Victim Support

INTERNET RESOURCES

International Crime Victims Survey (ICVS) http://www.unicri.it/services/library_documentation/publications/icvs/

The International Crime Victimization Survey involves more than two decades worth of data collection efforts spanning more than 70 countries and 300,000 individuals. Aside from violent and property victimization, the ICVS also measures sexual victimization.

International Victimology Institute Tilburg (INTERVICT) http://www.victimology.nl

The International Victimology Institute Tilburg is one of the leading research institutions focused solely on victimological inquiry. Moreover, the institute concentrates on interdisciplinary efforts in the investigation of victimization based upon the multifaceted nature of victimology.

Mothers of Srebrenica http://www.haguejusticeportal.net/index.php?id=9659

Maintained by The Hague, the Mothers of Srebrenica webpage provides a description about the civil suit filed on behalf of roughly 6,000 women impacted in 1995 by the Srebrenica genocide.

Victim Support Europe http://victimsupporteurope.eu/

Victim Support Europe focuses on the assistance of victims through the enhancement of services and victims' rights within Europe.

World Society of Victimology (WSV) http://www.worldsocietyofvictimology.org/ and www.world-society-victimology.de

The World Society of Victimology is one of the leaders in international victimology. The society functions as a nongovernmental organization (that provides consultations, and is associated with, the United Nations) that promotes comparative victimological research and cooperation between nations to further the assistance of victims.

15

CONTEMPORARY ISSUES IN VICTIMOLOGY

VICTIMS OF HATE CRIMES, HUMAN TRAFFICKING, AND TERRORISM

Cindy was living in rural China and going to school when she was offered the opportunity to work at a restaurant in Ghana that friends of her neighbor and her husband had opened. Cindy dropped out of school and went with the couple to Ghana. Instead of working in a restaurant, however, Cindy fell victim to a Chinese sex trafficking ring. She was taken to live in a brothel, and her passport and return ticket were taken from her. She was forced to engage in commercial prostitution and was beaten anytime she refused. The money she made from prostitution was taken from her by her traffickers, who told her that she owed money for her travel expenses and accommodations (U.S. Department of State, 2010).

What happened to Cindy is, unfortunately, probably more common than we realize. It is known as human trafficking—a contemporary issue in the field of victimology. It is a type of victimization in which a victim is targeted because of what he or she can provide in terms of services, work, or sex. Other types of victimization that we are becoming aware of involve people being targeted because of an offender's hate or bias. Terrorism also often creates victims because of the desire to harm a particular group or person. This chapter deals with these emerging issues in victimology.

■ VICTIMS OF HATE CRIMES

Some victims are targeted because of their qualities—not because of what they can provide in terms of services, work, or sex, but because the offender wants to attack them out of hate or bias. Qualities that an offender may target are sexual orientation, race, and religion. When victims are targeted under these circumstances, they are classified as **hate crime** or **bias crime** victims.

What Is Hate Crime Victimization?

Beginning in 1990 with the passage of the **Hate Crime Statistics Act** (28 U.S.C. 534), the attorney general is required to collect data on hate crimes perpetrated based on race, religion, sexual orientation, or ethnicity. This requirement was expanded via the Violent Crime Control and Law Enforcement Act of 1994 to include hate crimes based on disability. It was not until 2009, when Congress passed the **Matthew Shepard and James Byrd, Jr. Hate Crime Prevention Act,** that crimes motivated by bias against gender and gender identity and crimes committed by and against juveniles were included in the hate crimes data collection efforts. To meet these mandates, the attorney general has charged the Federal Bureau of Investigation (FBI) with data collection (Harlow, 2005). In doing so, the FBI acquires data from law enforcement agencies about the crimes of murder, nonnegligent manslaughter, forcible rape, aggravated assault, simple assault, intimidation, arson, destruction of property, damage of property, and vandalism of property that are hate or bias motivated. Currently, the FBI defines hate crimes as any of the above mentioned offenses or offenses that law enforcement agencies currently report on through their Uniform Crime Reports (UCRs) or National Incident-Based Reporting System data collection programs that are perpetrated based on race, religion, sexual orientation, ethnicity, disability, gender, and gender identity (FBI, 2010). How do the police know, though, if a crime should be considered a hate crime? Obviously, a crime that is reported to the police is supposed to be included in the statistics they report to the FBI through the UCR data collection. It is up to the police agency, however, to determine if the incident will be classified as a hate crime. Law enforcement, then, has to use their judgment to classify incidents—it is not enough that a victim is part of a protected class (e.g., a racial or ethnic minority). To determine hate crime status, law enforcement use victim and witness information as well as information from the investigation. Information they consider may include the following (Nolan, McDevitt, Cronin, & Farrell, 2004):

- Hate speech the offender used
- Hate symbols left by the offender (e.g., a swastika painted on a synagogue)
- Timing of incident to occur on day of significance for victim's or suspect's group
- Previous history of hate crime perpetration by the suspect or suspect is a known member of organized hate group
- Previous history of hate crime incidents at or around location of current incident
- Absence of other obvious motives of victimization

We will discuss the extent of hate crime victimization based on the data collected from the FBI below, but before we do, a discussion about how hate crime is defined in the National Crime Victimization Survey (NCVS) is warranted.

As you know, the NCVS asks individuals about their victimization experiences during the previous 6 months. Beginning in the July 2000 data collection, persons were asked in the incident report if they suspected that they were victimized because of one or more of their personal characteristics: race, ethnicity, religion, sexual orientation, and disability (Harlow, 2005). That question served as a hate crime **screen question.** If they answered affirmatively, they were also asked if they had any evidence that the incident was a crime of hate, bigotry, or prejudice. Evidence would include the offender used "derogatory language, the offender left hate symbols, or the police confirmed that a hate crime had taken place" (Harlow, 2005, p. 2). If they answered yes to a hate crime screen question and yes to a question regarding evidence of hate, bigotry, or prejudice motivation, then the incident was classified as a hate crime victimization.

Extent of Hate Crime Victimization

According to the statistics compiled by the FBI, in 2012, 7,151 people were victims of hate crimes in the United States (FBI, 2012b). Similar to other victimizations, there are differences when comparing data from the UCR with data from the NCVS. Keep in mind that UCR statistics reflect official data compiled by the FBI based on law enforcement agencies, which must make an official determination that a crime they are made aware of is, in fact, a hate crime before reporting it to the FBI as such. The NCVS data rely on the victim's assessment of the incident being motivated by bias. One of the key differences is the extent of hate crime victimizations in the NCVS as compared with the UCR. In 2012, there were 293,800 nonfatal hate crime victimizations in the United States according to the NCVS (Wilson, 2014). Although the NCVS measures both victimizations reported to the police and those not reported, victims indicated that about 40% of these incidents were, in fact, reported to the police (Wilson, 2014).

PHOTO 15.1

On the night of October 6–7, 1998, Matthew Shepard was beaten, pistol-whipped, robbed, and tied to a tree by two men in Laramie, Wyoming. He died on October 12, 1998, from his injuries. At the trial, it was revealed that he was targeted due to his sexual orientation. In 2009, the Matthew Shepard and James Byrd, Jr. Hate Crime Prevention Act was passed.

Photo Credit: © Mike Stewart/Sygma/Corbis.

Who Are Hate Crime Victims?

Individual Characteristics

One of the interesting findings from the NCVS survey data is that rates of hate crime victimization are similar across demographic groups. One difference that emerged in 2012, however, is that Hispanics experienced a higher rate of violent hate crime victimization than persons who are White or Black (Wilson, 2014). Hate crime victimization rates do not vary according to educational attainment. There are, however, some characteristics associated with an increased hate crime victimization risk. Persons who are young (17 or younger, 18–24) have higher hate crime victimization rates than persons who are 25–34 and older age groups (Wilson, 2014).

Type of Hate Crime Victimization Experienced

Of the victimizations reported in the UCR, the most common motivation for the offense was the victim's race. In fact, almost half (49%) of all hate crime victims were targeted for this characteristic. The next most common motivation was the victim's sexual orientation (20%), followed by religious bias (17%), ethnicity/national origin (12%), and disability (2%) (FBI, 2012b).

Within these categories, the FBI's data further delineate the characteristics of victims who were targeted. In terms of racially motivated bias crimes, an overwhelming majority of victims, 66%, were targeted because of an offender's anti-Black bias. Twenty-two percent of victims were targeted because of anti-White bias on the part of the offender. See Table 15.1 for more details regarding the percentage of victims targeted. Of the victims targeted for anti-religious reasons, most were targeted because of anti-Jewish bias. In fact, 60% of victims of anti-religious hate crime were victimized for this reason. As seen in Table 15.1, other victims are targeted for anti-Islamic bias, anti-Catholic bias, anti-Protestant bias, anti-atheist/agnostic bias, and for biases against other religions. Victims targeted due to sexual-orientation bias were most commonly victimized as a result of anti-male homosexual bias (55%), with more than one quarter of victims being targeted because of an offender's anti-homosexual bias.

Table 15.1 displays other common reasons victims were targeted. Victims of hate crimes were also targeted because of an offender's bias toward their ethnicity or national origin. Most typically, these crimes occurred because of an anti-Hispanic bias—60% of victims who were targeted because of ethnicity or national origin bias. The remaining victims in this category were targeted because of other ethnicities or national origins. Finally, offenders may target victims due to a bias against persons with disabilities. Most commonly, victims are targeted due to an anti-mental disability bias. See Table 15.1 for the percentage of victims who were targeted due to disability bias (FBI, 2012b).

Table 15.1 ■ Reasons Hate Crime Victims Reported Being Victimized, UCR 2012

Type of Bias	% Victims Experienced
Offender's racial bias (n = 3,297)	
Anti-Black bias	66.1
Anti-White bias	22.4
Anti-Asian/Pacific Islander bias	4.1
Bias against group of individuals in which more than one race was represented	4.1
Anti-American Indian/Alaska Native bias	3.3
Offender's religious bias (n = 1,166)	
Anti-Jewish bias	59.7
Anti-Islamic bias	12.8
Bias against other religions	9.2
Bias against multiple religions, groups	7.6
Anti-Catholic bias	6.8
Anti-Protestant bias	2.9
Anti-Atheist/Agnostic bias	1.0
Offender's sexual-orientation bias (n = 1,318)	
Anti-male homosexual bias	54.6
Anti-homosexual bias	28.0
Anti-female homosexual bias	12.3
Anti-bisexual bias	3.1
Anti-heterosexual bias	2.0
Offender's ethnicity/national origin bias (n = 822)	
Anti-Hispanic bias	59.4
Bias against other ethnicities/national origins	340.6
Offender's disability bias (n = 102)	
Anti-mental disability bias	80
Anti-physical disability bias	20

Source: Hate Crime Statistics. (2012). Hate crime statistics: Victims. Retrieved from http://www2.fbi.gov/ucr/hc2009/victims.html.

Data from NCVS indicate that ethnicity was the most common motivation (51% of incidents) for hate crime victimizations (Wilson, 2014). The second most common motivation victims reported for why they were targeted was their race (46%) (Wilson, 2014). The next most common reason victims reported being a hate crime victim was because of their association with persons with certain characteristics. In 34% of incidents, this reason was identified (Wilson, 2014). In 28% of incidents, a victim's religion provoked the victimization (Wilson, 2014). Gender was mentioned in about 1 in 4 hate crime victimizations, and about 1 in 8 hate crime victimizations were motivated by sexual orientation (Wilson, 2014).

RIPPED FROM THE HEADLINES

A man was run over by Joseph Caleca, a 55-year-old man, who was driving a pickup truck. Mr. Caleca yelled "anti-Muslim" comments to the man before hitting and running over him with his truck. Mr. Caleca was arraigned on second-degree attempted murder and first-degree assault charges that were charged as hate crimes. He was held without bail. Does this hate crime comport with the "typical" hate crime? Why or why not?

Source: Adapted from Yan, E. (2014, August 19). DA: Joseph Caleca charged with hate crimes after hitting, dragging Sandeep Singh in Queens. Retrieved from http://www.newsday.com/news/new-york/joseph-caleca-charged-with-hate-crimes-after-hitting-dragging-man-in-queens-nypd-says-1.9095507.

Special Case: Sexual-Orientation-Bias-Motivated Hate Crime Victimization

Although the FBI's UCR data collection and NCVS data both include information about sexual-orientation-based victimization experiences, other efforts have been made to identity the extent to which persons are victimized due to their sexual orientation or gender identity as well as the effects this specific type of hate crime victimization has on victims. One of the major sources of information on this type of hate crime victimization is the National Coalition of Anti-Violence Programs (NCAVP, 2010), which collects data from a network of some 38 antiviolence organizations that "monitor, respond to, and work to end hate and domestic violence, HIV-related violence, pick-up crimes, rape, sexual assault, and other forms of violence that affect LGBTQ (lesbian, gay, bisexual, transgendered, and queer) communities" (p. 1). Individuals who contact these anti-violence organizations and report victimizations will then be included in the NCAVP report of anti-LGBTQ hate violence. Based on this report, in 2013, there were 2,001 victims of anti-LGBTQ hate violence (NCAVP, 2014). There were 18 homicides of LGBTQ people in the same year according to the NCAVP (2014) report. Notice that both of these estimates are higher than what was found when examining hate crime statistics in the UCR. Other research using survey data estimates that about 20% of gay, lesbian, and bisexual individuals have experienced a victimization based on their sexual orientation during their adult life (Herek, 2009). This research based on a national probability sample of sexual minority adults found that gay males are more likely than other sexual minorities to experience anti-gay violence (Herek, 2009). Over half of gay males and lesbians (63% and 55%, respectively) in the sample reported experiencing verbal abuse because of their sexual orientation (Herek, 2009).

TARA'S STORY OF EXPERIENCING ANTI-LGBTQ VICTIMIZATION

Tara, 24, White, queer, non-transgender woman

I was going to the community center like I did every week for work meetings, and this man that always stared at me and yelled that he would "turn me straight" was there. After my meeting, I was walking to my car and the man followed me and raped me. The whole time he was talking about making me a straight girl like I should be. I called NCAVP after my nightmares about that night started coming back, and I would get panic attacks when I had to go to work. They gave me support and got me connected with a counselor that has really helped me to work on healing from this.

Source: National Coalition of Anti-Violence Programs. (2010). Hate violence against the lesbian, gay, bisexual, transgender and queer communities in the United States in 2009. Retrieved from http://www.avp.org/documents/NCAVP2009HateViolenceReportforWeb_000.pdf.

Characteristics of Hate Crime Victimizations

Of the hate crime victimizations known to the police that occurred in 2012, 59% were crimes against the person (FBI, 2012b). Of these, 40% were simple assaults, 38% were intimidations, and 21% were aggravated assaults (FBI, 2012b). Only 10 murders and 15 rape hate crime offenses were reported to the police (FBI, 2012b). Of the crimes against property, 75% were acts of destruction, damage, or vandalism (FBI, 2012b).

Findings from the NCVS also show that hate crimes were most commonly associated with violent victimizations. Rape/sexual assault, robbery, and assault together accounted for 63% of the hate crime victimizations in 2012 (Wilson, 2014). Hate crime victimizations were more likely to be violent victimizations than were non-hate crime victimizations (Wilson, 2014). More than half of all hate crime victimizations were simple assaults (Wilson, 2014).

Persons who indicated in the NCVS that they had experienced a hate crime victimization were asked if they told the police about the incident. About 40% of hate crime victimizations were reported to the police (Wilson, 2014). Research on hate crime victimization reporting indicates that minority victims are less likely than nonminority victims to report hate crime victimizations (Zaykowski, 2010). Overall reporting rates may be linked to the victim–offender relationship—about 4 in 10 violent hate crime victimizations were perpetrated by strangers (Wilson, 2014). Not all research on reporting has found that reporting is equally likely for hate crime victimizations and non-hate crime victimizations. When comparing hate crime victimizations based on sexual orientation to non-hate crime victimizations among individuals living in Sacramento, California, hate crimes were less likely to be reported to the police (Herek, Gillis, & Cogan, 1999). This lack of reporting may be due to the response that victims receive from the police. In the NCAVP (2014) report, the majority of victims who reported to the police indicated that the police response was something other than courteous. Of those who indicated negative police behavior, 32% of persons who reported their victimization to the police reported hostile attitudes from the police and 25% said the police used slurs and biased language. Slightly more than 11% of those who said the police engaged in negative behavior reported that the police were physically abusive (NCAVP, 2014).

Risk Factors for Hate Crime Victimization

Obviously, given what hate crime victimizations are, certain groups are at risk due to their characteristics. It is, in fact, personal characteristics or what an offender perceives to be personal characteristics—race, sexual orientation, religion, gender identity—that motivate hate crime victimizations. For example, a recent study found that gay men, lesbians, bisexuals, and people who have had a same-sex partner are 1.5 to 2 times more likely to experience violence as are people in the general population (Roberts, Austin, Corliss, Vandermorris, & Koenen, 2010). It also has been noted that for anti-LGBTQ hate crime victimizations, people may be targeted because offenders perceive that they are unlikely to notify the police due to the systemic discrimination they have faced (NCAVP, 2010).

Not all people who have characteristics covered in hate crime laws, however, are at risk of being victimized. Routine activities and lifestyles theory may be useful to understand why some people are victimized and others are not. According to this perspective, motivated offenders are ubiquitous and do not need to be explained (Cohen & Felson, 1979; Hindelang, Gottfredson, & Garofalo, 1978). Being a suitable target increases risk, though, as does a lack of capable guardianship. A person who has characteristics an offender "hates" is likely to activate an already motivated offender. For hate crimes, a motivated offender can simply see a person whom he or she perceives to have the characteristics the offender does not like. When this target lacks capable guardianship, a hate crime victimization is likely to occur.

In addition to individual risk factors, hate crime victimization may be a response to perceived threat—violations of territory or property, violations of what is sacred, and violations of status (Ehrlich, 1992). Following this threat explanation, economic competition by minorities has been proposed as a reason why racially and ethnically motivated hate crimes occur (Finn & McNeil, 1987). In addition, there may be community-level factors related to hate crime victimization. Lyons (2007), for instance, found that anti-Black hate crimes were more likely to occur in communities that were organized, while anti-White hate crimes occurred more frequently in disorganized communities. Accordingly, it may not be individual characteristics or routine activities per se that place individuals or groups at risk of hate crime victimization but, rather, underlying cultural or structural conditions.

Consequences of Hate Crime Victimization

We have discussed the innumerable consequences that come with many types of victimization, but the consequences of hate crime victimization deserve special consideration given that such victims are targeted because of characteristics they often cannot change. There is little doubt in victims' minds that their experience was born of hate. Think about how hard this must be to digest and live with afterward—it may result in a person seeing the world as particularly hostile and unsafe. Further, such a victimization may be particularly difficult to forgive (West & Wiley-Cordone, 1999). Because of hate motivation, the community also faces unique consequences.

Consequences for Individuals

Hate crime victimization likely comes with a heavy price for victims. Remember that hate crime victimizations are more likely than non-hate crime victimizations to be violent (Wilson, 2014). In addition, in 20% of hate crimes, victims report sustaining an injury (Wilson, 2014). In short, there are often physical consequences associated with hate crime victimization.

Along with these physical consequences, victims of hate crimes also commonly experience psychological consequences. As noted, victims are often unlikely to be capable of changing the characteristic for which they were targeted. As such, they may fear revictimization and feel that there is little they can do to prevent a subsequent attack. Fear may not be all that victims experience. Hate crime victimization has been linked to distress symptoms such as depression, stress, and anger (Roberts et al., 2010). For example, lesbians, gay men, and bisexuals who have experienced a bias crime victimization reported higher levels of fear of crime and perceived vulnerability and less belief in the benevolence of people compared with victims of non-bias crimes and nonvictims (Herek et al., 1999). For hate crime victimizations based on sexual orientation, another consequence is posttraumatic stress disorder (PTSD). In fact, gay men, lesbians, bisexuals, and persons who have had same-sex partners and who have been violently victimized are twice as likely to experience PTSD in response to the experience as are people in the general population (Roberts et al., 2010). This heightened response to hate crime victimization for gay, lesbian, and bisexual individuals may be due to the fact that their sexual orientation is an important part of their self-concept and also the reason they were victimized (Herek et al., 1999).

Consequences for the Community

When a hate crime victimization occurs, especially if it is made public, others in the community who share characteristics of the victim may become fearful that they will also become a target. This fear may cause individuals to change their behaviors and may limit their activities (West & Wiley-Cordone, 1999). To the extent that people identify with the victim, they may also experience **secondary victimization** whereby they suffer similar psychological consequences to those of the direct victim (West & Wiley-Cordone, 1999). The community may find that people are less likely to visit as tourists or to move there, and real estate values may plummet after publicized hate crime incidents (West & Wiley-Cordone, 1999).

Responses to Hate Crime Victimization

Legislation

It was not until the 1980s that hate crime victimization received widespread formal attention from the criminal justice system and the media. As special-interest groups began documenting victimizations that they perceived to be motivated by hate or bias, a movement toward recognizing hate crimes as a specialized category of crime took hold. In part, this movement resulted in the passage of legislation that attached enhanced penalties to crimes motivated by hate and that mandated the collection of data.

The first federal law specifically addressing hate crimes, as previously mentioned, was the Hate Crime Statistics Act (Pub. L. 101-275), which mandated the collection of data on hate crimes perpetrated based on race, religion, sexual orientation, or ethnicity. As noted, this requirement was expanded to include hate crimes based on disability via the Violent Crime Control and Law Enforcement Act of 1994 (Pub. L. No. 103-322). This law also directed the U.S. Sentencing Commission to develop or amend federal sentencing guidelines to provide enhancement of at least three offense levels for those offenses determined by judges beyond a reasonable doubt to be hate crimes. But how were hate crimes treated in federal court before 1990? There was not specific federal legislation that dealt with hate crimes. Rather, Title 18, U.S.C., Section 245 was used to hold people accountable for willfully injuring, intimidating, or interfering with, or attempting to do so by force or threat of force, people because of race, color, religion, or national origin during the course of federally protected activities—such as when attending school, participating as a juror, participating in an activity or program administered by the state or local government, or as a patron of any public accommodation. Although it served to protect certain classes of people, if a federally protected activity was not being engaged in at the time of the offense, the federal government could not intervene unless another federal interest was involved. This limit was removed with the passage of the Matthew Shepard and James Byrd, Jr. Hate Crime Prevention Act. This created a federal hate crimes law that eliminated the government's need to prove that victims were participating in a federally protected activity. Instead, crimes in which the federal government would otherwise have jurisdiction are included (e.g., the offender traveled with the victim across state lines). There are other federal laws in place that serve to prevent bias-motivated crimes, such as the **Church Arson Prevention Act of 1996,** which prohibits damage to religious property because of the religious, racial, or ethnic characteristics of the property, or the obstruction of or attempt to obstruct by force or threat of force a person exercising religious beliefs.

In addition to these pieces of federal legislation, states are also free to enact hate crime legislation to criminalize behavior that occurs within their borders. As recently as mid-year 2009, all but four states had hate crime legislation that included crimes based on individual characteristics (National Center for Victims of Crime, 2008b). See Table 15.2 for an example of California's hate crime law provisions.

Table 15.2 ■ California's Hate Crime Law Provisions, Cal Pen Code § 422.6

Who Is Protected?

Any person who is injured or threatened or has property damaged because of actual or perceived "race, color, religion, ancestry, national origin, disability, gender, or sexual orientation."

What Is the Penalty?

Persons who commit hate crime(s) as described above shall be punished by imprisonment for no more than one year or may be subject to a fine for no more than $5,000 and or both imprisonment and the fine. In addition, the court may order that community service be completed, not to exceed 400 hours, that is performed over a period of no more than 350 days (with consideration of his or her employment or school attendance).

Source: FindLaw. (2011). Cal. Pen. Code § 422.6: California Code. Retrieved from http://codes.lp.findlaw.com/cacode/PEN/3/1/11.6/2/s422.75.

Criminal Justice System Response

The criminal justice system is also set up to address this special type of crime victimization. As mentioned, the police are required to record and report data on hate crimes that occur. Research on compliance with the Hate Crime Statistics Act is somewhat sobering. King (2007) reported that police compliance with the requirements is less likely in jurisdictions that have greater populations of Black residents. This is particularly salient when considered in conjunction with the fact that racially motivated hate crimes are more likely to occur in these same areas. He further found that in the South, the correlation between the size of the Black population and police compliance with the reporting requirements of the Hate Crime Statistics Act was negative—in areas with high Black populations, adherence was low (King, 2007). Why do you think police are less likely to meet the requirements of federal reporting in these areas? What are the implications for these communities?

Also, most states have some type of hate crime legislation that specifically designates crimes motivated by hate as a special type of crime deserving of a special penalty. Remember, though, that even without hate crime laws, criminal behavior is criminal behavior, and a hate crime statute need not be in place for police to make an arrest when there is reason to do so. To address hate crimes, some police departments have specialty units (Levin & Amster, 2007). Boston was the first city, in 1978, to create a special unit whose mission was to respond to community disorders, including hate- or bias-motivated crimes (Levin & Amster, 2007). New York City founded a similar unit in 1980 (Levin & Amster, 2007). Many other jurisdictions today have similar units designed to address hate crimes, which have produced positive impacts on hate crime (Levin & Amster, 2007).

Once a crime is identified as being bias motivated, the prosecutor makes the decision whether to charge it as a hate crime. Some research suggests that prosecutors use their discretion, as they do when making charging decisions in other cases, when making this important decision. In fact, research shows that prosecutors are likely to charge bias crimes only when they are clearly bias motivated and when evidence overtly shows this bias (Bell, 2002; Phillips, 2009). Those cases in which bias is but one motive are unlikely to be charged as bias crimes—only "clean" cases, in which bias is the singular motive, are likely to be charged as bias crimes by a prosecutor (Maroney, 1998). Thus, when you consider that police must initially determine whether a crime is a hate crime (and only after the victim has decided to report) and then the prosecutor must determine whether to charge it as a hate crime—but only after the first step has been taken by the police—it should make sense that few hate crime victimizations actually result in formal charges in the criminal justice system.

Even if a case is not formally charged, hate crime victims can receive assistance from other sources. Victims of hate crimes can access traditional services designed for crime victims. That is, they are eligible to receive victim compensation; as long as they meet eligibility requirements, they can receive services from Victim/Witness Assistance Programs, they can agree to participate in victim–offender mediation or reconciliation programs, and they can exercise any rights granted to them in the jurisdiction in which they were victimized. Along with these traditional services, they can also seek assistance from special interest organizations and groups (e.g., Kansas City Anti-Violence Project).

■ VICTIMS OF HUMAN TRAFFICKING

Human trafficking has become a hot issue domestically and internationally, particularly in the past two decades. Interestingly, although media and governmental attention have grown dramatically over this time period, human trafficking is not a new victimization; it has its roots in slavery. Throughout history, we see examples of various forms of slavery, and America was not immune to the practice. Even though laws were passed in the United States to abolish slavery in 1863, these laws did not specifically address the issue of recruiting people for prostitution in another country and did not end the selling or forcing of African Americans into labor to pay debts (Logan, Walker, & Hunt, 2009). In other words, although race-based slavery was condemned, other forms of enslavement and trafficking were under way and were not similarly abolished (Logan et al., 2009).

What Is Human Trafficking?

Trafficking was not a federal crime until 2000, although the behaviors that are now prohibited may have been criminalized in other statutes. The Trafficking Victims Protection Act of 2000 (Pub. L. 106-386) defines human trafficking as

> (1) sex trafficking in which a commercial sex act is induced by force, fraud, or coercion, or in which the person induced to perform such act has not attained 18 years of age; or (2) the recruitment, harboring, transportation, provision, or obtaining of a person for labor or services, through the use of force, fraud, or coercion for the purpose of subjection to involuntary servitude, peonage, debt bondage, or slavery.

This definition is not the only one. The United Nations Protocol to Prevent, Suppress, and Punish Trafficking in Persons (2000) defines trafficking as

> the recruitment, transportation, transfer, harbouring or receipt of persons, by means of the threat or use of force or other means of coercion, of abduction, of fraud, of deception, of the abuse of power or of a position of vulnerability or of the giving or receiving of payments or benefits to achieve the consent of a person having control over another person, for the purpose of exploitation. Exploitation shall include, at a minimum, the exploitation of the prostitution of others or other forms of sexual exploitation, forced labour or services, slavery or practices similar to slavery, servitude or the removal of organs. (Article 2, Statement of Purpose)

The type of human trafficking related to sexual exploitation is known as **sex trafficking**. The type of human trafficking used to exploit someone for labor is known as **labor trafficking**. Persons do not have to be transported across international borders to be trafficked. Trafficking can be done within a country's borders. When this occurs, it is known as **domestic human trafficking**. When persons are transported into another country, it is called **transnational human trafficking**. Take note, however, that the actual transport of a person is not necessary for an incident to be considered human trafficking—you can become a victim of trafficking within your own home. If you were held against your will in your home and were made to perform sex acts on persons who came to the house, you would be a victim of sex trafficking.

Let's look at the different types of trafficking a little more closely. Sex trafficking occurs when a person is coerced, forced, or deceived into prostitution. If the initial decision to participate in prostitution was consensual, but the person is forced or coerced into continuing, then he or she is a victim of sex trafficking (U.S. Department of State, 2010). In this way, an initial consensual decision to engage in prostitution does not preclude a person from being considered a sex trafficking victim if that person wants to quit but is forced to continue. Persons can be forced to work in sex clubs, dance in strip clubs, work in massage parlors, or be otherwise enslaved or forced into other types of commercial sex work (e.g., street prostitution, pornography). Age is also a consideration when determining sex trafficking status. In the United States, if the victim is under the age of 18, there does not have to be force, fraud, or coercion in order for sex trafficking to occur. The victim simply being under the age of 18 and being recruited, harbored, transported, or obtained for the purpose of a commercial sex act is "enough" for sex trafficking to occur (Shared Hope International, 2011). Sex trafficking can also occur within debt bondage, another form of human trafficking discussed next.

Labor trafficking can be further divided into several types—bonded labor, forced labor, and involuntary domestic servitude. **Bonded labor,** also referred to as **debt bondage,** is the most common method of enslaving victims (U.S. Department of Health and Human Services [DHHS], 2011b). This type of labor trafficking occurs when a person is enslaved to work off a debt he or she owes when the terms or conditions of the debt were not previously known or properly defined or when the services the victim provides are not calculated in a reasonable fashion and "counted" toward the debt owed (DHHS, 2011b). The second type of labor trafficking is **forced labor,** which occurs when victims are forced to work under the threat of violence or punishment, their freedom is restricted, and some level of ownership over them is exercised (DHHS, 2011b). The third type of labor trafficking is **involuntary domestic servitude.** This type of trafficking involves victims who are forced to work as domestic workers. Often, these victims work in isolation on private property, which makes their situations difficult to detect since authorities may not be able to enter and inspect these locations (U.S. Department of State, 2010). Think back to Cindy's story at the beginning of this chapter. What type of human trafficking did she experience? How do you know?

Extent of Human Trafficking

As you may imagine, it is quite difficult to know the true extent to which people are trafficked within the United States and internationally. Generally, it is widely accepted that most human trafficking goes undetected, so reliance on official data sources most likely grossly underestimates the extent of human trafficking. The reasons that most human trafficking remains undetected are many. First, human trafficking is, by its nature, underground and hidden (Schauer & Wheaton, 2006). It is a type of victimization that occurs out of sight of most people and, therefore, is difficult to detect. Second, many countries do not treat trafficking seriously, and in some countries, law enforcement and other officials actively participate in human trafficking. Third, most victims do not report their victimizations to authorities. Many victims are unable to report and others are unwilling to report. Victims are often taught to fear law enforcement and other groups that would be able to help them (U.S. Department of State, 2010). Other victims receive threats of further harm if they report their victimizations to authorities. Fourth, victims are often a mobile population—they are frequently moved from one location to the next—and, thus, counting them is difficult at best (Schauer & Wheaton, 2006). Fifth, the definition of what constitutes human trafficking is not clear in every jurisdiction, despite formal definitions put forth by the United Nations (Gozdziak & Collett, 2005). Likewise, not all countries collect data about the number of human trafficking victims within their borders.

Despite these hindrances, there have been efforts to determine the extent to which humans are trafficked. The U.S. Department of State (2014) publishes the Trafficking in Persons Report (TIP Report), which provides information about trafficking throughout the world using information from U.S. embassies, government officials, nongovernmental and international organizations, reports, research trips to regions included in the report, and information submitted to the State Department's e-mail address for the TIP Report. From this report, it is estimated that 12.3 million persons are in forced labor, bonded labor, and forced prostitution in the world, and as many as 2 million children are in the global commercial sex trade (U.S. Department of State, 2010). It is estimated that between 600,000 and 4 million persons each year are trafficked worldwide (McCabe & Manian, 2010). In 2013 alone, 46,570 victims were identified in the TIP Report. Although much of the attention surrounding human trafficking is on sex trafficking, according to the TIP Report, there are more people trafficked for the purposes of forced labor than for commercial sex (U.S. Department of State, 2010). In fact, it is estimated that for every one person forced into prostitution, there are nine people forced into labor (U.S. Department of State, 2010). The TIP report also provides information on prosecutions and convictions related to trafficking. In 2013, there were 9,460 prosecutions included in the TIP report and 5,776 convictions (U.S. Department of State, 2014).

Domestic trafficking within the United States also has been investigated. As part of the Trafficking of Victims Protection Reauthorization Act of 2005 (Pub. L. 109-164), biennial reporting on human trafficking is now required. In response to this requirement, the U.S. Department of Justice has supported the creation of the Human Trafficking Reporting System, which provides information on investigations opened by federally funded human-trafficking task forces in the United States (Banks & Kyckelhahn, 2011). Based on this data collection, from January 2008 and June 2010, there were 2,515 investigations opened by these agencies, 389 of which were confirmed to be human trafficking (527 total victims) (Banks & Kyckelhahn, 2011). The vast majority of these incidents (82%) were sex trafficking incidents.

Who Is Trafficked?

For the same reasons it is difficult to know the true extent to which human trafficking occurs, it is also difficult to know who the "typical" victim of trafficking is. As a result, the description of who is most likely to be a human trafficking victim is likely only as reliable as the data available. Nevertheless, it is estimated that females make up 56% of all victims of human trafficking worldwide (U.S. Department of State, 2010). In the United States, males make up the most of the confirmed human trafficking incidents reported by task forces (Banks & Kyckelhahn, 2011). Females make up a larger percentage of victims of sex trafficking (94%) than of labor trafficking (69%) in the United States, as reported by task forces (Banks & Kyckelhahn, 2011). In terms of who is trafficked in the United States, data indicate that the majority are immigrants (Logan et al., 2009). Worldwide, about half of all victims of trafficking are under the age of 18 (McCabe & Manian, 2010). Trafficking appears to be more prevalent in some areas of the world than in others. In Asia and the Pacific, the prevalence of trafficking is estimated to be 3 persons per 1,000 inhabitants, compared with the worldwide estimate of 1.8 per 1,000 inhabitants (U.S. Department of State, 2010).

Russia supplies most of the women and girls for sex trafficking (Schauer & Wheaton, 2006). This means that Russia is a popular **source country** for sex trafficking. Other former Soviet bloc countries are also popular source countries for the sex trafficking industry (Schauer & Wheaton, 2006). The countries that receive victims of human trafficking are known as **destination countries.** Germany is the top destination country for sex trafficking of women and girls (Schauer & Wheaton, 2006). The United States is the second most popular destination country for sex trafficking, with most victims coming from Asia, Mexico, and former Soviet bloc countries (Schauer & Wheaton, 2006). Other popular destination countries are Italy, the Netherlands, Japan, Greece, India, Thailand, and Australia (Schauer & Wheaton, 2006). See the Focus on International Issues Box to read about Denmark and Sweden and their sex trafficking problems and how each country has responded to this particular type of victimization.

Anyone can also become a victim of labor trafficking. Victims can be children or adults and women or men. Even so, women and children are more likely to become victims of labor trafficking than are others (DHHS, 2011b). Victims may work in legitimate jobs such as domestic, factory, or construction work, while others may be involved in illegal activities such as distributing drugs (DHHS, 2011b).

FOCUS ON INTERNATIONAL ISSUES

Sweden and Denmark, while both Scandinavian countries, could not be more different in how they responded to the growing problem of sex trafficking in the mid-1990s. In 1995, Sweden passed a law that made it illegal to buy sex, but not illegal to sell sex, thus recognizing that women who sell sex are coerced into doing so either by circumstance or force. Those caught buying sex can face hefty fines, public notification, and potential prison time. Police believe that it has had an impact on trafficking, with sex traffickers choosing to not bring women into Sweden because there is little to gain financially and too much risk. Police estimate that there are only about 200 prostitutes working in Stockholm, a city of more than 2 million people. This is quite different than the conditions found in Copenhagen, Denmark. Instead of instituting tough laws against buying sex, Denmark decriminalized prostitution in 1999, leading to a growth in Copenhagen's red light district. Most of the women who are engaged in prostitution are not Danish, but are African or Eastern European. Estimates are that the majority of them have been or are vulnerable to trafficking. When police identify a possible victim of trafficking, they place him or her in a safe house for a reflection period that lasts up to 100 days. If the victims have not cooperated at the end of this time, they are deported (if they are in the country illegally). The problems in Copenhagen have led politicians to debate adopting an approach similar to Sweden's.

Source: Adapted from The battle against sex trafficking: Sweden vs. Denmark. (2011, March 20). The CNN Freedom Project: Ending Modern Day Slavery. Retrieved from http://thecnnfreedomproject.blogs.cnn.com/2011/03/30/sex-trafficking-countries-take-different-approaches-to-same-problem.

Risk Factors for Human Trafficking

Individual Risk Factors

One of the most pervasive factors placing persons at risk of being trafficked is living in extreme poverty. People living in some countries face little opportunity for gainful employment, and women in these countries especially face economic and social oppression (Schauer & Wheaton, 2006). Persons living in extreme poverty and/or those who are oppressed are vulnerable to accepting promises of work in other countries—work that sometimes turns into labor trafficking when they are forced into debt bondage upon arrival in the destination country. This desire for work may be the impetus for females willingly going with traffickers to other countries only to find that they owe their traffickers exorbitant amounts of money for falsified documents used to enter the country. They may also realize that the only work "available" to them is sex work (Miller, Decker, Silverman, & Raj, 2007). In the TIP report, certain occupations are also identified as being particularly dangerous for trafficking such as working in agriculture, fishing and aquaculture, logging, and mining. Persons working in these fields may find themselves at risk for environmental harms, and their jobs often occur in remote locations. Further, they often are not covered by local labor laws, and governments do not provide sufficient oversight (U.S. Department of State, 2014).

Country-Level Risk Factors

Not only are there factors that may place individuals at risk for being trafficked, either by making them suitable targets or by pushing them into choices that lead them into trafficking victimization, but characteristics about countries also can make trafficking more or less likely. Countries characterized by high levels of civil unrest and violence are more likely to have trafficking networks operating within them (Logan et al., 2009). Similarly, countries that provide little opportunity for social mobility and few economic opportunities are likely to have more victims of trafficking (DHHS, 2011b). In addition, some countries have greater levels of acceptance of trafficking and their governments do little to address this problem, even sometimes working to facilitate trafficking and not punishing traffickers (Logan et al., 2009). In countries where government officials and law enforcement are corrupt and easily bought off, traffickers are likely to pay off these officials. For example, in Bosnia and Herzegovina, victims have reported police officers actually participating in their transport and their traffickers giving "something" to the Border Police (Rathgeber, 2002). The role of women in many countries also contributes to their likelihood of being trafficked. Women who live in cultures that objectify and stigmatize them while at the same time barring them from legitimate employment opportunities may be more likely to be victims of trafficking than those who live in cultures where women are treated with more respect and allowed entry into legitimate employment (Schauer & Wheaton, 2006).

Consequences for Victims of Human Trafficking

There are obvious physical health consequences for persons who have been trafficked. They are often harmed physically while being held against their will. In addition, victims who are trafficked for labor are often forced to work long hours in deplorable conditions, which can take a toll on their bodies. These physical effects can be both immediate and long-lasting. Victims of labor trafficking may be exposed to dangerous working conditions and, as a result, may suffer health problems such as back pain, hearing loss, cardiovascular and respiratory problems, and limb amputations (DHHS, 2011b).

Health consequences also have been identified for victims of sex trafficking. In a study of women who had received services in Europe for sexual exploitation, 90% of the victims reported some type of sexual violence while they were trafficked, and 76% indicated they had been physically abused during their trafficking experience (Zimmerman et al., 2008). In addition to experiencing violence, the majority of these 192 women and adolescent girls reported experiencing headaches, dizzy spells, back pain, memory difficulty, stomach pain, pelvic pain, and gynecological symptoms during the previous 2 weeks (Zimmerman et al., 2008). Other research on victims of sex trafficking has noted forced or coerced use of drugs or alcohol (Zimmerman et al., 2003).

In addition to these physical health consequences, the mental health outcomes of trafficking victims have been examined. Reported psychological effects of labor trafficking include shame, anxiety disorders, PTSD, phobias, panic attacks, and depression (DHHS, 2011b). Women and girls trafficked for sex exploitation reported high levels of depression, anxiety, hostility (Zimmerman et al., 2003, 2008), PTSD, suicidal ideation, and suicide attempts (Zimmerman et al., 2003).

Response to Human Trafficking Victims

International Response

In 2000, the United Nations adopted the Protocol to Prevent, Suppress, and Punish Trafficking in Persons, Especially Women and Children (called the **Palermo Protocol**). This international protocol called for the criminalization of human trafficking and outlined how governments should respond to the problem of trafficking. Specifically, the Palermo Protocol identified that governments should include elements of prevention, criminal prosecution, and victim protection—the "3P" paradigm of governmental response (U.S. Department of State, 2010). Despite the Palermo Protocol being adopted more than 10 years ago, there are still 62 countries that have not convicted a trafficker under laws in compliance with the Palermo Protocol (U.S. Department of State, 2010). In addition, in 2013 only 31 countries were rated in Tier 1 of the TIP Report, indicating that they are in full compliance with the Trafficking Victims Protection Act's minimum standards (U.S. Department of State, 2014). See Table 15.3 for a list of these countries.

Victims who have traveled to foreign countries also have special needs tied to their immigration status. According to the Palermo Protocol, governments should not simply deport human trafficking victims if they are found to be in countries illegally. Despite this mandate, 104 countries do not have laws, policies, or regulations to prevent such deportation (U.S. Department of State, 2010). So how do countries deal with victims of human trafficking who are in foreign countries? One response is **repatriation** of foreign victims, although this should be done only if it serves the victims' best interests. It is possible that returning victims to their places of citizenship will put them back in the same context and conditions that led to their being trafficked originally, and some face violence or death upon return to their home countries (U.S. Department of State, 2010).

Table 15.3 ■ Countries in Tier 1		
Armenia	Iceland	Norway
Australia	Ireland	Poland
Austria	Israel	Slovak Republic
Belgium	Italy	Slovenia
Canada	Korea, South	Spain
Chile	Luxembourg	Sweden
Czech Republic	Macedonia	Switzerland
Denmark	Netherlands	Taiwan
Finland	New Zealand	United Kingdom
France	Nicaragua	United States of America
Germany		

United States Governmental/Criminal Justice Response

The United States has recognized that trafficked persons who are non-U.S. citizens have special needs regarding immigration and citizenship. To address this issue, victims can become **certified** so they can receive the same benefits and services from federal and/or state programs generally provided to refugees (DHHS, 2011a). To become certified, victims of human trafficking must meet three criteria: (1) be a victim of a severe form of trafficking according to the Trafficking Victims Protection Act of 2000; (2) be willing to assist in the investigation and prosecution of trafficking cases (or be unable to because of physical or psychological trauma); and (3) have completed a bona fide application for a T visa or received Continued Presence from the Department of Homeland Security to be able to contribute to the prosecution of human traffickers. A **T visa** allows victims of human trafficking to become temporary residents of the United States. After 3 years, persons with T visas may be eligible for permanent resident status (DHHS, 2011a).

One way in which trafficking has been addressed in the United States is through the adoption of formal law enforcement task forces and investigative entities. For example, an FBI initiative to disrupt human trafficking in the United States and abroad began in 2004. The FBI works with more than 71 human trafficking task force working groups throughout the United States. Since 2004 the FBI has doubled the number of open human trafficking investigations and quadrupled the number of prosecutions and convictions (FBI, n.d.-a). Research on trafficking task forces indicates that areas that have these task forces have higher detection rates and are more likely to succeed in prosecuting traffickers (Farrell, McDevitt, & Fahy, 2008). The FBI also employs victim specialists who work with victims of human trafficking to assist them with legal needs as well as other services such as child care, immigration issues, employment, education, and job training (FBI, n.d.-a).

Often, law enforcement officers must arrest victims for the crimes in which they are involved, such as prostitution (Shared Hope International, 2011). Even if doing so keeps the victim safe and frees him or her from his or her captor, this criminalization of the victim's behavior can have serious consequences since it brings the victim into the formal criminal justice system. For example, arresting a victim may actually make him or her ineligible for some victim services, such as victim compensation (Shared Hope International, 2011). To remedy this situation, some states have passed laws that make minors immune to prosecution for prostitution—for example, there is a presumption that minors are coerced into committing prostitution by another person (Shared Hope International, 2011). Victims, as defined by U.S. law, do have the right not to be held in detention or to be charged with crimes in relation to the trafficking offense, so long as they are willing to cooperate with the criminal investigation and prosecution of their trafficking offenders (Logan et al., 2009). If the victim is unwilling to assist in the formal criminal justice process, then he or she may not be protected from charges or deportation (Logan et al., 2009).

Victim Services

Along with the growing response to the problem of human trafficking, numerous resources for victims have been developed and instituted. Victims of trafficking often experience a higher level of distress than other victims, since when they seek assistance or are discovered they often have few, if any, resources of their own (Logan et al., 2009). Despite this need, victims of trafficking have fewer resources available to them than do victims of other crimes (Logan et al., 2009).

One option that may be available for victims is to be taken to a protective shelter. However, there is not enough space for all victims to use this option. For example, in the United States, there are fewer than 100 beds in facilities that specialize in treating victims of sex trafficking who are under the age of 18 (Shared Hope International, 2011). Reports from other countries also show a shortage of open beds in safe houses. For example, in Bosnia and Herzegovina, women victims have slept in chairs at police stations while waiting to be questioned instead of being taken to a safe house for the night (Rathgeber, 2002). It is also important to consider that female victims should be interviewed by female police officers who are specially trained in how to respond to victims of trafficking (Rathgeber, 2002). In the United States and abroad, victims should also be offered support counselors or advocates if they testify in court (Rathgeber, 2002). As human trafficking continues to receive attention as a serious problem throughout the world, the resources available to victims will, hopefully, continue to expand to meet their unique needs.

■ VICTIMS OF TERRORISM

Perhaps no victimization event in the past 20 years has impacted people in the United States more profoundly than the terrorist attacks that took place on September 11, 2001, in which almost 3,000 people lost their lives when planes were hijacked and crashed into the World Trade Center, into the Pentagon, and in Shanksville, Pennsylvania (National Commission on Terrorist Attacks upon the United States, 2004). An event so cataclysmic and profound, fortunately, does not happen very often. But people are impacted by terrorism throughout the world in less publicized incidents. This section discusses the extent to which terrorism victimization occurs, to whom it occurs, the impact it has, and how victims of terrorism can be assisted.

PHOTO 15.2

The aftermath of the World Trade Center attacks on 9/11.

Photo Credit: © Bernd Obermann/Corbis.

Extent of Terrorism Victimization

Outside Lahore High Court in GPO Chowk, Lahore, Punjab, Pakistan, on January 10, 2008, a suicide bomber detonated an improvised explosive device that was strapped to his body as he approached a group of riot police. In this single incident, 17 police officers were killed, along with 8 civilians. Eighty other people were wounded, and at least six vehicles were destroyed (National Counterterrorism Center [NCTC], 2009). Despite its severity, you probably did not hear about it, given that it was but one of the many terrorist attacks against noncombatants that occurred during that year.

It is difficult to know to what extent people are victimized by terrorism throughout the world. Not all incidents are recorded or reported—many may occur in remote areas of the world. The most comprehensive data available on terrorism incidents in the world are reported by the National Counterterrorism Center (NCTC), which are required by the U.S. State Department to compile statistical information on terrorism incidents—"the number of individuals . . . killed, injured, or kidnapped by each terrorist group during the preceding calendar year as reported in open source media" (NCTC, 2012, p. v). According to this report, over 10,000 terrorist attacks occurred worldwide in 2011. These attacks resulted in almost 45,000 persons being victimized—indicating that multiple people were harmed in many of the incidents—in 70 different countries (NCTC, 2012). U.S. citizens were relatively safe from terrorism in 2011—17 citizens were killed, 14 were injured, and 3 were kidnapped worldwide (NCTC, 2012).

Who Are Victims of Terrorism?

Of the 45,000 persons victimized by terrorism in 2012, over 50% of those who were killed were civilians. Although it is difficult to know exactly who the victims are in all cases, data indicate that police officers made up 18% of all those who were killed (NCTC, 2012). Other commonly targeted people are government officials, employees, and contractors—making up about 5% of terrorist victims in total (NCTC, 2012). Most of the victims of terrorism in 2009 were Muslims (NCTC, 2010). Sadly, children are disproportionately victimized by terrorism (NCTC, 2009).

Researchers examining data on terrorism collected from other sources have also attempted to identify the characteristics of persons who are most likely to be victims of terrorism. In a study of terrorism that occurred in Uruguay, Northern Ireland, Spain, Germany, Italy, and Cyprus, it was found that most victims were between the ages of 20 and 39 years, were males, and were members of security forces (Hewitt, 1988). Research on terrorism victims in Northern Ireland confirms this finding regarding males being the most likely victims (Fay, Morrissey, & Smyth, 1999). Other research examining Israeli civilians killed in Israel via acts of terror between September 1993 and the end of 2003 found that the majority of victims were male. Further, persons aged 17 to 24 composed 30% of fatalities attributed to terrorism in Israel even though they made up only 14% of the population (Feniger & Yuchtman-Yaar, 2010). In Israel, most of the fatalities were Jewish; this finding is contrary to the NCTC (2012) report, which found that, at least in 2012, Muslims were the largest group of victims in cases in which religious affiliation could be identified.

Characteristics of Terrorism Victimizations

In 2011, most of the terrorism incidents were perpetrated via armed attacks, bombings, and kidnappings (NCTC, 2012). Suicide attacks composed a small fraction of all terrorist activities recorded in the NCTC report (2,279 out of the 10,283 attacks). Of all attacks, terrorists most commonly used improvised explosive devices, firearms, and explosives (NCTC, 2012). Of the terrorist attacks that resulted in deaths, over half were caused by bombings (NCTC, 2012). Armed attacks caused the second most deaths (NCTC, 2012).

Terrorist attacks impact persons throughout the world, but some areas were disproportionately hit. The Near East and South Asia experienced over three fourths of all the terrorist attacks in 2012 (NCTC, 2012). Afghanistan alone experienced 2,872 attacks and 3,353 deaths—it was the country with the most terrorist attacks and deaths in 2012 (NCTC, 2012). In comparison, there were 480 attacks in the Western Hemisphere due to terrorism; most of these attacks occurred in Colombia (NCTC, 2012). See Table 15.4 for the breakdown of deaths for the top 15 countries resulting from terrorism in 2012.

Interestingly, when analysis of terrorism data is expanded across time from 1970 to 2006, a somewhat different picture emerges. Latin America was the region that experienced the greatest percentage of fatal and nonfatal attacks, followed by Western Europe (LaFree, Morris, & Dugan, 2010). Moreover, data show that terrorism grew during the 1970s, with a peak in 1992 and another in 2006 (Dugan, LaFree, Cragin, & Kasupski, 2008).

Risk Factors for Terrorism Victimization

One of the scariest things about terrorism is its unpredictability. Although some terrorism is targeted at specific groups or individuals, other terrorist activities are targeted more generally at "enemy" groups (Feniger & Yuchtman-Yaar, 2010). This type of terrorism appears to be indiscriminate, targeting anonymous individuals who belong or appear to belong to a group, but the precise identities of the individuals do not matter (Feniger & Yuchtman-Yaar, 2010). Obviously, some people are more at risk of being victimized than others, given that they belong to what has been identified as an "enemy" group. In addition, the amount of time that people spend in public spaces has been linked to terrorism victimization risk, particularly for indiscriminate forms of terrorism (Feniger & Yuchtman-Yaar, 2010).

These factors make sense when considered from a routine activities theory perspective. Persons who are suitable targets (i.e., deemed part of the "enemy" group) and who lack capable guardianship are at risk of being victims of terrorism when they come into contact in time and space with motivated offenders. Similarly, places that are suitable targets and are without capable guardianship are more likely to be targeted. As noted in the NCTC (2010) report, the United States has implemented strategies to track motivated offenders, harden targets, and create capable guardianship since 9/11; since then, the United States has not suffered a major attack, although other factors such as political forces are also noted as likely playing a role in terrorism activity.

Table 15.4 ◼ Deaths From Terrorism, 2012 Top 15 Countries	
Country	**Number of Deaths**
Afghanistan	3,353
Iraq	3,063
Pakistan	2,033
Somalia	1,101
Nigeria	593
India	497
Colombia	305
Thailand	238
Russia	189
Sudan	189
Philippines	188
Yemen	158
Congo, DR	99
Norway	91
Syria	52

Consequences of Terrorism on Victims

The loss of human life is inarguably the most tangible consequence of terrorism; however, terrorism has far-reaching impacts on victims and, as you will see, on those who are exposed to terrorism but not directly victimized. Along with physical injury, victims of terrorism are likely to be psychologically impacted by their experience. Basic assumptions about the world may change for victims. They may no longer believe that the world is a safe place where good things happen to good people; instead, they may realize that evil things can and do happen even to good people (Gonzales, Schofield, & Gillis, 2001). In addition to this impact on people's worldview, survivors may suffer from PTSD, anxiety disorders (North et al., 1999), major depression, panic disorder, and agoraphobia (Gabriel et al., 2007).

Following the attacks in Mumbai, India, in November 2008 that killed 164 people and injured at least 308 people, acute stress disorder was assessed in victims admitted to one of the public hospitals. Of the 74 victims, 30% were found to be suffering from acute stress disorder (Balasinorwala, 2009). Survivors of the 1995 Oklahoma City terrorist bombing also experienced negative consequences postdisaster. In a study of 50 of the survivors, 22% experienced bombing-related PTSD (Tucker et al., 2010). Persons who were injured in the March 11, 2004, terrorist attacks in Madrid had prevalence rates of PTSD in the 2 months after the attacks that were 40 times higher than expected given previous rates of PTSD in the Spanish adult population before the attacks (Gabriel et al., 2007).

Acts of terrorism also affect people who are not directly victimized. People may hear about the terrorism in the media, or they may know someone who was harmed. Think back to 9/11—it was difficult to turn the television on in the days and weeks that followed without seeing a news story or update about the events. This exposure, while informative, also could have been damaging (Slone & Shoshani, 2008). Indeed, research shows that persons not directly involved in terrorist attacks still may experience psychological trauma afterward. Research on Americans following the 9/11 terrorist attacks showed that between 3 and 5 days after the event, 44% of people surveyed experienced substantial stress reactions (e.g., repeated disturbed memories, thoughts, or dreams about what happened; difficulty concentrating) (Schuster et al., 2001). Further research investigating the impacts of 9/11 showed that almost 6% of persons surveyed reported PTSD symptoms 6 months after the attacks (Silver, Holman, McIntosh, Poulin, & Gil-Rivas, 2002). Terrorism also has indirect impacts on children. In a study that screened children after the Oklahoma City bombing, it was found that 34% of middle and high school students were worried about their own safety and the safety of their family 2 months later (Gurwitch, Pfefferbaum, & Leftwich, 2002).

Persons who lose loved ones in terrorist attacks may be hit especially hard. A common response is the desire to take revenge on the attacker, although actually taking action along these lines is quite rare (Miller, 2004). More common is a feeling of vulnerability and fear that may lead to isolation, changing daily routines, installing alarms, refusing to be alone or to go out at night, or carrying weapons for safety (Miller, 2004). They may have "survivor's guilt" or feel as though they should have somehow foreseen the attack or kept their loved one safe (Miller, 2004). They may suffer from a loss of appetite, difficulty sleeping, gastrointestinal problems, cardiovascular disease, anxiety, and depression (Miller, 2004).

Responses to Victims of Terrorism

Persons who are victimized by terrorism may access many of the same services available to other types of crime victims, but they may not view themselves in the same light as someone who is the victim of a more traditional crime. As you may imagine, they may not turn to the formal criminal justice system for assistance as might a person who has experienced, for example, a household robbery. Nonetheless, there is awareness that victims of terrorism have special needs and rights that deserve attention.

In the United States, by definition, terrorist acts are federal crimes (Reno, Marcus, Leary, & Turman, 2000). As such, the federal government has developed numerous resources for victims of terrorism. One set of resources centers on legislation. Following the Iran hostage crisis, two pieces of legislation were passed to provide a remedy to the victims. The **Hostage Relief Act of 1980** (Pub. L. 96-449) provided victims, their spouses, and dependent children benefits such as compensation for medical costs, deferral of taxes and penalties, and reimbursement for educational and training costs. It did not, however, provide money to compensate for wages lost during captivity. To remedy this, then president Reagan signed into law the **Victims of Terrorism Compensation Act** in 1986 (title VIII of Pub. L. 99-399).

Other pieces of legislation have been passed in response to specific terrorism acts, such as the **Aviation Security Improvement Act** (Pub. L. 101-604); however, the most grand-sweeping pieces of legislation dealing with terrorism were passed in response to the 9/11 attacks. The **Victims of Terrorism Tax Relief Act (2001)** (Pub. L. 107-134) mandates that qualifying payments made to the families of victims of "qualified disasters" for disaster-related expenses are not taxable.

Further, death benefits would not be counted as taxable income if the death was a result of the Oklahoma City bombing, the attacks on 9/11, or anthrax-related attacks between September 11, 2001, and January 1, 2002. Crime victim compensation was also extended to victims of 9/11 and their families through the **Air Transportation Safety and System Stabilization Act (2001)** (Pub. L. 107-42). This act established a compensation fund for victims who were killed or physically harmed; they, their spouses, and/or their dependents may receive benefits from the fund. Awards vary for individuals and families (e.g., compensation based on loss of future earnings), and only economic losses that victims could be compensated for in their state in a tort claim are covered (Levin, 2002). In addition, a presumptive amount of noneconomic damages was set—$250,000 for each deceased person, plus $100,000 for a widowed spouse and for each dependent child (Levin, 2002). On average, each family was predicted to be awarded $1.85 million (Levin, 2002). Research on the victims of 9/11 and their families shows that a total of $8.7 billion in benefits has been provided to civilians killed or seriously injured in the 9/11 attacks and their families (Dixon & Stern, 2004). Of this, about $6 million was funded through the Victims Compensation Fund, with awards ranging from $250,000 to $7.1 million (Dixon & Stern, 2004). Other persons also received compensation, such as emergency responders and businesses, and insurance companies and charities also provided compensation to victims. Figure 15.1 shows the amounts that different groups of victims received in quantified benefit payments from different sources.

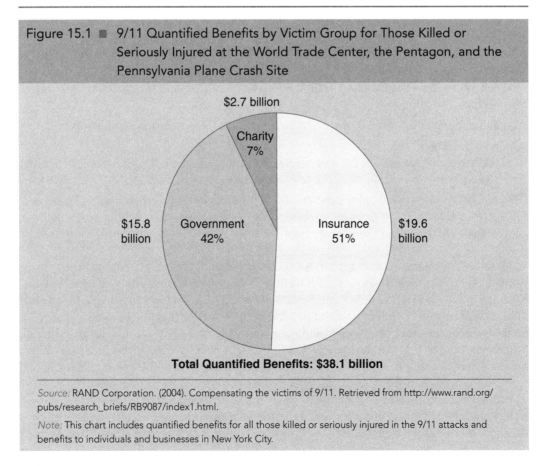

Figure 15.1 ■ 9/11 Quantified Benefits by Victim Group for Those Killed or Seriously Injured at the World Trade Center, the Pentagon, and the Pennsylvania Plane Crash Site

$2.7 billion

Charity 7%

$15.8 billion — Government 42%

Insurance 51% — $19.6 billion

Total Quantified Benefits: $38.1 billion

Source: RAND Corporation. (2004). Compensating the victims of 9/11. Retrieved from http://www.rand.org/pubs/research_briefs/RB9087/index1.html.

Note: This chart includes quantified benefits for all those killed or seriously injured in the 9/11 attacks and benefits to individuals and businesses in New York City.

Beyond financial compensation, the Office for Victims of Crime has identified several recommendations for services and policies for victims of terrorism in the United States. Specifically, this agency recommends that

- unnecessary delays in death notification should be avoided;
- release of victim remains and death notification should be handled in a sensitive manner;
- directly after a terrorism event, a "compassion center" should be established where victims and their families can go for information, crisis counseling, and privacy;
- mental health assessment and services should be provided;
- victim compensation and other services' applications should be streamlined—services should be made available in a timely manner, paperwork should be minimized, and agencies should coordinate services;
- states should establish emergency funds that can be used quickly in cases of terrorism;
- citizens who are victimized outside the United States should be eligible for compensation and services;
- federal personnel who work with victims of terrorism should receive training on victims' rights laws and services;
- the FBI should keep victims informed of the state of the investigation and events in the case, and identification of victims and access to victim contact information must be established and maintained;
- federal agencies should have a team that can be mobilized on-site to provide support to terrorism victims;
- prosecuting offices need to keep victims apprised of their cases and services while providing support;
- victims should be provided with a media liaison through the U.S. Department of Justice to help with media requests so they can avoid added trauma; and
- federal agencies that employ persons who may be targeted by terrorism should provide information about procedures for responding to employees and their families in the event of victimization (Reno et al., 2000).

Victims of terrorism in other countries are also afforded rights and protections. The Council of Europe's Guidelines on the Protection of Victims of Terrorist Acts (2005, as cited in Kilchling, n.d.) outlines that timely compensation should be given to victims of terrorism and their close family for direct physical and psychological harm. Further, the European Union has provided that victims of terrorism and their family members be protected during criminal proceedings and be provided restitution (Kilchling, n.d.). Victims of terrorism in Israel are also afforded access to compensation for property damage and bodily injuries. Family members of persons killed by terrorism can also be compensated (Kilchling, n.d.).

Although there are other contemporary issues in the field of victimology, human trafficking, hate crime victimization, and terrorism victimization are emerging areas of study that impact not just the United States but the global community as well. As these areas garner further attention, developing methodologies to determine the true extent to which each type of victimization occurs should be at the forefront. Identifying victims is critical to developing policies and implementing services to assist them.

SUMMARY

- The two major types of human trafficking are sex trafficking and labor trafficking. Human trafficking can be domestic or transnational.
- Much like other forms of sexual victimization, sex trafficking considers the age of the victim. In the United States, persons under 18 do not have to be forced or coerced for their victimization to be considered sex trafficking.
- Labor trafficking includes bonded labor and debt bondage, which are the most common forms of trafficking.
- Depending on the cultural gender role of women, one country may be more susceptible to human trafficking than another.
- Government officials sometimes participate in trafficking, and many countries do not treat trafficking seriously; trafficking is often difficult to detect, and estimates of its extent likely underestimate the problem.
- The Trafficking in Persons Report provides estimates of the extent of human trafficking in the United States.
- Females are more likely to be victims of human trafficking than are men. Poverty is one of the most salient risk factors for human trafficking.
- Countries characterized by high levels of civil unrest and violence are more likely to have trafficking networks operating within them. Countries that do not have opportunities for upward social mobility are also more likely to have human trafficking problems.
- Victims of human trafficking experience not only physical health consequences but also mental health problems such as shame, anxiety disorders, posttraumatic stress disorder, phobias, panic attacks, and depression.
- As an international response to human trafficking, the "3P" paradigm—prevention, criminal prosecution, and victim protection—was developed.
- A critical issue with foreign victims of human trafficking is that returning them to their legal home countries could put them at risk for revictimization.
- Victims who meet certain criteria can become certified and obtain a T visa allowing them temporary resident status in the United States.
- Some states have laws of protection for victims who are arrested for the crimes they commit while being trafficked.
- There is a lack of adequate space in protective shelters for victims of human trafficking (e.g., the United States has fewer than 100 beds for victims under age 18 in facilities that specialize in treating human trafficking).
- When victims are targeted out of hate or bias related to race, perceived race, religion, or sexual orientation, it is considered a hate crime.
- Generally, there are differences across gender, race, and ethnic groups for types of persons who are victimized, but this is not the case with hate crime victims.
- Hate crimes are sometimes committed due to the offender perceiving a threat from the victim.
- Because victims of hate crimes usually cannot change the characteristic for which they were targeted, there is a real fear of revictimization.
- If and when a hate crime is made public to the community, there may be some communal consequence, such as tourists deciding not to visit.

- The criminal justice system, specifically prosecutors, use discretion when determining whether the crime committed was a hate crime.
- About 10,000 terrorist attacks occurred worldwide in 2011.
- In 2012, most of the incidents of terrorism were perpetrated via armed attacks, bombings, and kidnappings.
- Obviously, some individuals are more at risk of terrorism victimization than others, given that they belong to a group identified as an "enemy." In addition, the amount of time people spend in public spaces has been linked to terrorism victimization risk, particularly for indiscriminate forms of terrorism.
- Along with physical injury, victims of terrorism are likely to be psychologically impacted by their experiences. Victims may experience posttraumatic stress disorder, depression, anxiety, agoraphobia, and panic disorders.
- The Air Transportation Safety and System Stabilization Act (2001) made it possible for victims of terrorism to be compensated for their losses.
- Victims of terrorism in other countries are also afforded rights and protections.

DISCUSSION QUESTIONS

1. What are some country-level factors that place women at risk of experiencing human trafficking? How do women's roles in their countries protect them or make them more likely to be trafficked?

2. What are some ways the government protects minors who are victims of human trafficking?

3. As it pertains to reporting hate crimes, why do you think the estimates from the Uniform Crime Reports are so different from those of the National Coalition of Anti-Violence Programs?

4. Why do you think some research shows minority victims as more likely to report their hate crimes than nonminority victims?

5. Could it be argued that being a member of security forces puts one at greater risk for terrorism victimization? Why or why not?

KEY TERMS

hate crime

bias crime

Hate Crime Statistics Act (1990)

Matthew Shepard and James Byrd, Jr. Hate Crime Prevention Act

screen question

anti-LGBTQ hate violence

secondary victimization

Church Arson Prevention Act of 1996

sex trafficking

labor trafficking

domestic human trafficking

transnational human trafficking

bonded labor

debt bondage

forced labor

involuntary domestic servitude

source country

destination countries

Palermo Protocol

repatriation

certified

T visa

Hostage Relief Act of 1980

Victims of Terrorism Compensation Act

Aviation Security Improvement Act

Victims of Terrorism Tax Relief Act (2001)

Air Transportation Safety and System Stabilization Act (2001)

INTERNET RESOURCES

"Hate Crime Statistics 2013: Victims" (http://www.fbi.gov/about-us/cjis/ucr/hate-crime/2013/topic-pages/victims/victims_final)

The U.S. Department of Justice uses the Uniform Crime Reports to generate current statistics on the victims of hate crime (i.e., race, age, religious belief, sexual preference, etc.). The types of hate crime that occurred in 2013, as well as the statistical tables that depict those crimes, are available on this website. The types of offenders that typically commit hate crimes are also detailed.

"Hate Crimes in the United States" (http://www.civilrights.org/hatecrimes/united-states/)

The Leadership Conference on Civil and Human Rights website provides detailed information about hate crimes in the United States. You can find information about the extent of hate crimes in general, but the website also provides statistics and descriptions about hate crimes against specific groups, such as the homeless, immigrants, children, and specific religious adherents. Links to other resources are also provided.

Humantrafficking.org (http://www.humantrafficking.org/countries/united_states _of_america)

This website provides information about what the government is currently doing to stop human trafficking. Several awareness campaigns are listed with detailed information about the prevention of human trafficking. Also provided are links to other countries that deal with human trafficking and information on what projects they currently use to combat this form of victimization.

"Terrorism" (http://www.fema.gov/hazard/terrorism/index.shtm)

The Federal Emergency Management Agency website provides general information about terrorism, explosions, threats, and homeland security. There are links to emergency contacts for victims. The section on disaster survivors would be most helpful for those who have experienced terrorism victimization. It is clear from this website that the U.S. government is involved in homeland security and ensuring the public is protected.

U.S. Department of State (http://www.state.gov/)

This website provides detailed information about our country's security as well as the security protocols of other countries with which the Unites States currently allies. It also includes information on counterterrorism, along with country reports on terrorism activities and responses. Go here for information about disputes, terrorism, and other international affairs that impact our security.

abandonment: When an elderly person is left by the caregiver in charge of him or her

account hijacking: Taking over someone else's existing account without consent

acute battering phase: The second phase in the cycle of violence, in which the abuser engages in major and often serious physically assaultive behavior

age-graded theory of adult social bonds: Proposes that marriage and employment can help one desist from criminal behavior

Air Transportation Safety and System Stabilization Act (2001): Compensation for victims of 9/11 who were killed or injured and their families

Anti-Car Theft Act (1992): Made carjacking a federal offense and provided funding to link motor vehicle databases

Anti-Car Theft Improvements Act of 1996: Upgraded state motor vehicle departments' databases to help identify stolen cars

anti-LGBTQ hate violence: Violence committed against people because of their sexual orientation or identity

Antiterrorism and Effective Death Penalty Act (1996): Required restitution for violent crimes and increased funds available to victims of terrorism

anxiety: An affective disorder or state often experienced as irrational and excessive fear and worry, which may be coupled with feelings of tension and restlessness, vigilance, irritability, and difficulty concentrating

Aviation Security Improvement Act: Legislation passed in response to terrorism

avoidance or constrained behaviors: Restrictions that people place on their own behaviors to protect themselves from harm

avoidance/numbing symptoms: Regular avoidance of stimuli associated with the traumatic event and numbness of response

baseless allegations: There is not enough evidence to prove an assault occurred

behavioral self-blame: When a person believes she or he did something to cause victimization

behavioral strategies: Actions workers can take to reduce their chances of victimization

Benjamin Mendelsohn: "Father of victimology"; coined the term *victimology* in the mid-1940s

bereavement: The state of being sad after an individual you have cared for has passed

bias crime: A crime committed against a person because of characteristics such as race, religion, or sexual orientation

bonded labor: Person is enslaved to work off a debt when the conditions of the debt were not previously known

boost: What happens during and after the first incident influences the risk of experiencing a subsequent victimization incident

bounding: Giving a time frame to reference in order to aid recall

British Crime Survey (BCS): A victimization survey conducted in England and Wales, now known as the Crime Survey for England and Wales (CSEW), in which persons are asked about victimizations that occurred during the previous 12 months

bullying: Intentional infliction of injury repeatedly over time by a more

powerful perpetrator over a less powerful victim

burglary: Entering a structure unlawfully to commit a felony or theft

CAN-SPAM Act of 2003: Made sending spam e-mail a crime in certain circumstances

capable guardianship: Means by which a person or target can be effectively guarded to prevent a victimization from occurring

carjacking: The taking of an occupied vehicle by an armed offender

castle doctrine: Persons do not have a duty to retreat prior to using force in self-defense, but these events are limited only to those occurring within or on an individual's personal property

certified: Allows victims of human trafficking access to the same services usually given to refugees

characterological self-blame: Person ascribes blame to a nonmodifiable source, such as one's character

Child Abuse Prevention and Treatment Act (1974): Provided definitions for child abuse and neglect and established mandatory reporting laws

child sexual abuse: Unwanted or forced sexual contact with a child, engaging children in sex work, or exposing children to sexually explicit material

Child Victims' Bill of Rights (1990): Gave victims' rights to children who were victims and witnesses

Church Arson Prevention Act of 1996: Prevents damaging religious buildings and preventing people from practicing their religious beliefs through threats or force

civil litigation: Victims may sue their offenders in civil court to recoup costs and to compensate for emotional harm

civil rights movement: Advocated against racism and discrimination, noting that all Americans have rights that are protected by the U.S. Constitution

classification: Inmates are assessed and placed in appropriate institutions based on needs and characteristics

Code of Hammurabi: Early Babylonian code that emphasized the restoration of equity between the offender and the victim

code of the streets: Respect is seen as a commodity that must be maintained, even through violence

coerced sexual contact: The offender uses psychological or emotional coercion to touch, grope, rub, pet, lick, or suck the breasts, lips, or genitals of the victim

cohabitation: Couples live together but are not married

comparative research: An approach to knowing social reality through the examination for similarities and differences between data gathered from more than one nation

Conflict Tactics Scale (CTS): Measurement tool used to gauge levels and use of various conflict tactics in intimate relationships

conjugal visits: Visits on prison grounds that allow married inmates to spend private time with their spouses

control deficit: When the amount of control a person exercises is outweighed by the control he or she is subject to

control ratio: Control surplus and control deficit considered together

control surplus: When the control one has exceeds the amount of control one is subject to

control-balance theory: The amount of control one possesses over others and the amount of control to which one is subject; the ratio of control influences the risk of engaging in deviant behavior

costs of crime/victimization: Mental, physical, and monetary loss that victims of crime incur

Crime Control Act (1990): Created a federal bill of rights for victims

Crime Survey for England and Wales: Victimization survey conducted in England and Wales every year. Persons aged 16 years and over are asked about victimization experiences over the previous 12 months. The survey uses a two-stage measurement design

crime switching: Examination in the recurring literature to see the patterns of types of victimizations that occur. Crime switching occurs when a person experiences two different types of victimizations

Crime Victims with Disabilities Act of 1998: Required the National Crime Victimization Survey to collect information on people with disabilities

criminal homicide: The purposeful, knowing, reckless, or negligent killing of one human being by another

criminal intent incidents: Offender has no real relationship to the business where the crime occurs

cross border victim: Anyone who has suffered directly from a crime that took place in a country different than one the victims lives in

customer/client incidents: A person with a legitimate reason for being at a business becomes violent while at that business

cyberbullying: Bullying over the Internet, by cell phone, or through another form of digital technology

cycle of violence: A common pattern of abuse that involves different phases: tension building phase, acute battering phase, and honeymoon phase; first developed by Lenore Walker in 1979

dark figure of crime: Crime that is not reported to the police

death or casualty notification: The process by which family members of the deceased are notified of their loved one's passing

debt bondage: Person is enslaved to work off a debt when the conditions of the debt were not previously known

Declaration of Basic Principles of Justice for Victims of Crime and Abuse of Power: Victims' rights charter

defensive or protective behaviors: Behaviors to guard against victimization, such as purchasing a weapon

deinstitutionalization: Closing of institutions for mentally disordered people

delayed repeat victimization: Repeat victimization incident that occurs more than 30 days after the initial incident

deliberate indifference: Prison officials know inmates' health or safety are at risk but disregard those risks

deliberation: An act that was planned after careful thought

delinquent peers: People involved in delinquency with whom a person spends time; having such peers increases one's likelihood of victimization

dependency theory: As the dependence of the elderly increases, their rates of abuse and neglect increase

dependency-stress model: Theory that disabled children are more dependent on caregivers, which causes more stress that can lead to abuse

depression: A mood disorder characterized by sleep disturbances, changes in eating habits, feelings of guilt and worthlessness, and irritability. These symptoms interfere with a person's everyday life.

deprivation: One of the explanations of prison behavior is that the prison experience is depriving, thus prisoners act in ways to adapt to these deprivations

destination countries: Countries that receive victims of human trafficking

developmental disability: Serious, chronic impairment of major activities such as self-care, language, learning, mobility, and capacity for independent living

direct bullying: Physical and verbal actions performed in the presence of the victim

direct costs: Monies and the value of goods and services taken as a result of identity theft

direct property losses: When victims' possessions are taken or damaged

diversion: Offender not formally charged if she or he completes required programs

domestic human trafficking: Trafficking that occurs within a country's borders

drug or alcohol facilitated rape: Victim is given drugs or alcohol without his or her knowledge or consent and then raped while under the influence

dual arrest: An arrest in which both the offender and the victim are arrested

dumpster dive: Going through trash to find papers with personal identifying information

dynamic causal perspective: The occurrence of victimization and offending are linked together whereby one directly causes the other

economic costs: Financial costs associated with victimization

Elder Justice Act 2010: Provided funding for Adult Protective Services and for the prevention and detection of elder abuse

eldercide: A murder that involves a victim who is 65 years of age or older

emotional abuse: Behavior such as yelling at or verbally degrading a partner or child; can also take the form of belittling, shaming, humiliating, ignoring, rejecting, or limiting physical contact

emotional or psychological elder abuse: Causing emotional pain by ridiculing, demeaning, humiliating, etc., an elderly person

environmental design: Making the workplace more secure and less of a target for crime

excusable homicide: Accidental or unintentional killings

express malice: Actual malice (such as when a person in a fight shoots the other person, showing an intention to cause serious injury)

false allegations: Report of a sexual assault that did not happen

family or community group conferencing: Victim, offender, family, friends, and supporters talk about the impact and consequences of a crime

family structure: Household style or shape

fatality reviews: Community-based programs that seek to review the circumstances of the homicide to gain a better understanding of the cause of death

fear of crime: An emotional response to being afraid of being victimized

Federal Crime Victims with Disabilities Awareness Act of 1998: Required that statistics on disabled victims of crime be collected through the National Crime Victimization Survey

Federal Victim Witness Protection Act (1982): Developed and implemented guidelines for how officials respond to victims and witnesses

felony murder: The often unintentional killing during the commission of another felony

femicide: The intentional murder of a female because of her sex

filicide: The killing of a child by a parent or a caretaker

financial exploitation: Illegal or improper use of an elderly person's property, assets, or funds

first degree murder: Murder committed with deliberate premeditation and malice

forced labor: Victims are held and forced to work under threat of violence or punishment

forceful physical strategies: Physical resistance by the victim against the offender, such as shoving, biting, hitting, etc.

forceful verbal strategy: Verbal attempts to scare the offender or attract the attention of others

forcible rape: Offender uses or threatens to use force to achieve penetration

gender-based violence: Acts of violence (i.e., physical, sexual, and/or psychological) that are directed at an individual because of their gender

gene x environment interaction: Genes interact with environmental features to shape behavior

general theory of crime: Proposes that a person with low self-control will engage in crime if given the opportunity

guardian ad litem (GAL): An adult who represents a child's best interests in court, often in child abuse or neglect cases

Gun-Free Schools Act (2004): Mandates that schools receiving federal funding must suspend for at least 1 year any student who brings a gun to school

Hans von Hentig: Developed a victim typology based on characteristics of the victim that increase risk of victimization

hate crime: A crime committed against a person because of characteristics such as race, religion, or sexual orientation

Hate Crime Statistics Act (1990): Requires that the attorney general collect statistics on hate crimes

hierarchy rule: If more than one Part I offense occurs in the same incident report, only the most serious offense will be counted in the reporting process

home invasion: Burglary of a residence in which the offender uses force against the residents

homicide: The killing of one human being by another

homicide survivors: People whose loved ones have been murdered

homicide-suicide: Characterized by the perpetrator killing himself after murdering his intimate partner honeymoon phase: The third phase in the cycle of violence, in which the abuser is calm and loving and most probably begging his partner for forgiveness

honor killings: Homicides that are perpetrated by males against females to ensure that honor (which can be his own, his family's, or his community's) is maintained

honor violence: Violence committed against a female to protect or regain the honor of the perpetrator, or that of the family or community

Hostage Relief Act of 1980: Provided funding to help hostage victims, their spouses, and their children

hostile work environment sexual harassment: Sexual harassment that occurs when sex-related behavior creates an intimidating, hostile, or offensive working environment or interferes with a person's performance at work

hot spots: Areas that are crime prone

hyperarousal: Persistent arousal symptomology; for example, not being able to sleep, being hypervigilant, and having problems concentrating

identity theft: Using another's personal identity information to commit fraud

Identity Theft and Assumption Deterrence Act (1998): Made identity theft a federal offense

Identity Theft Penalty Enhancement Act (2004): Created the crime of aggravated identity theft for identity theft associated with certain felonies

Identity Theft Supplement (ITS): Supplement to the National Crime Victimization Survey in which data on extent of account hijacking, and use and misuse of personal information was collected

importation: One of the explanations of prison behavior is that inmates bring with them certain individual-level characteristics (e.g., gender, race, abuse history) to prison that influence their prison experience

implied/constructive malice: When death occurs due to negligence rather than intent

incapacitated rape: Rape occurs when victim is unable to consent because of being unconscious, drugged, or otherwise incapacitated

incident report: Detailed questions about a victimization experience

incivilities: Low-level breaches of community standards that show that conventionally accepted norms and values have eroded in an area

indirect bullying: Subtle actions such as isolating, excluding, and making obscene gestures; often called social bullying

indirect costs: Legal bills, bounced checks, and other costs associated with identity theft

indirect/secondary victimization: When a loved one is victimized there are costs associated with this victimization for those who care about that person. When a person experiences these costs or consequences, he or she experiences indirect or secondary victimization.

infanticide: A type of filicide, involves homicides in which the victim is under one year of age

injury: A negative health outcome of intimate partner violence

International Crime Victims Study (ICVS): A comparative study of criminal victimization across various countries

International Self Report Delinquency Study (ISRD): A comparative study on juvenile delinquency and victimization among adolescents residing primarily in Europe

international victimization studies: Studies that utilize randomized samples from several countries that are representative of the populations from which they are taken

International Victimology Institute Tilburg (INTERVICT): The International Victimology Institute Tilburg is one of the leading research institutions focused solely on victimological inquiry. Moreover, the institute concentrates on interdisciplinary efforts in the investigation of victimization based on the multifaceted nature of victimology.

International Violence Against Women Survey (IVAWS): Coordinated by the UN Interregional Crime and Justice Research Institute, the European Institute for Crime Prevention and Control, and Statistics Canada, the IVAWS collects data from women on violence they have experienced at the hands of men, including the details and consequences of their victimization, as well as background information on the survey participants and their male partners

intimate partner: A husband or wife, an ex-husband or ex-wife, a boyfriend or girlfriend, or a dating partner

intimate partner homicide: A homicide involving spouses, ex-spouses, persons in current or de facto relationships, boyfriends or girlfriends, or partners of same-sex relationships

intimate terrorism: A type of intimate partner violence where males utilize coercion through physical, psychological, and emotional abuse to control females. Women seeking assistance from police or shelters have likely experienced this form of intimate partner violence

intrusive recollection: Reexperiencing trauma through recurring or intrusive recollections or nightmares, feeling as though the event were recurring, and/or intense psychological distress when exposed to cues that symbolize or resemble a component of the traumatic event

involuntary domestic servitude: Victims are forced to work as domestic workers

involuntary/negligent manslaughter: Death resulting from gross negligence (ignoring the possible danger or potential harm to other people)

Jeanne Clery Disclosure of Campus Security Policy and Campus Crime Statistics Act (1990): Requires schools to publish an annual crime report, report warnings of threats, and protect the rights of victims and offenders in cases handled on campus

Justice for All Act (2004): Enforced victims' rights and provided funds to test the backlog of rape kits

justifiable homicide: The killing of a felon by a peace officer in the line of duty or the killing (during the commission of a felony) of a felon by a private citizen

labor trafficking: Human trafficking with the goal of exploiting someone for labor

learned helplessness: Victims believe they are unable to change the situation and stop trying to resist

lex talionis: An eye for an eye

life-course perspective: Examines the development of and desistance from offending and other behaviors over time

local victimization studies: Surveys that are restricted to the population of a specific region or city

Long-Term Care Ombudsman Program: Receives complaints about elderly mistreatment in long-term care facilities

lost productivity: Being unable to work, go to school, or complete everyday tasks because of being victimized

mandatory arrest policies: Require arrest by police officers when there is probable cause that a crime was committed and enough evidence exists for an arrest

mandatory reporting law: Requires certain professionals, such as doctors, to report suspected cases of child abuse

manslaughter: Killing of a person that results from negligence and without willful intent

Marvin Wolfgang: Used Philadelphia homicide data to conduct the first empirical investigation of victim precipitation

mass murder: The killing of four or more victims in one location in one incident

matricide: The killing of one's mother

Matthew Shepard and James Byrd, Jr. Hate Crime Prevention Act (2009): Included gender-based hate crimes and hate crimes by and against juveniles in data collection

Max Planck Institute of Foreign and International Criminal Law: Located in Germany, The Max Planck Institute of Foreign and International Criminal Law provides a moderate level of attention toward victimological research including on attitudes, rights, and compensations for victims

medical care costs: Costs associated with treating victims of crime

Menachem Amir: Studied victim provocation in rapes

mental health care costs: Psychiatric care required as a result of being victimized

Minneapolis Domestic Violence Experiment: Conducted in 1984 by Lawrence Sherman and Richard Berk to examine the deterrent effect of arrest on domestic violence perpetrators

misdemeanor: A crime that usually is less serious than a felony and carries a maximum penalty of a year in jail

motivated offenders: People who will commit crime if given an opportunity

motor vehicle theft: The unlawful taking of another's vehicle

Motor Vehicle Theft Law Enforcement Act (1984): Required manufacturers to put identification numbers on car parts to make them easier to trace when stolen

Motor Vehicle Theft Prevention Act of 1994: Developed a voluntary, national motor vehicle theft prevention program

National Child Abuse and Neglect Data System (NCANDS): Annual analysis of data on child abuse reports submitted to child protective services

National College Women Sexual Victimization Study (NCWSV): A nationally representative study of sexual victimization among college women, conducted in 1997

National Crime Survey: First-ever government-sponsored victimization survey; relied on victims to recall their own victimization experiences

National Crime Victimization Survey (NCVS): National survey of households that is used to generate annual estimates of victimization in the United States

National Elder Abuse Incidence Study: Measured the incidence of mistreatment of people over age 60 in domestic settings

National Incidence Study (NIS): Report on cases investigated by child protective services and cases identified by professionals in the community

National Inmate Survey: Self-report survey on inmates' rates of victimization

National Social Life, Health, and Aging Project: Self-report survey of elderly people about their experiences of abuse

National Study of Drug or Alcohol Facilitated, Incapacitated, and Forcible Rape: A nation study of three types of rape

National Survey of Youth in Custody: Survey of youth in state and private correctional facilities

national victimization studies: Surveys that utilize a representative random sample in one country (e.g., National Crime Victimization Survey in the United States).

National Violence Against Women Survey (NVAWS): Telephone survey of 8,000 men and 8,000 women about violence they have experienced

near-repeat victimization: A victimization that occurs near a place that was recently victimized

neglect: When a child's basic needs are not met; also, when someone with the responsibility of caring for an elderly person fails to fulfill their caretaking obligations

neighborhood context: Features of neighborhoods that impact risk for victimization

New Fair and Accurate Credit Transactions Act of 2003: Enacted provisions to prevent identity theft and help victims

no-drop prosecution: The victim is not able to drop the charges against the offender and the prosecutor's discretion in deciding to charge is curtailed

noncontact sexual abuse: Forms of sexual victimization that do not involve touching or penetration; includes verbal and visual abuse

nonforceful physical strategies: Nonforceful physical attempts to stop an assault, such as trying to escape the attack by running away

nonforceful verbal strategy: Nonaggressive attempts to get the offender to stop, such as talking to or pleading with the offender

notification: The right of victims to be kept apprised of key events in their cases

Occupational Safety and Health Administration (OSHA): Federal agency in the U.S. Department of Labor that provides guidelines for workplace health and safety

offenders: Individuals who engage in crime but have no victimization history. Also referred to as pure or exclusive offenders.

Older Americans Act of 1965: Protected the rights of and provided funding for the elderly

organizational and administrative controls: Strategies that administrators and agencies can implement to reduce the risk of workplace victimization in their organizations

Palermo Protocol: Criminalized human trafficking and established

procedures for government response

parricide: The murder of one's parent

parity hypothesis: The idea that, to stop an incident, the victim's level of self-protection should match the offender's level of attack

participation and consultation: Rights given to victims to encourage participation in the criminal justice system; also provide victims the right to discuss their cases with the prosecutor and/or judge before key decisions are made

patriarchy: A form of social organization in which the man is dominant and is allowed to control women and children

patricide: The killing of one's father

peacemaking circle: Gathering of victim, offender, community members, and sometimes criminal justice officials to promote healing

perceived risk: The perceived likelihood that a person will be victimized

permissive arrest policies: Policies that do not mandate or presume that an arrest will be made by law enforcement when warranted; allow police to use their discretion

personal relationship incidents: Perpetrator has a relationship with the victim and targets him or her while at work

phishing: Use of fake websites and e-mails to trick people into providing personal information

physical abuse: Injury or physical harm of another person, such as a child

physical bullying: Hitting, punching, shoving, or other physical forms of violence

physical elder abuse: Nonaccidental harm of an elderly person causing pain, injury, or impairment

physical incivilities: Disorderly physical surroundings in an area

physical injury: Physical harm suffered that may include bruises, soreness, scratches, cuts, broken bones, contracted diseases, and stab or gunshot wounds

physical violence: Includes hitting, slapping, kicking, punching, choking, and throwing objects at another person

poly-victimization: When a person, usually in childhood or during the same developmental time period, experiences multiple forms of victimization

population heterogeneity perspective: Rather than victim or offender directly influencing one another, the relationship is influenced by a stable underlying personality trait(s) or environment(s)

posttraumatic stress disorder (PTSD): Psychiatric anxiety disorder caused by experiencing traumatic events such as war, violence, etc.

power: A person's ability to impose his or her will on another person

power of attorney abuse: Misusing access to an elderly person's money

premeditation: The act was considered beforehand

presumptive arrest policies: Arrest policies that presume an arrest will be made when probable cause exists to do so

principle of homogamy: People who share characteristics of offenders are more at risk of victimization, given that they are more likely to come into contact with offenders

Prison Rape Elimination Act of 2003: Requires the Bureau of Justice Statistics to analyze incidence and effects of prison rape

pro-arrest policies: Require arrests in specific situations in which certain criteria are met

protective behaviors: When a person engages in behaviors such as buying a gun or installing an alarm to protect against victimization

protective custody: Secure inmate housing in which inmates are separated from others

protective order: Order secured to keep one person away from another

quid pro quo sexual harassment: Sexual harassment that occurs when employment-related outcomes hinge on compliance with request for sexual favors

rape: Nonconsensual contact between the penis and the vulva or anus, or penetration of the vulva or anus, or contact between the mouth and penis, vulva, or anus, or penetration of another person's genital or anal opening with a finger, hand, or object, accompanied by force or threat of force

rape shield laws: Prohibit the defense from using the victim's sexual history in court

recurring victimization: When a person or place is victimized more than once in any way

repatriation: Returning trafficking victims to their native countries

repeat victimization: When a person is victimized more than once in the same way

reporting: Disclosing the victimization to the police

residential mobility: The percentage of persons 5 years and older living in a different house from 5 years before

resistance strategy: Something the victim does to try to stop or prevent an attack

response latency: In sexual victimization research, the time it takes for a person to identify a situation as risky, such as a situation is dangerous or that a man has gone too far

restitution: Money or services paid to victims of crimes by the offenders

restorative justice: A movement recognizing that crime is a harm caused not just to the state but to the victim and his or her community.

It seeks to use all entities in response to crime and allows for input from the offender, the victim, and community members harmed by the offense in making a determination of how to repair the harm caused by the offender.

retribution: A criminal is punished because he or she deserved it, and the punishment is equal to the harm caused

revictimization: When a person is victimized more than once over the course of the life span

right to a speedy trial: Victims' interests are considered when judges rule on postponement of trial dates

right to protection: Safety measures provided to victims

risk heterogeneity (the "flag" explanation): Characteristics about a person that, if left unchanged, place him or her at greater risk of being victimized repeatedly

risky lifestyles: Engaging in risky behaviors that expose people to situations likely to increase their victimization risk

routine activities and lifestyle theory: A person's routine activities and lifestyle place him or her at risk of being victimized. Risk is highest when motivated offenders, lack of capable guardianship, and suitable targets coalesce in time and space.

safe haven laws: Allow mothers or caregivers in crisis to leave their babies at designated locations anonymously without risk of punishment

school victimization: Victimization of students on school grounds, buildings, buses, or at school events or functions

screen questions: Used to cue respondents or jog their memories as to whether they experienced any of seven types of criminal victimization in the previous 6 months

screening: Questions asked by a medical professional to determine if

a victimization occurred, identifying victims in order to provide them service referrals

second degree murder: Murder committed with malice, but without premeditation and deliberation

secondary victimization: When people identify with the victim and suffer psychological consequences similar to the victim's

self-blame: Victims believe they are responsible for their own victimization

self-esteem: Beliefs and emotions about a person's own self-worth or value

self-neglect: When an elderly person fails to care for or adequately protect himself or herself

self-protective action: Something the victim does to try to stop or prevent an attack; generally classified into one of four types: forceful physical, nonforceful physical, forceful verbal, or nonforceful verbal

self-worth: A person's own perception of his or her worth or value

sentencing circle: Gathering of victim, offender, community members, and sometimes criminal justice officials to determine the offender's sentence

serial murder: A series of three or more killings committed by the same perpetrator or perpetrators

series victimization: Incidents that occur in which respondents cannot distinguish enough identifying details or even recall each incident

sex crime units: Special units within police departments trained to examine victims and collect evidence in sexual assault cases

sex trafficking: Human trafficking for the purpose of sexual exploitation

sexual assault nurse examiner (SANE): Registered nurses specially trained in examining victims of sexual assault and collecting forensic evidence

sexual assault response team (SART): Coordinate medical and criminal justice responses to rape and sexual assault victims

sexual coercion: Offender manipulates victim to engage in unwanted sex

sexual elder abuse: Sexual contact with an elderly person without his or her consent

Sexual Experiences Survey (SES): Widespread measurement tool developed by Koss that measures rape, sexual coercion, and sexual contact

sexual victimization: Encompasses any type of victimization involving sexual behavior perpetrated against an individual

sexual violence: Includes unwanted sexual contact, sexual coercion, and rape

shaken baby syndrome: Brain hemorrhages, skull fractures, and retinal hemorrhages caused by shaking

shoulder surfing: When offenders get information such as credit card numbers by watching or listening to someone enter them

situational couple violence: A type of intimate partner violence where violence is not a form of control, but rather males and females are both likely to be victims and perpetrators of IPV

skimming: Using devices to extract personal information from ATM machines

social distance: Feelings people have about others with whom they spend time

social incivilities: Disruptive social behaviors in an area

social interactionist perspective: Proposes that distressed individuals behave aggressively, which then elicits an aggressive response from others

social learning: People learn behavior by observing others engaging in it and by having their own behavior reinforced

source country: A country that supplies trafficking victims

specialized victimization surveys: Focusing on a specific type of victimization

spousal or marital privilege laws: Provide an exception that victims may not have to testify against their abusers if they are legally married to them

spree murder: The killing of multiple victims at two or more separate locations but with no cooling-off period in between so that each event is emotionally connected

spyware: Software that surreptitiously collects information from unsuspecting people's computers

stand your ground laws: Persons do not have a duty to retreat prior to using force in self-defense, regardless of where the event is taking place

state dependence: The way a victim and offender respond to an incidence of victimization effects their likelihood of being involved in future victimization

statutory rape: When a person below the age of consent has sex

Stephen Schafer: Argued that victims have a functional responsibility not to provoke others into victimizing or harming them and that they also should actively attempt to prevent that from occurring

stressor: A traumatic event

structural density: The percentage of units in structures of five or more units

subintentional homicide: The victim facilitates her or his own death

by using poor judgment, placing himself or herself at risk, living a risky lifestyle, or using alcohol or drugs

suitable targets: Victims chosen by offenders based on their attractiveness in the situation/crime

symptomology: Exhibiting symptoms of a mental disorder

system costs: Costs paid by society in response to victimization (e.g., law enforcement, insurance costs)

T visa: Allows victims of human trafficking to become temporary citizens of the United States

target hardening: Making it more difficult for an offender to attack a certain target

tension-building phase: The first phase in the cycle of violence, in which positive and charming behavior on the part of the abuser lasts until pressures and more serious events generate tension

theft: The taking of another person's property

theory of low self-control: Proposes that people who have low self-control are more likely to be involved in crime and delinquency

time-course: A term used in the revictimization literature to indicate how close in time a subsequent victimization incident occurs to an initial incident

transnational human trafficking: When victims are transported from one country to another

unfounded: Assault is determined to be untrue or a case lacks evidence to move forward

Uniform Crime Reports (UCR): Annual reports of the amount of crime reported to or known by the police in a year

unwanted sexual contact: Person is touched in an erogenous zone, but it does not involve attempted or completed penetration

unwanted sexual contact with force: Person is touched in an erogenous zone, but not penetrated, through use or threat of force

verbal abuse: Offender makes offensive sexual comments or noises to victim

verbal bullying: Direct name calling and threatening

vicarious victimization: The effect one person's victimization has on others

victims: Individuals who have been victimized, but do not perpetrate crime (also called "pure" or "exclusive" victims)

victim compensation: The right of victims to have monies that they lost due to victimization repaid to them by the state

victim facilitation: When a victim unintentionally makes it easier for an offender to commit a crime

victim impact statement (VIS): Statement made to the court by the victim or his or her family about the harm caused and the desired sentence for the offender

victim precipitation: The extent to which a victim is responsible for his or her own victimization

victim proneness: When a person is victimized a subsequent time, he or she might experience the same type of victimization previously experienced

victim provocation: When a person does something that incites another person to commit an illegal act

victimization theory: Generally, a set of testable propositions designed to explain why a person is victimized

victim–offender: An individual who has experienced both offending and victimization

victim–offender mediation programs: Sessions led by a third party in which the victim and offender meet face-to-face to come to a mutually satisfactory agreement as to what should happen to the offender—often

through the development of a restitution plan

victim–offender overlap: Victims that are offenders and vice versa

victimology: The scientific study of victims and victimization

Victims Bill of Rights Act: Legislation proposed in Canada to provide crime victims with rights at the federal level

Victims of Crime Act (1984): Created the Office for Victims of Crime and provided funds for victim compensation

Victims of Terrorism Compensation Act (1986): Provided money to compensate for wages lost during captivity

Victims of Terrorism Tax Relief Act (2001): Payments made to victims of qualifying disasters and death benefits for those lost in terrorist acts such as 9/11 cannot be taxed

Victim Support Europe: An international organization that focuses on the assistance of victims through the enhancement of services and victims' rights within Europe

victim/witness assistance programs (VWAPs): Provide aid to victims during the investigation and criminal justice process

victims' rights: Rights given to victims to enhance their privacy, protection, and participation

Victims' Rights and Restitution Act (1990): Guaranteed victims the right to restitution

Victims' Rights Clarification Act (1997): Allowed victims to make impact statements and attend their offenders' trials

victims' rights movement: Movement centered on giving victims a voice in the criminal justice system and providing them rights

violence: The intentional physical harm of another person

Violence Against Women Act (1994): Gave money to programs for prevention and treatment of female victims

Violence Against Women Act (2000): Provided funding for rape prevention and education and domestic violence victims and included Internet stalking as a crime

Violent Crime Control and Law Enforcement Act (1994): Increased funds for victim compensation and created the national sex offender registry

violent resistance: A type of intimate partner violence that involves females fighting back against intimate terrorism

voluntary manslaughter: Intentional infliction of injury that is likely to and actually does cause death

visual abuse: Victim is forced to view sexual acts, pictures, and/or videos

women's movement: Recognized the need for female victims of crime to receive special attention and help due to the fact that victimizations such as sexual assault and domestic violence are byproducts of sexism, traditional sex roles, emphasis on traditional family values, and the economic subjugation of women

worker-on-worker incidents: When a current or former employee attacks another employee

workplace victimization: Victimization that occurs while a person is on duty or at work

World Society of Victimology (WSV): A nongovernmental organization (that provides consultations, and is associated with, the United Nations) that promotes comparative victimological research and cooperation between nations to further the assistance of victims

zero-tolerance policies: Specific, established punishments for students involved in fighting, violence, or bringing weapons to school

■■REFERENCES

Abbey, A. (2002). Alcohol-related sexual assault: A common problem among college students. *Journal of Studies on Alcohol, 14,* 118–128.

Abramsky, T., Watts, C. H., Garcia-Moreno, C., Devries, K., Kiss, L., Ellsberg, M., … Heise, L. (2011). What factors are associated with recent intimate partner violence? Findings from the WHO multi-country study on women's health and domestic violence. *BMC Public Health, 11,* 109.

Addington, L. A. (2013). Who you calling old? Measuring "elderly" and what it means for homicide research. *Homicide Studies, 17*(2), 134–153.

Administration on Aging. (2012). *Complaint summary: Nursing facility totals and percents for FY 2012.* Washington, DC: U.S. Department of Health and Human Services, Administration on Aging. Retrieved from http://www.aoa.gov/AoARoot/AoA_Programs/Elder_Rights/Ombudsman/National_State_Data/2012/Index.aspx

The Advocates for Human Rights. (2010). *Victims' rights.* Retrieved from http://www.stopvaw.org/victims_rights_and_responding_to_victims_needs

Afifi, T. O., & Brownridge, D. A. (2008). Physical abuse of children born to adolescent mothers: The continuation of the relationship into adult motherhood and the role of identity. In T. I. Richardson & M. V. Williams (Eds.), *Child abuse and violence* (pp. 19–42). Hauppauge, NY: Nova Science.

Agnew, R. (2005). *Why do criminals offend? A general theory of crime and delinquency.* Los Angeles, CA: Roxbury.

Agnew, R. (2006). *Pressured into crime: An overview of general strain theory.* New York, NY: Oxford University Press.

Aisenberg, E., & Herrenkohl, T. (2008). Community violence in context: Risk and resilience in children and families. *Journal of Interpersonal Violence, 23*(3), 296–315.

Akers, R. L. (1973). *Deviant behavior: A social learning approach.* Belmont, CA: Wadsworth.

Aldrich, H., & Kallivayalil, D. (2013). The impact of homicide on survivors and clinicians. *Journal of Loss and Trauma, 18*(4), 362–377.

Allen, M. (2007). *Lesbian, gay, bisexual and trans (LGBT) communities and domestic violence: Information and resources.* Harrisburg, PA: National Resource Center on Domestic Violence. Retrieved from http://new.vawnet.org/Assoc_files_VAWnet/NRC_LGBTDV-Full.pdf

Allen, N. H. (1980). *Homicide: Perspectives on prevention.* New York, NY: Human Sciences Press.

American Psychiatric Association. (2000). *Diagnostic and statistical manual of mental disorders* (4th ed., text revision). Washington, DC: American Psychiatric Association.

Amick-Mcmullan, A., Kilpatrick, D. G., & Resnick, H. S. (1991). Homicide as a risk factor for PTSD among surviving family members. *Behavior Modification, 15*(4), 545–559.

Amick-McMullan, A., Kilpatrick, D. G., & Veronen, L. J. (1989). Family survivors of homicide victims: A behavioral analysis. *The Behavior Therapist, 12,* 75–79.

Anand, G. (2012, May 29). Stolen phones market thrives. *The Hindu.* Retrieved from http://www.thehindu.com/news/cities/Thiruvananthapuram/article3468842.ece

Angel, C. (2005). *Crime victims meet their offenders: Testing the impact of restorative justice on victims' post-traumatic stress symptoms* (PhD dissertation). University of Pennsylvania, Philadelphia.

Appelbaum, P., Robbins, P., & Monahan, J. (2000). Violence and delusions: Data from the MacArthur Violence Risk Assessment Study. *American Journal of Psychiatry, 157,* 566–572.

Applebaum, D. R., & Burns, G. L. (1991). Unexpected childhood death: Posttraumatic stress disorder in surviving siblings and parents. *Journal of Clinical Child Psychology, 20,* 114–120.

Archer, J. (1999). Assessment of the reliability of the Conflict Tactics Scale: A meta-analytic review. *Journal of Interpersonal Violence, 14,* 1263–1289.

Archer, J. (2000). Sex differences in aggression between heterosexual partners: A meta-analytic review. *Psychological Bulletin, 126,* 651–680.

Arseneault, L., Moffitt, T. E., Caspi, A., Taylor, P. J., & Silva, P. A. (2000). Mental disorders and violence in the total birth cohort: Results from the Dunedin study. *Archives of General Psychiatry, 57,* 979–986.

Arseneault, L., Walsh, E., Trzesniewski, K., Newcombe, R., Caspi, A., & Moffitt, T. E. (2006). Bullying victimization uniquely contributes to adjustment problems in young children: A nationally representative cohort study. *Pediatrics, 118,* 130–138.

Azrael, D., Braga, A. A., & O'Brien, M. (2013). *Developing the capacity to understand and prevent homicide: An evaluation of the Milwaukee Homicide Review Commission.* Retrieved from https://www.ncjrs.gov/pdffiles1/nij/grants/240814.pdf

Bachman, R. (1994). Violence and theft in the workplace. *Crime data brief: National Crime Victimization Survey* (p. 1). Washington, DC: Bureau of Justice Statistics.

Bachman, R., & Meloy, M. L. (2008). The epidemiology of violence against the elderly: Implications for primary and secondary prevention. *Journal of Contemporary Criminal Justice*, 24, 186–197.

Badgley, R. F., Allard, H. A., McCormick, N., Proudfoot, P. M., Fortin, D., Ogilvie, D., … Sutherland, S. (1984). *Sexual offences against children. Catalogue no. J2–50/1984E.* Ottawa, Canada: Department of Supply and Services.

Baladerian, N. J. (1991). Sexual abuse of people with developmental disabilities. *Sexuality and Disability, 9,* 323–335.

Balasinorwala, V. P. (2009). Acute stress disorder in victims after terror attacks in Mumbai, India. *British Journal of Psychiatry, 195,* 462.

Bandes, S. (1999). Victim standing. *Utah Law Review,* 331–348.

Banks, D., & Kyckelhahn, T. (2011). *Characteristics of suspected human trafficking incidents,* 2008–2010 (Report No. NCJ 233732). Washington, DC: Bureau of Justice Statistics, U.S. Department of Justice.

Banyard, V. L., Moynihan, M. M., & Plante, E. G. (2007). Sexual violence prevention through bystander education: An experimental evaluation. *Journal of Community Psychology, 35,* 463–481.

Banyard, V. L., Plante, E. G., & Moynihan, M. M. (2007). *Rape prevention through bystander education: Final report to NIJ for grant 2002-WG-BX-0009.* Retrieved from http:// www.ncjrs.gov/pdffiles1/nij/grants/208701.pdf

Banyard, V. L., Williams, L. M., & Siegel, J. A. (2001). The long-term mental health consequences of child sexual abuse: An exploratory study of the impact of multiple traumas in a sample of women. *Journal of Traumatic Stress, 14,* 697–715.

Barberet, B., Fisher, B. S., & Taylor, H. (2004). *University student safety in the East Midlands.* London, UK: Home Office.

Barnes, J. C., & Beaver, K. M. (2012a). Extending research on the victim-offender overlap: Evidence from a genetically informative analysis. *Journal of Interpersonal Violence,* 1–23. doi:10.1177/0886260512441259.

Barnes, J. C., & Beaver, K. M. (2012b). Marriage and desistance from crime: A consideration of gene–environment correlation. *Journal of Marriage and Family, 74*(1), 19–33.

Barnett, O. W., & LaViolette, A. D. (1993). *It could happen to anyone: Why battered women stay.* Newbury Park, CA: Sage.

Barrett, K. A., O'Day, B., Roche, A., & Carlson, B. L. (2009). Intimate partner violence, health status, and health care access among women with disabilities. *Women's Health Issues, 19,* 94–100.

Barton, G., & Vevea, B. (2010, July 10). 2 court systems didn't make link to Milwaukee assault suspect: Restraining orders not reviewed for criminal conduct. *Milwaukee Journal Sentinel.* Retrieved from http://www.jsonline.com/news/milwaukee/98177914.html

Baskin, D. R., Sommers, I., & Steadman, H. J. (1991). Assessing the impact of psychiatric impairment on prison violence. *Journal of Criminal Justice, 19,* 271–280.

Bassett, L. (2014, June 25). *NRA fights for convicted stalkers' gun rights.* Retrieved from http://www.huffingtonpost.com/2014/06/25/nra-stalkers-_n_5530097.html

Basu, K. (2014, January 30). *Laws to help MD. crime victims take effect Tuesday.* Retrieved from http://www.heraldmailmedia.com/news/local/laws-to-help-md-crime-victims-take-effect-tuesday/article_883b9c33-1b54-5cae-ac77-58639e311187.html

Battle against sex trafficking: Sweden vs. Denmark. (2011, March 20). *The CNN Freedom Project: Ending modern day slavery.* Retrieved from http://thecnnfreedomproject.blogs.cnn.com/2011/03/30/sex-traffick-ing-countries-take-different-approaches-to-same-problem/

Baum, K., Catalano, S., Rand, M., & Rose, K. (2009). *Stalking victimization in the United States.* Washington, DC: U.S. Department of Justice, Bureau of Justice Statistics.

Baum, K., & Klaus, P. (2005). *Violent victimization of college students, 1995–2002* (NCJ Report No. 206836). Washington, DC: Bureau of Justice Statistics.

Baum, R., & Moore, K. (2002). *Lesbian, gay, bisexual and transgender domestic violence in 2001.* New York, NY: National Coalition of Anti-Violence Programs.

Bayliss, K., & Chang, D. (2013, November 5). Man shoots, kills 2 armed robbers: Police. Retrieved from http://www.nbcphiladelphia.com/news/local/2-Shot-Killed-in-Attempted-Robbery-230539261.html

Beaver, K. M., Boutwell, B. B., Barnes, J. C., & Cooper, J. A. (2009). The biosocial underpinnings to adolescent victimization: Results from a longitudinal sample of twins. *Youth Violence and Juvenile Justice, 7,* 223–238.

Beaver, K. M., Wright, J. P., DeLisi, M., Daigle, L. E., Swatt, M. L., & Gibson, C. L. (2007). Evidence of a gene x environment interaction in the creation of victimization: Results from a longitudinal sample of adolescents. *International Journal of Offender Therapy and Comparative Criminology, 51,* 620–645.

Beaver, K. M., Wright, J. P., DeLisi, M., Walsh, A., Vaughn, M. G., Boisvert, D., & Vaske, J. (2007). A gene x gene interaction between DRD2 and DRD4 is associated with conduct disorder and antisocial behavior in males. *Behavioral and Brain Functions, 3,* 30.

Beck, A. J., & Harrison, P. M. (2010). *Sexual victimization in prisons and jails reported by inmates, 2008–09.* Washington, DC: Bureau of Justice Statistics, U.S. Department of Justice.

Beck, A. J., Harrison, P. M., & Guerino, P. (2010). *Special report: Sexual victimization in juvenile facilities reported by youth, 2008–09.* Washington, DC: Bureau of Justice Statistics, U.S. Department of Justice. Retrieved from http://bjs.ojp.usdoj.gov/content/pub/pdf/svjfry09.pdf

Beitchman, J. H., Zucker, K. J., Hood, J. E., da Costa, G. A., Akman, D., & Cassavia, E. (1992). A review of the long-term effects of child sexual abuse. *Child Abuse and Neglect, 16,* 101–118.

Bell, J. (2002). *Policing hatred: Law enforcement, civil rights, and hate crime.* New York: New York University Press.

Benjamin, J., Li, L., Patterson, C., Greenberg, B. D., Murphy, D. L., & Hamer, D. H. (1996). Population and familial association between D4 dopamine receptor gene and measures of novelty seeking. *Nature Genetics, 12,* 81–84.

Bennett, J. (2010, October 4). From lockers to lockup: School bullying in the digital age can have tragic consequences. But should it be a crime? *Newsweek.* Retrieved from http://www.newsweek.com/2010/10/04/phoebe-prince-should-bullying-be-a-crime.html?GT1=43002

Bennett, K. J. (2003). Legal and social issues surrounding closed-circuit television of child victims and witnesses. *Journal of Aggression, Maltreatment and Trauma, 8,* 233–271.

Benson, M. L., Fox, G. L., DeMaris, A., & Van Wyk, J. (2003). Neighborhood disadvantage, individual economic distress and violence against women in intimate relationships. *Journal of Quantitative Criminology, 19,* 207–235.

Berdahl, J. L. (2007). Harassment based on sex: Protecting social status in the context of gender hierarchy. *Academy of Management Review, 32,* 641–658.

Bernasco, W. (2008). Them again? Same-offender involvement in repeat and near repeat burglaries. *European Journal of Criminology, 5,* 411–431.

Berg, M. T. (2012). The overlap of violent offending and violent victimization: Assessing the evidence and explanations. In M. DeLisi & P. J. Conis (Eds.), *Violent offenders: Theory, research, policy, and practice* (pp. 17–38). Burlington, MA: Jones & Bartlett Learning.

Berg, M. T., & Loeber, R. (2011). Examining the neighborhood context of the violent offending-victimization relationship: A prospective investigation. *Journal of Quantitative Criminology, 27,* 427–451.

Berg, M. T., Stewart, E. A., Schreck, C. J., & Simons, R. L. (2012). The victim–offender overlap in context: Examining the role of neighborhood street culture. *Criminology, 50,* 359–390.

Berg, S. (2009). Identity theft causes, correlates, and factors: A content analysis. In F. Schmalleger & M. Pittaro (Eds.), *Crimes of the Internet* (pp. 225–250). Upper Saddle River, NJ: Pearson–Prentice Hall.

Berios, D. C., & Grady, D. (1991). Domestic violence: Risk factors and outcomes. *Western Journal of Medicine, 155,* 133–135.

Bettencourt, B. A., & Miller, N. (1996). Gender differences in aggression as a function of provocation: A meta-analysis. *Psychological Bulletin, 119,* 422–447.

Blaauw, E., Winkel, F. W., Arensman, E., Sheridan, L., & Freeve, A. (2002). The toll of stalking: The relationship features of stalking and psychopathology of victims. *Journal of Interpersonal Violence, 17,* 50–63.

Black families fear racism at Euros. (2012, May 25). *Black families fear racism at Euros.* Retrieved from http://www.iol.co.za/sport/soccer/cup-competitions/black-families-fear-racism-at-euros-1.1305217#.T-ndXmXwKHg

Black, M. C., Basile, K. C., Breiding, M. J., Smith, S. G., Walters, M. L., Merrick, M. T., ... Stevens, M. R. (2011). *The National Intimate Partner and Sexual Violence Survey (NISVS): 2010 summary report.* Atlanta, GA: National Center for Injury Prevention and Control, Centers for Disease Control and Prevention.

Block, C. R. (2003). How can practitioners help an abused woman lower her risk of death? *National Institute of Justice, 250,* 4–7.

Blumenthal, J. A. (2009). Affective forecasting and capital sentencing: Reducing the effect of victim impact statements. *American Criminal Law Review, 46,* 107–126.

Bond, L., Carlin, J. B., Thomas, L., Ruin, K., & Patton, G. (2001). Does bullying cause emotional problems? A prospective study of young teenagers. *British Medical Journal, 323,* 480–484.

Bond, P. G., & Webb, J. R. (2010). Child abuse, neglect, and maltreatment. In B. S. Fisher & S. P. Lab (Eds.), *Encyclopedia of victimology and crime prevention* (Vol. 1, pp. 75–83). Thousand Oaks, CA: Sage.

Bonderman, J. (2001). *Working with victims of gun violence.* Washington, DC: United States Department of Justice Office for Victims of Crime.

Bonnie, R. J., & Wallace, R. B. (2003). *Elder mistreatment: Abuse, neglect and exploitation in aging America.* Washington, DC: National Academies Press.

Bookwala, J., Frieze, I., Smith, C., & Ryan, K. (1992). Predictors of dating violence: A multivariate analysis. *Violence and Victims, 7,* 297–311.

Bouffard, L. A., & Koeppel, M. D. H. (2014). Understanding the potential long-term physical and mental health consequences of early experiences of victimization. *Justice Quarterly, 31,* 568–587.

Branson-Potts, H. (2014, August 24). Suge Knight, 2 others shot at Chris Brown party on sunset strip. *LA Times.* Retrieved from http://www.latimes.com/local/lanow/la-me-ln-suge-knight-chris-brown-20140824-story.html

Breetzke, G. D., & Pearson, A. L. (2014). The fear factor: Examining the spatial variability of recorded crime on the fear of crime. *Applied Geography, 46,* 45–52.

Breitenbecher, K. H. (2001). Sexual assault on college campuses: Is an ounce of prevention enough? *Applied and Preventative Psychology, 9,* 23–52.

Breitenbecher, K. H., & Gidycz, C. A. (1998). An empirical evaluation of a program designed to reduce the risk of multiple sexual victimization. *Journal of Interpersonal Violence, 13,* 472–488.

Briere, J., & Spinazzola, J. (2005). Phenomenology and psychological assessment of complex posttraumatic states. *Journal of Traumatic Stress, 18*(5), 401–412.

Brochman, S. (1991, July 30). Silent victims: Bringing male rape out of the closet. *The Advocate, 582,* 38–43.

Broidy, L. M., Daday, J. K., Crandall, C. S., Sklar, D. P., & Jost, P. F. (2006). Exploring demographic, structural, and behavioral overlap among homicide offenders and victims. *Homicide Studies, 10*(3), 155–180.

Browne, A., & Finkelhor, D. (1986). The impact of child sexual abuse: A review of the research. *Psychological Bulletin, 99,* 66–77.

Browning, S., & Erickson, P. (2009). Neighborhood disadvantage, alcohol use, and violent victimization. *Youth Violence and Juvenile Justice, 7,* 331–349.

Brownridge, D. A. (2006). Partner violence against women with disabilities: Prevalence, risk, and explanations. *Violence Against Women, 12,* 805–822.

Brunton-Smith, I., & Sturgis, P. (2011). Do neighborhoods generate fear of crime? An empirical test using the British Crime Survey. *Criminology, 49,* 331–369.

Bui, H. I. (2001). *In the adopted land: Abused immigrant women and the criminal justice system.* Westport, CT: Praeger.

Bunch, J., Clay-Warner, J., & McMahon-Howard, J. (2014). The effects of victimization on routine activities. *Criminal Justice and Behavior, 41,* 574–592.

Bune, K. L. (2007, February 4). *Marital privilege law sends wrong message.* Retrieved from http://www.officer.com/article/10250193/marital-privilege-law-sends-wrong-message

Bureau of Justice Statistics. (2006a). *Criminal victimization in the United States: Statistical tables.* Washington, DC: U.S. Department of Justice.

Bureau of Justice Statistics. (2006b). *National Crime Victimization Survey.* Washington, DC: United States Department of Justice.

Bureau of Justice Statistics. (2007). *National Crime Victimization Survey (NCVS).* Washington, DC: United States Department of Justice.

Bureau of Justice Statistics. (2010, February). *Criminal victimization in the United States, 2007: Statistical tables.* Washington, DC: U.S. Department of Justice, Bureau of Justice Statistics.

Bureau of Justice Statistics. (2011). *Criminal victimization in the United States, 2008: Statistical tables.* Washington, DC: U.S. Department of Labor, Bureau of Justice Statistics.

Bureau of Labor Statistics. (2010). *Fact sheet: Workplace shootings.* Washington, DC: Bureau of Labor Statistics, U.S. Department of Labor. Retrieved from http://www.bls.gov/iif/oshwc/cfoi/osar0014.htm

Bureau of Labor Statistics. (2011, August 25). *National census of fatal occupational injuries in 2010 (preliminary results).* Washington, DC: Bureau of Labor Statistics, U.S. Department of Labor. Retrieved from http://www.bls.gov/news.release/pdf/cfoi.pdf

Bureau of Labor Statistics. (2014). *National census of fatal occupational injuries in 2012* [Data Table A-2]. Washington, DC: Bureau of Labor Statistics, U.S. Department of Labor. Retrieved from http://www.bls.gov/iif/oshwc/cfoi/cftb0260.pdf

Buschur, C. (2010). Expert testimony. In B. S. Fisher & S. P. Lab (Eds.), *Encyclopedia of victimology and crime prevention* (Vol. 1, pp. 364–365). Thousand Oaks, CA: Sage.

Buzawa, E. (2007). Victims of domestic violence. In R. C. Davis, A. J. Lurigio, & S. Herman (Eds.), *Victims of crime* (3rd ed., pp. 55–74). Thousand Oaks, CA: Sage.

Buzawa, E. S., & Buzawa, C. G. (1993). Opening the doors: The changing police response to domestic violence. In R. G. Dunham & G. P. Alpert (Eds.), *Critical issues in policing* (pp. 551–567). Prospect Heights, IL: Waveland.

Campbell, J. C., Webster, D., Koziol-McLain, J., Block, C. R., Campbell, D., Curry, M. A., ... Wilt, S. A. (2003). Assessing risk factors for intimate partner homicide. *National Institute of Justice Journal, 250,* 14–19.

Campbell, R., Patterson, D., & Lichty, L. F. (2005). The effectiveness of sexual assault nurse examiner (SANE) programs: A review of the psychological, medical, legal, and community outcomes. *Trauma, Violence, and Abuse, 6,* 313–329.

Cantwell, H. B. (1999). The neglect of child neglect. In M. E. Helfer, R. S. Kempe, & R. D. Krugman (Eds.), *The battered child* (pp. 347–373). Chicago, IL: University of Chicago Press.

Carbone-Lopez, K., & Kruttschnitt, C. (2010). Risky relationships? Assortative mating and women's experiences of intimate partner violence. *Crime and Delinquency, 56,* 358–384.

Carter, S. D., & Bath, C. (2007). The evolution and components of the Jeanne Clery Act: Implications for higher education. In B. S. Fisher & J. J. Sloan (Eds.), *Campus crime: Legal, social and policy perspectives* (2nd ed., pp. 27–44). Springfield, IL: Charles C Thomas.

Casey, E. A., & Nurius, P. S. (2005). Trauma exposure and sexual revictimization risk. *Violence Against Women, 11,* 505–530.

Cass, A. I. (2007). Routine activities and sexual assault: An analysis of individual and school level factors. *Violence and Victims, 22,* 350–366.

Catalano, S. (2010). Victimization during household burglary. *National Crime Victimization Survey, 1–12.*

Catalano, S. (2013). *Intimate partner violence: Attributes of victimization, 1992–2011* (Report No. NCJ 243300). Washington, DC: U.S. Department of Justice, Bureau of Justice Statistics. Retrieved from http://www.bjs.gov/content/pub/pdf/ipvav9311.pdf

Catalano, S., Smith, E., Snyder, H., & Rand, M. (2009). *Female victims of violence.* Washington, DC: U.S. Department of Justice, Bureau of Justice Statistics. Retrieved from http://bjs.ojp.usdoj.gov/content/pub/pdf/fvv.pdf

Cattaneo, L. B., & Goodman, L. A. (2003). Victim-reported risk factors for continued abusive behavior: Assessing the dangerousness of arrested batterers. *Journal of Community Psychology, 31,* 349–369.

Cattaneo, L. B., & Goodman, L. A. (2005). Risk factors for reabuse in intimate partner violence: A cross-disciplinary critical review. *Trauma, Violence and Abuse: A Review Journal, 6,* 141–175.

Centers for Disease Control and Prevention. (2003). *Costs of intimate partner violence against women.* Atlanta, GA: Centers for Disease Control and Prevention, National Center for Injury Prevention and Control.

Centers for Disease Control and Prevention. (2006). *HIV statistics and surveillance.* Atlanta, GA: Centers for Disease Control and Prevention.

Centers for Disease Control and Prevention. (2010a). Developmental disabilities. Washington, DC: Department of Health and Human Services, Centers for Disease Control and Prevention. Retrieved from http://www.cdc.gov/ncbddd/dd/default.htm.

Centers for Disease Control and Prevention. (2010b). Intimate partner violence: Consequences. Retrieved from http://www.cdc.gov/ViolencePrevention/intimatepartnerviolence/consequences.html.

Centers for Disease Control and Prevention. (2014, June 13). Youth risk behavior surveillance: United States, 2013. *Surveillance Summaries, 63,* 1–168.

Centre for Justice and Reconciliation. (2008). *What is restorative justice?* (Briefing paper). Retrieved from http://www.pfi.org/cjr

Chalk, R., & King, P. (1998). *Violence in families: Assessing prevention and treatment programs.* Washington, DC: National Academy Press.

Chandek, M. S., & Porter, C. O. L. H. (1998). The efficacy of expectancy disconfirmation in explaining crime victim satisfaction with the police. *Police Quarterly, 1,* 21–40.

Chen, X. (2009). The link between juvenile offending and victimization: The influence of risky lifestyles, social bonding, and individual characteristics. *Youth Violence and Juvenile Justice, 7*(2), 119–135.

Child Abuse Prevention and Treatment Act of 1974, 42 U.S.C. §§ 5101–5106 (1974).

Child Welfare Information Gateway. (2008a). *Long-term consequences of child abuse and neglect.* Retrieved from http://www.childwelfare.gov/pubs/factsheets/long_term_consequences.cfm

Child Welfare Information Gateway. (2008b). *What is child abuse and neglect?* Retrieved from http://www.childwelfare.gov/pubs/factsheets/whatiscan.cfm

Child Welfare Information Gateway. (2009). *Parental substance use and the child welfare system*. Retrieved from http://www.childwelfare.gov/pubs/factsheets/parentalsubabuse.cfm

Child Welfare Information Gateway. (2010a). *Infant safe haven laws: Summary of state laws*. Retrieved from http://www.childwelfare.gov/systemwide/laws_policies/statutes/safehaven.cfm

Child Welfare Information Gateway. (2010b). *Mandatory reporters of child abuse and neglect: Summary of state laws*. Retrieved from http://www.childwelfare.gov/systemwide/laws_policies/statutes/manda.cfm

Chon, S. (2010, February 24). *Carr v. United States (08-1301)*. Ithaca, NY: Legal Information Institute, Cornell University Law School. Retrieved from http://topics.law.cornell.edu/supct/cert/08-1301

Chonco, N. R. (1989). Sexual assaults among male inmates: A descriptive study. *The Prison Journal, 69,* 72–82.

Clarke, R. V., & Harris, P. M. (1992). Auto theft and its prevention. In M. Tonry (Ed.), *Crime and justice: A review of research* (Vol. 16, pp. 1–52). Chicago, IL: University of Chicago Press.

Clarke, R. V., Perkins, E., & Smith, D. J., Jr. (2001). Explaining repeat residential burglaries: An analysis of property stolen. In G. Farrell & K. Pease (Eds.), *Repeat victimization. Crime prevention studies* (pp. 119–132). Monsey, NY: Criminal Justice Press.

Clarke, R. V. G. (1980). "Situational" crime prevention: Theory and practice. *British Journal of Criminology, 20*(2), 136–147.

Clarke, R. V. G. (1982). Crime prevention through environmental management and design. In J. Gunn & D. P. Farrington (Eds.), *Abnormal offenders, delinquency, and the criminal justice system* (pp. 213–230). Chichester, England: Wiley.

Classen, C., Pales, O. G., & Aggarwa, R. (2005). Sexual revictimization: A review of the empirical literature. *Trauma, Violence and Abuse, 6,* 103–129.

Clay-Warner, J. (2002). Avoiding rape: The effects of situational factors on rape. *Violence and Victims, 17,* 691–705.

Clery, H., & Clery, C. (2008). *What Jeanne didn't know*. Retrieved from http://www.securityoncampus.net/index.php?option=com_content&view=category&layout=blog&id=34&Itemid=53

CNN Wire Staff. (2011). Swiss social worker admits to 114 sexual assaults on disabled. *CNN World*. Retrieved from http://articles.cnn.com/2011-02-01/world/switzerland.sex.charges_1_sexual-assaults-so-cial-worker-information-on-similar-cases?_s=PM:WORLD

Cohen, L. E., & Felson, M. (1979). Social change and crime rate trends: A routine activities approach. *American Sociological Review, 44,* 588–608.

Coker, A. L., Cook-Craig, P. G., Williams, C. M., Fisher, B. S., Clear, E. R., Garcia, L. S., & Hegge, L. M. (2011). Evaluation of Green Dot: An active bystander intervention to reduce sexual violence on college campuses. *Violence Against Women, 17,* 777–796.

Coker, A. L., Smith, P. H., Bethea, L., King, M. R., & McKeown, R. E. (2000). Physical health consequences of physical and psychological intimate partner violence. *Archives of Family Medicine, 9,* 1–7.

Coker, A. L., Smith, P. H., Thompson, M. P., McKeown, R. E., Bethea, L., & Davis, K. E. (2002). Social support protects against the negative effects of partner violence on mental health. *Journal of Women's Health & Gender-Based Medicine, 5,* 465–476.

Coleman, K., & Straus, M. (1986). Marital power, conflict, and violence in a nationally representative sample of American couples. *Violence and Victims, 1,* 141–157.

College students at risk for identity theft. (2014, August 21). College students at risk for identity theft. *CNN News Wire*. Retrieved from http://www.ozarksfirst.com/story/d/story/college-students-at-risk-for-identity-theft/81271/LUzujp92oketdMheeMzevQ

Conron, K. J., Beardslee, W., Koenen, K. C., Buka, S. L., & Gortmaker, S. L. (2009). A longitudinal study of maternal depression and child maltreatment in a national sample of families investigated by child protective services. *Archives of Pediatric and Adolescent Medicine, 163,* 922–930.

Cooper, A., & Smith, E. L. (2011). Homicide trends in the United States, 1980–2008. *Bureau of Justice Statistics, Department of Justice*. Retrieved from http://www.bjs.gov/content/pub/pdf/htus8008.pdf

Copeland, A. R. (1985). Homicide in childhood: The Metro-Dade County experience from 1956 to 1982. *The American Journal of Forensic Medicine and Pathology, 6*(1), 21–24.

Cose, E. (1994, August 8). Truths about spouse abuse. *Newsweek,* 49.

Cox, R. W., Johnson, T. A., & Richards, G. E. (2009). Routine activity theory and Internet crime. In F. Schmalleger & M. Pittaro (Eds.), *Crimes of the Internet* (pp. 302–316). Upper Saddle River, NJ: Pearson–Prentice Hall.

Craig, W., Harel-Fisch, Y., Fogel-Grinvald, H., Dostaler, S., Hetland, J., Simons-Morton, B., ... The HBSC Violence and Injuries Prevention Focus Group, and the HBSC Bullying Writing Group (2009). A cross-national profile of bullying and victimization among adolescents in 40 countries. *International Journal of Public Health, 54*(Supp 2), 216–224.

Crandall, C., & Helitzer, D. (2003). *Impact evaluation of a sexual assault nurse examiner (SANE) program* (NIJ Document No. 203276). Washington, DC: National Institute of Justice.

Crime in England and Wales. (2010/2011) *Home Office statistical bulletin 2010/11*. London, UK: Home Office.

Cromwell, P. F., Olson, J. N., & Avary, D. W. (1991). *Breaking and entering: An ethnographic analysis of burglary*. Newbury Park, CA: Sage.

Cross, T. P., Walsh, W. A., Simone, M., & Jones, L. M. (2003). Prosecution of child abuse: A meta-analysis of rates of criminal justice decisions. *Trauma, Violence and Abuse, 4,* 323–340.

Custers, K., & Van den Bulck, J. (2013). The cultivation of fear of sexual violence in women: Processes and moderators of the relationship between television and fear. *Communication Research, 40,* 96–124.

Cyr, K., Clement, M., & Chamberland, C. (2014). Lifetime prevalence of multiple victimizations and its impact on children's mental health. *Journal of Interpersonal Violence, 29,* 616–634.

Daigle, L. E. (2010). Risk heterogeneity and recurrent violent victimization: The role of DRD4. *Biodemography and Social Biology, 56,* 137–149.

Daigle, L. E., Beaver, K. M., & Hartman, J. L. (2008). A life-course approach to the study of victimization and offending behaviors. *Victims and Offenders, 3,* 365–390.

Daigle, L. E., & Fisher, B. S. (2010). Rape. In B. S. Fisher & S. P. Lab (Eds.), *Encyclopedia of victimology and crime prevention* (Vol. 2, pp. 708–715). Thousand Oaks, CA: Sage.

Daigle, L. E., Fisher, B. S., & Cullen, F. T. (2008). The violent and sexual victimization of college women. *Journal of Interpersonal Violence, 23,* 1296–1313.

Daigle, L. E., Fisher, B. S., & Stewart, M. (2009). The effectiveness of sexual victimization prevention among college students: A summary of "what works." *Victims and Offenders, 4,* 398–404.

Dantas, S., Santos, A., Dinis-Oliveira, R. J., & Mahalhaes, T. (2014). Parricide: A forensic approach. *Journal of Forensic and Legal Medicine, 22,* 1–6.

Davies, K. (2010). Victim assistance programs, United States. In B. S. Fisher & S. P. Lab (Eds.), *Encyclopedia of victimology and crime prevention* (Vol. 2, pp. 968–969). Thousand Oaks, CA: Sage.

Davis, R. C., Henley, M., & Smith, B. (1990). *Victim impact statements: Their effects on court outcomes and victim satisfaction.* New York: New York City Victim Service Agency.

Davis, R. C., & Mulford, C. (2008). Victim rights and new remedies: Finally getting victims their due. *Journal of Contemporary Criminal Justice, 24,* 198–208.

Davis, R., O'Sullivan, C., Guthrie, P., & Ross, T. (2006). *Reducing repeat sexual revictimization: A field test with an urban sample.* New York, NY: Vera Institute of Justice.

Davis, R. C., Smith, B. E., & Davies, H. J. (2001). Effects of no-drop prosecution of domestic violence upon conviction rates. *Justice Research and Policy, 3,* 1–13.

Davis, R. C., Weisburd, D., & Taylor, B. (2008). Effects of second responder programs on repeat incidents of family abuse: A systematic review. *Campbell Systematic Reviews, 15.* doi:10.4073/csr.2008.15.

Dawkins, J. L. (1996). Bullying, physical disability and the pediatric patient. *Developmental Medicine and Child Neurology, 38,* 603–612.

Dawson, M., & Dinovitzer, R. (2001). Victim cooperation and the prosecution of domestic violence in a specialized court. *Justice Quarterly, 18,* 593–622.

Deess, P. (1999). *Victims' rights: Notification, consultation, participation, services, compensation, and remedies in the criminal justice process.* New York, NY: Vera Institute of Justice.

Deinstitutionalization. (2011). *Encyclopedia of mental disorders.* Retrieved from http://www.minddisorders.com/Br-Del/Deinstitutionalization.html

Department of Health and Human Services (DHHS) (2012). *Child maltreatment 2012.* Washington, DC: U.S. Department of Health and Human Services, Administration for Children and Families, Youth and Families, Children's Bureau. Retrieved from http://www.acf.hhs.gov/sites/default/files/cb/cm2012.pdf#page=16

Department of the Attorney General. (2006). *Compensation for victims of crime.* Retrieved from http://www.courts.dotag.wa.gov.au/_files/Compensation_for_VOC_brochure.pdf

Desai, S., Arias, I., Thompson, M. P., & Basile, K. C. (2002). Childhood victimization and subsequent adult revictimization assessed in a nationally representative sample of women and men. *Violence and Victims, 17,* 639–653.

Devoe, J. F., Bauer, L., & Hill, M. R. (2010, July). *Student victimization in U.S. schools: Results from the 2007 School Crime Supplement to the National Crime Victimization Survey.* Retrieved from http://nces.ed.gov/pubs2010/2010319.pdf

Devries, K. M., Child, J. C., Bacchus, L. J., Mak, J., Falder, G., Graham, K., … Heise, L. (2014). Intimate partner violence victimization and alcohol consumption in women: A systematic review and meta-analysis. *Addiction, 109,* 379–391.

DeYoung, C. G., Peterson, J. B., Seguin, J. R., Mejia, J. M., Pihl, R. O., Beitchman, J. H., … Palmour, R. M. (2006). The dopamine D4 receptor gene and moderation of the association between externalizing behavior and IQ. *Archives of General Psychiatry, 63,* 1410–1416.

Dixon, L., & Stern, R. K. (2004). Compensating the victims of 9/11 (Research brief). *RAND Corporation.* Retrieved from http://www.rand.org/pubs/research_briefs/RB9087.html

Dobash, R. E., & Dobash, R. P. (1979). *Violence against wives: A case against the patriarchy.* New York, NY: Free Press.

Dobash, R. E., & Dobash, R. P. (1992). *Women, violence and social change.* London, UK: Routledge.

Dobrin, A. (2001). The risk of offending on homicide victimization: A case control study. *Journal of Research in Crime and Delinquency, 38*(2), 154–173.

Dragiewicz, M. (2010). Conflict Tactics Scale (CTS/CTS2). In B. S. Fisher & S. P. Lab (Eds.), *Encyclopedia of victimology and crime prevention* (Vol. 1, pp. 136–139). Thousand Oaks, CA: Sage.

Dryden-Edwards, R. (2007). Anxiety. *eMedicineHealth.* Retrieved from http://www.emedicinehealth.com/anxiety/article_em.htm#Anxiety%20Overview

Dugan, L., LaFree, G., Cragin, K., & Kasupski, A. (2008). *Building and analyzing a comprehensive open source database on global terrorist events.* Washington, DC: U.S. Department of Justice. Retrieved from http://www.ncjrs.gov/pdffiles1/nij/grants/223287.pdf

Duhart, D. T. (2001). *National Crime Victimization Survey: Violence in the workplace, 1993–1999* (Special Report). Washington, DC: Bureau of Justice Statistics. Retrieved from http://bjs.ojp.usdoj.gov/content/pub/pdf/vw99.pdf

Du Mont, J., & Forte, T. (2014). Intimate partner violence among women with mental health-related activity limitations: A Canadian population based study. *BMC Public Health, 14,* 51.

Dunn, P. (2004). *Victim support in the United Kingdom: Its history and current work.* Retrieved from http://www.unafei.or.jp/english/pdf/RS_No63/No63_15VE_Dunn1.pdf

Dupont-Morales, T. (2009). Von Hentig's typologies. In J. K. Wilson (Ed.), *Praeger handbook of victimology* (pp. 308–309). Santa Barbara, CA: Praeger.

Eberhardt, S. (n.d.). *Core crimes defined in the Rome statute of the International Criminal Court.* Retrieved from http://www.iccnow.org/documents/FS-CICC-CoreCrimesinRS.pdf

Ebstein, R. P., Novick, O., Umansky, R., Priel, B., Osher, Y., Blaine, D., . . . Belmaker, R. H. (1996). Dopamine D4 receptor (D4DR) exon III polymorphism associated with the human personality trait of novelty seeking. *Nature & Genetics, 12,* 78–80.

Egan, S. K., & Perry, D. G. (1998). Does low self-regard invite victimization? *Developmental Psychology, 34,* 299–309.

Ehrlich, H. J. (1992). The ecology of anti-gay violence. In G. M. Herek & K. T. Berrill (Eds.), *Hate crimes: Confronting violence against lesbians and gay men* (pp. 105–122). Thousand Oaks, CA: Sage.

Eigenberg, H. M. (1989). Male rape: An empirical examination of correctional officers' attitudes toward rape in prison. *The Prison Journal, 68,* 39–56.

Elder, J. W. (1976). Comparative cross-national methodology. *Annual Review of Sociology,* Vol. 2, pp. 209–230.

Elias, R. (1984). Alienating the victim: Compensation and victim attitudes. *Journal of Social Issues, 40,* 103–116.

Erez, E., & Globokar, J. (2010). Victim impact statements. In B. S. Fisher & S. P. Lab (Eds.), *Encyclopedia of victimology and crime prevention* (Vol. 2, pp. 974–975). Thousand Oaks, CA: Sage.

Erez, E., Roeger, L., & Morgan, F. (1994). *Victim impact statements in South Australia: An evaluation.* Adelaide: Office of Crime Statistics, South Australian Attorney General's Department.

Erez, E., & Tontodonato, P. (1992). Victim participation in sentencing and satisfaction with justice. *Justice Quarterly, 9,* 393–417.

Ericksen, J., Dudley, C., McIntosh, G., Ritch, L., Shumay, S., & Simpson, M. (2002). Clients' experiences with a specialized sexual assault service. *Journal of Emergency Nursing, 28,* 86–90.

Ericson, N. (2001, June). *Addressing the problem of juvenile bullying* (OJJDP Fact Sheet #27). Washington, DC: U.S. Department of Justice, Office of Justice Programs, Office of Juvenile Justice and Delinquency Prevention. Retrieved from http://www.ncjrs.gov/pdffiles1/ojjdp/fs200127.pdf

Esbensen, F. A., Huizinga, D., & Menard, S. (1999). Family context and criminal victimization in adolescence. *Youth and Society, 31,* 168–198.

Escobar, G. (2010, November). *Prosecuting intimate partner violence: Do victim services affect case outcomes?* Paper presented at the ASC annual meeting, San Francisco. Retrieved from http://www.allacademic.com/meta/p431247_index.html

Espelage, D. L., & Swearer, S. M. (2003). Research on school bullying and victimization: What have we learned and where do we go from here? *School Psychology Review, 32,* 365–383.

Estrich, S. (1988). *Real rape: How the legal system victimizes women who say no.* Cambridge, MA: Harvard University Press.

European Union. (2014). *Victims.* Retrieved from http://ec.europa.eu/justice/criminal/victims/index_en.htm

Evans, D. N. (2014). *Compensating victims of crime.* New York, NY: Research & Evaluation Center, John Jay College of Criminal Justice, City University of New York. Retrieved from http://www.justicefellowship.org/sites/default/files/Compensating%20Victims%20of%20Crime_John%20Jay_June%202014.pdf

Ezell, M. E., & Tanner-Smith, E. E. (2009). Examining the role of lifestyle and criminal history variables on the risk of homicide victimization. *Homicide Studies, 13*(2), 144–173.

Family Violence Prevention Fund. (2010). *Intimate partner violence and healthy people 2010 fact sheet.* San Francisco, CA: Family Violence Prevention Fund. Retrieved from http://www.futureswithoutviolence.org/userfiles/file/Children_and_Families/ipv.pdf

Faraone, S. V., Doyle, A. E., Mick, E., & Biederman, J. (2001). Meta-analysis of the association between the 7-repeat allele of the dopamine D4 receptor gene and attention deficit hyperactivity disorder. *American Journal of Psychiatry, 158,* 1052–1057.

Farley, M., Cotton, A., Lynne, J., Zumbeck, S., Spiwak, F., Reyes, M. E., . . . Sezgin, U. (2003). Prostitution and trafficking in nine countries: An update on violence and posttraumatic stress disorder. In M. Farley (Ed.), *Prostitution, trafficking, and traumatic stress* (pp. 33–74). Binghamton, NY: The Haworth Maltreatment & Trauma Press.

Farmer v. Brennan, 92-7247, 511 U.S. 825 (1994).

Farrell, A., McDevitt, J., & Fahy, S. (2008). *Understanding and improving law enforcement responses to human trafficking, final report.* Rockville, MD: National Institute of Justice.

Farrell, G., & Pease, K. (2006). Preventing repeat residential burglary. In B. C. Welsh & D. P. Farrington (Eds.), *Preventing crime: What works for children, offenders, victims, and places* (pp. 161–178). Dordrecht, The Netherlands: Springer.

Farrell, G., Phillips, C., & Pease, K. (1995). Like taking candy: Why does repeat victimization occur? *British Journal of Criminology, 35,* 384–399.

Fattah, E. A. (2010). The evolution of a young, promising discipline: Sixty years of victimology, a retrospective and prospective look. In S. G. Shoham, P. Knepper, & M. Kett (Eds.), *International handbook of victimology* (pp. 43–94). Boca Raton, Florida: CRC Press.

Fay, M., Morrissey, M., & Smyth, M. (1999). *Northern Ireland's troubles: The human costs.* Sterling, VA: Pluto.

Federal Bureau of Investigation. (2006). *Crime in the United States, 2006.* Retrieved from http://www.fbi.gov/about-us/cjis/ucr/crime-in-the-u.s/2006/

Federal Bureau of Investigation. (2009). *Crime in the United States, 2009.* Retrieved from http://www.fbi.gov/about-us/cjis/ucr/crime-in-the-u.s/2009/crime2009

Federal Bureau of Investigation. (2010, November). *Crime statistics, 2009: Methodology.* Retrieved from http://www2.fbi.gov/ucr/hc2009/methodology.html

Federal Bureau of Investigation. (2011). *UCR program changes definition of rape.* Retrieved from http://www.fbi.gov/about-us/cjis/cjis-link/march-2012/ucr-program-changes-definition-of-rape

Federal Bureau of Investigation. (2012a). *Crime in the United States, 2012*. Retrieved from http://www.fbi.gov/about-us/cjis/ucr/crime-in-the-u.s/2012/crime-in-the-u.s.-2012

Federal Bureau of Investigation. (2012b). *Hate crime statistics, 2012: Victims*. Retrieved from http://www.fbi.gov/about-us/cjis/ucr/crime-in-the-u.s/2012/resource-pages/hate-crime-placeholder/hate-crime-statistics

Federal Bureau of Investigation. (2013a). *Burglary*. Retrieved from http://www.fbi.gov/about-us/cjis/ucr/crime-in-the-u.s/2012/crime-in-the-u.s.-2012/property-crime/burglary

Federal Bureau of Investigation. (2013b). *National Incident-Based Reporting System (NIBRS) user manual*. Retrieved from http://www.fbi.gov/about-us/cjis/ucr/nibrs/nibrs-user-manual

Federal Bureau of Investigation. (n.d.-a). *Human trafficking*. Retrieved from http://www.fbi.gov/about-us/investigate/civilrights/human_trafficking

Federal Bureau of Investigation. (n.d.-b). *National Incident Based Reporting System (NIBRS): General information*. Retrieved from http://www2.fbi.gov/ucr/faqs.htm

Federal Deposit Insurance Corporation. (2004, December 14). *Putting an end to account-hijacking identity theft*. Retrieved from http://www.fdic.gov/consumers/consumer/idtheftstudy/identity_theft.pdf

Federal Grants Wire. (2011). *Motor Vehicle Theft Prevention Act Program (16.597)*. Retrieved from http://www.federalgrantswire.com/motor-vehicle-theft-protection-act-program.html

Federal Trade Commission. (2004). *CAN-SPAM Act: A compliance guide for business*. Retrieved from http://business.ftc.gov/documents/bus61-can-spam-act-compliance-guide-business

Federal Trade Commission. (2014). *Consumer sentinel network data book: January–December 2013*. Retrieved from http://www.ftc.gov/system/files/documents/reports/consumer-sentinel-network-data-book-january-december-2013/sentinel-cy2013.pdf

Fedus, D. B. (2010). Elder abuse, neglect, and maltreatment. In B. S. Fisher & S. P. Lab (Eds.), *Encyclopedia of victimology and crime prevention* (Vol. 1, pp. 348–350). Thousand Oaks, CA: Sage.

Felson, R. B. (2002). Reasons for reporting and not reporting domestic violence to the police. *Criminology, 40,* 617–648.

Felson, R. B. (2006). Big people hit little people: Sex differences in physical power and interpersonal violence. *Criminology, 34,* 433–452.

Felson, R. M. (1992). Routine activities and crime prevention: Armchair concepts and practical action. *Studies on Crime and Crime Prevention, 1,* 30–34.

Feniger, Y., & Yuchtman-Yaar, E. (2010). Risk groups in exposure to terror: The case of Israel's citizens. *Social Forces, 88,* 1451–1462.

Ferraro, K. F. (1995). *Fear of crime: Interpreting victimization risk*. Albany: State University of New York Press.

Ferraro, K. F. (1996). Women's fear of victimization: Shadow of sexual assault? *Social Forces, 75,* 667–690.

Ferraro, K. F., & LaGrange, R. L. (1987). The measurement of fear of crime. *Sociological Inquiry, 5,* 70–101.

FindLaw. (2011). CAL. PEN. CODE § 422.6: California Code—Section 422.6. Retrieved from http://codes.lp.findlaw.com/cacode/PEN/3/1/11.6/2/s422.6

FindLaw for Legal Professionals. (2011). Farmer v. Brennan, U.S. 1994. Retrieved from http://caselaw.lp.findlaw.com/cgi-bin/getcase.pl?court=US&vol=000&invol=U10394

Finkelhor, D., Ormrod, R. K., & Turner, H. A. (2007a). Poly-victimization and trauma in a national longitudinal cohort. *Development and Psychopathology, 19,* 149–166.

Finkelhor, D., Ormrod, R. K., & Turner, H. A. (2007b). Poly-victimization: A neglected component in child victimization trauma. *Child Abuse and Neglect, 31,* 7–26.

Finkelhor, D., Ormrod, R. K., & Turner, H. A. (2009). Lifetime assessment of poly-victimization in a national sample of children and youth. *Child Abuse & Neglect, 33,* 403–411.

Finkelhor, D., Turner, H. A., Ormrod, R. K., & Hamby, S. (2009). Violence, abuse and crime exposure in a national sample of children and youth. *Pediatrics, 124,* 1–14.

Finn, M. A., Muftić, L. R., & Marsh, E. (2014). Exploring the overlap between victimization and offending among women in sex work. *Victims & Offenders: An International Journal of Evidence-based Research, Policy, and Practice.* doi:10.1080/15564886.2014.918069.

Finn, P. (2000). Labeling automobile parts to combat theft. *FBI Law Enforcement Bulletin, 69,* 10–14.

Finn, P., & McNeil, T. (1987). *The response of the criminal justice system to bias crimes*. Cambridge, MA: Abt Associates.

Fischer, K., & Rose, M. (1995). When "enough is enough": Battered women's decision making around court orders of protection. *Crime & Delinquency, 41,* 414–429.

Fishbein, D. (2001). *Biobehavioral perspectives in criminology*. Belmont, CA: Wadsworth/Thomson Learning.

Fisher, B. S., & Cullen, F. T. (2000). Measuring the sexual victimization of women: Evolution, current controversies, and future research. In D. Duffee (Ed.), *Criminal justice 2000: Measurement and analysis of crime and justice* (Vol. 4., pp. 317–390). Washington, DC: National Institute of Justice.

Fisher, B. S., Cullen, F. T., & Turner, M. G. (1998). *The extent and nature of sexual victimization among college women: A national-level analysis; Final report*. Washington, DC: U.S. Department of Justice, National Institute of Justice.

Fisher, B. S., Cullen, F. T., & Turner, M. G. (2000). *The sexual victimization of college women*. Washington, DC: U.S. Department of Justice, Bureau of Justice Statistics and National Institute of Justice.

Fisher, B. S., Daigle, L. E., & Cullen, F. T. (2010a). *Unsafe in the Ivory Tower: The sexual victimization of college women*. Thousand Oaks, CA: Sage.

Fisher, B. S., Daigle, L. E., & Cullen, F. T. (2010b). What distinguishes single from recurrent sexual victims? The role of lifestyle-routine activities and first-incident characteristics. *Justice Quarterly, 27,* 102–129.

Fisher, B. S., Daigle, L. E., Cullen, F. T., & Santana, S. A. (2007). Assessing the efficacy of the protective action-sexual victimization completion nexus. *Violence and Victims, 22,* 18–42.

Fisher, B. S., Daigle, L. E., Cullen, F. T., & Turner, M. G. (2003). Reporting sexual victimization to the police: Results from a national-level study of college women. *Criminal Justice and Behavior, 30,* 6–38.

Fisher, B. S., Karjane, H. M., Cullen, F. T., Blevins, K. R., Santana, S. A., & Daigle, L. E. (2007). Reporting sexual assault and the Clery Act: Situating findings from the National Campus Sexual Assault Policy Study within college women's experiences. In B. S. Fisher & J. J. Sloan (Eds.), *Campus crime: Legal, social and policy perspectives* (2nd ed., pp. 65–86). Springfield, IL: Charles C Thomas.

Fisher, B. S., Sloan, J. J., Cullen, F. T., & Lu, C. (1998). Crime in the Ivory Tower: The level and sources of student victimization. *Criminology, 36,* 671–710.

Fishman, G., Hakim, S., & Shachmurove, Y. (1998). The use of household survey data: The probability of property crime victimization. *Journal of Economic and Social Measurement, 24,* 1–13.

Fleming, J., Mullen, P. E., Sibthorpe, B., & Bammer, G. (1999). The long-term impact of childhood sexual abuse in Australian women. *Child Abuse and Neglect, 23,* 145–159.

Fliege, H., Lee, J., Grimm, A., & Klapp, B. F. (2009). Risk factors and correlates of deliberate self-harm behavior: A systematic review. *Journal of Psychosomatic Research, 66,* 477–493.

Focht-New, G., Clements, P. T., Barol, B., Faulkner, M. J., & Service, K. P. (2008). Persons with developmental disabilities exposed to interpersonal violence and crime: Strategies and guidance for assessment. *Perspectives in Psychiatric Care, 44,* 3–13.

Ford, J. D., Elhai, J. D., Connor, D. F., & Frueh, B. C. (2010). Poly-victimization and risk of posttraumatic, depressive, and substance use disorders and involvement in delinquency in a national sample of adolescents. *Journal of Adolescent Health, 46,* 545–552.

Ford, T. (2012, May 22). Domestic violence is biggest threat to west Africa's women, IRC says. *The Guardian.* Retrieved from http://www.guardian.co.uk/global-development/2012/may/22/domestic-violence-west-africa-irc

Forrester, D., Chatterton, M., & Pease, K. (1988). *The Kirkholt Burglary Prevention Project, Rochdale.* London, UK: Home Office.

Foshee, V. A., Bauman, K. E., & Linder, G. F. (1999). Family violence and perpetration of adolescent dating violence: Examining social learning and social control processes. *Journal of Marriage and the Family, 61,* 331–343.

Fox, K. A., Nobles, M. R., & Akers, R. L. (2011). Is stalking a learned phenomenon? An empirical test of social learning theory. *Journal of Criminal Justice, 39,* 39–47.

Four charged in starvation death of child with autism. (2014, August 27). *7 News.* Retrieved from http://www.wsvn.com/story/26388305/4-charged-in-starvation-death-of-child-with-autism

Franklin, C. A. (2011). An investigation of the relationship between self-control and alcohol-induced sexual assault victimization. *Criminal Justice and Behavior, 38,* 263–285.

Frye, V. (2001). Examining homicide's contribution to pregnancy-associated deaths. *Journal of the American Medical Association, 285,* 1510–1511.

Frye, V., Hosein, V., Waltermaurer, E., Blaney, S., & Wilt, S. (2005). Femicide in New York City: 1990 to 1999. *Homicide Studies, 9*(3), 204–228.

Fuentes, M. E., & Gatz, M. (1983, November). *Fear of crime in the elderly: Its relation to leaving one's abode, self reported health and sense of personal control.* Paper presented at the Annual Scientific Meeting of the Gerontological Society, San Francisco, CA.

Gabor, T., & Mata, G. (2004). Victimization and repeat victimization over the life span: A predictive study and implications for policy. *International Review of Victimology, 10,* 193–221.

Gabriel, R., Ferrando, L., Corton, E. S., Mingote, C., Garcia-Cambo, E., Liria, A. F., & Galea, S. (2007). Psychopathological consequences after a terrorist attack: An epidemiological study among victims, the general population, and police officers. *European Psychiatry, 22,* 339–346.

Gadsden mother convicted of aggravated child abuse of 22-month-old son. (2011, April 8). *The Gadsden Times.* Retrieved from http://www.gadsdentimes.com/article/20110408/NEWS/110409788

Gardella, J. H., Nichols-Hadeed, C. A., Mastrocinque, J. M., Stone, J. T., Coates, C. A., Sly, C. J., & Cerulli, C. (2014). Beyond Clery Act statistics: A closer look at college victimization based on self-report data. *Journal of Interpersonal Violence.* doi:10.1177/0886260514535257.

Garner, J., & Maxwell, C. (2009). Prosecution and conviction rates for intimate partner violence. *Criminal Justice Review, 34,* 44–79.

Gartner. com. (2006). *Gartner says number of phishing e-mails sent to U.S. adults nearly doubles in just two years* (Press release). Retrieved from http://www.gartner.com/it/page.jsp?id=498245

Garvin, M. (2010). Victims' rights movement, United States. In B. S. Fisher & S. P. Lab (Eds.), *Encyclopedia of victimology and crime prevention* (Vol. 2, pp. 1019–1020). Los Angeles, CA: Sage.

Gibson, C. L. (2012). An investigation of neighborhood disadvantage, low self-control, and violent victimization among youth. *Youth Violence and Juvenile Justice, 10,* 41–63.

Gibson, L. E., & Leitenberg, H. (2001). The impact of child sexual abuse and stigma on methods of coping with sexual assault among undergraduate women. *Child Abuse and Neglect, 25,* 1343–1361.

Gidycz, C. A., Lynn, S. J., Rich, C. L., Marioni, N. L., Loh, C., Blackwell, L. M., … Pashdag, J. (2001). The evaluation of a sexual assault risk reduction program: A multisite investigation. *Journal of Consulting and Clinical Psychology, 69,* 1073–1078.

Gidycz, C. A., Orchowski, L. M., & Berkowitz, A. D. (2011). Preventing sexual aggression among college men: An evaluation of a social norms and bystander intervention program. *Violence Against Women, 17*(6), 720–742.

Goldkamp, J. S., Weiland, D., Collins, M., & White, M. (1996). *Role of drug and alcohol abuse in domestic violence and its treatment: Dade County's domestic violence experiment, appendices to the final report.* Washington, DC: U.S. Department of Justice.

Goldman, R. (2010, March 29). *Teens indicted after allegedly taunting girl who hanged herself.* Retrieved from http://abcnews.go.com/Technology/TheLaw/teens-charged-bullying-massgirl-kill/story?id=10231357

Gonzales, A. R., Schofield, R. B., & Gillis, J. W. (2001). *Responding to victims of terrorism and mass violence crimes: Coordination and collaboration between American Red Cross workers and crime victim service providers.* Washington, DC: U.S. Department of Justice, Office for Victims of Crime. Retrieved from http://www.ojp.usdoj.gov/ovc/publications/infores/redcross/ncj209681.pdf

Goodlin, W. E., & Dunn, C. S. (2010). Three patterns of domestic violence in households: Single victimization, repeat victimization, and co-occurring victimization. *Journal of Family Violence, 25,* 107–122.

Goodman, L., Thompson, K., Weinfurt, K., Corl, S., Acker, P., Mueser, K., & Rosenberg, S. D. (1999). Reliability of reports of violent victimization and PTSD among men and women with SMI. *Journal of Traumatic Stress, 12,* 587–599.

Goodman, L. A., Salyers, M. P., Mueser, K. T., Rosenberg, S. D., Swartz, M., Essock, S. M., ... Vidaver, R. M. (2001). Recent victimization in women and men with severe mental illness: Prevalence and correlates. *Journal of Traumatic Stress, 14,* 615–632.

Gottfredson, M. R., & Hirschi, T. (1990). *A general theory of crime.* Stanford, CA: Stanford University Press.

Gover, A., MacDonald, J., & Alpert, G. (2003). Combating domestic violence: Findings from an evaluation of a local domestic violence court. *Criminology & Public Policy, 3,* 109–132.

Gozdziak, E. M., & Collett, E. A. (2005). Research on human trafficking in North America: A review of literature. *International Migration, 43,* 1–2.

Greenfeld, L., & Henneberg, M. (2000). *Alcohol, crime, and the criminal justice system.* Paper commissioned for the Alcohol Policy XII Conference, Washington, DC.

Grills, A. E., & Ollendick, T. H. (2002). Peer victimization, global self-worth, and anxiety in middle school children. *Journal of Clinical Child and Adolescent Psychology, 31,* 59–68.

Groff, E. R. (2007). Simulation for theory testing and experimentation: An example using routine activity theory and street robbery. *Journal of Quantitative Criminology, 23,* 75–103.

Grothaus, R. S. (1985). Abuse of women with disabilities. In S. E. Brown, D. Connors, & N. Stern (Eds.), *With the power of each breath: A disabled woman's anthology* (1st ed., pp. 124–132). Pittsburg, PA: Cleiss.

Gruszczynska, B., Lucia, S., & Killias, M. (2012). Juvenile victimization from an international perspective. In J. Junger-Tas, I. H. Marshall, D. Enzmann, M. Killias, M. Steketee, & B. Gruszczynska (Eds.), *Many faces of youth crime* (pp. 95–116). New York, NY: Springer.

Gundy-Yoder, A. V. (2010). Victims' rights legislation, federal, United States. In B. S. Fisher & S. P. Lab (Eds.), *Encyclopedia of victimology and crime prevention* (Vol. 2, pp. 1012–1013). Thousand Oaks, CA: Sage.

Gurwitch, R. H., Pfefferbaum, B., & Leftwich, M. T. J. (2002). The impact of terrorism on children: Considerations for a new era. *Journal of Trauma Practice, 1,* 101–124.

Guterman, N. B., & Lee, Y. (2005). The role of fathers in risk for physical child abuse and neglect: Possible pathways and unanswered questions. *Child Maltreatment, 10,* 136–149.

Hahn, J. W., McCormick, M. C., Silverman, J. G., Robinson, E. B., & Koenen, K. C. (2014). Examining the impact of disability status on intimate partner violence victimization in a population sample. *Journal of Interpersonal Violence.* doi:10.1177/0886260514534527.

Hancocks, P. (2012, February 20). *2 teens sent to prison for S. Korean bullying suicide.* Retrieved from http://articles.cnn.com/2012-02-20/asia/world_asia_south-korea-bulling-sentence_1_prison-terms-suicide-note-online-games?_s=PM:ASIA

Hanson, K. A., & Gidycz, C. A. (1993). Evaluation of a sexual assault prevention program. *Journal of Consulting and Clinical Psychology, 61,* 1046–1052.

Hard, S. (1986). *Sexual abuse of the developmentally disabled: A case study.* Paper presented at the National Conference of Executives of Associations for Retarded Citizens, Omaha, NE.

Harlow, C. W. (2005). *Hate crimes reported by victims and police* (Special report, NCJ 20991). Washington, DC: U.S. Department of Justice, Bureau of Justice Statistics.

Harper, D. W., & Voigt, L. (2007). Homicide followed by suicide: An integrated theoretical perspective. *Homicide Studies, 11*(4), 295–318.

Harper, S. (2014, April 3). *PM announces historic legislation to create a Canadian Victims Bill of Rights.* Retrieved from http://www.pm.gc.ca/eng/news/2014/04/03/pm-announces-historic-legislation-create-canadian-victims-bill-rights#sthash.XxHkKWsX.dpuf

Harrell, E. (2014). *Crimes against persons with disabilities, 2009–2012 statistical tables* (Report No. NCJ 244525). Washington, DC: Bureau of Justice Statistics, U.S. Department of Justice.

Harrell, E., & Langton, L. (2013). *Victims of identity theft, 2012* (Report No. NCJ 243779). Washington, DC: Bureau of Justice Statistics, U.S. Department of Justice.

Harrell, E., & Rand, M. (2010). *Disabilities and victimization: NCVS statistical overview.* Retrieved from http://bjs.ojp.usdoj.gov/content/pub/pdf/capd08.pdf

Hart, T. C. (2007). Violent victimization of college students: Findings from the National Crime Victimization Survey. In J. Sloan & B. Fisher (Eds.), *Campus crime: Legal, social, and policy perspectives* (2nd ed., pp. 129–146). Springfield, IL: Charles C Thomas.

Hartley, D., Biddle, E., & Jenkins, L. (2005). Societal cost of workplace homicides in the United States. *American Journal of Industrial Medicine, 47,* 518–527.

Hartman, J. L., & Alligood, K. (2010). Protection/restraining orders. In B. S. Fisher & S. P. Lab (Eds.), *Encyclopedia of victimology and crime prevention* (Vol. 2, pp. 688–689). Thousand Oaks, CA: Sage.

Hartman, J. L., & Belknap, J. (2003). Beyond the gatekeepers: Court professionals' self-reported attitudes about experiences with misdemeanor domestic violence cases. *Criminal Justice and Behavior, 30,* 349–373.

Hart, T. C., & Rennison, C. (2003). *Reporting crime to the police, 1992–2000.* Washington, DC: United States Bureau of Justice Statistics.

Hay, C., Meldrum, R., & Mann, K. (2010). Traditional bullying, cyber bullying, and deviance: A general strain theory approach. *Journal of Contemporary Criminal Justice, 26,* 130–147.

Haynie, D. L. (1998). Explaining the gender gap in fear of crime over time, 1970–1995: A methodological approach. *Criminal Justice Review, 23,* 29–50.

Haynie, D. L., Nansel, T., Eitel, P., Crump, A. D., Saylor, K., Yu, K., & Simmons-Morton, B. (2001). Bullies, victims, and bully/victims: Distinct groups of at-risk youth. *Journal of Early Adolescence, 21,* 29–49.

Headden, S. (1996, July 1). Guns, money & medicine. *U.S. News & World Report, 121,* 31–40.

Heide, K. M. (2013). Patricide and steppatricide victims and offenders: An empirical analysis of US arrest data. *International Journal of Offender Therapy and Comparative Criminology.* doi:10.1177/0306624X13495168.

Henning, K., Renauer, B., & Holdford, R. (2006). Victim or offender? Heterogeneity among women arrested for intimate partner violence. *Journal of Family Violence, 21,* 351–368.

Hensley, C., Koscheski, M., & Tewksbury, R. (2005). Examining the characteristics of sexual assault targets in maximum security prisons. *Journal of Interpersonal Violence, 40,* 667–697.

Hensley, C., Tewksbury, R., & Castle, T. (2003). Characteristics of prison sexual assault targets in male Oklahoma correctional facilities. *Journal of Interpersonal Violence, 18,* 595–606.

Herek, G. M. (2009). Hate crimes and stigma-related experiences among sexual minority adults in the United States: Prevalence estimates from a national probability sample. *Journal of Interpersonal Violence, 24,* 54–74.

Herek, G. M., Gillis, J. R., & Cogan, J. C. (1999). Psychological sequelae of hate crime victimization among lesbian, gay, and bisexual adults. *Journal of Consulting and Clinical Psychology, 67,* 945–951.

Herek, G. H., Gillis, J. R., Cogan, J. C., & Glunt, E. K. (1997). Hate crime victimization among lesbians, gay, and bisexual adults: Prevalence, psychological correlates, and methological issues. *Journal of Interpersonal Violence, 12,* 195–215.

Herkov, M. J., & Biernat, M. (1997). Assessment of PTSD symptoms in a community exposed to serial murder. *Journal of Clinical Psychology, 53,* 809–815.

Herman, S. (2004, April 28). *Supporting and protecting victims: Making it happen.* Retrieved from http://www.victimsofcrime.org/media/newsroom/speeches-and-testimony/support-and-protecting-victims-making-it-happen

Hewitt, C. (1988). The costs of terrorism: A cross-national study of six countries. *Studies in Conflict and Terrorism, 11,* 169–180.

Heyman, R. E., & Smith, A. (2002). Do child abuse and interparental violence lead to adulthood family violence? *Journal of Marriage and Family, 64,* 864–870.

Hiday, V. A. (1997). Understanding the connection between mental illness and violence. *International Journal of Law and Psychiatry, 20,* 399–417.

Hiday, V. A., Swartz, M. S., Swanson, J. W., Borum, R., & Wagner, H. R. (1999). Criminal victimization of persons with severe mental illness. *Psychiatric Services, 50,* 62–68.

Hiday, V. A., Swartz, M. S., Swanson, J. W., Borum, R., & Wagner, H. R. (2002). Impact of outpatient commitment on victimization of people with severe mental illness. *American Journal of Psychiatry, 159,* 1403–1411.

Hindelang, M. J., Gottfredson, M. R., & Garofalo, J. (1978). *Victims of personal crime: An empirical foundation for a theory of personal victimization.* Cambridge, MA: Ballinger.

Hirschel, D. (2008, July 25). *Domestic violence cases: What research shows about arrest and dual arrest rates.* Washington, DC: National Institute of Justice.

Hirschel, D., Buzawa, E., Pattavina, A., Faggiani, D., & Reuland, M. (2007, May). *Explaining the prevalence, context, and consequences of dual arrest in intimate partner cases.* Washington, DC: U.S. Department of Justice.

Hirschel, J., Dean, C., & Lumb, R. (1994). The relative contribution of domestic violence to assault and injury of police officers. *Justice Quarterly, 11,* 99–117.

Hodge, P. D. (1999). National law enforcement programs to prevent, detect, investigate and prosecute elder abuse and neglect in healthcare facilities. *Journal of Elder Abuse and Neglect, 9,* 23–41.

Holt, T. J., & Bossler, A. M. (2009). Examining the applicability of lifestyle-routine activities theory for cybercrime victimization. *Deviant Behavior, 30,* 1–25.

Holtfreter, K., Reisig, M. D., Mears, D. P., & Wolfe, S. E. (2014). *Financial exploitation of the elderly in a consumer context.* Washington, DC: National Institute of Justice.

Howard, D. E., Griffin, M. A., & Boekeloo, B. O. (2008). Prevalence and psychosocial correlates of alcohol-related sexual assault among university students. *Adolescence, 43,*733–750.

Howell, E., Bieler, S., & Anderson, N. (2014). *State variation in hospital use and cost of firearm assault injury, 2010.* Washington, DC: Urban Institute.

Howley, S., & Dorris, C. (2007). Legal rights for crime victims in the criminal justice system. In R. C. Davis, A. J. Lurigio, & S. Herman (Eds.), *Victims of crime* (3rd ed., pp. 299–314). Thousand Oaks, CA: Sage.

Howton, A. J. (2010). Sexual assault response team (SART). In B. S. Fisher & S. P. Lab (Eds.), *Encyclopedia of victimology and crime prevention* (Vol. 2, pp. 855–856). Thousand Oaks, CA: Sage.

Hudson, C. G. (2005). Socioeconomic status and mental illness: Tests of the social causation and selection hypotheses. *American Journal of Orthopsychiatry, 75,* 3–18.

Human Rights Watch. (2001). *Violence against women and honor crimes.* Retrieved from http://www.hrw.org/press/2001/04/un_oral12_0405.htm

Human Rights Watch. (2012, July 20). World court: Important victory for Habré victims. *Human Rights Watch.* Retrieved from http://www.hrw.org/news/2012/07/20/world-court-important-victory-habr-victims

Identity Theft and Assumption Deterrence Act of 1998, Pub. L. 105-318 (1998).

Insurance Information Institute. (2011, June). *Auto theft*. Retrieved from http://www.iii.org/media/hottopics/insurance/test4/

Insurance Institute for Highway Safety. (2013, August 8). *Ford F-250 has highest theft rate of any 2010–2012 model. Status Report, 48*. Retrieved from http://www.iihs.org/iihs/sr/statusreport/article/48/6/3

International Court of Justice. (n.d.-a). *The court*. Retrieved from http://www.icj-cij.org/court/index.php?p1=1

International Court of Justice. (n.d.-b). *How the court works*. Retrieved from http://www.icj-cij.org/court/index.php?p1=1

International Day of Innocent Children Victims of Aggression. (2012). *SOS Children's Villages Canada*. Retrieved from http://www.soschildrensvillages.ca/news/news/child-protection-news/child-rights-news/pages/inno-cent-children-aggression-298.aspx

International Victimology Institute Tilburg. (2014). *About INTERVICT*. Retrieved from Tilburg University website: https://www.tilburguniversity.edu/research/institutes-and-research-groups/intervict/about/

Irwin, J. (1980). *Prisons in turmoil*. Boston, MA: Little, Brown.

Iyengar, R. (2007, August 7). The protection battered spouses don't need (Editorial). *New York Times*. Retrieved from http://www.nytimes.com/2007/08/07/opinion/07iyengar.html

Jacques, S., & Wright, R. (2008). Intimacy with outlaws: The role of relational distance in recruiting, paying, and interviewing underworld research participants. *Journal of Research in Crime and Delinquency, 45*(1), 22–38.

Janoff-Bulman, R. (1979). Characterological versus behavioral self-blame: Inquiries into depression and rape. *Journal of Personality and Social Psychology, 37*, 1798–1809.

Jaquier, V. (2010). The role of the gay male and lesbian community. In B. S. Fisher & S. P. Lab (Eds.), *Encyclopedia of victimology and crime prevention* (Vol. 1, pp. 313–314). Thousand Oaks, CA: Sage.

Jenkins, E. L. (2010). Workplace violence, United States. In B. S. Fisher & S. P. Lab (Eds.), *Encyclopedia of victimology and crime prevention* (Vol. 2, pp. 1078–1084). Thousand Oaks, CA: Sage.

Jennings, W. G., Park, M., Tomscih, E., Gover, A., & Akers, R. L. (2011). Assessing the overlap in dating violence perpetration and victimization among South Korean college students: The influence of social learning and self-control. *American Journal of Criminal Justice, 36*, 188–206.

Jennings, W. G., Piquero, A. R., & Reingle, J. M. (2012). On the overlap between victimization and offending: A review of the literature. *Aggression and Violent Behavior, 17*(1), 16–26.

Jerin, R. A., Moriarty, L. J., & Gibson, M. A. (1996). Victim service or self-service: An analysis of prosecution-based victim-witness assistance programs and services. *Criminal Justice Policy Review, 7*, 142–154.

Jesperson, A., Lalumiere, M. L., & Seto, M. C. (2009). Sexual abuse history among adult sex offenders: A meta-analysis. *Child Abuse and Neglect, 33*(3), 179–192.

Johnson, H., Ollus, N., & Nevala, S. (2008a, Feb. 28). *Getting the facts to make the change: The International Violence Against Women Survey*. Retrieved from http://www.un.org/womenwatch/daw/csw/csw52/stmt/dawparallelevents/IVAWS%20Holly%20Johnson.pdf

Johnson, H., Ollus, N., & Nevala, S. (2008b). Methodology of the International Violence Against Women Survey. In H. Johnson, N. Ollus, & S. Nevala (Eds.), *Violence against women* (pp.17–31). New York, NY: Springer.

Johnson, I., & Sigler, R. (2000). Forced sexual intercourse among intimates. *Journal of Family Violence, 15*, 95–108.

Johnson, M. P. (2006). Conflict and control: Gender symmetry and asymmetry in domestic violence. *Violence Against Women, 12*, 1003–1018.

Johnson, M. P. (2011). Gender and types of intimate partner violence: A response to an anti-feminist literature review. *Aggression and Violent Behavior, 16*, 289–296.

Johnson, S. D., Bernasco, W., Bowers, K. J., Elffers, H., Ratcliffe, J., Rengert, G., & Townsley, M. (2007). Space-time patterns of risk: A cross national assessment of residential burglary victimization. *Journal of Quantitative Criminology, 23*, 201–219.

Johnson, S. D., & Bowers, K. J. (2004). The burglary as clue to the future: The beginnings of prospective hot-spotting. *European Journal of Criminology, 1*, 237–255.

Johnson, M., & Kercher, G. (2009, January). *Personal victimization of college students*. Huntsville, TX: Crime Victims' Institute, Criminal Justice Center, Sam Houston State University. Retrieved from http://www.crimevictimsinstitute.org/documents/CSVictimizationFinal.pdf

Johnson, R. J., Rew, L., & Sternglanz, W. (2006). The relationship between childhood sexual abuse and sexual health practices of homeless adolescents. *Adolescence, 41*, 221–234.

Johnstone, G. (2002). *Restorative justice: Ideas, values, debates*. Portland, OR: Willan.

Jordan, C. (2004). Intimate partner violence and the justice system: An examination of the interface. *Journal of Interpersonal Violence, 19*, 1412–1434.

Jozkowski, K. N., & Sanders, S. A. (2012). Health and sexual outcomes of women who have experienced forced or coercive sex. *Women & Health, 52*, 101–188.

Junger-Tas, J., Haen Marshall, I., Enzmann, D., Killias, M., Steketee, & Gruszczynska, B. (2010). History and design of the ISRD Studies. Pp. 1-11. In Juvenile Delinquency in Europe and Beyond, edited by J. Junger-Tas, H. I. Marshall, D. Enzmann, M. Killias, M. Steketee, and B. Gruszcznska. New York: Springer.

Kang, S., Magura, S., Laudet, A., & Whitney, S. (1999). Adverse effect of child abuse victimization among substance-using women in treatment. *Journal of Interpersonal Violence, 14*, 657–670.

Kanno, H., & Newhill, C. (2009). Social workers and battered women: The need to study client violence in the domestic field. *Journal of Aggression, Maltreatment and Trauma, 18*, 46–63.

Karmodi, O. (2011, October 31). *Hit, kicked and bruised: Beatings at Russian women's prison caught on video*. Retrieved from http://observers.france24.com/content/20111031-russia-amur-hit-kicked-bruised-beatings-women-prison-caught-video

Kastsoris, N. C. (1990). The European Convention on the Compensation of Victims of Violent Crimes: A decade of frustration. *Fordham International Law Journal, 14*(1) 186–215.

Kaufman, M. T. (1998, April 18). Marvin E. Wolfgang, 73, dies; leading figure in criminology. *The New York Times*. Retrieved from http://www.nytimes.com/1998/04/18/us/marvin-e-wolfgang-73-dies-leading-figure-in-criminology.html

Keilitz, S., Hannaford, P., & Efkeman, H. (1997). *Civil protection orders: The benefits and limitations for victims of domestic violence*. Williamsburg, VA: National Center for State Courts. Retrieved from http://www.ncjrs.gov/pdffiles1/pr/172223.pdf

Kelley, B. T., Thornberry, T. P., & Smith, C. A. (1997). In the wake of child maltreatment. *Juvenile Justice Bulletin*. Washington, DC: Office of Juvenile Justice and Delinquency Prevention, U.S. Department of Justice

Kennard, K. L. (1989). The victim's veto: A way to increase victim impact on criminal case dispositions. *California Law Review, 77,* 417.

Kerley, K. R., Hochstetler, A., & Copes, H. (2009). Self-control, prison victimization, and prison infractions. *Criminal Justice Review, 34,* 553–568.

Kessler, R. C., Sonnega, A., Bromet, E., Hughes, M., & Nelson, C. B. (1995). Posttraumatic stress disorder in the National Comorbidity Survey. *Archives of General Psychiatry, 52,* 1048–1060.

Kilchling, M. (n.d.). *Victims of terrorism: An overview on international legislation on the support and compensation for victims of terrorists threats*. Retrieved from http://www.humsec.eu/cms/fileadmin/user_upload/humsec/SAc_06_PPP/PPP_Kilchling_victims_of_terrorism.pdf

Kilpatrick, D. G., & Acierno, R. (2003). Mental health needs of crime victims: Epidemiology and outcomes. *Journal of Traumatic Stress, 16,* 119–132.

Kilpatrick, D. G., Amick, A., & Resnick, H. S. (1990). *The impact of homicide on surviving family members*. Charleston: Crime Victims Research and Treatment Center, Medical University of South Carolina.

Kilpatrick, D.G., Edmunds, C., & Seymour, A. (1992). *Rape in America: A report to the nation*. Charleston, SC: National Victim Center & the Crime Victims Research and Treatment Center, Medical University of South Carolina.

Kilpatrick, D. G., Resnick, H. S., Ruggiero, K., Conoscenti, L. M., & McCauley, J. (2007). *Drug facilitated, incapacitated, and forcible rape: A national study*. Washington, DC: U.S. Department of Justice.

Kilpatrick, D. G., & Tidwell, R. (1989). *Victims' rights and services in South Carolina: The dream, the law, the reality*. Charleston: Crime Victims Research and Treatment Center, Medical University of South Carolina.

King, R. D. (2007). The context of minority group threat: Race, institutions and complying with hate crime law. *Law and Society, 41,* 36–41.

Kirchhoff, G. F. (2010). History and a theoretical structure of victimology. In S. G. Shoham, P. Knepper, & M. Kett (Eds.), *International handbook of victimology* (pp. 95–123). Boca Raton, Florida: CRC Press.

Klaus, P. A., & Maston, C. T. (2008). *Criminal victimization in the United States, 2006*. Washington, DC: Bureau of Justice Statistics. Retrieved from http://bjs.ojp.usdoj.gov/index.cfm?ty=pbdetail&iid=1094

Klein, L. (2010). Victim compensation. In B. S. Fisher & S. P. Lab (Eds.), *Encyclopedia of victimology and crime prevention* (Vol. 2, pp. 971–974). Thousand Oaks, CA: Sage.

Klevens, J., Duque, L. F., & Ramírez, C. (2002). The victim-perpetrator overlap and routine activities results from a cross-sectional study in Bogotá, Colombia. *Journal of Interpersonal Violence, 17*(2), 206–216.

Knauer, S. (2002). *Recovering from sexual abuse, addictions, and compulsive behaviors: "Numb", survivors*. Binghamton, NY: Haworth Social Work Practice Press.

Knowles, G. J. (1999). Male prison rape: A search for causation and prevention. *Howard Journal of Criminal Justice, 38,* 267–282.

Kochenderfer, B. J., & Ladd, G. W. (1996). Peer victimization: Cause or consequence of school maladjustment? *Child Development, 67,* 1305–1317.

Koen, A. (2014, September 3). *Scam victim opens up to warn others about elder abuse*. Retrieved from http://www.koaa.com/news/scam-victim-opens-up-to-warn-others-about-elder-abuse/

Koss, M. P. (1985). The hidden rape victim. *Psychology of Women Quarterly, 48,* 193–212.

Koss, M. P. (1988). Hidden rape. In A. W. Burgess (Ed.), *Rape and sexual assault* (pp. 3–25). New York, NY: Garland.

Koss, M. P., Abey, A., Campbell, R., Cook, S., Norris, J., Testa, M., … White, J. (2007). Revising the SES: A collaborative process to improve assessment of sexual aggression and victimization. *Psychology of Women Quarterly, 31,* 357–370.

Koss, M. P., Gidycz, C. A., & Wisniewski, N. (1987). The scope of rape: Incidence and prevalence of sexual aggression and victimization in a national sample of higher education students. *Journal of Consulting and Clinical Psychology, 55,* 162–170.

Kotz, P. (2010, January 28). *Phoebe Prince, 15, commits suicide after onslaught of cyber-bullying from fellow students*. Retrieved from http://www.truecrimereport.com/2010/01/phoebe_prince_15_commits_suici.php

Krasnoff, M., & Moscati, R. (2002). Domestic violence screening and referral can be effective. *Annals of Emergency Medicine, 40,* 485–492.

Kunst, M., Winkel, F. W., & Bogaers, S. (2010). Prevalence and predictors of posttraumatic stress disorder among victims of violence applying for state compensation. *Journal of Interpersonal Violence, 25,* 1634–1654.

LaFree, G., Morris, N. A., & Dugan, L. (2010). Cross-national patterns of terrorism: Comparing trajectories for total, attributed and fatal attacks, 1970–2006. *Global Perspectives, 50,* 622–649.

LaGrange, R. L., Ferraro, K. F., & Supancic, M. (1992). Perceived risk and fear of crime: Role of social and physical incivilities. *Journal of Research in Crime and Delinquency, 29,* 311–334.

Lahm, K. F. (2009). Physical and property victimization behind bars: A multilevel examination. *International Journal of Offender Therapy and Comparative Criminology, 53,* 348–365.

Langton, L., & Planty, M. (2010). Victims of identity theft, 2008. *National Crime Victimization Survey Supplement,* 1–19.

Lasley, J. R., & Rosenbaum, J. L. (1988). Routine activities and multiple personal victimization. *Sociology and Social Research, 73,* 47–50.

Laub, J. H., & Lauritsen, J. L. (1998). The interdependence of school violence with neighborhood and family conditions. In D. S. Elliott, B. A. Hamburg, & K. R. Williams (Eds.), *Violence in American schools* (pp. 127–158). New York, NY: Cambridge University Press.

Laumann, E. I., Leitsch, S. A., & Waite, L. J. (2008). Elder mistreatment in the United States: Prevalence estimates from a nationally representative study. *Journal of Gerontology, Social Sciences, 63,* S248–S254.

Lauritsen, J., & Davis Quinet, K. F. (1995). Repeat victimization among adolescents and young adults. *Journal of Quantitative Criminology, 11,* 143–166.

Lauritsen, J. L., Laub, J. H., & Sampson, R. J. (1992). Conventional and delinquent activities: Implications for the prevention of violent victimization among adolescents. *Violence and Victims, 7,* 91–108.

Lauritsen, J. L., Sampson, R. J., & Laub, J. H. (1991). The link between offending and victimization among adolescents. *Criminology, 29*(2), 265–292.

Layman, M., Gidycz, C. A., & Lynn, S. J. (1996). Unacknowledged versus acknowledged rape victims: Situational factors and posttraumatic stress. *Journal of Abnormal Psychology, 105,* 124–131.

Lehner-Zimmerer, M. (2011). Future challenges of international victimology. *African Journal of Criminology & Justice Studies, 4*(2), 13–27.

Levin, A. (2005). People with mental illness more often crime victims. *Psychiatric News, 40,* 16.

Levin, B., & Amster, S. (2007). Making hate history: Hate crime and policing in America's most diverse city. *American Behavioral Scientist, 51,* 319–348.

Levin, R. (2002). *September 11 Victim Compensation Fund: A model for compensating terrorism victims?* Retrieved from http://www.kentlaw.edu/honorsscholars/2002students/Levin.html

Levitt, S. D. (1999). The limited role of changing age structure in explaining aggregate crime rates. *Criminology, 37*(3), 581–598.

Levy, M. P., & Tartaro, C. (2010). Auto theft: A site-survey and analysis of environmental crime factors in Atlantic City, NJ. *Security Journal, 23,* 75–94.

Limber, S. P., & Small, M. A. (2003). State laws and policies to address bullying in U.S. schools. *School Psychology Review, 32,* 445–455.

Linden, R., & Chaturvedi, R. (2005). The need for comprehensive crime prevention planning: The case of motor vehicle theft. *Canadian Journal of Criminology and Criminal Justice, 47,* 251–270.

Lindgren, M., & Nikolić-Ristanović, V. (2011). *Crime victims: International and Serbian perspective.* Belgrade, Serbia: Organization for Security and Cooperation in Europe, Mission to Serbia, Law Enforcement Department.

Link, B., Monahan, J., Stueve, A., & Cullen, F. T. (1999). Real in their consequences: A sociological approach to understanding the association between psychotic symptoms and violence. *American Sociological Review, 64,* 316–332.

Littel, K. (2001). Sexual assault nurse examiner programs: Improving the community response to sexual assault victims. *Office for Victims of Crime Bulletin, 4,* 1–19.

Little, L. (2002). Middle-class mothers' perceptions of peer and sibling victimization among children with Asperger's syndrome and nonverbal learning disorders. *Issues in Comprehensive Pediatric Nursing, 25,* 43–57.

Littleton, H. L., Axson, D., Breitkopf, C. R., & Berenson, A. (2006). Rape acknowledgment and postassault experiences: How acknowledgment status relates to disclosure, coping, worldview, and reactions received from others. *Violence and Victims, 21,* 761–778.

Logan, T. K., Walker, R., & Hunt, G. (2009). Understanding human trafficking in the United States. *Trauma, Violence & Abuse, 10,* 3–30.

LoJack. (2011). *How it works.* Retrieved from http://www.lojack.com/why/pages/how-lojack-works.aspx

Lonsway, K. A., Archambault, J., & Berkowitz, A. B. (2007). *False reports: Moving beyond the issue to successfully investigate and prosecute non-stranger sexual assault.* San Luis Obispo, CA: EVAW International.

Lonsway, K. A., & Fitzgerald, L. F. (1994). Rape Myths. In Review. Psychology of Women Quarterly, 18, 133-64.

Lord, V. B. (1998). Characteristics of violence in state government. *Journal of Interpersonal Violence, 13,* 489–503.

Luckenbill, D. F. (1977). Criminal homicide as a situated transaction. *Social Problems, 25*(2), 176–186.

Lynch, D. R. (1997). The nature of occupational stress among public defenders. *Justice System Journal, 19,* 17–35.

Lyon, E., & Lane, S. (2009). *Meeting survivors' needs: A multi-state study of domestic violence shelter experiences.* Harrisburg, PA: National Resource Center on Domestic Violence and UConn School of Social Work.

Lyon, E., Lane, S., & Menard, A. (2008, October). Review of relevant literature. In E. Lyon & S. Lane, (Eds.), *Meeting survivors' needs: A multi-state study of domestic violence shelter experiences* (pp. 22–26). Harrisburg, PA: National Resource Center on Domestic Violence. Retrieved from http://new.vawnet.org/Assoc_Files_VAWnet/MeetingSurvivorsNeeds-FullReport.pdf

Lyons, C. J. (2007). Community (dis)organization and racially motivated crime. *American Journal of Sociology, 113,* 815–863.

Maier, S. L. (2008). Are rape crisis centers feminist organizations? *Feminist Criminology, 3,* 82–100.

Maldonado-Molina, M. M., Jennings, W. G., Tobler, A. L., Piquero, A. R., & Canino, G. (2010). Assessing victim-offender overlap among Hispanic youth. *Journal of Criminal Justice, 38,* 1191–1201.

Maldonado-Molina, M. M., Piquero, A. R., Jennings, W. G., Bird, H. R., & Canino, G. J. (2009). Trajectories of delinquent behaviors among Puerto Rican children and adolescents at two sites. *Journal of Research in Crime & Delinquency, 46,* 144–181.

Maltz, W. (2001). *The sexual healing journey: A guide for survivors of sexual abuse.* New York, NY: HarperCollins.

Marge, D. K. (2003). *A call to action: Ending crimes of violence against children and adults with disabilities: A report to the nation.* Syracuse, NY: State University of New York Upstate Medical University, Department of Physical Medicine and Rehabilitation.

Margolin, L. (1992). Child abuse by mothers' boyfriends: Why the overrepresentation? *Child Abuse & Neglect, 16,* 541–551.

Maroney, T. A. (1998). The struggle against hate crime: Movement at a crossroads. *NYU Law Review, 73,* 564–620.

Marshall, I. H., & Maljevic, A. (2013). Editors' introduction: Theoretical and methodological insights from the second International Self-Report Study of Delinquency (ISRD-2). *Journal of Contemporary Criminal Justice, 29*(1), 4–12.

Marshall, T. F. (1999). *Restorative justice: An overview.* London, UK: Home Office, Research Development and Statistics Division.

Martin, G., Bergen, H. A., Richardson, A. S., Roeger, L., & Allison, S. (2004). Sexual abuse and suicidality: Gender differences in a large community sample of adolescents. *Child Abuse & Neglect, 28,* 491–503.

Martin, S. L., Ray, N., Sotres-Alvarez, D., Kupper, L. L., Moracco, K. E., Dickens, P. A., … Gizlice, Z. (2006). Physical and sexual assault of women with disabilities. *Violence Against Women, 12,* 823–837.

Marx, B. P., Calhoun, K. S., Wilson, A. E., & Meyerson, L. A. (2001). Sexual revictimization prevention: An outcome evaluation. *Journal of Consulting and Clinical Psychology, 69,* 25–32.

Maryland Crime Victims' Resource Center. (2007). *MCVRC mission.* Retrieved from http://www.mdcrimevictims.org/

Maston, C. T. (2010, March 2). *Criminal victimization in the United States, 2007.* Washington, DC: Bureau of Justice Statistics. Retrieved from http://bjs.ojp.usdoj.gov/index.cfm?ty=pbdetail&iid=1743

Matthias, R. E., & Benjamin, A. E. (2003). Abuse and neglect of clients in agency-based and consumer-directed home care. *Health & Social Work, 28,* 174–184.

Max Planck Institute for Foreign and International Criminal Law. (2013). *History and development of the institute.* Retrieved from http://www.mpicc.de/ww/en/pub/organisation/ueberblick/institutsgeschichte.htm

Max-Planck-Institut für Strafrecht. (2014). *Victim rights and compensation in an international comparison: France, Austria, Germany.* Retrieved from http://www.mpicc.de/ww/en/pub/forschung/forschungsarbeit/kriminologie/archiv/victim_rights.htm

Maxwell, C., Garner, J., & Fagan, J. (2001). *The effects of arrest on intimate partner violence: New evidence from the Spouse Assault Replication Program.* Washington, DC: National Institute of Justice. Retrieved from http://www.ncjrs.gov/txtfiles1/nij/188199.txt

May, D. (2010). Victimization of school teachers/staff. In B. S. Fisher & S. P. Lab (Eds.), *Encyclopedia of victimology and crime prevention* (Vol. 2, pp. 833–835). Thousand Oaks, CA: Sage.

May, D. C., Rader, N. E., & Goodrum, S. (2010). A gendered assessment of the "threat of victimization": Examining gender differences in fear of crime, perceived risk, avoidance, and defensive behaviors. *Criminal Justice Review, 35,* 159–182.

McCabe, A., & Manian, S. (2010). *Sex trafficking: A global perspective.* Plymouth, UK: Lexington Books.

McCartney, J. R., & Campbell, V. A. (1998). Confirmed abuse cases in public residential facilities for persons with mental retardation: A multi-state study. *Mental Retardation, 36,* 465–473.

McClellan, D. S., Farabee, D., & Crouch, B. M. (1997). Early victimization, drug use, and criminality: A comparison of male and female prisoners. *Criminal Justice and Behavior, 24,* 455–476.

McCold, P., & Wachtel, B. (1998). *Restorative policing experiment: The Bethlehem Pennsylvania Police Family Group Conferencing Project.* Bethlehem, PA: Real Justice.

McCorkle, R. C. (1992). Personal precautions to violence in prison. *Criminal Justice and Behavior, 19,* 160–173.

McFarlane, J., Hughes, R. B., Nosek, M. A., Groff, J. Y., Swedlend, N., & Dolan Mullen, P. (2001). Abuse Assessment Screen-Disability (AAS-D): Measuring frequency, type, and perpetrator of abuse toward women with physical disabilities. *Journal of Women's Health and Gender-Based Medicine, 10,* 861–866.

McGarrell, E., Olivares, K., Crawford, K., & Kroovand, N. (2000). *Returning justice to the community: The Indianapolis Juvenile Restorative Justice Experiment.* Indianapolis, IN: Hudson Institute.

McMullin, D., Wirth, R. J., & White, J. W. (2007). The impact of sexual victimization on personality: A longitudinal study. *Sex Roles, 56,* 403–414.

Medica Zenica (2014). History. Retrieved from: http://medicazenica.org/uk/index.php?option=com_content&view=article&id=48&ltemid=30.

Mele, M. (2009). The time course of repeat intimate partner violence. *Journal of Family Violence, 24,* 619–624.

Menard, S. (2002, February). *Short- and long-term consequences of adolescent victimization.* Youth Violence Research Bulletin. Washington, DC: U.S. Department of Justice, Office of Juvenile Justice and Delinquency Prevention.

Mendelsohn, B. (1947, March). *New biopsychosocial horizons: Victimology.* Paper presented to the Psychiatric Society of Bucharest, Coltzea State Hospital, Hungary.

Mertl, S. (2012, June 12). Toronto Eaton Centre shooting shines light on Canada's gang problem. *The Daily Brew.* Retrieved from http://ca.news.yahoo.com/blogs/dailybrew/toronto-eaton-centre-shooting-shines-light-canada-gang-202058661.html

Messman-Moore, T. L., & Long, P. J. (2002). Alcohol and substance abuse disorders as predictors of child to adult sexual revictimization in a sample of community women. *Violence and Victims, 17,* 319–340.

Meyers, T. W. (2002). Policing and sexual assault: Strategies for successful victim interviews. In L. J. Moriarty & M. L. Dantzker (Eds.), *Policing and victims* (pp. 57–73). Upper Saddle River, NJ: Pearson.

Miller, E., Decker, M. R., Silverman, J. G., & Raj, A. (2007). Migration, sexual exploitation and women's health: A case report from a community health center. *Violence Against Women, 13,* 486–497.

Miller, H. V., & Miller, J. M. (2010). School-based bullying prevention. In B. S. Fisher & S. P. Lab (Eds.), *Encyclopedia of victimology and crime prevention* (Vol. 2, pp. 817–819). Thousand Oaks, CA: Sage.

Miller, L. (2004). Psychotherapeutic interventions for survivors of terrorism. *American Journal of Psychiatry, 58,* 1–16.

Miller, T. R., Cohen, M. A., & Wiersema, B. (1996). *Victim costs and consequences: A new look.* Washington, DC: United States National Institute of Justice.

Millett, L. S., Kohl, P. L., Jonson-Reid, M., Drake, B., & Petra, M. (2013). Child maltreatment victimization and subsequent perpetration of young adult intimate partner violence: An exploration of mediating factors. *Child Maltreatment, 18,* 71–84.

Ministére de la Justice. (n.d.). *Compensation of victims of criminal acts in France.* Retrieved from http://www.justice.gouv.fr/art_pix/indemnisation_victime_an.pdf

Minnesota Department of Health. (1998). Tools about sexual violence: General prevention tool #25; Effects of sexual victimization. *A place to start: A resource kit for preventing sexual violence.* St. Paul, MN: Minnesota Department of Health.

Mitchell, H., & Aamodt, M. G. (2005). The incidence of child abuse in serial killers. *Journal of Police and Criminal Psychology, 20*(1), 40–47.

Moracco, K. E., Runyan, C. W., & Butts, J. D. (1998). Femicide in North Carolina, 1991–1993: A statewide study of patterns and precursors. *Homicide Studies, 2*(4), 422–446.

Morgan, P. (2010). Workplace violence training and education. In B. S. Fisher & S. P. Lab (Eds.), *Encyclopedia of victimology and crime prevention* (Vol. 2, pp. 1076–1078). Thousand Oaks, CA: Sage.

Morrall, P., Hazelton, M., & Shackleton, W. (2011). Homicide and its effect on secondary victims: Peter Morrall and colleagues discuss the impact of violent crime on the families, friends and associates of its victims, and the potential forensic role of mental health nurses. *Mental Health Practice, 15*(3), 14–19.

Morton, E., Runyan, C. W., Moracco, K. E., & Butts, J. (1998). Partner homicide-suicide involving female homicide victims: A population based study in North Carolina, 1988–1992. *Violence and Victims, 12*(2), 91–106.

Mouzos, J. (1999). *Femicide: An overview of major findings.* Canberra: Australian Institute of Criminology. Retrieved from http://www.aic.gov.au/documents/B/1/3/%7BB1300A0C-4ED2-45D2-9407-28EE7F30FE28%7Dti124.pdf

Muftić, L. R., & Baumann, M. (2012). Female versus male perpetrated femicide: An exploratory analysis of whether offender gender matters. *Journal of Interpersonal Violence, 27*(14), 2824–2844.

Muftić, L. R., & Deljkić, I. (2012). Exploring the overlap between offending and victimization within intimate partner violence in Bosnia and Herzegovina. *International Criminal Justice Review, 22*(2), 192–211.

Muftić, L. R., & Finn, M. A. (2013). Health outcomes among women trafficked for sex in the United States: A closer look. *Journal of Interpersonal Violence, 28*(9), 1859–1885.

Muftić, L. R., Finn, M. A., & Marsh, E. (2013). The victim-offender overlap, intimate partner violence, and sex: Assessing differences among exclusive victims, exclusive offenders, and victim-offenders. *Crime & Delinquency.* doi:0.1177/0011128712453677.

Muftić, L. R., & Hunt, D. E. (2013). Victim precipitation: Further understanding the linkage between victimization and offending in homicide. *Homicide Studies, 17,* 239–254.

Muftić, L. R., & Moreno, R. D. (2010). Juvenile homicide victims: Differences and similarities by gender. *Youth Violence and Juvenile Justice: An Interdisciplinary Journal, 8*(4), 386–398.

Mukherjee, S., & Carcach, C. (1998). *Repeat victimization in Australia (Australian Institute of Criminology Research and Public Policy Series No. 15).* Griffith, Australian Capital Territories: Australian Institute of Criminology.

Murphy, S. A., Tapper, V. J., Johnson, L. C., & Lohan, J. (2003). Suicide ideation among parents bereaved by the violent deaths of their children. *Issues in Mental Health Nursing, 24,* 5–25.

Murphy, S. M., Kilpatrick, D. G., Amick-McMullan, A., Veronen, L. J., Paduhovich, J., Best, C. L., & Saunders, B. E. (1988). Current psychological functioning of child sexual assault survivors: A community study. *Journal of Interpersonal Violence, 3,* 55–79.

Mustaine, E. E. (2010). Stalking. In B. S. Fisher & S. P. Lab (Eds.), *Encyclopedia of victimology and crime prevention* (Vol. 2, pp. 900–904). Thousand Oaks, CA: Sage.

Mustaine, E. E., & Tewksbury, R. (1998). Predicting risks of larceny theft victimization: A routine activity analysis using refined lifestyle measures. *Criminology, 36,* 829–857.

Mustaine, E. E., & Tewksbury, R. (1999). A routine activity theory explanation for women's stalking victimizations. *Violence Against Women, 5,* 43–62.

Mustaine, E. E., & Tewksbury, R. (2000). Comparing the lifestyles of victims, offenders, and victim-offenders: A routine activity theory assessment of similarities and differences for criminal incident participants. *Sociological Focus, 33*(3), 339–362.

Mustaine, E. E., & Tewksbury, R. (2007a). Collateral consequences and community reentry for registered sex offenders with child victims: Are the challenges even greater? *Journal of Offender Rehabilitation, 46,* 113–131.

Mustaine, E. E., & Tewksbury, R. (2007b). The routine activities and criminal victimization of students: Lifestyle and related factors. In B. S. Fisher & J. J. Sloan (Eds.), *Campus crime: Legal, social, and policy perspectives* (pp. 147–166). Springfield, IL: Charles C Thomas.

Nannini, A. (2006). Sexual assault patterns among women with and without disabilities seeking survivor services. *Women's Health Issues, 16,* 372–379.

Nansel, T. R., Overpeck, M., Pilla, R. S., Ruan, J., Simons-Morton, B., & Scheidt, P. (2001). Bullying behaviors among U.S. youth: Prevalence and association with psychosocial adjustment. *Journal of the American Medical Association, 285,* 2094–2100.

Natarajan, M. (1996). Women police units in India: A new direction. *Police Studies, 19*(2), 63–75.

National Association of Crime Victim Compensation Boards. (2009). *National conference to mark 25 years of VOCA grants to states*. 25 Years of Serving Crime Victims: Celebrating VOCA National Conference, Washington, DC, September 30–October 2. Retrieved from http://www.nacvcb.org/NACVCB/files/ccLibraryFiles/Filename/000000000025/20092.pdf

National Association of State Boards of Education. (2010, December 3). Bullying, harassment and hazing. *State School Healthy Policy Database*. Retrieved from http://nasbe.org/healthy_schools/hs/state.php?state=Florida#

National Center for Higher Education Management Systems Information Center for Higher Education Policymaking and Analysis. (2009). *College participation rates: Percent of 18 to 24 year olds enrolled in college*. Retrieved from http://www.higheredinfo.org/dbrowser/index.php?submeasure=331&year=2009&level=nation&mode=data&state=0

National Center for Prosecution of Child Abuse, National District Attorneys Association. (2010, July). *NDAA presence of support person for child witness compilation*. Retrieved from http://www.ndaa.org/pdf/Presence%20of%20Support%20Persons%20for%20Child%20Witnesses%202010.pdf

National Center for Victims of Crime. (1999). *Victim impact statements*. Retrieved from http://www.victimsofcrime.org/help-for-crime-victims/get-help-bulletins-for-crime-victims/victim-impact-statements

National Center for Victims of Crime. (2008a). *Domestic violence: Why victims may stay*. Washington, DC: Author.

National Center for Victims of Crime. (2008b). *Hate and bias crimes*. Retrieved from http://www.victimsofcrime.org/library/crime-information-and-statistics/hate-and-bias-crime

National Center for Victims of Crime. (2008c). *Sexual assault*. Retrieved from http://www.ncvc.org/ncvc/main.aspx?dbName=DocumentViewer&DocumentID=32369

National Center for Victims of Crime. (2009). *About victims' rights*. Retrieved from https://www.victimlaw.org/victimlaw/pages/victimsRight.jsp

National Center for Victims of Crime. (n.d.-a). *Male rape*. Retrieved from http://www.ncvc.org/ncvc/main.aspx?dbName=DocumentViewer&DocumentID=32361

National Center for Victims of Crime. (n.d.-b). *Stalking facts*. Retrieved from http://www.victimsofcrime.org/library/crime-information-and-statistics/stalking

National Center on Domestic and Sexual Violence. (2011). *Family justice centers*. Retrieved from http://www.ncdsv.org/ncd_linksfamilyjustice.html

National Center on Elder Abuse. (2011). *Why should I care about elder abuse?* Retrieved from http://www.ncea.aoa.gov/ncearoot/Main_Site/pdf/publication/NCEA_WhatIsAbuse-2010.pdf

National Coalition of Anti-Violence Programs. (2010). *Hate violence against the lesbian, gay, bisexual, transgender and queer communities in the United States in 2009*. New York, NY: National Coalition of Anti-Violence Programs. Retrieved from http://www.avp.org/documents/NCAVP2009HateViolenceReportforWeb.pdf

National Coalition of Anti-Violence Programs. (2014). *Lesbian, gay, bisexual, transgender, queer, and HIV-affected hate violence in 2013*. New York, NY: National Coalition of Anti-Violence Programs. Retrieved from http://www.avp.org/storage/documents/2013_ncavp_hvreport_final.pdf

National Commission on Terrorist Attacks upon the United States. (2004, July 22). *The 9/11 Commission report*. Retrieved from http://www.9-11commission.gov/report/911Report.pdf

National Conference of State Legislatures. (2010). *Identity theft state statutes*. Retrieved from http://www.ncsl.org/?tabid=12538

National Council on Disability. (2007). *Breaking the silence on crime victims with disabilities in the United States (Joint statement by the National Council on Disability, the Association of University Centers, and the National Center for Victims of Crime)*. Retrieved from http://www.ilru.org/html/training/webcasts/archive/2007/05-30-NCVC.html

National Counterterrorism Center. (2009, April 30). *2008 report on terrorism*. Washington, DC: Office of the Director of National Intelligence, National Counterterrorism Center. Retrieved from http://www.fas.org/irp/threat/nctc2008.pdf

National Counterterrorism Center. (2010, April 30). *2009 report on terrorism*. Washington, DC: Office of the Director of National Intelligence, National Counterterrorism Center. Retrieved from http://www.nctc.gov/witsbanner/docs/2009_report_on_terrorism.pdf

National Counterterrorism Center. (2012, March). *2012 report on terrorism*. Washington, DC: Office of the Director of National Intelligence, National Counterterrorism Center. Retrieved from http://fas.org/irp/threat/nctc2011.pdf

National Court Appointed Special Advocates. (2010). *Evidence of effectiveness*. Retrieved from http://www.casaforchildren.org/site/c.mtJSJ7MPIsE/b.5332511/k.7D2A/Evidence_of_Effectiveness.htm

National Crime Victim Bar Association. (2007). *Civil justice for victims of crime*. Washington, DC: National Crime Victim Bar Association. Retrieved from http://www.cdcr.ca.gov/Victim_Services/docs/Civil%20Justice%20%20FINAL%20%28non-book%29.pdf

National Crime Victimization Survey, 2004–2008. Alcohol and crime: Data from 2002 to 2008. Retrieved from http://www.bjs.gov/content/acf/25_crimes_by_knownoffenders.cfm

National District Attorneys Association. (2008, November). *Legislation permitting the use of anatomical dolls in child abuse cases*. Retrieved from http://www.ndaa.org/pdf/statutes-anatomical-dolls-112008.pdf

National Institute for Occupational Safety and Health. (1995, May). *Preventing homicide in the workplace* (Publication No. 93-109). Washington, DC: Department of Health and Human Services.

National Institute on Drug Abuse. (1995). *NIDA notes* (Vol. 10). Bethesda, MD: National Institute on Drug Abuse. Retrieved from http://archives.drugabuse.gov/NIDA_Notes/NN95index.html

National Institute on Drug Abuse. (1998). *NIDA notes* (Vol. 13, No. 5). Bethesda, MD: National Institute on Drug Abuse.

Retrieved from http://archives.drugabuse.gov/NIDA_Notes/NN98index.html#Number5

National Research Council. (1996). *Understanding violence against women*. Washington, DC: National Academy Press.

National Victims' Constitutional Amendment Passage. (n.d.). *Victims' Rights Amendment introduced*. Retrieved from http://www.nvcap.org/

Neeves, S. (2008). *An examination of power differentials and intimate partner violence in lesbian relationships* (Unpublished master's thesis). Virginia Polytechnic Institute and State University, Blacksburg, VA. Retrieved from http://scholar.lib.vt.edu/theses/available/etd-05012008-211729/unrestricted/NeevesThesisIPVLesbian.pdf

Nettelbeck, T., & Wilson, C. (2002). Personal vulnerability to victimization of people with mental retardation. *Trauma, Violence and Abuse, 3*, 289–306.

New York Department of Criminal Justice. (2013). Retrieved from http://www.criminaljustice.ny.gov/crimnet/ojsa/crimereporting/forms/homicide.pdf

Nicholas, S., Povey, D., Walker, A., & Kershaw, C. (2005). *Crime in England and Wales 2004/2005*. London, UK: Great Britain Home Office Research Development and Statistics Directorate.

Nies, Y., James, S. D., & Netter, S. (2010, January 28). Mean girls: Cyberbullying blamed for teen suicides. *Good Morning America, ABC News*. Retrieved from http://abcnews.go.com/GMA/Parenting/girls-teen-suicide-calls-attention-cyberbullying/story?id=9685026#.UEd9kmNrWTw

Nolan, J. J., McDevitt, S., Cronin, S., & Farrell, A. (2004). Learning to see hate crimes: A framework for understanding and clarifying ambiguities in bias crime classification. *Criminal Justice Studies: A Critical Journal of Crime, Law, and Society, 17*, 91–105.

Noonan, M. E. (2010a). *Deaths in Custody Reporting Program: Mortality in local jails, 2000–2007* (Special report). Washington, DC: Bureau of Justice Statistics, U.S. Department of Justice.

Noonan, M. E. (2010b). *Deaths in Custody Reporting Program: Mortality in state prisons, 2000–2007* (Special report). Washington, DC: Bureau of Justice Statistics, U.S. Department of Justice.

Norris, J., Nurius, P. S., & Graham, T. L. (1999). When a date changes from fun to dangerous: Factors affecting women's ability to distinguish. *Violence Against Women, 5*, 230–250.

North, C. S., Nixon, S. J., Shariat, S., Mallonee, S., McMillen, J. C., Spitznagel, E. L., & Smith, E. M. (1999). Psychiatric disorders among survivors of the Oklahoma City bombing. *Journal of the American Medical Association, 282*, 755–762.

Nosek, M. A. (1996). Sexual abuse of women with physical disabilities. In D. M. Krotoski, M. A. Nosek, & M. A. Turk (Eds.), *Women with physical disabilities: Achieving and maintaining health and well-being* (pp. 153–173). Baltimore, MD: Paul H. Brookes.

Nugent, W. R., & Paddock, J. B. (1995). The effect of victim-offender mediation on severity of response. *Conflict Resolution Quarterly, 12*, 353–367.

O'Leary-Kelly, A. M., Bowes-Sperry, L., Bates, C. A., & Lean, E. R. (2009). Sexual harassment at work: A decade (plus) of progress. *Journal of Management, 35*, 503–536.

O'Malley, P. M., & Johnston, L. D. (2002). Epidemiology of alcohol and other drug use among American college students. *Journal of Studies on Alcohol and Drugs, 14*, 23–29.

Occupational Safety and Health Act of 1970, Pub. L. 91-596 (1970).

Occupational Safety and Health Administration. (n.d.). *Safety and health topics: Workplace violence*. Retrieved from http://www.osha.gov/SLTC/workplaceviolence/

Office for Victims of Crime. (2012, April). *Crime Victims Fund: OVC fact sheet*. Retrieved from http://www.ovc.gov/pubs/crimevictimsfundfs/index.html

Office for Victims of Crime. (2013). *2012 Victims of Crime Act performance report*. Washington, DC: Office for Victims of Crime, Office of Justice Programs, U.S. Department of Justice.

Office of Justice Programs. (2002, January). *Enforcement of protective orders* (Legal Series, Bulletin #4). Washington, DC: U.S. Department of Justice. Retrieved from https://www.ncjrs.gov/ovc_archives/bulletins/legalseries/bulletin4/ncj189190.pdf

Okun, L. E. (1986). *Woman abuse: Facts replacing myths*. Albany: State University of New York Press.

Olweus Bullying Prevention Program. (2011). *State and federal bullying information*. Retrieved from http://www.olweus.org/public/bullying_laws.page

Olweus, D. (1991). Bully/victim problems among schoolchildren: Basic facts and effects of a school-based intervention program. In D. J. Pepler & K. H. Rubin (Eds.), *The development and treatment of childhood aggression* (pp. 411–448). Hillsdale, NJ: Erlbaum.

Olweus, D. (1993a). *Bullying at school: What we know and what we can do*. New York, NY: Blackwell.

Olweus, D. (1993b). Victimization by peers: Antecedents and long-term outcomes. In K. H. Rubin & J. B. Asendorpf (Eds.), *Social withdrawal, inhibition, and shyness in childhood* (pp. 315–341). Hillsdale, NJ: Erlbaum.

Olweus, D. (2007). Bullies and victims at school: Are they the same pupils? *British Journal of Educational Psychology, 77*, 441–464.

Orel, N. A. (2010). Elder abuse, neglect, and maltreatment: Institutional. In B. S. Fisher & S. P. Lab (Eds.), *Encyclopedia of victimology and crime prevention* (Vol. 1, pp. 351–353). Thousand Oaks, CA: Sage.

Osborn, D. R., Ellingworth, D., Hope, T., & Trickett, A. (1996). Are repeatedly victimized households different? *Journal of Quantitative Criminology, 12*, 23–245.

Osborn, D. R., & Tseloni, A. (1998). The distribution of household property crimes. *Journal of Quantitative Criminology, 14*, 307–330.

Ousey, G. C., Wilcox, P., & Fisher, B. (2011). Something old, something new: Revising competing hypotheses of the victimization-offending relationship. *Journal of Quantitative Criminology, 27,* 53–84.

Outlaw, M. C., Ruback, R. B., & Britt, C. (2002). Repeat and multiple victimizations: The role of individual and contextual factors. *Violence and Victims, 17,* 187–204.

Pagelow, M. D. (1997). *Battered women: A historical research review and some common myths.* Binghamton, NY: Haworth Maltreatment & Trauma Press.

Parents of Murdered Children (POMC). (2014). *Problems of survivors.* Retrieved from http://www.pomc.com/problems.html

Paternoster, R., & Deise, J. (2011). A heavy thumb on the scale: The effect of victim impact evidence on capital decision making. *Criminology, 49,* 129–161.

Pawloski, J. (2011, January 8). Olympia-area man arrested in Thurston County's largest ever ID-theft case. *The Olympian.* Retrieved from http://www.theolympian.com/2011/01/07/1498356/id-theft-bust-larg-est-ever-in.html

Payne v. Tennessee, 501 U.S. 808 (1991).

Payne, B. J., & Gainey, R. R. (2009). *Family violence and criminal justice: A life-course approach (3rd ed.).* Providence, NJ: Matthew Bender.

Payne, B. K., & Cikovic, R. (1995). An empirical examination of the characteristics, consequences and causes of elder abuse in nursing homes. *Journal of Elder Abuse and Neglect, 7*(4), 61–74.

Pease, K. (1992). The Kirkholt Project: Preventing burglary on a British public housing estate. *Security Journal, 2,* 73–77.

Pease, K. (1998). *Repeat victimization: Taking stock* (Crime Detection and Prevention Series Paper 90). London, UK: Home Office.

Pellegrini, A. D. (1998). Bullies and victims in school: A review and call for research. *Journal of Applied Developmental Psychology, 19,* 165–176.

Perrault, S., Sauve, J., & Burns, M. (2010). Multiple victimization in Canada, 2004. *Canadian Centre for Justice Statistics Profile Series, 22.*

Petersilia, J. (2010). A retrospective view of corrections reform in the Schwarzenegger administration. *Federal Sentencing Reporter, 22,* 148–153.

Petersilia, J. R. (2001). Crime victims with developmental disabilities: A review essay. *Criminal Justice and Behavior, 28,* 655–694.

Pfohl, S. J. (1977). The "discovery" of child abuse. *Sociological Problems, 24,* 310–323.

Phillips, N. (2009). The prosecution of hate crimes: The limitations of hate crime typologies. *Journal of Interpersonal Violence, 24,* 883–905.

Pillemer, K., & Finkelhor, D. (1988). The prevalence of elder abuse: A random sample survey. *The Gerontologist, 28,* 51–57.

Piquero, A. R., & Hickman, M. (2003). Extending Tittle's control-balance theory to account for victimization. *Criminal Justice and Behavior, 30,* 282–301.

Piquero, A. R., MacDonald, J., Dobrin, A., Daigle, L. E., & Cullen, F. T. (2005). Self-control, violent offending, and homicide victimization: Assessing the general theory of crime. *Journal of Quantitative Criminology, 21,* 55–71.

Pizarro, J. M., Zgoba, K. M., & Jennings, W. G. (2011). Assessing the interaction between offender and victim criminal lifestyles & homicide type. *Journal of Criminal Justice, 39*(5), 367–377.

Planty, M., Langton, L., Krebs, C., Berzofsky, M., & Smiley-McDonald, H. (2013). *Female victims of sexual violence, 1994–2010* (Report No. NCJ 240655). Washington, DC: Bureau of Justice Statistics, U.S. Department of Justice.

Pleck, E. (1987). *Domestic tyranny: The making of American social policy against family.* New York, NY: Oxford University Press.

Polk, K. (1999). Males and honor contest violence. *Homicide Studies, 3*(1), 6–29.

Polvi, N., Looman, T., Humphries, C., & Pease, K. (1991). The time course of repeat burglary victimization. *British Journal of Criminology, 31,* 411–414.

Potter, R., & Thomas, P. (2001). *Engine immobilisers: How effective are they?* Melbourne, Australia: National Motor Vehicle Theft Reduction Council.

Powers, L. E., Curry, M. A., Oschwald, M., Maley, S., et al., (2002). Barriers and strategies in addressing abuse: A survey of disabled women's experiences. *Journal of Rehabilitation, 68,* 4–13.

Pratt, T. C., Turanovic, J. J., Fox, K. A., & Wright, K. A. (2014). Self-control and victimization: A meta-analysis. *Criminology, 52,* 87–116.

Preston, E. (2014, August 24). Crime forcing old family business out of neighborhood. *News Channel 3, Memphis, TN.* Retrieved from http://wreg.com/2014/08/24/crime-forcing-old-family-business-out-of-neighborhood/

Prevent Child Abuse America. (2000). *Current trends in child abuse reporting and fatalities: The 2000 fifty state survey.* Chicago, IL: National Center on Child Abuse Prevention Research.

Ptacek, J. (1999). *Battered women in the courtroom: The power of judicial responses.* Boston, MA: Northeastern University Press.

Pyrooz, D. C., Moule, R. K., & Decker, S. H. (2014). The contribution of gang membership to the victim-offender overlap. *Journal of Research in Crime and Delinquency, 51*(3), 315–348.

Pyrooz, D. C., Wolfe, S. E., & Spohn, C. (2011). Gang-related homicide charging decisions: The implementation of a specialized prosecution unit in Los Angeles. *Criminal Justice Policy Review, 22*(1), 3–26.

Raghavan, R., Bogart, L. M., Elliott, M. N., Vestal, K. D., & Schuster, M. A. (2004). Sexual victimization among a national probability sample of adolescent women. *Perspectives on Sexual and Reproductive Health, 36,* 225–232.

RAINN. (2009a). *Male sexual assault.* Retrieved from http://www.rainn.org/get-information/types-of-sexual-assault/male-sexual-assault

RAINN. (2009b). *Ohio mandatory reporting requirements regarding elders/disabled.* Retrieved from https://rainn.org/pdf-files-and-other-documents/Public-Policy/Legal-resources/2009-Mandatory-Report/Ohio09E.pdf

RAINN. (2011a). *Alabama mandatory reporting requirements regarding elders/disabled.* Retrieved from http://www.rainn.org/files/reportingdatabase/Alabama/AlabamaElderlyMandatoryReporting.pdf

RAINN. (2011b). *Georgia*. Retrieved from http://www.rainn.org/files/reportingdatabase/Georgia/GeorgiaHIV.pdf

Rand, M. (2008). *Criminal victimization, 2007*. Washington, DC: U.S. Department of Justice, Bureau of Justice Statistics.

Rand, M. (2009). *Criminal victimization, 2008*. Washington, DC: U.S. Department of Justice, Bureau of Justice Statistics.

Rand, M., & Rennison, C. (2004). *How much violence against women is there?* Washington, DC: National Criminal Justice Reference Service. Retrieved from https://www.ncjrs.gov/pdffiles1/nij/199702.pdf

Rand, M. R. (1997). *Violence-related injuries treated in hospital emergency departments* [Special report]. Washington, DC: Bureau of Justice Statistics.

RAND Corporation. (2004). Compensating the victims of 9/11 (Research Brief). *RAND Corporation*. Retrieved from http://www.rand.org/pubs/research_briefs/RB9087/index1.html

Raphael, J. (2008). Book Review: Taylor Jr., S., & Johnson, K. C. (2007). "Until proven innocent: Political correctness and the shameful injustices of the Duke Lacrosse rape case." *Violence Against Women, 14,* 370–375.

Ratcliffe, J. H., & Rengert, G. F. (2008). Near-repeat patterns in Philadelphia shootings. *Security Journal, 21,* 58–76.

Rathgeber, C. (2002). The victimization of women through human trafficking: An aftermath of war? *European Journal of Crime, Criminal Law and Criminal Justice, 10,* 152–163.

Rauma, D. (1984). Going for the gold: Prosecutorial decision making in cases of wife assault. *Social Science Research, 13,* 321–351.

Reaves, B. A. (2008, February). *Campus law enforcement, 2004–05* (Special Report NCJ 219374). Washington, DC: Bureau of Justice Statistics.

Redmond, L. (1989). *Surviving when someone you love was murdered: A professional's guide to group grief therapy for families and friends of murder victims*. Clearwater, FL: Psychological Consultation and Educational Services.

Reiss, A. (1980). Victim proneness in repeat victimization by type of crime. In S. Fienberg & A. Reiss (Eds.), *Indicators of crime and criminal justice: Quantitative studies* (pp. 41–53). Washington, DC: U.S. Department of Justice.

Rengert, G., & Wasilchick, J. (1985). *Suburban burglary: A time and place for everything*. Springfield, IL: Charles C Thomas.

Rennison, C. M. (1999). *Criminal victimization in 1998: Changes 1997–1998 with trends 1993–1998*. Washington, DC: Bureau of Justice Statistics.

Rennison, C. M. (2002). *Criminal victimization 2001: Changes 2000–2001 with trends 1993–2001*. Washington, DC: U.S. Government Printing Office.

Reno, J., Marcus, D., Leary, M. L., & Turman, K. M. (2000). *Responding to terrorism victims: Oklahoma City and beyond*. Washington, DC: U.S. Department of Justice, Office of Justice Programs, Office for Victims of Crime.

Renzetti, C. M., & Miley, C. H. (1996). *Violence in gay and lesbian domestic partnerships*. New York, NY: Haworth.

Resnick, H., Monnier, J., & Seals, B. (2002). Rape-related HIV risk concerns among recent rape victims. *Journal of Interpersonal Violence, 17*(7), 746–759.

Rice, K. J., & Smith, W. R. (2002). Socioecological models of automotive theft: Integrating routine activity and social disorganization approaches. *Journal of Research in Crime and Delinquency, 39*(3), 304–336.

Ricketts, M. (2010). School violence. In B. S. Fisher & S. P. Lab (Eds.), *Encyclopedia of victimology and crime prevention* (Vol. 2, pp. 835–840). Thousand Oaks, CA: Sage.

Rigby, K. (1997). Bullying and suicide among children. *Beyond Bullying News, 2,* 3–4.

Rigby, K., & Slee, P. (1993). Dimensions of interpersonal relating among Australian school children: Implications for psychological well-being. *Journal of Social Psychology, 131,* 615–627.

Riggs, D. S., Caulfield, M. B., & Street, A. E. (2000). Risk for domestic violence: Factors associated with perpetration and victimization. *Journal of Clinical Psychology, 56,* 1289–1316.

Rinehart, J. K., & Yeater, E. A. (2013). Using cognitive theory and methodology to inform the study of sexual victimization. *Trauma, Violence & Abuse*. doi:10.1177/1524838013515761.

Risser, H. J., Hetzel-Riggin, M. D., Thomsen, C. J., & McCanne, T. R. (2006). PTSD as a mediator of sexual revictimization: The role of re-experiencing, avoidance, and arousal symptoms. *Journal of Traumatic Stress, 19,* 687–698.

Ritsche, D. F. (2006, September). *Sex crime legislation* (Informational Bulletin 06-3). Madison: State of Wisconsin Legislative Reference Bureau.

Robers, S., Kemp, J., Rathbun, A., & Morgan, R. E. (2014). *Indicators of school crime and safety: 2013* (NCES 2014-042/NCJ 243299). Washington, DC: National Center for Education Statistics, U.S. Department of Education, and Bureau of Justice Statistics, Office of Justice Programs, U.S. Department of Justice.

Robers, S., Zhang, J., Truman, J., & Snyder, T. D. (2010, November). *Indicators of school crime and safety: 2010* (NCES 2011-002/NCJ 230812). Washington, DC: National Center for Education Statistics, U.S. Department of Education, and Bureau of Justice Statistics, Office of Justice Programs, U.S. Department of Justice.

Roberts, A., & Willits, D. (2013). Lifestyle, routine activities, and felony-related eldercide. *Homicide Studies, 17*(2), 184–203.

Roberts, A. L., Austin, S. B., Corliss, H. L., Vandermorris, M. D., & Koenen, K. C. (2010). Pervasive trauma exposure among U.S. sexual orientation minority adults and risk of posttraumatic stress disorder. *American Journal of Public Health, 100,* 2433–2441.

Robinson, L., de Benedictis, T., & Segal, J. (2011). *Elder abuse and neglect: Warning signs, risk factors, prevention, and help*. Retrieved from http://helpguide.org/mental/elder_abuse_physical_emotional_sexual_neglect.htm

Robinson, M. B. (1998). Burglary revictimization: The time period of heightened risk. *British Journal of Criminology, 38,* 78–87.

Roe-Sepowitz, D. E., Hickle, K. E., Pérez Loubert, M., & Egan, T. (2011). Adult prostitution recidivism: Risk factors and impact of a diversion program. *Journal of Offender Rehabilitation, 50*(5), 272–285.

Rosenbaum, M. E. (1986). The acquaintance process: Looking mainly backward. *Journal of Personality and Social Psychology, 51,* 1156–1166.

Rosenfeld, R., Fornango, R., & Baumer, E. (2005). Did Ceasefire, Compstat, and Exile reduce homicide? *Criminology and Public Policy, 4*(3), 419–449.

Rounds-Bryant, J., Kristiansen, P. L., Fairbank, J. A., & Hubbard, R. L. (1998). Substance use, mental disorders, abuse and crime: Gender comparisons among a national sample of adolescent drug treatment centers. *Journal of Child and Adolescent Substance Abuse, 7*(4), 19–34.

Rountree, P. W. (1998). A reexamination of the crime-fear linkage. *Journal of Research in Crime and Delinquency, 35,* 341–372.

Rowe, D. C., Stever, C., Chase, D., Sherman, S., Abramowitz, A., & Waldman, I. D. (2001). Two dopamine genes related to reports of childhood retrospective inattention and conduct disorder symptoms. *Molecular Psychiatry, 6,* 429–433.

Ruback, R. B., Menard, K. S., Outlaw, M. C., & Shaffer, J. N. (1999). Normative advice to campus crime victims: Effects of gender, age, and alcohol. *Violence and Victims, 14*(4), 381–396.

Rubin, A. J. (2012, June 1). Rape case, in public, cites abuse by armed groups in Afghanistan. *The New York Times.* Retrieved from http://www.nytimes.com/2012/06/02/world/asia/afghan-rape-case-is-a-challenge-for-the-government.html?pagewanted=all

Russell, D. E. H., & Harmes, R. A. (2001). *Femicide in global perspective.* New York, NY: Teachers College Press.

Rycus, J., & Hughes, R. (1998). *Field guide to child welfare: Placement and permanence* (Vol. IV). Washington, DC: Child Welfare League of America and Columbus, OH: Institute for Human Services.

S.1290-Protecting Domestic Violence and Stalking Victims Act of 2013 bill summary. Retrieved from https://beta.congress.gov/bill/113th-congress/senate-bill/1290

Saarento, S., Karna, A., Hodges, E. V. E., & Salmivalli, C. (2013). Student-, classroom-, and school-level risk factors for victimization. *Journal of School Psychology, 51,* 421–434.

Saisan, J., Smith, M., & Segal, J. (2011, June). *Child abuse and neglect: Recognizing and preventing child abuse.* Retrieved from http://www.helpguide.org/mental/child_abuse_physical_emotional_sexual_neglect.htm

Salasin, S. E., & Rich, R. F. (1993). Mental health policy for victims of violence: The case against women. In J. P. Wilson & B. Raphael (Eds.), *International handbook of traumatic stress syndromes* (pp. 947–955). New York, NY: Plenum.

Sampson, R. J. (1985). Neighborhood and crime: The structural determinants of personal victimization. *Journal of Research in Crime and Delinquency, 22*(1), 7–40.

Sampson, R. J., & Laub, J. H. (1993). *Crime in the making: Pathways and turning points through life.* Cambridge, MA: Harvard University Press.

Sampson, R. J., & Lauritsen, J. L. (1990). Deviant lifestyles, proximity to crime, and the victim-offender link in personal violence. *Journal of Research in Crime and Delinquency, 27*(2), 110–139.

Sampson, R. J., Raudenbush, S. W., & Earls, F. (1997). Neighborhoods and violent crime: A multilevel study of collective efficacy. *Science, 277,* 918–924.

Sanders, A. (2012). Two accused drug dealers call police to report armed robbery. Retrieved from http://www.wsav.com/story/21211356/two-accused-drug-dealers-call-police-to-report-armed-robbery

Schafer, S. (1968). *The victim and his criminal: A study in functional responsibility.* New York, NY: Random House.

Schauer, E. J., & Wheaton, E. M. (2006). Sex trafficking in the United States: A literature review. *Criminal Justice Review, 31,* 146–169.

Schmidt, J., & Steury, E. (1989). Prosecutorial discretion in filing charges in domestic violence cases. *Criminology, 27,* 487–510.

Schmidt, L. A., Fox, N. A., Rubin, K. H., Hu, S., & Hamer, D. H. (2002). Molecular genetics of shyness and aggression in preschoolers. *Personality and Individual Differences, 33,* 227–238.

Schneider, H. J. (2001). Victimological developments in the world during the past three decades (I): A study of comparative victimology. *International Journal of Offender therapy and Comparative Criminology, 45*(4), 449–468.

Schneider, K. (2012, June 3). Dozens of Calgary sex assault victims opt to wait. *Calgary Sun.* Retrieved from http://www.calgarysun.com/2012/06/03/doezns-of-calgary-sex-assault-victims-opt-to-wait

Schreck, C. J. (1999). Criminal victimization and low self-control: An extension and test of a general theory of crime. *Justice Quarterly, 16*(3), 633–654.

Schreck, C. J., & Fisher, B. S. (2004). Specifying the influence of family and peers on violent victimization: Extending routine activities and lifestyles theories. *Journal of Interpersonal Violence, 19*(9), 1021–1041.

Schuster, M. A., Stein, B. D., Jaycox, L. H., Collins, R. L., Marshall, G. N., Elliott, M. N., … Berry, S. H. (2001). A national survey of stress reactions after the September 11, 2001, terrorist attacks. *New England Journal of Medicine, 345,* 1507–1512.

Schwartz, M. D., & Pitts, V. L. (1995). Exploring a feminist routine activities approach to explaining sexual assault. *Justice Quarterly, 12*(1), 9–31.

Schweig, S., Malangone, D., & Goodman, M. (n.d.). *Prostitution diversion programs.* Retrieved from http://www.courtinnovation.org/sites/default/files/documents/CI_Prostitution%207.5.12%20PDF.pdf

Scott, K. D., Schafer, J., & Greenfield, T. K. (1999). The role of alcohol in physical assault perpetration and victimization. *Journal of Studies on Alcohol, 60,* 528–536.

Sedensky, S. J. (2013). *Report of the state's Attorney for the Judicial District of Danbury on the shootings at Sandy Hook Elementary School and 36 Yogananda Street, Newtown, Connecticut on December 14, 2012.* Retrieved from http://www.ct.gov/csao/lib/csao/Sandy_Hook_Final_Report.pdf

Sedlak, A. J., Mettenburg, J., Basena, M., Petta, I., McPherson, K., Greene, A., & Li, S. (2010). *Fourth National Incidence Study of* child abuse and neglect (NIS-4): Report to Congress executive summary. Washington, DC: U.S. Department of Health and Human Services, Administration for Children and Families.

Segura, L. (2012, September 12). Will Pennsylvania execute a man who killed his abusers? The Nation. Retrieved from http://www.thenation.com/blog/169881/will-pennsylvania-execute-man-who-killed-his-abusers

Seligman, M. E. P. (1975). Helplessness: On depression, development, and death (A series of books in psychology). New York, NY: W. H. Freeman.

Sexual Assault Laws of Alabama. (n.d.). Retrieved from http://www.ageofconsent.com/alabama.htm

Sexual Harassment, 29 C.F.R. § 1604.11 (1999).

Shanley, J. R., Risch, E. C., & Bonner, B. L. (2010). U.S. child death review programs: Assessing progress toward a standard review process. American Journal of Preventive Medicine, 39(6), 522–528.

Shared Hope International. (2011). Protected innocence legislative framework: Methodology. Retrieved from http://www.sharedhope.org/Portals/0/Documents/ProtectedInnocenceMethodologyFINAL.pdf

Shdaimah, C. S., & Wiechelt, S. A. (2012). Converging on empathy: Perspectives on Baltimore City's Specialized Prostitution Diversion Program. Women & Criminal Justice, 22(2), 156–173.

Shepherd, J. M. (2002). Reflections on a rape trial: The role of rape myths and jury selection in the outcome of a trial. Affilia, 17, 69–92.

Sherman, L. W.(1992). Policing domestic violence: Experiments and dilemmas. New York, NY: Free Press.

Sherman, L. W., & Berk, R. A. (1984). The specific deterrent effects of arrest for domestic assault. American Sociological Review, 49, 261–272.

Sherman, L. W., Gartin, P. R., & Buerger, M. E. (1989). Hot spots of predatory crime: Routine activities and the criminology of place. Criminology, 27, 27–55.

Sherman, L. W., Strang, H., Angel, C., Woods, D., Barnes, G., Bennett, S., & Inkpen, N. (2005). Effects of face-to-face restorative justice on victims of crime in four randomized, controlled trials. Journal of Experimental Criminology, 1(3), 367–395.

Siegel, J. A., & Williams, L. M. (2003). Risk factors for sexual victimization of women: Results from a prospective study. Violence Against Women, 9(8), 902–930.

Siegel, R. S., La Greca, A. M., & Harrison, H. M. (2009). Peer victimization and social anxiety in adolescents: Prospective and reciprocal relationships. Journal of Youth and Adolescence, 38(8), 1096–1109.

Sievers, V., Murphy, S., & Miller, J. (2003). Sexual assault evidence collection more accurate when completed by Sexual Assault Nurse Examiners: Colorado's experience. Journal of Emergency Nursing, 29, 511–514.

Silver, E. (2002). Mental disorder and violent victimization: The mediating role of involvement in conflicted social relationships. Criminology, 40, 191–212.

Silver, E., Arseneault, L., Langley, J., Caspi, A., & Moffitt, T. (2005). Mental disorder and violent victimization in a total birth cohort. American Journal of Public Health, 95, 2015–2021.

Silver, R. C., Holman, E. A., McIntosh, D. N., Poulin, M., & Gil-Rivas, V. (2002). Nationwide longitudinal study of psychological responses to September 11. Journal of the American Medical Association, 288, 1235–1244.

Silverman, J. G., Raj, A., Mucci, L. A., & Hathaway, J. E. (2001). Dating violence against adolescent girls and associated substance use, unhealthy weight control, sexual risk behavior, pregnancy and suicidality. Journal of the American Medical Association, 286, 572–579.

Simmons, D. (2014, August 20). Sexual assault evidence will be stored in state crime lab in Madison. Retrieved from http://host.madison.com/wsj/news/local/sexual-assault-evidence-will-be-stored-in-state-crime-lab/article_8ed49c37-65f6-5509-b831-0312009e4089.html

Sloan, J. J., & Shoemaker, J. (2007). State-level Cleary Act initiatives: Symbolic politics or substantive policy? In B. S. Fisher & J. J. Sloan (Eds.), Campus crime: Legal, social, and policy perspectives (pp. 102–121). Springfield, IL: Charles C Thomas.

Slone, M., & Shoshani, A. (2008). Indirect victimization from terrorism: A proposed post-exposure intervention. Journal of Mental Health Counseling, 30, 255–266.

SmartMotorist.com. (n.d.). History of auto-theft legislation. Retrieved from http://www.smartmotorist.com/auto-security-systems/history-of-auto-theft-legislation.html

Smith, B. L., Sloan, J. J., & Ward, R. M. (1990). Public support for the victims' rights movement: Results of a statewide survey. Crime and Delinquency, 36(4), 488–502.

Smith, D. L. (2008). Disability, gender, and intimate partner violence: Relationships from the behavioral risk factor surveillance system. Sexuality and Disability, 26, 15–28.

Smith, E. L., & Cooper, A. D. (2013). Homicide in the U.S. known to law enforcement, 2011. Retrieved from http://www.bjs.gov/content/pub/pdf/hus11.pdf

Smith, Gambrell & Russell, LLP. (2005). Workplace violence: Recognizing risk factors and formulating prevention strategies. Retrieved from http://www.sgrlaw.com/resources/trust_the_leaders/leaders_issues/ttl13/869/

Smith, N. E., & Batiuk, M. E. (1989). Sexual victimization and inmate social interaction. The Prison Journal, 69, 29–38.

The Smoking Gun. (2010, April 15). Ben Roethlisberger's bad play: Police reports detail NFL quarterback's unseemly night in Georgia. The Smoking Gun. Retrieved from http://www.thesmokinggun.com/documents/crime/ben-roethlisbergers-bad-play

Smolak, L., & Murnen, S. K. (2002). A meta-analytic examination of the relationship between childhood sexual abuse and eating disorders. International Journal of Eating Disorders, 31, 136–150.

Snyder, J. A., Fisher, B. S., Scherer, H. L., & Daigle, L. E. (2012). Unsafe in the camouflage tower: Sexual victimization and perceptions of military academy leadership. Journal of Interpersonal Violence. doi:10.1177/0886260512441252.

Sobsey, D. (1994). Violence and abuse in the lives of people with disabilities: The end of silent acceptance? Baltimore, MD: Paul H. Brookes.

Sobsey, D., & Doe, T. (1991). Patterns of sexual abuse and assault. *Journal of Sexuality and Disability, 9,* 243–259.

Soler-Baillo, J. M., Marx, B. P., & Sloan, D. M. (2005). The psychophysiological correlates of risk recognition among victims and non-victims of sexual assault. *Behaviour Research and Therapy, 43*(2), 169–181.

Spohn, C., & Holleran, D. (2004). On the use of the total incarceration variable in sentencing research. *Criminology, 42*(1), 211–240.

Stark, E. (1984, May). The unspeakable family secret. *Psychology Today,* 42–46.

State Government of Victoria. (2013). *Victims of crime: Compensation and expenses.* Retrieved from the Victims of Crime website: http://www.victimsofcrime.vic.gov.au/home/going+to+court/compensation+and+financial+assistance/

State police: Man robbed Ogletown business once, then tried again. (2014, January 25). *The News Journal.* Retrieved from http://www.delawareonline.com/story/news/crime/2014/01/25/state-police-man-robbed-ogletown-business-once-then-tried-again/4895479/

State v. Johnson, No. C4-92-251, 1993, Minn. App. LEXIS 617 (Minn. App. June 9, 1993).

Stepakoff, S. (1998). Effects of sexual victimization on suicidal ideation and behavior in U.S. college women. *Suicide and Life-Threatening Behavior, 28*(1), 107–126.

Stets, J., & Straus, M. (1990). Gender differences in reporting marital violence and its medical and psychological consequences. In M. Straus & R. Gelles (Eds.), *Physical violence in American families* (pp. 227–244). New Brunswick, NJ: Transaction.

Stiegel, L., Klem, E., & Turner, J. (2007). *Neglect of older persons: An introduction to legal issues related to caregiver duty and liability.* Retrieved from http://www.americanbar.org/content/dam/aba/migrated/aging/about/pdfs/neglect_of_older_persons.authcheckdam.pdf

Stiegel, L. A. (2008). *Durable power of attorney abuse: A national center on elder abuse fact sheet for consumers.* Retrieved from http://www.americanbar.org/content/dam/aba/migrated/aging/about/pdfs/durable_poa_abuse_fact_sheet_consumers.authcheckdam.pdf

Stöckl, H., Devries, K., Rotstein, A., Abrahams, N., Campbell, J., Watts, C., & Moreno, C. G. (2013). The global prevalence of intimate partner homicide: A systematic review. *The Lancet, 382*(9895), 859–865.

Stombler, M. (1994). "Buddies" or "slutties": The collective sexual reputation of fraternity little sisters. *Gender and Society, 8,* 297–323.

Storch, E. A. (2003). Reliability and factor structure of the sport anxiety questionnaire in fifth- and sixth-grade children. *Psychological Reports, 93,* 160.

Strang, H. (2002). *Repair or revenge: Victims and restorative justice.* Oxford, UK: Clarendon.

Straus, M. (1979). Measuring intrafamilial conflict and violence: The Conflict Tactics Scales. *Journal of Marriage and the Family, 41,* 75–88.

Straus, M. A. (2007). Conflict Tactics Scales. In N. A. Jackson (Ed.), *Encyclopedia of violence* (pp. 190–197). New York, NY: Routledge, Taylor & Francis Group.

Straus, M. A., & Gelles, R. J. (Eds.). (1990). *Physical violence in American families.* New Brunswick, NJ: Transaction.

Straus, M. A., Hamby, S. L., Boney-McCoy, S., & Sugarman, D. B. (1996). The revised Conflict Tactics Scale (CTS2): Development and preliminary psychometric data. *Journal of Family Issues, 17*(3), 283–316.

Students invent nail polish that could detect date rape drugs. (2014, August 25). *Fox News.* Retrieved from http://www.foxnews.com/health/2014/08/25/students-invent-nail-polish-that-could-detect-date-rape-drugs/

Sugarman, D. B., & Frankel, S. L. (1996). Patriarchal ideology and wife-assault: A meta-analytic review. *Journal of Family Violence, 11,* 13–40.

Sullivan, P. M., & Knutson, J. F. (2000). Maltreatment and disabilities: A population-based epidemiological study. *Child Abuse & Neglect, 24,* 1257–1273.

Sweeting, H., Young, R., West, P., & Der, G. (2006). Peer victimization and depression in early-mid adolescence: A longitudinal study. *British Journal of Educational Psychology, 76*(3), 577–594.

Sygnatur, E. F., & Toscano, G. A. (2000, Spring). Work-related homicides: The facts. *Compensation and Working Conditions,* 3–8.

Tabachneck, A., Norup, H., Thomason, S., & Motlagh, P. (2000). *VICC approved theft deterrent systems: A study into the impact of VICC approved theft deterrent systems on insurance theft claim frequency and loss cost.* Don Mills, Ontario: Vehicle Information Centre of Canada.

Talerico, K., Evans, L., & Strumpf, N. (2002). Mental health correlates of aggression in nursing home residents with dementia. *The Gerontologist, 42,* 169–177.

Tatara, T., Kuzmeskus, L. B., Duckhorn, E., & Bivens, L. (1998). *National Elder Abuse Incidence Study: Final report.* Washington, DC: Administration on Aging, U.S. Department of Health and Human Services. Retrieved from http://aoa.gov/AoA_Programs/Elder_Rights/Elder_Abuse/docs/ABuseReport_Full.pdf

Taylor, B. G., Davis, R. C., & Maxwell, C. D. (2001). The effects of a group batterer treatment program in Brooklyn. *Justice Quarterly, 18,* 170–201.

Taylor, R. B. (2001). *Breaking away from broken windows: Baltimore neighborhoods and the nationwide fight against crime, grime, fear, and decline.* Boulder, CO: Westview Press.

Taylor, T. J., Peterson, D., Esbensen, F., & Freng, A. (2007). Gang membership as a risk factor for adolescent violent victimization. *Journal of Research in Crime and Delinquency, 44,* 351–380.

Teasdale, B. (2009). Mental disorder and violent victimization. *Criminal Justice and Behavior, 36,* 513–535.

Teaster, P. B., Otto, J. M., Dugar, T. A., Mendiondo, M. S., Abner, E. L., & Cecil, K. A. (2006). *The 2004 survey of state adult protective services: Abuse of adults 60 years of age and older.* Retrieved from http://www.ncea.aoa.gov/ncearoot/main_site/pdf/2-14-06%20final%2060+report.pdf

Teplin, L. A., McClelland, G. M., Abram, K. M., & Weiner, D. A. (2005). Crime victimization in adults with severe mental illness: Comparison with the National Crime Victimization Survey. *Archives of General Psychiatry, 62,* 911–921.

Testa, M., Hoffman, J. A., & Livingston, J. A. (2011). Intergenerational transmission of sexual victimization vulnerability as mediated by parenting. *Child Abuse & Neglect, 35,* 363–371.

Tewksbury, R., & Mustaine, E. E. (2000). Routine activities and vandalism: A theoretical and empirical study. *Journal of Crime and Justice, 23,* 81–110.

Tewksbury, R., & Pedro, D. (2003). The role of alcohol in victimization. In L. J. Moriarty (Ed.), *Controversies in victimology* (pp. 25–42). Cincinnati, OH: Anderson.

Thompson, M. P., Kaslow, N. J., Price, A. W., Williams, K., & Kingree, J. B. (1998). Role of secondary stressors in the parental death–child distress relation. *Journal of Abnormal Child Psychology, 26*(5), 357–366.

Tittle, C. R. (1995). *Control balance: Toward a general theory of deviance.* Boulder, CO: Westview.

Tittle, C. R. (1997). Thoughts stimulated by Braithwaite's analysis of control balance theory. *Theoretical Criminology, 1*(1), 99–110.

Tjaden, P., & Thoennes, N. (1998, November). *Prevalence, incidence, and consequences of violence against women: Findings from the National Violence Against Women Survey. Research in Brief.* Washington, DC: U.S. Department of Justice, National Institute of Justice and U.S. Department of Health and Human Services, Centers for Disease Control and Prevention. Retrieved from https://www.ncjrs.gov/pdffiles/172837.pdf

Tjaden, P., & Thoennes, N. (2000a). *Full report of the prevalence, incidence and consequences of violence against women.* Washington, DC: National Institute of Justice, Centers for Disease Control and Prevention.

Tjaden, P., & Thoennes, N. (2000b). Prevalence and consequences of male-to-female and female-to-male intimate partner violence as measured by the National Violence Against Women Survey. *Violence Against Women, 6,* 142–161.

Tjaden, P., & Thoennes, N. (2006). *Extent, nature, and consequences of rape victimization: Findings from the National Violence Against Women Survey.* Rockville, MD: National Institute of Justice.

Tjaden, P., Thoennes, N., & Allison, C. J. (1999). Comparing violence over the life span in samples of same-sex and opposite-sex cohabitants. *Violence and Victims, 14,* 413–425.

Tobolowsky, P. (1999). Victim participation in the criminal justice process: Fifteen years after the President's Task Force on Victims of Crime. *Criminal and Civil Confinement, 25*(21), 21–105.

Toch, H. (1977). *Police, prisons, and the problem of violence.* Washington, DC: U.S. Government Printing Office.

Trafficking Victims Protection Act of 2000, Pub. L. 106-386 (2000).

Truman, J., Langton, L., & Planty, M. (2013). *Criminal victimization, 2012.* Washington, DC: U.S. Department of Justice, Bureau of Justice Statistics. Retrieved from http://www.bjs.gov/content/pub/pdf/cv12.pdf

Truman, J. L. (2011). *Criminal Victimization in the United States, 2011.* Washington, DC: U.S. Department of Justice, Office of Justice Programs, Bureau of Justice Statistics.

Truman, J. L., & Rand, M. R. (2010). *Criminal victimization, 2009.* Washington, DC: Bureau of Justice Statistics, Office of Justice Programs, U.S. Department of Justice. Retrieved from http://bjs.ojp.usdoj.gov/content/pub/pdf/cv09.pdf

Tseloni, A. (2000). Personal criminal victimization in the United States: Fixed and random effects of individual and household characteristics. *Journal of Quantitative Criminology, 16,* 415–442.

Tucker, P., Pfefferbaum, B., North, C. S., Kent, A., Jeon-Slaughter, H., & Parker, D. E. (2010). Biological correlates of direct exposure to terrorism several years postdisaster. *Annals of Clinical Psychiatry, 22,* 186–195.

Tunnell, K. (1992). *Choosing crime: The criminal calculus of property offenders.* Chicago, IL: Nelson-Hall.

Turner, H. A., Finkelhor, D., & Ormrod, R. (2010). The effect of adolescent victimization on self-concept and depressive symptoms. *Child Maltreatment, 15*(1), 76–90.

Tynes, B., & Giang, M. (2009). P01-298 Online victimization, depression, and anxiety among adolescents in the U.S. *European Psychiatry, 24*(1), S686.

Ulicyn, G. R., White, G., Bradford, B., & Matthews, R. M. (1990). Consumer exploitation by attendants: How often does it happen and can anything be done about it? *Rehabilitation Counseling Bulletin, 33,* 240–246.

Ullman, S. E. (2007). A 10-year update of "Review and critique of empirical studies of rape avoidance." *Criminal Justice and Behavior, 34,* 411–429.

Ullman, S. E., Relyea, M., Peter-Hagene, L., & Vasquez, A. L. (2013). Trauma histories, substance use coping, PTSD, and problem substance use among sexual assault victims. *Addictive Behavior, 38,* 2219–2223.

Umbreit, M., & Greenwood, J. (2000). *Guidelines for victim-sensitive victim offender mediation: Restorative justice through dialogue.* Washington, DC: Office for Victims of Crime, Office of Justice Programs.

Umbreit, M. S. (1994a). Crime victims confront their offenders: The impact of the Minneapolis Mediation Program. *Research on Social Work Practice, 4*(4), 436–447.

Umbreit, M. S. (1994b). *Victim meets offender: The impact of restorative justice and mediation.* Monsey, NY: Criminal Justice Press.

Umbreit, M. S. (2000). *Peacemaking and spirituality: A journey toward healing and strength.* Saint Paul: Center for Restorative Justice and Peacemaking, University of Minnesota. Retrieved from http://www.cehd.umn.edu/ssw/rjp/resources/Forgiveness/Peacemaking_and_Spirituality_Journey_Toward_Healing.pdf

Umbreit, M. S., Coates, R. B., & Kalanj, B. (1994). *Victim meets offender: The impact of restorative justice and mediation.* Monsey, NY: Willow Tree Press.

Umbreit, M. S., & Vos, B. (2000). Homicide survivors meet the offender prior to execution: Restorative justice through dialogue. *Homicide Studies, 4*(1), 63–87.

United Nations Office on Drugs and Crime. (2013). *Global study on homicide.* Retrieved from http://www.unodc.org/documents/gsh/pdfs/2014_GLOBAL_HOMICIDE_BOOK_web.pdf

United Nations. (1985). *Declaration of basic principles of justice for victims of crime and abuse of power.* Retrieved from http://www.un.org/documents/ga/res/40/a40r034.htm

United Nations. (2000). *Protocol to prevent, suppress and punish trafficking in persons, especially women and children, supplementing the United Nations convention against transnational organized crime.* Retrieved from http://www.uncjin.org/Documents/Conventions/dcatoc/final_documents_2/convention_%20traff_eng.pdf

U.S. Department of Health and Human Services. (1996, July). *Violence in the workplace: Risk factors and prevention strategies* (DHHS [NIOSH] Publication No. 96-100). Retrieved from http://www.cdc.gov/niosh/docs/96-100/

U.S. Department of Health and Human Services. (1999, April). *Blending perspectives and building common ground: A report to Congress on substance abuse and child protection.* Washington, DC: U.S. Government Printing Office. Retrieved from http://aspe.hhs.gov/hsp/subabuse99/subabuse.htm

U.S. Department of Health and Human Services. (2010). *Child maltreatment, 2009.* Washington, DC: U.S. Department of Health and Human Services. Retrieved from http:// www.acf.hhs.gov/programs/cb/pubs/cm09/cm09.pdf

U.S. Department of Health and Human Services. (2011a). *Certification for victims of trafficking fact sheet.* Retrieved from http://www.acf.hhs.gov/trafficking/about/cert_victims.pdf

U.S. Department of Health and Human Services. (2011b). *Labor trafficking fact sheet.* Retrieved from http://www.acf.hhs.gov/trafficking/about/fact_labor.pdf

U.S. Department of Justice. (n.d.). *Identity theft and identity fraud.* Retrieved from http://www.justice.gov/criminal/fraud/websites/idtheft.html

U.S. Department of State. (2010, June). *Trafficking in persons report* (10th ed.). Retrieved from http://www.state.gov/documents/organization/142979.pdf

U.S. Department of State. (2014, June). *Trafficking in persons report.* Retrieved from http://www.state.gov/documents/organization/226844.pdf

U.S. National Library of Medicine. (2011). *Shaken baby syndrome.* Washington, DC: National Institutes of Health. Retrieved from http://www.nlm.nih.gov/medlineplus/ency/article/000004.htm

Valenti-Hein, D., & Schwartz, L. (1995). *The sexual abuse interview for those with developmental disabilities.* Santa Barbara, CA: James Stanfield Company.

van Dijk, J. J. M., van Kesteren, J. N., & Smit, P. (2008). Background to the International Crime Victims Survey. In *Criminal victimisation in international perspective: Key findings from the 2004–2005 ICVS and EU ICS* (pp. 21–23). The Hague, The Netherlands: Boom Legal. Retrieved from http://rechten.uvt.nl/icvs/pdffiles/ICVS2004_05.pdf

Vandello, J. A., & Cohen, D. (2003). Male honor and female fidelity: Implicit cultural scripts that perpetuate domestic violence. *Journal of Personality and Social Psychology, 84*(5), 997–1010.

Vaske, J., Boisvert, D., & Wright, J. P. (2012). Genetic and environmental contributions to the relationship between violent victimization and criminal behavior. *Journal of Interpersonal Violence.* doi:0886260512441254.

Vecchio, J. M. (2013). Once bitten, thrice wise: The varying effects of victimization on routine activities and risk management. *Deviant Behavior, 34*(3), 169–190.

Verdugo, M. A., Bermejo, B. G., & Fuertes, J. (1995). Maltreatment of intellectually handicapped children and adolescents. *Child Abuse and Neglect, 19,* 205–215.

Victim Support. (2004, Jan). Victim support celebrates 40 years of helping victims of crime. Retrieved from http://www.gmpcc.org.uk/news/victim-support-celebrates-40-years-of-helping-victims-of-crime.

Victim Support Australia. (2003). *Services and rights for crime victims in Australasia: A brief profile.* Retrieved from http://www.victimsupport.org.au/nationalprofile.php

Victim Support Europe. (2014). *Victim of crime in another EU country? What you need to know.* Retrieved from http://www.victimsupport.im/wp-content/uploads/2014/05/Victim-of-crime-in-another-country.pdf

Victim Support UK. (2014). *Who we are.* Retrieved from https://www.victimsupport.org.uk

Victim-Offender Reconciliation Program Information and Resource Center. (2006). *About victim-offender mediation and reconciliation.* Retrieved from http://www.vorp.com/

Victims of Crime Assistance Act 2009. From: https://www.legislation.qld.gov.au/LEGISLTN/ACTS/2009/09AC035.pdfhttps://www.legislation.qld.gov.au/LEGISLTN/ACTS/2009/09AC035.pdf.

Violence Policy Center. (2008). *American roulette: Murder-suicide in the United States* (3rd ed.). Washington, DC: The Violence Policy Center. Retrieved from http://www.vpc.org/studies/amroul2008.pdf

Virginia Department of Corrections. (2010). *Victim services.* Retrieved from http://www.vadoc.state.va.us/victim

von Hentig, H. (1948). *The criminal and his victim: Studies in the sociobiology of crime.* New Haven, CT: Yale University Press.

Waalen, J., Goodwin, M., Spitz, A., Petersen, R., & Saltzman, L. (2000). Screening for intimate partner violence by health care providers: Barriers and interventions. *American Journal of Preventative Medicine, 19,* 230–237.

Wacker, J. L., Parish, S. L., & Macy, R. J. (2008). Sexual assault and women with cognitive disabilities: Codifying discrimination in the states. *Journal of Disability Policy Studies, 19,* 86–94.

Wahab, S. (2006). Evaluating the usefulness of a prostitution diversion project. *Qualitative Social Work, 5*(1), 67–92.

Walker, L. E. (1979). *The battered woman.* New York, NY: Harper & Row.

Wallace, H. (2007). *Victimology: Legal, psychological, and social perspectives* (2nd ed.). Boston, MA: Pearson.

Wallace, R. M. M. (1997). *International human rights: Text and materials.* London, UK: Sweet & Maxwell.

Walters, J. H., Moore, A., Berzofsky, M., & Langton, L. (2013). *Household burglary, 1994–2011* (Special Report No. NCJ 241754). Washington, DC: Bureau of Justice Statistics, U.S. Department of Justice.

Warr, M. (1984). Fear of victimization: Why are women and the elderly more afraid? *Social Science Quarterly, 65,* 681–702.

Warr, M. (1985). Fear of rape among urban women. *Social Problems, 32,* 238–250.

Warr, M., & Stafford, C. (1983). Fear of victimization: A look at the proximate causes. *Social Forces, 61,* 1033–1043.

Watts-English, T., Fortson, B. L., Gibler, N., Hooper, S. R., & De Bellis, D. (2006). The psychology of maltreatment in childhood. *Journal of Social Issues, 62,* 717–736.

Websdale, N. (2003). *Reviewing domestic violence deaths.* Retrieved from the National Institute of Justice website: https://www.ncjrs.gov/pdffiles1/jr000250g.pdf

Weese, B. (2011, March 14). Honour killings term angers Trudeau. *Toronto Sun.* Retrieved from http://www.torontosun.com/news/canada/2011/03/14/17610021.html

Weinberg, M. K., & Tronick, E. Z. (1998). Emotional characteristics of infants associated with maternal depression and anxiety. *Pediatrics, 102,* 1298–1304.

Weisburd, D., Mastrofski, S. D., McNally, A. M., Greenspan, R., & Willis, J. J. (2003). Reforming to preserve: Compstat and strategic problem solving in American policing. *Criminology & Public Policy, 2*(3), 421–456.

Weisel, D. L., Clarke, R. V., & Stedman, J. R. (1999). *Hot dots in hot spots: Examining repeat victimization for residential burglary in three cities: Final report.* Washington, DC: U.S. Department of Justice.

Wells, W., Wu, L., & Ye, X. (2011). Patterns of near-repeat gun assaults in Houston. *Journal of Research in Crime & Delinquency, 49,* 186–212.

Welsh, B. C., Loeber, R., Stevens, B. R., Stouthamer-Loeber, M., Cohen, M. A., & Farrington, D. P. (2008). Costs of juvenile crime in urban areas: A longitudinal perspective. *Youth Violence and Juvenile Justice, 6,* 3–27.

West, K., & Wiley-Cordone, J. (1999). Healing the hate: Innovations in hate crime prevention. *Illinois Council for the Prevention of Violence, 1,* 1–4.

Westerholm, R. (2014, July 31). *U.S. Senate announces anticipated bill-toughening penalties on schools that mishandle campus sexual assault.* Retrieved from http://www.universityherald.com/articles/10687/20140731/u-s-senate-announces-anticipated-bill-toughening-penalties-on-schools-that-mishandle-campus-sexual-assault.htm

Wevodau, A. L., Cramer, R. J., Kehn, A., & Clark, J. W. (2014). Why the impact? Negative affective change as a mediator of the effects of victim impact statements. *Journal of Interpersonal Violence,* 1–20. doi:10.1177/0886260514527170.

Widom, C. S. (1989a). Child abuse, neglect, and adult behavior. *American Journal of Orthopsychiatry, 59*(3), 355–367.

Widom, C. S. (1989b). The cycle of violence. *Science, 244,* 160–166.

Widom, C. S. (2000, January). Childhood victimization: Early adversity, later psychopathology. *National Institute of Justice Journal,* 2–9.

Widom, C. S., Czaja, S., & Dutton, M. A. (2014). Child abuse and neglect and intimate partner violence victimization and perpetration: A prospective investigation. *Child Abuse & Neglect, 38,* 650–663.

Wilcox, P., Jordan, C. E., & Pritchard, A. J. (2006). Fear of acquaintance versus stranger rape as a "master status": Towards refinement of the "shadow of sexual assault" hypothesis. *Violence and Victims, 21*(3), 355–370.

Wilcox, W. B., & Dew, J. (2008, January). *Protectors or perpetrators? Fathers, mothers, and child abuse and neglect* (Research Brief 7). New York, NY: Institute for American Values: Center for Marriage and Families.

Williams, K., Chambers, M., Logan, S., & Robinson, D. (1996). Association of common health symptoms with bullying in primary school children. *BMJ, 313,* 17–19.

Willness, C. R., Steel, P., & Lee, K. (2007). A meta-analysis of the antecedents and consequences of workplace sexual harassment. *Personnel Psychology, 60,* 127–162.

Wilson, A. E., Calhoun, K. S., & Bernat, J. A. (1999). Risk recognition and trauma related symptoms among sexually revictimized women. *Journal of Consulting and Clinical Psychology, 67,* 705–710.

Wilson, C., & Brewer, N. (1992). The incidence of criminal victimization of individuals with an intellectual disability. *Australian Psychologist, 27,* 114–117.

Wilson, C., Seaman, L., & Nettelbeck, T. (1996). Vulnerability to criminal exploitation: Influence of interpersonal competence differences among people with mental retardation. *Journal of Intellectual Disability Research, 40,* 10–19.

Wilson, H. W., & Widom, C. S. (2010). The role of youth problem behaviors in the path from child abuse and neglect to prostitution: A prospective examination. *Journal of Research on Adolescence, 20*(1), 210–236.

Wilson, M., & Daly, M. (1993). Spousal homicide risk and estrangement. *Violence and Victims, 8,* 3–16.

Wilson, M. M. (2014). *Hate crime victimization, 2004–2012–Statistical tables* (Report No. NCJ 244409). Washington, DC: Bureau of Justice Statistics, U.S. Department of Justice.

Wisconsin Coalition Against Sexual Assault. (2003). *People with disabilities and sexual assault: Information sheet series.* Madison: Wisconsin Coalition Against Sexual Assault. Retrieved from http://kyasap.brinkster.net/Portals/0/pdfs/Disabilitiesandsexualassault.pdf

Wisner, C., Gilmer, T., Saltman, L., & Zink, T. (1999). Intimate partner violence against women: Do victims cost health plans more? *Journal of Family Practice, 48,* 6439–6443.

Wittebrood, K., & Nieuwbeerta, P. (2000). Criminal victimization during one's life course: The effects of previous victimization and patterns of routine activities. *Journal of Research in Crime and Delinquency, 37,* 91–122.

Wolf, M., Holt, V., Kernic, M., & Rivara, F. (2000). Who gets protection orders for intimate partner violence? *American Journal of Preventative Medicine, 19,* 286–291.

Wolff, N., Blitz, C., & Shi, J. (2007). Rates of sexual victimization in prisoners with and without mental disorders. *Psychiatric Services, 58,* 1087–1094.

Wolff, N., Shi, J., & Siegel, J. A. (2009a). Patterns of victimization among male and female inmates: Evidence of an enduring legacy. *Violence and Victims, 24,* 469–484.

Wolff, N., Shi, J., & Siegel, J. A. (2009b). Understanding physical victimization inside prisons: Factors that predict risk. *Justice Quarterly, 26,* 445–475.

Wolfgang, M. E. (1957). Victim precipitated criminal homicide. *Journal of Criminal Law, Criminology, and Police Science, 48*(1), 1–11.

Wolfgang, M. E., & Ferracuti, F. (1967). *The subculture of violence: Towards an integrated theory in criminology.* London, UK: Tavistock Publications.

Wooldredge, J., & Steiner, B. (2013). Violent victimization among state prison inmates. *Violence and Victims, 28,* 531–551.

Wooldredge, J. D. (1998). Inmate lifestyles and opportunities for victimization. *Journal of Research in Crime and Delinquency, 35,* 480–502.

World Health Organization (2013). Violence against women: a 'global health problem of epidemic proportions': New clinical and policy guidelines launched to guide health sector response Retrieved from http://www.who.int/mediacentre/news/releases/2013/violence_against_women_20130620/en/.

Wright, R. T., & Decker, S. (1994). *Burglars on the job: Streetlife and residential break-ins.* Boston, MA: Northeastern University Press.

Würger, M. (2013). *Victim rights and compensation in an international comparison: France, Austria, Germany.* Retrieved from http://www.mpicc.de/ww/en/pub/forschung/forschungsarbeit/kriminologie/archiv/victim_rights .htm#metanav

Wyatt, G. E., Guthrie, D., & Notgrass, C. M. (1992). Differential effects of women's child sexual abuse and subsequent sexual revictimization. *Journal of Consulting and Clinical Psychology, 60,* 167–173.

Yan, E. (2014, August 19). *DA: Joseph Caleca charged with hate crimes after hitting, dragging Sandeep Singh in Queens.* Retrieved from http://www.newsday.com/news/new-york/joseph-caleca-charged-with-hate-crimes-after-hitting-dragging-man-in-queens-nypd-says-1.9095507

Yllo, K. A., & Straus, M. A. (1990). Patriarchy and violence against wives: The impact of structural and normative factors. In M. A. Straus & R. J. Gelles (Eds.), *Physical violence in American families* (pp. 383–389). New Brunswick, NJ: Transaction.

Young, M., & Stein, J. (2004). *The history of the crime victims' movement in the United States: A component of the Office for Victims of Crime oral history project.* Washington, DC: United States Department of Justice.

Young, M. A. (1989). Crime, violence, and terrorism. In R. Gist & B. Lubin (Eds.), *Psychological aspects of disaster* (pp. 61–85). New York, NY: Wiley.

Young, M. E., Nosek, M. A., Howland, C., Chanpong, G., & Rintala, D. H. (1997). Prevalence of abuse of women with physical disabilities. *Archives of Physical Medicine & Rehabilitation, 78*(12, Suppl 5), S34–S38.

Yun, I., Johnson, M., & Kercher, G. (2005). *Victim impact statements: What victims have to say.* Huntsville, TX: Sam Houston State University Crime Victims' Institute.

Zaykowski, H. (2010). Racial disparities in hate crime reporting. *Violence and Victims, 25,* 378–394.

Zielinski, D. (2009). Child maltreatment and adult socioeconomic well-being. *Child Abuse and Neglect, 33*(10), 666–678.

Zimmerman, C., Hossain, M., Yun, K., Gajdadziev, N., Tchomarova, M., Ciarrochi, R. A., … Watts, C. (2008). The health of trafficked women: A survey of women entering posttrafficking services in Europe. *American Journal of Public Health, 98,* 55–59.

Zimmerman, C., Yun, K., Watts, C., Shvab, I., Trappolin, L., Treppete, M., … Regan, L. (2003). *The health risks and consequences of trafficking in women and adolescents: Findings from a European study.* London, UK: London School of Hygiene and Tropical Medicine.

Zink, T. M., Fisher, B. F., Regan, S. L., & Pabst, S. (2005).The prevalence and incidence of intimate partner violence in older women in primary care practices. *Journal of General Internal Medicine, 20,* 884–888.

Zubrick, S. R., Silburn, L., Gurrin, H., Teoh, C., Shepherd, J., Carlton, J., & Lawrence, D. (1997). *Western Australian child health survey: Education, health and competence.* Perth: Australian Bureau of Statistics and the TVW Institute for Child Health Research.

OSHA. *See* Occupational Safety and Health Administration
Otto, J. M., 202
Outlaw, M. C., 35–36

Pain, suffering, and lost quality of life, 62
Palermo Protocol, 320
Parity hypothesis, 147
Parker, William (Billy) Ray, 107–108
Parricide, 118
Participation and consultation, 89
Patriarchy, 174
Patricide, 118
Payne v. Tennessee (1991), 100
Peacemaking circles, 103
Peer mediation, 245
Perceived risk, 66
Permissive arrest policies, 180
Personal relationship incidents, 252
Petersilia, J. R., 219
Phishing, 274
Physical abuse, 188, 189 (table)
Physical bullying, 241
Physical elder abuse, 199–200, 199 (photo)
Physical guardianship, 143
Physical incivilities, 69
Physical injury, 55
Physical violence, 164
Pillemer, K., 202
Piquero, A. R., 32
Pizarro, J. M., 48
Police responses to victimization:
    disabilities, victims with, 218–219
    hate crimes, 310–311, 314
    homicide, 128–129
    intimate partner violence, 178–180, 179 (photo)
    motor vehicle theft, 268
    sexual victimization, 152–154
    See also Justice system responses to victimization
Police units, all-female, 300, 300 (table)
Political victim (victim type), 5
Polk, K., 126
Polygraph examinations of sexual assault victims, 150
Poly-victimization, 73–74, 75 (table), 82
Ponomaryov, Lev, 227
Population heterogeneity perspective, 45–46
Posttraumatic stress disorder (PTSD):
    about, 57, 58 (table)
    hate crime victimization and, 312
    homicide survivors and, 64

Netherlands, 97
    recurring victimization and, 79
    terrorism victimization and, 325, 326
Poverty:
    child maltreatment and, 193, 196
    disabled victimization and, 218
    human trafficking and, 319
Power, 174
Power of attorney abuse, 200, 201
Powers, L. E., 214
Precipitative victim (victim type), 5
Premeditation, 109
President's Task Force on Victims of Crime, 10, 91, 101
Presumptive arrest policies, 180
Prevention, 13–14, 82–85
Prince, Phoebe, 243, 244
Principle of homogamy, 27, 41–42
Prison Rape Elimination Act (2003), 230, 231
Pro-arrest policies, 180
Project Exile, 129
Property victimization:
    about, 262
    household burglary, 270–272
    motor vehicle theft, 265–269, 266 (table), 267 (photo), 267 (table)
    recurring victimization, 76
    reporting, 66
    theft, 263–265
Prostitution courts, 51–52
Protective behaviors, 69
Protective custody, 232
Protective orders, 182–183
Protocol to Prevent, Suppress, and Punish Trafficking in Persons, 315, 320
Provocative victim (victim type), 5
PTSD. *See* Posttraumatic stress disorder

Quid pro quo sexual harassment, 256

Rape:
    definitions of, 136, 139, 140, 150
    fear of, 69
    myths, 157
    recurring victimization, 75, 76, 77, 83–84
    types of, 136–137
    victim precipitation and, 6–7
    See also Sexual victimization
Rape kits, 156 (photo)
Rape shield laws, 150
Reagan, Ronald, 10

Walker, Lenore, 177
War crimes, 293 (table)
Weapon use, 116–117, 146
Weiner, D. A., 222
Welsh, B. C., 59
West Africa, intimate partner violence
    in, 165
Wheeler, Mrs., 188
WHO. *See* World Health Organization
Widom, C. S., 174
Wiersma, B., 59
Williams, Calvin, 44
Williams, Terrance, 39–40, 41 (photo)
Wilson, C., 213, 218
Wilson, Genarlow, 137
Wisconsin, victims' rights in, 90
Wisniewski, N., 140–141
Wolff, N., 226, 228
Wolfgang, Marvin, 5–6, 6 (photo), 48, 125
Women. *See* Females
Women's movement, 8, 165
Worker-on-worker incidents, 252

Workplace victimization:
    consequences of, 257
    extent of, 252
    fatal, 254–255, 257
    occupations/workplaces with greatest risk,
        252–254, 255, 256 (photo)
    responses to, 257–259, 258 (table)
    risk factors for, 255–256
    sexual harassment, 256
    types of, 252
    victim characteristics, 252, 254–255
World Health Organization (WHO), 114–115, 119, 241
World Society of Victimology (WSV), 285
Wright, J. P., 46

Youth Risk Behavior Surveillance System, 241
Youth victimization, 287–289, 288 (table)
Youth with disabilities, 215–216

Zero-tolerance policies, 244
Zgoba, K. M., 48
Zychkov, Sergei, 227

■■ABOUT THE AUTHORS

Leah E. Daigle is associate professor in the Department of Criminal Justice and Criminology in the Andrew Young School of Policy Studies at Georgia State University. She received her Ph.D. in criminal justice from the University of Cincinnati in 2005. Her most recent research has centered on repeat sexual victimization of college women and responses women use during and after being sexually victimized. Her other research interests include the development and continuation of offending and victimization across the life course. She is author of *Victimology: A Text/Reader*, coauthor of *Criminals in the Making: Criminality Across the Life Course and Unsafe in the Ivory Tower: The Sexual Victimization of College Women*, which was awarded the 2011 Outstanding Book Award by the Academy of Criminal Justice Sciences. She has also published numerous peer-reviewed articles that have appeared in outlets such as *Justice Quarterly, Journal of Quantitative Criminology, Journal of Interpersonal Violence,* and *Victims and Offenders.*

Lisa R. Muftić is associate professor in the Department of Criminal Justice & Criminology within the College of Criminal Justice and the assistant director for the Crime Victims' Institute at Sam Houston State University. She received her Ph.D. in criminal justice from North Dakota State University in 2006. For the 2012–2013 academic year, she was appointed the U.S. Fulbright Scholar to Bosnia and Herzegovina where she was a visiting faculty member with the Faculty of Criminal Justice Sciences, Criminology and Security Studies at the University of Sarajevo. Dr. Muftić has extensive experience in the areas of violence against women, human trafficking, and international criminal justice issues, with special expertise regarding the situation in Bosnia and Herzegovina. Her published scholarship has appeared in well-respected refereed journals including *Justice Quarterly, Crime & Delinquency, Journal of Research in Crime & Delinquency, Violence Against Women, Journal of Interpersonal Violence,* and *Victims and Offenders.*